"Takin' it to the streets"

"Takin' it to the streets"

A Sixties Reader

Edited by
ALEXANDER BLOOM
WINI BREINES

New York   Oxford
OXFORD UNIVERSITY PRESS
1995

Oxford University Press

Oxford   New York
Athens   Auckland   Bangkok   Bombay
Calcutta   Cape Town   Dar es Salaam   Delhi
Florence   Hong Kong   Istanbul   Karachi
Kuala Lumpur   Madras   Madrid   Melbourne
Mexico City   Nairobi   Paris   Singapore
Taipei   Tokyo   Toronto

and associated companies in
Berlin   Ibadan

Published by Oxford University Press, Inc.,
198 Madison Avenue, New York, New York 10016

Oxford is a registered trademark of Oxford University Press

Library of Congress Cataloging-in-Publication Data
Takin' it to the streets : a sixties reader /
edited by Alexander Bloom and Wini Breines.
p.   cm.
ISBN 0-19-506623-5 (c).—ISBN 0-19-506624-3 (p)
1. United States—History—1961–1969—Sources.
2. United States—History—1961–1969.
3. United States—Civilization—1945——SOURCES.
4. United States—Civilization—1945–
I. Bloom, Alexander.
II. Breines, Wini.
E841.T28   1995   973.92—dc20   94-42021

9   8   7   6   5   4   3   2   1
Printed in the United States of America
on acid-free paper

For Our Parents

*Vivian Bloom, Betty Jacoby, Daniel Jacoby
and in Memory of Erwin Bloom*

And Our Children

*Stefan Bloom, Zachary Bloom,
Raphael Breines, and Natasha Museles*

ACKNOWLEDGMENTS

Each of us has written books before, but neither of us had ever edited an anthology. Our work on this reader leaves us with a new sense of the labor involved and a high respect for all who undertake such a task. We now know how much effort exists behind the scenes of a book like this, especially a volume of original historical documents.

We want to thank friends and colleagues who read our initial proposal and offered suggestions of additional articles, topics, and even chapters: Rosalyn Baxandall, William Chafe, David Farber, Marilyn Halter, Allen Hunter, Maurice Isserman, Michael Kazin, Rebecca Klatch, Glen Omatsu, Carol Petillo, and Barbara Tischler.

At various points along the way, individuals have provided guidance, helped us find sources, located authors, thought of alternative entries, suggested chapter titles, and read drafts. These include Bettina Aptheker, Rosalyn Baxandall, Stefan Bloom, Chris Bose, Paul Breines, Lillian Castillo-Speed, Bill Flores, Alma Garcia, Kim MacInnes, Elizabeth Martinez, Glen Omatsu, Mary Parda, Nelida Perez, Clara Rodriguez, and Peggy Stockman. Our research assistants diligently dug out articles, photocopied stacks of material, collated chapters, helped with permissions requests, counted words, and performed a great number of other tasks. We are indebted to them all: Raphael Breines, Amy DiTullio, Jennifer Haber, David Hyde, Sue Lamay, Claire Lang, Kathryn Maciasek, Kim MacInnes, Jennifer Medeiros, Ardith Pierce, Mallory Plukas, Hillary Smith, and Alex Thomas.

Everyone who undertakes a project like this recounts the nightmare of securing permissions to reprint selections. Our story is no different; amidst this effort, however, there have been numerous bright lights. A number of authors, magazines, and publishing houses have agreed to republication of their material without charge or for reduced fees so that we could present the wide variety of material we have chosen. They all have our sincerest appreciation.

Readers may note the absence of any material from *Rolling Stone.* That magazine, alone among all the potential contributors we contacted—left, center, and right—refused to allow material to be reprinted for any fee. We were able to find suitable replacements, but we are saddened at the evaporation of the sense of community from which a magazine such as *Rolling Stone* emerged. We are heartened that such community continues to exist in so many other quarters.

Finally, this book is dedicated to our parents and our children. Our parents transmitted a political tradition that made it easier for us to engage in political activity than it was for many of our contemporaries. With them there was less of a generation gap and more generational continuity. Our children's generation has often demonstrated great nostalgia for the 1960s. We hope that they and their peers will use the 1960s, not as contemporary escapism but for a sense of historical understanding that will serve them in its social and political application to today's world.

CONTENTS

3. "SAY IT LOUD, SAY IT PROUD":
BLACK NATIONALISM AND ETHNIC CONSCIOUSNESSS,
135

9. "WHEN THE MUSIC'S OVER":
ENDINGS AND BEGINNINGS, 559

"Takin' it to the streets"

"PAST AS PROLOGUE": THE 1950s AS AN INTRODUCTION TO THE 1960s

Images of the 1950s are distinct: white middle-class families, suburban homes, backyard barbecues, big American cars with tail fins, Little League and Girl Scouts, peace, prosperity, and harmony. So, too, the images of the 1960s: civil rights sit-ins, urban violence, antiwar demonstrations, black power salutes, hippie love-ins, draft card burnings, death and destruction in Vietnam, police riots in Chicago, obscenities, hostilities, killings at Kent State and Jackson State universities.

These decades stand in marked contrast in the collective memory, each reduced to recollections distilled from media imagery and popular stereotypes. The periods recede into history, reflections of the dominant values of their eras rather than accurate representations of the complexity of the times: the harmonious 1950s; the turbulent 1960s. We remember the eras in stark opposition, in snapshots that symbolize values and aspirations unrelated to one another.

As scholars look back at these eras, however, they understand them as complex and interrelated. The obvious tensions and anxieties of postwar America—the cold war, fear of the atom bomb, McCarthyism and the specter of the witch-hunt—are easily recalled; they undermine notions of a calm and peaceful era. Questions about race and gender have further demonstrated that the 1950s were not nearly so harmonious for minorities and women. We now understand more clearly the complexities of family life, the pressures on men and women resulting from rigid gender roles, the large numbers of Americans—of all races—who felt left out of the suburban dream of the good life. All these suggest an era far more anxious, questioning, and discordant than do bland images of postwar bliss.

At the other extreme, many events, attitudes, and activities of the 1960s do not seem appropriate in a country torn by discontent and division: the counterculture's focus on "love," the hedonistic embrace of new lifestyles, the enthusiasm of the 1968 presidential campaigns of Eugene McCarthy and Robert Kennedy. These intertwine with intense anger over war, assassinations, and turbulence in the streets and on college campuses. Instead of a singular negative picture of society in upheaval, we find a mixed portrait—enthusiasm coupled with hostility, optimism about a "greening of America" jumbled with a view of a quasi-fascist "Amerika." Again, the images depict a decade more complex than the snapshot suggests.

Memory compresses the past, so that it seems that life was pacific at one moment and the nation exploded in the next. Deeper analysis of the two eras reveals continuities between them. At the simplest level, political activities such as the civil rights movement began in the 1950s. Little Leaguers and Girl Scouts of the fifties grew up to become the college students of the sixties. Unhappiness over the prescribed roles white postwar brides were asked to play in their "suburban utopias" was a shared experience for many fifties housewives and proved a crucial impetus for the women's movement of the late sixties. Younger women sought new roles beyond limits that had been drawn for their mothers.

Beneath the surface complacency of American intellectual, social, and cultural life in the postwar years, many critics and iconoclasts offered critical analyses of American life or led their own lives in ways that were shocking to mainstream America. In a society that valued homogeneity, they were attacked as atypical outsiders. But in the 1960s, as nonconformity and radicalism grew more commonplace, 1950s apostates—from political analyst C. Wright Mills to poet Allen Ginsberg—found new audiences, and their work took on new significance.

These decades, then, are more complex, more ambiguous, and more interconnected than popular imagery suggests. The events and perspectives of the sixties did not spring full blown and brand new into American life. For the 1960s, the 1950s are past as prologue.

The cold war was at the heart of postwar America. Beyond the immediate tensions that developed between the United States and the Soviet Union, the degree to which cold war ideology, imperatives, and necessities permeated American life was extraordinary. The Soviet threat precipitated an enormous buildup in America's defenses. Immediately after World War II the government had scaled back military spending dramatically. Within a few years, however, it had grown to monumental size for a nation not at war. This arms buildup had a significant impact on domestic life as well. No longer protected by the oceans that separated them from most of the world, and with constant reminders of the perceived Soviet threat, Americans came to believe that nuclear war was likely.

Fears of Soviet bombs raining from the skies were matched by the specter of Soviet agents penetrating the fabric of American society. These supposed subversives were not only spies from the KGB, but American leftists working for Soviet interests. Extraordinary measures were taken to root out the suspected traitors. Investigations into "communist activities" were undertaken by various forces, from congressional committees to internal investigations by universities, school systems, and the entertainment industry. Civil liberties were constricted, thousands lost their jobs, books were banned, passports lifted—all rationalized under the rubric of the domestic fight against communism.

Public trials focused attention on the issue. In 1947 former State Department official Alger Hiss ran afoul of the House Un-American Activities Committee, especially one of its members, California freshman congressman Richard Nixon. Accused of passing secrets to a Soviet agent in the 1930s, Hiss proclaimed his innocence. After two trials, he went to jail for perjury. Nixon moved on to the Senate and the vice-presidency, with Eisenhower in 1952. When the Soviets detonated their own atomic bomb, cold war panic rose to new heights. Images of pervasive Soviet espionage led to suggestions that America's nuclear secrets had been stolen. Americans Julius and Ethel Rosenberg were charged with stealing one of those secrets. Tried in an atmosphere of intense anticommunism, they were convicted in 1951 and, ultimately, executed in 1953. At their sentencing, the judge not only cited them for espionage and treason, but held them responsible for starting the Korean war—illustrating the degree and intensity of anticommunist sentiment by the early 1950s.

In 1950, searching for an issue to spark his reelection bid, Wisconsin Senator Joseph McCarthy announced that he possessed the names of numerous individuals within the State Department who were "known communists." (The actual number McCarthy cited shifted over time as his assertion came under scrutiny.) Seizing upon the most important domestic issue of the first half of the 1950s, McCarthy tossed accusations wildly. His final charge, that the U.S. Army was trying to stop McCarthy's investigation of communist infiltration of American army posts, led to the 1954 televised public investigation known as the "Army-McCarthy Hearings," during which McCarthy's questionable tactics and meanspiritedness were exposed.

Condemned by the Senate, McCarthy faded from public view and died in 1957. But this did not mark the end of anticommunism. Anticommunist prerogatives remained at the heart of American foreign policy—from Cuba to Berlin to Southeast Asia—as well as a central concern of domestic American life. Institutions outside the government—Hollywood, labor unions, school districts, colleges and universities—had moved to follow the federal lead. Throughout the 1950s anticommunism shaped American events in international relations, domestic politics, and local activities. It precipitated a view, reinforced by the tensions of the cold war, that the world was a troubled place populated by agents of foreign powers bent on undermining the beneficence of American life. For student radicals and their generational peers, however, this sensibility had little place in a world in which other issues seemed much more pressing than Soviet expansionism or internal communist subversion.

The second crucial domestic issue of the 1950s proved much more important for the young sixties generation. Beginning in the middle 1950s, the movement for civil rights gained increasing public attention in its effort to end the legalized segregation of the races that existed in a large portion of the country. In the late nineteenth century, institutionalized segregation had created separate facilities for blacks and whites in schools, hotels, waiting rooms, restaurants, restrooms, drinking fountains, and buses. Blacks had been systematically disenfranchised, excluded from juries, and prohibited from marrying whites. Ruling in 1896 that facilities could be "separate" if they were "equal," the Supreme Court had deemed all this constitutional. Legal segregation spread not only throughout the Deep South but into

Kansas, southern Illinois, Missouri, Delaware, Maryland, and even the nation's capital.

While movements to attack segregation had begun early in the century, their success was limited until the 1950s. Focusing on education, the NAACP Legal Defense Fund had won a series of small victories in the 1930s and 1940s. Its assault on school segregation culminated in the 1954 Supreme Court decision, *Brown v. Board of Education of Topeka, Kansas,* which declared school segregation unconstitutional. While southern school districts managed for years to block or stall much of the desegregation of their schools, the decision nonetheless marked both a turning point in civil rights activities and the most important civil rights decision in the Court's history.

A new consciousness began to grow among many southern blacks. No longer were they willing to tolerate the unpunished physical abuse visited upon them by whites. The brutal murder in 1955 of fourteen-year-old Emmett Till epitomized the situation for many. His two assailants were acquitted by an all-white jury, despite being identified as Till's abductors. Future civil rights activist Anne Moody recalls, "I was fifteen years old when I began to hate people. I hated the white people who murdered Emmett Till. . . . But I also hated Negroes. I hated them for not standing up and doing something about the murders."

This sense of resistance prompted many blacks to adopt new behavior with regard to civil rights questions. In December 1955 riding home from work on a Montgomery, Alabama, bus, Rosa Parks refused to give up her seat to a white man. Parks's case became the springboard for organization of the black community of Montgomery into collective action to boycott the buses until the situation for blacks improved, and catapulted a young Montgomery minister, Martin Luther King, Jr., to national prominence. During the boycott King developed his philosophy of nonviolent direct action as the means for battling segregation. Ultimately victorious over the bus company, the boycott initiated a series of direct confrontations with segregated institutions, often spearheaded by King's newly developed civil rights organization, the Southern Christian Leadership Conference (SCLC).

School desegregation frequently captured national headlines. The 1957 order to desegregate Central High School in Little Rock, Arkansas, led to a clash between state and federal authorities. When mobs threatened the black students and Arkansas governor Orval Faubus called out the National Guard to prevent integration, President Eisenhower sent federal troops to Little Rock to facilitate desegregation and to insure the students' safety. The troops remained stationed in Little Rock for the entire school year.

By 1960, civil rights had become not only the most pressing domestic issue, but one that captured the attention of the young. In it, young blacks and then young whites found their first real political cause.

Throughout the postwar years, American popular culture, political figures, and social and religious leaders had trumpeted the virtues of contemporary society. No matter what one's class or race, individuals were influenced by a celebration of the domestic tranquility embodied in the white middle-class American family. Traditional gender-differentiated roles of American adults provided the structure within which children matured. Celebrated in popular novels, movies, and, especially, on television, the stereotypic white nuclear family appeared to offer prosperity, harmony, and security for everyone.

The images were continually reinforced. "Situation comedies," developed for the exploding television medium, offered one "typical" American family after another: the Cleavers on *Leave It to Beaver,* the Nelsons of *The Adventures of Ozzie and Harriet,* the Stones of *The Donna Reed Show,* and the Anderson clan who believed that *Father Knows Best.* White, middle-class, and suburban, these television families and countless others created by the media suggested that "real life" was to be found at home, and not at the workplace. In these depictions men served as breadwinners, women stayed home, and children's problems emerged as the major concern of the modern family. Fathers monopolized the earning power of the family as well as the rationality to settle family issues. They would return home from work to find slightly hysterical mothers unable to cope with the latest domestic crisis and settle the matter calmly.

Subsequent analyses suggest that this model of family life was not as widespread as the media made it appear. The number of working wives grew steadily during the 1950s, from 25 percent in 1950 to 32 percent in 1960. Urban families, families of color, poor families, single-parent families, gays and lesbians, and many white, middle-class families shaped their lives—by choice or by necessity—differently from the media model. The postwar period witnessed, for example, an enormous migration from the rural south to the urban north and west, necessitating adjustments to urban life for these new arrivals.

Working hard, they tried to save so they could move out of the city, hoping to assimilate to mainstream middle class culture. Even while the realities of their lives differed starkly from those depicted on television, the cultural image of a cheerful white, nuclear family shaped their plans and dreams.

Those who constructed their lives according to the sanctioned model often found them less fulfilling and more problematic than anticipated. Young people probably rebelled first. Postwar home life had been arranged to serve the new children who populated postwar America at an amazing rate. Thousands of suburban housing developments sprang up, offering many American families the chance to own their own homes. These segregated communities attracted young white couples with small children—working fathers, mothers at home, and kids at school. Parents began to fear that unregulated childhood activities might lead their progeny into the most-feared snare for fifties youth, juvenile delinquency. Structured activities grew rapidly: Little League, Cub Scouts, Boy Scouts, Brownies, Girl Scouts, music lessons, dance classes, and so on. Mothers became chauffeurs, shuttling children from one activity to another.

Young people will ultimately resist the efforts of adults to shape and control their maturation. The declaration by postwar white youth of their difference, if not their independence, from adults, might be symbolized by Elvis Presley. Hardly seen as a cultural revolution at the time, the emergence of rock 'n' roll in mainstream culture in the middle 1950s, epitomized by the enormous popular success of Elvis, marked the clearest differentiation between parents and children in the 1950s. Growing out of black music, rock 'n' roll grabbed white teenagers with its youth concerns—dating, cars, sex, school, summer, dancing—and the physical drive of its music. Over the years, rock music would stitch itself into the American cultural fabric first, as a sign of teenage rebellion and then, in the 1960s, of generational difference. When Elvis Presley first appeared on *The Ed Sullivan Show,* parents looked on aghast as girls swooned. Boys grew their sideburns longer and slicked their hair into ducktails.

If Elvis was the symbol for white teen rebellion—the one the mainstream media talked the most about—he had his counterparts in the black and Latino communities. For poor and ghetto youths, adolescent issues were joined with concerns about education, after-school work, both parents working outside the home, and lives not represented by "typical" media families. Young people throughout the culture began to question their place and their prospects, albeit in different settings. And everywhere music punctuated the emerging youth cultures. While adults frequently predicted the end of these music "fads," one singing group symbolically spoke for many young people when they proclaimed "rock 'n' roll is here to stay." The sixties would prove them right.

As young people grew older, the assumptions of their parents' lives were subjected to direct questioning. Without the background of depression and war, desire for material possessions and family stability proved much less strong for the younger generation. The virtues of suburban life seemed less appealing, the problems of America more compelling.

The only socially acceptable path available to a young middle class white woman was to become a wife and mother. For teenage girls, the eventual goal was to find a husband. Girls were not encouraged to think of their futures in terms of work or careers. But many middle-class girls were expected to go to college. In addition, while television and mainstream magazines glorified domesticity, the youth culture and images of movie stars communicated messages about the possibility of feminine sexuality outside of marriage. Finally, women had been joining the labor force in increasing numbers. For working women, accepting or rejecting traditional feminine roles was not a choice. Economic necessity made it much more difficult to conform to the much celebrated life of full-time mom. All these messages competed with narrow notions of femininity that led directly to marriage. Although the change was not yet obvious, girls' links to their families were loosening.

Middle-class men found their assigned roles less than fulfilling. The pressures to provide for their families brought about extraordinary strains. Rates of divorce, alcoholism, heart disease, and other personal and social disorders all increased. Many white middle-class housewives also found their prescribed places stifling and depressing. When Betty Friedan interviewed Smith College alumnae, she found many of them unhappy with their lives despite having achieved most of the goals they had once thought would bring happiness—husband, family, home, affluence. Feeling alone in their disappointment, they rarely spoke to anyone about their concerns, considering it a personal failing rather than the results of narrow expectations for women.

Many of their daughters, part of the college-bound generation already questioning the assumptions of fifties America, recognized that following in their mothers' footsteps would not bring them happiness. The oppressiveness of the "feminine mystique" wouldn't be fully articulated and analyzed until the second half of the 1960s, but its effects pervaded all of postwar American life, contradicting popular images of contented domesticity on the suburban homefront.

A white middle-class full-time housewife might be bored, but not many black women were privileged enough to be at home full-time. Most black men never had the opportunity to feel alienated in corporate white-collar jobs because such jobs were not available to them. Even the suburban communities that sprang up in the postwar years were segregated, enforced privately in the North by realtors and bankers rather than by the explicit laws that segregated the South. Class and race perpetuated exclusions while cultural images offered a steady diet of the beneficence of the "good life."

Young people—male and female, black and white, poor and prosperous—growing up in this world were ambivalent about reproducing their parents' lives and began to consider other paths to fulfillment. In the early 1960s this took the form of questioning the status quo, leading the way to the decade's social movements. This questioning and search for alternatives created one of the clear divisions between fifties parents and sixties children.

Among the pervasive images of the 1950s is the picture of the American intellectual—in the fifties phrase, "the egghead." In fact, intellectuals became more closely integrated into American life than in any previous era. Directly associated with this rise in intellectuals' prominence was the changing place of the university in American life. In the postwar years, spurred by economic prosperity and the GI Bill, which provided educational assistance to veterans, colleges and universities expanded in size and influence. Along with thousands of new college students, intellectuals, artists, and writers moved to college campuses. This coincided with a shift in intellectual temperament, as well. Once critics standing outside mainstream American life, many intellectuals now became supporters of the direction America was taking. They lent weight to the arguments concerning anticommunism and the cold war. These individuals had become central players in the postwar American consensus.

As with political and social life, intellectual and cultural life offered the same divided sense of surface harmony and subterranean rumblings. Once many intellectuals and artists had reveled in their Bohemianism and marginality. With their postwar respectability came derision for the avant-garde. They greeted new radical cultural eruptions not only with typical mainstream antagonism but with doubts about the authenticity of these endeavors. The most prominent group to endure this derision were the Beats, the coterie of poets and novelists who gathered in Greenwich Village in the late 1940s and early 1950s. With the publication of Allen Ginsberg's *Howl* (1956) and Jack Kerouac's *On the Road* (1957), the Beats gained public attention. They rejected materialism, 9-to-5 jobs, families, monogamy, and respectability, embracing instead explorations of feelings, sexuality, and immediate experience. The mass media dismissed them as self-indulgent, bongo-playing *Beatniks* (their emergence coinciding with the orbiting of the Russian satellite *Sputnik,* hence the added -*nik*). Many leading intellectuals took equally harsh aim, finding the Beats crude, foolish, and anti-intellectual.

Despite this scorn, Beat life attracted many young people. Living for immediate experience and a disdain for making money, Beats proved to be progenitors of the youth revolts of the 1960s. The sixties counterculture found cultural antecedents in the Beat movement. Allen Ginsberg became an important figure, while Kerouac's books continued to draw youthful readers. Neal Cassidy, the model for Kerouac's hero in *On the Road,* would reappear among the Merry Pranksters who followed novelist Ken Kesey in the drug culture of late sixties San Francisco.

There were other rumblings beneath the surface complacency of fifties culture—stirrings either ignored or dismissed by mainstream critics that would find new adherents in the tumultuous world of sixties culture. In 1947 an avant-garde theatrical group, The Living Theatre, was founded by Julian Beck and Judith Malina. Putting on plays in their living room and later in very small performance spaces, Beck and Malina worked in relative obscurity for most of the 1950s. By the 1960s, however, their notions of a radical theater and of pushing the boundaries of art meshed with the emerging cultural vision of the new era. The Living Theatre became one of the most central and infamous artistic institutions of the time.

In the visual arts as well, new modes emerged to contest the prevailing forms. In the late 1950s Pop Art sprang to public attention, and was initially derided as simplistic and silly. Cartoon figures, soup cans, soft sculptures of everyday objects—all these seemed unlikely subjects for artistic representation. Pop Art's creations and it practitioners, especially Andy Warhol, would nevertheless find growing audiences in the 1960s. Warhol's move from canvas to cinema also helped mark the emergence of film as a central independent art form of the decade.

A number of young novelists who began to write in the postwar years found few readers and little critical response, as their work appeared out of touch with prevailing sensibilities. The satiric wartime vision of Joseph Heller in *Catch-22* seemed inappropriate to a public accustomed to the searing realism of World War II novels such as Norman Mailer's *The Naked and the Dead* or James Jones's *From Here to Eternity*. By the 1960s, however, Heller's view of war found larger audiences as it connected with contemporary attitudes in general, and with the growing cynicism about Vietnam in particular. Similarly, the offbeat sensibilities expressed in the early novels of Kurt Vonnegut, Jr., were confusing to critics and readers in the fifties. Relegated to the science fiction section of bookstores, Vonnegut's view of American life would, like Heller's, acquire increasing numbers of devotees in the new decade.

A different literary corpus grew out of the African-American community: novels and plays that mirrored the growing prominence of racial concerns. Ralph Ellison's *Invisible Man*, published in 1952 and frequently cited as the most important American novel of the postwar years, swept across twentieth-century black history, from the segregated South to the black colleges and, finally, to the radical and radical movements of Harlem. James Baldwin's novels explored the northern black experience and homosexuality. On the stage, Lorraine Hansberry's *A Raisin in the Sun* depicted contemporary black family life, while LeRoi Jones's (later Amiri Baraka) *Dutchman*, *The Slave*, and *The Toilet* offered even more searing portraits of American racism.

Throughout the culture of the 1950s we can identify iconoclasts, the critics and artistic movements at odds with prevailing notions of American life. Often viewed as angry or misguided, or ignored altogether, postwar artistic rebels now appear to have represented stirrings of the cultural transformations to come. Some of the practitioners themselves—Ginsberg, Warhol, Beck and Malina, Heller, Vonnegut, Baldwin, and Baraka—would emerge as important figures in sixties culture. In other cases the works would find new and often larger audiences among the young. In body and spirit, these artists had begun to develop perspectives and styles that would attract disciples and audiences in the new decade.

By the early 1960s the postwar consensus had run its course. National and world events, from college campuses to Vietnam, brought many of the basic tenets of American life into sharp consideration. "We are people of this generation," began the Port Huron Statement, the 1962 founding statement of the new left Students for a Democratic Society, "bred in at least modest comfort, housed now in universities, looking uncomfortably to the world we inherit." This handful of students and countless others—women, blacks, Latinos, Native Americans, gays—found little in 1950s mainstream culture and politics to explain inequalities, restrictions, and discontent, or to enable them to analyze the new world. The underground critiques of the 1950s, as well as movements such as civil rights, offered the first hints of new perspectives and new possibilities. The young and some of the old—critics of the 1950s consensus or apostates from it—would joint to confront the new realities of the era. And "the sixties" began.

*   *   *

To understand the 1960s we look at the decade in its component parts. But to break the decade into those parts is to run the risk of losing the sense of the decade's coherence and of the interconnections among seemingly disparate events and issues. Some of the connections are obvious. For example, civil rights not only came out of the 1950s, but set the stage for much of what happened in the 1960s. The link between SNCC's Freedom Summer Project and the emergence of black power is evident. But SNCC's activities also inspired white northern students in the early days of the new left. Young women involved in the civil rights movement, filled with a zeal to promote equality and justice, began to question the situation of women of all colors.

Movements had impact in various directions, issues diverged and reunited, and individuals often shifted their energies from one area to another. And by the mid-1960s the emerging critique took on a wholeness that, while not fully articulated, was nonetheless understood by most. Cultural activities resonated with political analyses—rock 'n' roll, counterculture literature, and rural communes were as much a part of the transformation as were sit-ins, demonstrations, and civil disobedience. Politics resonated with cultural meanings—music, drugs, and lifestyle experimentation all shaped political action. Different aspects might seem to dominate at various times. For example, 1967 is remembered as the "summer of love," the height of the hippie experiment in San Francisco's Haight-Ashbury. The next summer, demonstrators filled the streets of Chicago during the Democratic Convention. Young people flocked to Woodstock in the summer of 1969. And the 1970 academic year ended for most college students with the killings at Kent State University and Jackson State University, and the ensuing National Student Strike. Cultural and political, social and personal—all were realms the came under scrutiny during the decade and out of which new alternatives emerged. Together they appeared to create the basis for a new society.

The structure of an anthology requires that we proceed in linear fashion. There is a chronological order to the chapters, each with its own central theme. Events set in motion in 1968 seemed so significant as a national experience that we have given them their own chapter, as we have the collection of reactions and backlashes produced by the movements of the 1960s.

This reader is longer than we anticipated when we began, but shorter than we would have ultimately liked it to be. Our first "final" table of contents had to be significantly edited to arrive even at this extended length. There are a number of pieces whose removal pained us deeply, while others are shorter than we would have liked. A wealth of material about this period remains available, to which these chapters can serve as introductions.

Nearly all of the documents come directly from the 1960s. There are articles by famous writers, by well-known radicals, and more than a few by individuals who think very differently in the 1990s than they did in the 1960s. There are also numerous documents by unknown and anonymous writers—members of committees who wrote leaflets, those who produced pamphlets for political organizations, unsung and passionate polemicists.*

No single document represents the entire decade. Some contradict each other. Some speak in distanced political terminology, others in extraordinarily personal voices. Taken together, these documents create something of the mosaic that was America in the 1960s. But a mosaic presumes order, planning, and a pattern. What we have instead is the emotional, political, and cultural eruption of a generation, an eruption that carried many members of an older generation along with it, and at the same time engendered hostile reactions from other quarters. It is intense, often contradictory, and always electric. What follows are documents from a decade such as America had not seen before.

*In the process of editing this anthology we have made every effort to contact the authors of each entry. We are exceptionally grateful to all those who have agreed to let us reprint their work. A few, however, have escaped our diligent efforts to find them. We would greatly appreciate hearing from these authors, so that we may acknowledge their work.

1

"KEEP ON WALKIN', KEEP ON TALKIN' ": CIVIL RIGHTS TO 1965

The movement to end segregation and second-class citizenship for African-Americans had dominated domestic politics and newspaper headlines in the second half of the 1950s. Courtroom struggles, school desegregation efforts, bus boycotts, and coordinated campaigns to attack segregation in southern cities had all become a part of American life—and would provide enormous inspiration for many of the movements of the 1960s. The two groups central to carrying out these efforts in the 1950s were those involved in judicial battles, spearheaded by the Legal Defense Fund of the National Association for the Advancement of Colored People (NAACP), and the southern ministerial network developed by Martin Luther King, Jr., most notably his Southern Christian Leadership Conference (SCLC).

In early 1960 a third force joined the civil rights struggle, heralding not only a new tactic but the involvement of new cadres of civil rights workers. The decision of four freshmen from North Carolina A&T in Greensboro to conduct a sit-in at the all-white lunch counter of the local Woolworth's initiated a change that would ripple through the South and the nation. Students at black colleges across the region organized to challenge segregated lunch counters and other facilities in their own communities.

By the spring of that year the movement among college students had erupted, leading to the creation of a group to coordinate these efforts and provide these students with an organization parallel to the

17

NAACP and SCLC. The Student Nonviolent Coordinating Committee (SNCC) would, over the next five years, move to the center of the civil rights struggle. In the the years after 1965 it would embrace positions more radical than its predecessors dared. SNCC drew college students from all over the country—black and white, male and female, northern and southern—into the civil rights movement.

Media focus on civil rights grew with the Freedom Rides in 1961. The campaign organized by a northern-based civil rights organization, the Congress on Racial Equality (CORE), aimed to desegregate the facilities that served interstate bus routes. Black and white "freedom riders" entered southern bus terminals and asked for food and shoeshines, sat in restricted waiting rooms, and otherwise confronted segregation. Violent attacks on the buses on which they rode and on the civil rights workers themselves dominated the press and forced the Kennedy administration to intervene and, ultimately, to take a more active role in civil rights than it had initially. By 1963 a national consensus on civil rights had been created, forged by the compelling figures of the civil rights movement, epitomized by Martin Luther King, Jr.; by the persuasive tactic of nonviolence; and by the brutal response of many white, southern authorities.

The August 1963 March on Washington brought together civil rights leaders from all the major organizations and thousands of individual Americans in a show of unity in support of the civil rights bill Kennedy had introduced in June. Even within this demonstration of unity, however, strains were beginning to show. SNCC's John Lewis had to be dissuaded from giving a speech critical of other civil rights groups, the Kennedy administration, and the major political parties. Other leaders feared he would shatter the harmony of the event. Lewis acceded to this argument and toned down his speech. Nonetheless, SNCC continued to push in its own direction in 1964, intent on challenging the legitimacy of the all-white Mississippi Democratic Party and its delegation to the Democratic National Convention. Ultimately, SNCC's actions would test the commitment of the national Democratic Party as well.

In the summer of 1964 SNCC brought hundreds of young volunteers to Mississippi, intending to register voters into the new Mississippi Freedom Democratic Party (MFDP). These civil rights workers faced continual harassment and physical violence. Three of their number—Michael Schwerner, James Cheney, and Andrew Goodman—were murdered by southern whites fanatically opposed to desegregation.

Despite the hardships and threats, the MFDP did meet in state convention and selected an alternative slate of delegates to the all-white regular Mississippians. At the Democratic Convention in Atlantic City, the MFDP delegation, led by Aaron Henry and Fannie Lou Hamer, hoped to sway the convention to accept its credentials. After compelling testimony, they were offered what they considered a meager compromise—two at-large seats. Rejecting the proposal, they left the convention and returned to Mississippi.

By 1965 civil rights activities had made remarkable strides in the areas of school desegregation, public facilities, and, with the Voting Rights Act, the franchise. But the defeat in Atlantic City left a gnawing sense of disillusionment and foreboding, ushering in an era when achievements would be won less easily and when other national concerns would take precedence among the nation's political leaders.

The Jackson Sit-In

ANNE MOODY

The decision of four North Carolina A&T freshmen to sit in at the lunch counter of the local Woolworth's initiated a new phase of civil rights activity. It also drew black college students from throughout the South into new actions. Among them was Anne Moody. This account of her participation in a Jackson, Mississippi, sit-in comes from her poignant and compelling memoir, Coming of Age in Mississippi.

I had become very friendly with my social science professor, John Salter, who was in charge of NAACP activities on campus. All during the year, while the NAACP conducted a boycott of the downtown stores in Jackson, I had been one of Salter's most faithful canvassers and church speakers. During the last week of school, he told me that sit-in demonstrations were about to start in Jackson and that he wanted me to be the spokesman for a team that would sit-in at Woolworth's lunch counter. The two other demonstrators would be classmates of mine, Memphis and Pearlena. Pearlena was a dedicated NAACP worker, but Memphis had not been very involved in the Movement on campus. It seemed that the organization had had a rough time finding students who were in a position to go to jail. I had nothing to lose one way or the other. Around ten o'clock the morning of the demonstrations, NAACP headquarters alerted the news services. As a result, the police department was also informed, but neither the policemen nor the newsmen knew exactly where or when the demonstrations would start. They stationed themselves along Capitol Street and waited.

To divert attention from the sit-in at Woolworth's, the picketing started at J.C. Penney's a good fifteen minutes before. The pickets were allowed to walk up and down in front of the store three or four times before they were arrested. At exactly 11 A.M., Pearlena, Memphis, and I entered Woolworth's from the rear entrance. We separated as soon as we stepped into the store, and made small purchases from various counters. Pearlena had given Memphis her watch. He was to let us know when it was 11:14. At 11:14 we were to join him near the lunch counter and at exactly 11:15 we were to take seats at it.

Seconds before 11:15 we were occupying three seats at the previously segregated Woolworth's lunch counter. In the beginning the waitresses seemed to ignore us, as if they really didn't know what was going on. Our waitress walked past us a couple of times before she noticed we had started to write our own orders down and realized we wanted service. She asked us what we wanted. We began to read to her from our order slips. She told us that we would be served at the back counter, which was for Negroes.

"We would like to be served here," I said.

The waitress started to repeat what she had said, then stopped in the middle of the sentence. She turned the lights out behind the counter, and she and the other waitresses almost ran to the back of the store, deserting all their white customers. I guess they thought that violence would start immediately after the whites at the counter realized what was going on. There were five or six other people at the counter. A couple of them just got up and walked away. A girl sitting next to me finished her banana split before leaving. A middle-aged white woman who had not yet been served rose from her seat and came over to us. "I'd like to stay here with you," she said, "but my husband is waiting."

The newsmen came in just as she was leaving. They must have discovered what was going on shortly after some of the people began to leave the store. One of the newsmen ran behind the woman who spoke to us and asked her to identify herself. She refused to give her name, but said she was a native of Vicksburg and a former resident of California. When asked why she had said what she had said to us, she replied, "I am in sympathy with the Negro movement." By this time a crowd of cameramen and reporters had gathered around us taking pictures and asking questions, such as Where were we from? Why did we sit-in? What organization sponsored it? Were we students? From what school? How were we classified?

I told them that we were all students at Tougaloo College, that we were represented by no particular organization, and that we planned to stay there even after the store closed. "All we want is service," was my reply to one of them. After they had finished probing for about twenty minutes, they were almost ready to leave.

At noon, students from a nearby white high school started pouring in to Woolworth's. When they first saw us they were sort of surprised. They didn't know how to react. A few started to heckle and the newsmen became interested again. Then the white students started chanting all kinds of anti-Negro slogans. We were called a little bit of everything. The rest of the seats except the three we were occupying had been roped off to prevent others from sitting down. A couple of the boys took one end of the rope and made it into a hangman's noose. Several attempts were made to put it around our necks. The crowds grew as more students and adults came in for lunch.

We kept our eyes straight forward and did not look at the crowd except for occasional glances to see what was going on. All of a sudden I saw a face I remembered—the drunkard from the bus station sit-in. My eyes lingered on him just long enough for us to recognize each other. Today he was drunk too, so I don't think he remembered where he had seen me before. He took out a knife, opened it, put it in his pocket, and then began to pace the floor. At this point, I told Memphis and Pearlena what was going on. Memphis suggested that we pray. We bowed our heads, and all hell broke loose. A man rushed forward, threw Memphis from his seat, and slapped my face. Then another man who worked in the store threw me against an adjoining counter.

Down on my knees on the floor, I saw Memphis lying near the lunch counter with blood running out of the corners of his mouth. As he tried to protect his face, the man who'd thrown him down kept kicking him against the head. If he had worn hard-soled shoes instead of sneakers, the first kick probably would have killed Memphis. Finally a man dressed in plain clothes identified himself as a police officer and arrested Memphis and his attacker.

Pearlena had been thrown to the floor. She and I got back on our stools after Memphis was arrested. There were some white Tougaloo teachers in the crowd. They asked Pearlena and me if we wanted to leave. They said that things were getting too rough. We didn't know what to do. While we were trying to make up our minds, we were joined by Joan Trumpauer. Now there were three of us and we were integrated. The crowd began to chant, "Communists, Communists, Communists." Some old man in the crowd ordered the students to take us off the stools.

"Which one should I get first?" a big husky boy said.

"That white nigger," the old man said.

The boy lifted Joan from the counter by her waist and carried her out of the store. Simultaneously, I was snatched from my stool by two high school students. I was dragged about thirty feet toward the door by my hair when someone made them turn me loose. As I was getting up off the floor, I saw Joan coming back inside. We started back to the center of the counter to join Pearlena. Lois Chaffee, a white Tougaloo faculty member, was now sitting next to her. So Joan and I just climbed across the rope at the front end of the counter and sat down. There were now four of us, two whites and two Negroes, all women. The mob started smearing us with ketchup, mustard, sugar, pies, and everything on the counter. Soon Joan and I were joined by John Salter, but the moment he sat down he was hit on the jaw with what appeared to be brass knuckles. Blood gushed from his face and someone threw salt into the open wound. Ed King, Tougaloo's chaplain, rushed to him.

At the other end of the counter, Lois and Pearlena were joined by George Raymond, a CORE field worker and a student from Jackson State College. Then a Negro high school boy sat down next to me. The mob took spray paint from the counter and sprayed it on the new demonstrators. The high school student had on a white shirt; the word "nigger" was written on his back with red spray paint.

We sat there for three hours taking a beating when the manager decided to close the store because the mob had begun to go wild with stuff from other counters. He begged and begged everyone to leave. But even after fifteen minutes of begging, no one budged. They would not leave until we did. Then Dr. Beittel, the president of Tougaloo College, came running in. He said he had just heard what was happening.

About ninety policemen were standing outside the store; they had been watching the whole thing through the windows, but had not come in to stop the mob or do anything. President Beittel went outside and asked Captain Ray to come and escort us out. The captain refused, stating the manager had to invite him in before he could enter the premises, so Dr. Beittel himself brought us out. He had told the police that they had better protect us after we were outside the store. When we got outside, the policemen formed a single line that blocked the mob from us. However, they were allowed to throw at us everything they had collected. Within ten minutes, we were picked up by Reverend King in his station wagon and taken to the NAACP headquarters on Lynch Street.

After the sit-in, all I could think of was how sick Mississippi whites were. They believed so much in the segregated Southern way of life, they would kill to preserve it. I sat there in the NAACP office and thought of how many times they had killed when this way of life was threatened. I knew that the killing had just begun. "Many more will die before it is over with," I thought. Before the sit-in, I had always hated the whites in Mississippi. Now I knew it was impossible for me to hate sickness. The whites had a disease, an incurable disease in its final stage. What were our chances against such a disease? I thought of the students, the young Negroes who had just begun to protest, as young interns. When these young interns got older, I thought, they would be the best doctors in the world for social problems.

SNCC: Founding Statement

The eruption of sit-ins throughout the South led to the calling of a general meeting of black student leaders in the spring of 1960. Under the leadership of SCLC's Ella Baker, these students formed their own organization, the Student Nonviolent Coordinating Committee (SNCC), with Baker as executive secretary.

We affirm the philosophical or religious ideal of nonviolence as the foundation of our purpose, the presupposition of our belief, and the manner of our action.

Nonviolence, as it grows from the Judeo-Christian tradition, seeks a social order of justice permeated by love. Integration of human endeavor represents the crucial first step towards such a society.

Through nonviolence, courage displaces fear. Love transcends hate. Acceptance dissipates prejudice; hope ends despair. Faith reconciles doubt. Peace dominates war. Mutual regards cancel enmity. Justice for all overthrows injustice. The redemptive community supersedes immoral social systems.

By appealing to conscience and standing on the moral nature of human existence, nonviolence nurtures the atmosphere in which reconciliation and justice become actual possibilities.

Although each local group in this movement must diligently work out the clear meaning of this statement of purpose, each act or phase of our corporate effort must reflect a genuine spirit of love and good-will.

The Freedom Rides

In 1961 James Farmer became national director of the Congress of Racial Equality (CORE), an older civil rights organization. Inspired by the new intensity of civil rights actions and aware of the Kennedy administration's unwillingness to enforce a Supreme Court decision desegregating the facilities that served interstate bus transportation, Farmer decided to focus attention on this issue. Organizing a group of black and white volunteers, including SNCC's John Lewis, these "Freedom Riders" set out on two buses to travel the South—from Washington south to Atlanta and then from Atlanta west to New Orleans. These recollections were collected by Howell Raines, now editorial page editor of the New York Times, *for his oral history of the civil rights movement,* My Soul Is Rested.

JAMES FARMER

I was impressed by the fact that most of the activity thus far had been of local people working on their local problems—Greensborans sitting-in in Greensboro and Atlantans sitting-in in Atlanta—. . . . We somehow had to cut across state lines and establish the position that we were entitled to act any place in the country, no matter where we hung our hat and called home, because it was our country.

So those were the two things: cutting across state lines, putting the movement on wheels, so to speak, and remaining in jail, not only for its publicity value but for the financial pressure it would put upon the segregators. We decided that a good approach here would be to move away from restaurant lunch counters. That had been the Southern student sit-in movement, and anything we would do on that would be anticlimactic now. We would have to move into another area and so we decided to move into the transportation, interstate transportation. . . .

Reprinted by permission of The Putnam Publishing Group from *My Soul Is Rested* by Howell Raines. Copyright © 1977 by Howell Raines.

So we, following the Gandhian technique, wrote to Washington. We wrote to the Justice Department, to the FBI, and to the President, and wrote to Greyhound Bus Company and Trailways Bus Company and told them that on May first or May fourth—whatever the date was, I forget now—we were going to have a Freedom Ride. Blacks and whites were going to leave Washington, D.C., on Greyhound and Trailways, deliberately violating the segregated seating requirements and at each rest stop would violate the segregated use of facilities. And we would be nonviolent, absolutely nonviolent, throughout the campaign, and we would accept the consequences of our actions. This was a deliberate act of civil disobedience. . . .

We got no reply from Justice. Bobby Kennedy, no reply. We got no reply from the FBI. We got no reply from the White House, from President Kennedy. We got no reply from Greyhound or Trailways. . . .

We had some of the group of thirteen sit at a simulated counter asking for coffee. Somebody else refused them service, and then we'd have others come in as white hoodlums to beat 'em up and knock them off the counter and club 'em around and kick 'em in the ribs and stomp 'em, and they were quite realistic, I must say. I thought they bent over backwards to be realistic. I was aching all over. . . . Then we'd reverse roles and play it over and over again and have lengthy discussions of it. . . . I felt, by the way, that by the time that group left Washington, they were prepared for anything, even death, and this was a possibility, and we knew it, when we got to the Deep South.

Through Virginia we had no problem. In fact they had heard we were coming, Greyhound and Trailways, and they had taken down the For Colored and For Whites signs, and we rode right through. Yep. The same was true in North Carolina. Signs had come down just the previous day, blacks told us. And so the letters in advance did something.

In South Carolina it was a different story. . . . John Lewis started into a white waiting room in some town in South Carolina . . . and there were several young white hoodlums, leather jackets, ducktail haircuts, standing there smoking, and they blocked the door and said, "Nigger, you can't come in here." He said, "I have every right to enter this waiting room according to the Supreme Court of the United States. . . ."

They said, "Shit on that." He tried to walk past, and they clubbed him, beat him, and knocked him down. One of the white Freedom Riders . . . Albert Bigelow, who had been a Navy captain during World War II, big, tall, strapping fellow, very impressive, from Connecticut—then stepped right between the hoodlums and John Lewis. Lewis had been absorbing more of the punishment. They then clubbed Bigelow and finally knocked him down, and that took some knocking because he was a pretty strapping fellow, and he didn't hit back at all. [They] knocked him down, and at this point police arrived and intervened. They didn't make any arrests. Intervened.

Well, we went through the rest of South Carolina without incident and then to Atlanta, Georgia, and there we met with Dr. King. We called him and told him we were coming, and he had dinner with us and wished us well. . . .

JOHN LEWIS

He had left the Freedom Ride in South Carolina to keep an appointment for a job interview. Returning to Nashville on May 14, he learned of the attacks in Anniston and Birmingham and that CORE, heeding Attorney General Robert Kennedy's request for a "cooling-off" period, had canceled the ride altogether. He and a group of sit-in veterans believed that if the Freedom Ride did not continue, segregationists would conclude that they could, indeed, defeat the Movement with violence and intimidation. Using money left over from the sit-in treasury and ignoring the advice of Nashville's SCLC affiliate, they bought tickets for Birmingham and announced that the Freedom Ride was on again. At the Birmingham city limit, a policeman halted their bus and informed the driver that he was taking charge of the vehicle. When the bus pulled into the station, the "Birmingham police department put up newspapers all around the bus windows so you couldn't see out, and no one could see in." Shielded from inspection, they waited until "Bull" Connor arrived on the scene and ordered them taken into "protective custody." Thus began one of the most bizarre episodes of the Movement.

So they took us all to the jail, the Birmingham city jail. Now this was on a Wednesday. We went to jail and stayed in jail Wednesday night. We didn't eat anything. We went on a hunger strike.

They were very, very nice. They didn't rough us up or anything like that, just very nice, as I recall. They put us in jail, segregated us . . . and that Thursday we stayed in jail all day. That Thursday night around midnight, "Bull" Connor and two reporters . . . and maybe one or two detectives came up to the jail, and "Bull" Connor said they were going to take us back to Nashville, back to the college campus where we belonged. We said, "Well, we don't want to go back. We have a right to be on this Freedom Ride. We have a right to travel. We plan to go to Montgomery, and from Montgomery we're going to Jackson and to New Orleans." And he insisted. And people just sorta went limp, so they had people literally to pick us up and place us into these cars. . . .

Anyway, they drove us on the highway, and "Bull" Connor was really funny. I was in the car that he was in and this young lady, Katherine Burke. He was really funny, he was really joking with us, saying that he was gonna take us back to Nashville, and we told him we would invite him to the campus, and he could have breakfast with us and that type of thing. He said he would like that. It was that type of conversation that we had going with "Bull" Connor.

We got to the Tennessee-Alabama line. . . . They dropped us off, saying . . . "You can take the bus back to Nashville." They literally left us there. We didn't know anybody, didn't know any place to go. . . .

What we did, we started walking down a road, and we saw a railroad track, and we crossed this railroad track and went to an old house. There was an elderly couple there, must have been in their late sixties, early seventies. We knocked on the door, and they let us in, and they was just really frightened. They'd heard about the Freedom Riders. . . .

They didn't really want to let us in, but they did, and we called Nashville and told 'em what had happened. Called Diane Nash on the telephone. She was in the local student movement office there in Nashville, and she wanted to know whether we wanted to continue the ride or whether we wanted a car to pick us up to bring us back to Nashville. We told her to send a car to take us back to Birmingham. We wanted to continue the ride.

In the meantime, we hadn't had anything to eat, and we were very hungry. 'Cause this is now Friday morning, and we hadn't had any-thing to eat since, I guess, early Wednesday. This man, this elderly man, got in his pickup truck and went around during the early morn-ing to two or three stores and bought something like bologna and bread and cornflakes. Anyway, we had a little meal there, and apparently some of the white people in the community came by, and he told 'em some of his relatives were visiting from Nashville. We waited around till the car from Nashville got there, and this was really something else. It was seven of us and the driver now, eight of us, got in that car on our way back to Birmingham, and we heard a reporter on the radio saying the students had been taken to the state line and apparently they were ... back in Nashville on their college campuses. ...

So we drove back to Birmingham, and Rev. Shuttlesworth and several other ministers from the Alabama Christian Movement for Human Rights met us there, and we went directly back to the Greyhound bus station. And we tried to get on the bus around, I recall, three o'clock, on the Greyhound bus from Birmingham to Montgomery, and apparently Greyhound canceled the bus taking off. We were going to try to get on one at five-something, and this bus driver said something that I'll never forget. He said, "I only have one life to give and I'm not going to give it to CORE or the NAACP."

> He and his group, along with about twenty fresh volunteers from Nashville, spent the night on the wooden benches of the bus station. Departing from their previous practice, the police repelled a white mob which gathered during the night. Finally a reporter who was covering the story brought a message: "Apparently you all are going to get a chance to go. Attorney General Kennedy has been in contact with Greyhound."

The same bus driver came out to the bus about eight-thirty on Saturday morning, and we got on a bus from Birmingham to Montgomery. And apparently the arrangement was that every so many miles there would be a state patrol car and there would be a plane. We did see—I don't know whether it was the arrangement or not—we did see a small plane flying up above the bus for so many miles and we did have the patrol car. ...*

It was a nice ride between Birmingham and Montgomery. A few miles outside of Montgomery you just didn't see anything. You didn't see the plane, didn't see the state patrol car. It seemed like everything

---

*In fact, an airplane and sixteen highway patrol cars accompanied the bus, despite Governor Patterson's public statement that "we are not going to escort those agitators. We stand firm on that position."

sort of disappeared, and the moment that we arrived in that station, it was the strangest feeling to me. It was something strange, that you knew something. It was really weird. It was an eerie feeling. There was a funny peace there, a quietness. You didn't see anything happening. Apparently, when you really look back, the mob there must have been so planned and was so out of sight . . . it just sorta appeared, just appeared on the scene.

You didn't see any sign of it as you went into the bus station?

None. Just didn't see anything. When we drove up, we didn't see anything. . . . We got most of the young ladies in a cab. So they got in a cab and the black cab driver didn't want to drive, because at that time there was two white students, young ladies from Peabody or Scarritt, and in Alabama there was a law that you couldn't have an integrated cab. So the two young ladies got out, and at that very time, this mob started all over the place. So everybody, all the young ladies, got away, and the two young white girls were running down the street trying to get away. That's when John Siegenthaler got hit.* And at that time, the rest of us, mostly fellas, just literally standing there because we couldn't run—no place to go really.†

This was out in the lot?

Just out in the lot. And if you've been at the bus station, there's a rail there. . . . Down below is the entrance to the courthouse, the Post Office building. So when the mob kept coming, several of the people, several of the fellas jumped over and were able to get in the

---

*Robert Kennedy's administrative assistant, sent to Alabama as an observer.

†Freedom Rider William Harbour: "There was nobody there. I didn't see anybody standin' around the bus station. I saw some taxicabs there. That was about it. So the bus driver opened the bus door up and just walked away from the bus. I guess in less than fifteen minutes, we had a mob of people, five or six hundred people with ax handles, chains and everything else. . . . Soon as we walked off the bus, John Lewis said to me, 'Bill, it doesn't look right. . . .'

"Everything happened so quick. There was a standstill for the first two or three minutes. . . . They were closin' in on us, and we were standin' still tryin' to decide what should we do in order to protect the whites we had with us. But then you had a middle-aged white female hollerin', 'Git them niggers, git them niggers . . . ,' and that urged the crowd on. From then on, they was constantly movin' in. I don't think she ever hit anybody or threw anything whatsoever. Just the idea she started, just kept pushin' and pushin' and pushin' . . . It started just like that."

basement of the Post Office, and the postmaster there opened it and made it possible for people to come in and escape the mob. And I said—I remember saying that we shouldn't run, we should just stand there, 'cause the mob was beating people. And the last thing that I recall, I was hit with a crate, a wooden crate what you have soda in, and was left lying in the street. And I remember the Attorney General of Alabama, MacDonald Gallion, serving this injunction that Judge Walter B. Jones had issued saying that it was unlawful for interracial groups to travel. While I was lying there on the ground, he brought this injunction.

Wake Up America

JOHN LEWIS

By summer 1963 national attention to civil rights had led to the Kennedy administration's introduction of a civil rights bill, ultimately passed in 1964. A March on Washington planned for August 1963 was transformed from a protest against government disinterest to a show of unity and support for the bill. Within the movement, however, strains were beginning to develop. SNCC's John Lewis initially intended a speech critical of both the government and other elements within the movement. He was persuaded to tone down his speech in the interest of harmony. His original text, reprinted below, details his critique of the proposed civil rights bill, as well as the concerns of SNCC about the direction of the movement.

We march today for jobs and freedom, but we have nothing to be proud of. For hundreds and thousands of our brothers are not here. They have no money for their transportation, for they are now receiving starvation wages . . . or no wages, at all.

Reprinted by permission, John Lewis

In good conscience, we cannot support the administration's civil rights bill, for it is too little, and too late. There's not one thing in the bill that will protect our people from police brutality.

This bill will not protect young children and old women from police dogs and fire hoses, for engaging in peaceful demonstrations. This bill will not protect the citizens of Danville, Virginia, who must live in constant fear in a police state. This bill will not protect the hundreds of people who have been arrested on trumped-up charges. What about the three young men—SNCC field secretaries—in Americus, Georgia, who face the death penalty for engaging in peaceful protest?

The voting section of this bill will not help thousands of black citizens who want to vote. It will not help the citizens of Mississippi, of Alabama, and Georgia, who are qualified to vote, but lack a 6th grade education. "One man, one vote," is the African cry. It is ours, too. (It must be ours.)

People have been forced to leave their homes because they dared to exercise their right to register to vote. What is in the bill that will protect the homeless and starving people of this nation? What is there in this bill to insure the equality of a maid who earns $5 a week in the home of a family whose income is $100,000 a year?

For the first time in 100 years this nation is being awakened to the fact that segregation is evil and that it must be destroyed in all forms. *Your presence today proves* that you have been aroused to the point of action.

We are now involved in a serious revolution. This nation is still a place of cheap political leaders who build their careers on immoral compromises and ally themselves with open forms of political, economic and social exploitation. What political leader here can stand up and say, "My party is the party of principles"? The party of Kennedy is also the party of Eastland. The party of Javits is also the party of Goldwater. Where is *our* party?

In some parts of the South we work in the fields from sunup to sundown for $12 a week. In Albany, Georgia, nine of our leaders have been indicted not by Dixiecrats but by the Federal Government for peaceful protest. But what did the Federal Government do when Albany's Deputy Sheriff beat Attorney C. B. King and left him half-dead? What did the Federal Government do when local police officials kicked and assaulted the pregnant wife of Slater King, and she lost her baby?

It seems to me that the Albany indictment is part of a conspiracy on the part of the Federal Government and local politicians in the interest of political expediency.

Moreover, we have learned—and you should know—since we are here for Jobs and Freedom—that within the past ten days a spokesman for the administration appeared in secret session before the committee that's writing the civil rights bill and opposed and almost killed a provision that would have guaranteed in voting suits for the first time fair federal district judges. And, I might add, this administration's bill, or any other civil rights bill—such as the 1960 civil rights act—will be totally worthless when administered by racist judges, many of whom have been consistently appointed by President Kennedy.

I want to know, which side is the Federal Government on?

The revolution is at hand, and we must free ourselves of the chains of political and economic slavery. The nonviolent revolution is saying, "We will not wait for the courts to act, for we have been waiting for hundreds of years. We will not wait for the President, the Justice Department, nor Congress, but we will take matters into our own hands and create a source of power, outside of any national structure that could and would assure us a victory." To those who have said, "Be Patient and Wait," we must say that, "Patience is a dirty and nasty word." We cannot be patient, we do not want to be free gradually, we want our freedom, and we want it now. We cannot depend on any political party, for both the Democrats and the Republicans have betrayed the basic principles of the Declaration of Independence.

We all recognize the fact that if any social, political and economic changes are to take place in our society, the people, the masses, must bring them about. In the struggle we must seek more than mere civil rights; we must work for the community of love, peace and true brotherhood. Our minds, souls, and hearts cannot rest until freedom and justice exist for *all the people.*

The revolution is a serious one. Mr. Kennedy is trying to take the revolution out of the street and put it in the courts. Listen, Mr. Kennedy, listen Mr. Congressman, listen fellow citizens, the black masses are on the march for jobs and freedom, and we must say to the politicians that there won't be a "cooling-off" period.

All of us must get in the revolution. Get in and stay in the streets of every city, every village and every hamlet of this nation, until true Freedom comes, until the revolution is complete. In the Delta of Mississippi, in Southwest Georgia, in Alabama, Harlem, Chicago, Detroit, Philadelphia and all over this nation—the black masses are on the march!

We won't stop now. All of the forces of Eastland, Barnett, Wallace, and Thurmond won't stop this revolution. The time will come when we will not confine our marching to Washington. We will march through the South, through the Heart of Dixie, the way Sherman did. We shall pursue our own "scorched earth" policy and burn Jim Crow to the ground—nonviolently. We shall crack the South into a thousand pieces and put them back together in the image of democracy. We will make the action of the past few months look petty. And I say to you, WAKE UP AMERICA!!

Letters from Mississippi

As part of its new grass-roots approach, SNCC proposed to send workers into Mississippi in the summer of 1964. The intention was to create an alternative to the all-white Mississippi Democratic Party and to challenge its delegation at the national Democratic Convention that summer in Atlantic City. Trained in nonviolence in Oxford, Ohio, these volunteers—men and women, black and white, northern and southern—traveled to Mississippi to register voters, teach illiterate adults and children to read, and establish the Mississippi Freedom Democratic Party. The MFDP would conform to the party's national regulations regarding openness to membership without racial and ethnic barriers. This would form the basis of the challenge at the national convention. The volunteers faced constant harassment, physical abuse, and, in the case of three, murder. These letters, collected by Elizabeth Sutherland, represent only a handful of the many sent back to families and friends that summer.

Dear Folks,

A great deal of tension and a great deal of camaraderie here at Oxford. Workshops and role-playing are constant. We staged one situation, a screaming mob lining the steps to the courthouse while a small band of registrants tried to get through. The inevitable happened—what will actually happen in Mississippi happened. The chanting mob (instructed to be as brutal as possible, and to pull no punches) turned into a clawing, pounding mob, and we volunteer registrants were down in our crouched-up ball. Casualties? A couple of scratches, a sprained ankle, and one cameraman who got swept up was a little bit shaken. It seems like brutal play, and it is. We've got to be ready for anything, and we must prepare for it ourselves. Once we get south we are nonviolent; we must get whatever there is in our systems out now, and we must also learn to take the worst. Some of the staff members walk around carrying sections of hose. This strangely terrible training in brutality may well save lives. (I must confess, I have not been able to take part in even the screaming of a mob scene, much less the pummeling. Wherever possible, I am among the victims.)

We have registration workshops, too. And lecturers came from all over the country to speak to us. And we sing. What "We Shall Overcome" is to the national movement, "We'll never turn back" is to the Mississippi workers. It is a slow song, measured out in grief and determination. The final verse goes,

> We have hung our head and cried,
> Cried for those like Lee*
> who died
> Died for you and died for me,
> Died for the cause of equality,
>> But we will never turn back
>> Until we've all been free
>> And we have equality, and we have equality.

Love,

Jim

Dear Dad,

The mood up here [in Oxford, Ohio] is, of course, very strained with those three guys who disappeared Sunday, dead, most likely. Saturday night, I ate dinner with the wife of one of them. She was telling me about all the great things she and her husband were working on.

---

*Herbert Lee, Negro voter registration worker killed in Liberty, Miss., in 1961.

She looks younger than me. What does she do now? Give up the movement? What a terrible rotten life this is! I feel that the only meaningful type of work is the Movement but I don't want myself or anyone I've met to have to die. I'm so shook up that death just doesn't seem so awful anymore, though. I'm no different from anyone else and if they're risking their lives, then so must I. But I just can't comprehend why people must die to achieve something so basic and simple as Freedom. . . .

Love,
Sylvie

Dear Folks:

Yesterday was non-violence day here. In the morning we heard Jim Lawson of Nashville, who gave us the word on non-violence as a way of life. Lawson speaks of a moral confrontation with one's enemies, catching the other guy's eye, speaking to him with love, if possible, and so on. . . . "Violence always brings more harm to the people who use it; economic and political forces have no place in the Movement . . . etc." These are the things Lawson came up with. . . . I feel very strongly that he does NOT represent the Movement.

Stokely Carmichael of SNCC rebutted him in the afternoon session: Nonviolence used to work. . . . There comes a point when you get tired of being beaten and going back the next day for your beating for 5 days in a row. You get tired of being asked whether you are a Negro or a nigger, and ending up on the floor of the police station screaming at the top of your lungs that yes, you are a nigger, boss. You get tired of seeing young women smashed in the face right in front of your eyes. Stokely does not advocate violence. No SNCC workers are armed, nor are there guns in any SNCC office. What he is saying is that love and moral confrontations have no place in front of a brute who beats you till you cry nigger.

My feelings, and I think these are common, is that nonviolence is a perverted way of life, but a necessary tactic and technique. It is harmful to the human person to feel that he must love a man who has a foot in his face. The only reason that I will not hit back is because then I will be in the hospital two weeks instead of one, and will be useless to the movement during that extra week when I can only read Gandhi's latest book on how to win friends and influence people. . . .

Bill

Dear John and Cleo,   Canton, July 10

Our hostesses are brave women. And their fear is not at all mixed with resentment of us, but that makes it none the easier for them. The other morning a local newscaster said that someone was reported to have offered someone else $400 to bomb all the houses where volunteers are staying. I'm not convinced that that particular story has any basis, but it touched off the terror that must lie latent always in our sisters' hearts. I overheard one of them on the telephone: "My guhls probly think I'm out of mah head; I been singin' all mornin, every song I knows—I just has to." And she had been, moaning "Lord have musee" in between the songs. I talked with her a little bit. She told me she knows people have suffered and died too long and that we must take risks now so it won't go on forever. But that doesn't make the risk any less painful to bear. She sleeps with a hatchet under her bed. She told me she used to have a gun under her pillow until one night when she almost accidentally shot a neighbor boy. . . .

Jo

Dear Mom   Holly Springs
When we walk up to a house there are always children out front. They look up and see white men in the car, and fear and caution cover their expressions. Those terrified eyes are never quite out of my mind; they drive me as little else could. The children run to their parents, hide behind them. We walk up, smile, say howdy, and hold out our hands. As we shake hands I tell them my name. They tell me their names and I say Mr.—, how do you do. It is likely the first time in the life of this farmer or housewife that a white man has shaken hands with them like that. This does not necessarily bode well to them. They think, if Mr. Charlie knew. . . . Many are sharecroppers, who must turn over a third to a half of the year's harvest to a man who does no work at all, but who owns the land they till. They may be evicted, and have often been for far less serious offenses. Nearly everyone black in Mississippi is at least a year in debt. The threat of suspended credit and foreclosure is a tremendous burden. . . .

Love,
Bob

July 29
Everyday this week—the 22nd to 29th—the men of the community hammered and poured cement. At noon, about 7 or 8 women all gathered at the center with fried chicken, fish, salad, gallons of Kool-Aid and apple turnovers, and served them to the men, we teachers, and each other. It is a thing of beauty to see us all work together. Tuesday and Wednesday was the laying of the sub-floor. Two men cut the wood, two or three teenage boys and girls lay the wood down and hammered it in, a few more are bringing more wood. We are a living

repudiation of the "too many cooks" theory. It should be up by Saturday, or at latest Tuesday. The land was given by a local man for "the sum of one dollar," and deeds were drawn up. The teenagers are selling refreshments to raise money for the center, as well as membership cards for a dollar. It will hold the library, a snackbar, office space and recreation area. . . .

August 5

About 4 men or teenagers armed with rifles and pistols stand guard. Every local car that goes by has to honk a specific number of times. . . . If anyone does attempt to bomb or burn the center, they haven't got a chance. I live only about 50 yards away so I take over coffee, cookies, cigarettes, tobacco, etc., to the guards and talk with them. . . .

Greenwood, June 29

We have heard rumors twice to the effect that the three men were found weighted down in that river. Both stories, though the same, were later completely dropped in an hour or so. How do you like that guy Gov. Johnson saying that they might be hiding in the North or maybe in Cuba for all he knew. . . .

Tchula, July 16

Yesterday while the Mississippi River was being dragged looking for the three missing civil rights workers, two bodies of Negroes were found—one cut in half and one without a head. Mississippi is the only state where you can drag a river any time and find bodies you were not expecting. Things are really much better for rabbits—there's a closed season on rabbits.

On August 7, James Chaney's funeral and memorial service took place in Meridian.

Dear Folks,   Laurel, August 11
. . . The memorial service began around 7:30 with over 120 people filling the small, wooden-pew lined church. David Dennis of CORE, the Assistant Director for the Mississippi Summer Project, spoke for COFO [Council of federated organizations, a coalition of civil rights groups]. He talked to the Negro people of Meridian—it was a speech to move people, to end the lethargy, to make people stand up. It went something like this:

"I am not here to memorialize James Chaney, I am not here to pay tribute—I am too sick and tired. Do YOU hear me, I am S-I-C-K and T-I-R-E-D. I have attended too many memorials, too many funerals. This has got to stop. Mack Parker, Medgar Evers, Herbert Lee, Lewis

Allen, Emmett Till, four little girls in Birmingham, a 13-year-old boy in Birmingham, and the list goes on and on. I have attended these funerals and memorials and I am SICK and TIRED. But the trouble is that YOU are NOT sick and tired and for that reason YOU, yes YOU, are to blame, Everyone of your damn souls. And if you are going to let this continue now then you are to blame, yes YOU. Just as much as the monsters of hate who pulled the trigger or brought down the club; just as much to blame as the sheriff and the chief of police, as the governor in Jackson who said that he 'did not have time' for Mrs. Schwerner when she went to see him, and just as much to blame as the President and Attorney General in Washington who wouldn't provide protection for Chaney, Goodman and Schwerner when we told them that protection was necessary in Neshoba County. . . . Yes, I am angry, I AM. And it's high time that you got angry too, angry enough to go up to the courthouse Monday and register—every one of you. Angry enough to take five and ten other people with you. Then and only then can these brutal killings be stopped. Remember it is your sons and your daughters who have been killed all these years and you have done nothing about it, and if you don't do nothing NOW baby, I say God Damn Your Souls. . . ."

Testimony Before the Democratic National Convention

FANNIE LOU HAMER AND RITA SCHWERNER

Despite the hardships and harassment, SNCC volunteers had registered enough voters in 1964 to hold a state convention and select a delegation to the Democratic Convention in Atlantic City. Their intention was to challenge the all-white regulars before the Credentials Committee, hoping to be seated in place of the segregationists. Televised hearings on August 22, the Saturday before the convention opening, featured the compelling testimony of Fannie Lou Hamer, vice chairmen of the delegation, and Rita Schwerner, widow of slain civil rights worker Michael Schwerner. Lyndon Johnson, wishing to defuse any hostility at a convention sure to nominate him, interrupted the telecast of Hamer's testimony with a presidential announcement. Further, he dispatched vice-presidential hopeful Hubert Humphrey, sponsor of the 1964 Civil Rights Bill, to negotiate a settlement. Humphrey and his aide, Walter Mondale, brokered a compromise that would have seated two members of the MFDP as "delegates-at-large," with a promise of stricter qualifications for 1968 delegations. While both Martin Luther King, Jr., and MFDP lawyer Joseph Rauh favored the compromise, the delegation turned it down. "We didn't come here for no two seats," Hamer proclaimed. They boarded a bus and returned home to Mississippi, disillusioned with Washington's commitment to civil rights.

REMARKS OF MRS. FANNIE LOU HAMER

MRS. HAMER: Mr. Chairman, and the Credentials Committee, my name is Mrs. Fannie Lou Hamer, and I live at 626 East Lafayette Street, Ruleville, Mississippi, Sunflower County, the home of Senator James O. Eastland, and Senator Stennis.

It was the 31st of August in 1962 that 18 of us traveled 26 miles to the county courthouse in Indianola to try to register to try to become first-class citizens.

We was met in Indianola by Mississippi men, Highway Patrolmens, and they only allowed two of us in to take the literacy test at the time. After we had taken this test and started back to Ruleville, we was held up by the City Police and the State Highway Patrolmen and carried back to Indianola where the bus driver was charged that day with driving a bus the wrong color.

After we paid the fine among us, we continued on to Ruleville, and Reverend Jeff Sunny carried me four miles in the rural area where I had worked as a timekeeper and sharecropper for 18 years. I was met there by my children, who told me the plantation owner was angry because I had gone down to try to register.

After they told me, my husband came, and said the plantation owner was raising cain because I had tried to register, and before he quit talking the plantation owner came, and said, "Fannie Lou, do you know—did Pap tell you what I said?"

And I said, "Yes, sir."

He said, "I mean that," he said, "If you don't go down and withdraw your registration, you will have to leave, . . . you might have to go because we are not ready for that in Mississippi."

And I addressed him and told him and said "I didn't try to register for you. I tried to register for myself."

I had to leave that same night.

On the 10th of September, 1962, 16 bullets was fired into the home of Mr. and Mrs. Robert Tucker for me. That same night two girls were shot in Ruleville, Mississippi. Also Mr. Joe McDonald's house was shot in.

And in June, the 9th, 1963, I had attended a voter registration workshop, was returning back to Mississippi. Ten of us was traveling by the Continental Trailway bus. When we got to Winona, Mississippi, which is Montgomery County, four of the people got off to use the washroom, and two of the people—to use the restaurant—two of the people wanted to use the washroom.

The four people that had gone in to use the restaurant was ordered out. During that time I was on the bus. But when I looked through the window and saw they had rushed out I got off of the bus to see what had happened, and one of the ladies said, "It was a State Highway Patrolman and a Chief of Police ordered us out."

I got back on the bus and one of the persons had used the washroom got back on the bus, too.

As soon as I was seated on the bus, I saw when they began to get the four people in a highway patrolman's car, I stepped off of the bus to see what was happening and somebody screamed from the car that the four workers was in and said, "Get that one there," and when I went to get in the car, then the man told me I was under arrest, he kicked me.

I was carried to the county jail, and put in the booking room. They left some of the people in the booking room and began to place us in cells. I was placed in a cell with a young woman called Miss Ivesta Simpson. After I was placed in the cell I began to hear sounds of licks and screams. I could hear the sounds of licks and horrible screams, and I could hear somebody say, "Can you say, yes, sir, nigger?

Can you say yes, sir?"

And they would say other horrible names.

She would say, "Yes, I can say yes, sir."

"So, she say it."

She says, "I don't know you well enough."

They beat her, I don't know how long, and after a while she began to pray, and asked God to have mercy on those people.

And it wasn't too long before three white men came to my cell. One of these men was a State Highway Patrolman and he asked me where I was from, and I told him Ruleville, he said, "We are going to check this."

And they left my cell and it wasn't too long before they came back. He said, "You are from Ruleville all right," and he used a curse word, and he said, "We are gonna make you wish you was dead."

I was carried out of that cell into another cell where they had two Negro prisoners. The State Highway Patrolmen ordered the first Negro to take the blackjack.

The first Negro prisoner ordered me, by orders from the State Highway Patrolman for me, to lay down on a bunk bed on my face, and I laid on my face.

The first Negro began to beat, and I was beat by the first Negro until he was exhausted, and I was holding my hands behind me at that time on my left side because I suffered from polio when I was six years old.

After the first Negro had beat until he was exhausted the State Highway Patrolman ordered the second Negro to take the blackjack.

The second Negro began to beat and I began to work my feet, and the State Highway Patrolman ordered the first Negro who had beat to set on my feet to keep me from working my feet. I began to scream and one white man got up and began to beat me in my head and tell me to hush.

One white man—my dress had worked up high, he walked over and pulled my dress down and he pulled my dress back, back up.

I was in jail when Medgar Evers was murdered.

All of this is on account we want to register, to become first-class citizens, and if the Freedom Democratic Party is not seated now, I question America, is this America, the land of the free and the home of the brave where we have to sleep with our telephones off of the hooks because our lives be threatened daily because we want to live as decent human beings, in America?

Thank you.

REMARKS OF MRS. RITA SCHWERNER

MRS. SCHWERNER: Mr. Chairman, thank you.

Members of the Credentials Committee: I am Rita Schwerner, and I am the widow of Michael Schwerner who was killed in Philadelphia, Mississippi, on June 21, of this year.

My husband and I went to Mississippi together in January of this year to establish a community center and to work on voter registration. We went to Meridian, where we worked. My husband was very active in the formation of the Mississippi Freedom Democratic Party. As the two of us became more well-known to the people in Meridian, we received many threats upon our lives. We eventually had to get an unlisted phone number because the threats became too terrifying late at night.

Starting in February, my husband and Mr. James Chaney started working in the area of Neshoba County, in the formation of the Mississippi Freedom Democratic Party and on voter registration. They were on numerous occasions followed by official cars of the County of Neshoba.

Late in the spring, my husband was jailed in Meridian on a phony traffic charge. When he got out of jail, he told me that the officials of the jail attempted to have him beaten by other white prisoners. The prisoners refused to beat him.

The two men with a third, Andrew Goodman, disappeared on June 21 of this year. At the time, I was out of the State for a period of about a week, attending an orientation session for summer registration workers, in Oxford, Ohio. I returned to the state of Mississippi about two days after the disappearance, in an effort to get somebody to help me to find my husband and his two companions.

In the course of this search, I went to Jackson. I was accompanied by Reverend Edwin King, whom you heard speak before you today. We went to the State Capitol building to attempt to see Governor Johnson of Mississippi. The door was slammed in my face by several unidentified men. When they finally agreed to let me into the Governor's office, a Senator Barber of the State Senate spoke with me very rudely, and said I could not see the Governor, then or at any other time, that the Governor was unavailable and he didn't know when he would be available, and I couldn't see him.

I then went with the Reverend King to the Governor's Mansion which is only a few blocks away. It happened that at the time we arrived at the Mansion, Governor Johnson was climbing the steps with Governor Wallace of Alabama. We followed after them and when there was a pause in the conversation the two men were carrying on with others who were around them, other State officials, the Mayor of Jackson also, Reverend King attempted to introduce me to Governor Johnson. The moment Governor Johnson heard my name and who I was, he turned on his heel and with the Governor of Alabama they walked into the Mansion and slammed the door in my face, and I was surrounded by State Highway patrolmen. A Highway patrolman by the name of Harbor told me that I could not see the Governor. They refused to relay my message, and they refused to relay my pleas.

When the bodies of my husband and the other two men were discovered some 2-1/2 weeks ago, I was informed of the discovery by the Federal authorities. The State authorities had in no way tried to do anything to help me. I have not been allowed to see any official report on the condition of the bodies of my husband, or the other two men. No official report has been released for anyone else to see, and I would like you to know that to this day the State of Mississippi and the County of Neshoba has not even sent to me a copy of the death certificate of my husband.

Thank you.

WOMEN IN THE MOVEMENT

In a movement that was continually occupied with equality and personal recognition based on ability, concerns over the relative status of men and women within civil rights organizations became logical topics of discussion.

SNCC Position Paper:
Women in the Movement

Women within SNCC began to identify obvious examples of bias, as enumerated in the 1964 position paper below.

1. Staff was involved in crucial constitutional revisions at the Atlanta staff meeting in October. A large committee was appointed to present revisions to the staff. The committee was all men.
2. Two organizers were working together to form a farmers league. Without asking any questions, the male organizer immediately assigned the clerical work to the female organizer although both had had equal experience in organizing campaigns.
3. Although there are women in Mississippi project who have been working as long as some of the men, the leadership group in COFO is all men.
4. A woman in a field office wondered why she was held responsible for day-to-day decisions, only to find out later that she had been appointed project director but not told.
5. A fall 1964 personnel and resources report on Mississippi projects lists the number of people in each project. The section on Laurel, however, lists not the number of persons, but "three girls."
6. One of SNCC's main administrative officers apologizes for appointment of a woman as interim project director in a key Mississippi project area.
7. A veteran of two years' work for SNCC in two states spends her day typing and doing clerical work for other people in her project.
8. Any woman in SNCC, no matter what her position or experience, has been asked to take minutes in a meeting when she and other women are outnumbered by men.
9. The names of several new attorneys entering a state project this past summer were posted in a central movement office. The first initial and last name of each lawyer was listed. Next to one name was written: (girl).
10. Capable, responsible, and experienced women who are in leadership positions can expect to have to defer to a man on their project for final decisionmaking

11. A session at the recent October staff meeting in Atlanta was the first large meeting in the past couple of years where a woman was asked to chair.

Undoubtedly this list will seem strange to some, petty to others, laughable to most. The list could continue as far as there are women in the movement. Except that most women don't talk about these kinds of incidents, because the whole subject is [not] discussable—strange to some, petty to others, laughable to most. The average white person finds it difficult to understand why the Negro resents being called "boy," or being thought of as "musical" and "athletic," because the average white person doesn't realize that *he assumes he is superior.* And naturally he doesn't understand the problem of paternalism. So too the average SNCC worker finds it difficult to discuss the woman problem because of the assumption of male superiority. Assumptions of male superiority are as widespread and deep rooted and every much as crippling to the woman as the assumptions of white supremacy are to the Negro. Consider why it is in SNCC that women who are competent, qualified, and experienced, are automatically assigned to the "female" kinds of jobs such as typing, desk work, telephone work, filing, library work, cooking, and the assistant kind of administrative work but rarely the "executive" kind.

The woman in SNCC is often in the same position as that token Negro hired in a corporation. The management thinks that it has done its bit. Yet, every day the Negro bears an atmosphere, attitudes and actions which are tinged with condescension and paternalism, the most telling of which are when he is not promoted as the equally or less skilled whites are. This paper is anonymous. Think about the kinds of things the author, if made known, would have to suffer because of raising this kind of discussion. Nothing so final as being fired or outright exclusion, but the kinds of things which are killing to the insides—insinuations, ridicule, over-exaggerated compensations.

This paper is presented anyway because it needs to be made know[n] that many women in the movement are not "happy and contented" with their status. It needs to be made known that much talent and experience are being wasted by this movement when women are not given jobs commensurate with their abilities. It needs to be known that just as Negroes were the crucial factor in the economy of the cotton South, so too in SNCC, women are the crucial factor that keeps the movement running on a day-to-day basis. Yet they are not given equal say-so when it comes to day-to-day decisionmaking. What can be done? Probably nothing right away. Most men in this movement are probably too threatened by the possibility of serious discussion on this subject. Perhaps this is because they have recently broken away from a matriarchal framework under which they may have grown up. Then too, many women are as unaware and insensitive to this subject as men, just as there are many Negroes who don't understand they are not free or who want to be part of white America. They don't understand that they have to give up their souls and stay in their place to be accepted. So too, many women, in order to be accepted by men, on men's terms, give themselves up to that caricature of what a woman is—unthinking, pliable, an ornament to please the man.

Maybe the only thing that can come out of this paper is discussion—amidst the laughter—but still discussion. (Those who laugh the hardest are often those who need the crutch of male supremacy the most.) And maybe some women will begin to recognize day-to-day discriminations. And maybe sometime in the future the whole of the women in this movement will become so alert as to force the rest of the movement to stop the discrimination and start the slow process of changing values and ideas so that all of us gradually come to understand that this is no more a man's world than it is a white world.

Sex and Caste: A Kind of Memo

CASEY HAYDEN AND MARY KING

This argument over the problems women faced within the civil rights movement was further developed in the "kind of memo" written in 1965 by white civil rights workers Casey Hayden and Mary King. Their document proved not

Reprinted by permission, Casey Hayden and Mary King.

only a spark for internal debate within SNCC, but an important step in the early development of the women's movement (see chapter 8).

We've talked a lot, to each other and to some of you, about our own and other women's problems in trying to live in our personal lives and in our work as independent and creative people. In these conversations we've found what seems to be recurrent ideas or themes. Maybe we can look at these things many of us perceive, often as a result of insights learned from the movement:

SEX AND CASTE

There seem to be many parallels that can be drawn between treatment of Negroes and treatment of women in our society as a whole. But in particular, women we've talked to who work in the movement seem to be caught up in a common-law caste system that operates, sometimes subtly, forcing them to work around or outside hierarchical structures of power which may exclude them. Women seem to be placed in the same position of assumed subordination in personal situations too. It is a caste system which, at its worst, uses and exploits women.

This is complicated by several facts, among them: (1) The caste system is not institutionalized by law (women have the right to vote, to sue for divorce, etc.); (2) Women can't withdraw from the situation (a la nationalism) or overthrow it; (3) There are biological differences (even though those biological differences are usually discussed or accepted without taking present and future technology into account so we probably can't be sure what these differences mean). Many people who are very hip to the implications of the racial caste system, even people in the movement, don't seem to be able to see the sexual caste system and if the question is raised they respond with: "That's the way it's supposed to be. There are biological differences." Or with other statements which recall a white segregationist confronted with integration.

WOMEN AND PROBLEMS OF WORK

The caste system perspective dictates the roles assigned to women in the movement, and certainly even more to women outside the movement. Within the movement, questions arise in situations ranging from relationships of women organizers to men in the community, to who cleans the freedom house, to who holds leadership positions, to who does secretarial work, and who acts as a spokesman for groups. Other problems arise between women with varying degrees of awareness of themselves as being as capable as men but held back from full participation, or between women who see themselves as needing more control of their work than other women demand. And there are problems with relationships between white women and black women.

WOMEN AND PERSONAL RELATIONS WITH MEN

Having learned from the movement to think radically about the personal worth and abilities of people whose role in society had gone unchallenged before, a lot of women in the movement have begun trying to apply those lessons to their own relations with men. Each of us probably has her own story of the various results, and of the internal struggle occasioned by trying to break out of very deeply learned fears, needs, and self-perceptions, and of what happens when we try to replace them with concepts of people and freedom learned from the movement and organizing.

INSTITUTIONS

Nearly everyone has real questions about those institutions which shape perspectives on men and women: marriage, child rearing patterns, women's (and men's) magazines, etc. People are beginning to think about and even to experiment with new forms in these areas.

MEN'S REACTIONS TO THE QUESTIONS RAISED HERE

A very few men seem to feel, when they hear conversations involving these problems, that they have a right to be present and participate in them, since they are so deeply involved. At the same time, very few men can respond non-defensively, since the whole idea is either beyond their comprehension or threatens and exposes them. The usual response is laughter. That inability to see the whole issue as serious, as the straitjacketing of both sexes, and as societally deter-mined, often shapes our own response so that we learn to think in their terms about ourselves and to feel silly rather than trust our inner feelings. The problems we're listing here, and what others have said about them, are therefore largely drawn from conversations among women only—and that difficulty in establishing dialogue with men is a recurring theme among people we've talked to.

LACK OF COMMUNITY FOR DISCUSSION

Nobody is writing, or organizing or talking publicly about women, in any way that reflects the problems that various women in the move-ment come across and which we've tried to touch above. Consider this quote from an article in the centennial issue of *The Nation:*

> However equally we consider men and women, the work plans for husbands and wives cannot be given equal weight. A woman should not aim for "a second-level career" because she is a *woman;* from girlhood on she should recognize that, if she is also going to be a wife and mother, she will not be able to give as much to her work as she would if single. That is, she should not feel that she cannot aspire to directing the laboratory simply because she is a woman, but rather because she is also a wife and mother; as such, her work as a lab technician (or the equivalent in another field) should bring both satis-faction and the knowledge that, through it, she is fulfilling an additional role, making an additional contribution.

And that's about as deep as the analysis goes publicly, which is not nearly so deep as we've heard many of you go in chance conversations.

The reason we want to try to open up dialogue is mostly subjective. Working in the movement often intensifies personal problems, especially if we start trying to apply things we're learning there to our personal lives. Perhaps we can start to talk with each other more openly than in the past and create a community of support for each other so we can deal with ourselves and others with integrity and can therefore keep working.

Objectively, the chances seem nil that we could start a movement based on anything as distant to general American thought as a sex-caste system. Therefore, most of us will probably want to work full time on problems such as war, poverty, race. The very fact that the country can't face, much less deal with, the questions we're raising means that the movement is one place to look for some relief. Real efforts at dialogue within the movement and with whatever liberal groups, community women, or students might listen are justified. That is, all the problems between men and women and all the problems of women functioning in society as equal human beings are among the most basic that people face. We've talked in the movement about trying to build a society which would see basic human problems (which are now seen as private troubles) as public problems and would try to shape institutions to meet human needs rather than shaping people to meet the needs of those with power. To raise questions like those above illustrates very directly that society hasn't dealt with some of its deepest problems and opens discussion of why that is so. (In one sense, it is a radicalizing question that can take people beyond legalistic solutions into areas of personal and institutional change.) The second objective reason we'd like to see discussion begin is that we've learned a great deal in the movement and perhaps this is one area where a determined attempt to apply ideas we've learned there can produce some new alternatives.

Selma

SHEYANN WEBB

Selma, Alabama, had been the scene of SNCC activities since 1963. It was only with the 1965 decision of Martin Luther King, Jr., to make it SCLC's next point of focus that events there took on major national proportions. The murder of civil rights demonstrator Jimmie Lee Jackson during a rally in nearby Marion led to the decision for a march from Selma to the state capitol in Montgomery. Led by SCLC's Hosea Williams and SNCC's John Lewis, the 600 marchers set off on Sunday, March 7. At the Pettus Bridge in downtown Selma, the peaceful marchers were confronted by state troopers and local police, who used tear gas and billy clubs to break up the march brutally. Fifty marchers were injured.

Splits developed between King and SNCC over the next step. While King waited for a federal court order sanctioning the march, SNCC leaders pushed for a response regardless of court action. Televised pictures of the attack on the marchers fixed national attention on Selma and prompted Lyndon Johnson's call for a voting rights bill.

With federal court approval, the march to Montgomery began again on March 21, arriving in the capital four days later. Returning by car to Selma only hours after the march, Viola Liuzzo, a white Detroit housewife, was shot and killed by Klansmen.

During the march, SNCC workers had left the highway to talk with black residents. Along the route, SNCC leader Stokely Carmichael and others spoke of the new focus the organization had chosen. By the time they reached Montgomery, the slogan "Black Power" had caught on like wildfire and would be a rallying call for the remainder of the decade.

The account of the march below comes from the recollections of Sheyann Webb, a 12-year-old girl involved in the Selma campaign.

Used by permission of The University of Alabama Press from *Selma, Lord, Selma: Girlhood Memories of the Civil-Rights Days,* by Sheyann Webb and Rachel West Nelson, as told to Frank Sikora, © 1980 The University of Alabama Press.

I was walking between some young white guy and a black woman; I think she must have been from Perry County. Before we had left the church we had sung *Ain't Gonna Let Nobody Turn Me 'Round* and several other songs, but as we got to the downtown and started toward the bridge we got quiet. I think we stopped for just a short time there, and I was told later some of the leaders talked about going another route—back through town and out State Highway 14—to get around the troopers who were across the bridge, on the side toward Montgomery. I don't know what was said for sure, but after just a little while we started again.

Now the Edmund Pettus Bridge sits above the downtown; you have to walk up it like it's a little hill. We couldn't see the other side, we couldn't see the troopers. So we started up and the first part of the line was over. I couldn't see all that much because I was so little; the people in front blocked my view.

But when we got up there on that high part and looked down we saw them. I remember the woman saying something like, "Oh, my Lord" or something. And I stepped out to the side for a second and I saw them. They were in a line—they looked like a blue picket fence—stretched across the highway. [Broad Street becomes United States Highway 80] There were others gathered behind that first line and to the sides, along the little service road in front of the stores and drive-ins, there was a group of white people. And further back were some of Sheriff Jim Clark's possemen on their horses. Traffic had been blocked.

At that point I began to get a little uneasy about things. I think everyone did. People quit talking; it was so quiet then that all you could hear was the wind blowing and our footsteps on the concrete sidewalk.

Well, we kept moving down the bridge. I remember glancing at the water in the Alabama River, and it was yellow and looked cold. I was told later that Hosea Williams said to John Lewis, "See that water down there? I hope you can swim, 'cause we're fixin' to end up in it."

The troopers could be seen more clearly now. I guess I was fifty to seventy-five yards from them. They were wearing blue helmets, blue jackets, and they carried clubs in their hands; they had those gas-mask pouches slung across their shoulders. The first part of the march line reached them and we all came to a stop. For a few seconds we just kept standing, and then I heard this voice speaking over the bullhorn saying that this was an unlawful assembly and for us to disperse and go back to the church.

I remember I held the woman's hand who was next to me and had it gripped hard. I wasn't really scared at that point. Then I stepped out a way and looked again and saw the troopers putting on their masks. *That* scared me. I had never faced the troopers before, and nobody had ever put on gas masks during the downtown marches. But this one was different; we were out of the city limits and on a highway. Williams said something to the troopers asking if we could pray—I didn't hear it but was told later he asked if we could—and then I heard the voice again come over the bullhorn and tell us we had two minutes to disperse.

Some of the people around me began to talk then, saying something about, "Get ready, we're going to jail," words to that effect.

But I didn't know about that; the masks scared me. So the next thing I know—it didn't seem like two minutes had gone by—the voice was saying, "Troopers advance and see that they are dispersed." Just all of a sudden it was beginning to happen. I couldn't see for sure how it began, but just before it did I took another look and saw the line of troopers moving toward us; the wind was whipping at their pants legs.

All I knew is I heard all this screaming and the people were turning and I saw this first part of the line running and stumbling back toward us. At that point, I was just off the bridge and on the side of the highway. And they came running and some of them were crying out and somebody yelled, "Oh, God, they're killing us!" I think I just froze then. There were people everywhere, jamming against me, pushing against me. Then, all of a sudden, it stopped and everyone got down on their knees, and I did too, and somebody was saying for us to pray. But there was so much excitement it never got started, because everybody was talking and they were scared and we didn't know what was happening or was going to happen. I remember looking toward the troopers and they were backing up, but some of them were standing over some of our people who had been knocked down or had fallen. It seemed like just a few seconds went by and I heard a shout. "Gas! Gas!" And everybody started screaming again. And I looked and I saw the troopers charging us again and some of them were swinging their arms and throwing canisters of tear gas. And beyond

them I saw the horsemen starting their charge toward us. I was terrified. What happened then is something I'll never forget as long as I
live. Never. In fact, I still dream about it sometimes.

I saw those horsemen coming toward me and they had those awful
masks on; they rode right through the cloud of tear gas. Some of
them had clubs, others had ropes or whips, which they swung about
them like they were driving cattle.

> Judge Frank M. Johnson, Jr.'s order permitting the Selma-to-Montgom-
> ery march set off a frantic chain of events not only in Selma but,
> indeed, across the nation. Hundreds of people—the famous and the
> nameless—hurried to Selma to take part in the historic fifty-mile walk
> across part of the Alabama Black Belt. In Washington, President Lyndon
> Johnson ordered the Alabama National Guard federalized to provide
> protection; he also ordered paratroopers to be prepared to join in the
> march, should trouble occur. In Selma, preparations were being made
> to ensure the availability of adequate food supplies, tenting and bed-
> ding, portable sanitary facilities, and campsites. By Saturday morning,
> March 20, the George Washington Carver Homes were awash with
> people. The march was to begin the following day, just two weeks after
> the rout at the bridge.

Our house was full of people. They'd sleep in sleeping bags on
the living room floor, in the upstairs hallway, anywhere there was
space. It was that way everywhere. You had to stand in line to get into
the bathroom.

What I remember most about those days just before the march
was the large groups of people always out by the church singing
freedom songs. They'd go on all through the night. I'd fall asleep
listening to them.

Nothing like this had ever happened before in America; people
from all over had come to join us because we were successful in
dramatizing that there were wrongs in the South and the time had
come to change them. It was more than the right to vote; it was also
the way we had been treated.

Until Dr. King came to Selma, we had been too afraid even to ask
if we could be free; folks were too timid to ask to vote.

But Judge Frank Johnson's order was going to change that. Not
since Abraham Lincoln had a white man done so much to help us.
And President Johnson was helping.

So as we gathered at the church on that Sunday [March 21], it was more than just a march to dramatize our desire to vote. It meant that we would get out in the sunshine and let everyone know that we were Americans, too; and that we were southerners, too; and that we were Alabamians and citizens of Selma, too.

So all this was coming about—this right to be free from fear—in Selma and it was coming about because of the courage of poor, ordinary black people who knew the time was here.

I remember on that Sunday that there were thousands of people gathered around the church. But from all those people I remember they got me and Rachel and we sang a song while some people recorded it for a record company [Folkways]. And later, before we started, a photographer took a picture of me and Rachel sitting on Dr. King's lap.

What I remember so much about that day was the happiness of the people. I had never seen them like that before. When we finished singing *We Shall Overcome,* we started off and went to the bridge and there were soldiers with rifles and bayonets everywhere, protecting us. Well, when we crossed that bridge and started on down the road for Montgomery, the people just seemed like something had been lifted from their shoulders. They were so proud, but it was a pride that was dignified. We had always maintained that dignity.

It was such a beautiful, sunshiny day. And I walked along with Rachel for awhile and we kept looking up at the sky. And there was a sign that somebody was carrying—a placard or banner, I mean—which said the whole thing that was on my mind.

It said that we weren't marching fifty miles; instead, we were marching to cover three hundred years.

My family and Rachel's family were all with us that day and we went about ten miles down the road. We were singing *Ain't Gonna Let Nobody Turn Me 'Round* as we came up to some buses pulled off alongside the road. We stopped there, and that's when Dr. King saw us.

"Are you marching all the way?" he asked, and the way he said it and the way he was smiling told me he was quite proud.

And I told him, "I don't know 'cause my momma said I had to come back home. She didn't give me permission."

"Aren't you tired?" he says.

And me and Rachel shrugged and grinned, and I said, "My feet and legs be tired, but my soul still feels like marchin'."

So he said that we had walked far enough for little girls and he wanted us to get on the bus and go back to Selma. So we said we'd do that and he touched us on the head and went on down the road.

I remembered standing there a long time and watching those people marching along. I would never forget that sight.

And I said to Rachel, "It seem like we marchin' to Heaven today." And she says, "Ain't we?"

We all drove over to Montgomery that following Thursday for the big rally in front of the Alabama Capitol. We had parked on the edge of the city and joined in the march for the last few miles, and it was just an endless stream of people moving through a light rain. I remember the huge throng of people—some said there were twenty-five thousand, some said as many as fifty thousand—just massed there in front, and Dr. King speaking to us, telling us that we had been on a long journey for freedom. He ended with the words, "Glory, glory, hallelujah," and repeated it several times, and each time everyone would cheer and it ended with a deafening roar.

As I look back on it, I think the real victory wasn't the fact that we went to Montgomery and had that rally. The real victory was just winning the *right* to do that. That fifty-mile march was symbolic. The real triumph had been on March the seventh at the bridge and at the church afterwards, when we turned a brutal beating into a nonviolent victory.

On that day of the rally in Montgomery, we had stayed for part of the entertainment in which some singers such as Peter, Paul, and Mary and Harry Belafonte had performed; but it was raining so hard that we finally drove back home.

It was later that night that we went to the church [Brown Chapel] and someone came in with the news that a woman had been shot to death in Lowndes County.

Viola Gregg Liuzzo, thirty-eight, of Detroit, Michigan, had transported a car full of marchers back to Selma that night and, accompanied by a young black man, Leroy Moton, was making the return trip to Montgomery. A car carrying armed Klansmen had followed her, pursuing at speeds up to eighty miles per hour. Overtaking her in Lowndes County, they had sped around and fired several shots into her car; one bullet struck her in the head, killing her almost instantly. Leroy Moton survived the attack and managed to bring the car to a halt alongside Highway 80.

I didn't know Mrs. Liuzzo; she was one of the hundreds of people who had come to Selma for the big march. I remember when they told us the news that night, everyone seemed sort of shocked. We were all tired and drained of emotion. We had just made this monumental march to Montgomery, this pilgrimage to seek the right to be fully free, and we felt we had finally won it. The killing would not stop that. But it did make us realize that death and violence might still be a part of our lives and [that] the resistance might not stop. The bullets that had been fired at her car could have been aimed at any of the hundreds of cars making the trip that night. It had been a senseless crime, a cowardly action. The church was quiet. All we could do was shake our heads.

I think it was the next day that there was a memorial service for this woman who had come to help us. It was also reported that day that four Ku Klux Klansmen had been arrested for the murder. And we also learned that they had been in Selma that night, driving right by Brown Chapel, looking for blacks to attack. . . . Only the presence of armed troops probably kept them from attacking some of us.

2

"MY GENERATION":
THE STUDENT MOVEMENT AND
THE NEW LEFT

The early new left and student movement is usually dated from the publication in 1962 of The Port Huron Statement, the manifesto of ideas, values, and analyses produced by a small group of students affiliated with the main new left student organization of the sixties, Students for a Democratic Society (SDS). While The Port Huron Statement became the most important document of the early student movement, campus activity had been taking place since the late fifties at large state universities like Wisconsin, Michigan, and the University of California, Berkeley, and at elite East Coast schools such as Harvard and Swarthmore. Early new left activists were, for the most part, white, middle-class college students critical of their country's values and political direction. They were profoundly influenced by the early civil rights movement, especially SNCC. Both the early civil rights and student movements were idealistic, hopeful, and committed to a democracy in which everyone could participate.

White northern students were inspired to aid the civil rights movement in the South (see chapter 1) and on their own campuses. That activism led to an attempt at UC Berkeley to raise money for SNCC, which led in turn to the first widely heralded campus action of the 1960s, the Free Speech Movement. Students began to look at their own institutions and to realize how profoundly undemocratic they were. Colleges seemed, in the students' view, committed to producing unquestioning "sheep" who would obediently take their places in society rather than to fostering intellectual and political exploration. International changes, particularly the anticolonial movements in Asia and Africa, provoked a reevaluation of the role of the United States in the world. For black and student groups, analyses of America no longer fixed only on Mississippi and Alabama, but included Africa, Indochina, and the entire Third World.

The early student movement was more homogeneous than the mass movement of the second half of the decade, and more leftist in orientation. Many early new leftists wrote and organized on behalf of an American version of socialism that, they believed, would lead to a more equal and decent society for all. But to be active in student radicalism did not require a socialist perspective. Many who identified themselves as nonsocialist radicals were critical of materialist and conformist values and sought a more meaningful life within the economic frame of contemporary American society.

The middle-class basis of the student movement troubled some movement members. Arguing that students were too privileged, they felt that the only way to facilitate social change was to drop out of college and organize the poor. They received encouragement in this effort from SNCC. As black consciousness developed, SNCC members argued that white people should organize against racism in their own communities. To this end, in the early 1960s SDS initiated the Economic Research and Action Projects (ERAP), community-organizing projects in poor neighborhoods of northern cities.

By the middle of the decade the Vietnam War became an issue on numerous campuses (see chapter 4). The war, in conjunction with civil rights, drew thousands of students into the movement in the second half of the sixties, expanding the new left in ways those at Port Huron could only have dreamed about.

The early years of the student movement are often looked back upon nostalgically because of the feelings of optimism among activists. Young people were hopeful about democratic social change in America, believing in President Kennedy's rhetoric about democracy and participation and in the moral superiority of the civil rights movement and Martin Luther King, Jr., its most visible spokesperson. They believed the United States could be made to live up to its promise. Taking their lead from radical sociologist C. Wright Mills, new left theorists recognized the importance of the student movement and began to articulate analyses built on the significance of youth and students in the political transformation that would make America a better society. The rapid growth of the movement seemed to promise the imminent possibility of radical democratic change.

BEGINNINGS

The Port Huron Statement

Written in 1960 by a core group of the fledgling SDS, the statement became a manifesto for the new left. Its embrace of participatory democracy and egalitarianism; its portrayal of American society as undemocratic, bureaucratic, and militaristic; and its vision of a community in which no one would suffer from isolation, alienation, or want, all struck a chord with thousands of young white college students. The analysis owed much to the writings of the radical sociologist C. Wright Mills, while the vision was inspired by the youthful radicalism of SNCC. (The statement is notable for the male orientation of its language, despite its radical perspective.)

INTRODUCTION: AGENDA FOR A GENERATION

We are people of this generation, bred in at least modest comfort, housed now in universities, looking uncomfortably to the world we inherit.

When we were kids the United States was the wealthiest and strongest country in the world; the only one with the atom bomb, the least scarred by modern war, an initiator of the United Nations that we thought would distribute Western influence throughout the world.

Freedom and equality for each individual, government of, by, and for the people—these American values we found good, principles by which we could live as men. Many of us began maturing in complacency.

As we grew, however, our comfort was penetrated by events too troubling to dismiss. First, the permeating and victimizing fact of human degradation, symbolized by the Southern struggle against racial bigotry, compelled most of us from silence to activism. Second, the enclosing fact of the Cold War, symbolized by the presence of the Bomb, brought awareness that we ourselves, and our friends, and millions of abstract "others" we knew more directly because of our common peril, might die at any time. We might deliberately ignore, or avoid, or fail to feel all other human problems, but not these two, for these were too immediate and crushing in their impact, too challenging in the demand that we as individuals take the responsibility for encounter and resolution.

While these and other problems either directly oppressed us or rankled our consciences and became our own subjective concerns, we began to see complicated and disturbing paradoxes in our surrounding America. The declaration "all men are created equal . . ." rang hollow before the facts of Negro life in the South and the big cities of the North. The proclaimed peaceful intentions of the United States contradicted its economic and military investments in the Cold War status quo.

We witnessed, and continue to witness, other paradoxes. With nuclear energy whole cities can easily be powered, yet the dominant nation-states seem more likely to unleash destruction greater than that incurred in all wars of human history. Although our own technology is destroying old and creating new forms of social organization, men still tolerate meaningless work and idleness. While two-thirds of mankind suffers undernourishment, our own upper classes revel amidst superfluous abundance. Although world population is expected to double in forty years, the nations still tolerate anarchy as a major principle of international conduct and uncontrolled exploitation governs the sapping of the earth's physical resources. Although mankind desperately needs revolutionary leadership, America rests in national stalemate, its goals ambiguous and tradition-bound instead of informed and clear, its democratic system apathetic and manipulated rather than "of, by, and for the people."

Not only did tarnish appear on our image of American virtue, not only did disillusion occur when the hypocrisy of American ideals was discovered, but we began to sense that what we had originally seen as the American Golden Age was actually the decline of an era. The worldwide outbreak of revolution against colonialism and imperialism, the entrenchment of totalitarian states, the menace of war, overpopulation, international disorder, supertechnology—these trends were testing the tenacity of our own commitment to democracy and freedom and our abilities to visualize their application to a world in upheaval.

Our work is guided by the sense that we may be the last generation in the experiment with living. But we are a minority—the vast majority of our people regard the temporary equilibriums of our society and world as eternally functional parts. In this is perhaps the outstanding paradox: we ourselves are imbued with urgency, yet the message of our society is that there is no viable alternative to the present. Beneath the reassuring tones of the politicians, beneath the common opinion that America will "muddle through," beneath the stagnation of those who have closed their minds to the future, is the pervading feeling that there simply are no alternatives, that our times have witnessed the exhaustion not only of Utopias, but of any new departures as well. Feeling the press of complexity upon the emptiness of life, people are fearful of the thought that at any moment things might be thrust out of control. They fear change itself, since change might smash whatever invisible framework seems to hold back chaos for them now. For most Americans, all crusades are suspect, threatening. The fact that each individual sees apathy in his fellows perpetuates the common reluctance to organize for change. The dominant institutions are complex enough to blunt the minds of their potential critics, and entrenched enough to swiftly dissipate or entirely repel the energies of protest and reform, thus limiting human expectancies. Then, too, we are a materially improved society, and by our own improvements we seem to have weakened the case for further change.

Some would have us believe that Americans feel contentment amidst prosperity—but might it not better be called a glaze above deeply felt anxieties about their role in the new world? And if these anxieties produce a developed indifference to human affairs, do they not as well produce a yearning to believe there *is* an alternative to the present, that something *can* be done to change circumstances in the school, the workplaces, the bureaucracies, the government? It is to this latter yearning, at once the spark and engine of change, that we direct our present appeal. The search for truly democratic alternatives to the present, and a commitment to social experimentation with them, is a worthy and fulfilling human enterprise, one which moves us and, we hope, others today. On such a basis do we offer this document of our convictions and analysis: as an effort in understanding and changing the conditions of humanity in the late twentieth century, an effort rooted in the ancient, still unfulfilled conception of man attaining determining influence over his circumstances of life.

VALUES

Making values explicit—an initial task in establishing alternatives—is an activity that has been devalued and corrupted. The conventional moral terms of the age, the politician moralities—"free world," "people's democracies"—reflect realities poorly, if at all, and seem to function more as ruling myths than as descriptive principles. But neither has our experience in the universities brought us moral enlightenment. Our professors and administrators sacrifice controversy to public relations; their curriculums change more slowly than the living events of the world; their skills and silence are purchased by investors in the arms race; passion is called unscholastic. The questions we might want raised—what is really important? can we live in a different and better way? if we wanted to change society, how would we do it?—are not thought to be questions of a "fruitful, empirical nature," and thus are brushed aside.

Unlike youth in other countries we are used to moral leadership being exercised and moral dimensions being clarified by our elders. But today, for us, not even the liberal and socialist preachments of the past seem adequate to the forms of the present. Consider the old slogans: Capitalism Cannot Reform Itself, United Front Against Fascism, General Strike, All Out on May Day. Or, more recently, No Cooperation with Commies and Fellow Travellers, Ideologies Are Exhausted, Bipartisanship, No Utopias. These are incomplete, and there are few new prophets. It has been said that our liberal and socialist predecessors were plagued by vision without program, while our own generation is plagued by program without vision. All around us there is astute grasp of method, technique—the committee, the ad hoc group, the lobbyist, the hard and soft sell, the make, the projected image—but, if pressed critically, such expertise is incompetent to explain its implicit ideals. It is highly fashionable to identify oneself by old categories, or by naming a respected political figure, or by explaining "how we would vote" on various issues.

Theoretic chaos has replaced the idealistic thinking of old—and, unable to reconstitute theoretic order, men have condemned idealism itself. Doubt has replaced hopefulness—and men act out a defeatism that is labelled realistic. The decline of utopia and hope is in fact one of the defining features of social life today. The reasons are various: the dreams of the older left were perverted by Stalinism and never re-created; the congressional stalemate makes men narrow their view of the possible; the specialization of human activity leaves little room for sweeping thought; the horrors of the twentieth century, symbolized in the gas ovens and concentration camps and atom bombs, have blasted hopefulness. To be idealistic is to be considered apocalyptic, deluded. To have no serious aspirations, on the contrary, is to be "tough-minded."

In suggesting social goals and values, therefore, we are aware of entering a sphere of some disrepute. Perhaps matured by the past, we have no sure formulas, no closed theories—but that does not mean values are beyond discussion and tentative determination. A first task of any social movement is to convince people that the search for orienting theories and the creation of human values is complex but worthwhile. We are aware that to avoid platitudes we must analyze the concrete conditions of social order. But to direct such an analysis we must use the guideposts of basic principles. Our own social values involve conceptions of human beings, human relationships, and social systems.

We regard *men* as infinitely precious and possessed of unfulfilled capacities for reason, freedom, and love. In affirming these principles we are aware of countering perhaps the dominant conceptions of man in the twentieth century: that he is a thing to be manipulated, and that he is inherently incapable of directing his own affairs. We oppose the depersonalization that reduces human beings to the status of things—if anything, the brutalities of the twentieth century teach that means and ends are intimately related, that vague appeals to "posterity" cannot justify the mutilations of the present. We oppose, too, the doctrine of human incompetence because it rests essentially on the modern fact that men have been "competently" manipulated into incompetence—we see little reason why men cannot meet with increasing skill the complexities and responsibilities of their situation, if society is organized not for minority, but for majority, participation in decision-making.

Men have unrealized potential for self-cultivation, self-direction, self-understanding, and creativity. It is this potential that we regard as crucial and to which we appeal, not to the human potentiality for violence, unreason, and submission to authority. The goal of man and society should be human independence: a concern not with image of popularity but with finding a meaning in life that is personally authentic; a quality of mind not compulsively driven by a sense of powerlessness, nor one which unthinkingly adopts status values, nor one which represses all threats to its habits, but one which has full, spontaneous access to present and past experiences, one which easily unites the fragmented parts of personal history, one which openly faces problems which are troubling and unresolved; one with an intuitive awareness of possibilities, an active sense of curiosity, an ability and willingness to learn.

This kind of independence does not mean egotistic individualism—the object is not to have one's way so much as it is to have a way that is one's own. Nor do we deify man—we merely have faith in his potential.

Human relationships should involve fraternity and honesty. Human interdependence is contemporary fact; human brotherhood must be willed, however, as a condition of future survival and as the most appropriate form of social relations. Personal links between man and man are needed, especially to go beyond the partial and fragmentary bonds of function that bind men only as worker to worker, employer to employee, teacher to student, American to Russian.

Loneliness, estrangement, isolation describe the vast distance between man and man today. These dominant tendencies cannot be overcome by better personnel management, nor by improved gadgets, but only when a love of man overcomes the idolatrous worship of things by man. As the individualism we affirm is not egoism, the selflessness we affirm is not self-elimination. On the contrary, we believe in generosity of a kind that imprints one's unique individual qualities in the relation to other men, and to all human activity. Further, to dislike isolation is not to favor the abolition of privacy;

the latter differs from isolation in that it occurs or is abolished according to individual will.

We would replace power rooted in possession, privilege, or circumstance by power and uniqueness rooted in love, reflectiveness, reason, and creativity. As a *social system* we seek the establishment of a democracy of individual participation, governed by two central aims: that the individual share in those social decisions determining the quality and direction of his life; that society be organized to encourage independence in men and provide the media for their common participation.

In a participatory democracy, the political life would be based in several root principles:

> that decision-making of basic social consequence be carried on by public groupings;

> that politics be seen positively, as the art of collectively creating an acceptable pattern of social relations;

> that politics has the function of bringing people out of isolation and into community, thus being a necessary, though not sufficient, means of finding meaning in personal life;

> that the political order should serve to clarify problems in a way instrumental to their solution; it should provide outlets for the expression of personal grievance and aspiration; opposing views should be organized so as to illuminate choices and facilitate the attainment of goals; channels should be commonly available to relate men to knowledge and to power so that private problems—from bad recreation facilities to personal alienation—are formulated as general issues.

The economic sphere would have as its basis the principles:

> that work should involve incentives worthier than money or survival. It should be educative, not stultifying; creative, not mechanical; self-directed, not manipulated, encouraging independence, a respect for others, a sense of dignity, and a willingness to accept social responsibility, since it is this experience that has crucial influence on habits, perceptions, and individual ethics;

> that the economic experience is so personally decisive that the individual must share in its full determination;

> that the economy itself is of such social importance that its major resources and means of production should be open to democratic participation and subject to democratic social regulation.

Like the political and economic ones, major social institutions—cultural, educational, rehabilitative, and others—should be generally organized with the well-being and dignity of man as the essential measure of success.

In social change or interchange, we find violence to be abhorrent because it requires generally the transformation of the target, be it a human being or a community of people, into a depersonalized object of hate. It is imperative that the means of violence be abolished and the institutions—local, national, international—that encourage non-violence as a condition of conflict be developed.

These are our central values, in skeletal form. It remains vital to understand their denial or attainment in the context of the modern world.

THE STUDENTS

In the last few years, thousands of American students demonstrated that they at least felt the urgency of the times. They moved actively and directly against racial injustices, the threat of war, violations of individual rights of conscience, and, less frequently, against economic manipulation. They succeeded in restoring a small measure of controversy to the campuses after the stillness of the McCarthy period. They succeeded, too, in gaining some concessions from the people and institutions they opposed, especially in the fight against racial bigotry.

The significance of these scattered movements lies not in their success or failure in gaining objectives—at least, not yet. Nor does the significance lie in the intellectual "competence" or "maturity" of the students involved—as some pedantic elders allege. The significance is in the fact that students are breaking the crust of apathy and overcoming the inner alienation that remain the defining characteristics of American college life.

If student movements for change are still rarities on the campus scene, what is commonplace there? The real campus, the familiar campus, is a place of private people, engaged in their notorious "inner emigration." It is a place of commitment to business-as-usual, getting ahead, playing it cool. It is a place of mass affirmation of the Twist, but mass reluctance toward the controversial public stance. Rules are accepted as "inevitable," bureaucracy as "just circumstances," irrelevance as "scholarship," selflessness as "martyrdom," politics as "just another way to make people, and an unprofitable one, too."

Almost no students value activity as citizens. Passive in public, they are hardly more idealistic in arranging their private lives: Gallup concludes they will settle for "low success, and won't risk high failure." There is not much willingness to take risks (not even in business), no setting of dangerous goals, no real conception of personal identity except one manufactured in the image of others, no real urge for personal fulfillment except to be almost as successful as the very successful people. Attention is being paid to social status (the quality of shirt collars, meeting people, getting wives or husbands, making solid contacts for later on); much, too, is paid to academic status (grades, honors, the med school rat race). But neglected generally is real intellectual status, the personal cultivation of the mind.

"Students don't even give a damn about the apathy," one has said. Apathy toward apathy begets a privately constructed universe, a place of systematic study schedules, two nights each week for beer, a girl or two, and early marriage; a framework infused with personality, warmth, and under control, no matter how unsatisfying otherwise.

Under these conditions university life loses all relevance to some. Four hundred thousand of our classmates leave college every year.

But apathy is not simply an attitude; it is a product of social institutions, and of the structure and organization of higher education itself. The extracurricular life is ordered according to *in loco parentis* theory, which ratifies the Administration as the moral guardian of the young.

The accompanying "let's pretend" theory of student extracurricular affairs validates student government as a training center for those who want to spend their lives in political pretense, and discourages initiative from the more articulate, honest, and sensitive students. The bounds and style of controversy are delimited before controversy begins. The university "prepares" the student for "citizenship" through perpetual rehearsals and, usually, through emasculation of what creative spirit there is in the individual.

The academic life contains reinforcing counterparts to the way in which extracurricular life is organized. The academic world is founded on a teacher-student relation analogous to the parent-child relation which characterizes *in loco parentis*. Further, academia includes a radical separation of the student from the material of study. That which is studied, the social reality, is "objectified" to sterility, dividing the student from life—just as he is restrained in active involvement by the deans controlling student government. The specialization of function and knowledge, admittedly necessary to our complex technological and social structure, has produced an exaggerated compartmentalization of study and understanding. This has contributed to an overly parochial view, by faculty, of the role of its research and scholarship; to a discontinuous and truncated understanding, by students, of the surrounding social order; and to a loss of personal attachment, by nearly all, to the worth of study as a humanistic enterprise.

There is, finally, the cumbersome academic bureaucracy extending throughout the academic as well as the extracurricular structures, contributing to the sense of outer complexity and inner powerlessness that transforms the honest searching of many students to a ratification of convention and, worse, to a numbness to present and future catastrophes. The size and financing systems of the university enhance the permanent trusteeship of the administrative bureaucracy, their power leading to a shift within the university toward the value standards of business and the administrative mentality. Huge foundations and other private financial interests shape the underfinanced colleges and universities, making them not only more commercial, but less disposed to diagnose society critically, less open to dissent. Many social and physical scientists, neglecting the liberating heritage of higher learning, develop "human relations" or "morale-producing" techniques for the corporate economy, while others exercise their intellectual skills to accelerate the arms race.

Tragically, the university could serve as a significant source of social criticism and an initiator of new modes and molders of attitudes. But the actual intellectual effect of the college experience is hardly distinguishable from that of any other communications channel—say, a television set—passing on the stock truths of the day. Students leave college somewhat more "tolerant" than when they arrived, but basically unchallenged in their values and political orientations. With administrators ordering the institution, and faculty the curriculum, the student learns by his isolation to accept elite rule within the university, which prepares him to accept later forms of minority control. The real function of the educational system—as opposed to its more rhetorical function of "searching for truth"—is to impart the key information and styles that will help the student get by, modestly but comfortably, in the big society beyond.

THE SOCIETY BEYOND

Look beyond the campus, to America itself. That student life is more intellectual, and perhaps more comfortable, does not obscure the fact that the fundamental qualities of life on the campus reflect the habits of society at large. The fraternity president is seen at the junior manager levels; the sorority queen has gone to Grosse Pointe; the serious poet burns for a place, any place, to work; the once-serious and never-serious poets work at the advertising agencies. The desperation of people threatened by forces about which they know little and of which they can say less; the cheerful emptiness of people "giving up" all hope of changing things; the faceless ones polled by Gallup who listed "international affairs" fourteenth on their list of "problems" but who also expected thermonuclear war in the next few years; in these and other forms, Americans are in withdrawal from public life, from any collective effort at directing their own affairs.

Some regard these national doldrums as a sign of healthy approval of the established order—but is it approval by consent or manipulated acquiescence? Others declare that the people are withdrawn because compelling issues are fast disappearing—perhaps there are fewer breadlines in America, but is Jim Crow gone, is there enough work and work more fulfilling, is world war a diminishing threat, and what of the revolutionary new peoples? Still others think the national quietude is a necessary consequence of the need for elites to resolve complex and specialized problems of modern industrial society—but, then, why should *business* elites help decide foreign policy, and who controls the elites anyway, and are they solving mankind's problems? Others, finally, shrug knowingly and announce that full democracy never worked anywhere in the past—but why lump qualitatively different civilizations together, and how can a social order work well if its best thinkers are skeptics, and is man really doomed forever to the domination of today?

There are no convincing apologies for the contemporary malaise. While the world tumbles toward the final war, while men in other nations are trying desperately to alter events, while the very future qua future is uncertain—America is without community impulse, without the inner momentum necessary for an age when societies cannot successfully perpetuate themselves by their military weapons, when democracy must be viable because of its quality of life, not its quantity of rockets.

The apathy here is, first, *subjective*—the felt powerlessness of ordinary people, the resignation before the enormity of events. But subjective apathy is encouraged by the *objective* American situation—the actual structural separation of people from power, from relevant knowledge, from pinnacles of decision-making. Just as the university influences the student way of life, so do major social institutions create the circumstances in which the isolated citizen will try hopelessly to understand his world and himself.

The very isolation of the individual—from power and community and ability to aspire—means the rise of a democracy without publics. With the great mass of people structurally remote and psychologically hesitant with respect to democratic institutions, those institutions themselves attenuate and become, in the fashion of the vicious circle, progressively less accessible to those few who aspire to serious participation in social affairs. The vital democratic connection between community and leadership, between the mass and the several elites, has been so wrenched and perverted that disastrous policies go unchallenged time and again. . . .

THE UNIVERSITY AND SOCIAL CHANGE

There is perhaps little reason to be optimistic about the above analysis. True, the Dixiecrat-GOP coalition is the weakest point in the dominating complex of corporate, military, and political power. But the civil rights, peace, and student movements are too poor and socially slighted, and the labor movement too quiescent, to be counted with enthusiasm. From where else can power and vision be summoned? We believe that the universities are an overlooked seat of influence.

First, the university is located in a permanent position of social influence. Its educational function makes it indispensable and automatically makes it a crucial institution in the formation of social attitudes. Second, in an unbelievably complicated world, it is the central institution for organizing, evaluating, and transmitting knowledge. Third, the extent to which academic resources presently are used to buttress immoral social practice is revealed, first, by the extent to which defense contracts make the universities engineers of the arms race. Too, the use of modern social science as a manipulative tool reveals itself in the "human relations" consultants to the modern corporations, who introduce trivial sops to give laborers feelings of "participation" or "belonging," while actually deluding them in order to further exploit their labor. And, of course, the use of motivational research is already infamous as a manipulative aspect of American politics. But these social uses of the universities' resources also demonstrate the unchangeable reliance by men of power on the men and storehouses of knowledge: this makes the university functionally tied to society in new ways, revealing new potentialities, new levers for change. Fourth, the university is the only mainstream institution that is open to participation by individuals of nearly any viewpoint.

These, at least, are facts, no matter how dull the teaching, how paternalistic the rules, how irrelevant the research that goes on. Social relevance, the accessibility to knowledge, and internal openness—these together make the university a potential base and agency in a movement of social change.

1. Any new left in America must be, in large measure, a left with real intellectual skills, committed to deliberativeness, honesty, reflection as working tools. The university permits the political life to be an adjunct to the academic one, and action to be informed by reason.
2. A new left must be distributed in significant social roles throughout the country. The universities are distributed in such a manner.
3. A new left must consist of younger people who matured in the postwar world, and partially be directed to the recruitment of younger people. The university is an obvious beginning point.
4. A new left must include liberals and socialists, the former for their relevance, the latter for their sense of thoroughgoing reforms in the system. The university is a more sensible place than a political party for these two traditions to begin to discuss their differences and look for political synthesis.
5. A new left must start controversy across the land, if national policies and national apathy are to be reversed. The ideal university is a community of controversy, within itself and in its effects on communities beyond.

6. A new left must transform modern complexity into issues that can be understood and felt close up by every human being. It must give form to the feelings of helplessness and indifference, so that people may see the political, social, and economic sources of their private troubles and organize to change society. In a time of supposed prosperity, moral complacency, and political manipulation, a new left cannot rely on only aching stomachs to be the engine force of social reform. The case for change, for alternatives that will involve uncomfortable personal efforts, must be argued as never before. The university is a relevant place for all of these activities.

But we need not indulge in illusions: the university system cannot complete a movement of ordinary people making demands for a better life. From its schools and colleges across the nation, a militant left might awaken its allies, and by beginning the process towards peace, civil rights, and labor struggles, reinsert theory and idealism where too often reign confusion and political barter. The power of students and faculty united is not only potential; it has shown its actuality in the South, and in the reform movements of the North.

The bridge to political power, though, will be built through genuine cooperation, locally, nationally, and internationally, between a new left of young people and an awakening community of allies. In each community we must look within the university and act with confidence that we can be powerful, but we must look outwards to the less exotic but more lasting struggles for justice.

To turn these possibilities into realities will involve national efforts at university reform by an alliance of students and faculty. They must wrest control of the educational process from the administrative bureaucracy. They must make fraternal and functional contact with allies in labor, civil rights, and other liberal forces outside the campus. They must import major public issues into the curriculum—research and teaching on problems of war and peace is an outstanding example. They must make debate and controversy, not dull pedantic cant, the common style for educational life. They must consciously build a base for their assault upon the loci of power.

As students for a democratic society, we are committed to stimulating this kind of social movement, this kind of vision and program in campus and community across the country. If we appear to seek the unattainable, as it has been said, then let it be known that we do so to avoid the unimaginable.

Letter to the New Left

C. WRIGHT MILLS

First published in 1960, this essay by the radical sociologist had a profound impact on the new left. Mills criticizes the self-congratulatory dominant academic discourse of the postwar American academy, and suggests that there is a need for social and political analyses by the left that focus on systemic and structural issues. Most important, he raises questions about the Marxist theorization of the working class as the agent of social change from capitalism to socialism, and suggests that perhaps students and intellectuals have a central role to play.

We have frequently been told by an assorted variety of dead-end people that the meanings of left and of right are now liquidated, by history and by reason. I think we should answer them in some such way as this:

The *Right,* among other things, means what you are doing: celebrating society as it is, a going concern. *Left* means, or ought to mean, just the opposite. It means structural criticism and reportage and theories of society, which at some point or another are focussed politically as demands and programs. These criticisms, demands, theories, programs are guided morally by the humanist and secular ideals of Western civilization—above all, the ideals of reason, freedom and justice. To be "left" means to connect up cultural with political criticism, and both with demands and programs. And it means all this inside *every* country of the world.

Only one more point of definition: absence of public issues there may well be, but this is not due to any absence of problems or of contradictions, antagonistic and otherwise. Impersonal and structural changes have not eliminated problems or issues. Their absence from many discussions is an ideological condition, regulated in the first place by whether or not intellectuals detect and state problems as

Reprinted by permission, *The New Left Review,* where the article first appeared in 1960.

potential *issues* for probable publics, and as *troubles* for a variety of individuals. One indispensible means of such work on these central tasks is what can only be described as ideological analysis. To be actively left, among other things, is to carry on just such analysis.

To take seriously the problem of the need for a political orientation is not, of course, to seek for A Fanatical and Apocalyptic Vision, for An Infallible and Monolithic Lever of Change, for Dogmatic Ideology, for A Startling New Rhetoric, for Treacherous Abstractions, and all the other bogeymen of the dead-enders. These are, of course, "the extremes," the straw men, the red herrings used by our political enemies to characterize the polar opposite of where they think they stand.

They tell us, for example, that ordinary men cannot always be political "heroes." Who said they could? But keep looking around you; and why not search out the conditions of such heroism as men do and might display? They tell us that we are too "impatient," that our "pretentious" theories are not well enough grounded. That is true, but neither are our theories trivial. Why don't they get to work to refute or ground them? They tell us we "do not really understand" Russia and China today. That is true; we don't; neither do they. We at least are studying the question. They tell us we are "ominous" in our formulations. That is true: we do have enough imagination to be frightened, and we don't have to hide it. We are not afraid we'll panic. They tell us we are "grinding axes." Of course we are: we do have, among other points of view, morally grounded ones, and we are aware of them. They tell us, in their wisdom, that we do not understand that The Struggle is Without End. True: we want to change its form, its focus, its object.

We are frequently accused of being "utopian" in our criticisms and in our proposals and, along with this, of basing our hopes for a new left *politics* "merely on reason," or more concretely, upon the intelligentsia in its broadest sense.

There is truth in these charges. But must we not ask: What now is really meant by *utopian*? And is not our utopianism a major source of our strength? *Utopian* nowadays, I think, refers to any criticism or proposal that transcends the up-close milieux of a scatter of individuals, the milieux which men and women can understand directly and which they can reasonably hope directly to change. In this exact sense, our theoretical work is indeed utopian—in my own case, at least, deliberately so. What needs to be understood, and what needs to be changed, is not merely first this and then that detail of some institution or policy. If there is to be a politics of a new left, what needs to be analyzed is the *structure* of institutions, the *foundation* of policies. In this sense, both in its criticisms and in its proposals, our work is necessarily structural, and so—*for us,* just now—utopian.

This brings us face to face with the most important issue of political reflection and of political action in our time: the problem of the historical agency of change, of the social and institutional means of structural change. There are several points about this problem I would like to put to you.

First, the historic agencies of change for liberals of the capitalist societies have been an array of voluntary associations, coming to a political climax in a parliamentary or congressional system. For social-ists of almost all varieties, the historic agency has been the working class—and later the peasantry, or parties and unions composed of members of the working class, or (to blur, for now, a great problem) of political parties acting in its name, "representing its interests."

I cannot avoid the view that both these forms of historic agency have either collapsed or become most ambiguous. So far as structural change is concerned, neither seems to be at once available and effec-tive as *our* agency any more. I know this is a debatable point among us, and among many others as well; I am by no means certain about it. But surely, if it is true, it ought not to be taken as an excuse for moaning and withdrawal (as it is by some of those who have become involved with the end-of-ideology); and it ought not to be bypassed (as it is by many Soviet scholars and publicists, who in their reflections upon the course of advanced capitalist societies simply refuse to admit the political condition and attitudes of the working class).

Is anything more certain than that in 1970—indeed, at this time next year—our situation will be quite different, and—the chances are high—decisively so? But of course, that isn't saying much. The seem-ing collapse of our historic agencies of change ought to be taken as a problem, an issue, a trouble—in fact, as *the* political problem which *we* must turn into issue and trouble.

Second, it is obvious that when we talk about the collapse of agencies of change, we cannot seriously mean that such agencies do not exist. On the contrary, the means of history-making—of decision and of the enforcement of decision—have never in world history been so enlarged and so available to such small circles of men on both sides of The Curtains as they now are. My own conception of the shape of power, the theory of the power elite, I feel no need to argue here. This theory has been fortunate in its critics, from the most diverse political viewpoints, and I have learned from several of these critics. But I have not seen, as of this date, an analysis of the idea that causes me to modify any of its essential features.

The point that is immediately relevant does seem obvious: what is utopian for us, is not at all utopian for the presidium of the Central Committee in Moscow, or the higher circles of the Presidency in Washington, or, recent events make evident, for the men of SAC and CIA. The historic agencies of change that have collapsed are those which were at least thought to be open to *the left* inside the advanced Western nations, to those who have wished for structural changes of these societies. Many things follow from this obvious fact; of many of them, I am sure, we are not yet adequately aware.

Third, what I do not quite understand about some new-left writers is why they cling so mightily to "the working class" of the advanced capitalist societies as *the* historic agency, or even as the most important agency, in the face of the really impressive historical evidence that now stands against this expectation.

Such a labor metaphysic, I think, is a legacy from Victorian Marxism that is now quite unrealistic.

It is an historically specific idea that has been turned into an a-historical and unspecific hope.

The social and historical conditions under which industrial workers tend to become a-class-for-themselves, and a decisive political force, must be fully and precisely elaborated. There have been, there are, there will be such conditions. These conditions vary according to national social structure and the exact phase of their economic and political development. Of course we cannot "write off the working class." But we must *study* all that, and freshly. Where labor exists as an agency, of course we must work with it, but we must not treat it as The Necessary Lever, as nice old Labour Gentlemen in Britain and elsewhere tend to do.

Although I have not yet completed my own comparative studies of working classes, generally it would seem that only at certain (earlier) stages of industrialization, and in a political context of autocracy, *etc.*, do wage workers tend to become a class-for-themselves, *etc.* The *etceteras* mean that I can here merely raise the question.

It is with this problem of agency in mind that I have been studying, for several years now, the cultural apparatus, the intellectuals, as a possible, immediate, radical agency of change. For a long time, I was not much happier with this idea than were many of you; but it turns out now, at the beginning of the 1960's, that it may be a very relevant idea indeed.

In the first place, is it not clear that if we try to be realistic in our utopianism—and that is no fruitless contradiction—a writer in our countries on the left today *must* begin with the intellectuals? For that is what we are, that is where we stand.

In the second place, the problem of the intelligentsia is an extremely complicated set of problems on which rather little factual work has been done. In doing this work, we must, above all, not confuse the problems of the intellectuals of West Europe and North America with those of the Soviet bloc or with those of the underdeveloped worlds. In each of the three major components of the world's social structure today, the character and the role of the intelligentsia is distinct and historically specific. Only by detailed comparative studies of them in all their human variety can we hope to understand any one of them.

In the third place, who is it that is getting fed up? Who is it that is getting disgusted with what Marx called "all the old crap?" Who is it that is thinking and acting in radical ways? All over the world—in the bloc, and in between—the answer is the same: it is the young intelligentsia.

I cannot resist copying out for you, with a few changes, some materials I recently prepared for a 1960 paperback edition of a book of mine on war:

"In the spring and early summer of 1960, more of the returns from the American decision and default are coming in. In Turkey, after student riots, a military junta takes over the state, of late run by Communist Container Menderes. In South Korea, too, students and others knock over the corrupt American-puppet regime of Syngman Rhee. In Cuba, a genuinely left-wing revolution begins full-scale economic reorganization, without the domination of U.S. corporations. Average age of its leaders: about 30—and certainly a revolution without Labor As Agency. On Taiwan, the eight million Taiwanese under the American-imposed dictatorship of Chiang Kai-shek, with his two million Chinese, grow increasingly restive. On Okinawa, a U.S. military base, the people get their first chance since World War II ended to demonstrate against U.S. seizure of their island; and some students take that chance, snake-dancing and chanting angrily to the visiting President: 'Go home, go home—take away your missiles.' (Don't worry, 12,000 U.S. troops easily handle the generally grateful crowds; also the President is 'spirited out' the rear end of the United States compound—and so by helicopter to the airport.) In Japan, weeks of student rioting succeed in rejecting the President's visit, jeopardizing a new treaty with the U.S.A., and displacing the big-business, pro-American Prime Minister, Kishi. And even in our own pleasant South-land, Negro and white students are—but let us keep that quiet: it really *is* disgraceful.

"That is by no means the complete list; that was yesterday; see today's newspaper. Tomorrow, in varying degree, the returns will be more evident. Will they be evident enough? They will have to be very obvious to attract real American attention: sweet complaints and the voice of reason—these are not enough. In the slum countries of the world today, what are they saying? The rich Americans, they pay attention only to violence—and to money. You don't care what they say, American? Good for you. Still, they may insist; things are no longer under the old control; you're not getting it straight, American: your country—it would seem—may well become the target of a world hatred the like of which the easy-going Americans have never dreamed. Neutralists and Pacifists and Unilateralists and that confusing variety of Leftists around the world—all those tens of millions of people, of course they are misguided, absolutely controlled by small conspiratorial groups of trouble-makers, under direct orders from Moscow and Peking. Diabolically omnipotent, it is *they* who create all this messy unrest. It is *they* who have given the tens of millions the absurd idea that they shouldn't want to remain, or to become, the seat of American nuclear bases—those gay little outposts of American civilization. So now they don't want U-2's on their territory; so now they want to contract out of the American military machine; they want to be neutral among the crazy big antagonists. And they don't want their own societies to be militarized.

"But take heart, American: you won't have time to get really bored with your friends abroad: they won't be your friends much longer. You don't need *them;* it will all go away; don't let them confuse you."

Add to that: In the Soviet bloc, who is it that has been breaking out of apathy? It has been students and young professors and writers; it has been the young intelligentsia of Poland and Hungary, and of Russia, too. Never mind that they have not won; never mind that there are other social and moral types among them. First of all, it has been these types. But the point is clear, isn't it?

That is why we have got to study these new generations of intellectuals around the world as real live agencies of historic change. Forget Victorian Marxism, except when you need it; and read Lenin again (be careful)—Rosa Luxemburg, too.

"But it is just some kind of moral upsurge, isn't it?" Correct. But under it: no apathy. Much of it is direct non-violent action, and it seems to be working, here and there. Now we must learn from the practice of these young intellectuals and with them work out new forms of action.

"But it's all so ambiguous—Cuba, for instance." Of course it is; history-making is always ambiguous. Wait a bit; in the meantime, help them to focus their moral upsurge in less ambiguous political ways. Work out with them the ideologies, the strategies, the theories that will help them consolidate their efforts: new theories of structural changes of and by human societies in our epoch.

"But it is utopian, after all, isn't it?" No, not in the sense you mean. Whatever else it may be, it's not that. Tell it to the students of Japan. Tell it to the Negro sit-ins. Tell it to the Cuban Revolutionaries. Tell it to the people of the Hungry-nation bloc.

Raising the Question of Who Decides

CASEY HAYDEN

Casey Hayden was active in SNCC and in the growing critique of the role of women within the civil rights movement (see chapter 1). This 1964 article articulates the importance of participatory democracy on the local level. The aim was to help poor people gain the kind of power they had never possessed and to think about democracy in new ways.

I'm not sure that there is a new left, and if there is I'm not sure I'm in it. I do know there are people around the country who've enabled me to keep working over the past few years. From that work I've come to have some thoughts which I'm glad to share, although I'm not sure how clear they'll be.

My work has been with the poor. The main thing I've learned has been to see the world from their perspective: from the bottom. Being on the bottom means not only that you have no power over the forces that shape your life; it also means that because you want to eat, you want some power.

From watching that struggle by the excluded and from watching them gain access to traditional routes to power (the vote, education) I've seen that entering those routes doesn't make any real change in their lives. This leads me to think that it's not the case that most people have power and a few are excluded. It's the case, rather, that no one has real power to shape his own life, but most people are comfortable enough not to care. It's only through trying to create change that we've learned how much change is necessary and how rigid the country is. To infuse dignity and equality into the lives of the poor would involve radical rearrangements in the economic patterns of ownership and control and in the now sterile and nearly meaningless patterns of representative democracy.

Within this context the question of whether there's a consensus in the country favorable to social progress is not nearly so important as the quality of mind that informs that consensus. I suppose most Americans think Negroes shouldn't be shot, that hungry people should be given some help through a poverty program or welfare. But if one assumes the people on the bottom are human beings and looks at the programs from their perspective, the programs are paternalistic and based on a very deeply-rooted ethnocentrism. The way the thinking seems to run is that the poor person who is supposed to be "helped" can't really manage his own life very well, much less anything else, and isn't capable of democratic decision-making. He has to be "lifted" to "our level" at which point he is "ready" for "democracy." This premise is the basis of welfare and poverty programs and extends to our dealings with most nonwhite or non-middle-class people (including American Indians, American Negroes, the Vietnamese). The reason for this attitude of ours, I think, is that rather than people changing institutions to meet their own needs and desires, people through institutions are shaped to meet the needs of those with power. It is to the benefit of American economic power (from the cotton interests in the South to the Rockefeller interests in South Africa) to foster the view that the poor aren't "qualified" for self-government. Liberals and intellectuals seem to try to modify this position somewhat, so that what emerges is the outlined view of the "lifting" of people so they'll be "ready." And being "ready" means being ready to fit into existing patterns of power relationships in the country, exercise a meaningless vote periodically, and, above all, not embarrass anyone (especially "America in the eyes of the world") by raising any basic questions about who should qualify as full human beings and how society can be shaped to assure a person's being treated as a human being.

So within the consensus the debate and solutions are very limited. You can talk about giving the Southern Negroes the vote but not the land, even though their relationship to the landowners is precisely what causes their condition. You can talk about giving welfare recipients larger budgets. But you can't suggest they should control the welfare department, even though it is the paternalism and the bureaucracy which degrade them and keep them in the cycle of poverty. In short, you can't talk about a kind of democracy in which those who are affected by decisions make those decisions, whether the institutions in question be the welfare department, the university, the factory, the farm, the neighborhood, the country.

That kind of power shift is what I think would make society healthy and whole, if that is what is meant by a prescription. But the more important question is, I think, how do we get there? Or, what should I work on? What should I do and how, given a consensus that I'm not part of? The first task, I think, is expanding the group of people really committed to democratic change: increasing the number of people committed to full-time organizing, enlarging the group who will work on political activities even though they aren't involved in a radical vocation, helping people relate their professions to the movement.

All of this is toward the end of creating institutions of power for those who have no power, whether they be in the universities, in the slums or citizens at large concerned about lack of control of the economy and foreign policy. In trying to build such institutions for the poor I think we've learned a few things about building and sustaining a radical movement: People need institutions that belong to them, that they can experiment with and shape. In that process it's possible to develop new forms for activity which can provide new models for how people can work together so participants can think radically about how society could operate. People stay involved and working when they can see the actual results of their thought and work in the organization, so power must be distributed equally if large numbers are to be organized. Traditional parliamentary methods are beyond the experience of many of the poor, and in addition their use tends to create factions and a "win" psychology rather than building a cohesive group. It's hard for many of the poor to function in large groups, where demagogic traditions tend to prevail, but everyone can participate in small groups. Leaders tend to yield more rapidly than the base to pressures for modifications of the group's goals because they have to meet outsiders directly in their capacity as spokesmen; rotating leadership and a strengthening of each person's faith in the value of his own opinions can halt leadership sellouts. Bureaucracies tend to assume power, as they have access to funds and information; electing administrations and leadership on a rotating basis helps assure democratic control of funds and knowledge. People then tend to resist society's arguments that they be "responsible" (*i.e.,* responsive to those with power) and they then tend to turn to each other for strength. Organizers, too, need their own organizations, which must provide emotional and intellectual, as well as material, subsistence.

These things we've learned from work in the movement in turn shape our view of what the world could be like. I've read about some of these ideas in articles about the New Left and they always sound very mystical. They're not, at least for me. They are rooted in experiences of organizing and are very concrete. They are the base for whatever ideas I have about how society could function more humanely.

The groups that are being organized are primarily vehicles for giving political power to the poor. Electoral and party politics can't give much real power at this point; so few people are ready to entertain ideas for needed changes that radicals can't get elected, and if they could they would be outvoted or otherwise curtailed in their activities. However, political candidacies are an organizing device and provide a forum for the ideas and methods of a new politics, one in which those who are elected are really responsible to a constituency. It may well be that in the next few years some courthouses in the South can be won, and then the people can see how far they can and will go with putting radical ideas into concrete political action. What will happen if a Negro tax assessor in Podunk, Alabama, finally taxes the textile mill there? And will the people be ready to set up their own communal factory in the vacant building when the company pulls out?

But by and large now we can only raise questions about who decides. That is beginning to happen, but not nearly so much as some writers for left journals would like to believe. That it's happening at all is what I consider hopeful. It's a small hope. I don't know if we can make those qualitative changes that must occur if people's lives are not to be spent asking for the right to a decent life or trading their integrity for material needs, rather than each of us giving to the other.

How to Help the Ones at the Bottom

JEAN SMITH

Jean Smith, a SNCC activist, describes in 1964 how local organizers in an extremely poor Mississippi community try to build institutions that will provide basic necessities and a future over which the people can have control.

It's too hard to find ways of giving people decent places to stay and livable incomes. It is hard because we're told that to decide to do this is also to make decisions about national fiscal policy and the social order and labor unions and the international balance of payments. And we cringe before these weighty matters. It's too hard to talk about providing what people need to live on, because someone always says that that will make them lazy and runs headlong into our American ideals of industry and upward mobility. Then what can you reply but, "yea, well, poverty is really relative and look at the hungry people in India"? You don't believe in laziness either.

I think people can get loose from the fear of deciding about things that are important by trying to consider and deal with the problems of people at the bottom. Facing them is like being on your way to a terribly important meeting on which your future hangs, seeing a kid get hit by a car, and realizing that no one will help him. You can't keep driving. Once we begin to deal with the problems of these people, we will be building a fund of ways to work and resources to draw on. So that when we move on to others (maybe to people who can't afford a toilet), we will have materials and insights to work with.

Figuring into this first set of people are the absolutely dirt-poor sharecroppers and day laborers in Mississippi, people whose ability to live through winter after winter with no money in those cold, crowded, rundown "shotgun houses" is a mystery. They can't do anything more on those plantations than work hard for nothing and die. There is no possibility that helping them would be removing them from a situation where they could help themselves and pull themselves up by their bootstraps. You just have to see little babies lying on floors with flies all over them and kids trying to study in rooms with eight other people, a TV, and one dim light bulb to be certain that, whatever juggling it may take, the country's resources ought to be employed to get for these people decent places to live and some incomes.

These workers, having been replaced by machines and chemicals, no longer have even the $3 a day that they once could make at picking and chopping cotton to pay for shoes for the children to go to school and for food and fuel. Nor do they have the prospect of work during the winter or next spring. Now that the bossmen don't need their labor, they are being pressured to move off the farms. They may try to make it through the year in Mississippi or they may pull together enough money for bus fare to Chicago. Whatever choice they make, they look out on a future of watching their kids grow up dumb and poor and hopeless. They can neither buy a house nor borrow money since you have to have money before you can get money. They could never get credit because they could never show that they were good risks.

What can we do? How can we get them houses that the rain doesn't come in and that the kids don't mind bringing their friends home to? How can we repair the damage to the young people of having to stay out of school, year after year, to hoe the cotton and get it in? How can we find incomes for people who now are not needed even at $3 a day?

BUILDING STRIKE CITY

Some of us in Mississippi have developed an approach to some of these problems. In Tribbett, Mississippi, eight families have been put off a plantation because they struck for wages higher than $3 a day. They have been living in tents for four months. We have pulled together architectural, building and private financial resources so that we can, with the help of the men in Strike City, build houses for the 60 people now in the tents. The houses will be owned at first by their self-governed neighborhood corporation and ultimately by them individually.

Other interested people have already made plans to build a community center there, and they will have a community garden with the vegetables they need. We can put up a cannery for the food and can operate a reupholstering shop (after they get some furniture—now there are only beds). We hope to involve a number of the people in a building-trades training program and still others in learning and in teaching in programs of literacy and basic education. All of these would bring incomes in the form of stipends and salaries into the community. We expect to see a program of preschool education for the younger children. There are about 30 children there; nearly all of them are below the grade levels normal for their ages; many quit school long ago. Tribbett is located near Greenville, which is among the Delta towns most likely to offer employment in the coming years. For example, an MDTA training project for 800 people was just announced for Greenville. These efforts fit together in such a way that these people, who are at the bottom, will, through possessing their own homes and some income, have the means to stay in Mississippi and to move against the poverty and hopelessness that surround the lives of most of the Negro people in the state today.

Our work in Tribbett grew out of our effort to set up a three-part program for economic change: a Foundation which gives money to people to build a house; a brick factory which will make the materials to build a house; and a training program which will offer basic training in literacy and math, and vocational training. The thinking is that the first things people need, when they have to leave a plantation or some other place where their work is no longer needed, is a place to stay and some kind of income.

The Foundation is key to the entire scheme. It will be the only place a person without a job or collateral can get the money to build a home. With it we will be breaking the circle of privileges that lead to privileges. The Foundation will have a broad membership of poor people who will choose a board to handle its day-to-day operations. Money will be put into the hands of poor people to use as a base to move against their poverty. They will decide on how grants will be given and to whom.

This approach will be a lot different from that of current poverty spending. In Mississippi, poverty funds end up primarily in the hands of businessmen (rent-a-car men, airlines men, shoestore men) who have no desire to do anything for poor people, who, in fact, want them to leave the state and take their voting power with them. So it is as if the money was never there. The people are still without bathtubs; their teeth are still rotten; and the shoes that were bought still have to be replaced in three months. What also happens is that the poverty programs, by making people into field captains and aides, sap the energies of people who would be doing real work toward relieving their poverty. Since poor people don't run the programs (because most of them aren't "qualified"), they can't use them to make real changes in their style of living. And the poverty people are too busy going to meetings and driving up and down highways to do much else. In contrast, within the Foundation, money and resources will go to poor people to use as their own base of power to change the things that make them poor, to get themselves out of those shotgun houses, to find ways of creating incomes for themselves. When the Foundation (which will be statewide) turns money and resources over to groups of people (as in the case of Tribbett), these groups will form community governments which will do the work in their communities of building the homes, of running the health-care centers for old people, of running the vocational training. So that on several levels people will be moving, in ways that count.

The brick factory will sell bricks for what it costs to make them, to people who have got grants from the Foundation. The capital for it will have to come from government or outside private loans or grants, and we are still badly in need of technical assistance in setting it up. The factory is important because nowhere in Mississippi do Negroes run any important businesses. For it to be a success and to run on its own merits will mean to the young people who are now trying to save up the bus fare to Chicago that Negroes can make some future for themselves in the state. It will be important, too, because it can be the financial base for beginning other viable businesses in the state run by poor people.

The training program will be developed over the next six months by doing research into what kinds of things people already know and what kinds of skills other people will be paying for. When we look at what people can make money doing, we will be particularly concerned to find out where, in the state, businesses will be moving in or expanding. Knowing this we shall be able to style useful training programs and to plan the location of new housing (built through the Foundation) near towns which will be growing, and hiring people. It is pretty certain one of the areas of training will be in the building trades. Building is increasing all over the state and it pays well. We expect that this training will be especially effective in that it will fit into the building of people's own homes. In wanting to do a good job on their own houses, people will develop their skills more soundly than if they were trained by building a wall and tearing it down. Training in literacy and math will be worked into the overall scheme. Stipends will be arranged throughout the training so that people will have money to live on.

We saw that kid on the highway and this is what we thought we could do.

COMMUNITY ORGANIZING

Hoping to spread their movement for a new society beyond campuses and the arenas of civil rights actions, SDS initiated ERAP, community-organizing projects in poor northern neighborhoods.

The Politics of "The Movement"

TOM HAYDEN

Tom Hayden, author of the original draft of The Port Huron Statement and an SDS leader, became one of the most active and identifiable members of the emerging new left. Here in 1966 he argues for a new society based on an interracial movement of the poor that would include students and middle-class insurgents. This changed the traditional radical notion of a distinct proletariat- or working class–based movement. The new perspective served as the theoretical argument behind the ERAP projects.

The Mississippi Convention challenge points towards a new kind of politics and a new kind of organizing, which has at least an outside chance of truly changing American society. This stirring we call the Movement.

The Movement tries to oppose American barbarism with new structures and opposing identities. These are created by people whose need to understand their society and govern their own existence has somehow not been cancelled out by the psychological damage they have received. For different reasons such needs survive among the poor, among students and other young people, and finally among millions of other Americans not easily grouped except by their modest individual resistance to the system's inhumanity. It is from these ranks that the Movement is being created. What kind of people, more exactly, are they, and what kind of organizational strategy might they develop?

Reprinted by permission, Tom Hayden.

1. AN INTERRACIAL MOVEMENT OF THE POOR

The Mississippi sharecroppers are the most visible and inspiring representations of an awakening that is taking place among the poor in America. Their perspective centers on Negro freedom, of course, but they are committed deeply to the idea of a movement of all the powerless and exploited. In certain ways theirs is a radicalism unique because of Black Belt conditions. Their strength comes from a stable system of family life and work. Politics is new and fresh for them; they have not experienced the hollow promises of an opportunistic liberal-Negro machine. Their opposition's naked brutality keeps them constantly in a crisis framework. The broadening of their movement into Arkansas, Alabama, Louisiana, Georgia, the Carolinas and Virginia, already underway, can be expected to challenge fundamentally the national coalition directing the Democratic party. Already the Democrats are trying to groom moderate and liberal politicians to provide an "alternative" to the segregationists and the independent FDP. Probably this effort will succeed, in the sense that political moderates will begin to compete for electoral power and leadership of the civil rights forces, mostly basing their strength in the cities, among privileged Negroes. The FDP, as a structure, may be absorbed into the national party, if only because it has no other, more effective place to go. But since the new Southern power structure will not solve the problems of poverty and race which have plagued the North for generations, there is very little chance that this movement of poor people will be entirely co-opted or crushed.

In the black ghettoes of the North, the Movement faces heavier obstacles. There work is often deadening, family life distorted: "proper" political channels are sewers; people are used to, and tired of, party organizers exploiting them. The civil rights movement does not touch these hundreds of ghettoes in any significant way because of the middle class nature of its program and leadership. However, the Harlem rent strikes and the activities of Malcolm X are clear evidence that there are in the ghettoes people prepared to take action. Some of them are of Southern background; some are housewives with wasted talents; some are youth with no future for their energy; some are junkies and numbers men with little loyalty to their particular game. Different as the forms of their discontent may be, the discontent itself is general to the ghetto and can be the spring for action. Under present conditions, political movements among these people are likely to be based on a race consciousness which is genuine and militant—and which is also vital because of the failure of whites to act in favor of equal rights. The ghetto race consciousness, however, is intertwined with the consciousness of being both poor and powerless. Almost of necessity, the demands that the ghetto poor put forward are also in the interest of the white poor, as well as of middle class professionals who depend on the expansion of the public sectors of the economy.

But will white working class and poor people take up these issues, which the "Negro problem" by its nature tends to raise? The negative evidence is plentiful. Poor whites, such as those in parts of the South who are truly irrelevant to the modern economy, tend to see their plight (sometimes with accuracy) as personal rather than social: a function of sickness, bad luck, or psychological disorder. Poverty is not seen clearly as the fate of a whole interracial class, but only as the fate of individuals, each shamed into self-blame by their Protestant ideology. Working class whites, on the other hand, are more likely to be conscious of their problems as a group, but they tend to defend their scarce privileges—jobs, wages, education for their children—against what they see as the onslaught of Negro competition. While "backlash" did not split the alliance of white working people with the Democratic party in 1964, it does serve as a barrier to an alliance with the Negro poor. But it is foolish to be rigid about these notions. Whites *are* being organized, on a mass basis, in areas of Appalachia where there exists a common culture and an industrial union tradition, and where the blame for misery can be laid to the coal operators, the conservative United Mine Workers, and the government. They also have been organized in Cleveland, where they face the "welfare situation" together. . . .

The crucial importance of community work can only be grasped if one understands the sorts of ideas the American poor have about themselves. They operate with a kind of split consciousness. On the one hand, poor people know they are victimized from every direction. The facts of life always break through to expose the distance between American ideals and personal realities. This kind of knowledge, however, is kept undeveloped and unused because of another knowledge imposed on the poor, a keen sense of dependence on the oppressor. This is the source of that universal fear which leads poor people to act and even to think subserviently. Seeing themselves to blame for their situation, they rule out the possibility that they might be qualified to govern themselves and their own organizations. Besides fear, it is their sense of inadequacy and embarrassment which destroys the possibility of revolt. At the same time, this set of contradictory feelings results in indirect forms of protest all the time: styles of dress and language, withdrawal from political life, defiance of the boss's or the welfare worker's rules and regulations.

There can be no poor people's movement in any form unless the poor can overcome their fear and embarrassment. I think the release comes from a certain kind of organizing which tries to make people understand their own worth and dignity. This work depends on the existence of "material issues" as a talking and organizing point—high rents, voting rights, unpaved roads, and so on—but it moves from there into the ways such issues are related to personal life. The organizer spends hours and hours in the community, listening to people, drawing out their own ideas, rejecting their tendency to depend on him for solutions. Meetings are organized at which people with no "connections" can be given a chance to talk and work out problems together—usually for the first time. All this means fostering in everyone that sense of decision-making power which American society works to destroy. Only in this way can a movement be built which the Establishment can neither buy off nor manage, a movement too vital ever to become a small clique of spokesmen.

An organizational form that suggests the style of such a movement is the "community union," involving working-class and poor people in local insurgency. Open and democratic, the community union offers a real alternative to the kind of participation permitted in civil rights groups, trade unions and Democratic party machines. It might take a variety of forms: block clubs, housing committees, youth groups, etc. The union's insistence on the relevance of "little people," as well as its position outside and against the normal channels, would create a rooted sense of independence among the members.

The problem of politics among the poor is severe. In the first place, their potential electoral power is low because of their location in gerrymandered political districts, their rapid movement from house to house, and the complicated and discriminatory electoral procedures in many cities. Beyond these problems lies the obvious and well-grounded cynicism of the poor about elections. Given all these conditions, it is barely conceivable that a poor person could be elected to an important political office. Even were this possible, it would be on a token basis, and the elected official would be under strong pressure to conform to the rules of the game. Thus, the orthodox idea of politics is contradictory to building a movement. The movement needs to discover a politics of its own. This might be done by electing people who will see their office as a community organizing tool, letting community people participate directly in decisions about how the office should be used. This experiment is being made in Atlanta where a SNCC field secretary, Julian Bond, was elected in June 1965 to the State Legislature. Or what might be done is to contest the basic class and racial injustices of American politics, demanding that poverty areas be granted political representation, or running freedom elections to dramatize the lack of representation for the boxed-in poor. This sort of thing would probably mobilize more poor people than orthodox electoral activity. The mobilization would be "practical" from the standpoint of getting modest reforms; more important, it would point toward the need to rearrange American political institutions to fit the needs of excluded people. . . .

To summarize: the Movement is a community of insurgents sharing the same radical values and identity, seeking an independent base of power wherever they are. It aims at a transformation of society led by the most excluded and "unqualified" people. Primarily, this means building institutions outside the established order which seek to become the genuine institutions of the total society. Community unions, freedom schools, experimental universities, community-formed police review boards, people's own anti-poverty organizations fighting for federal money, independent union locals—all can be "practical" pressure points from which to launch reform in the conventional institutions while at the same time maintaining a separate base and pointing towards a new system. Ultimately, this movement might lead to a Continental Congress called by all the people who feel excluded from the higher circles of decision-making in the country. This Congress might even become a kind of second government, receiving taxes from its supporters, establishing contact with other nations,

holding debates on American foreign and domestic policy, dramatizing the plight of all groups that suffer from the American system.

If it is hard to imagine this kind of revolutionary process in the
United States, it might be because no previous model of revolution
seems appropriate to this most bloated and flexible of the advanced
societies. There may be no way to change this country. At least there
is no way we can bank on. Both technological change and social
reform seem to rationalize the power of the system to drain the heart
of protest. The Movement at least suggests that we bank on our own
consciousness, what there is of our own humanity, and begin to work.

Cleveland: Conference of the Poor

CONNIE BROWN

*A community organizer affiliated with ERAP, Connie Brown describes an
important 1964 conference at which community people from organizing projects
in the Northeast, Midwest, and South came together to discuss their common issues.*

Last fall, after the community organizing projects of the Economic
Research and Action Projects (ERAP) of Students for a Democratic
Society had been underway for three months, it occurred to some of
the staff that people from the eight communities should have a chance
to come together and talk over their problems and the programs of
their organizations. The experience of meeting and talking with other
poor people from different cities could demonstrate better than any
amount of discussion back home the similarity of the problems that
poor people face everywhere, and the necessity of a national move-

Reprinted by permission, James Weinstein.

ment of poor people. So the Community People's Conference was conceived at an ERAP staff meeting, and Cleveland chosen as the most convenient location. From that point on, the conference was planned and executed entirely by community people, with consultation going on by mail and telephone from project to project.

On February 19th, 150 poor people, white and Negro, came to Cleveland from Baltimore, Boston, Newark, Chester, Hazard, Kentucky, Chicago, Detroit and Mississippi. The conference opened with speeches by members of each organization on the general problems facing a poor people's movement. Small unstructured discussion groups occupied the rest of the day, with a March on downtown Cleveland in the late afternoon. An informal party that evening, a church service and dinner the next day, the conference was over.

Brief and simple as it was, the conference was a profound and startling experience for all who attended it. What had been abstractions in an ERAP staff discussion became realities. Negroes and poor whites listened to each other talk about problems of welfare, unemployment, housing and about the powerlessness of the unorganized poor. For two days, barriers of fear and distrust were dissolved. People were able to feel the idea of an interracial movement of the poor as an emotional reality.

In the South, everyone knows there is a freedom movement, and when it comes to a particular town, people can become part of it knowing they are part of something large and real. When the movement comes to a Southern town, it brings a history and a culture with it and gives strength to the people who become part of it, even if their town is physically isolated. Our movement is just beginning. It lacks the songs, the stories, the backlog of experience that provide so much of the force of the Southern movement. The Cleveland Conference, simply by bringing together from across the North 150 people who are doing the same things and who think the same way, created in them the sense of a national movement. That sense is real because they have it now—and important because it gives them strength to organize more and more people back home. And it has not disappeared in the months since the conference, although the realities of day-to-day work on the block have toned it down.

Four Negroes from rural Mississippi were at the conference. Perhaps because of the extreme youth of the Northern organizations, the personal strength of these Mississippi Negroes, their experience in organizing, their dramatic tales of oppression and brutality in many ways dominated the conference. There was a mixed response on the part of Northern whites and Negroes to the situation of Mississippi Negroes as it was presented to them by Mrs. Fannie Lou Hamer. The sympathy and horror shared by all gave rise in some to the feeling that "we should realize how much better off we are up here." The second attitude, and the prevailing one, was that things are just as bad up North, except that "they keep it hidden." In a discussion of welfare, people saw that payments get higher the further north you go. To some, this meant that things get better as you go north—to others, that things get worse, because the poor are being bought off, and their vision clouded by minor concessions. In the South, said Mrs. Unita Blackwell of Mayersville, Mississippi, everything is "wide open," but that does not mean it is worse.

A Negro man, from a Northern city, talked about programs to get drop-outs back into school. He said that where he lives, you have to have a high school diploma to get a job as a janitor. In his view, the efforts of the poor should be directed toward doing anything necessary to enter the small cracks in American society open to them. His acceptance of the situation he described, and his desire to accommodate himself to it constitute what is commonly termed adjustment. The relation, in his city and everywhere, between "education" and employment is totally absurd. His adjustment to it is absurd, too, but apparently necessary for survival both physical and mental. In order to survive in the Northern cities, to adjust, to enter the tiny crack, the poor man must blind himself to innumerable absurdities, and in doing so, he distorts his vision of himself and of the world he lives in. In the South, where things are "wide open," it is difficult for the poor Negro to blind himself. Presumably for this reason, the people from Mississippi were able to cut through again and again to the absurdities that lie at the root of the innumerable adjustments that the Northern poor people did not even know they had made. The man with the drop-out program regarded himself as sensible, and his program as constructive. Mrs. Blackwell thought he was crazy, his high school crazy, his program destructive. "We've got to stop letting ourselves be brainwashed." People have to "cut loose" from the thin but powerful strings that tie them to a society that offers them almost nothing, and which itself is as morally bankrupt in the North as in the South. And now, she said, people have an alternative. They can be part of the movement. People were exhilarated by the force and clarity of her message—but more than that, both organizers and poor people were *changed* by it. And the importance of her message must not be underestimated, for it concerns the central issue of the development of a radical movement—the forging of a new identity, in which the first step must be release from the values and expectations which are imposed on all of us.

At the end of the conference some one initiated a collection for the Mississippi delegation. Mrs. Blackwell stood up suddenly, and said that the taking up of money meant to her the drawing of a line between the Northern and Southern poor, and put the northerners who were giving money in the same category as the middle-class liberals who were quieting their consciences through donations. "To give money is to turn your backs on us. We need money, but so do you. And more than money, we need you to go back to your cities and organize a movement that will be part of our movement." Almost everyone understood what she was saying and took it to heart. By the end of the week-end, these people had come to regard themselves as the seed of a national poor people's movement. That feeling took expression in the desire for another larger conference, soon; and in the idea of a single national organization or party, which seemed logical. The notion of 150 scattered people forming a national party seems premature, to say the least, and stems from a sense of importance and power on the part of these people which may appear ludicrously exaggerated. At this point the question of the formation of a national party is unimportant to our real work, except as it is the literal expression of an important feeling. What is to be stressed and given deep consideration is what happened inside of these people at the conference. Listen to what they have to say:

> I think the conference was very nice. And I learned a lot and it gave me courage to go out and do things when I have time between my job. And we talked about rent strikes. I think it is good to get our peoples more organized better I mean all people, white or colored. And I think what I learned from Fannie, I learned a lot from her, the stories she told me how the peoples was doing in Mississippi. We just as worse off as them in Mississippi, but the most of ours is behind closed doors. But the people begin to wake up and started doing something about these things. . . . I feel that everything was for our good, and we ought to stop talking about what we going to do, and do it.

At this conference each and every one were given the opportunity to communicate and understand one another and their problems from city to city. Besides this, one was allowed to see and feel the love that people have for one another, even in this troubled and corrupted world. We were showed that regardless of color, race, or creed we all can live together as one. Just as God intended it to be.

This conference gave me a stronger desire to do my part to help towards this long and hard struggle for our rights. No one should be able to say now, that we can't fight the various high authorities. We can. That is, if we do it together. Anyone that talked with and listened to Mrs. Hamer and others from Mississippi and other places from various parts of the country should now feel that all things are possible. But first of all there has to be unity. . . . We *will* move out discrimination, we *will* lessen all of this unemployment, we *will* make our landlords get rid of rats and roaches, we *will* make it so that we the Negroes and poor whites will not be pushed aside, we *will* put in to office who we all want and not just a few. These and all other things I feel we can do united together.

I was quite thrilled with the feeling that I got out to the Cleveland Conference. For the first time in my life I had a chance to sit and talk with poor people black and white. And we all faced pretty much the same problems. We discussed our problems with one another, and we shared ideas with one another about how to solve our problems and how to fight for a better future, and I think we all agree that the only way we could get a better future is to organize ourselves and stand up and fight. All through the meeting, both black and white was like sisters and brothers.

For me personally, there was a lot of things that happened there that were different than what happened all my life, like black and white together. I was always against it, but I saw it there, and I don't know who to give the credit to: SDS? the Conference? NCUP (Newark Community Union Project)? I never thought it would happen. In the South we always had to beg or stand back and get things last, but here we walked up and asked. Newark is just like the south, right here they look down on you, give you a funny eye, make you feel different—it made me feel like I didn't have to be scared or nothing. I could say anything I wanted. Deep down in my heart I feel we are one and two or three kinds of people. A lot happened there that made people feel that they could talk for themselves and didn't have to feel that they were being pushed around no more. So much happened there, so many good things, that's how I feel about it. At the conference, the way we went into little rooms and talk about our towns made me realize the need to work for rent control in New Jersey. We've been talking about it in the neighborhood but I know now that we can work and fight for it.

THE FREE SPEECH MOVEMENT

While there had been demonstrations and campus actions over the first few years of the decade, it was the eruption in September 1964 of the Free Speech Movement (FSM) at the University of California, Berkeley, that marked the beginning of a student movement that gained national attention.

The Wedding Within the War

MICHAEL ROSSMAN

In his account of the autumn 1964 events of FSM, excerpted below, Michael Rossman, a participant, captures the importance and the excitement of the campus demonstration.

When we get back to school this fall, Dean Towle of the Administration hands down this order. For years there had been these tables on the edge of the campus, at Bancroft and Telegraph, where organizations handed out literature, solicited members, and collected funds. They were there, because they used to be on campus—right in the heart of campus, Dwinelle Plaza—but the Administration pushed them off. We used to be able to stand up under the Dwinelle Oak and talk, and advocate things. They stopped that too.

So Dean Towle said, "No more tables. They block the flow of traffic." So we say—I mean the students, because I didn't get into this until later—so we say, "Gee, we don't think they block traffic; tell you what, we'll put up the money to get an independent organization to make a survey of the traffic flow." The Administration doesn't reply to this. So we start to hold meetings. Suddenly, a week later, the reason changes. We can't have tables because of the Kerr Directives, which have always been there. Always for like three years! The tables had been on campus for at least fifteen! "They've always been there," they tell us, "and we're just getting around to realizing what they really mean." So just out of thin air, they give this additional thing—well, anyway, it becomes illegal, by the Administration's rules, to hand out literature there. Let alone advocate things, let alone collect money and members.

Meetings go on, more students keep getting upset. A week later, suddenly, the Directives are reinterpreted again. The Administration tells us we can have tables at Bancroft to distribute information. Just information. Well, that suggested the tables hadn't blocked traffic in the first place. But the Administration never got around to admitting this.

But this wasn't enough, we still couldn't advocate things. There were so many contradictions. The University is spending quite a bit of money advocating Proposition 2, a bond issue, but they won't let us advocate against Proposition 14, a fair-housing ordinance. Insurance men come into the card files, which are open to the public, and collect our names, and try to sell us insurance, but we can't collect names of people who want to help in the South. The Peace Corps recruits members on campus to help overseas; we can't recruit people who want to help in this country. The University sends out United Crusade envelopes to employees—I've worked for it, your superior asks you for your envelope back. They keep check lists of who brings envelopes full of money and who doesn't. But you can't collect money on campus to send some clothes down to Negroes in the South who have been evicted.

So all this was rather upsetting, and people still weren't satisfied. So a vigil was held, all night, on the steps of Sproul, the Administration building. I finally got interested enough to go to a vigil again. It was the worst one I'd seen; I mean I didn't like the people in it at all. They seemed to be the young kids who hang out on Telegraph Avenue; there was a lot of wine, guitars, it all seemed pretty rowdy. I felt very alienated, so I went home at 2 A.M. Still, a hundred or so stayed all night. And the next day or so, the Administration got around to saying, "Well, you can advocate things." They reinterpreted the Directives again. They never gave a reason for these successive reinterpretations.

Well, this still wasn't enough to restore our effectiveness. The University had shoved all these organizations off-campus and then graciously permitted them these tables in the last three or four years. And this is how the organizations kept alive. What it meant for them to be denied the "privilege" to collect money and to recruit members on campus—a right that exists at every state and junior college in California—was that they'd die. And in particular this meant CORE and SNCC. . . .

For the first time ever, all the political groups on the campus united in opposing what the Administration was doing. Not only the various socialist splinter groups, and CORE and SNCC, and the Young Democrats, who have never been very radical. Also the Young Republicans, Students for Goldwater, and even the Intercollegiate Society of Individualists, whom my political friends think of as young fascists. It was really a United Front, very strange political bedfellows. Because after all, here was a Constitutional issue.

And people said, don't be unreasonable, be moderate. Compromise is the central thing in a democracy. The Administration has come forward to meet your demands a bit; why don't you give a bit on these last two things? But it wasn't a question of giving *a bit* on them. For six years they had been trying to wipe out the organizations. This was not a new thing, and these were not two minor points.

And I want to make a point about tactics. There are a lot of people around, even in this community, who look on the Civil Rights demonstrations in the City as very unfortunate. They say, "How terrible: these kids get a cause, and they rush in and they perform hasty actions." But every single civil disobedience thing that has happened was preceded by months, sometimes over a year, of patient negotiation. And it was like this here. We had been negotiating not for two weeks. We had been negotiating for six years. . . .

In all those previous times, what we did, we negotiated. We did everything through the approved channels. We wrote letters to our Congressmen, letters to the local newspapers, letters to the *Daily Cal,* letters to the University administrators. We went in and saw them individually, and as group representatives, and in groups. Nothing happened. Nothing ever happened. We negotiated, we set up committees, we signed petitions, sometimes they had 5,000 signatures on them. We circulated petitions in the faculty. The faculty set up committees. We picketed. And what did we get for these six years, every time there was a repressive measure? We got nothing. We got back in those years not one inch of the ground that was taken away from us. We were nice all the way; we were very unhappy, but we were nice.

So it's Tuesday, I guess, that they say, "To hell with it. We give up. We're going to set up the tables on campus. We're going to set up the tables, and we're going to ask for money. We're going to ask for members." So they set them up, and some people sat down at them. And the Administration came along and took their names, and summoned them to see the Dean. By some coincidence, the five students were CORE and SNCC members. By some coincidence they were precisely the leaders in the movement. There were a lot of people sitting at the tables, but the Administration picked these. It happens, and there's not much you can say about it. You learn to expect it. You learn to expect to get beaten every step of the way.

That afternoon, the Dean of Men wanted to see the five students. But by this time over 400 students had signed a piece of paper that said, "I sat at the table too. I want equal treatment. Suspend me too." And somehow the five got into their heads that they weren't five any more; they were 400. And they all went and said this to the Dean, and asked him about all the other people who had been sitting there when the five leaders' names were taken. And he said, "Well, I'm sorry. We can only deal with observed violations, not unobserved violations." They said, "How can we negotiate if our leaders have been suspended?" So he canceled the negotiating meeting that had been set up for 4:00.

Well, what can you say? They stayed in Sproul Hall and began a small sit-in. There were a hundred there at midnight when they got word that the five had been suspended from school, "indefinitely," and three more too. The three weren't even notified; they didn't know why, people thought it was for helping organize the afternoon protest. It was very confused, and after a while everyone went home.

So the next morning I was sitting around on the Terrace, wondering what was going to happen. Everyone felt sure something would. Lo and behold, they bring the tables out again and set them up right in front of the Administration building. And they sit down at the tables again and put out membership lists and start collecting donations.

This time, there's a "non-student" sitting at one of the tables. He's a member of one of the organizations, he graduated last year, in mathematics. And the University police come along and arrest him. He goes limp; what else can you do? And so four cops carry him to this police car that's sitting in the middle of the Plaza. And a crowd starts gathering, and some people sit down in front of the police car, and behind the police car. The police don't like this. Luckily at this stage it was only campus cops, and as cops go, campus cops are pretty nice. As cops go. In a while it is noon, there are 3,000 people around this police car in Sproul Plaza. Around the car hundreds are sitting down; they don't want it to be moved.

Then somebody gets on top of the car—the cops let him—to talk to the crowd, it was unhappy. And then this incredible dialogue began. People got up on top of that car from before noon Wednesday, they were talking until two in the morning. All different points of view were offered. The top of that car was a platform thrown open to anybody who wanted to come up and say what he had to say. I have never heard anything like this in my life. It was a continuous dialogue that went on for fifteen straight hours.

And people stopped and listened to it. And people voted. If you've never seen 3,000 people voting, it's a very strange thing; 3,000 people in, as the newspapers described it, "a mob scene." So many people on a political issue had never been seen on campus, a large political demonstration on campus is maybe 300. Several faculty members told me that the Chancellor became absolutely hysterical—they used those words—and complained "he would not listen to reason." It seems to me that the rest of the Administration was pretty hysterical too. . . .

So it's Thursday night, and there are still well over a thousand of us. And by this time we realize simply that we have to hold that car. That car is the only thing we've gotten in six years. It's our car; it isn't the cops' car any more. And so we start bringing sleeping bags. And the dialogue on top of the car continues. People are getting up there and talking, and people are listening. And people are voting on this, and people are voting on that.

It's almost enough to make you believe that if it were given a chance, the democratic process might work. It just might work. People quoted books as if books were relevant. They talked about the Greeks, and they talked about theories of politics, as if it all *meant* something. And listening to them, I almost believed for the first time in years that it did mean something.

And we're sitting there near midnight when this kid Mario Savio—he's twenty-one, I'm twenty-four, a kid too—comes running up; I had never seen him before the last few days. He was one of the leaders, one of the suspended students. He talked pretty good; I gather he's a junior in philosophy. He's got a good heart, he talks straight sense, and he's got an infinite amount of patience. Anyway, he'd been up and down on the car during the day, and now he comes running up because some people jumped him, right off campus. It turns out, this huge flood of fraternity boys has come down. The paper says there were 200 of them. But there were not 200, there were over a thousand. I have been estimating crowds for a long time. We're seated, packed in, and they surround us and stand around, yelling and throwing tomatoes and eggs. And throwing dozens of lit cigarettes into our ranks. When you're sat down like that you can't move, and they're trampling people at the edges. Some of their own people got up to the car and spoke to calm them down, and they threw eggs even at their own people, and Jew-baited them. And they were screaming at us, "Get off the car, get off the car." They wanted the car like freed, and I think they wanted blood. And they were calling us Communists, and, you know, we should go home and take a bath. God, would we have loved to go home and take a bath. A bath and a shave, and sleep. But you can't. Because if you go home, there'll be nobody there. And always before, we've gone home, and there's been nobody left.

Meanwhile, the Alameda County Sheriff's Department men are standing in the background in their nice blue uniforms. And some of them are egging the fraternity boys on. We appealed that they should form a line between them and us, they should stop this, because it was an incredibly explosive situation. And they yelled back, "We don't see that it's explosive." Faculty members appealed for the same thing and got the same answer. So it stayed on being explosive.

It was like out of a fairy tale. Mario and a girl named Jackie were standing up there on top of the car and trying to *reason* with them. Mario in particular, who'd been up I don't know how many hours and had been talking all day, is trying to explain to them our position. And they keep yelling and throwing things at him, and then he starts talking, and they start chanting, "Get off the car," so nobody can hear him. And he waits till they're done, and he tries again, and again, and again. This goes on for hours. To explain; to explain; to ask them to come up and talk.

And meanwhile we're sitting there, scared to death. I'm not particularly cowardly, but they grow them big in the fraternities, and there are an awful lot of them. Somehow, tension bleeds away a little, and then this priest comes and for the first time there is silence. He climbs on top of the car, and some of the fraternity kids yell at him. But others silence them. Roughly he says, "This is a bad deal. There's a lot of hate here, and hate is bad. If you hate enough, it means murder. I want you to think of that." Then he gets down, and an Administration representative comes and says, "Go away."

After that, after hours and hours of speaking, we just shut up. They would yell, "Get off the car," and this little ruffle of "Shhh!" would go through the thousand or so of us. We sat there with our mouths shut for half an hour, and finally they just went away. Next morning, of course, the papers recorded a lot of conviviality between them and us; talked about panty raids and such things. I just want to say, it wasn't like that.

There was very little chance for sleep after all that. There were few fortunate enough to have sleeping bags. Some of us tried to sleep on the lawn, and got sopping when the automatic sprinkler system went on at five. Most got an hour and were grateful. I went and got my recorder and played with some guitars on the steps. When the sun came up people folded their blankets, picked up leaflets, and swept up all around the Plaza and the steps; it's a thing with us.

It's eight in the morning and it's a beautiful day; it's a beautiful Friday. And the sun starts coming up. And the sun keeps coming up. And the sun keeps up there all day, and we melt like wax. There's just nothing to protect you, you sit there, and you stink; you sweat;

you feel faint; and you just sit there, packed around the car, and there's nothing else you can do. By now there were maybe 400 of us, and hardly any more all day who sat down. But by God, we had that car. It was all we had, and we were going to keep it until we were forced to give it up.

As soon as day begins the dialogue on top of the car resumes. Everybody gets up and talks about our three demands. And people give history; and people give facts. At noontime, when the crowd of onlookers swells to about three thousand, we ask them, come sit down with us. A few do. Meanwhile all this time Jack, the guy, is still in the cop car, they give him a beer can to piss in. . . .

So we sat in the sun, and the dialogue continues, and there's so much information: historical résumés, California State Supreme Court decisions, and such. And somebody who'd been active in the old days, a law student, Michael Tigar, got up on top of the car. Those of us who had been active with him were very glad to see him. And he tells us about this book that Clark Kerr wrote in the late fifties, called *The Managerial Revolution,* and he gives us a summary of Kerr's thesis: There are the managed and the managers. The University is part of the managerial society. It's this big ship; and the ship has got a captain; and the captain is the President; and what he says goes. And Tigar says, "We thought the only place this kind of thinking was left in the world after the 1920s was in Mussolini's Italy." But he goes on talking about this book, as if it really meant something to talk about a book, as if these ideas and a rational counter-argument to them had some real use, which is very hard to believe after you've been around a University for eight years and gotten concerned about things, and had the spirit beaten down in you. At the end, Tigar says, "I don't want to be coarse, but there's one thing that's got to be said. People have been talking like this is just a little thing. But I want to say, even if they cut 'em off one at a time, it's still castration." And that's the truth, and it was good to hear someone say it in so many words.

I was ready to drop, everyone was. I went to lie down on a lawn for a while, but I asked a friend to wake me because the word was that something was going to happen that night. The next day was Parents' Day at the University. And, wow, publicity for the University was bad enough without all the parents coming along and seeing a crowd of 400 beatniks sitting around a cop car and this guy still in it.

But I couldn't get to sleep, because I was too keyed up. Because the only way you can keep going after you've been going like this for a couple of days, is on nervous energy. And the moment you let loose of it you're dead, and so it takes hours to unwind.

Forty minutes later, a friend comes over and says, come quick, something's going to happen, and I go to the car. There are very few of us, and slowly other people start collecting around us, but they're standing. We're the only ones who are sitting. And we scrunch up close to the car, because the word is that they're going to come and try to take Jack away. Meanwhile all day there've been these negotiations maybe going on; we've heard nothing, we figured they'd break down. We sit there for two hours. People are passing out sandwiches; both days we collected money and outside people made sandwiches and brought them in, and offered other help. And people bring us reports of sympathy demonstrations in other colleges. All this is very nice when you feel very much alone.

Comes 6:30, 7:00, there's this incredible scene. There are 500 of us at most seated around the car, and maybe 3,000 spectators. Some of them are with us but afraid to get arrested, maybe another 300, we can't tell. But the great majority are the kids who were heckling us the previous night, the Greeks and others. They fill the steps of Sproul; they're clustered in the Student Union; they're on the roof of the cafeteria; they're perched in trees. I have never seen so many at one time. And they want blood.

Meanwhile, in back of Sproul Hall, there are 500 policemen, with boots, with night sticks in hand, and with steel helmets. And the hecklers are there, screaming for blood. "We want blood," they yell. I'd seen this sort of thing before, but never in such magnitude, never 500 cops gathered together. And we're there, and we're singing. There are 400 people willing to go to jail; we're singing because we're scared to death.

Well, the jail part doesn't so much bother me. I mean, I've got a teaching assistantship to lose and a career and things like that, but these are minor points. And they really are. Somebody was going to get killed. This is not a melodrama. Somebody was going to get killed, if the cops came in. That's why I was there. I didn't realize at first how many they'd have. Then when I found out, I figured—somebody's going to get killed.

Because there were all sorts of people sitting there, these ninety pound girls and pregnant women, no kidding, pregnant women, packed in, unable to move. And we try to tell them what it's going to be like. "If you're wearing rings or you're wearing pierced earrings, take them off. Don't leave buttons pinned to your chest. When they get to you, go limp. If you lock arms they'll club you apart." In between the fraternity boys are yelling to bring on the cops. If that had started, I do believe we would have had not only 500 cops on our backs, but 2,000 fraternity boys.

But what can you do when you're in one of these things but lie there and take it? You tuck your chin to your chest so they can't get you under it, and you pray very selfishly that you're not going to be the one that gets hurt. And you hold on to the guy next to you for dear life. But you don't feel anything. You don't even feel hate. You know you dare not raise a finger to them.

It's sort of symbolic of the whole thing, these last six years. They take away everything, your papers, your rights, your friends, and you put up a polite protest, but you've just got to lie there and take it. And you walk a picket line clad in the same clothes that you went to your fellowship interview in, and they taunt you and spit on you. And you smile. And you don't get mad at them. Not because you're such a nice guy. You don't get mad at them because you can't afford to, because if you let what they're saying reach you, you'll crack in half. You can't do a damned thing about it. You've just got to sit there and take it, lie on the ground and let the cops tromp on you with their boots. . . .

. . . [A]ll you can do is hope that next time a few more will be aware that there are some issues around, and be willing to sit down for what they believe. If you don't know there are issues around, that's your tough luck; the "powers that be" try to keep you from learning. But I know enough to make me so sick at heart, so that for a long time I wasn't interested in learning any more. I couldn't take it. That's all there is to say. I know why there weren't 3,000 sitting down. I'll be damned if I know why even 300 were there waiting to get mashed.

I'm not even sure why I was there. I was there because I couldn't not be there, but that doesn't explain it. We were sitting there, they were shouting for our blood, and people were being very nice to each other, holding each other's things, handing each other sandwiches, bucking each other up. And I suddenly remembered, in the last three years I've walked maybe five or six picket lines, one of them was not too long ago, in Oakland, around the *Tribune*. There were maybe seventy kids, not particularly well dressed. The cops were there, giving them a hard time, and so were the hecklers.

And these goddamned kids were singing; they were singing, "There is love in that land." Did they believe it? I don't know. Then they sang, "There's free speech in that land." We sang that last night. God. These are maybe the only people around who believe *anything.* But can they really believe there is love in that land? After reading the *Tribune's* editorials?

There's so much hate around. There was so much hate yesterday, and so much last night. We were sitting there surrounded by hate, and singing about "There is love in that land." And after you've been at it two or three days, after you haven't slept, after you've sat there in the goddamned sun, with people yelling for your blood, knowing that you've been getting the boot steadily for the past six years—you get delirious. You honest to God get delirious. And you can almost believe what you're singing. You can almost con yourself into believing that these things mean something. That there is love in that land. That there is free speech, and all those other crazy abstractions, in that land.

An End to History

MARIO SAVIO

Mario Savio, a leader of FSM, seemed to articulate the pent-up feelings and frustrations of many students. In one of the most famous speeches of the early new left, Savio told a huge campus rally to resist the Berkeley administration:

"There's a time when the operation of the machine becomes so odious, makes you so sick at heart, that you can't take part, you can't even tacitly take part. And you've got to put your bodies upon the gears and

Reprinted by permission, Mario Savio.

upon the wheels, upon the levers, upon all the apparatus and you've got to make it stop. And you've got to indicate to the people who run it, to the people who own it, that unless you're free, the machine will be prevented from working at all."

In the essay below, written in 1964, Savio enunciates many new left themes: the hierarchical and bureaucratic nature of American society and of the University of California, the alienation of students, the limitation of speech to that which is not critical political speech, the existence of racial injustice, and the links between the civil rights movement and the student movement.

Last summer I went to Mississippi to join the struggle there for civil rights. This fall I am engaged in another phase of the same struggle, this time in Berkeley. The two battlefields may seem quite different to some observers, but this is not the case. The same rights are at stake in both places—the right to participate as citizens in democratic society and the right to due process of law. Further, it is a struggle against the same enemy. In Mississippi an autocratic and powerful minority rules, through organized violence, to suppress the vast, virtually powerless, majority. In California, the privileged minority manipulates the University bureaucracy to suppress the students' political expression. That "respectable" bureaucracy masks the financial plutocrats; that impersonal bureaucracy is the efficient enemy in a "Brave New World."

In our free speech fight at the University of California, we have come up against what may emerge as the greatest problem of our nation—depersonalized, unresponsive bureaucracy. We have encountered the organized status quo in Mississippi, but it is the same in Berkeley. Here we find it impossible usually to meet with anyone but secretaries. Beyond that, we find functionaries who cannot make policy but can only hide behind the rules. We have discovered total lack of response on the part of the policy makers. To grasp a situation which is truly Kafkesque, it is necessary to understand the bureaucratic mentality. And we have learned quite a bit about it this fall, more outside the classroom than in.

As bureaucrat, an administrator believes that nothing new happens. He occupies an ahistorical point of view. In September, to get the attention of this bureaucracy which had issued arbitrary edicts suppressing student political expression and refused to discuss its action, we held a sit-in on the campus. We sat around a police car and kept it immobilized for over thirty-two hours. At last, the administrative bureaucracy agreed to negotiate. But instead, on the following Monday, we discovered that a committee had been appointed, in accordance with usual regulations, to resolve the dispute. Our attempt to convince any of the administrators that an event had occurred, that something new had happened, failed. They saw this simply as something to be handled by normal University procedures.

The same is true of all bureaucracies. They begin as tools, means to certain legitimate goals, and they end up feeding their own existence. The conception that bureaucrats have is that history has in fact come to an end. No events can occur now that the Second World War is over which can change American society substantially. We proceed by standard procedures as we are.

The most crucial problems facing the United States today are the problem of automation and the problem of racial injustice. Most people who will be put out of jobs by machines will not accept an end to events, this historical plateau, as the point beyond which no change occurs. Negroes will not accept an end to history here. All of us must refuse to accept history's final judgment that in America there is no place in society for people whose skins are dark. On campus students are not about to accept it as fact that the university has ceased evolving and is in its final state of perfection, that students and faculty are respectively raw material and employees, or that the university is to be autocratically run by unresponsive bureaucrats.

Here is the real contradiction: the bureaucrats hold history as ended. As a result significant parts of the population both on campus and off are dispossessed, and these dispossessed are not about to accept this ahistorical point of view. It is out of this that the conflict has occurred with the university bureaucracy and will continue to occur until that bureaucracy becomes responsive or until it is clear the university can not function.

The things we are asking for in our civil rights protests have a deceptively quaint ring. We are asking for the due process of law. We are asking for our actions to be judged by committees of our peers. We are asking that regulations ought to be considered as arrived at legitimately only from the consensus of the governed. These phrases are all pretty old, but they are not being taken seriously in America today, nor are they being taken seriously on the Berkeley campus.

I have just come from a meeting with the dean of students. She notified us that she was aware of certain violations of University regulations by certain organizations. University friends of SNCC, which I represent, was one of these. We tried to draw from her some statement on these great principles, consent of the governed, jury of one's peers, due process. The best she could do was to evade or to present the administration party line. It is very hard to make any contact with the human being who is behind these organizations.

The university is the place where people begin seriously to question the conditions of their existence and raise the issue of whether they can be committed to the society they have been born into. After a long period of apathy during the fifties, students have begun not only to question but, having arrived at answers, to act on those answers. This is part of a growing understanding among many people in America that history has not ended, that a better society is possible, and that it is worth dying for.

This free speech fight points up a fascinating aspect of contemporary campus life. Students are permitted to talk all they want so long as their speech has no consequences.

One conception of the university, suggested by a classical Christian formulation, is that it be in the world but not of the world. The conception of Clark Kerr, by contrast, is that the university is part and parcel of this particular stage in the history of American society; it stands to serve the need of American industry; it is a factory that turns out a certain product needed by industry or government. Because speech does often have consequences which might alter this perversion of higher education, the university must put itself in a position of censorship. It can permit two kinds of speech, speech which encourages continuation of the status quo, and speech which advocates changes in it so radical as to be irrelevant in the foreseeable future. Someone may advocate radical change in all aspects of American society, and this I am sure he can do with impunity. But if someone advocates sit-ins to bring about changes in discriminatory hiring practices, this cannot be permitted because it goes against the status quo of which the university is a part. And that is how the fight began here.

The administration of the Berkeley campus has admitted that external, extra-legal groups have pressured the University not to permit students on campus to organize picket lines, not to permit on campus any speech with consequences. And the bureaucracy went along. Speech with consequences, speech in the area of civil rights, speech which some might regard as illegal, must stop.

Many students here at the University, many people in society, are wandering aimlessly about. Strangers in their own lives, there is no place for them. They are people who have not learned to compromise, who for example have come to the University to learn to question, to grow, to learn—all the standard things that sound like clichés because no one takes them seriously. And they find at one point or other that for them to become part of society, to become lawyers, ministers, businessmen, people in government, that very often they must compromise those principles which were most dear to them. They must suppress the most creative impulses that they have; this is a prior condition for being part of the system. The University is well structured, well tooled, to turn out people with all the sharp edges worn off, the well-rounded person. The University is well equipped to produce that sort of person, and this means that the best among the people who enter must for four years wander aimlessly much of the time questioning why they are on campus at all, doubting whether there is any point in what they are doing, and looking toward a very bleak existence afterward in a game in which all of the rules have been made up, which one cannot really amend.

It is a bleak scene, but it is all a lot of us have to look forward to. Society provides no challenge. American society in the standard conception it has of itself is simply no longer exciting. The most exciting things going on in America today are movements to change America. America is becoming ever more the Utopia of sterilized, automated contentment. The "futures" and "careers" for which American students now prepare are for the most part intellectual and moral wastelands. This chrome-plated consumers paradise would have us grow up to be well-behaved children. But an important minority of men and women coming to the front today have shown that they will die rather than be standardized, replaceable and irrelevant.

Free Speech Movement Leaflets

A brief selection of leaflets distributed during the Free Speech Movement provide a sense of the activities and enthusiasm.

To the Students of Political Science 113

". . . by our silence or by the stand we take, we too shall enter the fray." Some of you have heard me speak these words of Camus before; I speak them again today, only now not as the prelude to a lecture but rather to the expression of an obligation deeply felt. It has been said that with so worthy a cause, the protesting students deserved better of their leaders. I have no doubt we all do. But the luxury rarely falls to any one man, however rational or learned, himself to set the precise terms to a debate engaged in by his fellows. The fact is that I can no longer suit my actions to whatever hopes I might previously have held for seeing some of those terms changed. Even to be silent is still to enter the fray. I have been witnessing the astonishing scene at Sproul Hall since the early hours of morning. And as I have tried to absorb the significance of what was taking place before my eyes, it became clear to me that I simply was incapable of violating the palpable air of protest which today surrounds every building on this campus.

There will be no class today.

Norman Jacobson
Associate Professor of Political Science

"Do Not Fold, Bend, Mutilate, or Spindle"

In the tumultuous months of the 1964 fall semester, Berkeley activists produced numerous leaflets, position papers, and ruminations about the situation on their campus. This anonymous statement, and the two that follow, appeared in the FSM Newsletter, *one of the publications that sprang into existence in the wake of campus action.*

At the beginning, we did not realize the strength of the forces we were up against. We have learned that we must fight not only Dean Towle, Chancellor Strong, and President Kerr, but also the Board of Regents with their billions of dollars and Governor Brown with his army of cops.

But neither did they realize the forces they were up against. At the beginning, they thought they had only to fight a hundred or so "beatniks," "Maoists," and "Fidelistas." But they put eight hundred of the "hard core" in jail and found they still had to face thousands of other students and faculty members.

The source of their power is clear enough: the guns and the clubs of the Highway Patrol, the banks and corporations of the Regents. But what is the source of our power?

It is something we see everywhere on campus but find hard to define. Perhaps it was best expressed by the sign one boy pinned to his chest: "I am a UC student. Please don't bend, fold, spindle or mutilate me." The source of our strength is, very simply, the fact that we are human beings and so cannot forever be treated as raw materials—to be processed. Clark Kerr has declared, in his writings and by his conduct, that a university must be like any other factory—a place where workers who handle raw material are themselves handled like raw material by the administrators above them. Kerr is confident that in his utopia "there will not be any revolt, anyway, except little bureaucratic revolts that can be handled piecemeal."

As President of one of the greatest universities in the world, one which is considered to lie on the "cutting edge of progress," Kerr hopes to make UC a model to be proudly presented for the consideration of even higher authorities.

By our action, we have proved Kerr wrong in his claim that human beings can be handled like raw material without provoking revolt. We have smashed to bits his pretty little doll house. The next task will be to build in its stead a real house for real people.

Catch-801

MARVIN GARSON

Marvin Garson, an FSM activist, drew on Joseph Heller's Catch-22, *a novel attracting considerable attention among the young, in analyzing the Berkeley situation.*

Joseph Heller's authoritative work on constitutional law offers the following definition of Catch-22: "Catch-22 says they have a right to do anything we can't stop them from doing." This fundamental section has been construed by American law enforcement authorities to override any conflicting provisions in our Constitution.

Many students, inexperienced in the ways of the law, thought that they had been subjected to irregular and illegal procedures. One student, for instance, said to a sheriff's deputy, "You can't do this," even though the deputy had, in fact, just done it.

In the booking room at Oakland City Jail, a pay telephone hangs on the wall. Next to it is a very clear sign saying that prisoners have a right to two completed phone calls immediately after being booked. We were told we could make only one phone call. Those who protested were threatened with loss of their one phone call.

Reprinted by permission, Marvin Garson.

Our bond had already been posted, which set us free according to the law. Instead of telling us we were free, they took us to the Alameda County Prison Farm at Santa Rita.

In another part of Santa Rita, fifty girls who wanted to telephone were told to wait in a cage. After a few hours, the wardens told them that they couldn't telephone; but if they handed in signed slips saying they had already telephoned, they would be let out of the cage.

Like the police, the University Administration has the right to do anything we can't stop them from doing. They tried to exercise that right in September by taking away our tables. We were entitled to those tables; even they admit it, now that it doesn't matter so much. They ordered the police to arrest one of our people sitting at a table; *but we stopped them from doing it.* On October 2, we first realized that Catch-22 is the fundamental law of California and the world, so we began to act accordingly to protect ourselves.

When the Regents met, they confirmed the principle by saying they had a right to do anything they wanted except take away the tables, because we had stopped them from doing *that.*

Then Chancellor Strong sent letters to four of us, saying that he was preparing to do anything to them that he wanted. ("The Committee's recommendation will be advisory to me.") So we responded by doing our best to stop Chancellor Strong.

Governor Brown has called us Anarchists. Nonsense. We have acted, and will continue to act, in accordance with the basic law of our country, the law which Governor Brown applied to us when we were in the hands of his deputies in the Alameda County Prison Farm at Santa Rita.

Freedom Is a Big Deal

BARBARA GARSON

Another FSM activist, Barbara Garson, later gained national attention for her satire MacBird, *a parody of* Macbeth, *in which Lyndon Johnson and wife, Lady Bird, substitute for Shakespeare's originals.*

It seems very likely now that the University will liberalize its regulations on free speech and political activity. No doubt, hidden restrictions will be wrapped in the new rules.

The administration, of course, will deny that it yielded to direct pressure but we can take great pride in having for once, reversed the world-wide drift from freedom. We did not teach Clark Kerr the moral error of his ways; we simply showed him that in this case, blatantly repressing us was more trouble than it was worth.

But must we always make this massive effort in order to effect a minor change? The answer is yes. Yes, because power still lies with the administration. Our lives at school are still ruled and regulated by officials who are not responsible to us. Our recent rebellion did not attempt to change this. Indeed this change can not be made on one campus.

Yet I dream of someday living in a democracy. On campus, committees of students and faculty will make the minimum regulations needed to administer (not rule) our academic community. I hope to see democracy extended to the offices and factories, so that everyone may have the satisfaction of making the decisions about the use of his productive energies.

I look past government by the grunted consent of the governed. Someday we will participate actively in running our own lives in all spheres of work and leisure.

Reprinted by permission, Barbara Garson.

Memories of FSM

BETTINA APTHEKER

Aptheker, a leader of FSM, recalls her experiences as a woman in the early days of the student movement. This speech was given in Berkeley in 1984 at a twentieth reunion of FSM participants.

I have some things I'd like to say to you about women in the 60s.

You know there were scores of documentaries, anthologies, histories, memoirs . . . about the sixties. . . . And most of them, the vast majority, have been written or edited by men. And often they have not included even the most minimal representation of the ideas, reflections, experiences, and articulations of women. We have, therefore, only a partial history of the sixties. It's not that what is written is wrong, it's that it's partial. It only reflects part of that movement. One of the things I have noticed about these anthologies and materials that have been produced is that they tend to dwell excessively on issues of power and control. I have often thought that if we were to put together an anthology of women activists from the sixties, with memoirs and ideas and thoughts and reflections and experiences, they would dwell in part on issues of power and control and politics, but they would also talk about the dailyness of struggle, of making connections, and of a long, slow process of meaningful change. They would also talk about other issues that are far more painful and far less pretty to look at, but they are absolutely essential for us. Within my experience in the student movement, in the civil rights movement, in the anti-war movements, it was women, primarily, who staffed the offices, answered the telephones, assembled the mailings, ran the mimeograph machines, often all night. And it was the men who held

Reprinted by permission, Bettina Aptheker.

the press conferences and established the parameters of publicity around the movements. This reflected the sexual division of labor that exists in this society. But if we're a radical movement, about the business of changing society, we need to change how we go about our business of making change. On a more difficult note, it was also the case that there were women who in one way or another found themselves in situations of performing sexual favors for important movement leaders. That's a fact; that happened. It is also a fact that women activists were also more seriously abused, physically and sexually, both by the police, which is to be expected, and also by men within the movement, which . . . is no longer tolerable. It is impossible to conceive of making significant social change in this society and in this world at the same time that one has personal relationships in which women are sexually or physically abused by men. It's not acceptable. And we cannot make any kind of permanent change if we do not take the issues of women's personal experiences and place them onto a political plane where we understand the nature and dimension of women's oppression.

A favorite accusation of the right wing press during the Free Speech Movement was that Mario, wonderful Mario, I love Mario, that Mario, however, was an innocent, if misguided, youth who had been seduced, by me, the villainess and evil woman, into criminal and seditious acts. It was generally assumed, even in the mainstream press, that Mario and I were lovers. So much so that when Mario announced his engagement to someone else, I was bombarded with questions from a dozen reporters. How was I taking the news? Was I upset? Was I crushed? What revenge would I visit upon this sainted fellow? This is really true, this really happened.

Now it wasn't until the women's liberation movement in the 70s that I could begin to process this and figure it out in terms of the sexism that was involved. . . . And that it was just a variation on the old theme of a woman as either a virgin or a whore with nothing in between. You know, so that it was this same notion . . . that I was somehow this evil, and, of course, the fact that I was a Communist helped. The other thing about this was that it was also very painful for me, because you see, I loved Mario and I had a wonderful friendship with Mario, and Mario was the first man with whom I had an intimate friendship that was not sexual. And that was very important to me, and I was very confused about my sexual identity and who I was, and all of those kinds of issues. So the relationship was crucial for me, and to have it broadcast in that way with such innuendoes . . . was very difficult for me. And it was clarifying when the women's movement came along and I began to understand what the politics of that accusation were.

This leads to another point. . . . Because of my upbringing and experience in the revolutionary and Communist circles in which I was raised, and I was an only child, very cherished by my parents, I was not a gendered female in traditional ways, in a traditional sense. You know, gender is socially constructed. See you are born one sex or another, you all know that, I mean you're either one or the other. But your gender, how you are socialized, is culturally constructed. So, I was raised in a family where . . . baseball was my presiding passion as a child. I was completely crushed at the age of ten when I found out that I couldn't play in Little League because they didn't accept girls; it was a devastating experience for me. It really was. And I was taught in my family and in the circles in which I grew up to speak, to write what I thought, to speak my views and that I was as capable and as intelligent as anyone else. I didn't have a socialization that made me unable to speak in public, or unable to act. And when I hit Berkeley (I was, after all, [Herbert] Aptheker's daughter), I was ushered in to the inner circles of the revolutionary movement, despite my sex. And I became part of that. In fact, I was treated as one of the boys. Now you see there was a problem here for me, because I wasn't a boy. So I want to describe to you what happened, and this is something we need to work on. What happened for me was that I was treated as a pal by the men in the movement. I was neutered sexually. In other words, I didn't have any other kind of social existence, social life, anything else. Or, the other . . . experience was that I became an object of sexual prey. If I was perceived female, and not one of the boys, then I became an object of sexual prey. So I had . . . two extremes that I was trying to cope with, which were very confusing and very difficult. And again, it wasn't until the women's movement that I could understand what had taken place there, and to see that there were ways of changing what seemed to be a natural ordering of relationships.

I internalized certain aspects of the oppression of women by believing that there were men, there were women, and then there was me. Because I didn't seem to fit anywhere. And I didn't want to be like other women. Because I saw other women as being subordinated, and unable to speak and unable to present their views. So I didn't want to identify with women. And therefore I participated in the oppression of women in the FSM, for which I apologize. I didn't know, but I have learned, and what I want to do is take the experience and I want to give it back to you, all right?

So it is that female activists of the 60s encounter each other years later with a kind of awed respect. It doesn't matter where we have been or what our political allegiances are now. The first greeting is a tender caress of memory, the second an almost incoherent staccato representation of key junctures in the arrangement of twenty years. We are everywhere now, scattered among workers, poets, artists, teachers, and children. And even within the secondary and, at times, humiliating roles women were forced to play within the movement of the 60s, we were part of it. And we could, and did, march in the morning, and in apprehending the sound of those streets flooded with people we heard the echo of our own liberation. It was the first and enduring piece of evidence. What we learned in the 60s, the great secret, as it were, is that people have both the inherited wisdom and the collective strength to change the conditions of their lives. That we have identified ourselves as women and gotten that point is shifting the balance of power in the world.

Women in the 60s were central to the process of social change, using the resources and materials we had available to us. Part of our purpose in remembering our lives twenty years ago is our determination that we will never again permit the lives, experience, history of women to be erased. We will never again permit that to happen. There will be a continuity, and our children and our children's children will have a record of what women have done. And I call upon you to remember the women of the Free Speech Movement, whose names I can only recall some of, some of whom are here tonight [gives names], who organized, picketed, staffed, and were jailed in the Free Speech Movement. Let their names live in your memory and know what their lives have been about, and where they have been, and what they have done, and let you pass that on to your children.

I want to say something else about this. Which is that because of a collision of racism and sexism in this society, the work of black women in the South in the civil rights movement has been substantially erased. And I want you to remember the names of the women who were active, and organized, and maintained the civil rights movement in the South in those early days of the 60s and before. From Rosa Parks, who refused to move to the back of the bus in Montgomery, Alabama, to Mary Church Terrill who ... at the age of eighty six, filed suit against the Thompson restaurants in the city of Washington, DC, which was a segregated city. Mary Church Terrill sued the Thompson restaurants, and it was her case that broke the back of segregation in Washington, DC, a year before the Supreme Court decision that ordered the desegregation of public schools. I want you to remember the committee of one hundred black women in Montgomery, Alabama, who were the ones that organized and provided the transportation for the black community in Alabama during that bus boycott so that folks could get to and from work and the doctor and the grocery store and everything else in the dailyness of their lives that they had to do. It was black women who were the backbone of that movement. And I want you to remember May Mallory, and I want you to remember Ruby Doris Robinson, and I want you to remember Fannie Lou Hamer.

So we understand that we're not going to allow this history to be erased again. And we understand that we're also not going to allow the history of lesbian women to be erased again. Not ever again. There was a continuity, and there was a history, and it is going to be maintained. . . .

A very wonderful woman named Florence Luscombe demonstrated for women's suffrage many, many years ago. She said, "There is no end to what you can accomplish, if you don't care who gets the credit." May peace be with you. Thank you.

NEW LEFT THINKING AT MID-DECADE

After the initial flush of Port Huron, ERAP, and FSM, student and new left leaders began, in the mid-sixties, to attempt the development of an increasingly sophisticated theoretical position upon which to expand and further the

In White America: Radical Consciousness and Social Change

GREGORY CALVERT

Gregory Calvert, a president of SDS, gave this important speech in February 1967 at an SDS gathering in Princeton, New Jersey. He contends that the only real revolutionaries are those struggling for their own liberation. This was a significant argument in the ongoing new left debate over which groups were the potential agencies of social change in a capitalist society. Many white middle-class students felt guilty about their privilege, and Calvert suggests that students' activism on their own behalf was authentically oppositional.

I am going to speak today about the problem of consciousness in American society and about the possibility of developing radical or revolutionary consciousness. I approach the problem of organizing from this viewpoint because 1) the objective conditions of oppression in America seem to be manifest and 2) because those objective conditions are not perceived, and 3) because the major problem to which organizers must address themselves in this period is the problem of false consciousness.

Let me posit a first principle: All authentically revolutionary movements are struggles for human freedom.

Contrary to what was suggested here last evening, revolutionary mass movements are not built out of a drive for the acquisition of more material goods. That is a perversion and vulgarization of revolutionary thought and a misreading of history. Revolutionary movements are freedom struggles born out of the perception of the contradictions between human potentiality and oppressive actuality. Revolutionary consciousness interprets those social economic and political structures which maintain the existing gap between potentiality and actuality as the objective conditions of oppression which must be transformed.

Reprinted by permission, Gregory Calvert. Ph.D.

Revolutionary consciousness sees the transformation of those oppressive conditions as the act of liberation and sees the realization of the previously frustrated human potentiality as the achievement of freedom. The bonds of oppression are broken and the new reality is constructed.

What is fundamental to this process is the mass perception of the contradiction between potentiality and actuality. In a given historical situation that contradiction may take the concrete form of economic deprivation in the face of the possibility of material abundance and the struggle for liberation may take the form of a drive to eliminate the conditions which prevent the achievement of that abundance. In a situation of economic abundance, the drive for freedom will rest on different perceptions and will set different goals. But the struggle in either case is a struggle for freedom, the form of which depends on the given stage of historical development—that is, on the level of development of human potentiality.

There is only one impulse, one dynamic which can create and sustain an authentic revolutionary movement. The revolutionary struggle is always and always must be a struggle for freedom. No individual, no group, no class is genuinely engaged in a revolutionary movement unless their struggle is a struggle for their own liberation.

Radical or revolutionary consciousness perceives contradiction . . . not between oneself, what one is, and the underprivileged but as the gap between "what one could be" and the existing conditions for self-realization. It is the perception of oneself as unfree, as oppressed—and finally it is the discovery of oneself as *one of the oppressed* who must unite to transform the objective conditions of their existence in order to resolve the contradiction between potentiality and actuality. Revolutionary consciousness leads to the struggle for one's own freedom in unity with others who share the burden of oppression. It is, to speak in the classical vocabulary, class consciousness because it no longer sees the problem as someone else's, because it breaks through individualization and privatization, because the recognition of one's own unfreedom unites one in the struggle of the oppressed, because it posits a more universally human potentiality for all men in a liberated society.

The problem in white America is the failure to admit or recognize unfreedom. It is a problem of false consciousness, that is, the failure to perceive one's situation in terms of oppressive (class) relationships.

Only when white America comes to terms with its own unfreedom can it participate in the creation of a revolutionary movement.

When we have talked about the "new radicalism," about the "freedom movement," with a passionate conviction, we have been talking about a movement which involves us, you and me, in a gut-level encounter with, disengagement from, and struggle against the America which keeps us in bondage. It may have begun in a very personalistic fashion, out of a private sense of our individual alienation from the U.S. corporate-liberal capitalist monster and from "the bomb" which was its logical but unthinkable conclusion. But, it has and must move beyond the level of our own bewilderment, confusion, and despair about America. It moves to the final realization of our common oppression.

We should realize that Marx was quite correct when he said the true revolutionary consciousness was class consciousness. What he meant by that was that in order to change society people must realize that they are united in common struggle for their own liberation from objective conditions of oppression. . . . [H]e was saying to people that their struggle was the struggle of unfree men—not for individual salvation—but a struggle for collective liberation of all unfree, oppressed men.

What has held the new radicalism together, what has given it its life and vitality, has been the conviction that the gut-level alienation from America-the-Obscene-and-the-Dehumanized was a sincere and realistic basis for challenging America. What has often left the new radicals impotent and romantic is their failure to understand the dynamics of the society which produced their gut-level alienation, that is their failure to understand that what seemed humanly and emotionally real could be understood in terms of a fundamental and critical analysis of American corporate-liberal capitalism. There was a crying out of their own being against America, but a failure to understand why that revolt was authentically related to the necessity and the possibility of revolutionizing America.

That situation has begun to change. The new radicals are beginning to produce an analysis of America which enables them to understand themselves and the greater reality of American society in a way which authenticates their own revolt as a realistic basis for understanding the way in which we can be freed. It begins to relate the anarchist demand, "I want freedom," to the revolutionary socialist analysis which points the way to collective liberation.

If the analysis is correct and if false consciousness is the major obstacle to organizing a revolutionary movement, then it would seem to follow that our primary task at this stage of development is the encouragement or building of revolutionary consciousness, of consciousness of the conditions of unfreedom. A question immediately arises however— . . . since the society can buy people off with goods, are there other sufficiently potent radicalizing experiences apart from economic deprivation which radicals can work with?

This is an important and complex question. It is perhaps the failure of the old left to arrive at a satisfactory answer to that question which was responsible for its fervent attachment to the concept of the inevitability of the collapse of capitalism—the catastrophic event which would reveal both the objective contradictions of the system and create the proper subjective response on the part of the exploited.

Without necessarily ruling out the possibility of such an economic cataclysm in the capitalist world, the new left is hardly notable for its faith in the inevitability of the event. Thus deprived of the *deus ex machina* which the old left was certain existed in the wings, we new leftists have been driven by a special urgency which gives rise to a variety of inventive activities designed to reveal to people their unfreedom and to offer them alternatives and hope. Certainly the organizing of the new radicals has been one of their most characteristic features. . . . The whole notion of the "new working class" provides a powerful tool for understanding the present structure of advanced industrial capitalism.

First, it breaks through the "myth of the great American middle class." Not only are millions of Americans held captive by that notion, but it has also been a major psychological obstacle for most radicals. If white America is mostly middle class, and if being middle class means not being oppressed, then there is no possibility for finding the resources upon which a radical movement can be built in white America. What we have come to understand is that the great American middle class is not middle class at all. . . . The vast majority of those whom we called the middle class must properly be understood as members of the "new working class": that is, as those workers who fill the jobs created by a new level of technological development within the same exploitive system.

Secondly, it enables us to understand the special role of students in relation to the present structure of industrial capitalism. Students are the "trainees" for the new working class and the factory-like multiversities are the institutions which prepare them for their slots in the bureaucratic machinery of corporate capitalism. We must stop apologizing for being students or for organizing students. Students are in fact a key group in the creation of the productive forces of this super-technological capitalism. We have organized them out of their own alienation from the multiversity and have raised the demand for "student control." That is important: because that is precisely the demand that the new working class must raise when it is functioning as the new working class in the economic system. It is that demand which the system cannot fulfill and survive as it is. That is why it is potentially a real revolutionary demand in a way that demands for higher wages can never be.

Thirdly, we can see that it was a mistake to assume that the only radical role which students could play would be as organizers of other classes. It is still important, vitally important that student organizers continue to involve themselves in ghetto organizing, in the organizing of the underclass. That work is a vital part of the movement and it is first from ghetto community organizing that the demand for control was clearly articulated. But it is now important to realize that we must organize the great majority of students as the trainees of the new working class. We must speak to them of the way in which the new working class is created—of the meaningless training which is passed off as education and of the special coercive devices like the Selective Service System with its student deferments designed to channel them into the multiversity.

Finally, we must be sensitive to those places in the social strata where false consciousness is being broken down, where the middle-class myth is crumbling, where groups are beginning to struggle for their own freedom. In terms of the concept of the new working class, certain groups have begun to respond: social workers; teachers, the medical profession. All of these are service groups, it is true, and, interestingly, there is in all these areas a characteristic contradiction between a high level of articulated aspiration and increasingly oppressive conditions. We need radicals in all those areas in order to articulate more clearly the political ramifications of the demands for control and meaningful work. . . .

We must be sensitive to the fact that a mass movement in America will take time to develop and that it requires the involvement of a broad range of social strata, old and new working class, students and underclass. What counts is that America is beginning to break up, that the myth of the great American middle class is crumbling, that white Americans as well as black Americans are beginning to recognize their common oppression and are raising their demands for freedom which can be the basis of a movement which could revolutionize America.

Student Power: A Radical View

CARL DAVIDSON

In 1966 Carl Davidson, an SDS leader, argues that students could be relevant radicals.

What can students do?

Organizing struggles over dormitory rules seems frivolous when compared to the ghetto rebellions. And white students are no longer wanted or necessary in the black movement. Organize against the war? Of course. But we have pride in being a multifaceted movement, organizing people around the issues affecting their lives.

Change your life. The war hardly affects most students. In some sense, we are a privileged elite, coddled in a campus sanctuary. Draft resistance tables in the student union building—the arrogance of it all. We organize students against the draft when the Army is made up of young men who are poor, black, Spanish-American, hillbillies, or working class. Everyone except students. How can we be so stupid when we plan our strategies?

Students are oppressed. Bullshit. We are being trained to be oppressors and the underlings of oppressors. Only the moral among us are being hurt. Even then, the damage is only done to our sensitivities. Most of us don't know the meaning of a hard day's work. . . .

Student power! Classes are large and impersonal. Reduce the size of the class in counter-insurgency warfare from 50 to 5. Students and professors should "groove" on each other. We want to control student rules, tribunals, and disciplinary hearing "ourselves." One cop is so much like another.

Student radicals cannot leave the campus because they might lose their 2-S deferments. Organize in the white community. What white community can be organized by an organizer with a 2-S?—Hippies, students, and middle class suburbanites. What sections of the white community are exploited and oppressed?—The poor and the working class. That's where we're at, brothers and sisters.

Yet, there is a student movement. Something is afoot on the nation's campuses. What can we do with it?

We have to look at the university more carefully, but, at the same time, keep it in its proper perspective. The university is connected structurally with the larger society. Nevertheless, we cannot build socialism on one campus. Most attempts in reforming the university have ricocheted immediately against the necessity of transforming the society as well.

Which is as it should be. Our analysis of the university as a service station and job-training factory adjunct to American corporate capitalism would hardly be relevant otherwise. If this is the case, however, where do student politics fit into the picture?

In the past few years, the student revolt has been primarily directed against the form of our education: i.e., class size, grading, participation in rule-making, etc. We have emphasized these aspects over and above the "content" and "ends" of our "training"; and, as a result, we have failed in eliciting a seriousness and sense of direction in our work.

Being a student is not an eternal condition. Rather, we are a flow of manpower with the need of being whipped into shape before entering a lifelong niche in the political economy. While this process has precious little to do with education, there is nothing wrong with it in itself. I have no objection to the "training" of schoolteachers. And our knowledge factories do an effective job of that.

Rather, my objectives focus on how they are being trained and for what ends. Perhaps the implications of these questions can be seen if we examine an institution like student government.

My objection to student government is not that it is "unreal" or "irrelevant." Quite the opposite. Student government is quite effective and relevant in achieving its purpose. Beginning in grade school, we all went through the "let's pretend" process of electing home room officers. In high school, student council was the name of the game. And so on into college.

Throughout it all, none of us ever doubted the fact that forms of our self-government had any power. We all knew the teacher, or the principal, or the administration, or the regents had the final and effective say-so in most of our affairs.

But think about it for a minute. Did not the process effectively achieve its purpose?

We learned to acquiesce in the face of arbitrary authority. We learned to surrender our own freedom in the name of something called "expertise."

We learned that elections should be personality-oriented popularity contests; that issues with which we ought to be concerned should only be the most banal.

Most of all, we learned about "responsibility" and "working inside the system." Was all of this not an adequate preparation for "life in the real world?" Are national, state, and local elections any different?

The farce of it all is only evidenced by comparing the reality of our political lives with the ideals we are given to revere. Even so, we were also taught to smirk at "idealism."

We learned our lessons well, so well in fact, that some of us have embraced a cynicism so deep that the quality of our lives has been permanently impaired. Perhaps a majority of us have been castrated by the existing order; a generation's young manhood and womanhood manifesting nothing beyond the utter destruction of seriousness. Give a flower to a cop. Join the marines and be a man. James Bond is the fraternity man of the year.

Student government reeks of the worst aspect of this syndrome. Because of that, it may be a good place for initiating on the campus the movement for human liberation already in progress off the campus.

We have no blueprints. Only some guidelines. Administrators are the enemy. Refuse to be "responsible." Have more faith in people than in programs. Refuse to accept the "off-campus-on-campus" dichotomy. Finally, demand seriousness by dealing with serious issues—getting the U.S. out of Vietnam, getting the military off the campus, enabling people to win control over the quality and direction of their lives.

In short, make a revolution.

"SAY IT LOUD, SAY IT PROUD": BLACK NATIONALISM AND ETHNIC CONSCIOUSNESS

The optimism growing out of a decade of successes in the battles against Jim Crow segregation and institutionalized racism began to wane in the middle 1960s. The failure of the Mississippi Freedom Democratic Party to win its challenge at the 1964 Democratic National Convention foretold difficulties to come. National focus began to turn away from civil rights as other issues, particularly the war in Vietnam, moved to the center of the political stage. Northern blacks looked at a decade of civil rights successes and found little improvement in their own situation. Finally, voices that had been building in the black community, offering an alternative vision to the position favored by the major civil rights organizations, began to permeate both the movements and the media.

The second half of the 1960s saw a different pattern develop on questions of race and saw new constituencies join in the struggles to define and maintain ethnic identity and end racial discrimination. Central to all these movements was a growing sense of personal identity and cultural heritage. The voice of Malcolm X, minister for the Nation of Islam and later leader of his own movement, proved compelling in the black community. Misunderstood by the white press and misidentified as "black racism," the message of black nationalism and arguments that self-defense should replace nonviolent resistance found favor among many African-Americans.

These sentiments meshed with the growing frustrations of many blacks in northern urban ghettos. Despite civil rights legislation and a decade of struggle against southern segregation, northern blacks continued to face poverty, discrimination, and de facto segregation. This frustration exploded in rebellion during the latter 1960s in many urban ghettos, including Watts, Harlem, Newark, and Detroit.

Even some southern civil rights leaders felt it was time to readjust their positions and tactics. During the Selma march of 1965, SNCC leader Stokely Carmichael proclaimed the new goal of "Black Power." Again misunderstood by the white press, Black Power aimed to bring control of black communities to their black citizens. It paralleled growing sentiments in the black community about the need to maintain ethnic identity in the course of civil rights activities and to avoid assimilation into a white society that drained the black experience of its true meaning. African-American culture and history, it was suggested, needed to be protected and integrated into the American black experience.

In the North, blacks organized in new ways to respond to the needs and problems of their communities. In Oakland, California, young blacks formed the Black Panther Party, intending to create a militant, community-based organization to protect blacks from harassment and to provide internal organizational structure for the ghetto. Adopting the emerging style of both civil rights and new left organizations, the Black Panthers exhibited a newfound posture of militancy and black identity. The Panthers, like the other militant organizations, would run afoul of both the press and national and local law-enforcement authorities.

While Martin Luther King, Jr., did not adopt the style or perspective of the younger black militants, he did begin to move beyond the issues of southern life that had inspired SCLC for a decade. Attempting to combat racism in the North, his campaign in the white Chicago suburb of Cicero proved telling, as many northern whites responded with the same racial epithets and hostility exhibited by southern whites. King's perspective began to expand as well. After steadfastly refusing to become involved in issues other than civil rights, he now spoke of the relationship between race and other issues, notably Vietnam (see chapter 4) and poverty. The Poor People's March, planned for the summer of 1968, aimed to bring many of America's poor to Washington to lobby for economic as well as political justice. King himself would be murdered only months before the beginning of the march. Assassinated in Memphis in April 1968, his death sparked a wave of urban riots throughout the nation.

Racial issues crossed into a variety of other areas of American life, including sports. Heavyweight champion Muhammad Ali (born Cassius Clay, but changed with his conversion to the Nation of Islam) was stripped of his title when he refused induction into the military, arguing that his religion made him a conscientious objector. Black athletes were asked to boycott the 1968 Olympics. Some did, while others demonstrated their sense of black pride after winning medals.

Finally, questions about racial identity and personal place within American society moved not only African-Americans but other racial minorities as well. Latino communities, from Chicanos in California and Texas to Puerto Ricans in New York, began to articulate a new sense of race pride. Identified as "Caucasians" in census polling, they nonetheless had experienced discrimination in housing and employment, as well as a secondary status for their native language. Similarly, Asian-Americans and American Indians each began to express the combined sentiments of personal frustration with white society and ethnic identification with their own culture and heritage. And within all these movements, questions began to surface about the distinct role of women of color.

The racial struggles of the second half of the 1960s would not produce as many clear victories as the first decade of civil rights activities. But questions of race would broaden the discussion—with new issues and new groups, ultimately including white ethnic minorities as well. Contemporary concerns about ethnic identity, cultural diversity, and bilingualism stem directly from the issues developed during these years.

BLACK NATIONALISM AND BLACK PRIDE

The Ballot or the Bullet

MALCOLM X

While attention focused on civil rights activities in the South, many African-Americans were increasingly drawn to the black nationalist themes of the Nation of Islam and, in particular, its most compelling spokesman, Malcolm X. Born Malcolm Little, he became a Black Muslim while in prison in the late 1940s. By the end of 1963 he had broken with Nation of Islam leader Elijah Muhammad, made a pilgrimage to Mecca, and begun to develop his own movement, The Organization of Afro-American Unity. The speech excerpted below was given in Cleveland in April 1964, during this last period of his life. On February 21, 1965, Malcolm X was assassinated while speaking in Harlem.

Although I'm still a Muslim, I'm not here tonight to discuss my religion. I'm not here to try and change your religion. I'm not here to argue or discuss anything that we differ about, because it's time for us to submerge our differences and realize that it is best for us to first see that we have the same problem, a common problem—a problem that will make you catch hell whether you're a Baptist, or a Methodist, or a Muslim, or a nationalist. Whether you're educated or illiterate, whether you live on the boulevard or in the alley, you're going to catch hell just like I am. We're all in the same boat and we all are going to catch the same hell from the same man. He just happens to be a white man. All of us have suffered here, in this country, political oppression at the hands of the white man, economic exploitation at the hands of the white man, and social degradation at the hands of the white man.

Now in speaking like this, it doesn't mean that we're anti-white, but it does mean we're anti-exploitation, we're anti-degredation, we're anti-oppression. And if the white man doesn't want us to be anti-him, let him stop oppressing and exploiting and degrading us. Whether we are Christians or Muslims or nationalists or agnostics or atheists, we must first learn to forget our differences. If we have differences, let us differ in the closet; when we come out in front, let us not have anything to argue about until we get finished arguing with the man. If the late President Kennedy could get together with Khrushchev and exchange some wheat, we certainly have more in common with each other than Kennedy and Khrushchev had with each other.

If we don't do something real soon, I think you'll have to agree that we're going to be forced either to use the ballot or the bullet. It's one or the other in 1964. It isn't that time is running out—time has run out! 1964 threatens to be the most explosive year America has ever witnessed. The most explosive year. Why? It's also a political year. It's the year when all of the white politicians will be back in the so-called Negro community jiving you and me for some votes. The year when all of the white political crooks will be right back in your and my community with their false promises, building up our hopes for a letdown, with their trickery and their treachery, with their false promises which they don't intend to keep. As they nourish these dissatisfactions, it can only lead to one thing, an explosion; and now we have the type of black man on the scene in America today who just doesn't intend to turn the other cheek any longer.

Don't let anybody tell you anything about the odds are against you. If they draft you, they send you to Korea and make you face 800 million Chinese. If you can be brave over there, you can be brave right here. These odds aren't as great as those odds. And if you fight here, you will at least know what you're fighting for.

I'm not a politician, not even a student of politics; in fact, I'm not a student of much of anything. I'm not a Democrat, I'm not a Republican, and I don't even consider myself an American. If you

and I were Americans, there'd be no problem. Those Hunkies that
just got off the boat, they're already Americans; Polacks are already
Americans; the Italian refugees are already Americans. Everything
that came out of Europe, every blue-eyed thing, is already an American. And as long as you and I have been over here, we aren't Americans yet.

Well, I am one who doesn't believe in deluding myself. I'm not
going to sit at your table and watch you eat, with nothing on my plate,
and call myself a diner. Sitting at the table doesn't make you a diner,
unless you eat some of what's on that plate. Being here in America
doesn't make you an American. Being born here in America doesn't
make you an American. Why, if birth made you American, you
wouldn't need any legislation, you wouldn't need any amendments
to the Constitution, you wouldn't be faced with civil-rights filibustering
in Washington, D.C., right now. They don't have to pass civil-rights
legislation to make a Polack an American.

No, I'm not an American. I'm one of the 22 million black people
who are the victims of Americanism. One of the 22 million black
people who are the victims of democracy, nothing but disguised hypocrisy. So, I'm not standing here speaking to you as an American, or a
patriot, or a flag-saluter, or a flag-waver—no, not I. I'm speaking as
a victim of this American system. And I see America through the eyes
of the victim. I don't see any American dream; I see an American
nightmare. . . .

We need new friends, we need new allies. We need to expand the
civil-rights struggle to a higher level—to the level of human rights.
Whenever you are in a civil-rights struggle, whether you know it or
not, you are confining yourself to the jurisdiction of Uncle Sam. No
one from the outside world can speak out in your behalf as long as
your struggle is a civil-rights struggle. Civil rights comes within the
domestic affairs of this country. All of our African brothers and our
Asian brothers and our Latin-American brothers cannot open their
mouths and interfere in the domestic affairs of the United States.
And as long as it's civil rights, this comes under the jurisdiction of
Uncle Sam . . .

Right now, in this country, if you and I, 22 million African-Americans—that's what we are—Africans who are in America. You're nothing but Africans. Nothing but Africans. In fact, you'd get farther
calling yourself African instead of Negro. Africans don't catch hell.

You're the only one catching hell. They don't have to pass civil-rights bills for Africans. An African can go anywhere he wants right now. All you've got to do is tie your head up. That's right, go anywhere you want. Just drop being a Negro. Change your name to Hoogagagooba. That'll show you how silly the white man is. You're dealing with a silly man. A friend of mine who's very dark put a turban on his head and went into a restaurant in Atlanta before they called themselves desegregated. He went into a white restaurant, he sat down, they served him, and he said, "What would happen if a Negro came in here?" And there he's sitting, black as night, but because he had his head wrapped up the waitress looked back at him and says, "Why, there wouldn't no nigger dare come in here." . . .

The political philosophy of black nationalism means that the black man should control the politics and the politicians in his own community; no more. The black man in the black community has to be re-educated into the science of politics so he will know what politics is supposed to bring him in return. Don't be throwing out any ballots. A ballot is like a bullet. You don't throw your ballots until you see a target, and if that target is not within your reach, keep your ballot in your pocket. The political philosophy of black nationalism is being taught in the Christian church. It's being taught in the NAACP. It's being taught in CORE meetings. It's being taught in SNCC meetings. It's being taught in Muslim meetings. It's being taught where nothing but atheists and agnostics come together. It's being taught everywhere. Black people are fed up with the dillydallying, pussyfooting, compromising approach that we've been using toward getting our freedom. We want freedom *now,* but we're not going to get it saying "We Shall Overcome." We've got to fight until we overcome. . . .

It's time for you and me to stop sitting in this country, letting some cracker senators, Northern crackers and Southern crackers, sit there in Washington, D.C., and come to a conclusion in their mind that you and I are supposed to have civil rights. There's no white man going to tell me anything about *my* rights. Brothers and sisters, always remember, if it doesn't take senators and congressmen and presidential proclamations to give freedom to the white man, it is not necessary for legislation or proclamation or Supreme Court decisions to give freedom to the black man. You let that white man know, if this is a country of freedom, let it be a country of freedom; and if it's not a country of freedom, change it.

We will work with anybody, anywhere, at any time, who is genuinely interested in tackling the problem head-on, nonviolently as long as the enemy is nonviolent, but violent when the enemy gets violent.

The Watts Riots

A decade's activity around questions of race had done little to improve the economic condition of blacks living outside the Deep South. The resulting frustration, combined with ongoing hostilities between community members and local police, often led to urban tensions and riots. In the summer of 1965 the Los Angeles ghetto of Watts exploded in a six-day rampage of burning, looting, arrests, and death.

Violence in the City—An End or a Beginning?

THE MCCONE COMMISSION REPORT ON WATTS

and

Watts: The Aftermath

PAUL BULLOCK

The report of the governor's commission that investigated the riots attempted to identify solutions to urban problems, as well as discuss responsibility for the events. Rereading this report evokes a sense of irony, as many of its suggestions went unheeded in subsequent years and the problems it identified rekindled urban conflagration a quarter century later in Los Angeles's South Central riots of 1992. Portions of the report are reprinted here, along with several interviews with Watts residents conducted by Paul Bullock. These are set off in italics.

In the ugliest interval, which lasted from Thursday through Saturday, perhaps as many as 10,000 Negroes took to the streets in marauding bands. They looted stores, set fires, beat up white passerby whom they hauled from stopped cars, many of which were turned upside down and burned, exchanged shots with law enforcement officers, and stoned and shot at firemen. The rioters seemed to have been caught up in an insensate rage of destruction. By Friday, the disorder spread to adjoining areas, and ultimately an area covering 46.5 square miles had to be controlled with the aid of military authority before public order was restored.

When the spasm passed, thirty-four persons were dead, and the wounded and hurt numbered 1,032 more. Property damage was about $40,000,000. Arrested for one crime or another were 3,952 persons, women as well as men, including over 500 youths under eighteen. The lawlessness in this one segment of the metropolitan area had terrified the entire county and its 6,000,000 citizens.

SOWING THE WIND

In the summer of 1964, Negro communities in seven eastern cities were stricken by riots. Although in each situation there were unique contributing circumstances not existing elsewhere, the fundamental causes were largely the same:

> Not enough jobs to go around, and within this scarcity not enough by a wide margin of a character which the untrained Negro could fill.
>
> Not enough schooling designed to meet the special needs of the disadvantaged Negro child, whose environment from infancy onward places him under a serious handicap.
>
> A resentment, even hatred, of the police, as the symbol of authority. . . .

When the rioting came to Los Angeles, it was not a race riot in the usual sense. What happened was an explosion—a formless, quite senseless, all but hopeless violent protest—engaged in by a few but bringing great distress to all.

Nor was the rioting exclusively a projection of the Negro problem. It is part of an American problem which involves Negroes but which equally concerns other disadvantaged groups. In this report, our major conclusions and recommendations regarding the Negro problem in Los Angeles apply with equal force to the Mexican-Americans, a community which is almost equal in size to the Negro community and whose circumstances are similarly disadvantageous and demand equally urgent treatment. That the Mexican-American community did not riot is to its credit; it should not be to its disadvantage.

The Dull Devastating Spiral of Failure

In examining the sickness in the center of our city, what has depressed and stunned us most is the dull, devastating spiral of failure that awaits the average disadvantaged child in the urban core. His home life all too often fails to give him the incentive and the elementary experience with words and ideas which prepares most children for school. Unprepared and unready, he may not learn to read or write at all; and because he shares his problem with 30 or more in the same classroom, even the efforts of the most dedicated teachers are unavailing. Age, not achievement, passes him on to higher grades, but in most cases he is unable to cope with courses in the upper grades because they demand basic skills which he does not possess. ("Try," a teacher said to us, "to teach history to a child who cannot read.")

Frustrated and disillusioned, the child becomes a discipline problem. Often he leaves school, sometimes before the end of junior high school. (Although two-thirds of those who enter the three high schools in the center of the curfew area do not graduate.) He slips into the ranks of the permanent jobless, illiterate and untrained, unemployed and unemployable. All the talk about the millions which the government is spending to aid him raise his expectations but the benefits seldom reach him.

Reflecting this spiral of failure, unemployment in the disadvantaged areas runs two to three times the country average, and the employment available is too often intermittent. A family whose breadwinner is chronically out of work is almost invariably a disintegrating family. Crime rates soar and welfare rolls increase, even faster than the population.

What can be done to prevent a recurrence of the nightmare of August? It stands to reason that what we and other cities have been doing, costly as it all has been, is not enough. Improving the conditions of Negro life will demand adjustments on a scale unknown to any great society. The programs that we are recommending will be expensive and burdensome. And the burden, along with the expense, will fall on all segments of our society—on the public and private sectors, on industry and labor, on company presidents and hourly employees, and most indispensably, upon the members and leaders of the Negro community. For unless the disadvantaged are resolved to help themselves, whatever else is done by others is bound to fail.

The consequences of inaction, indifference, and inadequacy, we can all be sure now, would be far costlier in the long run than the cost of correction. If the city were to elect to stand aside, the walls of segregation would rise ever higher. The disadvantaged community would become more and more estranged and the risk of violence would rise. The cost of police protection would increase, and yet, would never be adequate. Unemployment would climb; welfare costs would mount apace. And the preachers of division and demagoguery would have a matchless opportunity to tear our nation asunder.

The Frye Arrests

On August 11, 1965, California Highway Patrolman Lee W. Minikus, a Caucasian, was riding his motorcycle along 122nd street, just south of the Los Angeles City boundary, when a passing Negro motorist told him he had just seen a car that was being driven recklessly. Minikus gave chase and pulled the car over at 116th and Avalon, in a predominantly Negro neighborhood, near but not in Watts. It was 7:00 P.M.

The driver was Marquette Frye, a 21-year-old Negro, and his older brother, Ronald, 22, was a passenger. Minikus asked Marquette to get out and take the standard Highway Patrol sobriety test. Frye failed the test, and at 7:05 P.M., Minikus told him he was under arrest. He radioed for his motorcycle partner, for a car to take Marquette to jail, and a tow truck to take the car away.

They were two blocks from the Frye home, in an area of two-story apartment buildings and numerous small family residences. Because it was a very warm evening, many of the residents were outside.

Ronald Frye, having been told he could not take the car when Marquette was taken to jail, went to get their mother so that she could claim the car. They returned to the scene about 7:15 P.M. as the second motorcycle patrolman, the patrol car, and tow truck arrived. The original group of 25 to 50 curious spectators had grown to 250 to 300 persons.

Mrs. Frye approached Marquette and scolded him for drinking. Marquette, who until then had been peaceful and cooperative, pushed her away and moved toward the crowd, cursing and shouting at the officers that they would have to kill him to take him to jail. The patrolmen pursued Marquette and he resisted.

The watching crowd became hostile, and one of the patrolmen radioed for more help. Within minutes, three more highway patrolmen arrived. Minikus and his partner were now struggling with both Frye brothers. Mrs. Frye, now belligerent, jumped on the back of one of the officers and ripped his shirt. In an attempt to subdue Marquette, one officer swung at his shoulder with a night stick, missed, and struck him on the forehead, inflicting a minor cut. By 7:23 P.M., all three of the Fryes were under arrest, and other California Highway Patrolmen and, for the first time, Los Angeles police officers had arrived in response to the call for help.

Officers on the scene said there were now more than 1,000 persons in the crowd. About 7:25 P.M., the patrol car with the prisoners, and the tow truck pulling the Frye car, left the scene. At 7:31 P.M., the Fryes arrived at a nearby sheriff's substation. . . .

As the officers were leaving the scene, someone in the crowd spat on one of them. They stopped withdrawing and two highway patrolmen went into the crowd and arrested a young Negro woman and a man who was said to have been inciting the crowd to violence when the officers were arresting her. . . .

Following these arrests, all officers withdrew at 7:40 P.M. As the last police car left the scene, it was stoned by the now irate mob.

As has happened frequently in riots in other cities, inflated and distorted rumors concerning the arrests spread quickly to adjacent areas. The young woman arrested for spitting was wearing a barber's smock, and the false rumor spread throughout the area that she was pregnant and had been abused by police. Erroneous reports were also circulated concerning the treatment of the Fryes at the arrest scene.

The crowd did not disperse, but ranged in small groups up and down the street, although never more than a few blocks from the arrest scene. Between 8:15 P.M. and midnight, the mob stoned automobiles, pulled Caucasian motorists out of their cars and beat them, and menaced a police field command post which had been set up in the area. By 1:00 A.M., the outbreak seemed to be under control but, until early morning hours, there were sporadic reports of unruly mobs, vandalism, and rock throwing. Twenty-nine persons were arrested.

Let me see, first night when it got started . . . we just saw a whole lot of people starting to run; I thought maybe somebody was fighting or something like that, or there had been an accident, so Henry and I went down to investigate. I saw a lot of police. I saw cars turned over on the street, and bricks, bottles, and a whole lot of glass lying around. I looked at Henry . . . and started laughing. So we decided to go on down further. I looked around, a whole big crew of policemen just ran by us. They were running opposite directions; I didn't know what was happening. I just turned back to Henry, and we thought we'd come home before we got killed. . . . We passed by another group of policemen, and they stopped us. They asked us where we was going. Henry told him we were on our way home, and he asked us where we live, and we responded and told him, and he told us where were we going and where were we coming from. Of course, Henry and I were scared, so I said, "We just got off work. . . ." We took a couple more steps, and he grabbed me by my shoulders, and I turned around and asked him what was wrong with him, and he swung at me with his night stick, but he missed. And I grabbed his arm and knocked his arm down, and I was going to hit him. Then a whole police gang got around him, and they had us circled. We just stood there, and he says, "Where did you say you was going?" I say, "I'm going along," and he says, "Let me see you get along". . . . He swung at me again, and he hit me on the leg. Then immediately I knew what was he talking about, you know.

We started running, and we got down by the corner. We were going to be smart, so I called him a name, and we took off again. We were in an open field, and we looked around, and a whole bunch of lights were flashing over that way, and we paused for a moment, then we looked back over there again, and there were nine or ten police cars behind us. So me and Henry started running again, and all of a sudden we thought, "here is the law." We thought somebody was shooting at us, and they got to ricocheting kind of close. I finally realized that we was being shot at, so me and Henry, we hit the dirt and we were crawling across this big old open field. They was shining a big old spotlight, trying to find us. . . . I looked up and I just saw a fire; the air was just full of smoke, and I glanced over and I saw a large fire over toward where I live at; I just saw things burning, burning, burning. Everywhere I looked, I saw a fire.

On Thursday morning, there was an uneasy calm, but it was obvious that tensions were still high. A strong expectancy of further trouble kept the atmosphere tense in the judgment of both police and Negro leaders. The action by many individuals, both Negro and white, during Thursday, as well as at other times, to attempt to control the riots are commendable. We have heard many vivid and impressive accounts of the work of Negro leaders, social workers, probation officers, churchmen, teachers, and businessmen in their attempts to persuade the people to desist from their illegal activities, to stay in their houses and off the street, and to restore order. . . .

Shortly before midnight, rock-throwing and looting crowds for the first time ranged outside the perimeter. Five hundred police officers, deputy sheriffs and highway patrolmen used various techniques, including fender-to-fender sweeps by police cars, in seeking to disperse the mob. By 4:00 A.M. Friday, the police department felt that the situation was at least for the moment under control. At 5:09 A.M., officers were withdrawn from emergency perimeter control. . . .

The first death occurred between 6:00 and 7:00 P.M. Friday, when a Negro bystander, trapped on the street between police and rioters, was shot and killed during an exchange of gunfire.

Friday was the worst night. The riot moved out of the Watts area and burning and looting spread over wide areas of Southeast Los Angeles several miles apart. At 1:00 A.M. Saturday, there were 100 engine companies fighting fires in the area. Snipers shot at firemen as they fought new fires. That night, a fireman was crushed and killed on the fire line by a falling wall, and a deputy sheriff was killed when another sheriff's shotgun was discharged in a struggle with rioters.

Friday night, the law enforcement officials tried a different tactic. Police officers made sweeps on foot, moving en masse along streets to control activity and enable firemen to fight fires. By midnight Friday, another 1,000 National Guard troops were marching shoulder to shoulder clearing the streets. By 3:00 A.M. Saturday, 3,356 guardsmen were on the streets, and the number continued to increase until the full commitment of 13,900 guardsmen was reached by midnight on Saturday. . . .

Despite the new tactics and added personnel, the area was not under control at any time on Friday night, as major calls of looting, burning, and shooting were reported every two to three minutes. On throughout the morning hours of Saturday and during the long day, the crowds of looters and patterns of burning spread out and increased still further until it became necessary to impose a curfew on the 46.5 square-mile area on Saturday.

We was walking down from 107th and Graham, from the Teen Post, on Friday night, and at this time, the police was riding four deep with shotguns hanging out the window. They stopped us; they stopped us all at once and told us to put our hands against the wall, and we had this truant officer with us named Jim. He was supposed to have been a probation officer. They made him get up beside the wall, and we was all up beside the wall till . . . this one boy name Ricky . . . said, "What did we do? We didn't do nothing." So the police kicked him, then took his jacket, took this big stick he had out and poked Ricky with it. He told Ricky, "You are getting smart." Ricky didn't say nothing; Ricky just couldn't say nothing; he had all the wind out of him. Then he [the cop] came over to me, and he started talking to me; he said, "You want to get smart?" I said, "No, sir. I ain't said nothing, sir," just like that. So he went where Henry was; he put his knee up on Henry's butt and told Henry to straighten up and kick, open his legs up, you know, and I thought he was beating on his behind, myself, so I started laughing. So he came back to me and asked what was funny. I told him, "Nothing." He grabbed me in the back of my neck, and he slugged me down; he told me, and he told all of us, to go. He told all of us to get on home where we was going. He said, "You are going to walk down the street; you are not going to look back, and you aren't going to think no nasty names in your mind to call us, are you? And I said, "No, sir, we are going on home." So we were going home.

So this . . . Mexican-American Johnny Garcia, he was walking down the street, and he was walking minding his own business; the police flashed a light in his face and told him to stop, and he was walking and looking at him. He told him to come here, and the Mexican fellow was walking over, blocking the light out of his eyes. By the time he got up the him, the police hit him, wham, wham, slapped him upside and pushed him, told him to get on, just like that. We felt like running; we all started running and started laughing about it, and later we got together, we called ourselves camouflaged police that night. We started throwing bricks and bottles; that was what started us; that's what really started us. Like we get dog dukey, put it in a bottle, throw it on them, messing them up, that was what we did after they did that. We weren't thinking about it at first, you know.

The Beginning of Control

Much of the Saturday burning had been along Central Avenue. Again using sweep tactics, the guardsmen and police were able to clear this area by 3:30 P.M. Guardsmen rode "shotgun" on the fire engines and effectively stopped the sniping and rock throwing at firemen. Saturday evening, road blocks were set up in anticipation of the curfew. The massive show of force was having some effect although there was still riot activity and rumors spread regarding proposed activity in the south central area.

When the curfew started at 8:00 P.M., police and guardsmen were able to deal with the riot area as a whole. Compared with the holocaust of Friday evening, the streets were relatively quiet.

During the day Sunday, the curfew area was relatively quiet. Because many markets had been destroyed, food distribution was started by churches, community groups, and government agencies. Governor Brown, who had returned Saturday night, personally toured the area, talking to residents. Major fires were under control but there were new fires and some rekindling of old ones. By Tuesday, Governor Brown was able to lift the curfew and by the following Sunday, only 252 guardsmen remained.

That Sunday . . . when everything had cooled off, and the National Guards had arrived. And I had this radio, this FM, I had looted out of the store, my personal self, and we was sitting off in the project . . . over by Bob's liquor store on 103rd, they said everybody . . . had to make a curfew at eight o'clock. We didn't believe this curfew. So we's sitting down drinking up wine. Everybody got something else; they got wine, whiskey, beer, and everything; everybody sitting out at the project socializing, talking about what they looted, what they stole, and all this. So this man comes over, this colored dude comes over with a tape recorder; he gets to talking about what's our names, you know, and all this stuff. We had a fifth of corn whisky. He asked us all our names. We gave him all phony names. He said, "I know this is phony." I said, "If you know it, why do you want to ask?" He was supposed to have been a newspaper reporter, or something . . . tennis shoes, levis; he had a tape recorder. I thought he was losing his mind, you know.

All of a sudden, we heard shots, five minutes to eight, just boom, boom, boom, boom. I just grabbed my radio. I had to go over to my friend's house to stay all night, because I couldn't get out, and I saw everybody at Bob's liquor store. National guard had one of those big, old 21 BM's, whatever you want to call it, just sitting it up on the air, just blow out a whole light pole . . . with one shot, blowed the whole light out and people standing like fools, standing over there on the property shooting at him with little, old .45's and the Guards had great big machine guns, and tearing the brick walls up, tearing the whole wall up with three or four shots. . . .

Let me tell you, and this is the truth. I saw a 1964 or '65 Dodge with a Caucasian, it got stopped on Wilmington right at 105th. . . . They stopped him early in the morning, Monday, must be about 6:30 or 7:30 in the morning, and they opened the trunk of that man's car. He had rifles for an army; he had rifles; he had machine guns; they opened up the back of his seat, he had so many bullets that he could start anything he wanted. He was over there selling that stuff to them colored peoples. That is the truth, and the National Guard catch him, held him there until the police came. . . . White people, they did a hell of a lot in the riot.

The Basis of Black Power

SNCC

In the spring of 1966 SNCC elected Stokely Carmichael as its president and changed the focus of its organizational efforts. SNCC had already begun to talk about "Black Power" during the 1965 march from Selma to Montgomery (see chapter 1). By 1966 the slogan became its rallying cry and the basis of its political program. In an effort to explain what Black Power meant—rather than its being defined by a white press that confused its message with black separatism—SNCC circulated the following position paper.

The myth that the Negro is somehow incapable of liberating himself, is lazy, etc., came out of the American experience. In the books that children read, whites are always "good" (good symbols are white), blacks are "evil" or seen as savages in movies, their language is referred to as a "dialect," and black people in this country are supposedly descended from savages.

Any white person who comes into the movement has the concepts in his mind about black people, if only subconsciously. He cannot escape them because the whole society has geared his subconscious in that direction.

Miss America coming from Mississippi has a chance to represent all of America, but a black person from either Mississippi or New York will never represent America. Thus the white people coming into the movement cannot relate to the black experience, cannot relate to the word "black," cannot relate to the "nitty gritty," cannot relate to the experience that brought such a word into existence, cannot relate to chitterlings, hog's head cheese, pig feet, hamhocks, and cannot relate to slavery, because these things are not a part of their experience. They also cannot relate to the black religious experience, nor to the black church, unless, of course, this church has taken on white manifestations.

WHITE POWER

Negroes in this country have never been allowed to organize themselves because of white interference. As a result of this, the stereotype has been reinforced that blacks cannot organize themselves. The white psychology that blacks have to be watched, also reinforces this stereotype. Blacks, in fact, feel intimidated by the presence of whites, because of their knowledge of the power that whites have over their lives. One white person can come into a meeting of black people and change the complexion of that meeting, whereas one black person would not change the complexion of that meeting unless he was an obvious Uncle Tom. People would immediately start talking about "brotherhood," "love," etc.; race would not be discussed.

If people must express themselves freely, there has to be a climate in which they can do this. If blacks feel intimidated by whites, then they are not liable to vent the rage that they feel about whites in the presence of whites—especially not the black people whom we are trying to organize, i.e., the broad masses of black people. A climate has to be created whereby blacks can express themselves. The reasons that whites must be excluded is not that one is anti-white, but because the effects that one is trying to achieve cannot succeed because whites have an intimidating effect. Ofttimes the intimidating effect is in direct proportion to the amount of degradation that black people have suffered at the hands of white people.

ROLES OF WHITES AND BLACKS

It must be offered that white people who desire change in this country should go where that problem (racism) is most manifest. The problem is not in the black community. The white people should go into white communities where the whites have created power for the express purpose of denying blacks human dignity and self-determination. Whites who come into the black community with ideas of change seem to want to absolve the power structure of its responsibility for what it is doing, and saying that change can only come through black unity, which is the worst kind of paternalism. This is not to say that whites have not had an important role in the movement. In the case of Mississippi, their role was very key in that they helped give blacks the right to organize, but that role is now over, and it should be.

People now have the right to picket, the right to give out leaflets, the right to vote, the right to demonstrate, the right to print.

These things which revolve around the right to organize have been accomplished mainly because of the entrance of white people into Mississippi, in the summer of 1964. Since these goals have now been accomplished, whites' role in the movement has now ended. What does it mean if black people, once having the right to organize, are not allowed to organize themselves? It means that blacks' ideas about inferiority are being reinforced. Shouldn't people be able to organize themselves? Blacks should be given this right. Further, white participation means in the eyes of the black community that whites are the "brains" behind the movement, and that blacks cannot function without whites. This only serves to perpetuate existing attitudes within the existing society, i.e., blacks are "dumb," "unable to take care of business," etc. Whites are "smart," the "brains" behind the whole thing.

How do blacks relate to other blacks as such? How do we react to Willie Mays as against Mickey Mantle? What is our response to Mays hitting a home run against Mantel performing the same deed? One has to come to the conclusion that it is because of black participation in baseball. Negroes still identify with the Dodgers because of Jackie Robinson's efforts with the Dodgers. Negroes would instinctively champion all-black teams if they opposed all white or predominantly white teams. The same principle operates for the movement as it does for baseball: a mystique must be created whereby Negroes can identify with the movement.

Thus an all-black project is needed in order for the people to free themselves. This has to exist from the beginning. This relates to what can be called "coalition politics." There is no doubt in our minds that some whites are just as disgusted with this system as we are. But it is meaningless to talk about coalition if there is no one to align ourselves with, because of the lack of organization in the white communities. There can be no talk of "hooking up" unless black people organize blacks and white people organize whites. If these conditions are met, then perhaps at some later date—and if we are going in the same direction—talks about exchange of personnel, coalition, and other meaningful alliances can be discussed.

In the beginning of the movement, we had fallen into a trap whereby we thought that our problems revolved around the right to eat at certain lunch counters or the right to vote, or to organize our communities. We have seen, however, that the problem is much deeper. The problem of this country, as we had seen it, concerned all blacks and all whites and therefore if decisions were left to the young people, then solutions would be arrived at. But this negates the history of black people and whites. We have dealt stringently with the problem of "Uncle Tom," but we have not yet gotten around to Simon Legree. We must ask ourselves, who is the real villain—Uncle Tom or Simon Legree? Everybody knows Uncle Tom, but who knows Simon Legree? So what we have now in SNCC is a closed society, a clique. Black people cannot relate to SNCC because of its unrealistic, nonracial atmosphere; denying their experiences of America as a racist society. In contrast, the Southern Christian Leadership Conference of Martin Luther King, Jr., has a staff that at least maintains a black facade. The front office is virtually all black, but nobody accuses SCLC of being racist.

If we are to proceed toward true liberation, we must cut ourselves off from white people. We must form our own institutions, credit unions, co-ops, political parties, write our own histories.

To proceed further, let us make some comparisons between the Black Movement of the early 1900s and the movement of the 1960s—i.e., compare the National Association for the Advancement of Colored People with SNCC. Whites subverted the Niagara movement (the forerunner of the NAACP) which, at the outset, was an all-black movement. The name of the new organization was also very revealing, in that it presupposed blacks have to be advanced to the level of whites. We are now aware that the NAACP has grown reactionary, is controlled by the black power structure itself, and stands as one of the main roadblocks to black freedom. SNCC, by allowing the whites to remain in the organization, can have its efforts subverted in the same manner, i.e., through having them play important roles such as community organizers, etc. Indigenous leadership cannot be built with whites in the positions they now hold.

These facts do not mean that whites cannot help. They can participate on a voluntary basis. We can contract work out to them, but in
no way can they participate on a policy-making level.

BLACK SELF-DETERMINATION

The charge may be made that we are "racists," but whites who are
sensitive to our problems will realize that we must determine our
own destiny.

In an attempt to find a solution to our dilemma, we propose that
our organization (SNCC) should be black-staffed, black-controlled,
and black-financed. We do not want to fall into a similar dilemma
that other civil rights organizations have fallen into. If we continue
to rely upon white financial support we will find ourselves entwined
in the tentacles of the white power complex that controls this country.
It is also important that a black organization (devoid of cultism) be
projected to our people so that it can be demonstrated that such
organizations are viable.

More and more we see black people in this country being used
as a tool of the white liberal establishment. Liberal whites have not
begun to address themselves to the real problem of black people
in this country—witness their bewilderment, fear, and anxiety when
nationalism is mentioned concerning black people. An analysis of the
white liberal's reaction to the word "nationalism" alone reveals a very
meaningful attitude of whites of any ideological persuasion toward
blacks in this country. It means previous solutions to black problems
in this country have been made in the interests of those whites dealing
with these problems and not in the best interests of black people in
this country. Whites can only subvert our true search and struggles for
self-determination, self-identification, and liberation in this country.
Reevaluation of the white and black roles must NOW take place so
that whites no longer designate roles that black people play but rather
black people define white people's roles.

Too long have we allowed white people to interpret the importance
and meaning of the cultural aspects of our society. We have allowed
them to tell us what was good about our Afro-American music, art,
and literature. How many black critics do we have on the "jazz"
scene? How can a white person who is not part of the black psyche

(except in the oppressor's role) interpret the meaning of the blues to us who are manifestations of the songs themselves?

It must be pointed out that on whatever level of contact blacks and whites come together, that meeting or confrontation is not on the level of the blacks but always on the level of the whites. This only means that our everyday contact with whites is a reinforcement of the myth of white supremacy. Whites are the ones who must try to raise themselves to our humanistic level. We are not, after all, the ones who are responsible for a genocidal war in Vietnam; we are not the ones who are responsible for neocolonialism in Africa and Latin America; we are not the ones who held a people in animalistic bondage over 400 years. We reject the American dream as defined by white people and must work to construct an American reality defined by Afro-Americans.

WHITE RADICALS

One of the criticisms of white militants and radicals is that when we view the masses of white people we view the overall reality of America, we view the racism, the bigotry, and the distortion of personality, we view man's inhumanity to man; we view in reality 180 million racists. The sensitive white intellectual and radical who is fighting to bring about change is conscious of this fact, but does not have the courage to admit this. When he admits this reality, then he must also admit his involvement because he is a part of the collective white America. It is only to the extent that he recognizes this that he will be able to change this reality.

Another common concern is, how does the white radical view the black community, and how does he view the poor white community, in terms of organizing? So far, we have found that most white radicals have sought to escape the horrible reality of America by going into the black community and attempting to organize black people while neglecting the organization of their own people's racist communities. How can one clean up someone else's yard when one's own yard is untidy? Again we feel that SNCC and the civil rights movement in general is in many aspects similar to the anticolonial situations in the African and Asian countries. We have the whites in the movement corresponding to the white civil servants and missionaries in the colonial countries who have worked with the colonial people for a long period of time and have developed a paternalistic attitude toward them. The reality of the colonial people taking over their own lives and controlling their own destiny must be faced. Having to move aside and letting the natural process of growth and development take place must be faced.

These views should not be equated with outside influence or outside agitation but should be viewed as the natural process of growth and development within a movement; so that the move by the black militants and SNCC in this direction should be viewed as a turn toward self-determination.

It is very ironic and curious that aware whites in this country can champion anticolonialism in other countries in Africa, Asia, and Latin America, but when black people move toward similar goals of self-determination in this country they are viewed as racists and anti-white by these same progressive whites. In proceeding further, it can be said that this attitude derives from the overall point of view of the white psyche as it concerns the black people. This attitude stems from the era of the slave revolts when every white man was a potential deputy or sheriff or guardian of the state. Because when black people got together among themselves to work out their problems, it becomes a threat to white people, because such meetings were potential slave revolts.

It can be maintained that this attitude or way of thinking has perpetuated itself to this current period and that it is part of the psyche of white people in this country whatever their political persuasion might be. It is part of the white fear-guilt complex resulting from the slave revolts. There have been examples of whites who stated that they can deal with black fellows on an individual basis but become threatened or menaced by the presence of groups of blacks. It can be maintained that this attitude is held by the majority of progressive whites in this country.

BLACK IDENTITY

A thorough re-examination must be made by black people concerning the contributions that we have made in shaping this country. If this re-examination and re-evaluation is not made, and black people are not given their proper due and respect, then the antagonisms and contradictions are going to become more and more glaring, more and more intense, until a national explosion may result.

When people attempt to move from these conclusions it would be faulty reasoning to say they are ordered by racism, because, in this country and in the West, racism has functioned as a type of white nationalism when dealing with black people. We all know the habit that this has created throughout the world and particularly among nonwhite people in this country.

Therefore any re-evaluation that we must make will, for the most part, deal with identification. Who are black people, what are black people, what is their relationship to America and the world?

It must be repeated that the whole myth of "Negro citizenship," perpetuated by the white elite, has confused the thinking of radical and progressive blacks and whites in this country. The broad masses of black people react to American society in the same manner as colonial peoples react to the West in Africa, and Latin America, and had the same relationship—that of the colonized toward the colonizer.

Black Art and Black Liberation

LARRY NEAL

As part of the broadened focus of race questions, cultural and social concerns were added to the political issues that had been confronted for a decade. Renewed interest in an African heritage, appreciation for the contributions blacks had made to American culture, and a celebration of African-American life all joined to promote black pride and a desire to celebrate and perpetuate black culture. Larry Neal assessed this aspect of the African-American movement in a special 1969 issue of Ebony.

Reprinted by permission, Evelyn Neal.

I was born by the river in a little old tent
and just like the river I've been running ever since.
It's been a long time, but I know change is gonna come.

Sam Cooke

We bear witness to a profound change in the way we now see ourselves
and the world. And this has been an ongoing change. A steady, certain
march toward a collective sense of who we are, and what we must
now be about to liberate ourselves. Liberation is impossible if we fail
to see ourselves in more positive terms. For without a change of vision,
we are slaves to the oppressor's ideas and values—ideas and values
that finally attack the very core of our existence. Therefore, we must
see the world in terms of our own realities.

Black Power, in its most fundamental sense, stands for the principle
of Self-Definition and Self-Determination. Black Power teaches us that
we must have ultimate control over our own lives. It teaches us that
we must make a place on this Earth for ourselves, and that we must
construct, through struggle, a world that is compatible with our highest visions. . . .

Now along with the Black Power movement, there has been developing a movement among Black artists. This movement we call the
Black Arts. This movement, in many ways, is older than the current
Black Power movement. It is primarily concerned with the cultural
and spiritual liberation of Black America. It takes upon itself the task
of expressing, through various art forms, the Soul of the Black Nation.
And like the Black Power Movement, it seeks to define the world of
art and culture in its own terms. The Black Arts movement seeks to
link, in a highly conscious manner, art and politics in order to assist
in the liberation of Black people. The Black Arts movement, therefore,
reasons that this linking must take place along lines that are rooted
in an Afro-American and Third World historical and cultural sensibility. By ''Third World,'' we mean that we see our struggle in the context
of the global confrontations occurring in Africa, Asia and Latin
America. We identify with all of the righteous forces in those places
which are struggling for human dignity. . . .

We are constantly forced to see ourselves through white eyes. We
are made to evaluate our innermost impulses against theirs. And in
the process, we do ourselves great spiritual and psychological harm.
The Black Art movement seeks to give a total vision of ourselves. . . .

Black music, in all of its forms, represents the highest artistic achievement of the race. It is the memory of Africa that we hear in the churning energy of the gospels. The memory of the Motherland that lingers behind the Christian references to Moses, Jesus, and Daniel. The Black Holy Ghost roaring into some shack of a church in the South, seizing the congregation with an ancient energy and power. The Black Church, therefore, represents and embodies the transplanted African memory. The Black Church is the Keeper of that Memory, the spiritual bank of our almost forgotten visions of the Homeland. The Black Church was the institutionalized form that Black people used to protect themselves from the spiritual and psychological brutality of the slave-masters. She gave us a music, a literature and a very valid and essential poetry. And when she ceased to be relevant, for some of us, we sang the blues: *"They call it stormy Monday, but Tuesday's just as bad; call it stormy Monday, but Tuesday's just as bad. Wednesday's worse, but Thursday's also sad. . . ."*

At the pulsating core of their emotional center, the blues are the spiritual and ritual energy of the church thrust into eyes of life's raw realities. Even though they appear to concern themselves primarily with the secular experience, the relationships between males and females, between boss and worker, between nature and Man, they are, in fact, extensions of the deepest, most pragmatic spiritual and moral realities. Even though they primarily deal with the world as flesh, they are essentially religious. Because they finally celebrate life and the ability of man to control and shape his destiny. The blues don't jive. They reach way down into the maw of the individual and collective experience. . . .

Taken together, the blues represent an epic cycle of awesome propositions—one song (poem) after the other expressing the daily confrontations of Black people with themselves and the world. They are not merely entertainment. They act to clarify and make more bearable the human experience, especially when the context of that experience is oppressive. . . .

Therefore, no matter how you cut it, the blues and the people who create them are the Soul Force of the race, the emotional current of the Nation. And that is why Langston Hughes and Ralph Ellison based their esthetic on them. The Black Arts movement strives for the same kind of intimacy with the people. It strives to be a movement that is rooted in the fundamental experiences of the Nation.

The blues singer is not an alienated artist moaning songs of self-pity and defeat to an infidel mob. He is the voice of the community, its historian, and one of the shapers of its morality. He may claim to speak for himself only, but his ideas and values are, in fact, merely expressions of the general psychology of his people. He is the bearer of the group's working myths, aspirations, and values. And like the preacher, he has been called on by the Spirit to rap about life in the sharpest, the harshest terms possible. Also like the preacher, he may have gotten the calling early in life. He may have even sung in the church like Ray Charles and James Brown. . . .

The Black Arts movement is rooted in a spiritual ethic. In saying that the function of art is to liberate Man, we propose a function for art which is now dead in the West and which is in keeping with our most ancient traditions and with our needs. Because, at base, art is religious and ritualistic; and ritual moves to liberate Man and to connect him to the Greater Forces. Thus Man becomes stronger psychically, and is thus more able to create a world that is an extension of his spirituality—his positive humanity. We say that the function of art is to liberate Man. And we only have to look out of the window to see that we need liberation. Right on, Brothers. And God Shango, help us!

This is what's on Ameer Baraka's (LeRoi Jones) mind. He could have been the pawed-over genius of the white literary establishment. But he peeped that they were dead, and that they finally had nothing to give—the future ultimately did not include them. It was LeRoi who first used the term "Black Art" in a positive sense. In the Western world view, it is connected with the "evil," "dark" forces of witchcraft and demonology. It was LeRoi who first shifted and elevated its meaning, giving it new significance in the context of a Black esthetic. . . .

The Black Arts movement preaches that liberation is inextricably bound up with politics and culture. The culture gives us a revolutionary moral vision and a system of values and a methodology around which to shape the political movement. When we say "culture," we do not merely mean artistic forms. We mean, instead, the values, the life styles, and the feelings of the people as expressed in everyday life. The total liberation of Blues People can not be affected if we do not have a value system, a point of reference, a way of understanding what we see and hear every day around us. If we do not have a value system that is, in reality, more moral than the oppressor's, then we can not hope to change society. We will end up taking each other off, and in our confusion and ignorance, calling the murders of each other revolutionary. A value system helps us to establish models for Black people to emulate; makes it more possible for us to deeply understand our people, and to be understood by them. . . .

The new references of clothing and hair are essentially visions of ourselves perfected; they are sign posts on the road to eventual Self-Determination. For a sister to wear her hair natural asserts the sacred and essentially holy nature of her body. The natural, in its most positive sense, symbolizes the Sister's willingness to determine her own destiny. It is an act of love for herself and her people. . . .

If Black Revolutionary Cultural Consciousness is perverted by jive Negro hustlers and Madison Avenue freaks, it is our job to illustrate how that very perversion is consistent with the nature of the capitalistic, colonialistic and imperialistic monsters that now rule the planet. Merely to point out to Black people the economic and political nature of our oppression is not enough. Why is it not enough? It is so because people are *more* than just the sum total of economic and political factors. Man must exist on a more cosmic plane than that. . . .

The Blues God knows that he will cease to exist if his people cease to exist. He knows that being Black and Beautiful is not enough. He knows that the oppressor cares nothing about our beauty. . . .

This is what the Black Arts movement is all about. What I believe to be its most vital core. However, there *are* people out there bullcrapping, but that don't matter—the Black Boogaloo will blow them away. What we got to do is to dig into this thing that tugs at our souls—this blue yearning to make a way of our own.

The Black Panthers

The Black Panther Platform: "What We Want, What We Believe"

In 1966 two young blacks from Oakland, California, Huey Newton and Bobby Seale, organized the Black Panther Party, taking its name from the SNCC-organized political party in Lowndes County, Mississippi. These Black Panthers sought a militant community-based organization to deal with the problems in northern ghettoes. Their platform, "What We Want, What We Believe," took an aggressive stand against the problems of northern black life.

1. We want freedom. We want power to determine the destiny of our Black Community.

We believe that black people will not be free until we are able to determine our destiny.

2. We want full employment for our people.

We believe that the federal government is responsible and obligated to give every man employment or a guaranteed income. We believe that if the white American businessmen will not give full employment, then the means of production should be taken from the businessmen and placed in the community so that the people of the community can organize and employ all of its people and give a high standard of living.

3. We want an end to the robbery by the CAPITALIST of our Black Community.

We believe that this racist government has robbed us and now we are demanding the overdue debt of forty acres and two mules. Forty acres and two mules was promised 100 years ago as restitution for slave labor and mass murder of black people. We will accept the payment in currency which will be distributed to our many communities. The Germans are now aiding the Jews in Israel for the genocide of the Jewish people. The Germans murdered six million Jews. The American racist has taken part in the slaughter of over fifty million black people; therefore, we feel that this is a modest demand that we make.

4. We want decent housing, fit for shelter of human beings.

We believe that if the white landlords will not give decent housing to our black community, then the housing and the land should be made into cooperatives so that our community, with government-aid, can build and make decent housing for its people.

5. We want education for our people that exposes the true nature of this decadent American society. We want education that teaches us our true history and our role in the present-day society.

We believe in an educational system that will give to our people a knowledge of self. If a man does not have knowledge of himself and his position in society and the world, then he has little chance to relate to anything else.

6. We want all black men to be exempt from military service.

We believe that Black people should not be forced to fight in the military service to defend a racist government that does not protect us. We will not fight and kill other people of color in the world who, like black people, are being victimized by the white racist government of America. We will protect ourselves from the force and violence of the racist police and the racist military, by whatever means necessary.

7. We want an immediate end to POLICE BRUTALITY and MUR-DER of black people.

We believe we can end police brutality in our black community by organizing black self-defense groups that are dedicated to defending our black community from racist police oppression and brutality. The Second Amendment to the Constitution of the United States gives a right to bear arms. We therefore believe that all black people should arm themselves for self-defense.

8. We want freedom for all black men held in federal, state, county and city prisons and jails.

We believe that all black people should be released from the many jails and prisons because they have not received a fair and impartial trial.

9. We want all black people when brought to trial to be tried in court by a jury of their peer group or people from their black communities, as defined by the Constitution of the United States.

We believe that the courts should follow the United States Constitution so that black people will receive fair trials. The 14th Amendment of the U.S. Constitution gives a man a right to be tried by his peer group. A peer is a person from a similar economic, social, religious, geographical, environmental, historical and racial background. To do this the court will be forced to select a jury from the black community from which the black defendant came. We have been, and are being tried by all-white juries that have no understanding of the "average reasoning man" of the black community.

10. We want land, bread, housing, education, clothing, justice and peace. And as our major political objective, a United Nations-supervised plebiscite to be held throughout the black colony in which only black colonial subjects will be allowed to participate, for the purpose of determining the will of black people as to their national destiny.

When, in the course of human events, it becomes necessary for one people to dissolve the political bands which have connected them with another, and to assume, among the powers of the earth, the separate and equal station to which the laws of nature and nature's God entitle them, a decent respect to the opinions of mankind requires that they should declare the causes which impel them to the separation.

We hold these truths to be self-evident, that all men are created equal; that they are endowed by their Creator with certain unalienable rights; that among these are life, liberty, and the pursuit of happiness. That, to secure these rights, governments are instituted among men, deriving their just powers from the consent of the governed; that, whenever any form of government becomes destructive of these ends, it is the right of the people to alter or to abolish it, and to institute a new government, laying its foundation on such principles, and organizing its powers in such form, as to them shall seem most likely to effect their safety and happiness. Prudence, indeed, well dictate that governments long established should not be changed for light and transient causes; and, accordingly, all experience hath shown, that mankind are more disposed to suffer, while evils are sufferable, than to right themselves by abolishing the forms to which they are accustomed. But, when a long train of abuses and usurpations, pursuing invariably the same object, evinces a design to reduce them under absolute despotism, it is their right, it is their duty, to throw off such government, and to provide new guards for their future security.

Police and the Panthers

Documents from congressional investigations during the 1970s revealed the degree to which both the FBI and the CIA were disturbed by the actions of many groups, including the Black Panthers (see chapter 6). Harassment, disinformation, infiltration, and provocations all became part of the government attempt to discredit the Panthers, among other organizations. Frequent confrontations between police and Panthers left many dead. These personal accounts, collected by Henry Hampton and Steve Fayer for the Eyes on the Prize *documentary series, recount the shootings that killed Chicago Panther leader Fred Hampton.*

DEBORAH JOHNSON

The first thing that I remember after Fred and I had went to sleep was being awakened by somebody shaking Fred while we were laying in bed. Saying, "Chairman, Chairman, wake up! The pigs are vamping. The pigs are vamping." About the same time, I looked up and I saw what appeared to be flashes of light going across the entranceway to the back bedroom. It looked like a million flashes of light, because the apartment was pretty much dark. I rolled over to Fred—he still hadn't moved at this point, as I recall—and then slid down to Fred's right side, so that put me closest to the wall in the bedroom. The bed was pushed against the wall. Fred at some point raised his head up, looked out towards the entranceway to the bedroom, and laid his head back down. That's all the movement that Fred Hampton had that night.

Someone else was in the room with me and kept yelling out, "Stop shooting, stop shooting, we have a pregnant sister in here." Eventually the shooting stopped and they said we could come out. I remember crossing over Fred and telling myself over and over, Be real careful. Don't stumble, they'll try to shoot you. Just be real calm. Watch how you walk. Keep your hands up. Don't reach for anything. Don't even try to close your robe.

I'm walking out of the bedroom, there are two lines of policemen that I have to walk through on my right and my left. I remember focusing on their badge numbers and their faces. Saying them over and over in my head, so I wouldn't forget. As I walked through these two lines of policemen, one of them grabbed my robe and opened it and said, "Well, what do you know, we have a broad here." Another policeman grabbed me by the hair and pretty much just shoved me—I had more hair then—into the kitchen area. It was very cold that night. I guess that it snowed. The back door was open. Some people were on the floor in the kitchen area.

I heard a voice come from the dining room area. Someone said, "He's barely alive. He'll barely make it." The shooting, I heard some shooting start again.

> On December 4, 1969, State's Attorney Hanrahan told a press confer-
> ence that the Black Panthers had mounted a "vicious, unprovoked
> attack" on the police who had appeared at the Monroe Street apartment
> at 4:45 that morning to carry out a search for illegal weapons. Hanrahan
> later praised the fourteen officers—nine white, five black—for their
> "good judgment, considerable restraint, and professional discipline,"
> and urged all law-abiding citizens to do the same. Fred Hampton, shot
> in the arm, shoulder, and twice through the head, and Mark Clark,
> shot through the heart and lungs, were dead on arrival at the hospital.
> The seven survivors, including Deborah Johnson, were arrested and
> charged with attempted murder.

FLINT TAYLOR

The miracle in a sense was that the police left the apartment open so that we could go there. I think they thought they could do whatever they wanted to and get away with it as far as public opinion went. So they didn't seal the apartment. When I walked in, there was blood. It was like a Swiss-cheese type of effect, because they had ripped the apartment open with these submachine guns and automatic weapons. The walls were stitched with bullet holes. There was blood all over the place. The people who were with me had the presence of mind to get a cameraman down there, someone with a sixteen-millimeter camera. And we started to take the evidence. We didn't know what significance things had. So we took everything. We took every bullet, and there were shells all over the place.

Hanrahan had a story that Fred was up and firing away at the police in the back part of the apartment. Well, the bed that he was sleeping on had blood all over it—at the head and at other places. So obviously that totally disproved the theory that Fred was up, about, and firing away. But rather that he was murdered in his bed, which was what our people said. So we took the mattress, and we hid it. And we brought it back every day, so that people who came through the apartment could see it on the tours. So people could be shown the bed on which Fred was murdered, and here's how it proves that he's lying about Fred being involved in this serious shoot-out.

I think the police waited until the seventeenth of December to actually seal that apartment. So it was open for almost two weeks. And we spent the better part of those two weeks getting that evidence out of there. And the Panthers spent the better part of two weeks taking people who wanted to see the place through there. We would be talking to people when they went through, and while we were working, there'd be people walking through constantly. Maybe ten thousand people went through that apartment. From all over Chicago, but primarily from the black community, to see what had happened. And I'll never forget—I don't know what day it was or what—but I just remember some older black woman coming through there, shaking her head, and going, "It's nothing but a northern lynching."

On December 12, the *Chicago Sun-Times* reported that the photos released by the state's attorney's office to prove that the Panthers had shot at police depicted not bullet holes—as the *Chicago Tribune* had reported—but nail holes. This report lent credibility to the Panthers' claim that they had not attacked the police. . .

A federal grand jury that was convened in 1970 concluded that of the more than eighty shots fired during the raid, only one came from a Panther weapon. . . .

The Death of Martin Luther King, Jr.

As participants in the civil rights movement began to divide over tactics and targets, the influence of Martin Luther King, Jr., declined somewhat. His failed campaign in Chicago suggested that approaches appropriate for southern segregation might not be as successful with northern discrimination and racism. Further, King began to articulate his evolving sense that poverty, racism, and colonialism were all interwoven. The Poor People's March planned for the summer of 1968 would seek to call attention to these concerns. In the spring of that year, however, King traveled to Memphis to lend his support to striking garbage collectors and to recoup some of his diminished credibility. It was there, on April 4, that he was shot and killed by an assassin.

Requiem for Nonviolence

ELDRIDGE CLEAVER

The news of King's death sparked riots across the country. For activists such as Black Panther leader Eldridge Cleaver, his murder marked the death knell for the nonviolent phase of the civil rights movement.

The murder of Dr. Martin Luther King came as a surprise—and surprisingly it also came as a shock. Many people, particularly those in the black community who long ago abandoned nonviolence and opted to implement the slogan of Malcolm X—"black liberation by any means necessary"—have been expecting to hear of Dr. King's death for a long time. Many even became tired of waiting. But that Dr. King would have to die was a certainty. For here was a man who refused to abandon the philosophy and the principle of nonviolence in face of a hostile and racist nation which has made it indisputably clear that it has no intention and no desire to grant a redress of the grievances of the black colonial subjects who are held in bondage.

To black militants, Dr. King represented a stubborn and persistent stumbling block in the path of the methods that had to be implemented to bring about a revolution in the present situation. And so, therefore, much hatred, much venom and much criticism was focused upon Dr. King by the black militants. And the contradiction in which he was caught up cast him in the role of one who was hated and held in contempt, both by the whites in America who did not want to free black people, and by black people who recognized the attitude of white America and who wanted to be rid of the self-deceiving doctrine of nonviolence. Still, black militants were willing to sit back and watch, and allow Dr. King to play out his role. And his role has now been played out.

The assassin's bullet not only killed Dr. King, it killed a period of history. It killed a hope, and it killed a dream.

That white America could produce the assassin of Dr. Martin Luther King is looked upon by black people—and not just those identified as black militants—as a final repudiation by white America of any hope of reconciliation, of any hope of change by peaceful and nonviolent means. So that it becomes clear that the only way for black people in this country to get the things that they want—and the things that they have a right to and that they deserve—is to meet fire with fire.

That there is a holocaust coming I have no doubt at all. I have been talking to people around the country by telephone—people intimately involved in the black liberation struggle—and their reaction to Dr. King's murder has been unanimous: the war has begun. The violent phase of the black liberation struggle is here, and it will spread. From that shot, from that blood, America will be painted red.

America has said "No" to the black man's demand for liberation, and this "No" is unacceptable to black people. They are going to strike back, they are going to reply to the escalation of this racist government, this racist society. They are going to escalate their retaliation. And the responsibility for all this blood, for all this death, for all this suffering . . . well, it's beyond the stage of assigning blame. Black people are no longer interested in adjudicating the situation, in negotiating the situation, in arbitrating the situation. Their only interest now is in being able to summon up whatever it will take to wreak the havoc upon Babylon that will force Babylon to let the black people go. For all other avenues have been closed.

The assassin's bullet which struck down Dr. King closed a door that to the majority of black people seemed closed long ago. To many of us it was clear that that door was never open. But we were willing to allow those who wanted to to bang upon that door for entry, we were willing to sit back and let them do this. Indeed, we had no other choice. But now all black people in America have become Black Panthers in spirit.

And it is strange to see how, with each significant shot that is fired, time is speeded up. How the dreadful days that we all somehow knew were coming seem to cascade down upon us immediately, and the dreadful hours that we thought were years away are immediately upon us, immediately before us. And all eternity is gone, blown away, washed away in the blood of martyrs.

Is the death of Dr. King a sad day for America? No. It is a day consistent with what America demands by its actions. The death of Dr. King was not a tragedy for America. America should be happy that Dr. King is dead, because America worked so hard to bring it about. And now all the hypocritical, vicious madmen who pollute the government of this country and who befoul the police agencies of this country, all of the hypocritical public announcements following the death of Dr. King are being repudiated and held in contempt, not only by black people but by millions of white people who know that had these same treacherous, political gangsters made the moves that clearly lay within their power to make, Dr. King would not be dead, nonviolence would prevail and the terror would not be upon us. These people, the police departments, the legislatures, the government, the Democratic Party, the Republican Party, those commonly referred to as the Establishment or the power structure, they can be looked upon as immediate targets and symbols of blame. . . .

Last night I heard Lyndon Baines Johnson admonishing his people, admonishing black people to turn away from violence, and not to follow the path of the assassins. And of all the corn pone that he spouted forth one thing struck me and I felt insulted by it. He was ringing changes on a famous statement made by Malcolm X in his speech. "The Ballot or the Bullet." Malcolm X had prophesied that if the ballot did not prevail in gaining black people their liberation, then the bullet would be made to prevail. And Lyndon Johnson said last night that he was going to prove to the nation and to the American people that the ballot and not the bullet would prevail. Coming from him, it was a pure insult.

Those of us in the Black Panther Party who have been reading events and looking to the future have said that this will be the Year of the Panther, that this will be the Year of the Black Panther. And now everything that I can see leaves no doubt of that. And now there is Stokely Carmichael, Rap Brown, and above all there is Huey P. Newton. Malcolm X prophesied the coming of the gun, and Huey Newton picked up the gun, and now there is gun against gun. Malcolm X gunned down. Martin Luther King gunned down.

The Revolt of the Black Athlete

HARRY EDWARDS

The conspicuous position of black athletes in American culture contrasted sharply with the inferior place of African-Americans as a people. Seizing upon this disparity, black activists sought to illustrate the issue through a number of confrontations around athletic events. Heavyweight boxing champion Muhammad Ali, who had announced his conversion to the Nation of Islam and

Reprinted by permission of author, Harry Edwards, Ph.D., Professor of Sociology, University of California, Berkeley. Original source: Harry Edwards, *The Revolt of the Black Athlete*, New York: Free Press, 1969.

changed his name from Cassius Clay, refused induction into the armed forces
on religious grounds in 1967. He was stripped of his title. Ali's case ended
in a 1971 Supreme Court decision upholding his constitutional guarantees.
He did not regain the championship until 1974, however.

Not only was 1968 a presidential election year, but it was an Olympic
year as well. The Olympic Project for Human Rights was organized to use the
international spotlight of the Olympics to highlight race problems. A number
of American basketball players joined in a boycott of the Olympics, while track
and field athletes staged personal demonstrations on the victory stand. Harry
Edwards, black sociologist and former athlete, recounts the issues and ramifica-
tions of these activities.

Since the time of Jesse Owens it has been presumed that any poor
but rugged youngster who was able to jump racial fences into a college
haven was happy all day long. He—the All-American, the subsidized,
semiprofessional racer—was fortunate. Mostly, this is a myth. In 1960,
for example, I was recruited by San Jose State College, a prominent
"track school." Fine things were promised. "You'll be accepted here,"
the head coach and deans assured me. It developed that of 16 campus
fraternities (as Greek in name as Plato, who revered the democracy
of the Olympic Games) not one would pledge Harry Edwards (or
anyone of color). The better restaurants were out of bounds and
social activity was nil—I was invited nowhere outside "blood" circles.
Leaving California, I spent two years acquiring a Master's degree at
Cornell University. Returning to San Jose State as a teacher, I knocked
on door after door bearing "vacancy" signs, but Mr. Charley was so
sorry—the rental room suddenly wasn't available. The end-up: a cold
cement-floor garage, costing $75 a month. Not long after I came to
know Tommie Smith, whose 0:19.5 is the world 220-yard record and
whom this same state college uses to impress and procure other
speedsters and footballers of his race. "I have you beat," he said. "My
wife's pregnant. We have no decent house. So far 13 lovely people
have turned me down.". . .

During the spring months of 1968, the Olympic Committee for
Human Rights, in addition to mobilizing and counseling black athletes and students on various campuses, had continued its drive to
keep the Olympic Project for Human Rights in the forefront of public concern. . . .

Some athletes had to be convinced to compete. Typical of these were Tommie Smith and John Carlos. They had to be convinced that for them to boycott under the existing circumstances would be in a vain sacrifice. For unlike Lew Alcindor, the great black basketball star, they could easily have been replaced by Negroes more than willing to compete for the United States. . . .

Undoubtedly, there would be some defections in Mexico City. But if only one single black athlete staged a gesture of protest during the course of victory ceremonies in Mexico City, the millions of oppressed black people in America would have been remembered. . . .

Because of the overawing of some black athletes by the Olympic men's track and field coaching staff and by Avery Brundage, it became necessary to make certain changes with regard to the forms of protest outlined in the Statement to the Black Power Conference. The center of the protest did not, however, move from the victory stand. It was decided that each athlete would determine and carry out his own "thing," preferably focusing around the victory stand ceremonies. In this way, potential repercussions from a so-called "Black Power" conspiracy could be avoided and, also, each athlete would be free to determine his own course of protest. The results of this new strategy, devised for the most part by the athletes themselves, were no less than revolutionary in impact. . . .

The first test of support for the Olympic Project for Human Rights came when Jim Hines and Charles Greene took the victory stand after finishing a close 1-2 in the 100-meter dash. The two took the stand and stood stolidly, facing the flag. Neither made so much as an utterance in protest of black degradation in America. . . .

Then came the victory ceremonies for the 200-meter dash. Tommie Smith, the gold medalist, and John Carlos, the bronze medalist, had made it crystal clear that they intended to go through with their planned protest at the victory stand. Subtle attempts at intimidating the two had been made by members of both the U.S. Olympic Committee and the U.S. track and field coaching staff. But Carlos and Smith would not bend. They climbed the victory stand shoeless, each wearing a black glove. Smith had a black scarf tied around his neck. They were joined on the victory stand by Peter Norman, the silver medalist from Australia, who wore the official badge of the Olympic Project for Human Rights to underscore his support of the black liberation struggle. The men were presented with their medals and then each turned toward the flag of the country represented by the gold medal winner. The U.S. National Anthem was played. Smith and Carlos immediately raised their gloved fists and bowed their heads. In a taped interview with Howard Cosell, Smith explained the pair's protest gestures. He stated, "I wore a black right-hand glove and Carlos wore the left-hand glove of the same pair. My raised right hand stood for the power in black America. Carlos' raised left hand stood for the unity of black America. Together they formed an arch of unity and power. The black scarf around my neck stood for black pride. The black socks with no shoes stood for black poverty in racist America. The totality of our effort was the regaining of black dignity." Smith later confided to me that the gesture of the bowed head was in remembrance of the fallen warriors in the black liberation struggle in America—Malcolm X, Martin Luther King, Jr., and others.

The impact of the protest was immediate. The U.S. Olympic Committee, acting hastily and rashly, warned all other U.S. athletes, black and white, that "severe" penalties would follow any further protests. Smith and Carlos were given 48 hours to get out of Mexico and were suspended from the Olympic team.

LATINOS

Public declarations by African-Americans of race pride and ethnic heritage prompted members of other minority groups to reassess their own place and backgrounds. This was an especially compelling discussion among American Latinos, who had lived in a world that offered contradictory messages about their race and culture. Across the country, from Puerto Rican communities in New York to Hispanic enclaves in Texas and Chicano barrios in California, this discussion exploded.

Chicano Manifesto

ARMENDO B. RENDON

Being raised as a Latino in the United States meant dealing with a complex personal heritage. For Armando Rendon, this entailed coming to terms with his own background as well as understanding the degree to which many Latinos had been seduced into presenting themselves in a shallow imitation of white culture.

I am a Chicano. What that means to me may be entirely different from what meaning the word has for you. To be Chicano is to find out something about one's self which has lain dormant, subverted, and nearly destroyed.

I am a Chicano because of a unique fusion of bloods and history and culture. I am a Chicano because I sense a rising awareness among others like myself of a fresh rebirth of self and self-in-others.

I am a Chicano because from this revived and newly created personality I draw vitality and motivation more forceful and tangible than I ever did or could have from the gringo world.

I am a Chicano in spite of scorn or derision, in spite of opposition even from my own people, many of whom do not understand and may never fathom what Chicano means.

I am a Chicano, hopeful that my acceptance and assertion of Chicanismo will mean a better life for all my people, that it will move others into making the same act of will to accept and develop a new-found identity and power. . . .

There is a mystique among us Chicanos, something that we have searched for and now have found. It draws us together, welds from insecure, disparate groups and viewpoints a common focal thought, experience, and power. For so many years we have disclaimed or claimed this or that label, sought leadership even from the Anglo,

Reprinted by permission, Amando Rendon. Original source: Armando Rendon, *Chicano Manifesto,* New York: Macmillan Co., 1971.

founded any number of organizations, worried over internal issues, fought for prestige and position within our little groups; and all the while the Anglo kept us in subjugation.

To be Chicano is nothing new; it is as old as our people. But it is a new way of knowing your brown brother and of understanding our brown race. To be Chicano means that a person has looked deeper into his being and sought unique ties to his brothers in la raza.

I nearly fell victim to the Anglo. My childhood was spent in the West Side barrio of San Antonio. I lived in my grandmother's house on Ruiz Street just below Zarzamora Creek. I did well in the elementary grades and learned English quickly.

Spanish was off-limits in school anyway, and teachers and relatives taught me early that my mother tongue would be of no help in making good grades and becoming a success. Yet Spanish was the language I used in playing and arguing with friends. Spanish was the language I spoke with my abuelita, my grandmother, as I ate atole on those cold mornings when I used to wake at dawn to her clattering dishes in the tiny kitchen; or when I would cringe in mock horror at old folk tales she would tell me late at night.

But the lesson took effect anyway. When at the age of ten I went with my mother to California, to the San Francisco Bay Area where she found work during the war years, I had my first real opportunity to strip myself completely of my heritage. In California the schools I attended were all Anglo except for this little mexicanito. At least, I never knew anyone who admitted he was Mexican and I certainly never thought to ask. When my name was accented incorrectly, Réndon instead of Rendón, that was all right; finally I must have gotten tired of correcting people or just didn't bother. . . .

When my mother, who speaks both Spanish and English fluently, spoke to me in Spanish, I would respond in English. By the time I graduated from high school and prepared to enter college, the break was nearly complete. Seldom during college did I admit to being a Mexican American. Only when Latin American students pressed me about my surname did I admit my Spanish descent, or when it proved an asset in meeting coeds from Latin American countries.

My ancestry had become a shadow, fainter and fainter about me. I felt no particular allegiance to it, drew no inspiration from it, and elected generally to let it fade away. I clicked with the Anglo mind-set in college, mastered it, you might say. I even became editor of the campus biweekly newspaper as a junior, and editor of the literary magazine as a senior—not bad, now that I look back, for a tortillas-and-beans Chicano upbringing to beat the Anglo at his own game.

The point of my "success," of course, was that I had been assimilated; I had bought the white man's world. After getting my diploma I was set to launch out into a career in newspaper reporting and writing. There was no thought in my mind of serving my people, telling their story, or making anything right for anybody but myself. Instead I had dreams of Pulitzer Prizes, syndicated columns, foreign correspondent assignments, front page stories—that was for me. Then something happened.

A Catholic weekly newspaper in Sacramento offered me a position as a reporter and feature writer. I had a job on a Bay Area daily as a copyboy at the time, with the opportunity to become a reporter. But I'd just been married, and there were a number of other reasons to consider: there'd be a variety of assignments, Sacramento was the state capital, it was a good town in which to raise a family, and the other job lacked promise for upward mobility. I decided to take the offer. . . .

It was my own people who rescued me. There is a large Chicano population in Sacramento, today one of the most activist in northern California, but at the time factionalized and still dependent on the social and church organizations for identity. But together we found each other.

My job soon brought me into contact with many Chicanos as well as with the recently immigrated Mexicans, located in the barrios that Sacramento had allocated to the "Mexicans." I found my people striving to survive in an alien environment among foreign people. . . . I rediscovered my own people, or perhaps they redeemed me. . . . For the first time in many years I became reimmersed in a tough, macho ambiente (an entirely Mexican male environment). Only Spanish was spoken. The effect was shattering. It was as if my tongue, after being struck dumb as a child, had been loosened. . . . I was cast in a spiritual setting which was a perfect background for reviving my Chicano soul. Reborn but imperfectly, I still had a lot to learn about myself and my people. But my understanding deepened and renewed itself as the years went by. I visited bracero camps with teams of Chicanos; sometimes with priests taking the Sacraments; sometimes only Chicanos, offering advice or assistance with badly needed food and clothing, distributed through a bingo-game technique; and on occasion, music for group singing provided by a phonograph or a guitar. Then there were barrio organization work; migrant worker programs; a rural self-help community development project; and confrontation with antipoverty agencies, with the churches, with government officials, and with cautious Chicanos, too. . . .

I owe my life to my Chicano people. They rescued me from the Anglo kiss of death, the monolingual, monocultural, and colorless gringo society. I no longer face a dilemma of identity or direction. That identity and direction have been charted for me by the Chicano—but to think I came that close to being sucked into the vacuum of the dominant society.

Chicano is a beautiful word. Chicano describes a beautiful people. Chicano has a power of its own. Chicano is a unique confluence of histories, cultures, languages, and traditions.

Chicano is the one unique word of the Mexican American people. Its derivation is strictly internal; it owes nothing to the Anglo penchant for categorizing ethnic groups. In a way, Chicano is indefinable, more a word to be understood and felt and lived than placed in a dictionary or analyzed by Anglo anthropologists, sociologists, and apologists.

Chicano has the ring of pachuco slang, of shortening a word, which is typical of our Mexican American experience. It also echoes the harsher sounds of our native ancestors of the Mexican Valley, but is softened by the rounded-vowel endings of our Spanish forebears. It is the perfect word to characterize the mezcla that is la raza. It portrays the fact that we have come to psychological terms with circumstances which might otherwise cause emotional and social breakdowns among our people if we only straddle cultures and do not absorb them.

Chicano is a very special word. Chicano is a unique people. Chicano is a prophecy of a new day and a new world.

El Plan de Aztlán

Reassessments such as that of Armando Rendon led to a growing sense of Chicano self-identity. Political movements were not far behind. The First Chicano National Conference, held in Denver in 1969, produced "El Plan de Aztlan," a call for political action and race pride.

EL PLAN ESPIRITUAL DE AZTLÁN

In the spirit of a new people that is conscious not only of its proud historical heritage but also of the brutal "gringo" invasion of our territories, *we,* the Chicano inhabitants and civilizers of the northern land of Aztlán from whence came our forefathers, reclaiming the land of their birth and consecrating the determination of our people of the sun, *declare* that the call of our blood is our power, our responsibility, and our inevitable destiny.

We are free and sovereign to determine those tasks which are justly called for by our house, our land, the sweat of our brows, and by our hearts. Aztlán belongs to those who plant the seeds, water the fields, and gather the crops and not to the foreign Europeans. We do not recognize capricious frontiers on the bronze continent.

Brotherhood unites us, and love for our brothers makes us a people whose time has come and who struggle against the foreigner "gabacho" who exploits our riches and destroys our culture. With our heart in our hands and our hands in the soil, we declare the independence of our mestizo nation. We are a bronze people with a bronze culture. Before the world, before all of North America, before all our brothers in the bronze continent, we are a nation, we are a union of free pueblos, we are *Aztlán.*

Por La Raza todo. Fuera de La Raza nada.

PROGRAM

El Plan Espiritual de Aztlán sets the theme that the Chicanos (La
Raza de Bronze) must use their nationalism as the key or common
denominator for mass mobilization and organization. Once we are
committed to the idea and philosophy of El Plan de Aztlán, we can
only conclude that social, economic, cultural, and political independence is the only road to total liberation from oppression, exploitation, and racism. Our struggle then must be for the control of our
barrios, campos, pueblos, lands, our economy, our culture, and our
political life. El Plan commits all levels of Chicano society—the barrio,
the campo, the ranchero, the writer, the teacher, the worker, the
professional—to La Causa.

Nationalism

Nationalism as the key to organization transcends all religious, political, class, and economic factions or boundaries. Nationalism is the
common denominator that all members of La Raza can agree upon.

Organizational Goals

1. UNITY in the thinking of our people concerning the barrios,
the pueblo, the campo, the land, the poor, the middle class, the
professional—all committed to the liberation of La Raza.

2. ECONOMY: economic control of our lives and our communities can only come about by driving the exploiter out of our communities, our pueblos, and our lands and by controlling and developing
our own talents, sweat, and resources. . . .

3. EDUCATION must be relative to our people, i.e., history, culture, bilingual education, contributions, etc. Community control of
our schools, our teachers, our administrators, our counselors, and
our programs.

4. INSTITUTIONS shall serve our people by providing the service
necessary for a full life and their welfare on the basis of restitution, not
handouts or beggar's crumbs. Restitution for past economic slavery,
political exploitation, ethnic and cultural psychological destruction
and denial of civil and human rights. Institutions in our community

which do not serve the people have no place in the community. The institutions belong to the people.

5. SELF-DEFENSE of the community must rely on the combined strength of the people. The front line defense will come from the barrios, the campos, the pueblos, and the ranchitos. Their involvement as protectors of their people will be given respect and dignity. They in turn offer their responsibility and their lives for their people. Those who place themselves in the front ranks for their people do so out of love and carnalismo. . . .

6. CULTURAL values of our people strengthen our identity and the moral backbone of the movement. Our culture unites and educates the family of La Raza towards liberation with one heart and one mind. We must insure that our writers, poets, musicians, and artists produce literature and art that is appealing to our people and relates to our revolutionary culture. Our cultural values of life, family, and home will serve as a powerful weapon to defeat the gringo dollar value system and encourage the process of love and brotherhood.

7. POLITICAL LIBERATION can only come through independent action on our part, since the two-party system is the same animal with two heads that feed from the same trough. Where we are a majority, we will control; where we are a minority, we will represent a pressure group; nationally, we will represent one party: La Familia de La Raza!

Action

1. Awareness and distribution of El Plan Espiritual de Aztlán. Presented at every meeting, demonstration, confrontation, courthouse, institution, administration, church, school, tree, building, car, and every place of human existence.
2. September 16, on the birthdate of Mexican Independence, a national walk-out by all Chicanos of all colleges and schools to be sustained until the complete revision of the educational system: its policy makers, administration, its curriculum, and its personnel to meet the needs of our community.
3. Self-defense against the occupying forces of the oppressors at every school, every available man, woman, and child.
4. Community nationalization and organization of all Chicanos: El Plan Espiritual de Aztlán.
5. Economic program to drive the exploiters out of our community

and a welding together of our people's combined resources to control their own production through cooperative effort.

6. Creation of an independent local, regional, and national political party.

A nation autonomous and free—culturally, socially, economically, and politically—will make its own decisions on the usage of our lands, the taxation of our goods, the utilization of our bodies for war, the determination of justice (reward and punishment), and the profit of our sweat.

El Plan de Aztlán is the plan of liberation!

First National Chicana Conference

The emergence of a women's movement in the late 1960s (see chapter 8) coincided with that of the movement for Latino rights. The combined effort of the two movements led to direct questioning of the situation of Latino women and to plans for action. A brief selection from the final report of the first national meeting is reprinted here.

SEX AND THE CHICANA

We feel that in order to provide an effective measure to correct the many sexual hangups facing the Chicano community the following resolutions should be implemented:

I. Sex is good and healthy for both Chicano and Chicanas and we must develop this attitude.

II. We should destroy the myth that religion and culture control our sexual lives.

III. We recognize that we have been oppressed by religion and that the religious writing was done by *men* and interpreted by *men*. Therefore, for those who desire religion, they should interpret their Bible, or Catholic rulings according to their own feelings, what they think is right, without any guilt complexes.

IV. Mothers should teach their sons to respect women as human beings who are equal in every respect. *No double standard.*

V. Women should go back to the communities and form discussion and action groups concerning sex education.

VI. Free, legal abortions and birth control for the Chicano community, controlled by *Chicanas.* As Chicanas we have the right to control our own bodies.

VII. Make use of church centers, neighborhood centers and any other place available.

"Liberate your mind and the body will follow. . . ."

"*A quitarnos todos nuestros complejos sexuales para tener una vida mejor y feliz*" (Let's cast off all our sexual complexes to have a better and happier life). . . .

RELIGION

I. Recognize the *Plan de Aztlán*

II. Take over already existing Church resources for community use, i.e., health, Chicano awareness—public information of its resources, etc.

III. Oppose any institutionalized religion.

IV. Revolutionary change of Catholic Church or for it to get out of the way.

V. Establish communication with the barrio and implement programs of awareness to the Chicano movement.

César Chávez and the Farm Workers' Movement

Probably no movement among Latinos received more national attention than the struggle by César Chávez and the National Farm Workers Association (NFWA) to organize the migrant farm workers. Calling for a nationwide boycott of California grapes and a march from Delano, in California's Central Valley, to the state capitol in Sacramento—among other actions—Chavez and the NFWA combined issues of race and labor relations into a single movement.

The Tale of the Raza

LUIS VALDEZ

Chicano author Luis Valdez assessed the larger impact of this struggle for La Raza *(The Race), as well as for the workers.*

The revolt in Delano is more than a labor struggle. Mexican grape pickers did not march 300 miles to Sacramento, carrying the standard of the *Virgen de Guadalupe,* merely to dramatize economic grievances. Beyond unionization, beyond politics, there is the desire of a New World race to reconcile the conflicts of its 500-year-old history. *La Raza* is trying to find its place in the sun it once worshipped as a Supreme Being.

La Raza, the race, is the Mexican people. Sentimental and cynical, fierce and docile, faithful and treacherous, individualistic and herd-following, in love with life and obsessed with death, the personality of the *raza* encompasses all the complexity of our history. The conquest of Mexico was no conquest at all. It shattered our ancient Indian universe, but more of it was left above ground than beans and tortillas. Below the foundations of our Spanish culture, we still sense the ruins of an entirely different civilization.

Most of us know we are not European simply by looking in a mirror—the shape of the eyes, the curve of the nose, the color of skin, the texture of hair; these things belong to another time, another people. Together with a million little stubborn mannerisms, beliefs, myths, superstitions, words, thoughts—things not so easily detected— they fill our Spanish life with Indian contradictions. It is not enough to say we suffer an identity crisis, because that crisis has been our way of life for the last five centuries. . . .

Although he sometimes reminds one of Benito Juarez, César is our first real *Mexican-American* leader. Used to hybrid forms, the *raza* includes all Mexicans, even hyphenated Mexican-Americans; but divergent histories are slowly making the *raza* in the United States different from the *raza* in Mexico. We who were born here missed out on the chief legacy of the Revolution: the chance to forge a nation true to all the forces that have molded us, to be one people. Now we must seek our own destiny, and Delano is only the beginning of our active search. For the last hundred years our revolutionary progress has not only been frustrated, it has been totally suppressed. This is a society largely hostile to our cultural values. There is no poetry about the United States. No depth, no faith, no allowance for human contrariness. No soul, no mariachi, no chili sauce, no pulque, no mysticism, no *chingaderas*. . . .

The pilgramage to Sacramento was no mere publicity trick. The *raza* has a tradition of migrations, starting from the legend of the founding of Mexico. Nezahualcoyotl, a great Indian leader, advised his primitive *Chichimecas*, forerunners of the Aztecs, to begin a march to the south. In that march, he prophesied, the children would age and the old would die, but their grandchildren would come to a great lake. In that lake they would find an eagle devouring a serpent, and on that spot, they would begin to build a great nation. The nation was Aztec Mexico, and the eagle and the serpent are the symbols of the *patria*. They are emblazoned on the Mexican flag, which the marchers took to Sacramento with pride.

Then there is the other type of migration. When the migrant farm laborer followed the crops, he was only reacting to the way he saw the American *raza*: no unity, no representation, no roots. The pilgrimage was a truly religious act, a rejection of our past in this country and a symbol of our unity and new direction. It is of no lasting significance that Governor Brown was not at the Capitol to greet us. The unity of thousands of *raza* on the Capitol steps was reason enough for our march. Under the name of HUELGA we had created a Mexican-American *patria*, and César Chávez was our first *Presidente*.

Huelga means strike. With the poetic instinct of the *raza*, the Delano grape strikers have made it mean a dozen other things. It is a declaration, a challenge, a greeting, a feeling, a movement. We cried *Huelga!* to the scabs, *Huelga!* to the labor contractors, to the growers, to Governor Brown. With the Schenley and DiGiorgio boycotts, it was *Huelga!* to the whole country. It is the most significant word in our entire Mexican-American history. If the *raza* of Mexico believes in *La Patria,* we believe in *La Huelga.*

The route of the pilgrimage was planned so that the Huelga could reach all the farmworkers of the San Joaquin Valley. Dependent as we were on each farmworking town for food and shelter, we knew the *raza* would not turn us down. *"Mi case es suya,"* is the precept of Mexican hospitality: "My house is yours."

The Virgin of Guadalupe was the first hint to farmworkers that the pilgrimage implied social revolution. During the Mexican Revolution, the peasant armies of Emiliano Zapata carried her standard, not only because they sought her divine protection, but because she symbolized the Mexico of the poor and humble. It was a simple Mexican Indian, Juan Diego, who first saw her in a vision at Guadalupe. Beautifully dark and Indian in feature, she was the New World version of the Mother of Christ. Even though some of her worshippers in Mexico still identify her with Tonatzin, an Aztec goddess, she is a Catholic saint of Indian creation—a Mexican. The people's response was immediate and reverent. They joined the march by the thousands, falling in line behind her standard. To the Catholic hypocrites against the pilgrimage and strike the Virgin said *Huelga!*

The struggle for better wages and better working conditions in Delano is but the first, realistic articulation of our need for unity. To emerge from the mire of our past in the United States, to leave behind the divisive, deadening influence of poverty, we must have unions. To the farmworkers who joined the pilgrimage, this cultural pride was revolutionary. There were old symbols—Zapata lapel buttons—and new symbols standing for new social protest and revolt; the red thunderbird flags of the NFWA, picket signs, arm bands. . . .

The NFWA is a radical union because it started, and continues to grow, as a community organization. Its store, cafeteria, clinic, garage, newspaper and weekly meeting have established a sense of community the Delano farmworkers will not relinquish. After years of isolation in the *barrios* of Great Valley slum towns like Delano, after years of living in labor camps and ranches at the mercy and caprice of growers and contractors, the Mexican-American farmworker is developing his own ideas about living in the United States. He wants to be equal with all the working men of the nation, and he does not mean by the standard middle-class route. We are repelled by the human disintegration of peoples and cultures as they fall apart in this Great Gringo Melting Pot, and determined that this will not happen to us. But there will always be a *raza* in this country. There are millions more where we came from, across the thousand miles of common border between Mexico and the United States. For millions of farmworkers, from the Mexicans and Philippinos of the West to the Afro-Americans of the South, the United States has come to a social, political and cultural impasse. Listen to these people, and you will hear the first murmurings of revolution.

ASIAN-AMERICANS

Americans of Asian descent felt the same stirrings as did blacks and Latinos. In each case, however, the racial stereotyping contained elements unique to the minority population and led to slightly different perspectives.

The Emergence of Yellow Power

AMY UYEMATSU

Amy Uyematsu recounts the clear debt "yellow power" owed to its Black Power predecessor, but continues with discussions of the particular situation and style of Asian-Americans.

Asian Americans can no longer afford to watch the black-and-white struggle from the sidelines. They have their own cause to fight, since they are also victims—with less visible scars—of the white institutionalized racism. A yellow movement has been set into motion by the black power movement. Addressing itself to the unique problems of Asian Americans, this "yellow power" movement is relevant to the black power movement in that both are part of the Third World struggle to liberate all colored people.

PART I: MISTAKEN IDENTITY

The yellow power movement has been motivated largely by the problem of self-identity in Asian Americans. The psychological focus of this movement is vital, for Asian Americans suffer the critical mental crises of having "integrated" into American society—

> No person can be healthy, complete, and mature if he must deny a part of himself; this is what "integration" has required so far. —Stokely Carmichael & Charles V. Hamilton

The Asian Americans' current position in America is not viewed as a social problem. Having achieved middle-class incomes while presenting no real threat in numbers to the white majority, the main body of Asian Americans (namely, the Japanese and the Chinese) have received the token acceptance of white America.

Precisely because Asian Americans have become economically secure, do they face serious identity problems. Fully committed to a system that subordinates them on the basis of non-whiteness, Asian Americans still try to gain complete acceptance by denying their yellowness. They have become white in every respect but color.

However, the subtle but prevailing racial prejudice that "yellows" experience restricts them to the margins of the white world. Asian Americans have assumed white identities, that is, the values and attitudes of the majority of Americans. Now they are beginning to realize that this nation is a "White democracy" and that yellow people have a mistaken identity.

Within the past two years, the "yellow power" movement has developed as a direct outgrowth of the "black power" movement. The "black power" movement caused many Asian Americans to question themselves. "Yellow power" is just now at the stage of "an articulated mood rather than a program—disillusionment and alienation from white America and independence, race pride, and self-respect." Yellow consciousness is the immediate goal of concerned Asian Americans.

In the process of Americanization, Asians have tried to transform themselves into white men—both mentally and physically. Mentally, they have adjusted to the white man's culture by giving up their own languages, customs, histories, and cultural values. They have adopted the "American way of life" only to discover that this is not enough.

Next, they have rejected their physical heritages, resulting in extreme self-hatred. Yellow people share with the blacks the desire to look white. Just as blacks wish to be light-complected with thin lips and unkinky hair, "yellows" want to be tall with long legs and large eyes. The self-hatred is also evident in the yellow male's obsession with unobtainable white women, and in the yellow female's attempt to gain male approval by aping white beauty standards. Yellow females have their own "conking" techniques—they use "peroxide, foam rubber, and scotch tape to give them light hair, large breasts, and double-lidded eyes."

The "Black is Beautiful" cry among black Americans has instilled a new awareness in Asian Americans to be proud of their physical and cultural heritages. Yellow power advocates self-acceptance as the first step toward strengthening personalities of Asian Americans. . . .

The problem of self-identity in Asian Americans also requires the removal of stereotypes. The yellow people in America seem to be silent citizens. They are stereotyped as being passive, accommodating, and unemotional. Unfortunately, this description is fairly accurate, for Asian Americans have accepted these stereotypes and are becoming true to them.

The silent, passive image of Asian Americans is understood not in terms of their cultural backgrounds, but by the fact that they are scared. The earliest Asians in America were Chinese immigrants who began settling in large numbers on the West Coast form 1850 through 1880. They were subjected to extreme white racism, ranging from economic subordination, to the denial of rights of naturalization, to physical violence. During the height of anti-Chinese mob action of the 1880's, whites were "stoning the Chinese in the streets; cutting off their queues, wrecking their shops and laundries." The worst outbreak took place in Rock Springs, Wyoming, in 1885, when twenty-eight Chinese residents were murdered. Perhaps, surviving Asians learned to live in silence, for even if "the victims of such attacks tried to go to court to win protection, they could not hope to get a hearing. The phrase 'not a Chinaman's chance' had a grim and bitter reality."

Racist treatment of "yellows" still existed during World War II, with the unjustifiable internment of 110,000 Japanese into detention camps. When Japanese Americans were ordered to leave their homes and possessions behind within short notice, they co-operated with resignation and did not even voice opposition. . . .

Today the Asian Americans are still scared. Their passive behavior serves to keep national attention on the black people. By being as inconspicuous as possible, they keep pressure off of themselves at the expense of the blacks. Asian Americans have formed an uneasy alliance with white Americans to keep the blacks down. They close their eyes to the latent white racism toward them which has never changed.

Frightened "yellows" allow the white public to use the "silent Oriental" stereotype against the black protest: The presence of twenty million blacks in America poses an actual physical threat to the white system. Fearful whites tell militant blacks that the acceptable criterion for behavior is exemplified in the quiet, passive Asian American.

The yellow power movement envisages a new role for Asian Americans:

> It is a rejection of the passive Oriental stereotype and symbolizes the birth of a new Asian—one who will recognize and deal with injustices. The shout of Yellow Power, symbolic of our new direction, is reverberating in the quiet corridors of the Asian community.

I Forgot My Eyes Were Black

JAN MASAOKA

Like black and Latino women, Asian women felt the unique consequences of an identity created from both racial and sexual stereotypes. Jan Masaoka discusses the special position of Asian women, in terms of both white America and Asian men.

I sometimes think about my position as an Asian woman in a society geared to the needs of whites and men, and it's pretty weird. I can say that now I am content, even a little proud, with myself. After years of wanting to be white and a boy, I am progressing. . . .

I guess that one of the most difficult things for me to understand is how to relate to my boyfriend who is white. Sometimes I flash back on all the ideas my parents taught me such as the idea that to marry a white man was to sort of degrade myself, and it's really hard to know how to feel with these kinds of feelings.

I once read this poem by an Asian woman where she said that after looking into blue eyes for so long she forgot hers were black. I really feel this, and it's hard to understand: I identify so strongly with this man I love and that's inevitably tied up somewhat to the way he looks, which conflicts with me and my background and the way I look.

So I look at him and all the feelings I have get mixed up and make me upset and dizzy: loving him, hating myself for loving a white man, hating him because he's white, hating white people in general, feeling underneath that I'm superior to white people, and even deeper underneath that I'm inferior to white people, especially men, feeling guilty for not having an Asian boyfriend, feeling that I'm taking unfair advantage of my social and sexual mobility racially when Asian men don't have that mobility, and being afraid of what other people think about my going with a white man—it's just really frightening.

ASIAN WOMEN AND WHITE MEN

It seems to me that there are three reasons why it is more acceptable
for an Asian woman to be seen with a white man or marry one than
it is for an Asian man to marry a white woman. First, in this country,
people have become accustomed to seeing "war brides," and so the
sight of an Asian woman with a white man is a little more familiar.
Second, Asian women are rather "exotic" these days—you know us—
combs float through our hair as we rinse with coconut oil in front of
waterfalls every morning. Third, because this society puts the woman
in the "lower" position of the marriage, it seems more acceptable
for the "lower" race to be in the "lower" position rather than for
the "lower" Asian male to be in the "higher" male position of the
marriage. This is disgusting logic, but it sure causes problems!

Also, white men have always had the "privilege" in this country
of getting their kicks using women in any way they can, whether that
means using black slave women for pleasure and to breed more slaves
to sell, being unfaithful but forbidding it for their wives, or going out
with Third World women but ridiculing white women who go out
with Third World men.

I have a Japanese man friend who was once beat up by some white
boys for being on the street with a white girl. Actually, it was an
unusual situation in the first place since many white women won't go
out with Asian men because "I'm just not attracted to them." So,
where Asian men are sort of "restricted" to Asian women—maybe
even to their own nationality—Asian women are more or less free to
go out with white men. As a result, Asian men can resent Asian women
who do take advantage of that freedom, and we Asian women don't
know how to feel.

SEXUAL STANDARDS

We have such a hard time when the American media sets the standards
for desirability. The sexy American male is tall, blonde, big muscles,
hairy chest, etc. But the Asian males are short, dark, with wiry muscles
and not much hair on their chests. So they're self conscious and we
Asian women sometimes fall for the American stereotype while white

women hardly ever think of Asian men as potential boyfriends or anything.

On the other hand, the typical sexy American women are fair, with long, slender legs, big eyes and big breasts while Asian women are dark, have short stocky legs, almond eyes and small breasts. The American ideal is ridiculous and sick for American women, but it's much harder when you're Asian and know you'll never live up to that. When I was a little girl I thought that the epitome of beauty was blonde hair and blue eyes, a pretty common vision for little girls in America, I guess, but when I looked in the mirror, I just knew I was hopeless.

But the answer isn't to go back to the old Japanese or Chinese culture either. At my family reunions the women do all the cooking, serving, and all the cleaning up. The traditional Japanese family rejoiced when a son was born and was indifferent or resentful when a girl was born. Uh huh. We've got to make ourselves a new culture without any of that.

RACISM AND PRIVATE PROPERTY

Racism is now used to keep wars going: "Over 3/4 of a million Vietnamese have been killed by American bombs and guns, but so what? We've got to protect our interests in oil, agriculture, and finances." And we even see a trickier kind of racism in the peace movement: "Over 3/4 of a million Vietnamese have been killed by American bombs and guns, but what really counts is that 50,000 A*M*E*R*I*C*A*N boys have died, so we've got to end the war to bring our boys home."

Racism and sexism are two tools society uses to divide people who are getting the short end of the deal. The people who have all the money and power are more than happy to let the rest of us fight among ourselves instead of fighting them to get the share of this country's wealth we deserve. . . .

White capitalistic values come between Asian men and women when we really need to get together for our liberation as Asians. . . .

Since we and all Third World people have been oppressed as a people, perhaps we can understand more easily than they that our real enemy is not men, but a system geared to profit, and not the needs of all the people.

And if all of us who are put down and cheated by this system unite, we will fight a struggle that is, at last, truly *our* struggle—for we will be fighting for a society not decided by profit, race, or sex, but a society that *belongs* to the people.

AMERICAN INDIANS

National Indian Youth Council

As early as 1960, American Indian leaders had begun to organize around discontent with the position of Indians within American society and over the decline in race pride among Indian peoples, as demonstrated by the preamble to the constitution, founding resolution, and statement of purpose of the National Indian Youth Council.

PREAMBLE TO THE CONSTITUTION

We, the younger generation, at this time in the history of the American Indian, find it expedient to band together on a national scale in meeting the challenges facing the Indian people. In such banding for mutual assistance, we recognize the future of the Indian people will ultimately rest in the hands of the younger people, and Indian youth need be concerned with the position of the American Indian. We further recognize the inherent strength of the American Indian heritage that will be enhanced by a National Indian Youth Council. We, the undersigned, believing in a greater Indian America, in order to form a non-profit corporation for the purposes hereinafter enumerated, do hereby certify as follows:

FOUNDING RESOLUTION

WHEREAS, the National Indian Youth Council holds it to be in the best interest of Indian people for better understanding of conditions for all Indians to carry forward our policies to make clear the inherent sovereign rights of all Indians;

WHEREAS, in order to gain this end the National Indian Youth Council strongly opposes the termination of federal trusteeship over Indians, and;

WHEREAS, the National Indian Youth Council holds that it is morally and legally right that Indians have a voice in matters of jurisdiction directly or indirectly affecting Indians, and;

WHEREAS, the National Indian Youth Council recognizes the inherent rights guaranteed all people in statutes of the United States and holds Indians must exercise their rights:

Now therefore be it resolved, that the National Indian Youth Council endeavors to carry forward the policy of making their inherent sovereign rights known to all people, opposing termination of federal responsibilities at all levels, seeking full participation and consent on jurisdiction matters involving Indians, and staunchly supporting the exercise of those basic rights guaranteed American Indians by the statutes of the United States of America.

STATEMENT OF PURPOSE BY MELVIN D. THOM, CHAIRMAN

The history of the American Indian records the suppression of a proud people and meager redresses by the federal government. Today, the suppressed are still a proud people who have made many concessions to a changing world. Through the years, individuals, agencies and organizations have acted on behalf of the Indian people. These individuals and organizations have enjoyed a considerable extent of success; yet there remains an important role which can only be occupied by the Indian people themselves.

This role is one of understanding and assumption of leadership responsibilities for the values and beliefs which make our Indian people worthy of honor and pride. This role has been and is being filled by dedicated Indians. However, if we are to maintain and strengthen our position as America's original inhabitants, the younger generation of Indian people must participate in fostering of our values and beliefs.

A group of young Indians who first met at the American Indian Chicago Conference and later at Gallup, New Mexico on August 10–13, 1960, have formed the National Indian Youth Council which considered the above stated position. This group decided after considerable preliminary correspondence and deliberations that the NIYC shall be organized to develop greater leadership responsibilities, especially when our basic values and beliefs are jeopardized.

WITH THE BELIEF THAT WE CAN SERVE A REALISTIC NEED, THE NATIONAL INDIAN YOUTH COUNCIL DEDICATED ITS ACTIVITIES AND PROJECTS TO ATTAINING A GREATER FUTURE FOR OUR INDIAN PEOPLE. WE BELIEVE IN A FUTURE WITH HIGH PRINCIPLES DERIVED FROM THE VALUES AND BELIEFS OF OUR ANCESTORS. WE FURTHER BELIEVE IN A STRONG PLACE IN AMERICAN SOCIETY BEING HELD BY INDIAN BLOOD, AND THE DEVELOPMENT OF GREATER LEADERSHIP WITH INDIAN YOUTH.

The Indian people are going to remain Indians for a long time to come. However, every ethnic group of people who are to live within a changing world of good and bad influences must possess a sense of security within their own group. Being of Indian origin should always be held in high regard but never as a disadvantage. American Indians rightfully hold an esteemed and influential position based on their past and present record. Generosity, understanding of feelings, and values based on fairness is well-known to the Indian people and their friends. The adaptability of natural talents of our people are to be revered. Notwithstanding our present and potential achievements, there is and always will be need for the Indian people themselves to protect our birthright. We should never abuse the integrity of our people.

There are many particular problems and needs facing our people, which we acknowledge. A great amount of lip service has been given to "Indian problems and solutions"; so much that we are sometimes labeled as a problem people. Of course, this is not fair! The ultimate realization of man lies in being content with his livelihood and beliefs.

This goal can only be realized with individuals and leaders of strong character. It is the aim of the NIYC that we promote activities and projects for the development of upstanding leaders.

Our Council does not intend to draw lines with elaborate rules nor do we intend to propose any radical movement. WE CONSIDER RULES BASED ON INDIAN THINKING AS BEING SUFFICIENT. It is hoped that the overall purpose and goals will guide the organization to its success. We sincerely hope that all Indians will join us in establishing and maintaining a greater Indian America.

Watts and Little Big Horn

By 1966 connections could be drawn between events in American Indian history, such as Little Big Horn, and more recent occurrences in the black community, particularly the Watts riots. This editorial from the NCAI *[National Congress of American Indians]* Sentinel *suggests the growing links between the movements for racial equality and identity.*

There seems to be a sudden preoccupation with Indian Affairs in the newspapers, in Congress, and in the movies this month. We can't help feeling that a great deal of misunderstanding is being spread by people who are interested in Indians but who don't have the facts and aren't aware of the issues involved.

Basic to misunderstanding is the assumption that has silently been acknowledged as an eternal truth for most of American History: that somehow, in some way, perhaps tomorrow, the American Indian will ASSIMILATE and disappear. He will vanish!!!

This theory, the "ten little, nine little, eight little Indians" theory, celebrated in song and story by millions of non-Indian children for hundreds of years, should be laid to rest once and for all. It should

Reprinted by permission, National Congress of American Indians.

not form the basis of Indian policy and groups working with Indians should not base programs and program projections on the natural course of events working toward assimilation.

In El Paso, Texas, in March during the Executive Committee session of the NCAI we were greeted by a group of Tigua Indians, descendants of a group marched south from Isleta Pueblo by the Spanish in the middle 1600's. Somehow they had survived 300 years right inside El Paso, keeping their ceremonies, their form of government, their culture. Rather than assimilating or vanishing, the group has grown. Should we form a new rhyme? 10 little, 11 little, 12 little Indians?

In addition we are continually discovering surviving groups of Indians in parts of the east where they have managed to hold their group together for 400 years. Admittedly many of the traditions have long since vanished, the native languages have all but died, there are few full bloods left. But the important thing to remember is that they have survived and intend to remain together as long as possible.

In 1887 the Dawes Allotment Act was passed. It was highly advocated by the Churches whose battle cry had become "Send a red-blooded Christian after a Redskinned Heathen." The purpose of this Act? To assist in the eventual assimilation of Indians by giving them that most precious gift possible—160 acres and farm equipment!!! Today we have a fantastically complicated problem of fractional interests owning small pieces of land as a result of the great experiment in assimilation.

A recent study, *Beyond the Melting Pot,* points out that in New York City over a period of 3 generations the ethnic groups have remained characteristically themselves in spite of all sociological theories and programs devised to "melt them." Such efforts have by and large proved fruitless and the book frankly admits that all forms of social and political organization have been forced to adapt to the different groups rather than being able to force conformity from them.

Granted that assimilation has not and will not work, we still have a serious problem of making sufficient progress with, for and by Indians so that they are not made obsolete by the onrushing technology of today. We would suggest that new Indian policy be formed to take into account the differences in culture and outlook that Indians have with the rest of American society. And we would not suggest that we begin with a group of anthropologists talking about beads and braids and dances. When we advocate recognition of cultural differences we are thinking primarily of the ways that people act and react to situations, the way they view the world, and the values that they consider most important. For example, profit, while dearly worshipped by the rest of the society, is not particularly dear to tribal hearts. Tribal enterprises are operated more to provide employment and opportunity than to create dividends. The rest of society has a mania for "giving" to every noble cause. This is climaxed of course by the "One Great Hour of Sharing" initiated by the churches. Indians would rather share daily than give weekly, monthly, at income tax time, or by fund raising appeals. Indians truly believe that the gift without the giver is bare and with the giver it is sharing, not giving.

We would advocate, therefore, a program of acculturation rather than a temporary patchwork of assimilationist programs. Acculturation is, we feel, a program by which tribes can be encouraged to change behavior patterns by giving them the opportunity to develop programs incorporating their present values with new opportunities for human resource advancement. Teach HOW credit works by allowing tribal credit unions to be developed, teach HOW to manage land by allowing tribes more freedom in leasing and range management and land consolidation. Let them find programs which will work rather than being forced to submit to programs which do not work.

There is continual emphasis on bringing the poor into the "mainstream" of American society. Quite often this means the ridiculous assumption that poor, and especially rural, people must assume a value system that will always be foreign to them. There is not that much stability in the "mainstream" that a certain set of values will prove to be universally valid. And the "mainstream" itself must inevitably give way to innovations demanded by the poor to fit their needs.

We believe that the solution to Indian problems lies with development of human and natural resources of the people where they are—on reservations. Watts, California should be warning enough that it is too late to solve problems of rural folk people when they are penned up in an urban area without any hope for the future. We would not like to see Watts re-enacted in Billings, Albuquerque, Boise, Rapid City, Minneapolis, Spokane, Phoenix, Reno, Portland, Omaha, but it will unless problems are solved where they exist.

4

"HEY, HEY, LBJ!": VIETNAM AND THE ANTIWAR MOVEMENT

It is impossible to separate the antiwar movement from the student movement. It was among students that opposition to the war began and developed its massive following. For years students remained the most vocal and active group opposing American involvement in Vietnam. SDS called for the first demonstrations against American involvement in 1965; organizers were staggered when 25,000 people showed up in Washington to protest the war.

After initial eruptions over campus issues and other questions (see chapter 2), by 1965 campus activism began to focus on opposition to the war. Teach-ins offered day- and night-long forums of opinion and information about American policy in Southeast Asia. Opposition grew to campus recruiting by war-related industries, defense-related and -funded research, and campus Reserve Officer Training Corps (ROTC). Student protests against these institutions and representatives erupted on countless campuses. Off-campus, students demonstrated in front of the White House and the Pentagon, attempted to prevent government officials from speaking around the country, campaigned for candidates running against the war, and sought in numerous ways to convince others of the immorality and wrongheadness, to say nothing of the incredible destruction and probable failure, of American involvement.

Students were not alone in protesting the war. Civil rights activists, initially SNCC and later Martin Luther King, Jr., joined the active opposition to the war. Many black Americans' growing internationalism enabled them to identify with the Vietnamese whose homes and lives the American army seemed to be destroying. In addition, many blacks began to wonder why the American government appeared more concerned with freedom in Vietnam than in the United States. Finally, black soldiers accounted for a disproportionate number of those drafted and killed, while the social programs on which Lyndon Johnson and his administration had embarked were threatened as the war competed for government resources. Many radical civil rights activists arrived at the conclusion that black men should not fight in Vietnam (see chapter 3).

As opposition to the war grew, antidraft and resistance activities were among its more dramatic developments. At first small numbers of young men, many exempted from the draft because of their student status, announced they would not enter the army if drafted and would counsel other young men to resist. Nonviolent resistance to the war meant risking jail. As this movement grew, every large demonstration saw young men burn their draft cards, an increase in conscientious objection, and word of resisters leaving for Canada to escape the army or jail. Desertions from the army swelled, while some soldiers who remained on duty refused to be sent to Vietnam. Coffeehouses sprang up near military bases, established by movement activists as places where soldiers opposed to the war could find support and information. Civil rights became an issue within the army as well as the civilian world, as soldiers demanded better treatment and increased personal liberties.

Civil disobedience by those not directly threatened frequently focused on local draft boards. Offices were disrupted and files destroyed. Prominent in this activity was a movement among Catholic nuns and priests, including the widely reported action at the Catonsville, Maryland, draft board led by Revs. Daniel and Philip Berrigan. Churches frequently provided sanctuary for soldiers opposed to the war. In many cases, the courage and idealism of the civil rights movement was reproduced among antiwar activists.

The war in Vietnam created a crisis in American society. As doubts and opposition grew, the president and his advisers continually made decisions to become further involved by sending more soldiers and committing more money and resources, convinced that only one more escalation was needed to break the enemy's will to fight. Journalists reported in word and picture the brutal destruction of Vietnam and the price being paid by the Vietnamese people, as well as the perpetual instability and corruption of the South Vietnamese government. Violence, confusion, and cruelty became staples of American news. The brutality of the war was reinforced daily by television images. The war in Vietnam is considered the first televised war.

Debate over the war grew increasingly bitter. Already-existing societal divisions—between younger and older generations, between blacks and whites, between middle-class students and white working-class men, between the government and the people—were more deeply exacerbated. The dreadful experience of many GIs in Vietnam, coupled with often poor treatment upon returning home, added fuel to the anger, bitterness, and frustration. By the late 1960s the Vietnam war and the movement for racial equality—once priorities of the Johnson administration—were polarizing America. These movements embodied America's harshest antagonisms as well as its most idealistic hopes.

UNDERSTANDING THE WAR

American involvement in Vietnam was just one of the areas of international concern for Americans during the years following World War II. In fact, Southeast Asian issues were overshadowed until the early 1960s by events in Berlin, Korea, Suez, Hungary, and Cuba. By 1963, however, Americans became aware of the seriousness of the problem. Most had little sense of how the country got involved.

This Isn't Munich, It's Spain

BERNARD B. FALL

Bernard Fall, one of the first journalists to file reports critical of America's role in Vietnam, offers an early description (1965) of the extraordinary techno-logical war undertaken by the United States and its brutal impact on the people of Vietnam. Fall was killed in Vietnam.

. . . It is a brutal war. One million Vietnamese died in the long colonial encounter with the French—and already, in what may loosely be termed the "American period," the dead are near a quarter million, with perhaps another half million people seriously maimed. And other Vietnamese people are dying because they are starving; there are vast areas where people starve because food cannot get through—food blocked off by our side so it won't get to the Viet Cong, or taken by the Viet Cong to feed their forces. If the present war were to last as long as the French war, another million people may well die in Vietnam.

There are two theoretical casualties in this war. One is the "war of national liberation" concept of the Communists, and the other is the American theory of "counter-insurgency." At the heart of counter-insurgency is the idea that people matter—that we are in Vietnam to get people to fight for something *they* believe in rather than something *we* believe in. The new mix of air war and of land and seaborne firepower in Vietnam is one of technological counter-insurgency—if you keep up the kill rate you will eventually run out of enemies. Or at least armed enemies. Of course, the whole country will hate you, but at least they won't resist you. What you will get is simply a cessation of resistance—an acquiescence in one's fate rather than a belief that your side and your ideas have really prevailed.

I don't think we are buying Vietnamese stability in the long run out of the present operation. What we are buying is an example—for

Latin America and other guerrilla-prone areas. What we're really doing in Vietnam is killing the cause of "wars of liberation." And we may yet succeed.

The common explanation of America's Vietnam involvement is that the United States is being "tested"—that we have to stand up and stop communism right here. The analogy of Munich is suggested here—the failure of the British and French to stand up to the Nazis. But the situation in Vietnam isn't Munich; it is Spain. There is in Vietnam a test of wills, of course, as at Munich—but above all, there is a test of military technology and techniques and military ideas. One side believes it can win with a combination of guerrilla warfare and political ideology. The other side believes it can win with the massive use of military power. America may be able to prove, as the Germans and Italians did in Spain, that superior firepower will carry the day in such a situation. . . .

The impact of the war right now is not literally the killing of individuals by individuals—you do not often see heaps of the dead lying around. But what you do see is the impact on the countryside. In Asia vegetation is always lush, but now when you fly over parts of Vietnam you can see the dead, brown surface of the areas which have been sprayed with weed killers. You see the areas that were sprayed on purpose, and the places defoliated by accident. Ben Cat, a huge plantation near Saigon, was almost completely destroyed by accident; 3000 acres were transformed into the tropical equivalent of a winter forest. . . . A Catholic refugee village, Honai, along Highway 1 in South Vietnam . . . was sprayed by mistake. All its fruit trees died. United States Air Force planes were defoliating the jungle along Highway 1, but the wind shifted and blew the killer spray towards the villages instead. In a supreme irony, the jungle now stands in the background, lush and thick, while the villages are barren.

When I was there, the villagers were chopping down the trees. The only resource they had left was the remains of their dead fruit trees, to be sold in Saigon for firewood. . . .

Mao Tse Tung's theory that a guerrilla must live among the population like a fish in water worked in China against a politically and militarily ineffective enemy. This theory as a guideline for "wars of liberation" may be disproved in Vietnam. Mao's theory requires an effective political base in the country—but what is a political base

208

against B-52's? The United States, by massive bombing, seeks to deprive the guerrilla of his population—the fish of his water. We want the population to flee to our side—after all, on our side you at least can get food, and get away from the bombing.

The statistics behind this strategy are as brutal as the reality. The Viet Cong are credited with killing or kidnapping between 15,000 and 16,000 village officials during the course of the war, and probably killing another 5,000 in one way or another during the past year. American casualties are less than 1,000 dead and about 3,000 wounded. On the other hand, the official United States statistics of "enemy" killed since 1961 have now passed the 100,000 mark. In the week ending October 4, 1965, some 1,067 Communists were said to have been killed in South Vietnam. At that rate, there will be 50,000 "enemy" deaths in Vietnam this year alone.

One of the great and crucial questions in this war is how many of these casualties are Viet Cong, and how many are civilians? It is generally estimated that there are two wounded for every one killed on the battlefield. Thus by the end of this year the Viet Cong or somebody in its area of operations must be presumed to have suffered upwards of 400,000 casualties. Since the entire Viet Cong force is estimated at between 150,000 to 160,000, this means that we have "overkilled" the Viet Cong about two and a half times. Obviously this isn't true.

Official figures set the number of infiltrators to the Viet Cong from North Vietnam at five to six thousand a year; yet, despite the tremendous firepower thrown at the Communists and the high casualty count, the Viet Cong does not appear to lose appreciably in strength. The conclusion that must be reached is that many of the people being killed are not Viet Cong, even though they may be listed as such. A truly staggering amount of civilians are getting killed or maimed in this war.

The Vietnam conflict has become an impersonal, an American war. I was with an American airborne unit operating strictly on its own. There was not one Vietnamese with that unit. It was going strictly by its own mark and literally by its own light. The . . . "Skyraider," a World War II vintage bomber that is used quite effectively in Vietnam . . . is said to be the only airplane that carries its own weight in payload. An extremely solid and heavy plane, the "Skyraider" can withstand small arms and automatic weapons ground fire better than any other fighter bombers, including the jets. It is an amazing airplane—especially in the amount of destruction it can bring to bear. You have to know an airplane like this before you can really understand the tremendous impact of American firepower on the Vietnamese on the ground. This airplane can carry a bombload of 7,500 pounds under its wings. It can unload a variety of bombs—750-pounders, 500-pounders, 250-pounders, 100-pound general-purpose bombs. It also can drop 260-pound fragmentation bombs, 120-pound fragmentation bombs, or 100-pound white phosphorous bombs and napalm. The "Skyraider" has four 20-millimeter cannon as well.

This was the airplane I was to ride in on a raid on a Vietnamese fishing village. . . .

I took a photograph of a South Vietnamese prisoner cage inside a camp where Americans were present. No attempt was made to hide the cage, an iron frame covered completely with barbed wire. About four feet high, it is used for bringing prisoners to "reason." I was not told what kind of prisoners are put in the cage, but no matter who they are, this is a pretty violent process. The prisoner cannot stand up or sit down—if he moves out of a crouch he falls against the sharp barbed wire; there is so much wire that his body is punctured all over. This makes Christ's Crown of Thorns look like a child's toy. . . .

In this war, there is no respect for the wounded. The Communist prisoner [in a photograph] had been shot in the back. He was bleeding when I found him lying on the floor in a Vietnamese Army Command Post. A journalist from a New York paper came in and asked to photograph him. The South Vietnamese officer in the room raised the wounded man matter-of-factly and propped him against a table leg for the photographer. The prisoner grimaced in pain.

I told an American officer who was with the unit that the man was wounded and should get some attention. His answer: "Yes, I know he needs help, but there isn't anything I can do about it. He's in Vietnamese hands. That is why I walked away, don't you see?" I saw. I also walked away and said nothing.

In this war, there is no respect for hospitals, either. I saw a South Vietnamese civilian ambulance which had been raked with machine gun fire by the Viet Cong. All four patients and the driver were killed inside. This sort of brutality has become normal on both sides: Joseph Alsop reported recently, unblinkingly, that there had been three Viet Cong hospitals destroyed in Zone D along with "vast stocks of medicine." This followed on complaints from the North, now verified by non-Communist outside observers, that at least one hospital had been completely destroyed by bombers. Canadian officials who recently returned from North Vietnam also told me that the city of Vinh was "flattened." It used to have a population of 60,000. I can't believe that the whole city was a "military objective."

The answer to any attempt to raise the question of America's moral responsibility for such actions is the same excuse the Army officer gave me about the bleeding, unattended prisoner: the violation of rules is done by the Vietnamese. But that in itself is not an *excuse*. While it is true that South Vietnam is a sovereign entity, it is also true that it hardly operates independently of the United States. I spent 1946–48 at the Nuremberg trials as a young research analyst and in a number of cases I heard the Germans attempt to excuse atrocities as acts committed by troops of their allies. This wasn't considered an excuse and did not absolve the Germans of their responsibility. (By the way, both Vietnam and the United States have signed and ratified the 1949 Geneva Convention on War Victims.). . .

But, contrary to what had been expected, the Viet Cong have treated American prisoners quite correctly. From all the accounts I received from Intelligence in Vietnam, there is no evidence of torture of American prisoners by the Viet Cong, and released United States prisoners have confirmed this. . . .

The torture and terror utilized by the South Vietnamese is something else. It is, in the Pentagon phrase, "counterproductive." American officers in the field with Vietnamese troops make critical remarks about their behavior toward their own people—stealing, raping, burning down villages, generally kicking people around. In contrast to this random brutality, one of the most heralded of the Viet Cong's terror tactics, the selective assassination of village chiefs, could even be considered, in the military idiom, "productive." When Diem ended the 400 to 500 year tradition of the democratic election of village chiefs by each village, he made, to my mind, probably his most crucial mistake. He began making local appointments from Saigon, and the appointees—many of them outsiders—were met with open hostility by the villagers. Diem's men would have to go outside the village to the police post to sleep safely. Many of them were known to be gouging the villages. The hard fact is that when the Viet Cong assassinated these men, the Viet Cong were given a Robin Hood halo by the villagers.

The reality in Vietnam is that the international rules of war are not obeyed and, contrary to popular belief, the rules *do* apply to guerrilla wars as well. "War crimes" are recorded almost daily and sometimes by cameramen—the burning of villages, for example. There seems to be a predisposition on our side to no longer be able to see the Vietnamese as people against whom crimes can be committed. This is the ultimate impersonalization of the war. . . .

The incredible thing about Vietnam is that the worst is yet to come. . . .

The University on the Make

STANLEY K. SCHEINBAUM

As Vietnam grew in public consciousness, the relationship between American universities and the war effort also began to emerge. Warren Hinckle's detailed 1966 account of the role of academics at Michigan State University argued that they had been corrupted by their collaboration with the government's military activities and had surrendered their position of critical detachment. Stanley Scheinbaum provides a brief introduction to Hinckle's long analysis, which appeared in the new left magazine Ramparts.

During the summer of 1958, I cut my vacation short and rushed off to San Francisco to meet the four leading police figures of South Vietnam. Among them they controlled the Saigon police, the national police and the VBI, South Vietnam's equivalent of the FBI.

Within an hour of their arrival the youngest, a nephew of Ngo
Dinh Diem, conspiratorially drew me aside and informed me that
one of the others was going to kill the eldest of the group. The story
he told possessed plot and counter-plot. In essence, Michigan State
University was being used to invite these men to the United States
under the auspices of its foreign aid contract in Vietnam. The dirty
deed was to be done prophylactically in the States, uncluttered by
any complicating factors in Saigon.

At a time when relations between Diem and the U.S. were already
strained, the whole story might have been a trick to embarrass Washington. Or else my informant's facts could have been straight, and
failure to take action would have been equally embarrassing. The
upshot was some nocturnal maneuvers and a cross-country flight designed to separate the quartet by forcibly hospitalizing the supposed
target on the pretext he showed signs of T.B.

Nothing ever came of the episode. The intended target lived long
enough to be executed by Diem's successors for having assassinated
a variety of political prisoners himself.

The question is, why was I, of the Department of Economics at
MSU, involved in such ugliness?

I was coordinator of the Vietnam Project at Michigan State University, and I am no less culpable of the charges I make herein, or are
made in the following article, than are any of my former colleagues.
Looking back I am appalled how supposed intellectuals (Aren't acade-
micians supposed to be intellectuals?) could have been so uncritical
about what they were doing. There was little discussion and no protest
over the cancellation of the 1956 elections. Nor were any of us significantly troubled by the fact that our Project had become a CIA front.
(The University is still denying this in an odd mixture of embarrassment and loyalty.) On the campus a pitiful handful of faculty—usually mavericks and among the best teachers—questioned MSU's role
in assisting U.S. foreign policy. (One of these became an enthusiast
when the opportunity arose for him to make a leisurely trip to Saigon
on behalf of the Project.) From Saigon some professors did write
popular and troublesome articles criticizing Diem's oppressions.
Good, but even these bold ventures accepted U.S. policy as given with
no questions asked.

The Michigan State professors performed at all levels. They advised
on fingerprinting techniques, on bookkeeping, on governmental bud-

geting and on the very writing of South Vietnam's constitution. One was even instrumental in the choice of the President of South Vietnam. But in all this they never questioned U.S. foreign policy which had placed them there and which, thereby, they were supporting.

. . . MSU's involvement in Vietnam [shows] two critical failures in American education and intellectual life today. The first and more obvious is the diversion of the university away from its functions (and duties) of scholarship and teaching. The second has to do with the failure of the academic intellectual to serve as critic, conscience, *ombudsman*. Especially in foreign policy, which henceforth will bear heavily on our very way of life at home, is this failure serious.

For this failure has left us in a state of drift. We lack historical perspective. We have been conditioned by our social science training not to ask the normative question; we possess neither the inclination nor the means with which to question and judge our foreign policy. We have only the capacity to be experts and technicians to serve that policy. This is the tragedy of the Michigan State professors: we were all automatic cold warriors.

On every campus from Harvard to Michigan State, the story is the same. The social science professor, trained (not educated) to avoid the bigger problems, is off campus expertising for his government or industry client whose assumptions he readily adopts. His students are mechanistically led through the same social science materials by a less competent instructor or graduate assistant, and they will be as little exposed to questions of judgment and the application of wisdom as was the professor in the first place.

No doubt the problem is far more advanced at parvenu institutions like Michigan State than in the Ivy League. The struggle for status, recognition and money is an irresistible lure; the glamorous project is grabbed and sometimes even invented. Within the university only the exceptional faculty member seeks reward and promotions via scholarship and teaching. The easier and even the more prestigious route, is that of the new breed professor with his machine-stamped PhD who orbits in the university's stratosphere of institutes, projects and contracts. The student is lowest among his priorities. The work he emphasizes is of dubious value—by reason of his bias against considerations of value.

Where is the source of serious intellectual criticism that would help us avoid future Vietnams? Serious ideological controversy is dead and with it the perspective for judgment. Our failure in Vietnam was not one of technical expertise, but rather of historical wisdom. We at Michigan State failed to take a critical stance a decade ago. This was our first responsibility, and our incapacity gave rise to the nightmare described in the following pages.

THE ANTIWAR MOVEMENT

The Incredible War

PAUL POTTER

The first antiwar rally called by SDS—on April 17, 1965—attracted the surprising turnout of 25,000. At that demonstration, Paul Potter, then president of SDS, gave this powerful speech in front of the Washington Monument in which he first suggested that the American "system" was connected to the evolution of the war.

. . . The incredible war in Vietnam has provided the razor, the terrifying sharp cutting edge that has finally severed the last vestige of illusion that morality and democracy are the guiding principles of American foreign policy. The saccharine self-righteous moralism that promises the Vietnamese a billion dollars of economic aid at the very moment we are delivering billions for economic and social destruction and political repression is rapidly losing what power it might ever have had to reassure us about the decency of our foreign policy. The further we explore the reality of what this country is doing and planning in Vietnam the more we are driven toward the conclusion of Senator Morse that the United States may well be the greatest threat to peace in the world today. That is a terrible and bitter insight for people who grew up as we did—and our revulsion at that insight, our refusal to accept it as inevitable or necessary, is one of the reasons that so many people have come here today.

The President says that we are defending freedom in Vietnam. Whose freedom? Not the freedom of the Vietnamese. The first act of the first dictator, Diem, the United States installed in Vietnam, was to systematically begin the persecution of all political opposition, non-Communist as well as Communist. . . .

The pattern of repression and destruction that we have developed and justified in the war is so thorough that it can only be called cultural genocide. I am not simply talking about napalm or gas or crop destruction or torture, hurled indiscriminately on women and children, insurgent and neutral, upon the first suspicion of rebel activity. That in itself is horrendous and incredible beyond belief. But it is only part of a larger pattern of destruction to the very fabric of the country. We have uprooted the people from the land and imprisoned them in concentration camps called "sunrise villages." Through conscription and direct political intervention and control, we have destroyed local customs and traditions, trampled upon those things of value which give dignity and purpose to life. . . .

Not even the President can say that this is a war to defend the freedom of the Vietnamese people. Perhaps what the President means when he speaks of freedom is the freedom of the American people.

What in fact has the war done for freedom in America? It has led to even more vigorous governmental efforts to control information, manipulate the press and pressure and persuade the public through distorted or downright dishonest documents such as the White Paper on Vietnam. It has led to the confiscation of films and other anti-war material and the vigorous harassment by the FBI of some of the people who have been most outspokenly active in their criticism of the war. As the war escalates and the administration seeks more actively to gain support for any initiative it may choose to take, there has been the beginnings of a war psychology unlike anything that has burdened this country since the 1950s. How much more of Mr. Johnson's freedom can we stand? How much freedom will be left in this country if there is a major war in Asia? By what weird logic can it be said that the freedom of one people can only be maintained by crushing another?

In many ways this is an unusual march because the large majority of people here are not involved in a peace movement as their primary basis of concern. What is exciting about the participants in this march is that so many of us view ourselves consciously as participants as well in a movement to build a more decent society. There are students here who have been involved in protests over the quality and kind of education they are receiving in growingly bureaucratized, depersonalized institutions called universities; there are Negroes from Mississippi and Alabama who are struggling against the tyranny and repression of those states; there are poor people here—Negro and white—from Northern urban areas who are attempting to build movements that abolish poverty and secure democracy; there are faculty who are beginning to question the relevance of their institutions to the critical problems facing the society. Where will these people and the movements they are a part of be if the President is allowed to expand the war in Asia? What happens to the hopeful beginnings of expressed discontent that are trying to shift American attention to long-neglected internal priorities of shared abundance, democracy and decency at home when those priorities have to compete with the all-consuming priorities and psychology of a war against an enemy thousands of miles away?

The President mocks freedom if he insists that the war in Vietnam is a defense of American freedom. Perhaps the only freedom that this war protects is the freedom of the warhawks in the Pentagon and the State Department to experiment with counter-insurgency and guerrilla warfare in Vietnam.

Vietnam, we may say, is a laboratory run by a new breed of gamesmen who approach war as a kind of rational exercise in international power politics. It is the testing ground and staging area for a new American response to the social revolution that is sweeping through the impoverished downtrodden areas of the world. It is the beginning of the American counter-revolution. . . .

Thus far the war in Vietnam has only dramatized the demand of ordinary people to have some opportunity to make their own lives, and of their unwillingness, even under incredible odds, to give up the struggle against external domination. We are told, however, that the struggle can be legitimately suppressed since it might lead to the development of a Communist system, and before that ultimate menace all criticism is supposed to melt.

This is a critical point and there are several things that must be said here—not by way of celebration, but because I think they are the truth. First, if this country were serious about giving the people of Vietnam some alternative to a Communist social revolution, that opportunity was sacrificed in 1954 when we helped to install Diem and his repression of non-Communist movements. There is no indication that we were serious about that goal—that we were ever willing to contemplate the risks of allowing the Vietnamese to choose their own destinies. Second, those people who insist now that Vietnam can be neutralized are for the most part looking for a sugar coating to cover the bitter pill. We must accept the consequences that calling for an end of the war in Vietnam is in fact allowing for the likelihood that a Vietnam without war will be a self-styled Communist Vietnam. Third, this country must come to understand that creation of a Communist country in the world today is not an ultimate defeat. If people are given the opportunity to choose their own lives it is likely that some of them will choose what we have called "Communist systems." . . . Fourth, I must say to you that I would rather see Vietnam Communist than see it under continuous subjugation of the ruin that American domination has brought.

But the war goes on; the freedom to conduct that war depends on the dehumanization not only of Vietnamese people but of Americans as well; it depends on the construction of a system of premises and thinking that insulates the President and his advisors thoroughly and completely from the human consequences of the decisions they make. I do not believe that the President or Mr. Rusk or Mr. McNamara or even McGeorge Bundy are particularly evil men. If asked to throw napalm on the back of a ten-year-old child they would shrink in horror—but their decisions have led to mutilation and death of thousands and thousands of people.

What kind of system is it that allows good men to make those kinds of decisions? What kind of system is it that justifies the United States or any country seizing the destinies of the Vietnamese people and using them callously for its own purpose? What kind of system is it that disenfranchises people in the South, leaves millions upon millions of people throughout the country impoverished and excluded from the mainstream and promise of American society, that creates faceless and terrible bureaucracies and makes those the place where people spend their lives and do their work, that consistently puts material values before human values—and still persists in calling itself free and still persists in finding itself fit to police the world? . . .

We must name that system. We must name it, describe it, analyze it, understand it and change it. For it is only when that system is changed and brought under control that there can be any hope for stopping the forces that create a war in Vietnam today or a murder in the South tomorrow. . . .

If the people of this country are to end the war in Vietnam, and to change the institutions which create it, then the people of this country must create a massive social movement—and if that can be built around the issue of Vietnam then that is what we must do.

By a social movement I mean more than petitions or letters of protest, or tacit support of dissident Congressmen; I mean people who are willing to change their lives, who are willing to challenge the system, to take the problem of change seriously. By a social movement I mean an effort that is powerful enough to make the country understand that our problems are not in Vietnam, or China or Brazil or outer space or at the bottom of the ocean, but are here in the United States. What we must do is begin to build a democratic and humane society in which Vietnams are unthinkable, in which human life and initiative are precious. The reason there are twenty thousand people here today and not a hundred or none at all is because five years ago in the South students began to build a social movement to change the system. The reason there are poor people, Negro and white, housewives, faculty members, and many others here in Washington is because that movement has grown and spread and changed and reached out as an expression of the broad concerns of people throughout the society. The reason the war and the system it represents will be stopped, if it is stopped before it destroys all of us, will be because the movement has become strong enough to exact change in the society. Twenty thousand people, the people here, if they were serious, if they were willing to break out of their isolation and to accept the consequences of a decision to end the war and commit themselves to building a movement wherever they are and in whatever way they effectively can, would be, I'm convinced, enough. . . .

But that means that we build a movement that works not simply in Washington but in communities and with the problems that face people throughout the society. That means that we build a movement that understands Vietnam in all its horror as but a symptom of a deeper malaise, that we build a movement that makes possible the implementation of the values that would have prevented Vietnam, a movement based on the integrity of man and a belief in man's capacity to tolerate all the weird formulations of society that men may choose to strive for; a movement that will build on the new and creative forms of protest that are beginning to emerge, such as the teach-in, and extend their efforts and intensify them; that we will build a movement that will find ways to support the increasing numbers of young men who are unwilling to and will not fight in Vietnam; a movement that will not tolerate the escalation or prolongation of this war but will, if necessary, respond to the administration war effort with massive civil disobedience all over the country, that will wrench the country into a confrontation with the issues of the war; a movement that must of necessity reach out to all these people in Vietnam or elsewhere who are struggling to find decency and control for their lives.

For in a strange way the people of Vietnam and the people in this demonstration are united in much more than a common concern that the war be ended. In both countries there are people struggling to build a movement that has the power to change their condition. The system that frustrates these movements is the same. All our lives, our destinies, our very hopes to live, depend on our ability to overcome that system.

Trapped in a System

CARL OGLESBY

Speaking to an antiwar rally in October 1965, Carl Oglesby, president of SDS, condemned American foreign policy as systematic foreign intervention run by liberals whose interests were corporate profits. This speech became well known for its exposure of liberal anticommunism and its critique of liberal foreign policy.

Seven months ago at the April March on Washington, Paul Potter, then President of Students for a Democratic Society, stood in approximately this spot and said that we must name the system that creates and sustains the war in Vietnam—name it, describe it, analyze it, understand it, and change it.

Today I will try to name it—to suggest an analysis which, to be quite frank, may disturb some of you—and to suggest what changing it may require of us.

We are here again to protest a growing war. Since it is a very bad war, we acquire the habit of thinking it must be caused by very bad men. But we only conceal reality, I think, to denounce on such grounds the menacing coalition of industrial and military power, or the brutality of the blitzkrieg we are waging against Vietnam, or the ominous signs around us that heresy may soon no longer be permitted. We must simply observe, and quite plainly say, that this coalition, this blitzkrieg, and this demand for acquiescence are creatures, all of them, of a Government that since 1932 has considered itself to be fundamentally *liberal.*

The original commitment in Vietnam was made by President Truman, a mainstream liberal. It was seconded by President Eisenhower, a moderate liberal. It was intensified by the late President Kennedy, a flaming liberal. Think of the men who now engineer that war—those who study the maps, give the commands, push the buttons, and tally the dead: Bundy, McNamara, Rusk, Lodge, Goldberg, the President himself. They are not moral monsters. They are all honorable men. They are all liberals.

But so, I'm sure, are many of us who are here today in protest. To understand the war, then, it seems necessary to take a closer look at this American liberalism. Maybe we are in for some surprises. Maybe we have here two quite different liberalisms: one authentically humanist; the other not so human at all.

Not long ago I considered myself a liberal and if someone had asked me what I meant by that, I'd perhaps have quoted Thomas Jefferson or Thomas Paine, who first made plain our nation's unprovisional commitment to human rights. But what do you think would happen if these two heroes could sit down now for a chat with President Johnson and McGeorge Bundy?

They would surely talk of the Vietnam war. Our dead revolutionaries would soon wonder why their country was fighting against what appeared to be a revolution. The living liberals would hotly deny that it is one: there are troops coming in from outside, the rebels get arms from other countries, most of the people are not on their side, and they practice terror against their own. Therefore: *not* a revolution.

What would our dead revolutionaries answer? They might say: "What fools and bandits, sirs, you make then of us. Outside help? Do you remember Lafayette? Or the three thousand British freighters the French navy sunk for our side? Or the arms and men we got from France and Spain? And what's this about terror? Did you never hear what we did to our own Loyalists? Or about the thousands of rich American Tories who fled for their lives to Canada? And as for popular support, do you not know that we had less than one-third of our people with us? That, in fact, the colony of New York recruited more troops for the British than for the revolution? Should we give it all back?"

Revolutions do not take place in velvet boxes. They never have. It is only the poets who make them lovely. What the National Liberation Front is fighting in Vietnam is a complex and vicious war. This war is also a revolution, as honest a revolution as you can find anywhere in history. And this is a fact which all our intricate official denials will never change.

But it doesn't make any difference to our leaders anyway. Their aim in Vietnam is really much simpler than this implies. It is to safeguard what they take to be American interests around the world against revolution or revolutionary change, which they always call communism—as if that were that. In the case of Vietnam, this interest is, first, the principle that revolution shall not be tolerated anywhere, and second, that South Vietnam shall never sell its rice to China—or even to North Vietnam.

There is simply no such thing now, for us, as a just revolution—never mind that for two-thirds of the world's people the Twentieth Century might as well be the Stone Age; never mind the melting poverty and hopelessness that are the basic facts of life for most modern men; and never mind that for these millions there is now an increasingly perceptible relationship between their sorrow and our contentment.

Can we understand why the Negroes of Watts rebelled? Then why do we need a devil theory to explain the rebellion of the South Vietnamese? Can we understand the oppression in Mississippi, or the anguish that our Northern ghettoes makes epidemic? Then why can't we see that our proper human struggle is not with communism or revolutionaries, but with the social desperation that drives good men to violence, both here and abroad?

To be sure, we have been most generous with our aid, and in Western Europe, a mature industrial society, that aid worked. But there are always political and financial strings. And we have never shown ourselves capable of allowing others to make those traumatic institutional changes that are often the prerequisites of progress in colonial societies. For all our official feeling for the millions who are enslaved to what we so self-righteously call the yoke of communist tyranny, we make no real effort at all to crack through the much more vicious right-wing tyrannies that our businessmen traffic with and our nation profits from every day. And for all our cries about the international Red conspiracy to take over the world, we take only pride in the fact of our six thousand military bases on foreign soil.

We gave Rhodesia a grave look just now—but we keep on buying her chromium, which is cheap because black slave labor mines it.

We deplore the racism of Verwoerd's fascist South Africa—but our banks make big loans to that country and our private technology makes it a nuclear power.

We are saddened and puzzled by random back-page stories of revolt in this or that Latin American state—but are convinced by a few pretty photos in the Sunday supplement that things are getting better, that the world is coming our way, that change from disorder can be orderly, that our benevolence will pacify the distressed, that our might will intimidate the angry.

Optimists, may I suggest that these are quite unlikely fantasies? They are fantasies because we have lost that mysterious social desire for human equity that from time to time has given us genuine moral drive. We have become a nation of young, bright-eyed, hard-hearted, slim-waisted, bullet-headed make-out artists. A nation—may I say it?—of beardless liberals.

You say I am being hard? Only think.

This country, with its thirty-some years of liberalism, can send 200,000 young men to Vietnam to kill and die in the most dubious of wars, but it cannot get 100 voter registrars to go into Mississippi.

What do you make of it?

The financial burden of the war obliges us to cut millions from an already pathetic War on Poverty budget. But in almost the same breath, Congress appropriates one hundred forty million dollars for the Lockheed and Boeing companies to compete with each other on the supersonic transport project—that Disneyland creation that will cost us all about two billion dollars before it's done.

What do you make of it?

Many of us have been earnestly resisting for some years now the idea of putting atomic weapons into West German hands, an action that would perpetuate the division of Europe and thus the Cold War. Now just this week we find out that, with the meagerest of security systems, West Germany has had nuclear weapons in her hands for the past six years.

What do you make of it?

Some will make of it that I overdraw the matter. Many will ask: What about the other side? To be sure, there is the bitter ugliness of Czechoslovakia, Poland, those infamous Russian tanks in the streets of Budapest. But my anger only rises to hear some say that sorrow cancels sorrow, or that *this* one's shame deposits in *that* one's account the right to shamefulness.

And others will make of it that I sound mighty anti-American. To these, I say: Don't blame *me* for *that!* Blame those who mouthed my liberal values and broke my American heart. . . .

Liberalism faced a crisis. In the face of the collapse of the European empires, how could it continue to hold together our twin need for richness and righteousness? How can we continue to sack the ports of Asia and still dream of Jesus?

The challenge was met with a most ingenious solution: the ideology of anti-Communism. This was the bind: We cannot call revolution bad, because we started that way ourselves, and because it is all too easy to see why the dispossessed should rebel. So we will call revolution Communism. And we will reserve for ourselves the right to say what Communism means. We take note of revolution's enormities, wrenching them where necessary from their historical context and often exaggerating them, and say: Behold, Communism is a blood-bath. We take note of those reactionaries who stole the revolution, and say: Behold, Communism is a betrayal of the people. We take note of the revolution's need to consolidate itself, and say: Behold, Communism is a tyranny.

It has been all these things, and it will be these things again, and we will never be at a loss for those tales of atrocity that comfort us so in our self-righteousness. Nuns will be raped and bureaucrats will be disembowelled. Indeed, revolution is a *fury*. For it is a letting loose of outrages pent up sometimes over centuries. But the more brutal and longer-lasting the supression of this energy, all the more ferocious will be its explosive release.

Far from helping Americans deal with this truth, the anti-Communist ideology merely tries to disguise it so that things may stay the way they are. Thus, it depicts our presence in other lands not as a coercion, but a protection. It allows us even to say that the napalm in Vietnam is only another aspect of our humanitarian love—like those exorcisms in the Middle Ages that so often killed the patient. So we say to the Vietnamese peasant, the Cuban intellectual, the Peruvian worker: "You are better dead than Red. If it hurts or if you don't understand why—sorry about that."

This is the action of *corporate liberalism*. It performs for the corporate state a function quite like what the Church once performed for the feudal state. It seeks to justify its burdens and protect it from change. As the Church exaggerated this office in the Inquisition, so with liberalism in the McCarthy time—which, if it was a reactionary phenomenon, was still made possible by our anti-Communist corporate liberalism.

Let me then speak directly to humanist liberals. If my facts are wrong, I will soon be corrected. But if they are right, then you may face a crisis of conscience. Corporatism or humanism: which? For it has come to that. Will you let your dreams be used? Will you be a grudging apologist for the corporate state? Or will you help try to change it—not in the name of this or that blueprint or ism, but in the name of simple human decency and democracy and the vision that wise and brave men saw in the time of our own Revolution?

And if your commitment to human values is unconditional, then disabuse yourselves of the notion that statements will bring change, if only the right statements can be written, or that interviews with the mighty will bring change if only the mighty can be reached, or that marches will bring change if only we can make them massive enough, or that policy proposals will bring change if only we can make them responsible enough.

We are dealing now with a colossus that does not want to be changed. It will not change itself. It will not cooperate with those who want to change it. Those allies of ours in the Government—are they really our allies? If they *are*, then they don't need advice, they need *constituencies;* they don't need study groups, they need a *movement.* And if they are *not,* then all the more reason for building that movement with a most relentless conviction.

There are people in this country today who are trying to build that movement, who aim at nothing less than a humanist reformation. And the humanist liberals must understand that it is this movement with which their own best hopes are most in tune. We radicals know the same history that you liberals know, and we can understand your occasional cynicism, exasperation, and even distrust. But we ask you to put these aside and help us risk a leap. Help us find enough time for the enormous work that needs doing here. Help us build. Help us shape the future in the name of plain human hope.

SDS Call for a March on Washington

This SDS leaflet calling for a March on Washington in November 1965 highlights the organization's commitment to participatory democracy, as well as its antiwar position.

In the name of freedom, America is mutilating Vietnam. In the name of peace, America turns that fertile country into a wasteland. And in the name of democracy, America is burying its own dreams and suffocating its own potential.

Americans who can understand why the Negroes of Watts can rebel should understand too why Vietnamese can rebel. And those who know the American South and the grinding poverty of our Northern cities should understand that our real problems lie not in Vietnam but at home—that the fight we seek is not with Communism but with the social desperation that makes good men violent, both here and abroad.

THE WAR MUST BE STOPPED

Our aim in Vietnam is the same as our aim in the United States: that oligarchic rule and privileged power be replaced by popular democracy where the people make the decisions which affect their lives and share in the abundance and opportunity that modern technology makes possible. This is the only solution for Vietnam in which Americans can find honor and take pride. Perhaps the war has already so embittered and devastated the Vietnamese that that ideal will require years of rebuilding. But the war cannot achieve it, nor can American military presence, nor our support of repressive unrepresentative governments.

The war must be stopped. There must be an immediate cease fire and demobilization in South Vietnam. There must be a withdrawal of American troops. Political amnesty must be guaranteed. All agreements must be ratified by the partisans of the "other side"—the National Liberation Front and North Vietnam.

We must not deceive ourselves: a negotiated agreement cannot guarantee democracy. Only the Vietnamese have the right of nationhood to make their government democratic or not, free or not, neutral or not. It is not America's role to deny them the chance to be what they will make of themselves. That chance grows more remote with every American bomb that explodes in a Vietnamese village.

But our hopes extend not only to Vietnam. Our chance is the first in a generation to organize the powerless and the voiceless at home to confront America with its racial injustice, its apathy, and its poverty, and with that same vision we dream for Vietnam: a vision of a society in which all can control their own destinies.

We are convinced that the only way to stop this and future wars is to organize a domestic social movement which challenges the very legitimacy of our foreign policy; this movement must also fight to end racism, to end the paternalism of our welfare system, to guarantee decent incomes for all, and to supplant the authoritarian control of our universities with a community of scholars.

This movement showed its potential when 25,000 people— students, the poverty-stricken, ministers, faculty, unionists, and others—marched on Washington last April. This movement must now show its force. SDS urges everyone who believes that our warmaking must be ended and our democracy-building must begin, to join in a March on Washington on November 27, at 11 A.M. in front of the White House.

SNCC Position Paper on Vietnam

The relation between domestic struggles to end racism and the struggle of the Vietnamese people against the American army, as well as the struggles by people of color around the world, merged into a unified position as the war progressed. SNCC argues that the freedom struggle in the United States is an alternative to fighting in Vietnam.

"THE U.S. GOVERNMENT HAS DECEIVED US"

The Student Nonviolent Coordinating Committee has a right and a responsibility to dissent with United States foreign policy on any issue when it sees fit. The Student Nonviolent Coordinating Committee now states its opposition to United States' involvement in Vietnam on these grounds:

We believe the United States government has been deceptive in its claims of concern for the freedom of the Vietnamese people, just as the government has been deceptive in claiming concern for the freedom of colored people in such other countries as the Dominican Republic, the Congo, South Africa, Rhodesia, and in the United States itself.

We, the Student Nonviolent Coordinating Committee, have been involved in the black people's struggle for liberation and self-determination in this country for the past five years. Our work, particularly in the South, has taught us that the United States government has never guaranteed the freedom of oppressed citizens, and is not yet truly determined to end the rule of terror and oppression within its own borders.

We ourselves have often been victims of violence and confinement executed by United States governmental officials. We recall the numerous persons who have been murdered in the South because of their efforts to secure their civil and human rights, and whose murderers have been allowed to escape penalty for their crimes.

The murder of Samuel Young in Tuskegee, Alabama, is no different than the murder of peasants in Vietnam, for both Young and the Vietnamese sought, and are seeking, to secure the rights guaranteed them by law. In each case, the United States government bears a great part of the responsibility for these deaths.

Samuel Young was murdered because United States law is not being enforced. Vietnamese are murdered because the United States is pursuing an aggressive policy in violation of international law. The United States is no respecter of persons or law when such persons or laws run counter to its needs or desires.

We recall the indifference, suspicion and outright hostility with which our reports of violence have been met in the past by government officials.

We know that for the most part, elections in this country, in the North as well as the South, are not free. We have seen that the 1965 Voting Rights Act and the 1966 Civil Rights Act have not yet been implemented with full federal power and sincerity.

We question, then, the ability and even the desire of the United States government to guarantee free elections abroad. We maintain that our country's cry of "preserve freedom in the world" is a hypocritical mask behind which it squashes liberation movements which are not bound, and refuse to be bound, by the expediencies of United States cold war policies.

We are in sympathy with, and support, the men in this country who are unwilling to respond to a military draft which would compel them to contribute their lives to United States aggression in Vietnam in the name of the "freedom" we find so false in this country.

We recoil with horror at the inconsistency of a supposedly "free" society where responsibility to freedom is equated with the responsibility to lend oneself to military aggression. We take note of the fact that 16% of the draftees from this country are Negroes called on to stifle the liberation of Vietnam, to preserve a "democracy" which does not exist for them at home.

We ask, where is the draft for the freedom fight in the United States?

We therefore encourage those Americans who prefer to use their energy in building democratic forms within this country. We believe that work in the civil rights movement and with other human relations organizations is a valid alternative to the draft. We urge all Americans to seek this alternative, knowing full well that it may cost them their lives—as painfully as in Vietnam.

Declaration of Independence from the War in Vietnam

MARTIN LUTHER KING, JR.

During the first decade of the civil rights movement, Martin Luther King, Jr. had been hesitant to become involved in other political issues, for fear of weakening the cause for racial justice. By 1967, however, in a speech at Riverside Church in New York City that many considered momentous, he declares his opposition to the war.

Over the past two years, as I have moved to break the betrayal of my own silences and to speak from the burnings of my own heart. As I have called for radical departures from the destruction of Vietnam, many persons have questioned me about the wisdom of my path. At the heart of their concerns this query has often loomed large and loud: Why are *you* speaking about the war, Dr. King? Why are *you* joining the forces of dissent? Peace and civil rights don't mix, they say. Aren't you hurting the cause of your people, they ask. And when I hear them, although I often understand the source of their concern, I am nevertheless greatly saddened, for such questions mean that the inquirers have not really known me, my commitment or my calling. Indeed, their questions suggest that they do not know the world in which they live.

In the light of such tragic misunderstanding, I deem it of signal importance to try to state clearly why I believe that the path from Dexter Avenue Baptist Church—the church in Montgomery, Alabama, where I began my pastorage—leads clearly to this sanctuary tonight.

I come to this platform to make a passionate plea to my beloved nation. . . .

I wish not to speak with Hanoi and the NLF, but rather to my fellow Americans who, with me, bear the greatest responsibility in ending a conflict that has exacted a heavy price on both continents.

Since I am a preacher by trade, I suppose it is not surprising that I have seven major reasons for bringing Vietnam into the field of my moral vision. There is at the outset a very obvious and almost facile connection between the war in Vietnam and the struggle I, and others, have been waging in America. A few years ago there was a shining moment in that struggle. It seemed as if there was a real promise of hope for the poor—both black and white—through the Poverty Program. Then came the build-up in Vietnam, and I watched the program broken and eviscerated as if it were some idle political plaything of a society gone mad on war, and I knew that America would never invest the necessary funds or energies in rehabilitation of its poor so long as Vietnam continued to draw men and skills and money like some demonic, destructive suction tube. So I was increasingly compelled to see the war as an enemy of the poor and to attack it as such.

Perhaps the more tragic recognition of reality took place when it became clear to me that the war was doing far more than devastating the hopes of the poor at home. It was sending their sons and their brothers and their husbands to fight and to die in extraordinarily high proportions relative to the rest of the population. We were taking the young black men who had been crippled by our society and sending them 8000 miles away to guarantee liberties in Southeast Asia which they had not found in Southwest Georgia and East Harlem. So we have been repeatedly faced with the cruel irony of watching Negro and white boys on TV screens as they kill and die together for a nation that has been unable to seat them together in the same schools. So we watch them in brutal solidarity burning the huts of a poor village, but we realize that they would never live on the same block in Detroit. I could not be silent in the face of such cruel manipulation of the poor.

My third reason grows out of my experience in the ghettos of the North over the last three years—especially the last three summers. As I have walked among the desperate, rejected, and angry young men, I have told them that Molotov cocktails and rifles would not solve their problems. I have tried to offer them my deepest compassion while maintaining my conviction that social change comes most meaningfully through non-violent action. But, they asked, what about Viet-

nam? They asked if our own nation wasn't using massive doses of
violence to solve its problems, to bring about the changes it wanted.
Their questions hit home, and I knew that I could never again raise
my voice against the violence of the oppressed in the ghettos without
having first spoken clearly to the greatest purveyor of violence in the
world today—my own government.

For those who ask the question, "Aren't you a civil rights leader?"
and thereby mean to exclude me from the movement for peace, I
have this further answer. In 1957 when a group of us formed the
Southern Christian Leadership Conference, we chose as our motto:
"To save the soul of America." We were convinced that we could not
limit our vision to certain rights for black people, but instead affirmed
the conviction that America would never be free or saved from itself
unless the descendants of its slaves were loosed from the shackles
they still wear.

Now it should be incandescently clear that no one who has any
concern for the integrity and life of America today can ignore the
present war. If America's soul becomes totally poisoned, part of the
autopsy must read "Vietnam." It can never be saved so long as it
destroys the deepest hopes of men the world over.

And as I ponder the madness of Vietnam, my mind goes constantly
to the people of that peninsula. I speak now not of the soldiers of
each side, not of the junta in Saigon, but simply of the people who
have been living under the curse of war for almost three continuous
decades. I think of them, too, because it is clear to me that there will
be no meaningful solution there until some attempt is made to know
them and their broken cries.

They must see Americans as strange liberators. The Vietnamese
proclaimed their own independence in 1945 after a combined French
and Japanese occupation and before the communist revolution in
China. Even though they quoted the American Declaration of Independence in their own document of freedom, we refused to recognize
them. Instead, we decided to support France in its re-conquest of her
former colony.

Our government felt then that the Vietnamese people were not
"ready" for independence, and we again fell victim to the deadly
Western arrogance that has poisoned the internal atmosphere for so
long. With that tragic decision, we rejected a revolutionary government seeking self-determination, and a government that had been

established not by China (for whom the Vietnamese have no great love) but by clearly indigenous forces that included some communists. For the peasants, this new government meant real land reform, one of the most important needs in their lives.

For nine years following 1945 we denied the people of Vietnam the right of independence. For nine years we vigorously supported the French in their abortive effort to re-colonize Vietnam.

Before the end of the war we were meeting 80 per cent of the French war costs. Even before the French were defeated at Dien Bien Phu, they began to despair of their reckless action, but we did not. We encouraged them with our huge financial and military supplies to continue the war even after they had lost the will to do so.

After the French were defeated it looked as if independence and land reform would come again through the Geneva agreements. But instead there came the United States, determined that Ho should not unify the temporarily divided nation, and the peasants watched again as we supported one of the most vicious modern dictators—our chosen man, Premier Diem. The peasants watched and cringed as Diem ruthlessly routed out all opposition, supported their extortionist landlords and refused even to discuss reunification with the North. The peasants watched as all this was presided over by U.S. influence and then by increasing numbers of U.S. troops who came to help quell the insurgency that Diem's methods had aroused. When Diem was overthrown they may have been happy, but the long line of military dictatorships seemed to offer no real change—especially in terms of their need for land and peace.

The only change came from America as we increased our troop commitments in support of governments which were singularly corrupt, inept and without popular support. All the while, the people read our leaflets and received regular promises of peace and democracy—and land reform.

Now they languish under our bombs and consider us—not their fellow Vietnamese—the real enemy. They move sadly and apathetically as we herd them off the land of their fathers into concentration camps where minimal social needs are rarely met. They know they must move or be destroyed by our bombs. So they go.

They watch as we poison their water, as we kill a million acres of their crops. They must weep as the bulldozers destroy their precious trees. They wander into the hospitals, with at least 20 casualties from

American firepower for each Viet Cong–inflicted injury. So far we may have killed a million of them—mostly children.

What do the peasants think as we ally ourselves with the landlords and as we refuse to put any action into our many words concerning land reform? What do they think as we test out our latest weapons on them, just as the Germans tested out new medicines and new tortures in the concentration camps of Europe?* Where are the roots of the independent Vietnam we claim to be building?

Now there is little left to build on—save bitterness. Soon the only solid physical foundations remaining will be found at our military bases and in the concrete of the concentration camps we call "fortified hamlets." The peasants may well wonder if we plan to build our new Vietnam on such grounds as these. Could we blame them for such thoughts? We must speak for them and raise the questions they cannot raise. These too are our brothers.

Perhaps the more difficult but no less necessary task is to speak for those who have been designated as our enemies. What of the NLF—that strangely anonymous group we call VC or communists? What must they think of us in America when they realize that we permitted the repression and cruelty of Diem which helped to bring them into being as a resistance group in the South? How can they believe in our integrity when now we speak of "aggression from the North" as if there were nothing more essential to the war? How can they trust us when now we charge *them* with violence while we pour new weapons of death into their land?

How do they judge us when our officials know that their membership is less than 25 per cent communist and yet insist on giving them a blanket name?

Here is the true meaning and value of compassion and non-violence—when it helps us to see the enemy's point of view, to hear his questions, to know his assessment of ourselves. For from his view we may indeed see the basic weaknesses of our own condition, and if we are mature, we may learn and grow and profit from the wisdom of the brothers who are called the opposition.

---

*The press and some critics have quoted this sentence out of context. I had no intention of equating the U.S. and Nazi Germany. Indeed, recognition of American democratic traditions and the absence of them in Nazi Germany, makes it all the more disturbing if even some elements of similarity of conduct appear.

So, too, with Hanoi. In the North, where our bombs now pummel the land, and our mines endanger the waterways, we are met by a deep but understandable mistrust. In Hanoi there are men who led the nation to independence against the Japanese and the French, the men who sought membership in the French commonwealth and were betrayed by the weakness of Paris and the willfulness of the colonial armies. It was they who led a second struggle against French domination at tremendous costs, and then were persuaded at Geneva to give up, as a temporary measure, the land they controlled between the 13th and 17th parallels. After 1954 they watched us conspire with Diem to prevent elections which would have surely brought Ho Chi Minh to power over a united Vietnam, and they realized they had been betrayed again.

Ho Chi Minh has watched as America has spoken of peace and has built up its forces, and now he has surely heard the increasing international rumors of American plans for an invasion of the North. Perhaps only his sense of humor and irony can save him when he hears the most powerful nation of the world speaking of aggression as it drops thousands of bombs on a poor, weak nation more than 8000 miles from its shores.

At this point, I should make it clear that while I have tried here to give a voice to the voiceless of Vietnam and to understand the arguments of those who are called enemy, I am as deeply concerned about our own troops there as anything else. For it occurs to me that what we are submitting them to in Vietnam is not simply the brutalizing process that goes on in any war where armies face each other and seek to destroy. We are adding cynicism to the process of death, for our troops must know after a short period there that none of the things we claim to be fighting for are really involved. Before long they must know that their government has sent them into a struggle among Vietnamese, and the more sophisticated surely realize that we are on the side of the wealthy and the secure while we create a hell for the poor.

Somehow this madness must cease. I speak as a child of God and brother to the suffering poor of Vietnam and the poor of America who are paying the double price of smashed hopes at home and death and corruption in Vietnam. I speak as a citizen of the world, for the world as it stands aghast at the path we have taken. I speak as an American to the leaders of my own nation. The great initiative in this war is ours. The initiative to stop must be ours.

This is the message of the great Buddhist leaders of Vietnam. Recently, one of them wrote these words: "Each day the war goes on the hatred increases in the hearts of the Vietnamese and in the hearts of those of humanitarian instinct. The Americans are forcing even their friends into becoming their enemies. It is curious that the Americans, who calculate so carefully on the possibilities of military victory, do not realize that in the process they are incurring deep psychological and political defeat. The image of America will never again be the image of revolution, freedom and democracy, but the image of violence and militarism."

If we continue, there will be no doubt in my mind and in the mind of the world that we have no honorable intentions in Vietnam. It will become clear that our minimal expectation is to occupy it as an American colony, and men will not refrain from thinking that our maximum hope is to goad China into a war so that we may bomb her nuclear installations.

The world now demands a maturity of America that we may not be able to achieve. It demands that we admit that we have been wrong from the beginning of our adventure in Vietnam, that we have been detrimental to the life of her people.

In order to atone for our sins and errors in Vietnam, we should take the initiative in bringing the war to a halt.

Berrigan at Cornell

DANIEL BERRIGAN

The Reverend Daniel Berrigan, a leading antiwar activist, was a Jesuit priest who symbolized the growing religious opposition to the war. This talk, given at Cornell University, was published in 1968.

The question of the war is a very precious one to which I have given certain irreplaceable years of my life in my poetry and my relationship with others in all those things which define me. These are years I will not have again. I can't really go back and say that I made a good or bad choice. I just chose! I chose to be here rather than elsewhere in the largest sense. So it is clear to me that I operate from a sense that all things are obscurely joined and that to be really at a point of human death or anguish or hope is to be at the center of the picture. Maybe this is the act demanded of us: to take one choice that includes many other choices.

The choice that my brother and I have made was, given the times and the Church, a choice of conflict, undoubtedly with our own communities and our own faith and the things we had grown up with. But this act resulted in a great communion with all sorts of other people, of other faiths and traditions. We found a larger meaning to being Catholic Christians. Neither of us found a serious temptation to leave our commitments in any of these absurd ways that others are speaking of. We probably have certain resources available to us which allowed us to get beyond our own needs. We didn't need to be married—and I say this humbly, it's just that we could operate as celibates. We were not in such revolt against authority that we could not communicate with it. We didn't have any personal frenzy or revenge to work out.

The war is a nightmare and the only advantage my brother and I have is that our nightmare began earlier. It began four or five years ago. So, we are better prepared to live in this nightmare, not as nightmare figures but as men who declare that it is a nightmare and, therefore, can dissolve it. Let us begin living in reality once more. This requires what it required of any period of the Church where death is in command and where society is moving to exclude more and more people through jail or the army or exclusion from benefits.

The real news is that Rome is burning. The city in which we are asked to live is in flames. I am trying to get with a much bigger thing than this little churchy thing which has been proposed as a real thing. What I am trying to suggest is that neither the Church nor the State nor the University alone has been capable of dealing with the fact of death, mass extermination and nuclear overkill, the cold war and the despair of the developing peoples.

Christianity deepens in men without violating any area in which we are requested to be human beings. Christianity does not say get the hell out of your profession or income or anything else. But it does place these things in question; which is exactly where they should be—in question.

We will try to expose our conscience to the Catholic community and listen. If they will respect us, we will go ahead. If they do not respect us, we will go ahead. But we will not cut ourselves off, though we will not foreclose the possibility of their cutting us of. . . .

I speak as a minority figure. I've always been one. I try not to be romantic or obsessive about it but that is where I am. Around me is a minority group whether Christian or Jewish or humanist or secular. We represent, perhaps, only two percent of the community. From the point of view of anything now operating in society that remains true. Mine is an embattled, impoverished minority. My brother is just out of jail; he is in official disgrace. He is a cleric facing trial in war time and I am with him. The Society of Jesus, which is my community, which I love very much, which is the source of almost everything I have ever learned and valued is silent and will probably remain silent.

When I was in jail in Washington in November, I asked myself where the members of my community were. Why didn't a Jesuit come to see how I was or another member of the Catholic community? Why didn't someone come and say, "Where is Berrigan? I don't agree with what he is doing but he is my brother and, therefore, I must know how he is?" I look to my brothers in the Society for a communal effort toward redemption. But except for one priest, I was abandoned by the Society, and except for a fine Dominican chaplain, also by the Church. I was left to the community which grew up in that jail among the protestors—most of whom were not Catholics.

I don't want to make a great issue. I want to express my anguished longing which I am trying to be faithful to, to remain a priest in the Church and my Order. To invite my Order to a deeper understanding of itself, of the dead-end it is encountering by identifying through its silence with the structures of power, the war structures. This momentary evidence of power has nothing to do with real history, which is to say, the real Church. It may be necessary to be evicted from the Jesuits in order to do this. I have faced this and it is quite tolerable to me. I do not have any turn-off point at which I must say that my conscience must come to terms with what is officially acceptable. I must take the very absurd risk of saying that I could die in disgrace and die at peace in the hope that something would come later.

For the Church, I must say in all honesty, I have already outlined the choices and I have deliberately ignored the Catholic campus. I have ignored it because I believe it is unhistorical and finished. I have hoped not to be insensitive to the values of the best of these campuses but I am profoundly convinced that the time has come for them to integrate and reform themselves and make their values available to those who are passionately interested in entering into communion with the purity and depth of the Catholic tradition. And who, I might add, desperately need this resource.

We are facing a mysterious kind of new form of the immanence of God with regard to young people of very deep sacrificial possibility. I don't know whether it is inevitably connected with one period, one war, one crisis; or whether the times are really forming people who can be ready for whatever is going to happen. But let us rejoice in what is here. And what is here is a minority, extremely precious and exciting and full of promise for humanity with the Church.

RESISTANCE AND ANTIDRAFT ACTIVITY

The drafting of young men into the army became one of the focal points of opposition to the War in Vietnam.

Channeling

While the Selective Service System argued that its method of conscription was fair and only existed to provide the necessary number of soldiers, this 1965 government document suggests that there were other goals the army intended to achieve through the draft. Once secretly obtained, this document was widely distributed as evidence of indirect coercion of young educated men on behalf of the military.

One of the major products of the Selective Service classification process is the channeling of manpower into many endeavors, occupations, and activities that are in the national interest. This function is a counterpart and amplification of the System's responsibility to deliver manpower to the armed forces in such a manner as to reduce to a minimum any adverse effect upon the national health, safety, interest, and progress. By identifying and applying this process intelligently, the System is able not only to minimize any adverse effect but to exert an effect beneficial to the national health, safety, and interest.

The line dividing the primary function of armed forces manpower procurement from the process of channeling manpower into civilian support is often finely drawn. The process of channeling by not taking men from certain activities who are otherwise liable for service, or by giving deferment to qualified men in certain occupations, is actual procurement by inducement of manpower for civilian activities which are manifestly in the national interest.

While the best known purpose of Selective Service is to procure manpower for the armed forces, a variety of related processes take place outside delivery of manpower to the active armed forces. Many of these may be put under the heading of "channeling manpower." Many young men would not have pursued a higher education if there had not been a program of student deferment. Many young scientists, engineers, tool and die makers, and other possessors of scarce skills would not remain in their jobs in the defense effort if it were not for a program of occupational deferments. Even though the salary of a teacher has historically been meager, many young men remain in that job, seeking the reward of a deferment. The process of channeling manpower by deferment is entitled to much credit for the large number of graduate students in technical fields and for the fact that there is not a greater shortage of teachers, engineers, and other scientists working in activities which are essential to the national interest. . . .

Educators, scientists, engineers, and their professional organizations, during the last ten years particularly, have been convincing the American public that for the mentally qualified man there is a special order of patriotism other than service in uniform—that for the man having the capacity, dedicated service as a civilian in such fields as engineering, the sciences, and teaching constitute the ultimate in their expression of patriotism. A large segment of the American public has been convinced that this is true.

It is in this atmosphere that the young man registers at age 18 and pressure begins to force his choice. He does not have the inhibitions that a philosophy of universal service in uniform would engender. The door is open for him as a student to qualify if capable in a skill badly needed by his nation. He has many choices and he is prodded to make a decision. . . .

Throughout his career as a student, the pressure—the threat of loss of deferment—continues. It continues with equal intensity after graduation. His local board requires periodic reports to find out what he is up to. He is impelled to pursue his skill rather than embark upon some less important enterprise and is encouraged to apply his skill in an essential activity in the national interest. The loss of deferred status is the consequence for the individual who has acquired the skill and either does not use it or uses it in a nonessential activity.

The psychology of granting wide choice under pressure to take action is the American or indirect way of achieving what is done by direction in foreign countries where choice is not permitted. Here, choice is limited but not denied, and it is fundamental that an individual generally applies himself better to something he has decided to do rather than something he has been told to do. . . .

We Refuse to Serve

THE RESISTANCE

In 1967 a group of antiwar men centered in the San Francisco Bay Area declared their intention to stop all connection with the Selective Service System. They hoped to join with other groups advocating resistance to the war, arguing that noncooperation with a government conducting an immoral war was the only appropriate moral path.

I. WE REFUSE TO SERVE

In the past few months, in many parts of the country, a resistance has been forming . . . a resistance of young men—joined together in their commitment against the war. . . .

We will renounce all deferments and refuse to cooperate with the draft in any manner, at any level. We have taken this stand for varied reasons:

> opposition to conscription
>
> opposition only to the Vietnam war
>
> opposition to all wars and to all American military adventures.

We all agree on one point: the war in Vietnam is criminal and we must act together, at great individual risk, to stop it. Those involved must lead the American people, by their example, to understand the enormity of what their government is doing . . . that the government cannot be allowed to continue with its daily crimes. . . .

There are many ways to avoid the draft, to stay clear of this war. Most of us now have deferments . . . but all these individual outs can have no effect on the draft, the war, or the consciousness of this country. To cooperate with conscription is to perpetuate its existence, without which, the government could not wage war. We have chosen to openly defy the draft and confront the government and its war directly. . . .

IV. THE RESISTANCE

Since the United States is engaged in criminal activity in Vietnam.

Since the major instrument of that criminal activity is the American military establishment.

Since the machinery of the military cannot effectively function without the acquiescence of the people it is supposed to represent.

Since we are young Americans who still believe in the ideals our country once stood for,

The RESISTANCE has been formed to organize and encourage resistance to, disruption of, and noncooperation with all the war-making machinery of the United States.

The RESISTANCE is a nationwide movement with organizations in New York, Illinois, Massachusetts, Iowa, Ohio, Wisconsin, Michigan, Oregon, and California.

ON OCTOBER 16, 1967, WE WILL PUBLICLY AND COLLECTIVELY RETURN OUR DRAFT CARDS TO THE SELECTIVE SERVICE SYSTEM IN MAJOR CITIES THROUGHOUT THE COUNTRY. We will clearly challenge the government's right to use any young lives for its own nefarious purposes. Our challenge will continue, and we will openly confront the Selective Service System, until the government is forced to deal with our collective action. After October 16, we will organize campuses and communities for similar waves of resistance in December, March, etc. We have gone beyond the "We Won't Go" statements in that we are renouncing all deferments, joining the forces of those who can and those who cannot afford deferments, and forcing an immediate confrontation by practicing total noncooperation with the military establishment. By turning in rather than burning our draft cards, we will be proudly giving our names to the public at large, and to the powers that be. Our hope is that upon our example every young man in America will realize that *he* must decide whether to resist or acquiesce to the draft and the war. We are confident that many will resist. . . .

Vietnam and the Draft

In 1969, 250 college and university student-body presidents stated their refusal to serve in what they considered an immoral and unjust war.

Students have, for a long time, made known their desire for a peaceful settlement. The present negotiations, however, are not an end in themselves, but rather, the means to a complete cease-fire and American extrication. And until that cease-fire is reached, or until the Selective Service System is constructively altered, young men who oppose this war will continue to face the momentous decision of how to respond to the draft.

In December of 1966, our predecessors as student body presidents and editors, in a letter to President Johnson, warned that "a great many of those faced with the prospect of military duty find it hard to square performance of the duty with concepts of personal integrity and conscience."

Many of the draft age have raised this issue. In the spring of 1967, over 1000 seminarians wrote to Secretary of Defense McNamara suggesting the recognition of conscientious objection to particular wars as a way of "easing the coming confrontation between the demands of law and those whose conscience will not permit them to fight in Vietnam." In June of 1967, our predecessors submitted, along with a second letter to the President, a petition signed by over 10,000 draft-eligible students from nine campuses, calling for alternative service for those who cannot fight in Vietnam. There have been many other similar attempts to influence Congress and the Administration. Nonetheless, despite all our efforts, the Selective Service System has remained impervious to constructive change. Presently, thousands of fellow students face the probability of immediate induction into the armed forces.

Most of us have worked in electoral politics and through other channels to change the course of America's foreign policy and to remove the inequities of the draft system. We will continue to work in these ways, but the possible results of these efforts will come too late for those whose deferments will soon expire. We must make an agonizing choice: to accept induction into the armed forces, which we feel would be irresponsible to ourselves, our country, and our fellow man; or to refuse induction, which is contrary to our respect for law and involves injury to our personal lives and careers.

Left without a third alternative, we will act according to our conscience. Along with thousands of our fellow students, we campus leaders cannot participate in a war which we believe to be immoral and unjust. Although this, for each of us, is an intensely personal decision, we publicly and collectively express our intention to refuse induction and to aid and support those who decide to refuse. We will not serve in the military as long as the war in Vietnam continues.

A Time to Say No

MICHAEL FERBER

Michael Ferber, draft resister, spoke at a Boston church on October 16, 1967, the day the Resistance had called for young men to turn in their draft cards. Ferber was later tried, along with famed pediatrician Benjamin Spock and three others, for counseling men to refuse induction.

We are gathered in this church today in order to do something very simple: to say No. We have come from many different places and backgrounds and we have many different ideas about ourselves and the world, but we have come here to show that we are united to do one thing: to say No. Each of our acts of returning our draft cards is our personal No; when we put them in a single container or set fire to them from a single candle we express the simple basis of our unity.

But what I wish to speak about now is what goes beyond our saying No, for no matter how loudly we all say it, no matter what ceremony we perform around our saying it, we will not become a community among ourselves nor effective agents for changing our country if a negative is all we share. Albert Camus said that the rebel, who says no, is also one who says Yes, and that when he draws a line beyond which he will refuse to cooperate he is affirming the values on the other side of that line. For us who come here today, what is it that we affirm, what is it to which we can say Yes?

To be honest we have to admit that we in the Resistance still disagree about a great many things, whether we speak out about them or not. For example, here we all are in a church, and yet for some of us it is the first time we've been inside one for years. Here we are receiving the help of many clergymen, and yet some of us feel nothing but contempt for the organized religions that they represent. Some of us, therefore, feel a certain hypocrisy in being part of this service.

But it would not surprise me if many of the clergymen who are here today feel some of the same contempt for organized religion that our unreligious or anti-religious brothers feel. They know better than we do the long and bloody history of evils committed in the name of religion, the long history of compromise and . . . subservience to political power, the long history of theological hair-splitting and the burning of heretics, and they feel more deeply than we do the hypocrisy of Sunday (or Saturday) morning. Perhaps the things that made some of us leave the church are the very things that made some of them become ministers, priests, and rabbis, the very things that bring them here today. Many of them will anger their superiors or their congregations by being here but they are here anyway.

There is a great tradition within the church and synagogue which has always struggled against the conservative and worldly forces that have always been in control. It is a radical tradition, a tradition of urgent impulse to go to the root of the religious dimension of human life. This tradition in modern times has tried to recall us to the best ways of living our lives: the way of love and compassion, the way of justice and respect, the way of facing other people as human beings and not as abstract representatives of something alien and evil. It tries to recall us to the reality behind religious ceremony and symbolism, and it will change the ceremony and symbolism when the reality changes.

As a part of this service we will break bread together. We do this, however, not because some churches happen to take Communion; we do this for one of the root reasons for Communion itself: that men around the world and for all time have found it good to eat together when they are sharing in something important.

The radical tradition is still alive; it is present here in this church. Those of us who disregard organized religion, I think, are making a mistake if they also disregard this tradition and its presence today. This tradition is something to which we can say Yes.

There is another disagreement among us, or if not a disagreement then a difference in attitude toward what we are doing today. It is a difference that cuts through the other differences, perhaps because it is a little inside each of us, and it leads to a mistake that we are liable to make no matter how else we agree or differ. In religious terms, it is to dwell too much on the possibility of the Apocalypse; in political terms, it is to dwell too much on the possibility of a Utopian Society. We must not confuse the ceremony and symbolism of today's service with the reality that we are only a few hundred people with very little power. And we must not confuse the change inside each of us, important though that may be, with the change that we have yet to bring about in this country and the world. Neither the Revelation nor the Revolution is at hand, and to base our hopes and plans on them would be a tragic blunder.

Maybe all of us—Leftists or Liberals, Reformers or Revolutionaries, Radical Religionists or Hippies—maybe all of us are apocalyptarians, I don't know. Surely something else besides a cold rational calculation of sociological options has brought us here to this church. And surely we ate in this church partly to celebrate the occasion of our noncooperation (and many of us will celebrate in a somewhat different way at parties with friends tonight). But let us not be deceived. The sun will rise tomorrow as it does every day, and when we get out of bed the world will be in pretty much the same mess it is in today. American bombers will continue to drop incendiary bombs on the Vietnamese people and American soldiers will continue to "pacify" their villages. The ghettos will continue to be rotten places to live in. Black and Mexican farm workers will continue to get miserable wages. America's schools will continue to cripple the minds and hearts of its pupils.

And the American Selective Service System will continue to send
young men out to the slaughter.

Today is not the End. Today is the Beginning.

Antidraft Activity

*These three brief articles about antidraft and anticorporate activities come from
the many examples printed in the alternative press that was spawned by the
movements. Political actions against draft boards and corporations grew more
numerous in the late sixties as antiwar protestors' desperation kept pace with
the War's escalation.*

Draft Board Raids Up

An incomplete listing on draft board and Dow Chemical Co. raids
(the Dow raids are of the same genre and often are conducted by
the same people) shows that they have become much more frequent
as the Vietnam war has dragged on.

There was a kind of freak raid on a Minnesota draft board in
1966, but the one that is generally credited—or blamed—with starting
the movement was the four-person raid at the Baltimore Customs
House Oct. 21, 1967. Father Berrigan was among the raiders who
poured blood on the draft records.

The federal charges were destroying government property and
interfering with the Selective Service system's operation. These
charges have since become fairly standard wherever federal prosecution of draft board raids is undertaken.

The next step was the May 17, 1968, raid by the Catonsville 9—Catonsville is a Baltimore suburb—and this precipitated not only federal but also Maryland state charges, including arson. Most of the state charges eventually were dropped.

Next came the Sept. 14, 1968, raid by the Milwaukee 14. In this case, two of the raiders pleaded guilty to federal charges but eventually federal charges against all other defendants were dropped because it proved impossible to get an impartial jury.

The pace was stepped up this year. It went like this:

—March 22 the D.C. 9 invaded Dow Chemical's Washington office. They are charged with three federal felony counts—burglary, and two counts of property destruction—and come to trial Feb. 3 in a federal court in the District of Columbia.

—May 20, the Pasadena 3 invaded an induction center in that Los Angeles suburb, took 600 1-A files and burned them in a field. They got three years in federal prison.

—May 21, the Silver Spring 3 invaded a draft board in that Maryland suburb of Washington, threw paint on the files and destroyed equipment. Two of the three pleaded nolo contendere—one who'd broken bond was sent to jail while a second was sent to a federal youth center at Morgantown, W. Va.—and the third raider, a 17-year-old, got three years' probation.

—May 25, the Chicago 15 invaded a South Side Chicago draft board, took files down a fire escape and burned them. They await federal trial at the end of January; the state did not press charges.

—July 4, the New York 5, led by Maggie Geddes, invaded a Rockefeller Center draft board, shredded 6,500 1-A files, damaged 1-A keys on typewriters and destroyed cross-reference books. Miss Geddes was not arrested but the other four were. The federal case against them was dismissed but they could be re-indicted.

—Aug 2, in the Bronx and Aug. 15 in Jamaica, Long Island, the New York 8 invaded draft boards and damaged records. Later in the month they surfaced and accepted responsibility for the acts. No prosecution so far.

—In mid-October two Clevelanders set fire to draft board records in Akron and later surfaced in a Cleveland cathedral, claiming responsibility for the act. No prosecution so far.

—On Oct. 31, the Beaver 55—who were not 55 but only eight and were named whimsically by Tom Trost, one of the group—shredded records of 44 Indianapolis draft boards, according to their later statement. No prosecution so far.

—Nov. 7, the Washington Dow Chemical offices were hit again with files strewn and ink and chemicals splashed around. A short statement left in the office said it was wrong to "put profit before people," invoked support for the Beaver 55, the D.C. 9 and the Ohio group and was signed, "D.C. 54 1/2."

The person who carried this out surfaced the next day; he was one of the Akron draft board invaders. No prosecution so far.

—Nov. 7, the Boston 8 entered four Boston locations housing eight draft boards and shredded files. The Boston 8 surfaced the morning and afternoon of Nov. 15 in Washington and distributed Boston draft files around the mall and the reflecting pool between the Washington Monument and Lincoln Memorial. No prosecution so far.

—Nov. 7, the Beaver 55 invaded Dow Chemical's data center in Midland, Mich., and erased magnetic tapes filled with biological and chemical research. They surfaced at a Nov. 16 Washington press conference (which was widely unreported); five of the Beavers were arrested in Midland and held on $20,000 bond apiece under state charges.

—Nov. 11, the Silver Spring draft board was revisited by the youngest of the original Silver Spring 3, plus the two Clevelanders who had worked over the Akron draft board. They took out the files and left them on a railroad track. They were spotted and held on federal charges; bond is $10,000 apiece.

The trick in all this seems to be to not get caught and then surface at some distance from the deed and with sufficient vagueness so that no evidence is available for prosecution.

An Open Letter to the Corporations of America

The Dow Chemical Company became a special target of the antiwar movement because of its manufacture of napalm, a chemical widely used by the American military. Dropped by American planes, this jellylike substance killed and maimed by burning off the skin.

Today, March 22, 1969, in the Washington office of the Dow Chemical Company we spill human blood and destroy files and office equipment. By this action, we condemn you, the Dow Chemical Company, and all similar American Corporations.

We are outraged by the death-dealing exploitation of people of the Third World, and of all the poor and powerless who are victimized by your profit-seeking ventures. Considering it our responsibility to respond, we deny the right of your faceless and inhuman corporation to exist:

> you, corporations, who under the cover of stockholder and executive anonymity, exploit, deprive, dehumanize and kill in search of profit;
>
> you, corporations, who contain (or control) Americans and exploit their exaggerated need for security that you have helped create;
>
> you, corporations, who numb our sensitivity to persons, and capitalize on our concern for things.

Specifically, we warn you, Dow Chemical Company, that we will no longer tolerate your refusal to accept responsibility for your programmed destruction of human life.

> You, stockholders and company executives alike, are so willing to seek profit in the production of napalm, defoliants, nerve gas, as in the same spirit you co-operated with the I. G. Farben Company, a chemical manufacturer in Nazi Germany, during the Second World War.
>
> You, who without concern for development for other nations or for their rights of self-determination, maintain 100% control over subsidiaries in more than twenty nations.

You, who in the interest of profit, seek to make it in the military interest of the United States to suppress the legitimate national desires of other peoples. Your product is death, your market is war.

Your offices have lost their right to exist. It is a blow for justice that we strike today.

In your mad pursuit of profit, you and others like you are causing the psychological and physical destruction of mankind. We urge all to join us as we say "no" to this madness.

Statement of the DC 9

Beaver 55 Strikes Again

Over the weekend, St. Paul and Minneapolis, Minn. was the scene of a massive action to destroy U.S. ability to wage war in Vietnam.

A group calling itself Beaver 55 raided Selective Service offices in 3 separate locations. All 1-A and 1-A delinquent draft files along with ledger books and cross references were destroyed in local boards 27 thru 48 in Hennepin County and 87–98 in Ramsey County. The State office building housing all duplicate files was also ransacked and thousands of back-up files for those boards were destroyed. The group announced its support of the Provisional Revolutionary Government of South Vietnam and denounced the draft for "perpetuating and inflicting male chauvinism in our culture."

These actions will probably stop any possible induction from these local boards for up to a year. This will cripple almost 50% of the entire Selective Service System in the state. This is the largest and most effective strike against the Selective Service System of its kind and the first time a State office was invaded.

The group, Beaver 55, was responsible for actions against 44 draft boards in Indianapolis Oct. 31, and Dow Chemical Company November 7. It seems these actions are continuing as the group said they would.

In the War

The antiwar movement was not restricted to those outside of the military. Among those fighting the war, concern mounted as the years passed. Some refused to be shipped to Vietnam, others declined to return to their ships or companies after a leave.

Army Times

The alternative magazine Hard Times *reported in 1970 on the growing antiwar movement within the military.*

The GI "protest" movement is growing as dramatically, in its way, as the student radical movement did half-a-decade ago. But the military system is far more tough to crack than the university establishment. The biggest GI action to date—in mass if not militancy—was a march last month of 750 active-duty servicemen, most of them from the San Diego, Calif., Naval complex at Camp Pendleton, through nearby Oceanside.

The servicemen led a chanting crowd of about 5,000 people on the march through the town—the closest community to the sprawling Marine encampment. There was more than a march; at a rally afterwards, GIs announced the formation of "Movement for a Democratic Military," and read a list of 12 demands ranging from collective bargaining to support of the Black Panthers' "POWs for Panthers" prisoner exchange project with North Vietnam. The GI contingent was thoroughly integrated; one key organizer, a black Marine sergeant named Jack Anderson, had been bailed out two days before after

Reprinted by permission, James Ridgeway.

being beaten and jailed in a raid on the Los Angeles Black Panther Party headquarters. Press and town officials hardly knew how to respond (Washington newspapers carried a one-paragraph item the next day); but the classiest comment of the day came from the mayor of Oceanside: "It was like a great open sewer running through the streets of our city."

In the last month California has also seen the birth of another unusual kind of anti-military activity: the beginnings of political organizing among Reservists and National Guardsmen.

Until now, Reservists and Guardsmen have been anything but outspoken. They are the upper end of the Army's class hierarchy: Blacks and high school dropouts end up on the front lines in Vietnam: Upper-middle college graduates tend to wangle their way into Reserve and Guard units. There, they usually spend four and a half months on active duty at US training bases, and the rest of their six-year obligation period going to evening and weekend drills and an annual two-week summer camp. It's a bothersome routine, but a good deal more privileged—and safer—than crawling through the rice paddies of Southeast Asia.

The new organizing within the military comes in the form of a strongly-worded statement now being circulated by 50 officers and men from the National Guard and the Army, Navy, Air Force, Marine, and Coast Guard Reserves. They call for immediate total withdrawal from Vietnam, and demand "total withdrawal now of all the American soldiers advising the armies of dictatorships throughout Latin America and Asia. We don't want Guatemala, Thailand, or Bolivia to become the Vietnams of the 1970s. One Vietnam is enough; too many people have been killed already to preserve America's overseas empire."

Organizers of the campaign hope to gather several thousand signatures from around the country and use the total to publicize the extent of antiwar feeling inside the military. Guardsmen and Reservists can legally sign a statement like this; active duty soldiers believe they cannot. Readers in the Guard or Reserves interested in seeing the statement and adding their names should write Box 4398, Berkeley, Calif.

The Fort Hood Three

The Fort Hood Three were soldiers who refused to be shipped to Vietnam in 1966.

JOINT STATEMENT BY FORT HOOD THREE

The following statement was read to over 40 cameramen, reporters, and antiwar fighters at a press conference in New York on June 30th. The statement was prepared jointly and read by Pvt. Dennis Mora.

We are Pfc. James Johnson, Pvt. David Samas, and Pvt. Dennis Mora, three soldiers formerly stationed at Fort Hood, Texas in the same company of the 142 Signal Battalion, 2nd Armored Division. We have received orders to report on the 13th of July at Oakland Army Terminal in California for final processing and shipment to Vietnam.

We have decided to take a stand against this war, which we consider immoral, illegal and unjust. We are initiating today, through our attorneys, Stanley Faulkner of New York and Mrs. Selma Samols of Washington, D.C. an action in the courts to enjoin the Secretary of Defense and the Secretary of the Army from sending us to Vietnam. We intend to report as ordered to the Oakland Army Terminal, but under no circumstances will we board ship for Vietnam. We are prepared to face Court Martial if necessary.

We represent in our backgrounds a cross section of the Army and of America. James Johnson is a Negro, David Samas is of Lithuanian and Italian parents, Dennis Mora is a Puerto Rican. We speak as American soldiers.

We have been in the army long enough to know that we are not the only G.I.'s who feel as we do. Large numbers of men in the service either do not understand this war or are against it.

When we entered the army Vietnam was for us only a newspaper box score of G.I.'s and Viet Cong killed or wounded. We were all against it in one way or another, but we were willing to "go along with the program," believing that we would not be sent to Vietnam.

We were told from the very first day of our induction that we were headed for Vietnam. During basic training it was repeated often by sergeants and officers, and soon it became another meaningless threat that was used to make us take our training seriously.

But later on Vietnam became a fact of life when some one you knew wondered how he could break the news to his girl, wife, or family that he was being sent there. After he solved that problem, he had to find a reason that would satisfy him. The reasons were many—"Somebody's got to do it," "When your number's up, your number's up," "The pay is good," and "You've got to stop them someplace" were phrases heard in the barracks and mess hall, and used by soldiers to encourage each other to accept the war as their own. Besides, what could be done about it anyway? Orders are orders.

As we saw more and more of this, the war became the one thing we talked about most and the one point we all agreed upon. No one wanted to go and more than that, there was no reason for anyone to go.

The Viet Cong obviously had the moral and physical support of most of the peasantry who were fighting for their independence. We were told that you couldn't tell them apart—that they looked like any other skinny peasant.

Our man or our men in Saigon has and have always been brutal dictators, since Diem first violated the 1954 Geneva promise of free elections in 1956.

The Buddhist and military revolt in all the major cities proves that the people of the cities also want an end to Ky and U.S. support for him.

The Saigon Army has become the advisor to American G.I.'s who have to take over the fighting.

No one used the word "winning" anymore because in Vietnam it has no meaning. Our officers just talk about five and ten more years of war with at least 1/2 million of our boys thrown into the grinder. We have been told that many times we may face a Vietnamese woman or child and that we will have to kill them. We will never go there—to do that—for Ky!

We know that Negroes and Puerto Ricans are being drafted and end up in the worst of the fighting all out of proportion to their numbers in the population; and we have first hand knowledge that these are the ones who have been deprived of decent education and jobs at home.

The three of us, while stationed together, talked a lot and found we thought alike on one over-riding issue—the war in Vietnam must be stopped. It was all talk and we had no intentions of getting into trouble by making waves at that stage.

Once back in Texas we were told that we were on levy to Vietnam. All we had discussed and thought about now was real. It was time for us to quit talking and decide. Go to Vietnam and ignore the truth or stand and fight for what we know is right.

We have made our decision. We will not be a part of this unjust, immoral, and illegal war. We want no part of a war of extermination. We oppose the criminal waste of American lives and resources. We refuse to go to Vietnam!!!!!!

Antiwar Activity Within the Military

The alternative press reported actions and activities in the military that indicated growing discontent within the system. Five brief selections, from 1967–1970, are reprinted below. These provide some sense of the variety of activities inside, outside, and around the army.

The Pentagon Is Rising

It's difficult to write about what happened that night and not sound corny. You had to have been there and felt the vibrations to understand how real it was. We began pleading with the soldiers to "Join us," singing "Soldiers are our friends, we shall overcome," and chanting "We love you." Corny words, silly slogans, cliches that have long lost their meaning. But we were communicating with the soldiers, putting them through changes. And they, with their silent faces, were communicating with us, putting us through changes. For us it was a shock of recognition that despite their arms, their uniforms, and their orders to attack us, the soldiers were very much our brothers.

WIN Magazine, Review of October 21–22,
1967 Pentagon demonstration

A Lot of GIs

A lot of GIs are taking a lot of shit from the brass because they oppose the war, because they organize other GIs, because they smoke dope, because they refuse to take riot training, because they refuse to become automatons.

These same GIs come to the city looking for a little brotherliness, dope, support. And they get cold stares because they have short hair.

As if it needed to be said, hair don't mean shit. But for a brother to be able to come to a strange place and find friends does. Support our boys—bring one home now.

The Great Speckled Bird

A.W.O.L.

The desertion rate from the U.S. Army has increased 80% since 1967. When Lt. General A.O. Conner, Army personnel chief, was called before a House committee to explain this alarming development, he came up with this answer: "We are getting more kooks into the Army, for one thing. We are getting more young men who are coming in undisciplined, the product of a society that trains them to resist authority." But despite the rise in desertions, Gen. Conner said that the troop morale in Vietnam was "fabulous" and that the "vast majority of them are doing it beautifully—we do not have to be too concerned about our youth."

LNS

Oleo Strut Is Recruiting

The Oleo Strut is looking for new staff members. The Strut is a GI coffeehouse located in Killeen, Texas near Fort Hood. As well as the regular activities of a GI coffeehouse, we hope to have a radical bookstore, combination military law and radical books library in the near future.

Killeen is a small town with a population of 35,000 people totally dependant on the Army for its income. Fort Hood itself is a 39,000 man Armored Post staffed largely by Viet Nam returnees. There is no basic training, and almost everyone is just waiting to get out. Because Fort Hood is a riot control center and discipline is threatened by Nam vets, the propaganda and coercion are heavy.

The Oleo Strut staff is a collective. We live in one house and all work every day at the Strut. We have been working as a collective for 4 months and have been varyingly successful. Within the collective is a women's caucus. We discuss all problems and political questions that arise. We discipline ourselves individually and from the collective we discipline ourselves as a group and criticize each other for mistakes we make as staff members.

We feel that our most important work is developing GI organizers who are laying the groundwork for a mass movement in the Army. One of the best organizing tools that has been established at Fort Hood is the Fatigue Press which is put out by the GIs.

In conclusion then, we are looking for people (men, women, or couples) who are willing to:

1. make a commitment of at least six months, hopefully starting in October or November, or as soon as possible.
2. do shit work in the coffeehouse.
3. learn about military law and counsel on court-martials and CO applications.
4. learn and make changes according to the demands made by the working situation in Killeen and the Army.
5. view their work as long-range, and not look for regular victories. This is organizing, not activism and takes patience.
6. talk politics with guys in the Army and keep studying and learning new ways to build a movement.

If you feel that this is the kind of work you want to do, please write us immediately, so that we can begin discussions about joining the staff. Tell us about yourself and what you have been doing, and we will describe in greater detail the work that goes on in the Strut. . . .

San Francisco Express Times

Join the Foreign Legion

The 13,000 American civilians employed in South Vietnam have a "high incidence of alcoholism, psychopathic behavior and frank psychosis," according to Dr. John A. Talbott, just returned from a year in Saigon serving as an army psychiatrist.

"The US government and its private contract firms offer positions in Vietnam that appeal to the borderline personality, the person with severe character disorders and the social misfit."

The men seek jobs in Vietnam hoping to recover "their lost youth, their dashed hopes; primitive, mainly living without rules and bossy American women."

They hope that "Vietnamese women are compliant and feminine, with girlish, thin figures; they do not talk back and are readily available to Americans." Dr. Talbott's report appeared in the Journal of the American Psychiatric Assn.

EXPERIENCES OF WAR

My Lai

The March 16, 1968, massacre by American troops at My Lai of hundreds of Vietnamese civilians, including women and children, sent shock waves across the American home front when it came to light over a year later. One of the participants, Paul Meadlo, responds to questions about the events. This interview was published in the New York Times *in 1969.*

MEADLO: Captain Medina had us all in a group, and oh, he briefed us, and I can't remember all the briefing.

WALLACE: How many of them were you? A. Well, with the mortar platoon, I'd say there'd be about 60–65 people, but the mortar platoon wasn't with us, and I'd say the mortar platoon had about 20–25—about 25 people in the mortar platoon. So we didn't have the whole company in the Pinkville [My Lai], no we didn't.

Q: There weren't about 40–45—A. . . . right. . . .

Q: —that took part in all of this? A. Right.

Q: Now you took off from your base camp. A. . . . yes—Dolly.

Q: . . . Dolly. At what time? A. I wouldn't know what time it was. . . .

Q: . . . in the early morning. . . . A. . . . In the early morning. It was—it would have been a long time ago.

Q: And what had you been briefed to do when you got to Pinkville?

A: To search and to make sure that there weren't no N.V.A. in the village and expecting to fight—when we got there. . . .

Q: To expect to fight? A. To expect to fight.

Q: Un-huh. So you took off and—in how many choppers?

A: Well, I'd say the first wave was about four of us—I mean four choppers and. . . .

Q: How many men aboard each chopper?

A: Five of us. And we landed next to the village, and we all got in line and we started walking toward the village. And there was one man, one gook in the shelter, and he was all huddled up down in there, and the man called out and said there's a gook over here.

Q: How old a man was this? I mean was this a fighting man or an older man?

A: An older man. And the man hauled out and said that there's a gook over here, and then Sergeant Mitchell hollered back and said shoot him.

Q: Sergeant Mitchell was in charge of the 20 of you? A. He was in charge of the whole squad. And so then the man shot him. So we moved on into the village, and we started searching up the village and gathering people and running through the center of the village.

Q: How many people did you round up? A. Well, there was about 40—45 people that we gathered in the center of the village. And we placed them in there, and it was like a little island, right there in the center of the village, I'd say. And—

Q: What kind of people—men, women, children?

A: Men, women, children.

Q: Babies?

A: Babies. And we all huddled them up. We made them squat down, and Lieutenant Calley came over and said you know what to do with them, don't you? And I said yes so I took it for granted that he just wanted us to watch them. And he left, and came back about 10 to 15 minutes later, and said, how come you ain't killed them yet? And I told him that I didn't think you wanted us to kill them, that you just wanted us to guard them. He said, no, I want them dead. So—

Q: He told this to all of you, or to you particularly?

A: Well, I was facing him. So, but, the other three, four guys heard it and so he stepped back about 10, 15 feet, and he started shooting them. And he told me to start shooting. So I started shooting. I poured about four clips into the group.

Q: You fired four clips from your. . . . A. M-16.

Q: And that's about—how many clips—I mean how many—

A: I carried seventeen rounds to each clip.

Q: So you fired something like 67 shots—A. Right.

Q: And you killed how many? At that time?

A: Well, I fired them on automatic, so you can't—you just spray the arch on them and so you can't know how many you killed 'cause they were going fast. So I might have killed ten or fifteen of them.

Q: Men, women and children? A. Men, women and children.

Q: And babies?

A: And babies.

Q: Okay, then what? A. So we started to gather them up, more people, and we had about seven or eight people, that we was gonna put into the hootch, and we dropped a hand grenade in there with them.

Q: Now you're rounding up more?

A: We're rounding up more, and we had about seven or eight people. And we was going to throw them in the hootch, and well, we put them in the hootch and then we dropped a hand grenade down there with them. And somebody holed up in the ravine, and told us to bring them over to the ravine, so we took them back out, and led them over to—and by that time, we already had them over there, and they had about 70–75 people all gathered up. So we threw ours in with them and Lieutenant Calley told me, he said, Meadlo, we got another job to do. And so he walked over to the people, and he started pushing them off and started shooting. . . .

Q: Started pushing them off into the ravine?

A: Off into the ravine. It was a ditch. And so we started pushing them off and we started shooting them, so altogether we just pushed them all off, and just started using automatics on them. And then—

Q: Again—men, women, children? A. Men, women and children.

Q: And babies?

A: And babies. And so we started shooting them and somebody told us to switch off to single shot so that we could save ammo. So we switched off to single shot and shot a few more rounds. And after that, I just—we just—the company started gathering up again. We started moving out, and we had a few gooks that was in—as we started moving out, we had gooks in front of us that was taking point, you know. . . .

Q: Why did you do it? A. Why did I do it? Because I felt like I was ordered to do it, and it seemed like that, at the time I felt like I was doing the right thing, because like I said I lost buddies. I lost a damn good buddy, Bobby Wilson, and it was on my conscience. So after I done it, I felt good, but later on that day, it was getting to me.

Q: You're married? A. Right.

Q: Children? A. Two.

Q: How old? A. The boy is two and a half, and the little girl is a year and a half.

Q: Obviously, the question comes to my mind . . . the father of two little kids like that . . . how can he shoot babies? A. I didn't have the little girl. I just had a little boy at the time.

Q: Uh-huh. How do you shoot babies? A. I don't know. It's just one of them things.

Q: How many people would you imagine were killed that day? A. I'd say about 370.

Q: How do you arrive at that figure? A. Just looking.

Q: You say, you think, that many people, and you yourself were responsible for how many of them? A. I couldn't say.

Q: Twenty-five? Fifty? A. I couldn't say . . . just too many.

Q: And how many men did the actual shooting? A. Well, I really couldn't say that, either. There was other . . . there was another platoon in there and . . . but I just couldn't say how many.

Q: But these civilians were lined up and shot? They weren't killed by cross-fire? A. They weren't lined up . . . they [were] just pushed in a ravine or just sitting, squatting . . . and shot.

Q: What did these civilians—particularly the women and children, the old men—what did they do? What did they say to you? A. They weren't much saying to them. They [were] just being pushed and they were doing what they was told to do.

Q: They weren't begging or saying, "No . . . no," or—A. Right, they were begging and saying, "No, no." And the mothers was hugging their children and, but they kept right on firing. Well, we kept right on firing. They was waving their arms and begging. . . .

Q: Was that your most vivid memory of what you saw? A. Right.

Q: And nothing went through your mind or heart? A. Many a times . . . many a times. . . .

Q: While you were doing it? A. Not while I was doing it. It just seemed like it was the natural thing to do at the time. I don't know . . . I was getting relieved from what I'd seen earlier over there.

Q: What do you mean? A. Well, I was getting . . . like the . . . my buddies getting killed or wounded or—we weren't getting no satisfaction from it, so what it really was, it was just mostly revenge.

Q: You call the Vietnamese "gooks?" A. Gooks.

Q: Are they people to you? Were they people to you?

A: Well, they were people. But it was just one of them words that we just picked up over there, you know. Just any word you pick up. That's what you call people, and that's what you been called.

Q: Obviously, the thought that goes through my mind—I spent some time over there, and I killed in the second war, and so forth. But the thought that goes through your mind is, we've raised such a dickens about what the Nazis did, or what the Japanese did, but particularly what the Nazis did in the second world war, the brutalization and so forth, you know. It's hard for a good many Americans to understand that young, capable, American boys could line up old men, women and children and babies and shoot them down in cold blood. How do you explain that?

A: I wouldn't know.

Q: Did you ever dream about all of this that went on in Pinkville?

A: Yes I did . . . and I still dream about it.

Q: What kind of dreams? A. About the women and children in my sleep. Some days . . . some nights, I can't even sleep. I just lay there thinking about it.

Home Before Morning

LYNDA VAN DEVANTER

Only as the passions of the Vietnam experience have receded has America begun to go beyond the polarized feelings of the war and understand the complex experiences of individuals on all sides of the question. The complexities proved to be especially great for groups within the military. There is a growing body of literature about their experiences, from personal memoirs to fictional

Excerpted from *Home Before Morning: The Story of an Army Nurse in Vietnam,* by Lynda Van Devanter (Warner Books: New York, 1983). Used by permission. Copyright © 1983 by Lynda Van Devanter.

accounts to group portraits, such as Wallace Terry's oral history of African-American soldiers, Bloods. *Lynda Van Devanter, a nurse in Vietnam, recounts in her 1983 memoir how she still remains haunted by the destruction and misery she witnessed.*

Three A.M. Sometimes, when the nights are not easy, I can lie here alone in this big bed for hours, listening to the ticking clock or the sound of the crickets in the bushes beneath my window, part of me wanting desperately to get back to sleep, knowing that if I don't, tomorrow's meetings will be filled, for me, with little more than exhaustion.

I hate dragging myself through the deadening days that follow these long nights. I hate that sick morning feeling in my stomach that comes from being too tired. I hate the thought that, in my half-awake state, I will lose some of tomorrow.

But more than all that, I hate what I might face were I to once again allow myself the mixed blessing of sleep. It's not that I don't want to sleep, only that I'm afraid of tonight's kind of sleep, afraid of what it often brings.

In part, this night is my own fault. Lately, these difficult times have been almost nonexistent and, if I hadn't spent so many hours this afternoon reliving Vietnam with another troubled woman veteran, I would now be resting quietly. But at a 3 A.M. like this one, that thought offers little consolation.

They flew him in by chopper and there were streaks of dirt along his face. His sandy brown hair was uneven, with patches pressed down where the sweat-soaked straps of his helmet had been. With his eyes closed, he might have been just another tired soldier resting. However, the bloody mess that was once his body told a different story. Maybe, if there were time, he could be saved. But there were too many others.

In some ways, the bad nights must have been easier when Bill was here. He used to tell me that I ground my teeth in my sleep. He would touch my cheek and I'd stop for a while, only to start again later. He told me about the talking in my sleep and the moaning sounds I would make before waking in fear.

I would put my arms around him and hold myself tightly against his body, trying to draw enough strength to make him understand all that I had seen. It was useless. He could listen to me, yet I hadn't figured out how to say all that was inside, and probably, like the others, he wouldn't want to know anyway.

What did he do to help me on nights like this one? Did he hold me, return my frantic hugs with reassurance? Did he tuck my head into his hollow formed by his shoulder and tell me it would be all right? Did he make me feel protected? Did he take away any of the pain? Could he? Could anyone?

Maybe the nights are worse since we separated. Or were they just as bad when he was here?

I don't remember.

The boy couldn't have been more than ten years old, the kind of kid who would have been sitting down by a stream, dangling his feet in the water, holding the end of a fishing line, enjoying a lazy summer day—if he hadn't stepped on the land mine. When his mother carried him onto the compound, there were two bloody stumps where his legs had been.

Any shrink worth his ninety dollars an hour would probably say I should "face the pain and deal with it." In fact, I've heard those words more than once. They even sound like something I might say to the women who come to me for counseling, looking for someone to take away their pain, their voices breaking as they recount the horrors of their own personal hells while I sit there listening, trying to assure them that they are not crazy.

"I understand," I say. "You're not alone. Many of us have seen the same things. Together, we can get past the problems. It's hard work, but it can be done."

Occasionally, the words work. But it's on nights like this that they and I must face the realization that we are alone, that ours is a solitary pain, to be felt in hundreds of 3 A.M.s when those around us are sleeping peacefully.

There was a time when I didn't understand that, when I didn't know how alone I was, how alone we all were. It was a time when I thought I would be able to talk about—exorcise—all the memories of hours spent in the operating rooms of Pleiku and Qui Nhon, working with surgeons as we tried to save the lives of boys who would never again be whole. I wanted to tell someone I loved—my parents, a friend, a relative, anyone—about the rocket attacks and all the nights I slept under my bunk; about the weeks we had more casualties than we could handle and how hard we worked even when we knew it was hopeless; about the tiny children with their arms and legs blown off; about the terrible oppression of the monsoon and the nights we knew we would die. Vietnam was the worst time of my life, yet it was also, in many ways, the most important and the most intense. For years, I tried to talk about it. Nobody listened.

Who would have wanted to listen? Mine were not nice, neat stories. There was love, but no cute little love stories; heroes, but no grand, heroic war stories; winners, but you had to look hard to tell them from the losers. On our battlefields, there were no knights in shining armor rescuing damsels in distress. The stories, even the funny ones, were all dirty. They were rotten and they stank. The moments, good and bad, were permeated with the stench of death and napalm.

And when that year was over, when the "Freedom Bird" took me back to "the world," I learned that my war was just beginning.

They wheeled her in on a gurney. She'd already gone into labor. With the bullet wound in her belly, a normal childbirth would be out of the question. So we cut into her, and found a perfectly formed live baby boy. He had a gunshot wound in his belly. . . .

. . . He was only eighteen years old. I put his hand in mine. "I'm a nurse," I said. "You are in an American hospital. We're going to make you as comfortable as possible." It was what we said to all the ones we classified as expectants, those we expected to die. It was simply a matter of time.

Against my better judgment, I decide to try once more for sleep, hopefully a peaceful one this time. I crawl over to the dry empty side of the bed—Bill's side—and lie down. Eyes closed, breathing slowly, I attempt to calm myself. It works. I am drifting, resting normally, this time possibly until morning. It is peaceful, so peaceful.

The dreams come slowly. I can hear birds and the sound of water lapping against my air mattress as I lie in the middle of a pool. The sun is setting, casting long shadows. Some men and women are sitting on the grass nearby. They are laughing and talking. Behind them, the top of a makeshift chapel rises above a wooden fence. The building is dwarfed by twin radar screens on the hill to the right. Near the screens, a soldier sits in a guard tower. I can hear the tanks rolling across the compound. Suddenly, it's all interrupted by a rocket attack and mud is oozing through the walls of the operating room, while we work frantically to put some soldier's leg back together. There's an explosion.

Everything goes black.

After a few moments in the darkness, I hear the insistent ring of a telephone outside my door. It's 3 A.M. in Pleiku. The fighting in the Central Highlands is heavy, with the continuous sound of rifles, mortars, and artillery off in the distance. I've been sleeping under my cot, having been awakened an hour earlier by a rocket attack. In my exhaustion, not even the concussion of explosions nearby could keep me awake. But the telephone sets me in motion.

Still half asleep, I hold the receiver to my ear. "Incoming wounded! Get everyone down here on the double." The adrenalin flows as I run through the hooch, waking the other nurses—"Mickie, get up!" "Oh, no! Not again!" Banging on their doors—"Coretta, casualties." "Don't those V.C. ever rest?" Racing against time, while the sound of the med-evac choppers grows louder—"Jill." "Leave me alone, Van. I'm tired." "Let's go, kiddo, we're on!" A groan, and I hear her moving.

Back in my room, I can hear running footsteps on the hall floor as I remove my nightgown and hustle into fatigues. *Bastards! Won't they ever let us sleep?* I throw my flak jacket over one shoulder, my helmet onto my head, and race to the doorway of the hooch, my untied bootlaces dragging on the floor. By the time I reach the outside steps, my fatigue shirt is buttoned and the flak jacket is joisted onto my other shoulder, one snap fastened to keep it from flapping. Others are running ahead of me toward the emergency room, their silhouettes sharply outlined by the flashing light of flares, exploding artillery rounds, and rockets. My heart is beating wildly. Miles away, red tracers rain down from Cobra gunships. The ARVN tanks are moving around the edges of our compound. Overhead, a helicopter begins its descent with more wounded as doctors, nurses, and medics push gurneys to the landing pad. The roar of the rotor blades becomes deafening.

I run to the ER, grab a gurney, and wheel it out. The first dust-off is already lifting off, heading back into combat for more casualties, while a second chopper comes in quickly to take its place. As soon as the bird touches down, the medical personnel and flight crew work frantically to unload the damaged human cargo. The pilot is a twenty-one-year-old kid nicknamed Shortstop, because he's barely five foot six. He has an oversized baby face that is usually dominated by his cute, puffy red cheeks. Those cheeks are now a pasty white as he yells from his seat, "Get those fuckers moving. We gotta get back there quick!" There's blood down the left side of Shortstop's flight suit. I notice it as I'm helping another nurse drag a litter from the chopper onto a gurney.

"Come on, assholes, we don't have all day!" Shortstop screams.

I jump back on the chopper and grab his left shoulder. I have to yell to be heard above the engine. "You're hit."

"No shit, Dick Tracy."

"Let someone look at it."

"Later, Van. It's a fucking mess out there right now. Get the fuck off my goddamned machine so I can go back to work." Although he protests, I quickly wrap a pressure dressing around his arm to stop the bleeding. It takes only a few extra seconds.

With all the wounded cleared out, I jump to the ground. Short-stop's chopper is lifting off even before my feet have touched the earth. It is the last time I will ever see him alive.

I run to catch up with a corpsman pushing the last gurney as another chopper lands behind me. More medical personnel start off-loading new wounded, but by now my full attention is on the soldier at my side. As we roll through the doors of the ER, I am using my scissors to cut his uniform off so we can examine his sucking chest wound. The corpsman pushes the soldier's litter against a wall and I hang his IV bottle. In the light, it quickly becomes apparent that this guy has more than just a chest wound. There's a through and through gunshot wound in his left shoulder and hundreds of smaller wounds—multiple frag wounds—covering his entire body. They probably came from a rocket, mine, or grenade. Although he doesn't say a word, I can see the fear in his eyes. I give him a shot of morphine and try to offer some reassurance before moving along to another case. This one will survive. "Don't worry," I say. "We've got the best doctors in the world here. You'll be better before you know it.'' My words don't ease the pain, but I know the morphine soon will.

One of the ER doctors comes up behind me with a clipboard as I'm drawing some blood to be typed and crossmatched for later transfusion. "What do we have here, Van?"

"A sucking chest wound," I answer. "GSW T and T in the left shoulder and MFWs front and back. Blood pressure eighty over fifty, pulse one fifty."

"Okay, we'll send him in as soon as he's stabilized."

I begin moving through the seemingly endless flow of wounded soldiers, working with the doctors, making quick, superficial examinations to determine which will be first into the operating rooms, which ones can wait for treatment, and which ones will be left to die because we lack the time or resources to save them. The emergency room is filled with the moaning and screaming of boys and men who have been rudely confronted with their own mortality, their mangled and twisted bodies contorted by more than physical pain. Mixed among their cries are the urgent, but professional voices of the medical people.

"Get another IV into this one, he's shocky."

"Somebody help me!"

"They're only MFWs of the legs. He can wait."

"I want my mother."

"Type and cross this one for fifteen units."

"Don't let me die."

"Wheel that one over to the expectant room."

To the average person, the scene in the ER might appear to be one of absolute chaos. But the actual precision of this system is amazing, especially for the Army. Everyone knows exactly what to do and does it without question, giving the best possible care in the shortest amount of time, to keep as many people alive as possible.

As I finish one soldier's examination, a weak hand grabs my arm. "Hey, Van?"

I turn to find Bennie Dickenson, a twenty-year-old field medic from the 4th Division lying on a gurney. Almost every man in his platoon has been killed or wounded tonight. Bennie has a gaping hole in his left side, exposing half of his chest, another in his belly, and a bloody stump where his left used to be. Around the stump is a tourniquet that he probably applied by himself. He might make it, but he'd need to get to an operating room quickly.

In spite of his pain, Bennie's voice is calm and well modulated, sounding like that of a precise and highly trained medic, and not that of a man with half his body blown away.

"I apologize for the unexpected visit," he says. "I wanted to surprise you guys to see if you really work as hard as you say."

I am speechless—I've partied with Bennie, compared stories about our respective childhoods, and more than once, I've considered saying yes to his half-joking requests for a date. His best friend, Phil Conklin, is an OR technician here, and Bennie frequently spends his free time at our hospital, playing cards and chess with Phil or conning us out of extra medical supplies that he can take to the field. Phil and Bennie have gone through grammar school, high school, and basic training together. They even worked it so they arrived in Vietnam on the same day. But their different medical specialties landed them in different assignments, a problem that Phil had wanted to correct by having Bennie apply for a transfer to our hospital. By the time the skids were greased, Bennie was so worried about "his boys" in the platoon that he refused to budge. Like most field medics, he's been their mother hen almost since the day he arrived. He worries that no one can care for them as well as he can.

I wipe the sweat from his forehead. "Van, could you please do me a big favor?" he asks.

"Sure, Bennie. You need some morphine?"

"No, thanks. It's Petrocelli over there." He lifts his arm weakly and points to a brawny, dark-haired kid about five feet away. "I ran out of plasma before he got hit and he's lost at least three or four units of blood. He looks like he's going into shock. Could you get an extra IV into him?"

"Sure thing."

As soon as I take care of Petrocelli, I come back to Bennie. It's difficult to keep my hands from shaking as I cut away his uniform and examine his open belly. I've worked on friends before, but it's never easy.

"Don't waste your time on me, Van. Take care of my guys first."

I ignore his suggestion and continue the exam, trying to see him as merely another case, and not as a person who was telling me jokes only four days earlier.

"When you get to Spezak, you better turn him over," Bennie says. "He's got some frags in his back. And I think he might have something going on in his belly, because it was rigid. Better get a surgeon to open him up quick."

He continues, "When you get Mitchell into the OR, tell the gas passer to be careful putting him under. The crazy fucker just finished eating six cans of beans and dicks before we got hit."

I cut away what's left of Bennie's fatigue pants and can see a long deep wound down to the bone in the back of his "good" leg. I cover it and him with a clean sheet. I touch his cheek before moving on to another casualty. He smiles weakly. He knows that his chances are not good. He probably knew it from the moment he was hit.

Five minutes later, with the choppers still bringing in wounded, I am called to scrub for surgery. On my way to the operating room, I walk past Phil Conklin as he pushes a dead body toward the morgue. He's muttering to himself and trying to hold back tears. "Stupid fucking hero."

I glance down and see Bennie's face. I too want to cry; to mourn not only Bennie, but the thousands like him who have come through this hospital. But tonight, neither Phil Conklin nor I, nor any of the other personnel at the 71st Evacuation Hospital will shed a tear for Bennie Dickenson. There isn't enough time to cry while so many others are depending on us to keep them alive.

When I wake again, my body is shaking and the sheets under me are saturated with sweat. I stare at the bedroom ceiling and try to tell myself that it's all over, that Vietnam is behind me. In spite of my best efforts, a single word keeps screaming inside my head:

Why?

There are hours left until daybreak. The sun is half a lifetime away. In a moment, when the tears stop, I will climb out of bed, head downstairs for a drink, and try, once more, to figure out where it all began.

5

"EIGHT MILES HIGH":
THE COUNTERCULTURE

The lessons of the student movement and the new left were not to be contained within domestic politics and foreign affairs. Activists, young people, and even some older Americans began to see the implications for new and expanded thinking in areas beyond the political—on cultural questions and the way people lived life itself. And, equally important, these cultural and social endeavors would have an impact on society and influence the political process. The transformation of American life was to be felt everywhere: politics, culture, personal life.

In the world of the arts, individuals began to sense their role in this evolving transformation. Art, they came to see, should not only reflect the changing political realities, it should influence them. In fact, all these efforts came to be seen as parts of a whole; politics, art, and personal life were all components of an interactive movement aimed at transforming the way people lived. Art was politics. This was not like the 1930s, when artists sought to aid in the radical transformation of the working class. Artists had always believed that their work could tap the deepest recess of the human unconscious and touch lives profoundly. The artists of the counterculture set out to make this understanding explicit, both to capture the spirit and to further the cause—and in the process to express the joy of it all.

The lines between fact and fiction blurred in many instances, as did those between audience and performer. Insight as well as analysis provided meaning, form as well as content. For many, rock music

275

provided a perfect example of the melding of these themes. Derived from the youth culture of the 1950s, nothing in the 1960s seemed more clearly to separate the young from the old. Part romantic escape, part physical reaction, and part cultural anthem, rock music served as the steady underbeat of much of the political activity of the times. Lyrics often embodied direct meaning, but just as often the music carried the sentiment as much as the words. Rock 'n' roll became, for John Sinclair, "a weapon of cultural revolution."

Other art forms also responded. Fiction, theatre, dance, and the visual arts took up the vision and sensibility of the age, expressing in their individual forms the new sense of both political rebellion and exploration of the unconscious. From poetry to plays, novels to films, art forms began to incorporate, represent, and then attempt to further the transformation already underway. Unlike past eras of political art, however, these efforts rarely came with a political agenda or cultural position attached. Like the music, the message was either understood implicitly or there was no point in explaining it. "I'll tell you about the magic and it'll free your soul," sang the Lovin' Spoonful, "but it's like trying to tell a stranger about rock 'n' roll."

Just as the lines between art and politics blurred, so, too, did the lines between political and social movements. Again, these activities were perceived to be parts of a greater whole. If social change was the goal, then people's personal lives would have to change as well. First in Northern California and then elsewhere, young people began to construct living arrangements on a new basis. The hippie movement developed a more communitarian and antimaterial approach to living. Combining innocence and naiveté with a utopian vision, young people in the Haight-Ashbury district of San Francisco sought to live more integrated, more cooperative lives. Groups such as the Diggers carried out these ideals. Free food, free clinics, free lodging, free rock concerts emerged as counterculture institutions.

And so did drugs. Unlike the more recent notion of drugs as a means of escape from reality, the drug culture that developed in the 1960s believed that drugs—particularly marijuana and LSD—would provide deeper insights into reality and human existence. Drugs might tap into the unconscious, offer hallucinatory visions of greater truths, or allow the users to see themselves more fully. Drugs could break down barriers, free inhibitions, further human interaction. Public events like the Human Be-In in San Francisco's Golden Gate Park offered a collective experience for large numbers of people seeking to be part of this new reality.

When the drug culture reared its uglier side, particularly with the appearance of violence and organized crime in Haight-Ashbury, hippies sought to transpose their communitarian ideals to new contexts. Rural and urban communes provided smaller structures in which groups of individuals could still build their lives around cooperative endeavors.

If one movement embodies the interconnections among the political, cultural and social elements of the era, it was the Youth International Party, or Yippies. Founded by Abbie Hoffman and Jerry Rubin, the Yippies sought to live out all the components of the counterculture. The combination of politics and theatre was well demonstrated when Yippies dumped hundreds of one-dollar bills from the visitor's gallery of the New York Stock Exchange. Stockbrokers abandoned the ticker tape to scurry after the bills, briefly halting the Exchange's activity and presenting a striking depiction of the material basis of contemporary American life. Yippie activities at the Chicago Democratic Convention of 1968—nominating an actual pig for president and mock-threatening to dump LSD into the water supply of the city—similarly reflected their approach of combining political action and street theatre (see chapter 7).

In recent times, the pieces that created the whole that was the counterculture have been scattered in the popular imagination. One element, the music of the rock band The Grateful Dead, continues to draw young people more than twenty-five years after the Haight-Ashbury summer in which the Dead emerged. Hippies, however, have been stereotyped into ridiculousness, becoming objects of disdain. Some of the works of art, film, and literature that emerged are now narrowly evaluated solely within the context of their literary genres, disconnected from the elements that bound the various movements together.

In retrospect, the counterculture was naive, radical, and utopian, insightful and self-conscious, and linked deeply to other more explicitly political elements of sixties life. Its impact, like that of all art and social movements, has been varied. It produced some works of art worthy of praise and some worthy of dismissal. Its emphasis on the natural, on ecology and conservation, and on finding personal fulfillment in a materially based culture speak to deeply rooted concerns about American life. Other aspects reflect youthful self-indulgence more than revolutionary transformation. But beneath it all was the notion that how one lived one's life and the power of art in the world were as crucial to an emerging social transformation as any political activity—and, more important, that they were all one.

A LITERATURE OF THE COUNTERCULTURE

The literary forms that emerged with the counterculture embodied the techniques of impressionism, personal exploration, and random insight. Some older authors whose work had been neglected in the 1950s—such as Joseph Heller and Kurt Vonnegut, Jr.—found new audiences with their sardonic view of American life. Younger authors began to explore new forms, often hailed as experimental or criticized as self-indulgent.

Trout Fishing in America

RICHARD BRAUTIGAN

San Francisco poet and novelist Richard Brautigan was one of the first writers to emerge from the heart of the counterculture. His Trout Fishing in America, *published in 1967, brief sections of which are reprinted here, confused readers desiring a direct narrative, but appealed to an audience looking for seriousness in frivolity and insight in the occasional aside.*

THE COVER FOR TROUT FISHING IN AMERICA

The cover for *Trout Fishing in America* is a photograph taken late in the afternoon, a photograph of the Benjamin Franklin statue in San Francisco's Washington Square.

Born 1706—Died 1790, Benjamin Franklin stands on a pedestal that looks like a house containing stone furniture. He holds some papers in one hand and his hat in the other.

Then the statue speaks, saying in marble:

PRESENTED BY
H.D. COGSWELL
TO OUR
BOYS AND GIRLS
WHO WILL SOON
TAKE OUR PLACES
AND PASS ON.

Around the base of the statue are four words facing the directions of this world, to the east WELCOME, to the west WELCOME, to the north WELCOME, to the south WELCOME. Just behind the statue are three poplar trees, almost leafless except for the top branches. The statue stands in front of the middle tree. All around the grass is wet from the rains of early February.

In the background is a tall cypress tree, almost dark like a room. Adlai Stevenson spoke under the tree in 1956, before a crowd of 40,000 people.

There is a tall church across the street from the statue with crosses, steeples, bells and a vast door that looks like a huge mousehole, perhaps from a Tom and Jerry cartoon, and written above the door is "Per L'Universo."

Around five o'clock in the afternoon of my cover for *Trout Fishing in America,* people gather in the park across the street from the church and they are hungry.

It's sandwich time for the poor.

But they cannot cross the street until the signal is given. Then they all run across the street to the church and get their sandwiches that are wrapped in newspaper. They go back to the park and unwrap the newspaper and see what their sandwiches are all about.

A friend of mine unwrapped his sandwich one afternoon and looked inside to find just a leaf of spinach. That was all.

Was it Kafka who learned about America by reading the autobiography of Benjamin Franklin . . .

Kafka who said, "I like the Americans because they are healthy and optimistic."

KNOCK ON WOOD (PART ONE)

As a child when did I first hear about trout fishing in America? From whom? I guess it was a stepfather of mine.

Summer of 1942.

The old drunk told me about trout fishing. When he could talk, he had a way of describing trout as if they were a precious and intelligent metal.

Silver is not a good adjective to describe what I felt when he told me about trout fishing.

I'd like to get it right.

Maybe trout steel. Steel made from trout. The clear snow-filled river acting as foundry and heat.

Imagine Pittsburgh.

A steel that comes from trout, used to make buildings, trains and tunnels.

The Andrew Carnegie of Trout!

The Reply of Trout Fishing in America:

I remember with particular amusement, people with three-cornered hats fishing in the dawn.

KNOCK ON WOOD (PART TWO)

One spring afternoon as a child in the strange town of Portland, I walked down to a different street corner, and saw a row of old houses, huddled together like seals on a rock. Then there was a long field that came sloping down off a hill. The field was covered with green grass and bushes. On top of the hill there was a grove of tall, dark trees. At a distance I saw a waterfall come pouring down off the hill. It was long and white and I could almost feel its cold spray.

There must be a creek there, I thought, and it probably has trout in it.

Trout.

At last an opportunity to go trout fishing, to catch my first trout, to behold Pittsburgh.

It was growing dark. I didn't have time to go and look at the creek. I walked home past the glass whiskers of the houses, reflecting the downward rushing waterfalls of night.

The next day I would go trout fishing for the first time. I would get up early and eat my breakfast and go. I had heard that it was better to go trout fishing early in the morning. The trout were better for it. They had something extra in the morning. I went home to prepare for trout fishing in America. I didn't have any fishing tackle, so I had to fall back on corny fishing tackle.

Like a joke.

Why did the chicken cross the road?

I bent a pin and tied it onto a piece of white string.

And slept.

The next morning I got up early and ate my breakfast. I took a slice of white bread to use for bait. I planned on making doughballs from the soft center of the bread and putting them on my vaude-villean hook.

I left the place and walked down to the different street corner. How beautiful the field looked and the creek that came pouring down in a waterfall off the hill.

But as I got closer to the creek I could see that something was wrong. The creek did not act right. There was a strangeness to it. There was a thing about its motion that was wrong. Finally I got close enough to see what the trouble was.

The waterfall was just a flight of white wooden stairs leading up to a house in the trees.

I stood there for a long time, looking up and looking down, following the stairs with my eyes, having trouble believing.

Then I knocked on my creek and heard the sound of wood.

I ended up by being my own trout and eating the slice of bread myself.

The Reply of Trout Fishing in America:

There was nothing I could do. I couldn't change a flight of stairs into a creek. The boy walked back to where he came from. The same thing once happened to me. I remember mistaking an old woman for a trout stream in Vermont, and I had to beg her pardon.

"Excuse me," I said. "I thought you were a trout stream."

"I'm not," she said. . . .

A WALDON POND FOR WINOS

The autumn carried along with it, like the roller coaster of a flesh-eating plant, port wine and the people who drank that dark sweet wine, people long since gone, except for me.

Always wary of the police, we drank in the safest place we could find, the park across from the church.

There were three poplar trees in the middle of the park and there was a statue of Benjamin Franklin in front of the trees. We sat there and drank port.

At home my wife was pregnant.

I would call on the telephone after I finished work and say, "I won't be home for a little while. I'm going to have a drink with some friends."

The three of us huddled in the park, talking. They were both broken-down artists from New Orleans where they had drawn pictures of tourists in Pirate's Alley.

Now in San Francisco, with the cold autumn wind upon them, they had decided that the future held only two directions: They were either going to open up a flea circus or commit themselves to an insane asylum.

So they talked about it while they drank wine.

They talked about how to make little clothes for fleas by pasting pieces of colored paper on their backs.

They said the way that you trained fleas was to make them dependent upon you for their food. This was done by letting them feed off you at an appointed hour.

They talked about making little flea wheelbarrows and pool tables and bicycles.

They would charge fifty-cents admission for their flea circus. The business was certain to have a future to it. Perhaps they would even get on the Ed Sullivan Show.

They of course did not have their fleas yet, but they could easily be obtained from a white cat.

Then they decided that the fleas that lived on Siamese cats would probably be more intelligent than the fleas that lived on just ordinary alley cats. It only made sense that drinking intelligent blood would make intelligent fleas.

And so it went on until it was exhausted and we went and bought another fifth of port wine and returned to the trees and Benjamin Franklin.

Now it was close to sunset and the earth was beginning to cool off in the correct manner of eternity and office girls were returning like penguins from Montgomery Street. They looked at us hurriedly and mentally registered: winos.

Then the two artists talked about committing themselves to an insane asylum for the winter. They talked about how warm it would be in the insane asylum, with television, clean sheets on soft beds, hamburger gravy over mashed potatoes, a dance once a week with the lady kooks, clean clothes, a locked razor and lovely young student nurses.

Ah, yes, there was a future in the insane asylum. No winter spent there could be a total loss.

The Glass Mountain

DONALD BARTHELME

Donald Barthelme had been writing experimental short stories and novels throughout the 1960s. Possessing a more established literary reputation than Brautigan, Barthelme's stories appeared most frequently in The New Yorker, *as well as in* Esquire, Harper's, *and* The Paris Review. *"The Glass Mountain," from 1970, offers a style different from that of Brautigan, but shares the random, impressionistic approach of much of sixties writing.*

1. I was trying to climb the glass mountain.
2. The glass mountain stands at the corner of Thirteenth Street and Eighth Avenue.
3. I had attained the lower slope.
4. People were looking up at me.
5. I was new in the neighborhood.
6. Nevertheless I had acquaintances.
7. I had strapped climbing irons to my feet and each hand grasped a sturdy plumber's friend.
8. I was 200 feet up.
9. The wind was bitter.
10. My acquaintances had gathered at the bottom of the mountain to offer encouragement.
11. "Shithead."
12. "Asshole."
13. Everyone in the city knows about the glass mountain.
14. People who live here tell stories about it.
15. It is pointed out to visitors.
16. Touching the side of the mountain, one feels coolness.
17. Peering into the mountain, one sees sparkling blue-white depths.
18. The mountain towers over that part of Eighth Avenue like some splendid, immense office building.

19. The top of the mountain vanishes into the clouds, or on cloudless days, into the sun.
20. I unstuck the righthand plumber's friend leaving the lefthand one in place.
21. Then I stretched out and reattached the righthand one a little higher up, after which I inched my legs into new positions.
22. The gain was minimal, not an arm's length.
23. My acquaintances continued to comment.
24. "Dumb motherfucker."
25. I was new in the neighborhood.
26. In the streets were many people with disturbed eyes.
27. Look for yourself.
28. In the streets were hundreds of young people shooting up in doorways, behind parked cars.
29. Older people walked dogs.
30. The sidewalks were full of dogshit in brilliant colors: ocher, umber, Mars yellow, sienna, viridian, ivory black, rose madder.
31. And someone had been apprehended cutting down trees, a row of elms broken-backed among the VWs and Valiants.
32. Done with a power saw, beyond a doubt.
33. I was new in the neighborhood yet I had accumulated acquaintances.
34. My acquaintances passed a brown bottle from hand to hand.
35. "Better than a kick in the crotch."
36. "Better than a poke in the eye with a sharp stick."
37. "Better than a slap in the belly with a wet fish."
38. "Better than a thump on the back with a stone."
39. "Won't he make a splash when he falls, now?"
40. "I hope to be here to see it. Dip my handkerchief in the blood."
41. "Fart-faced fool."
42. I unstuck the lefthand plumber's friend leaving the righthand one in place.
43. And reached out.
44. To climb the glass mountain, one first requires a good reason.
45. No one has ever climbed the mountain on behalf of science, or in search of celebrity, or because the mountain was a challenge.
46. Those are not good reasons.
47. But good reasons exist.
48. At the top of the mountain there is a castle of pure gold, and in a room in the castle tower sits . . .
49. My acquaintances were shouting at me.
50. "Ten bucks you bust your ass in the next four minutes!"

51. . . . a beautiful enchanted symbol.
52. I unstuck the righthand plumber's friend leaving the lefthand one in place.
53. And reached out.
54. It was cold there at 206 feet and when I looked down I was not encouraged.
55. A heap of corpses both of horses and riders ringed the bottom of the mountain, many dying men groaning there.
56. "A weakening of the libidinous interest in reality has recently come to a close." (Anton Ehrenzweig)
57. A few questions thronged into my mind.
58. Does one climb a glass mountain, at considerable personal discomfort, simply to disenchant a symbol?
59. Do today's stronger egos still *need* symbols?
60. I decided that the answer to these questions was "yes."
61. Otherwise what was I doing there, 206 feet above the power-sawed elms, whose white meat I could see from my height?
62. The best way to fail to climb the mountain is to be a knight in full armor—one whose horse's hoofs strike fiery sparks from the sides of the mountain.
63. The following-named knights had failed to climb the mountain and were groaning in the heap: Sir Giles Guilford, Sir Henry Lovell, Sir Albert Denny, Sir Nicholas Vaux, Sir Patrick Grifford, Sir Gisbourne Gower, Sir Thomas Grey, Sir Peter Coleville, Sir John Blunt, Sir Richard Vernon, Sir Walter Willoughby, Sir Stephen Spear, Sir Roger Faulconbridge, Sir Clarence Vaughan, Sir Hubert Ratcliffe, Sir James Tyrrel, Sir Walter Herbert, Sir Robert Brakenbury, Sir Lionel Beaufort, and many others.
64. My acquaintances moved among the fallen knights.
65. My acquaintances moved among the fallen knights, collecting rings, wallets, pocket watches, ladies' favors.
66. "Calm reigns in the country, thanks to the confident wisdom of everyone." (M. Pompidou)
67. The golden castle is guarded by a lean-headed eagle with blazing rubies for eyes.
68. I unstuck the lefthand plumber's friend, wondering if—
69. My acquaintances were prising out the gold teeth of not-yet-dead knights.
70. In the streets were people concealing their calm behind a façade of vague dread.
71. "The conventional symbol (such as the nightingale, often associated with melancholy), even though it is recognized only through agreement, is not a sign (like the traffic light) because, again, it

presumably arouses deep feelings and is regarded as possessing properties beyond what the eye alone sees." (*A Dictionary of Literary Terms*)

72. A number of nightingales with traffic lights tied to their legs flew past me.

73. A knight in pale pink armor appeared above me.

74. He sank, his armor making tiny shrieking sounds against the glass.

75. He gave me a sideways glance as he passed me.

76. He uttered the word *"Muerte"* as he passed me.

77. I unstuck the righthand plumber's friend.

78. My acquaintances were debating the question, which of them would get my apartment?

79. I reviewed the conventional means of attaining the castle.

80. The conventional means of attaining the castle are as follows: "The eagle dug its sharp claws into the tender flesh of the youth, but he bore the pain without a sound, and seized the bird's two feet with his hands. The creature in terror lifted him high up into the air and began to circle the castle. The youth held on bravely. He saw the glittering palace, which by the pale rays of the moon looked like a dim lamp; and he saw the windows and balconies of the castle tower. Drawing a small knife from his belt, he cut off both the eagle's feet. The bird rose up in the air with a yelp, and the youth dropped lightly onto a broad balcony. At the same moment a door opened, and he saw a courtyard filled with flowers and trees, and there, the beautiful enchanted princess." (*The Yellow Fairy Book*)

81. I was afraid.

82. I had forgotten the Bandaids.

83. When the eagle dug its sharp claws into my tender flesh—

84. Should I go back for the Bandaids?

85. But if I went back for the Bandaids I would have to endure the contempt of my acquaintances.

86. I resolved to proceed without the Bandaids.

87. "In some centuries, his [man's] imagination has made life an intense practice of all the lovelier energies." (John Masefield)

88. The eagle dug its sharp claws into my tender flesh.

89. But I bore the pain without a sound, and seized the bird's two feet with my hands.

90. The plumber's friends remained in place, standing at right angles to the side of the mountain.

91. The creature in terror lifted me high in the air and began to circle the castle.

92. I held on bravely.

93. I saw the glittering palace, which by the pale rays of the moon looked like a dim lamp; and I saw the windows and balconies of the castle tower.

94. Drawing a small knife from my belt, I cut off both the eagle's feet.

95. The bird rose up in the air with a yelp, and I dropped lightly onto a broad balcony.

96. At the same moment a door opened, and I saw a courtyard filled with flowers and trees, and there, the beautiful enchanted symbol.

97. I approached the symbol, with its layers of meaning, but when I touched it, it changed into only a beautiful princess.

98. I threw the beautiful princess headfirst down the mountain to my acquaintances.

99. Who could be relied upon to deal with her.

100. Nor are eagles plausible, not at all, not for a moment.

The Living Theatre

PIERRE BINER

Experimental theatre was not new to the 1960s. For decades—in locales such as Paris, New York, Vienna, Berlin, and San Francisco—theatre companies had pushed the limits of theatrical convention, in form and content. Theater had been avant-garde, political, unstructured, interactive. In the 1960s it was all of these and more.

The Living Theatre, probably the most famous dramatic company of the era, had been formed in the late 1940s by Julian Beck and Judith Malina. Still running the company in the sixties, Beck and Malina gained wide notoriety with experimental productions that attempted to incorporate the introspective vision of the counterculture. In addition, they aimed to obliterate the line between audience and actor. Paradise Now, *the company's most infamous and provocative piece, is here described by French critic Pierre Biner, from his book on* The Living Theatre.

It is said that the Living Theatre actor merely plays himself on stage. Instead of saying, as a traditional actor: "I am the embodiment of Richard III," or as a Brechtian actor: "I am Mother Courage, . . ." the actor in the Living Theatre says: "I am Julian Beck and I play Julian Beck." Even presenting oneself as an individual, however, requires maintaining oneself continually in the process of becoming. To touch with your rays other beings, you must be a sun. What the Living Theatre wants to accomplish in *Paradise Now* is a realization in each spectator that a transformation of his whole being is both possible and urgent; that he may pass from an imperfect state to lesser and lesser imperfection. . . .

Paradise Now—does any play have a more beautiful title? When the spectator enters he is handed a chart that illustrates the structure of the production—the "map" conceived by the company. It is to be read horizontally from left to right, then vertically; each horizontal "rung" is numbered, and consists of three states—a Rite, a Vision, and an Action—which represent the actual sequence of events on stage. Pertinent information relating to each rung is given on the margins of the chart. Schematically, the play begins at the foot of the chart and moves on upward. The "Action" segment of the eighth (last) rung is called the Street.

The end of the play is left open. Some critics wanted to take the play for the revolution and the paradise the play speaks of. It is not so. Even if the audience feels, when they truly enter the structure and add to its beauty by their actions, a physical and mental exaltation bordering on ecstasy, the play remains nevertheless a *didactic practicing of joy*.

The Living Theatre strives to communicate the very taste of revolution. All social orders are maintained by tacit and hypocritical agreement among their members, the relationship between performer and audience in traditional theatre being but one example among many. *Paradise Now* audiences, however, suddenly discover that they are no longer the "privileged class" to whom the play is "presented," but are needed by the actors for the very accomplishment of the play. It is not only the actors who become creators in *Paradise Now,* but, what is still more revolutionary, the spectators as well! . . .

"The purpose of the play," Judith and Julian declare, "is to lead to a state of being in which non-violent revolutionary action is possible.". . .

RUNG I

The Rite of Guerrilla Theatre. While the audience is taking their seats, the actors file silently into the theatre. Approaching people here and there, separately, they declare in tones ranging from anguished confidence to neutral objectivity, "I am not allowed to travel without a passport." Whatever the reaction, verbal or otherwise, the actor repeats the sentence without engaging in conversation. The little statement becomes more intense; the actor remains detached from the surrounding people. After about two minutes of this all the actors let out a great shout—releasing, in effect, the mute cry that has welled up within everyone during the foregoing action. (Sometimes a spectator, in touching demonstration of the need to communicate, tries to help the actor. The actor, however, refuses all dialogue, for he is bent on the task of depicting the present world, which is everything but a Paradise. To speak at this point would only deny the present frustration.) When silence is restored, the actors utter another sentence in the same manner: "I don't know how to stop the wars." There is another joint shout; then the statement becomes: "You can't live if you don't have money." The next sentence is: "I am not allowed to smoke marijuana." The last: "I am not allowed to take my clothes off." Here, instead of ending with another yell, the actor angrily undresses in the midst of the audience, taking off as much clothing as the law allows. . . .

RUNG II

The Rite of Prayer. Here the actors affirm the sanctity of everything that man's eyes look upon. They are among the audience at the end of Action I and they advance toward the audience and, touching clothing, hair, noses, etc., they proclaim the name of each accompanied by the adjective "holy."

By celebrating the holiness of all things, the company indicated the essential bond that unites all men. They say "holy," not "sacred," rejecting interference by those who would grant themselves the right to decide the sanctity of certain men and objects at the expense of others. Holiness pre-dates the enthronement of priests; it resides in the deepest being of each man and each object that compose the universe. (The Rite lasts about five minutes.). . . .

RUNG III

The Rite of Study. Seated in yoga position in a spiral formation, the actors trace improvised shapes related to the *mudras*—the hundred or so Tantric gestures of hands and fingers, each of which has a precise meaning—in the air with their arms and hands, drawing on the "energy centers" in their bodies. This ritual generates energy among its participants, which energy here impels each actor to say his lines. The individual actor thus does not know the precise moment that he will speak, for that moment depends upon his reception of the energy released by the *mudras*. The order in which the lines are spoken varies accordingly from performance to performance. . . .

The *mantras* recited here are all definitions of liberty: "To be free is to be free / of money / of hatred / of punishment / to eat / of prejudice / of violence," etc. When the energy runs out, the actors freeze in their last *mudra*. . . .

RUNG IV

The Rite of Universal Intercourse. The actors lie on the stage and caress the bodies of those nearest them while the spectators gather around. Then some divide into couples. . . . Although the couples usually consist of a man and a woman, this is not mandatory. Owing to legal strictures, they do not perform the act of love, but embrace tightly. The stage is suffused with quiet, contemplative joy. In this Rite the company strikes down the barrier of sexual taboo and seeks to demonstrate that every human body is a source of pleasure and beauty. . . .

"Sensation and pleasure are aroused in the genital organs and in the erotic chambers of the mind. Body contact without game playing. The Rite of Prayer, expression of the holiness of all things, is expanded here," as Judith and Julian put it. (All political change is illusory if the mind simply falls back in its old ruts.) Discovery and use of the body, so that feelingful physical awareness can be unified with thought, is an essential Revolutionary Voyage. . . .

RUNG V

The Rite of the Mysterious Voyage. What happens in this rite is entirely real. In the center of the circle of actors sits a subject who undergoes a struggle with demonic forces that he is allowing to enter him. The surrounding community of actors does not restrain him, but with cries and movements of heads and torsos tries to maintain him in a state of abandon, a self-willed trance. The idea is that if the community can help the subject boldly to confront and attack these forces, he will emerge from the ordeal purified. The company with their collective energy sustains and propels him in his struggle against fear and the unknown. The subject is literally out of his mind, his body wracked by convulsive movements. Some of the spectators are astonished to see the subject and the actors at the end of the trance radiant, re-charged with energy, and exhibiting joy in voice and gesture.

At the end of the voyage the subject signals to the rest of the company, physically indicating his state of being at the moment—how he feels, where he is at. . . .

RUNG VIII

The Rite of I and Thou. In a motif inspired by the Tibetan *Book of the Dead,* the actors go through the act of dying, being reborn, and forming the tree of knowledge. They speak the word "Om" and follow it with a gloomy "Rrr. . . ." inhaling as deeply as possible. The five stages in this voyage are 1) weakening; 2) feeling death seize the throat, change of breathing; 3) feeling the arrest of cell renewal by oxygen combustion, disintegration of being; 4) loss of vision (the eyes film over); 5) taking leave of the world.

When an actor nears death's door, he signals to the others the degree of his fright and his state of mind and receives their signals in return. Then couples form, the actors touch each other, the sound changes, and life is reborn in the exchange of energies. The actors leave death's door to construct the tree of knowledge. . . .

The Street. There are no archangels at the door to this Paradise. What the brain acquires through study interferes with life. (The Living Theatre preserves the vision of Paradise, but renounces the myth of Eden.) The jubilation that infects the spectators and actors at this point was most manifest in the incredible procession that followed the second performance of *Paradise Now* at Avignon. It ended at close to two in the morning. In the street, spectators surrounded the actors in a compact circle of about two hundred people. An intense bond of communication united them, despite the fact that most of them did not know each other. A humming sound rose spontaneously from the crowd, and as if propelled by an invincible force, it split into ranks and with linked arms marched the length of two long streets before breaking up in front of the Cloister.

Some of these spectators decided to embark on the quest for the Paradise, which is earthly, yet without limits. For the true Revolution is permanent and the only boundary of the voyage they would undertake is their physical departure from this earth.

ROCK AROUND THE CLOCK

The rock 'n' roll rebellion of the 1950s had faded by the early 1960s. The spontaneous combustion that marked the emergence of Elvis Presley, Buddy Holly, Jerry Lee Lewis, Chuck Berry, and Little Richard had been replaced by a blander, more packaged form of popular music. In England, however, a new music movement was beginning to simmer. When the Beatles erupted on the music scene in Britain in 1962 and in America a year later, rock 'n' roll stormed its way back not only as the music of the young, but as the rhythm behind the emerging political and social upheavals.

San Francisco Bray

RICHARD GOLDSTEIN

While the sixties rock 'n' roll revival began in England, it was not long before a new American rock scene emerged. Not surprisingly, it developed in San Francisco. Rock critic Richard Goldstein surveys the San Francisco music scene in 1965 just before its major bands—The Jefferson Airplane, Big Brother and the Holding Company, Country Joe and the Fish, and The Grateful Dead—began to receive national attention, and rock venues like The Fillmore and the Avalon Ballroom became institutions of counterculture life.

The new music from San Francisco, most of it unrecorded at this writing, is the most potentially vital in the pop world. It shoots a cleansing wave over the rigid studiousness of rock. It brings driving spontaneity to a music that is becoming increasingly conscious of form and influence rather than effort. It is a resurgence which could drown the castrati who make easy listening and devour all those one-shot wonders floating above stagnant water. . . .

Talent scouts from a dozen major record companies are now grooving with the tribes at the Fillmore and the Avalon. Hip San Francisco is being carved into bits of business turf. The Jefferson Airplane belong to RCA. The Grateful Dead has signed with Warner Brothers in an extraordinary deal which gives them complete control over material and production. Moby Grape is tinkering with Columbia. And a fistful of local talent is being wined and dined like the last available *shikse* in the promised land.

All because San Francisco is the Liverpool of the West. Not many breadmen understand the electronic rumblings from beneath the Golden Gate. But youth power still makes the pop industry move, and record executives know a fad sometimes needs no justification for success except its presence in a void. There is the feeling now, as pop shepherds watch the stars over their grazing flock, that if the San

Reprinted by permission, Richard Goldstein.

Francisco sound isn't the next Messiah, it will at least give the profits a run for their money.

"The important thing about San Francisco rock & roll," says Ralph Gleason, "is that the bands here all sing and play live, and not for recordings. You get a different sound at a dance, it's harder and more direct.". . .

San Francisco is far and away the most turned-on city in the Western world. "The cops are aware of the number of heads here," says Bill Graham who owns the Fillmore and manages the Jefferson Airplane. "The law thinks it will fade out, like North Beach: What can they do? To see a cop in the Haight . . . it's like the English invading China. Once they own it, how are they going to police it?"

With safety in numbers, the drug and rock undergrounds swim up the same stream. The psychedelic ethic—still germinating and still unspoken—runs through the musical mainstream in a still current. When Bob Weir, rhythm guitarist with the Grateful Dead, says "the whole scene is like a contact high," he is not talking metaphor. Musical ideas are passed from group to group like a joint. There is an almost visible cohesion about San Francisco rock. With a scene that is small enough to navigate and big enough to make waves, with an establishment that all but provides the electric current, no wonder San Francisco is Athens. This acropolis has been carefully, sturdily built, and it is not going to crumble because nobody wants to see ruins messing up the skyline.

Bob Weir of the Grateful Dead insists: "We're not singing psychedelic drugs, we're singing music. We're musicians, not dope fiends." He sits in the dining-room of the three-story house he shares with the group, their women, and their community. The house is one of those masterpieces of creaking, curving spaciousness the Haight is filled with. Partially because of limited funds, but mostly because of the common consciousness which almost every group here adapts as its ethos, the Grateful Dead live and work together. They are acknowledged as the best group in the Bay Area. Leader Jerry Garcia is a patron saint of the scene. Ken Kesey calls him "Captain Trips."

Together, the Grateful Dead sound like live thunder. There are no recordings of their music yet, which is probably just as well because no album could duplicate the feeling they generate in a dancehall. I have never seen them live, but I spent an evening at the Fillmore listening to tapes. The music hits hard and stays hard, like early Rolling

Stones, but distilled and concentrated. When their new album comes out, I will whip it on to my record-player and if they have left that boulder sound at some palatial studio and come out with a polished pebble, I will know they don't live together in the Haight anymore.

But right now a group called the Grateful Dead is playing live and living for an audience of anybody's kids in San Francisco. Theirs is the Bay Area sound. Nothing convoluted in the lyrics, just rock lingua franca. Not a trace of preciousness in the music; just raunchy funky chords. The big surprise about the San Francisco sound has nothing to do with electronics or some zany new camp. Musicians in this city have knocked all the civility away. They revel in the dark, grainy sound of roots. . . .

What really matters about San Francisco is what mattered about Liverpool three years ago. The underground occupies a pivotal place in the city's life. The Fillmore and the Avalon are jammed every weekend with beaded, painted faces and flowered shirts. The kids don't come from any mere bohemian quarter. Hip has passed the point where it signifies a commitment to rebellion. It has become the style of youth in the Bay Area, just as long hair and beat music were the Liverpool Look.

San Francisco is a lot like the grimy English seaport these days. In 1964, Liverpool rang with a sound that was authentically expressive and the city never tried to bury it. This is what is happening in San Francisco today. . . .

The underground is open, unencumbered and radiating. The rest of the country will get the vibrations, and they will pay for them.

Which everyone thinks is groovy. The Grateful Dead are willing to sing their twenty-minute extravaganza, "Midnight Hour," for anyone who will listen, and if people pay, so much the better. But Bob Weir insists: "If the Industry is gonna want us, they're gonna take us the way we are. Then, if the money comes in, it'll be a stone gas."

Love, Janis

JANIS JOPLIN

Janis Joplin, lead singer for Big Brother and the Holding Company, emerged as one of the most important musical figures of the San Francisco scene. Before her death from drugs in 1970, Joplin had formed her own band and gained a national reputation. These two letters, written to her family during her first days in San Francisco and at the beginning of Big Brother's success, demonstrate both the small scale of rock music as compared with its status today, and the headiness and enthusiasm that marked this period.

June 6, 1966

Mother & Dad . . .

With a great deal of trepidation, I bring the news. I'm in San Francisco. Now let me explain—when I got to Austin, I talked to Travis Rivers who gave me a spiel about my singing w/a band out here. Seems Chet Helms, old friend, now is Mr. Big in S.F. Owns 3 big working Rock & roll bands with bizarre names like Captain Beefheart & his Magic Band, Big Brother & the Holding Co. etc. Well, Big Brother et al needs a vocalist. So I called Chet to talk to him about it. He encouraged me to come out—seems the whole city had gone rock & roll (and it has!) and assured me fame & fortune. I told him I was worried about being hung up out here w/no way back & he agreed to furnish me w/a bus ticket back home if I did just come & try. So I came.

I don't really know what's happening yet. Supposed to rehearse w/ the band this afternoon, after that I guess I'll know whether I want to stay & do that for awhile. Right now my position is ambivalent—I'm glad I came, nice to see the city, a few friends, but I'm not at all sold on the idea of becoming the poor man's Cher. So I guess we'll see.

I just want to tell you that I *am* trying to keep a level head about everything & not go overboard w/enthusiasm. I'm sure you're both convinced my self-destructive streak has won out again but I'm really trying. I do plan on coming back to school—unless, I must admit, this turns into a good thing. Chet is a very important man out here now & he wanted me specifically, to sing w/this band. I haven't tried yet so I can't say what I'm going to do—so far I'm safe, well fed, and nothing has been stolen. . . .

April 1967

Dear Mother, family

Things are going so good for us & me personally I can't quite believe it! I never ever thought things could be so wonderful! Allow me to explain. First of all, the group—we're better than ever (please see enclosed review from S.F. Examiner) and working all the time. Just finished 3 weeks straight engagements, 6 nights a week, & we're booked up weekends for well over a month. And we're making a thousand or over for a weekend. For single nights we're getting from $500–$900. Not bad for a bunch of beatniks, eh? And our reputation is still going uphill. It's funny to watch—you can tell where you are by the people that are on your side. Y'know, the scene-followers, the people "with the finger on the pulse of the public." One of the merchants on Haight St. has given all of us free clothes (I got a beautiful blue leather skirt) just because 1) she really digs us & 2) she thinks we're going to make it & it'll be good publicity. Our record is enjoying a fair reception—much better than our first one which was much, much better. We made #29 in Detroit but we don't really know what's happening because we never hear from Mainstream. It's a long & involved story but we really feel like we've been used & abused by our record co & we'd like to get out of the contract but don't know whether we can. We talked to a lawyer about it & he seemed fairly negative & we can't even get ahold of our record co. to talk about it. So until further news, we're hung up. There's a slim possibility we might go to Europe & play this summer. There's a hippie boat going back and forth & rock bands get free passage if they play on the way over. And Chet, head of the Family Dog, is trying to organize dances over there & if he does, we'd have a place to work. Probably won't work but it sure would be groovy. Speaking of England, guess who was in town last week—Paul McCartney!!! (he's a Beatle). And he came to see us!!! SIGH Honest to God! He came to the Matrix & saw us & told some people that he dug us. Isn't that exciting!!!! Gawd, I was so thrilled—I still am! Imagine—Paul!!!! If it could only have been George. . . . Oh, well. I didn't get to see him anyway—we heard about it afterwards. Why, if I'd known that he was out there, I would have jumped right off the stage & made a fool of myself.

Now earlier, I spoke of how well things are going for me personally—it's really true. I'm becoming quite a celebrity among the hippies &

everyone who goes to the dances. Why, last Sunday we played a Spring
Mobilization for Peace benefit & a simply amazing thing happened. As
the boys were tuning, I walked up to the front of the stage to set up
the microphones &, as I raised the middle mike up to my mouth, the
whole audience applauded! Too much! And then as we're getting ready
to play, a girl yelled out "Janis Joplin lives!" Now you can't argue with
that, and they clapped again. Also, a rock publication named *World
Countdown* had a collage on its cover using photographs of important
personages in & about the scene & I'm in there. Also they're bringing
out a poster of me! Maybe you've read in *Time* magazine about the
personality posters. They're big, very big photographs, Jean Harlow,
Einstein, Belmondo, Dylan, & Joplin. Yes, folks, it's me wearing a se-
quined cape, thousands of strings of beads & topless. But it barely
shows because of the beads. Very dramatic photograph & I look really
beautiful!! If it wouldn't embarrass you, I'll send you one. I'm thrilled!!
I can be Haight-Ashbury's first pin-up. . . .

LoveXXX
Janis

Nothing Would Ever Be the Same

DANNY SUGERMAN

*The Los Angeles-based band The Doors may not have been, as some have
subsequently claimed, the quintessential sixties rock group. There was no
denying, however, that Doors' lead singer Jim Morrison conveyed a unique
and potent stage presence. Sexuality, introspection, power, and raw emotion
combined to create a different kind of rock experience. Rock writer Danny
Sugerman recalls his first encounter with that presence.*

Reprinted by permission, Danny Sugerman. Original source: Danny Sugerman, *Wonder-
land Avenue: Tales of Glamour and Excess,* New York: Morrow, 1989.

Nothing in my life prepared me for the arrival of Jim Morrison.

I had gotten my seat, up front, up close in front of the front row, sitting cross-legged with dozens of other members of the audience, pressed tightly together. They sat alert, as if awaiting a lecture, not a concert. They knew something I didn't. I tried to be cool. I made some room for myself and tried to fit in. . . .

Then it happened.

I heard a scream, long, pained, thick and husky: loud enough and strong enough to wake me up. In his black leather, with long brown hair and angelic features, the singer was a phantom, staggering across the stage, about to fall but somehow keeping his balance, bellowing a long-winded series of screams and grunts. The rest of the band looked unconcerned. The keyboardist's eyes were closed, his head slowly winding from side to side in time with the music. The drummer was raising his hands and drumsticks in the air and bringing them down with an exaggerated motion. The guitarist stood stone still.

The lead singer was still yelling, but slower now, in time with the music, hard grunts.

He stopped, as if regaining awareness, and looked right in our faces, held our stare as the music began to build. He dropped back, and leapt forward, throwing his face at ours, his eyes agog, terrorized, tearing at the microphone. Hands a blur, on the verge of insanity, and he screamed again, the sound of a thousand curtains torn. The audience, who were already on the edge of their seats, were bolted and locked in the Doors' current. Jim crumpled on to the stage in a lifeless heap; the music pounding. I thought he was dead, electrocuted, maybe shot.

He rose from the ground slowly and did a beautiful leap straight up, as if jettisoned. He landed easily but staggered a bit as he approached the microphone. He touched it slowly, and blinked, opened his mouth to sing, but thought of something else and closed his mouth. (Has he forgotten the words?) The music continued, repeating itself, waiting for him to enter. The audience was frozen in expectation and attention. Morrison just rode it all, letting the music build and build, blind to stares. Then just when it felt like the room would blow its roof off, he slipped the words in, closing his eyes he sang:

> When the music's over
> When the music's over, turn out the lights

It was the end. It was the end of the world as I had known it. Nothing would ever again be the same for me.

Rock and Roll Is a Weapon of Cultural Revolution

JOHN SINCLAIR

In their first American hit, in 1964, the Beatles had sung "I Want to Hold Your Hand." By 1970 The Jefferson Airplane chanted, "Got a Revolution, Got to Revolution!" In the years between, rock music became more than a form of popular culture. Individuals such as John Sinclair found in its very existence a central component of the cultural revolution. Sinclair, manager of the Detroit political rockers MC5, attempted to merge politics and music to a greater extent than most, as his 1968 article makes clear.

"The duty of the revolutionary is to make the revolution." The duty of the musician is to make the music. But there is an equation that must not be missed: MUSIC IS REVOLUTION. Rock and roll music is one of the most vital revolutionary forces in the West—it blows people all the way back to their senses and makes them feel good, like they're *alive* again in the middle of this monstrous funeral parlor of western civilization. And that's what the revolution is all about—we have to establish a situation on this planet where all people can feel good all the time. And we will not stop until that situation exists.

Rock and roll music is a weapon of cultural revolution. There are not enough musicians around today who are hip to this fact. Too many of your every-day pop stars feel that music is simply a means by which they can make a lot of money or gain a lot of cheap popularity or whatever—dollars and ego power, both of which are just a killer ruse, in fact I would have to say the killer ruse of all time. Money is the biggest trick of all, next to the so-called ego, which comes out of the same scene as money anyway. I mean the ego developed strictly as an economic function, when there got to be too many people on the planet for the planet's natural resources and there wasn't enough for everybody any more. Then people had to start separating themselves out from the tribe and see themselves as individuals, because if there ain't enough for everybody then everybody's got to try to make sure he or she has got enough, and there's always somebody else around who wants to take it away from you. . . .

Think about it. If all the kids in high schools who can't stand that shit would stop going—all of you—then where would the schools be? They have to have you there. If you aren't there they won't be able to eat—they won't have a job any more. Your parents will go crazy too. . . .

If you're living at home, start planning for what you'll be doing when you split. Get together with your people who are waiting to split and plan a scene for when you can be together. Start practicing now, on your parents' money and time. Save up your money if you get any so you can buy your supplies and equipment when you split.

Don't waste your time pissing and moaning about how shitty everything is. Start getting it together so you can change it. Everybody knows what a drag it is. You're not telling anybody anything they can use. Exchange information. Get down. And when you *have* split, get your thing together so you'll be able to have a better time than just sitting around smoking bogus dope, dropping bogus speed-filled acid, shooting smack, and listening to brainwash low-energy jams. Tripping out is a dead end and a drag. *You always come down.* If you engage yourself in a total revolutionary program of self-reliance and serving the people any way you can, you will have a guaranteed good time forever (except for when they lock you up from time to time) and will help other people get it together too.

It isn't enough just to drop out though—you have to create new forms which will enable you to sustain yourselves while you're doing your work. The commune is the life-form of the future, it is *the* revolutionary organizational life-form, and the communal relationship must be realized in everything you do. Rock and roll is the best example. That's why I said at the beginning of this rant, that MUSIC IS REVO-

LUTION, because it is immediate, total, fast-changing and on-going. Rock and roll not only is a weapon of cultural revolution, it is the *model* of the revolutionary future. At its best the music works to free people on all levels, and a rock and roll band is a working model of the post-revolutionary production unit. The members of a rock and roll family or tribe are totally interdependent and totally committed to the same end—they produce their music collectively, sharing both the responsibility and the benefits of their work equally. They work on the frontiers of modern technology to produce a new form which is strictly contemporary in all its implications. *There is no separation.* And that's what it's all about. . . .

Capitalism is obsolete—it is based on the two horrible notions of private property and competition, both of which have to go right now. And the point is, that it's time for them to go, because there's no more room for that old-time shit in the world today. People have got to get it together, not apart. People are now stuck in bullshit jobs, bullshit schools, bullshit houses, bullshit marriages, bullshit social and economic scenes, and there's no need for it anymore. Most of the jobs that presently exist are useless and anti-human, and they'll be done away with immediately once the people are in power and the machines are freed to do all the work.

Likewise most of the products of the present consumer economy—they're bullshit and will no longer exist. Eighty-seven different brands of toothpaste! Millions of junky automobiles! That's all they are—junk—that people have been hooked on by the junk pushers of capitalism. The whole thing is ridiculous! Everything has to be free or else!

It is extremely important for urban groups to organize themselves around some form of popular cultural activity like a rock and roll band, a community newspaper, guerrilla theatre groups, a health clinic, or whatever you can put together. The cultural forms will give you access to the mass media and to mass audiences of pre-revolutionary youth who are just sitting around waiting to get totally turned on. High school groups can organize around newspapers and posters and bands and present a united front in their dealings with administrators and other old creeps. . . . It's time to turn on, tune in and *take over!* Up against the ceiling, motherfucker!

To Dance

TOM ROBBINS

Rock 'n' roll shows in San Francisco and elsewhere became multimedia sensual experiences. Lights, music, incense, and dancing combined to create an experience encompassing all the senses. Dance became liberating and expressive. Novelist Tom Robbins, not yet famous for Another Roadside Attraction *and* Even Cowgirls Get the Blues, *offered this brief paean to dance in 1967.*

We, all of us, have a need to identify our bodily rhythms with those of the cosmos.

The wind in a forest of fir. The spilling of grain in the fields. The migration of bird and seed. The trek of atom and star.

That is why we dance.

Dance began as a co-ordination of motor impulses with universal energies which man only instinctively perceived. It developed into a playful Dionysian rite designed to help man get outside of himself, or rather, to get outside of the ego so that he might discover the self.

Dance is a fundamental human need. To deny that need is to become hostile, neurotic and menopausal. Everyone should dance every day. Dance at a discotheque. Dance in your living room. Dance in bed. Stick flowers in your typewriter and dance at the office. Dance at the supermarket with a smoking banana in your teeth. Dance in the streets. Dance in church. "Dance beneath a diamond sky with one hand waving free."

Shiva danced to release the countless souls of men from the snare of illusion. The Hopi danced in the desert and made rain. Muhammad Ali danced at the Houston induction center in his shorts and socks. To arrest a human being for dancing is in itself an immoral act. A law which prohibits dancing is a crime against man and a sin against God.

Reprinted by permission, Tom Robbins.

Dance. Next time you are at a light show be especially sure to
dance. So dance. Dance and if you should ever be arrested for dancing,
dance in the paddy wagon. Dance in your jail cell and dance in court.
Maybe the judge will dance with you.

> The place of the dance is within the heart.
> To dance is to love again.

Notes of Andy Warhol: His Life and Work as Death in America

DOTSON RADER

*Film became the chic visual art form of the 1960s. While movies had existed
since the turn of the century, the seriousness with which cinema was now taken
put it on an equal plane with the other visual arts. European directors gained
wide followings in America. Film schools became centers of counterculture life;
The Doors, for example, came together while studying film at UCLA. Offering
a vehicle for impression and introspection, film became an art form appropriate
for the artistic sensibilities of the era.*

*In the late 1950s Andy Warhol joined with other painters in changing
the face of American art with what became known as Pop Art—superrealistic
depictions of American culture, such as Warhol's paintings of Campbell's soup
cans. In the 1960s Warhol (temporarily) abandoned painting for filmmaking
and created The Factory, a scene of constant action and creation over which
Warhol presided. He produced a series of films that enthralled some while
enraging others. In this 1971 article, Dotson Rader describes Warhol's films
and his world.*

When I leave Andy Warhol, those occasions when I have been with him and he has been open, I go home and I have an urge to call him on the phone to find out if he is all right, if he made it home OK. I sometimes worry about him as I worry would about a child, although a bereaved child, who by some terror has been weakened irreparably and is vulnerable. You see, I hate to leave him. I want to stay the night in bed with him, to sleep with him to be certain that he makes it through to morning. For he is possessed of death. It is no longer unexpected. . . .

One night this winter Brigid Polk, Andy with one of his boys, and I had dinner together at a restaurant in the East twenties in New York. Earlier, at his Factory, he had run his tape recorder and shot pictures of us with his Polaroid camera, and as we walked to the restaurant, about fifteen blocks from the Factory, the tape machine went on recording our conversation. At the dinner table, Andy ate with one hand and with the other he held the mike awkwardly and recorded what we said. The owner of the restaurant had a pet chimpanzee, and Brigid had him bring the animal to the table. . . .

Andy through his friends invents his family, and his friends generally run to two types. The first is the beautiful, gentle, and shy young men and women who wander into his studio, into his life, or whom he finds on beaches and in the street, or who his friends bring to him much as people bring each other gifts; and these young people are decorous and watchful, unimpassioned and unimpressed, narcissistic, introverted, like passive children come to rest; and Andy likes to look at them, arrange them in a room much the way one arranges flowers or exquisite, precious objects. He is comfortable with them for he is also shy and gentle and exists half-bored on the edge of death. That is, when I see him, as when I see some of the extraordinary beauty around him, I look and I catch myself astonished that he still exists, that he survives, that he exists at all, that he is not extinguished already, for he conveys, as does beauty, enormous fragility and darkly shadowed threat of expiration. I wonder why he has not been broken yet, how he has made it through this far. Again, he is like the beautiful, silent youth around him, whose numbers always change. One arrives each day and is surprised only that they are still there.

I said he treats them like objects. That is not quite true. For he treats objects with indifference, and he is never indifferent to life. I meant he arranges them as objects, appreciates them for their being, for what they are beside their essence. *Because* they are. In his house in the East 80s in Manhattan, the walls are bare and painted white (like the walls in the Factory), and there is almost no furniture. His considerable collection of contemporary painting is arranged in casual piles on the floor. When he wants to look at a particular painting he will pull if from the pile and lean it against the wall and look at it. He is offended by the tyranny of objects, having to look at what he does not feel like looking at simply because it is there in the room, hanging against the wall. He is conscious that objects survive our death.

Beautiful young people, then, he likes to have around. He does not like them to talk much, for talk is tiring and it prevents the play of the imagination. He never is bored watching beautiful and strange people. He once said that he wanted to have a television talk show so he could present twenty or so new people a night and have them sit and be pretty or chatter and entertain, and then the next night twenty more new people. The show would be an excuse to bring people together, and to watch and direct them, much as his movies are a similar excuse for a similar pastime.

His other friends, the other type, are talkative, gossipy. Warhol loves gossip. I have seen him sit for hours listening to gossip about people he did not know and had never heard of before, interrupting occasionally with an Ah or Really? or Marvelous!, fascinated by the talk. By now it must be obvious: Warhol is a voyeur. And that is why he is, as Observer, a metaphor for the age. He is someone who has literally gone through death and is returned and is astonished by his good luck. He wants to sit and watch. He is in awe of death and life. . . .

He said he made his famous Campbell soup cans and Brillo boxes because he liked the design and colors, and because his rooms were empty and they filled the space interestingly. He also said that he filmed his movie *Lonesome Cowboys* because "everybody [his friends] could be in it together. They look nice together. They won't always be like that. They won't be together all the time. This way it doesn't change. This way it never has to change." Death is banished.

In June, 1968, a day before Bobby Kennedy was assassinated, Valerie Solanas, a twenty-eight year old failed writer, came to the Factory to try and sell Warhol a script. She had met him twice before. She was not his friend. That year Solanas had formed the Society for Cutting Up Men (S.C.U.M.), and in her manifesto she had written,

"Life in this society being at best an utter bore and no aspect of society being at all relevant to women, there remains to civic-minded, responsible, thrill-seeking females only to overthrow the government, eliminate the money system, institute complete automation, and eliminate the male sex."

Solanas came to the Factory at noon and asked to see Warhol. Paul Morrissey told her that Andy was never in until after 4 o'clock. She waited outside. When Andy arrived at 4:30 the two of them came up the elevator together. Andy told her that she looked nice, for he had never seen her in a skirt and makeup before. Inside the Factory Andy took a phone call from Vival, and while he sat on the desk speaking to her, Solanas shot him. He fell to the floor. She walked over to his body and put a pistol under his armpit against his chest and fired down into his body, the bullet ripping through his chest and stomach. And then she fled.

Andy was in the hospital for three months. His operation lasted five hours. He survived. Through sheer will he survived. Through sheer will he had become an artist, invented himself, through sheer will abandoned it, gave it up and became a movie maker. Why did he give up painting? "It took too long to do. I don't think it's interesting anymore. I think movies are the paintings for today, for everybody."

Andy Warhol was born in Philadelphia in 1928 or 1930 (he is confused as to the date, his mother does not remember), the son of Czech immigrants named Warhola. Andy's father was a coal miner and when Andy was quite young the family moved to Pittsburgh to be near the mines. Warhol attended Catholic schools and later Carnegie Institute of Technology. When Andy was ten years old his father died. Andy took a series of menial jobs, working for a time in a five-and-dime store.

Andy has always been very close to his mother, who is a devout Catholic, and she was very interested in drawing and encouraged her son to learn commercial art. In the early 1950's Warhol and his mother moved to New York City, where he began his career as a commercial artist and illustrator. He won his initial attention as the artist for the I. Miller shoe ads which appeared daily in the newspapers. Every day he drew shoes and his mother lettered the ads. During this period he illustrated a number of books, and published four of his own books, one by his mother titled *Andy Warhol's Mother's Book of Cats,* which contained her drawings of cats in heaven, sleeping, playing, having innocent sex, with Andy's lettering. Around this time he also tried to get permission to illustrate Truman Capote's first book, *Other Voices, Other Rooms,* but the publisher, never having heard of Warhol, refused.

In 1960–61, Warhol began his Pop Art paintings for the Stable Gallery in Manhattan. They made him famous overnight. The paintings were a series of comic strip characters, Superman, Dick Tracy and the like, and two major paintings of Coca-Cola bottles—major in the sense that they were the first utilization of commercial art as high art, art as parody, the isolation and elevation of advertising trivia to art.

The following year, Andy asked a woman friend what he should paint now. "What do you like best?" she asked him. "Money!" he replied. "Well, paint money then." He did a series of paintings of dollar bills. This was followed by his enormously successful Campbell soup cans and Brillo boxes, which made him internationally famous. . . .

At a party several years ago an American playwright and his male lover were confronted by a disgruntled woman, who shouted at the astonished pair, "There they are, covered in blood and sperm!" What she said could be applied generally to the underground arts in America. They are, to a large extent, dominated by the homosexual imagination, an imagination caught between the symbolic polarity of blood and sperm. Warhol, in [his] three films, has broken with that imagination in an attempt to describe the difficulty of making one's manhood in America. . . .

Warhol's young men strive to remain within human limits. Their dilemma arises when people refuse to acknowledge their integrity and equality. Their search is for a valid manhood. It is hopeless, and yet they refuse to give over to transcendence or fantasy. Their lives are gradually reduced to impotency and gesture. In a deadly, unjust nation, where the Buyers possess the earth, they are defenseless. For they have gone into the world vulnerable, without the shield of adequate or appropriate myth or legend or fantasy or belief. Vulnerable, their manhood escapes them.

HIPPIES

By the time it was discovered by the popular media, the hippie lifestyle was already in decline. To this day, hippies remain the object of parody and scorn. But at the time their lifestyle seemed a social counterpoint to the political movements under way.

What Is A Hippie?

GUY STRAIT

Guy Strait, in this 1967 essay, attempts to define what true hippies were and how their choices related to the traditional world they chose to abandon.

It is strange and disturbing to watch the straight community's angry, sometimes violent reaction to the hippies. There are many reasons for this. The principal one is appearance. The hippies dress strangely. They dress this way because they have thrown a lot of middle-class notions out the window and with them the most sensitive middle-class dogma: the neutral appearance.

The straight world is a jungle of taboos, fears, and personality games. People in that jungle prey on each other mercilessly. Therefore to survive in any jungle requires good protective coloring: the camouflage of respectable appearance. The anonymity of middle-class dress is like a flag of truce. It means (whether true or not): "I'm not one of the predators." It is in the nature of an assurance of harmlessness. Unusual or bright-colored clothing, then becomes an alarm, a danger signal to the fearful and their armed truce with the rest of mankind. They see it as a challenge. They are fearful, unsure of themselves, and fear sours into anger. It is but a step to thinking that the anger is "good." The oldest fallacy in the world is that anything that makes you angry must be bad.

The sin of the hippies is that they will not play the straight game of camouflage. Their non-participation, in effect, exposes them as another tribe, whose disregard of straight taboos of dress makes them seem to be capable of anything, and therefore a danger. That danger moreover is felt clear up to city hall, that shrine of Squaredom. Why else, I submit, does the Health Department of this city have such a tender solicitude about the living conditions of human beings at the Haight when they have ignored the conditions at Hunter's Point, the Mission and the Fillmore?

Many people cannot understand the hippies' rejection of everything that is commonly expected of the individual in regard to employment and life goals: steady lucrative employment, and the accumulation through the years of possessions and money, building (always building) security for the future. It is precisely this security hypochondria, *this checking of bank books rather than pulses,* this worrying over budgets instead of medicine cabinets, that drives the youth of today away. It is this frantic concern with money that also drives the young into the Haight-Ashbury. They have seen their parents slave for years, wasting away a lifetime to make sure that the house was paid off, that the kids got through school in order to get "good" jobs so that they could join the frantic scramble, later on. The parents' reward for this struggle is that they wind up old and tired, alienated from their children and just as often each parent from the other. They have thought so long in terms of money and possessions, that they have forgotten how to think in terms of people. So they think of "my son," and "my daughter," and talk to their children as one would speak from a great distance to a check book.

"But you've got to build a future for yourself. If you don't support yourself, no one else is going to!" The tired, lined face argues to the young. "It's a hard world." And pray tell who makes it hard, participating in the scramble for material "security?" Who makes it difficult by insisting that everyone must participate in that scramble or suffer social censure? Listen to the tone of those who lecture about the "economic realities" of life. Are they presenting impartial facts? Or do they sound like someone expounding church doctrine? It is the latter. The conventional folk of our society, the "normal" people, so called, believe in the rat race. Competition is holy. Keeping up with the Joneses is a mandate from God. The requirement of keeping up a respectable front is the principal article of faith.

It has been demonstrated over and over again throughout history by the best possible people that very little is required for happiness. It is the fight for money and possessions and the prestige they bring that sets people at odds, and *that* is what makes the world hard. We are the richest nation in the world, with the highest living standard. By our own fond illusions about prosperity we should also be the happiest. Are we? Suicides, racial violence, and the exodus of the young from comfortable homes suggest otherwise. The terrible truth is that our prosperity is the bringer of misery. We have been brainwashed by the advertising industry into being the most dissatisfied people in the world. We are told we must all be handsome or beautiful, sexually devastating, and owners of a staggering amount of recreational gadgetry or doomed to frustration. The result is that most of us are frustrated. It is exactly this that the hippie avoids like poison. He wants no part of self-defeating goals.

It is very likely that the hippie will go hungry and suffer exposure, and perhaps freak out. But he considers these far less dangerous than the kind of dehumanization society tried to wreak on him before his rebellion. He has escaped from a culture where the machine is god, and men judge each other by mechanical standards of efficiency and usefulness. He sees a madness in the constant fight to sell more washing machines, cars, toilet paper, girdles, and gadgets than the other fellow. He is equally horrified at the grim ruthlessness of the men who participate in that fight.

The Human Be-In

HELEN SWICK PERRY

Probably the most famous "happening" of the hippie era was the great Human Be-In held in San Francisco's Golden Gate Park on January 14, 1967. Helen Swick Perry remembers it as "the first coming together of the militant political movement on the Berkeley campus and the humanistic search in the Haight-Ashbury." She had been studying mental health concerns in the area, under the aegis of the University of California Medical Center. The Haight-Ashbury experience offered her the chance to study the issues faced by adolescents—concerns heightened by the problems of war, civil rights, and questions of gender identification.

The gathering was scheduled as an all-day affair, "come any time," so we began our trek at about noon from Stanyan Street on the edge of Golden Gate Park and walked into the Polo Field where the gathering was to take place—some thirty blocks from the center of the neighborhood. By that time, there was a steady stream of people walking in, winding over the hillocks and through the glades as far as the eye could see. And facing us as we moved along with this human stream of communicants was a stream of people who had been there and were winding their way home; they all seemed enchanted, happy, and smiled like a welcoming committee upon us, as they trundled along with baby carriages and picnic hampers. It would seem almost as if they had been to early morning mass, which had turned out to be a huge picnic. Their costumes were varied and imaginative, or again they wore ordinary street clothes; but each person had his sign of participation somewhere upon him—a young boy with a nasturtium stuck behind his ear, a gray-haired woman with a flower tied on her cane with a ribbon.

But it was the Polo Field itself that presented a new world. It was a medieval scene, with banners flying, bright and uncommitted; the

Reprinted by permission, Helen Swick Perry.

day was miraculous, as days can be in San Francisco at their best, and the world was new and clean and pastoral. Children wandered around in the nude. People sat on the grass with nothing to do, sometimes moving up near to the small platform where a poetry-reading might be going on, or where a band might be playing. There was no program; it was a happening. Sounds and sights turned me on, so that I had the sensation of dreaming. The air seemed heady and mystical. Dogs and children pranced around in blissful abandon, and I became aware of a phenomenon that still piques my curiosity: The dogs did not get into fights, and the children did not cry. . . .

We sat on the grass most of the afternoon without any knowledge of what particular band was playing, what poet was reading his poems. Clusters of people would move up toward the platform at the east end of the Polo Field to listen to some favorite performers and then drift back again. From time to time, the loud-speaker on the platform would be raised in volume and everyone would become quiet, while an important announcement was made. The announcements concerned lost children. "The Hell's Angels have a little girl here behind the platform and she has curly hair. She says her name is Mary. She wants to see her mother." For that particular tribe of young men on motorcycles had also appeared at the Be-In, replete with a station wagon, bearing apparently all kinds of refreshments, liquids and solids. They were well equipped for the task of serving as a clearing house for lost and strayed children, since they had walkie-talkies and were well organized. Whether their services had been sought in advance, or whether they were commandeered on the spot, no one seemed to know; in hippie language, it happened. When a call would go out for "Timmie's mother," we all smiled and watched until finally from the huge throng a young woman would be seen moving serenely toward the Hell's Angels caravan, whereupon we would all settle back to our task of being. Late in the afternoon, when we walked by the caravan, we felt as if we were looking at a heavenly nursery, that indeed the formidably dressed young men were angels; and the children looked so happy and admiring of their benefactors that it was difficult to imagine that any of the mothers were urgently needed that afternoon.

In the midst of the afternoon, out of a clear noiseless sky, a man attached to a billowy parachute that looked like a huge cloud drifted down from the sky above; no one announced it but the message seemed to go soundlessly throughout that huge crowd of tens of thousands of people; and we all looked up into the sky with a single ripple of turned heads and eyes. No airplane was heard, there was no sign of where he came from, and we all treated it as a latter-day miracle. Slowly people got to their feet in awe and wonder, mixed with absolute delight; and no one asked, "How did he do it?" or "Wasn't that a clever stunt?"—remarks that people who did not attend the Be-In asked later, for the event captivated the entire city. Those of us who were there when it happened were children again: We wanted to believe in magic that would match the day; and the man floating down on a white cloud was clearly a fairy-tale happening.

Beyond that, it was difficult to sort out what happened. It was a religious rite in which nothing particular happened. And yet it was a day that marked for me at least the end of something and the beginning of something else. There was clearly a renewal of the spirit of man, unplanned, non-political. But then what do we mean by political? For at the end of the day, as the sun was sinking into the ocean beyond the Park, someone from the loud-speaker suggested that it would be nice to leave the Park clean, to practice kitchen yoga, and that is what happened. The litter of so many people, all the sandwich wrappings, the wine bottles, and the endless paper products so characteristic of the rubbish of our decade, disappeared, so that the police reported afterwards, with a sense of wonderment, that no other group of people of such size in the memory of any living person had ever left an area so clean before, whether stadium or park. It was another miracle—and in some ways this was more disturbing to the square community than a ton of refuse would have been.

Wine, incense, food, and pot clearly intertwined that day; but none of these was necessary, as I can testify. We had not planned to stay so long, so we were without food; and we had no drugs. But it was the people that turned me on—the spectacle of people from so many walks of life, some come in curiosity, some in search of something, some in worship of the idea, some to be initiated into a new rite: It was people being together, unprogrammed, uncommitted, except to life itself and its celebration.

Afterwards, walking slowly toward the car, we did not have much to say; we did not walk back through the Park, but along the street bordering it, hoping perhaps to board a bus for the long return trip to where the car was parked. Half of the city seemed to be waiting at the bus stops, so we abandoned that attempt. Most of the people looked tired and droopy, but our eyes met in a secret delight. We had in common the sound of a different drummer.

The Digger Papers

Emerging out of the counterculture scene of Haight-Ashbury, San Francisco, the Diggers attempted to weld a political movement to the communal lifestyle of the hippies. Antimaterial and fostering cooperation and the free exchange of services, the Diggers sought to create the world they envisioned. Free clinics, meals, lodging, concerts, and other activities sprang up all over the Bay Area. "The Digger Papers" was their blueprint for a very different society.

Our state of awareness demands that we uplift our efforts from competitive game playing in the underground to the comparative roles *of free families* in *free cities*.

We must pool our resources and interact our energies to provide the freedom for our individual activities.

In each city of the world there is a loose competitive underground composed of groups whose aims overlap, conflict, and generally enervate the desired goal of autonomy. By now we all have guns, know how to use them, know our enemy, and are ready to defend. We know that we ain't gonna take no more shit. So it's about time we carried ourselves a little heavier and got down to the business of creating free cities within the urban environments of the western world.

Free Cities are composed of Free Families (e.g., in San Francisco: Diggers, Black Panthers, Provos, Mission Rebels and various revolutionist gangs and communes) who establish and maintain services that provide a base of freedom for autonomous groups to carry out their programs without having to hassle for food, printing facilities, transportation, mechanics, money, housing, working space, clothes, machinery, trucks, etc.

At this point in our revolution it is demanded that the families, communes, black organizations and gangs of every city in America co-ordinate and develop Free Cities where everything that is necessary can be obtained for free by those involved in the various activities of the individual clans.

Every brother should have what he needs to do his thing.

FREE CITY

An outline . . . a beginning.

> Each service should be performed by a tight
> gang of brothers whose commitment should enable
> them to handle an overload of work with ability
> and enthusiasm. "Tripsters" soon get bored, hopefully
> before they cause an economic strain.

FREE CITY SWITCHBOARD/INFORMATION CENTER

should coordinate all services, activities, and aid and direct assistance where it is most needed. Also provide a reference point for legal aid, housing, machinery, etc.; act as a mailing address for dislocated groups or individuals and guide random energies where they are most needed. (The work load usually prevents or should prevent the handling of messages from parents to their runaway children . . . that should be left up to the churches of the community.)

FREE FOOD STORAGE AND DISTRIBUTION CENTER

should hit every available source of free food—produce markets, farmers markets, meat packing plants, farms, dairies, sheep and cattle ranches, agricultural colleges, and giant institutions (for the uneaten vats of food)—and fill up their trucks with the surplus by begging, borrowing, stealing, forming liaisons and communications with delivery drivers for the left-overs from their routes . . . best method is to work in two shifts: morning group picks up the foodstuffs and the afternoon shift delivers it to the list of Free Families and the poor peoples of the ghettoes, everyday, hard work.

This gang should help people pool their welfare food stamps and get their old ladies or a group to open a free restaurant for people on the move and those who live on the streets. Giant scores should be stored in a garage-type warehouse equipped with freezers and its whereabouts known only to the Free Food Gang. This group should also set up and provide help for canning, preserving, bread baking, and feasts and anything and everything else that has to do with food.

FREE CITY GARAGE AND MECHANICS

to repair and maintain all vehicles used in the various services, the responsibility for the necessary tools and parts needed in their work is entirely theirs and usually available by maintaining friendly relations with junkyards, giant automotive schools, and generally scrounging around those areas where auto equipment is easily obtained. The garage should be large enough and free of tripsters who only create more work for the earnest mechanics.

FREE CITY BANK AND TREASURY

this group should be responsible for raising money, making free money, paying rents, for gasoline, and any other necessary expenses of the Free City Families. They should also organize and create small rackets (cookie sales, etc.) for the poor kids of the ghettoes and aid in the repair and maintenence of the machinery required in the performance of the various services.

FREE CITY LEGAL ASSISTANCE

high style, hard nosed, top class lawyers who are willing to defend the rights of the Free City and its services . . . no honky, liberal bleeding heart, guilt-ridden advocates of justice, but first class case-winners . . . turn on the best lawyers who can set up air-tight receivership for

free money and property, and beat down the police harassment and
brutality of your areas.

FREE CITY HOUSING AND WORK SPACE

rent or work deals with the urban gov't to take over spaces that have
been abandoned for use as carpentry shops, garages, theatres, etc.,
rent whole houses, but don't let them turn into crash pads. Set up
hotels for new arrivals or transients by working out deals with small
hotel owners for free rooms in exchange for light house-work, porter
duties, etc. Big warehouses can be worked on by environmental artists
and turned into giant free dance-fiesta-feast palaces.

A strong trio of serious business-oriented cats should develop this
liberation of space within the cities and be able to work with the
lawyers to make deals and outmaneuver urban bureaucracies and
slum landlords . . . one of the main targets for space are the churches
who are the holders of most real-estate and they should be approached
with no-bullshit hard-line.

FREE CITY STORES AND WORKSHOPS

nothing in these stores should be throwaway items . . . space should
be available for chicks to sew dresses, make pants to order, re-cut
garments to fit, etc. The management should all be life-actors capable
of turning bullshitters into mud. Important that these places are first
class environments with no trace of salvation army/st. vinnie de paul
charity rot. Everything groovy. Everything with style . . . must be first
class. *It's all free because it's yours!*

FREE MEDICAL THING

should be established in all poverty areas and run by private physicians
and free from any bureaucratic support. The Free City Bank should
try to cover the expenses, and pharmaceutical houses should be hit
for medical supplies, etc. Important that the doctors are *brothers* and
do not ask to be salaried or are not out to make careers for themselves

(witness Dr. David Smith of the Hippie Free Clinic in San Francisco who is far from a brother . . . very far).

FREE CITY HOSPITAL

should be a house converted into bed space and preferably with a garden and used for convalescence and people whose funds have been blown or who have just been released from a state institution and who need the comfort and solace of their people rather than the cold alienated walls of an urban institution.

FREE CITY ENVIRONMENTAL AND DESIGN GANG

gangs of artists from universities and art institutes should be turned on and helped in attacking the dank squalor of the slums and most of the Free City Family dwellings . . . paint landscapes on the sides of tenements . . . fiberglass stairwells . . . make crazy. Tight groups of good painters, sculptors, designers who comfortably construct environments for the community. Materials and equipment can be hustled from university projects and manufacturers, etc.

FREE CITY SCHOOLS

schools designed and run by different groups according to the consciousness of their Free Families (e.g., Black Man's Free School, Anarchist's Creative Arts School, etc.). The schools should utilize the space liberated for them by the Free City Space Gang.

FREE CITY NEWS AND COMMUNICATION COMPANY

providers of a daily newspaper, monthly magazine, free Gestetner and printing of notices for other groups and any special bulletins and

propaganda for the various families of the Free City. The machinery
should be kept in top condition and supplied by any of the various
services. Paper can be scavenged at large mills and cut down to proper
working size.

FREE CITY EVENTS ... FESTIVAL PLANNING COMMITTEES

usually involves several Families interacting to sponsor tours for the
kids ... Balls, Happenings, Theatre, Dance, and spontaneous experiments in joy ... Park Events usually are best set up by hiring a 20-
foot flat-bed truck for the rock band to use as a stage and to transport
their equipment; people should be advised by leaflets to bring food
to exchange with their neighbors; banners, props, balloons, kites, etc.
should be handled by a committee; an electrician should be around
to run the generator and make sure that the P.A. systems work; hard
work made easy by giving responsible people the tough jobs.

CO-OPERATIVE FARMS AND CAMPSITES

the farms should be run by experienced hands and the Free Land
settled on by cottage industrial people who will send their wares into
the Free City. The farms must produce vital food for the families ...
some free land that is no good for farming should be used as campsites
and/or cabin areas for citizens who are in need of country leisure,
as well as kids who could use a summer in the woods.

SCAVENGER CORPS AND TRANSPORT GANG

is responsible for garbage collection and the picking up and delivery
of items to the various services, as well as liberating anything they
think useful for one project or an other. They are to be responsible
for the truck fleet and especially aware of the economic strain if trucks
are mis-used by tripsters.

FREE CITY TINKERS AND GUNSMITHS, ETC.

will repair and keep things going in the houses . . . experienced repair men of all sorts, electricians, and carpenters. They should maintain a warehouse or working space for their outfit.

FREE CITY RADIO, TV AND COMPUTER STATIONS

demand Free time on radio and TV stations; demand a Free City frequency to set up your own stations; rent computers to call the punches for the revolution or use them in any constructive way possible.

FREE CITY MUSIC

Free Music
Where is the place that your music comes from
do you know
What determines the rest between phrases
The Interval that grows from the cluster
of sounds around it
Hanging behind the beat
Clipping the front of it
That's the gift
The thing that blows through a body responds to spirit and a mind that
doesn't lock itself
It's that thing
We're all made of, forget about, and then try to grab again
That thing that's all there and all free
The fretless infinite string banjo has invented new means of music which it
must buy from itself to sing

YIPPIES

The union of sixties politics and the counterculture attitudes found its fullest expression in the Youth International Party, or Yippies, founded by Jerry Rubin and Abbie Hoffman.

Yippie Manifesto

The combination of political confrontation, guerrilla theatre, and thumb-nosing attitudes is expressed in this 1968 Yippie statement of principles.

Come into the streets on Nov. 5, election day. Vote with your feet. Rise up and abandon the creeping meatball! Demand the bars be open. Make music and dance at every red light. A festival of life in the streets and parks throughout the world. The American election represents death, and we are alive.

Come all you rebels, youth spirits, rock minstrels, bomb throwers, bank robbers, peacock freaks, toe worshippers, poets, street folk, liberated women, professors and body snatchers: it is election day and we are everywhere.

Don't vote in a jackass-elephant-cracker circus. Let's vote for ourselves. Me for President. We are the revolution. We will strike and boycott the election and create our own reality.

Can you dig it: in every metropolis and hamlet of America boycotts, strikes, sit-ins, pickets, lie-ins, pray-ins, feel-ins, piss-ins at the polling places.

Nobody goes to work. Nobody goes to school. Nobody votes. Everyone becomes a life actor of the street doing his thing, making the revolution by freeing himself and fucking up the system.

Ministers dragged away from polling places. Free chicken and ice cream in the streets. Thousands of kazoos, drums, tambourines, triangles, pots and pans, trumpets, street fairs, firecrackers—a symphony of life on a day of death. LSD in the drinking water.

Let's parade in the thousands to the places where the votes are counted and let murderous racists feel our power.

Force the National Guard to protect every polling place in the country. Brush your teeth in the streets. Organize a sack race. Join the rifle club of your choice. Freak out the pigs with exhibitions of snake dancing and karate at the nearest pig pen.

Release a Black Panther in the Justice Department. Hold motorcycle races a hundred yards from the polling places. Fly an American flag out of every house so confused voters can't find the polling places. Wear costumes. Take a burning draft card to Spiro Agnew.

Stall for hours in the polling places trying to decide between Nixon and Humphrey and Wallace. Take your clothes off. Put wall posters up all over the city. Hold block parties. Release hundreds of greased pigs in pig uniforms downtown.

Check it out in Europe and throughout the world thousands of students will march on the USA embassies demanding to vote in the election cause Uncle Pig controls the world. No domination without representation.

Let's make 2–300 Chicago's on election day.

On election day let's pay tribute to rioters, anarchists, Commies, runaways, draft dodgers, acid freaks, snipers, beatniks, deserters, Chinese spies. Let's exorcise all politicians, generals, publishers, businessmen, Popes, American Legion, AMA, FBI, narcos, informers.

And then on Inauguration Day Jan. 20 we will bring our revolutionary theater to Washington to inaugurate Pigasus, our pig, the only honest candidate, and turn the White House into a crash pad. They will have to put Nixon's hand on the bible in a glass cage.

Begin now: resist oppression as you feel it. Organize and begin the word of mouth communication that is the basis of all conspiracies. . . .

Every man a revolution! Every small group a revolutionary center! We will be together on election day. Yippie!!!

Do It

JERRY RUBIN

For Yippies, democracy and theatre were in the streets. Jerry Rubin describes several Yippie actions, including their demonstration at the New York Stock Exchange and their call to students across America.

The secret to the yippie myth is that it's nonsense. Its basic informational statement is a blank piece of paper.

The left immediately attacked us as apolitical, irrational, acidhead freeks who were channeling the "political rebellion of youth" into dope, rock music and be-ins. The hippies saw us as Marxists in psychedelic clothes using dope, rock music and be-ins to radicalize youth politically at the end of a policeman's club.

The hippies see us as politicos and the politicos see us as hippies. Only the right wing sees us for what we actually are.

The slogan of the yippies is: *"Rise up and abandon the creeping meatball!"* The straight press thought that *"creeping meatball"* meant Lyndon Baines Johnson and that we wanted to throw him out of office.

We just laughed, because we love LBJ. LBJ was our leader, founder, guru. Where would we be without LBJ?

Everybody has his own creeping meatball—grades, debts, pimples. Yippies are a participatory movement. There are no ideological requirements to be a yippie. Write your own slogan. Protest your own issue. Each man his own yippie.

All you have to do to be a yippie is to be a yippie.

Yippie is just an excuse to rebel.

* * *

The Stock Exchange official looks worried. He says to us, "You can't see the Stock Exchange."

We're aghast. "Why not?" we ask.

"Because you're hippies and you've come to demonstrate."

"Hippies?" Abbie shouts, outraged at the very suggestion. "We're Jews and we've come to see the stock market."

VISION: *The next day's headlines:*
NEW YORK STOCK MARKET BARS JEWS.

We've thrown the official a verbal karate punch. He relents.

The stock market comes to a complete standstill at our entrance at the top of the balcony. The thousands of brokers stop playing Monopoly and applaud us. What a crazy sight for them—longhaired hippies staring down at them.

We throw dollar bills over the ledge. Floating currency fills the air. Like wild animals, the stockbrokers climb all over each other to grab the money.

"This is what it's all about, real live money!!! Real dollar bills! People are starving in Biafra!" we shout.

We introduce a little reality into their fantasy lives.

While throwing the money we spot the cops coming. The cops grab us and throw us off the ledge and into the elevators. The stockbrokers below loudly boo the pigs.

We find ourselves in front of the stock market at high noon. The strangest creeps you ever saw are walking around us: people with short hair, long ties, business suits and brief cases.

They're so serious.

We start dancing "Ring Around the Rosey" in front of the Stock Exchange.

And then we begin burning the things they worship: dollar bills!

Straight people start yelling: "Don't! Don't do that!"

One man rushes to get a burning $5 bill out of Abbie's hand, but it's too late. The money is *poof!*

A crowd assembles; emotions are high. The police come to break it up. We split into the subway.

Three weeks later *The New York Times* reports: "The New York Stock Exchange last night installed bullet-proof glass panels and a metal grillwork ceiling on its visitors' gallery for what an exchange spokesman said were 'reasons of security.'

"Last August 24 a dozen or so hippies threw dollar bills from the gallery—a display many exchange members do not want to see repeated."

* * *

School addicts people to the heroin of middle-class life: busy work for grades (money) stored in your records (banks) for the future (death). We become replaceable parts for corporate Amerika!

School offers us cheap victories—grades, degrees—in exchange for our souls. We're actually supposed to be happy when we get a better grade than somebody else! We're taught to compete and to get our happiness from the unhappiness of others.

For us education is the creation of a free society. Anyone who wants to teach should be allowed to "teach." Anybody who wants to learn should be allowed to "learn." There is no difference between teachers and students, because we teach and learn from each other!

The professors and the students are the dropouts—people who have dropped out of Life. The dropouts from school are people who have dropped into Living. Our generation is making history in the streets, so why waste our lives in plastic classrooms?

High school students are the largest oppressed minority in Amerika.

We know what *freedom is* when we hear the bell dismissing school. *"School's out, I'm free at last!"*

Teachers know that unless they control our toilet training, we'd never stay in class. You gotta raise your hand to get permission to go take a shit. The bathrooms are the only liberated areas in school.

DROP OUT!

Why stay in school? To get a degree? *Print your own!* Can you smoke a diploma?

We are going to invade the schools and free our brothers who are prisoners. We will burn the buildings and the books. We will throw pies in the faces of our professors.

We will give brooms and pails to the administrators so they can be useful and sweep the place up. Fuck bureaucrats, especially the "nice" Deans of Men who put one hand around our shoulders while the other hand gropes for our pants. We'll take all the records, grades, administrative shit and flush it down the toilet.

The same people who control the universities own the major capitalist corporations, carry out the wars, fuck over black people, run the police forces and eat money and flesh for breakfast. They are absentee dictators who make rules but don't live under them.

Universities are feudal autocracies.

Professors are house niggers and students are field niggers.

Demonstrations on campuses aren't "demonstrations"—they're jail breaks. Slave revolts.

The war on the campuses is similar to the war in Vietnam: a guerrilla people's war.

By closing down 100 universities in one day, we, the peasants, can level the most powerful blow possible against the pigs who run Amerikan society.

We'll force the President of the United States to come on his hands and knees to the conference table.

We're using the campus as a launching pad to foment revolution everywhere.

Ronnie Reagan, baby, you're right!

COMMUNES

The Alternative

WILLIAM HEDGEPATH

By the late sixties many of the grander utopian visions of the counterculture had given way to smaller dreams. William Hedgepath, in the introduction to his 1970 study of communal life in America, describes the path that took many out of places like Haight-Ashbury and into the hundreds of smaller communes that began springing up at decade's end.

They left. Not in a mass organized way or because some dark figure came to town and told them to, but rather left because they sensed some itch in the back of the teeth or in the root of the brain that put upon them each, singly, an awful awareness that wherever they had come from was no longer now the place to stay. Somehow it was just no longer home. So they up and drifted doggedly outward from the settings they had known: out of surburban ranch-style two-car-garage cottages; out of high-rise condominiums and anonymous urban rat-warrens and sensible Southern middle-class brick bungalows and grain-belt clapboard dwellings. Up and out the door now and down the path, beyond the gate and—slam—they'd gone. . . .

To whatever extent they have a shared an at least semi-coherent philosophy, it's one whose origins lay in the blossoming, and subsequent wilting, of the "flower children" phase of the hippie revolution: so carefully scrutinized, analyzed, and televised in the Haight-Ashbury district of San Francisco while it was still titillating to the public—and so diligently documented and filed away as a faintly disagreeable historical event when it began to bore.

The Haight, like most other valuable social phenomena, probably reached it's creative peak before people anywhere else were able to learn what *was* going on. What was going on prior to, say, the legendary summer of 1967, was the beginning of an intensely gentle, profoundly subversive shift in the whole system. . . .

It came to represent not merely a place but a state of mind, a different approach to the world—and eventually a full-scale testing tank for whole fresh shapes of human life and new reasons for doing things. Something wildly radical was being awakened: the senses—feeling, seeing, hearing, smelling, soaking up, "grokking." People rediscovered here the perfect wholeness of their own bodies; in the doing of which, it dawned on them for the first time, too, just how ungodly fragmented and sealed off from themselves they had always lived before. . . .

One year after 1967's "summer of love," Hashbury was acknowledged as a violent, animalized slum, awash with hard-drug pushers, old junkies, . . . and with drifting clumps of disillusioned young runaways who hadn't gotten the word before they left home that this was no longer the "love capital of the world," and who still felt obliged, therefore, to wander the streets trying sadly to generate something colorful, or at least suitably eccentric. . . .

Finally, the omniscient *New York Times* felt secure enough to hoot forth the headline "LOVE IS DEAD," over a last-word-on-the-subject sort of story which let it be known that: "The hippie movement is over—the alternative to the 'computerized society' has proved to be as unsatisfactory to its adherents as the society that gave birth to it."

So . . . with that and a few other such pronouncements, the press and the public retooled for new explorations into fresh areas of social outrage, and the Haight was allowed to continue its slow rot in relative privacy. . . .

Missing in all of the epitaphs, though—and totally overlooked— was the fact that these young people's mass readjustment to their parents' world simply didn't take place. Another, and quieter, alternative had appeared. Even while hippie stories were fading from the headlines to the back pages and then out of the public eye altogether, hip communes of every genre imaginable were silently cropping out of the earth by the hundreds. And in time, the faint word-of-mouth rumored murmurations about their whereabouts had swollen into enough of a knowledgeable whisper among alienated young folks to set them off in collective exodus once again. This time, however, the young migrants were a little less noisy, a little more sophisticated and a damn sight more serious about why they were leaving and what they were headed for.

It was not just displaced veteran hip gypsies who set forth on this second wave; now they were joined by the thousands more hippie-symps and until-just-recently straight kids who were finally sensing the *Angst* of living in official America. Each was, in his own way, either originally motivated or now propelled by some set of ineffable but strong vibrations—by a vague interplay of biological, geographical, social, historical and mystical forces. More importantly, there was a vibrant sense of something shared in the separate and uncoordinated driftings of all these individuals. As children, they had been quietly coaxed along with the blind, carrot-on-a-stick faith that someday, someday when they were older, they might be able to make sense out of things. And now here they were, and they couldn't. It was as if they'd become infected somehow *en masse* with the germ of the death of their own childhood, whose symptoms erupted in varying shades of the amorphous yearning that finally pushed them, wordless, out-wards, out the door and away. And so it was—not quite certain as to the origins of their motives or specific goals, but eyes bright with stone-serious fantasy—they left. And their leaving seemed to satisfy, for the moment at least, that unquenchable itch that had grown up within them to run way the hell off beyond the farthest highway somewhere and start their own country. . . .

It's Haight-Ashbury and New York's East Village turned loose on the land: wildly-dressed children moving now across the countryside with all their tragical intuitions in tow. The unwritten hip gospel seems every bit as demon-filled and apocalyptic as the Old Testament, and its young believers all carry that quality within them like an emblem affixed to their vital organs. They are, in varying degrees, doom-ridden, claustrophobic, paranoic, occult . . . and hopeful. They are also without guile. And guilelessly they tend to place their faith and base their hope in a few simple gut-felt profundities of grave purity: That (1) Somewhere along the evolutionary line civilization slipped up, freaked out and grew into a self-consuming, arthritic gargoyle; that (2) We've got to go "back to the land," where things are clean, and start from almost-scratch again; and that (3) In time, and with God on our side and with honorable intentions and hard work and honesty among ourselves and faith in beauty's righteousness, the whole world's eventually going to turn on, or blow up.

So there is, then, a serious, mass-level motive behind this migration—in a sense, something of a public-spirited attitude. And those communes lying out there somewhere in the fierce, snaky reaches of the wilderness are by no means seen as hideouts—cop-outs—from the world. Rather, they are outposts, testing grounds, self-experimental laboratories, starting points for whole hallucinatory metropolises: Super turn-on—a culture shaped, at last, as a physical extension of the way people really are: a wildly different pattern of social life that more rightly fits the human form.

Some of the communes that have stuck it out for more than a year or so are regarded as little cities along the hip circuit, complete with cryptic or charismatic names like Olympali, Drop City, Libre, The Hog Farm, The New Buffalo, Lama, Wheeler's Free, etc. Others—not necessarily less durable or serious-purposed—may exist as simple groupings of like-minded souls, known (if known at all) not by a name but rather by vague sets of verbal directions as to how to reach them (or at least how to get within, say, 20 square miles of where they might be—or once were) if, in fact, they haven't meanwhile upped and moved off or been chased away or else just disbanded, with their various members latching, purely at random, onto any of the 500-plus *other* communes scattered throughout the open countryside.

But along the unofficial network of communes, that stretches from New England to California (with most of them found west of the Mississippi), something well over 10,000 out-and-out hippies as well as just generally disaffected young people are either settled or still shifting from one sort of community to another. The types range from highly-transient urban crash pads to those that are fairly large, self-contained and rural. And within that range is a vast variation.

The simplist of the urban type, for example, usually consists of an apartment or house where a steady turn-over of new dropouts may exist in a loosely cooperative arrangement before either: (a) going back home; or (b) contracting some disease (and going back home); or (c) pushing onward to a more stable commune. The more stable of those communes that are able to function in cities generally tend toward a sort of space-age religious zealotry, complete with their own built-in avatars, fanatical-eyed young followers and well-ordered sets of loony notions about how to avoid the Apocalypse. Other of the city-centered type may be single-purpose communal groupings: collections of individuals who live together to share some special passion or practical function, such as rock music, art, draft resistance, printing posters, putting out underground newspapers or subsisting philosophically on indiscriminate screwing.

The most radical departures from straight civilization, though, are the communes lying out in the open country. These can be "classified" according to their chief activity. Some, like the New Buffalo in northern New Mexico, are tribal alliances of mostly city-born young people determined to farm and generally befriend the earth. A few, like the Lama Foundation, also in New Mexico, resemble semireligious retreats or Hindu *ashrams,* bent on teaching new styles of perception with, most usually, a strict ban on drug use. A few more are bizarre-exploratory like the Animal Farm in upper New York State, which takes in members willing to self-experiment creatively with human eugenics. Others, like Drop City, conceive themselves as rural "decompression chambers" for over-urbanized kids fresh off the road. And still more, like Wheeler's Free near Occidental, California (and countless other of the communes that don't have names) are wildly primitive stretches of rude landscape where unorganized agglomerations of hip gypsies live in scattered tents or in caves or abandoned cars or out under the trees.

In whatever form it may take, the new communal movement, on the whole, is an updated attempt to practicalize an ancient ideal—the pooling of souls and resources with some special vision in mind. And, too, regardless of how estranged from straight society they may feel, the new communitarians bring with them their ingrained Americanistic impulses to make things work. Along with this, they bring a mystical sort of faith that through work and through their anarchical mode of life they can rediscover their own functionalism as human beings. ("Now, by God, we're gonna do things *our* way.") Though many of them aren't aware of it, their visionary and migratory impulses form a common bond with the early Christians, who themselves were guided—as almost all communal efforts since then have been inspired—by Acts 2:44–46: "And all that believed were together, and had all things in common; and sold their possessions and goods and parted them to all men, as every man had need . . . and did eat their meat with gladness and singleness of heart."

⑥

"LOVE IT OR LEAVE IT":
THE BACKLASH AGAINST
THE MOVEMENTS

Tuning in the nightly news, picking up the morning paper, listening to friends and neighbors complain about "the kids" and "the minorities" and "the government"—"average" Americans wondered what was going on. They had bought into the postwar ethos—worked hard, saved, believed in the promise of American life. Communism was the international evil and social conformity the rule in the fifties. But now, all around them, individuals and movements emerged to challenge nearly every value to which they subscribed, from foreign policy on a global stage to school policy on a local one. Something was happening and they didn't know what it was. And more important, it unnerved them. Using the frame of reference they knew, the culture of post-World War II America, they tried to make sense of it.

Over the course of the sixties, the part of white America outside of the sweep of events looked on in anger, envy, and frustration as elements within American society seemed bent on undermining what they held dear—or thought they were supposed to hold dear. Working-class whites began to fear that advances by minorities would limit their economic opportunities. Americans steeped in anticommunism believed anti-Vietnam demonstrators had capitulated to Ho Chi Minh and the "international communist conspiracy." The perceived political "anarchy" of the student demonstrations mixed with visions of a "sexual anarchy" that appeared to result from free love, premarital sexuality, and gender equality. The sexual openness of the counterculture changed the rules of the game. Women as well as men were seen as capable of active sexuality. Further, sex was no longer the reward at the end of a preordained path—be it the sexual attractiveness material success was supposed to provide or a woman's "gift" to her husband upon marriage—but part of normal human activity. Individuals who had lived their lives by the constraining values of postwar life saw the proponents of the counterculture dismiss those values and flaunt the dismissal in the process.

The responses, however, far exceeded the actions that created them. Few of the antiwar demonstrators were overtly procommunist. Advances within the black community were slowing by the mid-1960s. As American mores began to shift, the idea of sexual liberation proved more attractive than repellent. The changes in society actually brought about more of a balance between personal beliefs and public pronouncements than a radical transformation. *Playboy* magazine, for example, had been a creation of 1950s America, and a hugely successful one at that. Sexuality in the postwar world had been constrained and channeled, not nonexistent. In the 1960s these constraints seemed to be lifting, but new guidelines had not yet been drawn. Without the old sense of order, many Americans felt disoriented and threatened.

Probably no issue epitomized the struggle more than the nationwide preoccupation with hair—in particular, men's hair. In retrospect the issue seems astonishingly silly, but at the time it was amazingly intense. The trend toward longer hair for men probably started with the Beatles' arrival in America. By later standards the Beatles seemed well groomed and well dressed. But as young men began to grow their hair longer and longer, hair length turned into one of the most apparent cultural badges of distinction. "Long-haired hippies" became a frequent epithet. Court cases dealt with the civil rights of men who felt they had been discriminated against because of the length of their hair. Beneath objections about cleanliness, safety, or etiquette was the matter of gender confusion. To many conventional Americans, long hair on men seemed an effeminate attribute. Yet these same men seemed to be indulging in the sort of sexual activity that fifties men had reserved for their fantasies. This kind of confusion called basic assumptions into question and rendered traditional explanations inadequate to account for what people observed around them.

A host of other identifiable styles developed among men and women of the counterculture and the student movement, all aimed at challenging basic presumptions. Everything from their secondhand clothes to their interests in Eastern philosophy seemed at odds with the values and assumptions of postwar America. Those who espoused traditional values not only disagreed with the new vision, they could not understand it. Based on their own worldview, these actions seemed incomprehensible. Why were secondhand clothes preferred over new ones? Why run-down apartments over clean homes in suburbia? How could anyone not support American soldiers in combat? How could students show so little respect for administrators of the colleges they attended? How could you hear the words to the song when the music was so loud?

When commentators tried to assess what has happening, they reverted to familiar presuppositions and vocabulary. Student radicals were tools of the communists, incipient fascists, or undisciplined adolescents. Even rock 'n' roll was seen as part of a communist plot or an example of teenage arrogance. But along with these analyses—perhaps encouraged by them—emerged political movements as well, seeking to turn growing anger and confusion into political power. The frustration felt by many Americans found outlet in attachments to politicians seeking to use for their own ends reactions against the student movement, black activism, and the counterculture.

One generation grew to political awareness based on the flaws it perceived in American society. But many in an older generation focused their political awareness on the movements themselves, and were led to believe that if these movements succeeded, average Americans—especially average white Americans—would lose out.

OPPOSING THE STUDENTS

Various American politicians understood the antagonism the student movement was beginning to engender in mainstream America. They lacked a vocabulary, however, for accurate identification of the problem and the sources of frustration. Here three American political figures take different approaches in attempting to define the young radicals.

If Mob Rule Takes Hold in the U.S.

RICHARD NIXON

Former Vice President Richard Nixon set out in 1966 to recapture the Republican nomination for president in 1968. Nixon had lost a razor-thin election to John Kennedy in 1960 and watched Barry Goldwater lose overwhelmingly to Lyndon Johnson in 1964. Considered finished in American politics after losing the race for governor of California in 1962, Nixon would ultimately triumph. Part of his revived viability came from the harsh "law and order" positions he took. While appearing to take the high ground against "mob rule," Nixon's words were subtly coded appeals to those fearful of student and minority unrest.

The polls still place the war in Vietnam and the rising cost of living as the major political issues of 1966. But, from my own trips across the nation, I can affirm that private conversations and public concern are increasingly focusing upon the issues of disrespect for law and race turmoil.

The recent riots in Chicago, Cleveland, New York and Omaha have produced in the public dialogue too much heat and very little light. The extremists have held the floor for too long.

One extreme sees a simple remedy for rioting in a ruthless application of the truncheons and an earlier call to the National Guard.

The other extremists are more articulate, but their position is equally simplistic. To them, riots are to be excused upon the grounds that the participants have legitimate social grievances or seek justifiable social goals.

I believe it would be a grave mistake to charge off the recent riots to unredressed Negro grievances alone.

To do so is to ignore a prime reason and a major national problem: the deterioration of respect for the rule of law all across America.

That deterioration can be traced directly to the spread of the corrosive doctrine that every citizen possesses an inherent right to decide for himself which laws to disobey and when to disobey them.

The doctrine has become a contagious national disease, and its symptoms are manifest in more than just racial violence. We see them in the contempt among many of the young for the agents of the law—the police. We see them in the public burning of draft cards and the blocking of troop trains.

We saw those symptoms when citizens in Chicago took to the streets to block public commerce to force the firing of a city official. We saw them on a campus of the University of California, where students brought a great university to its knees in protest of the policies of its administration.

Who is responsible for the breakdown of law and order in this country? I think it both an injustice and oversimplification to lay blame at the feet of the sidewalk demagogues alone. For such a deterioration of respect for law to occur in so brief a time in so great a nation, we must look to more important collaborators and auxiliaries.

It is my belief that the seeds of civil anarchy would never have taken root in this nation had they not been nurtured by scores of respected Americans: public officials, educators, clergymen and civil rights leaders as well.

When the junior Senator from New York [Robert Kennedy] publicly declares that "there is no point in telling Negroes to obey the law," because to the Negro "the law is the enemy," then he has provided a rationale and justification for every Negro intent upon taking the law into his own hands. . . .

The agonies and indignities of urban slums are hard facts of life. Their elimination is properly among our highest national priorities, but within those slums, political phrases which are inflammatory are as wrong and dangerous as political promises which are irredeemable.

In this contest, men of intellectual and moral eminence who encourage public disobedience of the law are responsible for the acts of those who inevitably follow their counsel: the poor, the ignorant, and the impressionable.

Such leaders are most often men of good will who do not condone violence and, perhaps even now, see no relation between the civil disobedience which they counsel and the riots and violence which have erupted. Yet, once the decision is made that laws need not be obeyed—whatever the rationale—a contribution is made to a climate of lawlessness.

To the professor objecting to de facto segregation, it may be crystal clear where civil disobedience may begin and where it must end. But the boundaries have become fluid to his students. And today they are all but invisible in the urban slums.

In this nation we raise our young to respect the law and public authority. What becomes of those lessons when teachers and leaders of the young themselves deliberately and publicly violate the laws?

There is a crucial difference between lawful demonstration and protests on the one hand—and illegal demonstrations and "civil disobedience" on the other.

I think it is time the doctrine of civil disobedience was analyzed and rejected as not only wrong but potentially disastrous.

If all have a right to engage in public disobedience to protest real or imagined wrongs, then the example set by the minority today will be followed by the majority tomorrow.

Issues then will no longer be decided upon merit by an impartial judge. Victory will go to the side which can muster the greater number of demonstrations in the streets. The rule of law will be replaced by the rule of the mob. And one may be sure that the majority's mob will prevail.

From mob rule it is but a single step to lynch law and the termination of the rights of the minority. This is why it is so paradoxical today to see minority groups engaging in civil disobedience; their greatest defense is the rule of law. . . .

Civil disobedience creates a climate of disrespect for law. In such a climate the first laws to be ignored will be social legislation that lacks universal public support. In short, if the rule of law goes, the civil-rights laws of recent vintage will be the first casualties.

Historic advances in civil rights have come through court decisions and federal laws in the last dozen years.

Only the acceptances of those laws and the voluntary compliance of the people can transfer those advances from the statute books into the fabric of community life.

If indifference to the rule of law permeates the community, there will be no voluntary acceptance. A law is only as good as the will of the people to obey it. . . .

Across this nation today, civil disobedience and racial disorders are building up a wall of hate between the races which, while less visible, is no less real than the wall that divides freedom and slavery in the city of Berlin. . . . Continued racial violence and disorders in the cities of the nation will produce growing disenchantment with the cause of civil rights—even among its staunchest supporters.

It will encourage a disregard for civil rights laws and resistance to the legitimate demands of the Negro people.

Does anyone think that progress will be made in the hearts of men by riots and disobedience which trample upon the rights of those same men? But then it is not enough to simply demand that all laws be obeyed?

Edmund Burke once wrote concerning loyalty to a nation that "to make us love our country, our country ought to be lovely." There is an analogy in a commitment to the rule of law. For a law to be respected, it ought to be worthy of respect. It must be fair and it must be fairly enforced.

It certainly did nothing to prevent a riot when Negroes in Chicago learned that while water hydrants in their own area were being shut down, they were running free in white neighborhoods just blocks away.

Respect for the dignity of every individual is absolutely essential if there is to be respect for law.

The most common and justifiable complaint of Negroes and members of other minority groups is not that their constitutional rights have been denied, but that their personal dignity is repeatedly insulted.

As an American citizen, the American Negro is entitled to equality of rights, under the Constitution and the law, with every other citizen in the land. But, as important as this, the Negro has the right to be treated with the basic dignity and respect that belong to him as a human being.

Advocates of civil disobedience contend that a man's conscience should determine which law is to be obeyed and when a law can be ignored. But, to many men, conscience is no more than the enshrinement of their own prejudices. . . . But if every man is to decide for himself which to obey and which to ignore, the end result is anarchy.

The way to make good laws is not to break bad laws, but to change bad laws through legitimate means of protest within the constitutional process.

In the last analysis, the nation simply can no longer tolerate men who are above the law. For, as Lincoln said, "There is no grievance that is a fit object of redress by mob law."

Communist Infiltration

EDWIN WILLIS

Chair of the House Committee on Un-American Activities, Louisiana Congressman Edwin Willis reported to the full House in the spring of 1968 about "communist infiltration" of the student and antiwar movement. Willis's focus, like that of the committee he chaired, seemed a holdover from 1950s anticommunism. Yet his approach resonated with segments of the American population schooled to see all domestic political dissent as communist inspired.

Mr. Speaker, on March 31, 1967, the House Committee on Un-American Activities released its well-documented and timely report on the "Communist Origin and Manipulation of Vietnam Week, April 8–15, 1967."

This report gave valuable insight into the reasons why a planned nationwide student strike for the spring of 1967 never happened. Extensive planning and organization for the 1967 student strike fell by the wayside when dissident leftist elements withdrew their support in the critical months of organizing. In place of the strike, the Spring Mobilization Committee—now National Mobilization Committee— and the Student Mobilization Committee—SMC—engineered and staged simultaneous demonstrations in New York City and San Francisco on April 15, 1967. A week of campus anti-Vietnam war demonstrations prior to last April 15 was but an ugly prelude to the mass demonstrations on either coast.

At the culmination of Vietnam Week last year, the American citizen was left stunned. Indelibly stamped on his mind were the front page photos of his country's beloved flag being burned in New York City. Other photographs of the demonstrations showed an unruly mob waving flags of the Vietcong and raising large portraits of Ho Chi Minh.

Broadcasts of the demonstrations picked out the shrill voices raised in vilification of the American Government and even in denouncement of America's sons in service to their country. On April 15, 1967, demonstrations were clearly staged in defiance of the determination of our people to help resist Communist aggression in Southeast Asia. Those hysterical voices which screamed out over loudspeakers in eulogy of the Communist aggressor will not soon be forgotten by any decent American.

What began as a "Massive protest demonstration against U.S. Government policy" in Vietnam, was skillfully maneuvered into a carnival of unmistakable support for a Communist victory in Vietnam.

THE ABORTIVE 1967 "STRIKE" PROPOSAL

In the chain of events which led to the ultimate demonstrations last year in New York and San Francisco, the Communist Party— CPUSA—and the Communist organized and controlled W.E.B. Du-Bois Clubs of America—DCA—were the driving forces behind the plan to hold a nationwide student strike in sympathy with the Vietcong and the Communist North Vietnamese.

Bettina Aptheker Kurzweil, daughter of chief CPUSA theoretician Herbert Aptheker, and herself a dedicated party functionary and CPUSA national committee member, promoted the student strike idea—almost single-handedly—for more than a year. Factionalism among the several Communist, splinter, new left and "peace" groups—coupled with a series of individual power plays for the claim of leadership of the proposed student strike movement—proved nearly too much for the newly formed United Front to overcome.

However, a coalition of veteran Communist organizers "peace" agitators and special interest promoters, took control of the base of the strike movement and manipulated it into what was to become the notorious Vietnam Week demonstrations which took place throughout the country.

The mobilization this year exhibits principally the same individual Communist leadership that masterminded and engineered the Vietnam Week demonstrations of April 8–15, 1967.

The student strike and mass actions day April 27, 1968—will be the Communist run vehicle of irresponsible dissent and internal disruption within the United States. This dissent and disruption is designed to benefit the North Vietnamese enemy and the world Communist movement in general by undermining public support of the present U.S. policy of resisting Communist aggression in South Vietnam.

Communist organizations, the Communist press, Communist fronts and individual Communists have drawn together under the banner of the Student Mobilization Committee in a united front. The primary objective of this united front is to defeat American determination of continued support for U.S. policy in Vietnam. As secondary objectives, this united front hopes to first, depict the U.S. Government as "imperialistic" in its policy of assisting nations which are presently opposing Communist aggression throughout the world; and second, to exploit the current racial tensions in the United States by blaming continuing ghetto problems on the diversion of poverty funds in order to fight Communist aggression in Southeast Asia and elsewhere.

If the Communists are successful in inducing a significant number of college and high school students to strike on April 26, 1968, and to partake in the mass disruptive actions on April 27, 1968—for whatever reasons—the international Communist propaganda network will use this incident to attempt to: First, create widespread public demand for reversal of present U.S. foreign policy; second, propagandistically give aid and comfort to Communists everywhere in the world Communist movement, but particularly in Vietnam; and third, further dampen the resolve of America's allies who presently support U.S. policy in Vietnam, and make the war effort appear solely "America's problem."

Freedom vs. Anarchy on Campus

RONALD REAGAN

In 1966—after the eruption of the student movement—motion picture actor Ronald Reagan achieved what Richard Nixon had failed to do in 1962, winning the governorship of California. In the process he inherited the leadership of the Goldwater wing of the Republican Party. Although it would be fourteen years before Reagan gained the White House, his initial successes in the political arena came with his positioning himself against the student demonstrators. The 1968 radio address excerpted below demonstrates Reagan's hard-line stand against the student militants, as well as a call to political action from "the rest of us."

The people of California founded and generously support what has become the finest system of public higher education in the land.

Within this system there are now nine university campuses, nineteen State-college campuses and 81 community colleges, plus many fine independent colleges and universities which are also supported, for the most part, by the people of California.

The system has worked well.

Yes—on these campuses, generations of Californians have pursued knowledge within the widest range of disciplines. They have sampled widely of man's knowledge of man, of the history of his ideas and what he knows of the world around him.

This is the role of higher education in California. At least this has been the case up until recently.

Within the past five or six years, something new has been added—a violent strident something that has disturbed all of us; a something whose admitted purpose is to destroy or to capture and use society's institutions for its own purpose. I say "whose admitted purpose" because the leadership minces no words. It is boastful, arrogant and threatening.

Consider these words from a campus teacher:

"I think we agree that the revolution is necessary and that you don't conduct a revolution by attacking the strongest enemy first. You take care of your business at home first, then you move abroad. Thus we must make the university the home of the revolution."

From the capture of a police car and negotiations conducted in an atmosphere of intimidation, threats and fear; we went from free speech to filthy speech.

The movement spread to other campuses. There has been general incitement against properly constituted law enforcement authorities and general trampling of the will, the rights and freedom of movement of the majority by the organized, militant, and highly vocal minority.

Though the causes were cloaked in the dignity of academic and other freedoms, they are—in fact—a lusting for power. Some protesters even marched under banners that ranged from the black flag of anarchy, the red flag of revolution, to the flags of enemies engaged in killing young Americans—the North Vietnamese and the Viet Cong.

Academic freedom is one of the important freedoms to go in the new order envisioned by the New Left. There was no academic freedom in Hitler's Germany. There is no academic freedom in Mao's China or Castro's Cuba. And there is no academic freedom in the philosophies or the actions of the George Murrays, the Eldridge Cleavers or the Jerry Rubins.

It is therefore most imperative that we—the great and thoughtful majority of citizens of all races—keep our perspective. We must recognize the manipulations being carried out to frustrate our common interest in living together with dignity in one American society. And we must also recognize that those who exercise violence must be held accountable for their actions—and held equally accountable regardless of their color.

Nationwide, experience has shown that prompt dealing with disturbances leads to peace, that hesitation, vacillation and appeasement leads to greater disorder.

Isn't it logical, in view of past experience to ask that no campus official negotiate or hold conferences with any individual or group while such individual or group is disturbing or disrupting campus activities, violating any rule or regulation of the campus or its governing board, or committing any criminal offense? And, likewise, to insist that there shall be no consideration of the demands or requests of any such individual or group while their disruptive or disorderly conduct continues?

And finally, isn't it time to demand that when individuals have been arrested as a result of their participation in the disturbances and disorders, the chief campus officer—or such other person designated by him—shall sign a criminal complaint against such persons and shall co-operate in the prosecution of those individuals and shall immediately suspend them from the university? . . .

From which group will we—and, really, from which group will you young people now going to college—elect your future leaders? Will it be from the few, but militant, anarchists and others now trying to control and run our campuses? Or will we elect our future leaders from the majority of fine young men and women dedicated to justice, order and the full development of the true individual?

GEORGE WALLACE

The first political figure actually to turn the rising tide of frustration to his advantage was not one of the traditional conservatives, but former Alabama Governor George Wallace. Wallace initially achieved national attention as a segregationist who attempted to block the integration of the University of Alabama. Beginning in 1966, however, his appearances in white working-class communities of the North suggested that his appeal went beyond the regional.

In 1968 he ran as a third-party candidate for president. While Richard Nixon won the election, Wallace was able to gather nearly ten million votes.

Wallace

PETE HAMILL

Journalist Pete Hamill followed the 1968 Wallace campaign and reported on the appeal of the former Alabama governor in Ramparts, *a magazine with new left sympathies.*

At a bar munching sardines and crackers, a tall, lean man named Jim Lewis stared at himself in the mirror. He was wearing a plastic boater adorned with a Wallace-For-President bumper sticker.

"Sure, I'm for Wallace," he said, washing the sardines down with beer. "There ain't no one else but Wallace. He's the one, the only one who's sayin' he's really gonna change things in this country."

"You don't care for Humphrey or Nixon?"

"Just a couple of phonies. Couldn't change a gah-dam thing. . . ."

"What kind of change are you looking for?"

"Everythin'," said Jim Lewis, who is a carpenter. "Get these long-haired scum in the colleges straightened out. Stop the gah-dam knee-groes from riotin' an' lootin'. Stop taxin' us to pay for people for not workin'. Let our boys win that war in Viet-Nam. Hell, any plain fool knows what we gotta change."

"What makes you think Wallace can change all of that?"

Jim Lewis slowly turned his head and squinted the way John Wayne has squinted in every movie he's ever been in.

"George Wallace can do it," he said firmly, "because George Wallace is his own Man!"

They want change: the America they thought was theirs has become something else in their own lifetime, and they want to go back. Some of them have even been supporters of Robert Kennedy (a phenomenon first noted by Paul Cowan in *The Village Voice*), because they saw him as an agent of change; whatever America is in 1968, they want to change it and their instincts are true enough to tell them that Humphrey and Nixon will change nothing. So they have rallied to George Wallace, mainly because he says to them that change is simple. Just change the man at the top and we can all return to a year like 1910, when there were harvests in the Fall and feasts in the Spring, when kids went swimming in the old swimming hole and played baseball and football and respected God, Flag and Country. Most of all they want to return to a time in America when you lived in the same house all of your life and knew everybody you would ever care to know on the street where you were born. Dismiss these people as racists and bigots if you will, but you would be a bit too glib. A lot of people attracted to George Wallace are just people who think America has passed them by, leaving them confused and screwed-up and unhappy.

"There's some days when I get up and read the paper and feel like I'm gonna go out of my goddarn mind," a farm implement salesman named James Quigg told me in Springfield, Missouri. "When is all of this gonna end?"

"This is the greatest country in the world," she was saying. "People used to be happy here. I'm telling you. Maybe in the Depression we didn't have much money, but nobody starved. And we made our own fun. We read books to each other or played Monopoly at night and once a month we all went to a show. Kids today got too much. They don't do anything for themselves. And ever since this civil rights business started people have been unhappy."

Everywhere that Wallace went the speech was sure to go. In Little Rock and Milwaukee, in Springfield, Illinois, and Springfield, Missouri, in Cincinnati and Charleston. Only a phrase or two would change, and only the audiences were different. Wallace would stand before a cluster of microphones and cameras, his hands shifting from one pocket to another or stabbing the air for emphasis, and the speech would come rolling out—cocky, defiant, loaded with innuendo, sarcasm and country humor. The audiences were almost always filled with His People, and they would sing the national anthem and recite the Lord's Prayer and fill the plastic boaters with dollar bills when the Wallace girls came around, and some even signed the automated pledges for larger amounts which would be billed to them long after the candidate had left town, even after his campaign had been settled forever at the ballot boxes. But they were willing to give because they were the believers and because when that was settled they could hear The Speech.

"I want to talk to yawl about dissent," Wallace says. "I believe in dissent. I myself am a dissenter. I agree with the right to oppose the war in Viet-Nam and the right of dissent." The audience is quiet, unsure of what's coming. "But I do not agree with your right to advocate and work for a communist victory in Viet-Nam! There's a difference between dissent and treason! [Roar From The Crowd] And any good cabdriver here in Springfield [Milwaukee, Columbia, Charleston] knows that! [Big Roar] So I promise you when I'm elected President and someone waves a Viet Cong flag or raises blood, money, or other things for the enemy, we're gonna throw him under a good jail someplace!"

To visitors freshly arrived, his views on Viet-Nam seem surprising; the popular image of Wallace, at least in the East, would lead one to believe that he is a Super-Hawk who is fully prepared to unload the hydrogen bomb on the yellow vermin of Southeast Asia. But he actually says something quite different.

"Now about Viet-Nam," he says, "I don't think we should have gone to our Western European allies and the noncommunist nations of Southeast Asia, and if we decided to go in there at all, we should have told them we would not carry the military and economic burden alone. That they would have to share equally, and if they were still not interested, I would cut off every dime of foreign aid and make them pay back every cent they owe us datin' back to World War One. [Big Applause] So I would go to the joint Chiefs of Staff, and I would ask them, 'Can we win this war with conventional weapons?' And if they said yes, I would make full use of the country's conventional weapons to quickly end this war and bring our boys home." This always brings a roar from the crowd. Wallace never says what he would do if the Joint Chiefs told him the war was not winnable with conventional weapons. Some of his aides say that he would pull out "and to hell with it."

A lot of what he says on the other issues is reasonably mild. Even on law and order (or as he says it, "Lawn Awduh"). "The other two candidates—before the conventions I used to say they wasn't a dime worth of difference between 'em, especially on Lawn Awduh. Now I says they's not a dime worth of difference between them and me . . . and I'm the original!" Wallace is against increases in welfare spending and poverty programs which he feels are essentially used to bribe slum dwellers. But he is also against creating a national police force. "I said facetiously that we oughta turn the country over to the police for two years," he will say. "Well, you all know what I mean. I mean that we should give the police and firemen just two years of being able to enforce the law, without the Supreme Court standin' on their necks, and we could straighten this country out. We don't need new laws. All y'have to do is enforce the laws you got and if they [Read Blacks] don't obey them then throw them under a good jail someplace." This always brings a roar, and he follows it this way: "You know, if you were to be mugged or beaten or molested on the way home from heah tonight, the person that did it to you would be free before you got to the hospital. [Laughter] And on Monday they'd be charging some policeman with the crime!"

Wallace reserves his most withering scorn for those members of the federal bureaucracy who are charged with enforcing federal guidelines on desegregation, open housing and equal opportunities. These are the guideline writers, a contemptuous creed of Americans who are only slightly worse than their allies in perfidy, the pointed heads Who Can't Park A Bicycle Straight. These people have clogged the country's laws with so much bureaucratic verbiage that "the anarchists and seditionists" have been running amok on the streets of America.

Why Wallace?

MICHAEL NOVAK

Michael Novak, later known for his analysis of white ethnicity, captures some of the perspective and frustrations of the individuals who supported Wallace in 1968.

When the major candidates in an election year cry "unity!" it sets one to imagining the sources of disunity. It makes me think of Andy Restek, who runs the Texaco station in a Pennsylvania steel town. His brother Pete works in the mills. His other brother Steve, I think, is a manager at the local Sears or some other chain. In any case, I am told that all three Restek brothers are voting for Wallace this year. Why? I ask myself. And why do they hate the hippies so much, and praise the Chicago cops?

Andy Restek has two kids in college—one at State College, and one at the local branch of the University of Pittsburgh. He wipes the grease from his hands as he talks about them, and pushes back his heavy rimless glasses. He is rather proud that his children will all go to college—and a little ashamed to say that he is glad they won't be gas station attendants. He envisages Bob as a clerk in a bank (as he is, summers) and later as an officer; Bob's a pretty bright and impressive boy, with personality and presence. He hopes Sally will marry a nice solid fellow with sound ideas. Since Andy's parents came to America with nothing, he's rather passionately uncritical about the nation. He has a fairly comfortable house and nice lawn, a new Plymouth, and the youngest boy is a much touted junior halfback.

Andy served in Italy in 1944–45, and has served as an officer in the local VFW. He knows he has worked hard, and has succeeded. He lives in a better neighborhood than where he began, and he owns the station. He's been a good mechanic and has a lot of loyal customers. The neighborhood where his station is located, however, is run-down and the ugly houses that are not unoccupied (windows broken, doors boarded up) are inhabited by passive, silent blacks. There is no need to rehearse Andy's attitudes to blacks. "I'm no racist or bigot; it's only that. . . ." From that point onward he merely reports the evidence of his own senses, as his perception shapes that evidence: dirty, passive, strange, unreliable, careless. Andy points out that Harry Scott, the black man who works at the Esso station seven blocks away, has what it takes; he works hard, which only shows they can do it if they want, and proves that Andy isn't prejudiced. It's the majority of Negroes who are lazy that cause the trouble. Andy doesn't see any difference between the starting place of any black man and his own starting place. The only difference he perceives is one of initiative and brains.

Andy responds to Wallace, I suspect, because Wallace puts things exactly in the way Andy's experience has put them. Andy doesn't understand sociological or psychological or economic theories. But he catches the tone in which all those people on television or in the papers talk about such things. They don't say that they're out to destroy sound family values, or common sense, or tough, hard work and painfully acquired respectability. Educated people talk with a kind of code. They try to sound harmless, but you know they're trying to take your world from you. You can almost feel them screwing you; you see it in their complacent eyes. They know so much.

Andy trusts his own experience. He knows what he knows. And he likes his world, his home, his America.

He is very worried about Sally. He saw a picture of a longhaired boy in her wallet and threw her out of the house for several hours. He doesn't dare allow himself to think that she has been taking pot, but sometimes his stomach tightens. He tries to get her to cut her long hair and not to wear it straight, and hates when she merely tells him he's old-fashioned and doesn't respect his word as law. He blames himself for working too hard—American materialism, his pastor would say—and not being as strict with her as his parents had been with him. She would *never* have talked back to them that way. She hates church so much, and refuses to go to confession, that he knows there is trouble brewing. If she gets pregnant . . . he can't allow himself to think that, and strikes out in fury at every manifestation of the kind of youth he despises: shiftless, dirty, uninhibited, smart-alecky, superior, aiding our enemies. The outrage he feels is so deep he can't understand how anyone in his right mind would not scream out in anguish at what is happening to America. He wants authority to tighten up, in part to assuage his own guilt for having been too soft with his kids.

He watches with trepidation the books that Bob brings home. Bob is majoring in Business Administration and Finance. But Andy is suspicious of some of the poetry and novels he brings home, and books with words like "humanism" on the jacket. In Andy's experience, "humanism" has been one of the code words for softheaded thinking, pornography, and the collapse of authority.

Andy's brothers Pete and Steve largely agree. They grow bitter often when they get together. Their wives hate to hear them begin to talk politics. Even miniskirts—much as the men joke about them man-to-man—have become for them one more symbol of the collapse of values. And Hollywood and television and the liberal reporters. The hometown newspaper is solidly conservative; but the lurid ads for the movies still announce the general sickness. It's just like the priests say. Secularism is the collapse of all decency and morals and authority. We need a man who talks sense and isn't softheaded about authority, to clean this country up from coast to coast. That way, we can all have the America we worked so hard to build, which gave us what success we have.

Andy, Pete and Steve are all for the underprivileged, but (they say) let them prove themselves by work, the way we did. "Racism" and "bigot," they have come to think, are other code words by which the white-handed, effeminate Harvard men want to call the good people evil, and win the allegiance of the blacks for their own political and unstated purposes.

Impudence in the Streets

SPIRO T. AGNEW

With Richard Nixon as president, the so-called "silent majority" believed that it had a friend in the White House and a spokesman in Nixon's vice president, Spiro Agnew. Employed by the administration as its voice of anger and frustration with the students, antiwar demonstrators, and black activists, Agnew became popular with the right and with blue-collar constituencies, until he was forced from office in 1973, after pleading "no contest" to charges of income tax evasion stemming from an investigation into money received during his tenure as governor of Maryland.

This speech, given at a Republican dinner during the first year of Nixon's presidency, shows Agnew's blend of high moralizing about American values and patronizing characterizations of the students and demonstrators.

A little over a week ago, I took a rather unusual step for a Vice President. I said something. Particularly, I said something that was predictably unpopular with the people who would like to run the country without the inconvenience of seeking public office. I said I did not like some of the things I saw happening in this country. I criticized those who encouraged government by street carnival and suggested it was time to stop the carousel.

It appears that by slaughtering a sacred cow I triggered a holy war. I have no regrets. I do not intend to repudiate my beliefs, recant my words, or run and hide.

What I said before, I will say again. It is time for the preponderant majority, the responsible citizens of this country, to assert *their* rights. It is time to stop dignifying the immature actions of arrogant, reckless, inexperienced elements within our society. The reason is compelling. It is simply that their tantrums are insidiously destroying the fabric of American democracy.

By accepting unbridled protest as a way of life, we have tacitly suggested that the great issues of our times are best decided by posturing and shouting matches in the streets. America today is drifting toward Plato's classic definition of a degenerating democracy—a democracy that permits the voice of the mob to dominate the affairs of government.

Last week I was lambasted for my lack of "mental and moral sensitivity." I say that any leader who does not perceive where persistent street struggles are going to lead this nation lacks mental acuity. And any leader who does not caution this nation on the danger of this direction lacks moral strength.

I believe in Constitutional dissent. I believe in the people registering their views with their elected representatives, and I commend those people who care enough about their country to involve themselves in its great issues. I believe in legal protest within the Constitutional limits of free speech, including peaceful assembly and the right of petition. But I do not believe that demonstrations, lawful or lawful, merit my approval or even my silence where the purpose is fundamentally unsound. In the case of the Vietnam Moratorium, the objects announced by the leaders—immediate unilateral withdrawal of all our forces from Vietnam—was not only unsound but idiotic. . . .

So great is the latitude of our liberty that only a subtle line divides use from abuse. I am convinced that our preoccupation with emotional demonstration, frequently crossing the line to civil disruption and even violence could inexorably lead us across that line forever.

Ironically, it is neither the greedy nor the malicious but the self-righteous who are guilty of history's worse atrocities. Society understands greed and malice and erects barriers of law to defend itself from these vices. But evil cloaked in emotional causes is well disguised and often undiscovered until it is too late.

We have just such a group of self-proclaimed saviours of the American soul at work today. Relentless in their criticism of intolerance in America, they themselves are intolerant of those who differ with their views. In the name of academic freedom, they destroy academic freedom. Denouncing violence, they seize and vandalize buildings of great universities. Fiercely expressing their respect for truth, they disavow the logic and discipline necessary to pursue truth.

They would have us believe that they alone know what is good for America—what is true and right and beautiful. They would have us believe that their reflexive action is superior to our reflective action; that their revealed righteousness is more effective than our reason and experience.

Think about it. Small bands of students are allowed to shut down great universities. Small groups of dissidents are allowed to shout down political candidates. Small cadres of professional protestors are allowed to jeopardize the peace efforts of the President of the United States.

It is time to question the credentials of their leaders. And, if in questioning we disturb a few people, I say it is time for them to be disturbed. If, in challenging, we polarize the American people, I say it is time for a positive polarization.

It is time for a healthy in-depth examination of policies and constructive realignment in this country. It is time to rip away the rhetoric and to divide on authentic lines. It is time to discard the fiction that in a country of 200 million people, everyone is qualified to quarterback the government. . . .

Now, we have among us a glib, activist element who would tell us our values are lies, and I call them impudent. Because anyone who impugns a legacy of liberty and dignity that reaches back to Moses, is impudent.

I call them snobs for most of them disdain to mingle with the masses who work for a living. They mock the common man's pride in his work, his family and his country. It has also been said that I called them intellectuals. I did not. I said that they characterized themselves as intellectuals. No true intellectual, no truly knowledgeable person, would so despise democratic institutions. . . .

Finally—and most important—regardless of the issue, it is time to stop demonstrating in the streets and start doing something constructive about our institutions. America must recognize the dangers of constant carnival. Americans must reckon with irresponsible leadership and reckless words. The mature and sensitive people of this country must realize that their freedom of protest is being exploited by avowed anarchists and communists who detest everything about this country and want to destroy it.

This is a fact. These are the few; these are not necessarily leaders. But they prey upon the good intentions of gullible men everywhere. They pervert honest concern to something sick and rancid. They are vultures who sit in trees and watch lions battle, knowing that win, lose or draw, they will be fed.

Abetting the merchants of hate are the parasites of passion. These are the men who value a cause purely for its political mileage. These are the politicians who temporize with the truth by playing both sides to their own advantage. They ooze sympathy for "the cause" but balance each sentence with equally reasoned reservations. Their interest is personal, not moral. They are ideological eunuchs whose most comfortable position is straddling the philosophical fence, soliciting votes from both sides. . . .

This is what is happening in this nation. We *are* an effete society if we let it happen here. . . .

Will Congress settle down to the issues of the nation and reform the institutions of America as our President asks? Can the press ignore the pipers who lead the parades? Will the heads of great universities protect the rights of all their students? Will parents have the courage to say no to their children? Will people have the intelligence to boycott pornography and violence? Will citizens refuse to be led by a series of Judas goats down tortuous paths of delusion and self-destruction?

Will we defend fifty centuries of accumulated wisdom? For that is our heritage. Will we make the effort to preserve America's bold, successful experiment in truly representative government? Or do we care so little that we will cast it all aside?

Because on the eve of our nation's 200th birthday, we have reached the crossroads. Because at this moment totalitarianism's threat does not necessarily have a foreign accent. Because we have a home-grown menace, made and manufactured in the U.S.A. Because if we are lazy or foolish, this nation could forfeit its integrity, never to be free again.

Tony Imperiale Stands Vigilant for Law and Order

PAUL GOLDBERGER

The white backlash did not restrict itself to presidential politics or the speeches of the vice president. In communities around the country, local groups chan- neled their fears and frustrations into organizations aimed at protecting, they believed, their own neighborhoods and achievements—often "taking the law into their own hands." In 1968 Paul Goldberger profiled one such group, centered in Newark, New Jersey, and headed by Tony Imperiale.

It was a warm Sunday evening in May, and the crowd, jammed elbow-to-elbow in the tavern parking lot, was wildly enthusiastic. "Give 'em hell, Tony," an old man shouted. 'Tell 'em where to go."

Tony began quietly. "I didn't see any flags in the city of Newark lowered to half mast when Gov. Lurleen Wallace died," he said. "Why not, when they could do it for that Martin Luther Coon?" The audience cheered, and Tony gained momentum. "When is it gonna stop?" he cried. "Everybody says, 'Don't bother 'em now. Leave 'em alone, and they'll calm down.' Well, it took riots that burned down half of a town before we learned."

Tony is Anthony Imperiale—5 feet 6 1/4 inches, a tough-muscled 230 pounds, 39 years old. That evening in Nutley, N.J., five miles north of Newark, he was hailed as a savior by hundreds of white residents who are convinced that the Negro is taking away everything the white man has earned. Tony isn't going to give it up without a fight—and Tony is their man.

Imperiale is the organizer of Newark's North Ward Citizens' Committee, which claims a dues-paying membership of 200 and thousands of enthusiastic followers. In their leader's view, they are "defenders of law and order," banded together in the wake of last summer's Newark riots to stand up to Communist-inspired racial pressures. In the view of Gov. Richard J. Hughes, they are "vigilantes."

They own guns and take karate training from Imperiale, a Black Belt in the art. Ten of their radio-equipped cars patrol the North Ward each weekday night (17 on weekends) to ward off criminals and/or invaders from the adjacent Central Ward, the black ghetto. Chapters in five suburban towns, including Nutley, mount their own patrols. Imperiale used to boast loudly that the committee owned a helicopter and an armored car, and he insisted that members on patrol wear fatigues—but he has of late soft-pedaled these matters.

Last month the windows fronting the committee's cinder-block headquarters on North Seventh Street were shattered by three explosions. No one was injured in the 1:20 A.M. bombing, but it was a close call. "If a guy hadn't talked me into taking another drink at a bar I was in," Imperiale says, "me and my wife Louise would have been sitting right where the plate-glass window was torn out." He has few doubts about who placed the dynamite, and he has doubled the night patrols. He has also expressed uncertainty about his ability to control committee members: "If this kind of thing happens again, I won't be responsible for what these people here will do."

Tony Imperiale is not alone in America 1968. In Detroit there is Donald Lobsinger, chairman of a 6-year-old organization called Breakthrough. His formula for security: "Study, arm, store provisions and organize." In Warren, Mich., druggist Ronald Portnoy leads a group known as Fight Back. Its literature proclaims: "The only way to stop them is at the city limits." In Oakland, Calif., the leader of the Home Defense Association is Herbert Clark. It has published a manual recommending firearms and ammunition and containing chapters on "Defense of an Individual House" and "Neighborhood Perimeter Defense.". . .

Imperiale is of another stripe. Last month he sought election to a council that will oversee administration of the Federal Model Cities program in Newark. There were four posts open in each of 13 districts—248 candidates for 52 seats. Imperiale not only won in his district but polled more votes than any other candidate in the city. He called his victory "an affirmation of the people's desire for law and order." Now he is running for the City Council, and his eye is on the office now occupied by Mayor Hugh J. Addonizio.

The Imperiale platform is basically the same cry for law and order that sets crowds cheering wherever he speaks. Some of the planks:

"The American people are very gullible. They let the politicians yield to the radical. And the Communists take the radical and exploit him. . . . In the riots, billions of dollars of property was destroyed, and the Constitution of the United States was thrown into the gutter. When is Washington gonna put down their foot and say 'Look, law and order must prevail'?"

"We look at the policemen—they've been abused, they've been harassed, they've been rubbed under the nose with anything that these radicals wanted to do, and they got away with it. Because the quislings, the politicians with no guts, were selling the decent people out. . . . The first thing I'm gonna do is take politics out of the Police Department. . . . And I intend to fight any group who tries to tie the hands of the police by shouting 'police brutality' or this or that. I'm gonna fight you, tooth and nail.''

"They oughta register Communists, not guns.''

"Are there no poor whites? But the Negroes get all the antipoverty money. When pools are being built in the Central Ward, don't they think the white kids have got frustration? The whites are the majority. You know how many of them come to me, night after night, because they can't get a job? They've been told, 'We have to hire Negroes first.' ''. . .

In the view of Imperiale's constituency, he tells it like it is. The large majority of the ward's 43,000 residents are Italian-American, though there has been something of an influx of Negroes since the 1960 census, when the proportion of Negroes was 17.6 per cent. White Protestants have been leaving the area, and Roman Catholic population has increased and some Negro congregations have taken over property formerly owned by white Protestant churches.

It is a shabby neighborhood, once firmly middle-class, now in the grip of a slow but insistent deterioration. The percentage of owner-occupied homes has dipped. Many single-family homes have been converted to multiple-occupancy dwellings. There is a crowded, ticky-tacky feeling about it all.

Perhaps the most unhappy facet of the North Ward, however, is a pervasive—and in many ways valid—mental set. The people sense that their backs are to the wall, that conditions are worsening and no help is on the way. There are state and Federal funds being poured into Newark, but they are being spent elsewhere; for bad as the ward's problems may be, they don't compare to the problems of the city's black ghettos.

More than half of Newark's 400,000 residents are Negroes. A third of the city's housing is substandard; unemployment in black areas such as the Central Ward is officially set at 12 per cent, unofficially as high as 20 per cent; there are 17,000 households "living" on incomes of less than $3,000 a year. Newark leads all cities of the nation of its size in crime and venereal disease and maternal mortality rates.

When the city celebrated its tricentennial in 1966, it adopted the slogan, "Pride in Newark." But the statistics above don't lend themselves to being pointed to with pride; Tony Imperiale and his followers point to them with fear and anger, and the presence of black faces in their North Ward is a constant reminder that "it could happen here."

It is not, Imperiale insists, that he and the members of the committee are racists. He tells of inviting a Negro neighbor and his family over for a meal. When a Negro woman died in his neighborhood this summer, he took in her 7-year-old boy for several days; the boy still spends as much time with the Imperiales as with his own family, Imperiale says.

But Imperiale is quick to defend whites who attack Negroes entering the ward ("The colored just come looking for trouble"), and he is convinced that the Negro is incapable of dignified living ("Look at this," he says, pointing to a 15-year-old photograph of a North Ward neighborhood. "And look at it now, with garbage on the streets." A committee member adds, "They don't know how to live here; they have no pride." Later, a tour of the neighborhood turns up only a few signs of deterioration. "The garbage man must have just been here," the committee member quickly explains). . . .

Patrols start at headquarters, a one-story building that contains a small office with radio equipment and several telephones. Behind the office is a multipurpose room, once the karate school gymnasium, the walls of which are painted bright orange. A bulletin board is posted with clippings—pro and con—about the organization. Judo posters line one wall, and literature published by black militants is displayed on another. Street maps abound. A sign beside the door reads: "No profanity. Fine 25 cents."

The office is usually staffed by neighborhood housewives while their husbands patrol the streets and their young children play hide-and-go-seek around the building. They are, respectively, members of the North Ward Women's Auxiliary and the North Ward Junior Auxiliary. The most singular artifact in the office is a telephone directly connected to LeRoi Jones's Spirit House in the Central Ward. . . .

Most of the members of the patrol are young, and the cars they drive tend to be old. As dusk falls, the street in front of headquarters comes alive with the roar of faulty mufflers and the impatient engine revving of youth craving excitement. They wear black construction hats decorated with the committee's initials, N.W.C.C., embossed in white. They talk together with a kind of false bravado.

Imperiale gives the word, and the four-man patrols move out. They follow carefully planned routes, studying the scene, looking for signs of trouble. At first, the police used to stop the cars to search them for weapons, and some such searches still occur. "They never find any guns," says Imperiale, "because we never carry any. It would be stupid." The patrol is intended to prevent conflict, he says, not start it.

For Imperiale, a patrol consists of driving from one corner gathering of white youths to another. Invariably he is recognized, and he knows most of the boys by their first names. "Hi ya, Angelo." "Waddaya doin', Stevie?" He urges them to stay cool, stay out of trouble. Older residents often spot his elderly black Cadillac. "Go get 'em, Tony," they shout. "They're out to get you." The bombing of committee headquarters is fresh in their minds. . . .

Because of such patrols and the other activities of the committee, Imperiale believes, an all-out race war in the city and suburbs can be avoided. "It doesn't necessarily have to come to that," he says, "We're showing the radical blacks that there's whites that will stand up. We're proving that it can be prevented."

This optimistic outlook is not shared, however, by all of Imperiale's followers. Tom Benecchi, the former coordinator of the committee's Nutley chapter who has withdrawn to form his own group and do his own thing, views his role mainly as that of delaying race war, not preventing it. "It's bound to come," he says. "Some crazy colored bastard, a Negro militant, will start shooting at whites, and then some crazy white bastard will start shooting back. But maybe when they see 500 of us with guns, maybe then they'll think twice about coming into our town.". . .

COINTELPRO

While American politicians from Nixon to Reagan railed against black, student, and antiwar leaders, the Federal Bureau of Investigation, under director

J. Edgar Hoover, sought to undermine the movements more directly. In 1976 the United States Senate Select Committee to Study Governmental Operations reported to the American people about "COINTELPRO: The FBI's Covert Action Programs Against American Citizens." Included in these activities, some of which had begun as early as 1956, were systematic attempts to undermine, harass, and disrupt various political and racial organizations, including a number within the new left and the Black Power movements.

Who Were the Targets?

The first selection is from the introduction to the COINTELPRO report and offers a general description of the programs' targets, their aims, and some of their activities.

COINTELPRO is the FBI acronym for a series of covert action programs directed against domestic groups. In these programs, the Bureau went beyond the collection of intelligence to secret action designed to "disrupt" and "neutralize" target groups and individuals. The techniques were adopted wholesale from wartime counterintelligence, and ranged from the trivial (mailing reprints of *Reader's Digest* articles to college administrators) to the degrading (sending anonymous poisen-pen letters intended to break up marriages) and the dangerous (encouraging gang warfare and falsely labeling members of a violent group as police informers). . . .

Who were the targets?

THE FIVE TARGETED GROUPS

The Bureau's covert action programs were aimed at five perceived threats to domestic tranquility: the "Communist Party, USA" program (1956–71); the "Socialist Workers Party" program (1961–69); the

"White Hate Group" program (1964–71); the "Black Nationalist Hate Group" program (1967–71); and the "New Left" program (1968–71).

The Bureau's titles for its programs should not be accepted uncritically. They imply a precision of definition and of targeting that did not exist.

Even the names of the later programs had no real definition. The Black Nationalist Program, according to its supervisor, included "a great number of organizations that you might not today characterize as black nationalist but which were in fact primarily black." Indeed, the nonviolent Southern Christian Leadership Conference was labeled as a Black Nationalist "Hate Group." Nor could anyone at the Bureau even define "New Left," except as "more or less an attitude."

Protecting national security and preventing violence are the purposes advanced by the Bureau for COINTELPRO. There is another purpose for COINTELPRO which is not explicit but which offers the only explanation for those actions which had no conceivable rational relationship to either national security or violent activity. The unexpressed major premise of much of COINTELPRO is that the Bureau has a role in maintaining the existing social order, and that its efforts should be aimed toward combating those who threaten that order.

Under the COINTELPRO programs, the arsenal of techniques used against foreign espionage agents was transferred to domestic enemies. As William S. Sullivan, former Assistant to the Director, put it,

> This is a rough, tough, dirty business, and dangerous. It was dangerous at times. No holds were barred. . . . We have used [these techniques] against Soviet agents. They have used [them] against us. . . . [The same methods were] brought home against any organization against which we were targeted. We did not differentiate. This is a rough, tough, business.

The Bureau approved 2,370 separate counterintelligence actions. Their techniques ranged from anonymously mailing reprints of newspaper and magazine articles (sometimes Bureau-authored or planted) to group members or supporters to convince them of the error of their ways, to mailing anonymous letters to a member's spouse accusing the target of infidelity; from using informants to raise controversial issues at meetings in order to cause dissent, to the "snitch jacket" (falsely labeling a group member as an informant), and encouraging street warfare between violent groups; from contacting members of a legitimate group to expose the alleged subversive background of a fellow member, to contacting an employer to get a target fired; from attempting to arrange for reporters to interview targets with planted questions, to trying to stop targets from speaking at all; from notifying state and local authorities of a target's criminal law violations, to using the IRS to audit a professor, not just to collect any taxes owing, but to distract him from his political activities.

Initial group targets for "intensified attention" were the Southern Christian Leadership Conference, the Student Nonviolent Coordinating Committee, Revolutionary Action Movement, Deacons for Defense and Justice, Congress of Racial Equality, and the Nation of Islam. Individuals named targets were Stokely Carmichael, H. "Rap" Brown, Elijah Muhammad, and Maxwell Stanford. The targets were chosen by conferring with Headquarters personnel supervising the racial cases; the list was not intended to exclude other groups known to the field.

According to the Black Nationalist supervisor, individuals and organizations were targeted because of their propensity for violence *or* their "radical or revolutionary rhetoric [and] actions.". . .

The letter explaining the program lists five long-range goals for the program:

1. to prevent the "coalition of militant black nationalist groups," which might be the first step toward a real "Mau Mau" in America;
2. to prevent the rise of a "messiah" who could "unify and electrify" the movement, naming specifically Martin Luther King, Stokely Carmichael, and Elijah Muhammad;
3. to prevent violence on the part of black nationalist groups, by pinpointing "potential troublemakers" and neutralizing them "before they exercise their potential for violence";
4. to prevent groups and leaders from gaining "respectability" by discrediting them to the "responsible" Negro community, to the white community (both the responsible community and the "liberals"—the distinction is the Bureau's), and to Negro radicals; and
5. to prevent the long range growth of these organizations, especially among youth, by developing specific tactics to "prevent these groups from recruiting young people."

The Panther Directives The Black Panther Party ("BPP") was not included in the first two lists of primary targets (August 1967 and March 1968) because it had not attained national importance. By November 1968, apparently the BPP had become sufficiently active to be considered a primary target. A letter to certain field offices with BPP activity dated November 26, 1968, ordered recipient offices to submit "imaginative and hard-hitting counterintelligence measures aimed at crippling the BPP."

New Left The Internal Security Section had undergone a slow transition from concentrating on the "Old Left"—the CPUSA and SWP—to focusing primarily on the activities of the "New Left"—a term which had no precise definition within the Bureau. Some agents defined "New Left" functionally, by connection with protests. Others defined it by philosophy, particularly antiwar philosophy.

On October 28, 1968, the fifth and final COINTELPRO was started against this undefined group. The program was triggered in part by the Columbia campus disturbance. Once again, law enforcement methods had broken down, largely (in the Bureau's opinion) because college administrators refused to call the police on campus to deal with student demonstrations. . . .

According to the initiating letter, the counterintelligence program's purpose was to "expose, disrupt, and otherwise neutralize" the activities of the various New Left organizations, their leadership, and adherents, with particular attention to Key Activists, "the moving forces behind the New Left." The final paragraph contains an exhortation to a "forward look, enthusiasm, and interest" because of the Bureau's concern that "the anarchist activities of a few can paralyze institutions of learning, induction centers, cripple traffic, and tie the arms of law enforcement officials all to the detriment of our society." The internal memorandum recommending the program further sets forth the Bureau's concerns:

> Our nation is undergoing an era of disruption and violence caused to a large extent by various individuals generally connected with the New Left. Some of these activists urge revolution in America and call for the defeat of the United States in Vietnam. They continually and falsely allege police brutality and do not hesitate to utilize unlawful acts to further their so-called causes.

The document continues:

> The New Left has on many occasions viciously and scurrilously attacked the Director and the Bureau in an attempt to hamper our investigation of it and to drive us off the college campuses. . . .

Briefly the techniques are:

1. preparing leaflets designed to discredit student demonstrators, using photographs of New Left leadership at the respective universities. "Naturally, the most obnoxious pictures should be used";
2. instigating "personal conflicts or animosities" between New left leaders;
3. creating the impression that leaders are "informants for the Bureau or other law enforcement agencies";
4. sending articles from student newspapers or the "underground press" which show the depravity of the New Left to university officials, donors, legislators, and parents. "Articles showing the advocation of the use of narcotics and free sex are ideal";
5. having members arrested on marijuana charges;
6. sending anonymous letters about a student's activities to parents, neighbors, and the parents' employers. "This could have the effect of forcing the parents to take action";
7. sending anonymous letters or leaflets describing the "activities and associations" of New Left faculty members and graduate assistants to university officials, legislators, Boards of Regents, and the press. "These letters should be signed 'A Concerned Alumni,' or 'A Concerned Taxpayer' ";
8. using "cooperative press contacts" to emphasize that the "disruptive elements" constitute a "minority" of the students. "The press should demand an immediate referendum on the issue in question";
9. exploiting the "hostility" among the SDS and other New Left groups toward the SWP, YSA, and Progressive Labor Party;
10. using "friendly news media" and law enforcement officials to disrupt New Left coffeehouses near military bases which are attempting to "influence members of the armed forces";
11. using cartoons, photographs, and anonymous letters to "ridicule" the New Left; and
12. using "misinformation" to "confuse and disrupt" New Left activities, such as by notifying members that events have been canceled.

COINTELPRO and Homophobia

Included in the COINTELPRO report were several documents the Bureau had generated to undermine the credibility of antiwar activist David Dellinger, one of the defendants in the Chicago Conspiracy Trial (see chapter 7). What is striking about these efforts is the degree to which the FBI believed that questioning sexual orientation would be as damaging as questioning patriotism. This entire matter has taken on added irony as allegations about FBI Director J. Edgar Hoover's hidden homosexuality have come to light in recent years.

One FBI memorandum, entitled "Desperate Dave Dangles Dingus," referred to Dellinger as "speaking in his usual high-pitched voice" and described him as looking "more fairy-like than ever," while his followers "stood behind their Guru sniffling and fingering wilted flowers."

Another even more insulting document was an FBI-produced parody contest, "The Gigantic 'Pick the Fag' Contest." Included were pictures of Dellinger, Latin American revolutionary Che Guevera, Columbia student leader Mark Rudd, and philosopher Herbert Marcuse. The instructions read: "Simply pick the faggot from the following photos. Print your choice on the entry blank at the bottom of this page and pop it in the mail." Sexism joined homophobia in the phony prizes:

> Grand Prize . . . Seven full days in Hanoi—Expense Paid
>
> Second Prize . . . Fourteen full days in Hanoi
>
> Third Prize . . . A weekend with Josie Duke in a genuine fire-damaged Columbia University dormitory
>
> Fourth Prize . . . Two weekends with tubby little Josie!

COINTELPRO and Violence

FBI activities went beyond insensitivity and nastiness. Senate documents report attempts by the FBI to foster antagonisms within groups and to encourage violence between them. The following is a brief section from the COINTELPRO report focusing on efforts to exacerbate friction between the Black Panthers and a second black nationalist group, known as US. This antagonism did lead to violence and the deaths of several Panthers. The FBI then sought to exploit these deaths to further hostility between the groups.

ENCOURAGING VIOLENCE BETWEEN RIVAL GROUPS

The Bureau's attempts to capitalize on active hostility between target groups carried with them the risk of serious physical injury to the targets. As the Black Nationalist supervisor put it:

> It is not easy [to judge the risks inherent in this technique]. You make the best judgment you can based on all the circumstances and you always have an element of doubt where you are dealing with individuals that I think most people would characterize as having a degree of instability.

The Bureau took that risk. The Panther directive instructing recipient officers to encourage the differences between the Panthers and US, Inc. which were "taking on the aura of gang warfare with attendant threats of murder and reprisals," is just one example.

In November 1968, the FBI took initial steps in its program to disrupt the Black Panther Party in San Diego, California by aggravating the existing hostility between the Panthers and US. A memorandum from FBI director Hoover to 14 field offices noted a state of "gang warfare" existed, with "attendant threats of murder and reprisals," between the BPP and US in southern California and added:

> In order to fully capitalize upon BPP and US differences as well as to exploit all avenues of creating further dissension in the ranks of the BPP, recipient offices are instructed to submit imaginative and hard-hitting counterintelligence measures aimed at crippling the BPP.

As the tempo of violence quickened, the FBI's field office in San Diego developed tactics calculated to heighten tension between the hostile factions. On January 17, 1969, two members of the Black Panther Party—Apprentice "Bunchy" Carter and John Huggins— were killed by US members of the UCLA campus following a meeting involving the two organizations and university students. One month later, the San Diego field office requested permission from headquarters to mail derogatory cartoons to local BPP offices and to the homes of prominent BPP leaders around the country. The purpose was plainly stated:

> The purpose of the caricatures is to indicate to the BPP that the US organization feels that they are ineffectual, inadequate, and riddled with graft and corruption.

On April 4, 1969, there was a confrontation between US and BPP members in Southcrest Park in San Diego at which, according to an FBI memorandum, the BPP members "ran the US members off." On the same date, US members broke into a BPP political education meeting and roughed up a female BPP member. The FBI's Special Agent in Charge in San Diego boasted that the cartoons had caused these incidents:

> The BPP members . . . strongly objected being made fun of by cartoons being distributed by the US organization (FBI cartoons in actuality). . . . [Informant] has advised on several occasions that the cartoons are "really shaking up the BPP." They have made the BPP feel that US is getting ready to move and this was the cause of the confrontation at Southcrest Park on 4/4/69.

The fragile truce had ended. On May 23, 1969, John Savage, a member of the BPP in Southern California, was shot and killed by US member Jerry Horne, aka Tambuzi. The killing was reported in an FBI memorandum which stated that confrontations between the groups were now ranging from "mere harassment up to and including beating of various individuals." In mid-June, the San Diego FBI office informed Washington headquarters that members of the US organization were holding firearms practice and purchasing large quantities of ammunition.

Despite this atmosphere of violence, FBI headquarters authorized the San Diego field office to compose an inflammatory letter over the forged signature of a San Diego BPP member and to send it to the BPP headquarters in Oakland, California. The letter complained of the killing of Panthers in San Diego by US members, and the fact that a local BPP leader had a white girlfriend.

According to a BPP bulletin, two Panthers were wounded by US gunmen on August 14, 1969, and the next day another BPP member, Sylvester Bell, was killed in San Diego by US members. On August 30, 1969, the San Diego office of US was bombed. The FBI believed that the BPP was responsible for the bombing.

The San Diego office of the FBI viewed this carnage as a positive development and informed headquarters: "Efforts are being made to determine how this situation can be capitalized upon for the benefit of the Counterintelligence Program. . . ." The field office further noted:

> In view of the recent killing of BPP member Sylvester Bell, a new cartoon is being considered in the hopes that it will assist in the continuance of the rift between BPP and US.

COUNTER-COUNTERCULTURE

Americans were as perplexed by the counterculture as they were unnerved by the political movements. Rock 'n' roll epitomized the culture of the young for the older generation as much as it did for sixties youth.

Air Pollution?

When Newsweek *first tried to assess the new music in 1965, it focused on the sexual innuendo and drug references in song lyrics.*

> I can't get no satisfaction,
> I can't get no girlie action
> ... Ah try and ah try and ah try ...
> And I'm tryin' to make some girl. ...

Panted rather than sung by a leering quintet called the Rolling Stones, "Satisfaction" has dominated teen-age record sales and radio's Top Forty sound in the U.S. for the last six weeks. If these explicit lyrics dismay adults, they ought to hear the flip side, "The Under Assistant West Coast Promotion Man," which has a line sufficiently indecent to get it banned on some rock-'n'-roll stations.

Sexual innuendo, of course, is nothing new in popular music. It lent an added glitter to such old standards as Cole Porter's "Let's Do It" and "All of You." But the suggestive songs of today's commercial rock-'n'-roll groups are something different: they have no wit, for one thing, but more important they are frankly aimed at adolescents rather than the sophisticated Broadway audiences who first heard Porter.

Digging the Dirt: "Porter and Lorenz Hart did it with such class and taste that it sounded mature," contends disk jockey William B. Williams of WNEW in New York, who plays the standards. "Now there isn't any taste involved." "The average 14-year-old," adds Atlanta's Pat Hughes, "digs all the dirt."

Unhappily, too, there's more dirt to dig, for a kind of Gresham's law is at work today in pop music, and the tasteless themes of the Rolling Stones have begun to displace the innocently exuberant sounds of the Beatles (who only pleaded "I Want to Hold Your Hand"). The Stones continue to grind out visceral stuff like "King

Bee" (Buzzin' 'round your hive, together we can make honey . . . let me come inside . . .") and "I'm All Right," a crescendo of *do you feel it, do you FEEL it* and *c'mon, c'mon, c'mon, C'MON BABY.*

But dirty lyrics are sometimes hard to pin down. The words of the songs are teen argot to begin with, and they are inundated by an artillery of yeah yeah yeahs, then run through a battery of echo and "dubbing over" chambers and topped off by a pulsating, drown-'em-out percussionist. "It seems like the harder they are to understand, the dirtier you can bet they are," said a teen-age girl in Atlanta, who has given up on deciphering rock 'n' roll. Chicago disk jockeys refer to slurred-lyric songs as "mumblies"—"you can hear anything you want to in them," says one DJ.

The Kingsmen's "Louie Louie" is a particularly blatant recent example. A group of Princeton students heard that spinning the 45 version at 33 rpm furnished quite a shock even to strong stomachs. When the FCC looked into complaints, its investigators found the chant unintelligible at any speed. Some listeners discerned the same slurring technique to disguise the words in the Elchords' "Peppermint Stick."

Double Entendre: Knowing teenagers also listen for euphemisms in such alleged underground songs as Lee Dorsey's "Ride Your Pony," Ian Whitcomb's "You Turn Me On," and Tom Jones's smash, "What's New Pussycat?" Yet a new hit with suggestive credentials, "I Want Candy"—sung by the Strangeloves on the Bang label—proves, after careful scrutiny, innocent enough.

Songs with multiple meanings are not all based on sex: the Rooftop Singers' "Walk Right In" sounds to some ears, like an illusion to drug addiction; and the Byrds' hit of several weeks ago, "Mr. Tambourine Man," is reputedly about a pusher in New York's Greenwich Village—although Bob Dylan's original lyrics were tamed down somewhat for the pop version. "Puff," a whimsical fairy tune on the surface, which doting fathers bought for their 6-year-olds, sounded to some like a narcotics cryptogram:

> *Puff* [smoke], *the magic dragon,*
> [drag-in=inhale]
> *Lived by the sea* ["C"=cocaine].
> *And frolicked in the autumn mist*

In a land called Honah Lee
[argot for being high on heroin].
Little Jackie Paper [in which
marijuana is wrapped] *loved*
that rascal Puff.

Although Federal criminal status make it a crime to broadcast obscene, indecent or profane material, and the FCC can revoke a license for violation of that statute, radio stations are supposed to police their own content. "The record studios know they won't get onto the big stations with off-color songs," said Gene Williams, program director of WLS in Chicago. "We screen all the music up here before we play it, and we're pretty careful."

True, most stations hold reviewing sessions where officials and disk jockeys are supposed to toss out songs deemed in questionable taste; but apparently standards have been relaxed recently more and more. (DJ taste is not impeccable: in New York last week WABC fired Bob Dayton after he reported the anniversary of Hiroshima and then played a record of "Happy Birthday.") The stations feel they must be with it—and if the Rolling Stones' songs are not always decorous, they are in demand. "Unfortunately, the Stones now are hot. They could hum something and it would sell—that might be an improvement," says WLS's Clark Weber.

Lyric Agonies: Yet there are the stirrings of audience unease. The PTA Magazine, which tries to act as a guide for parents who still have some control over their children's entertainment, recently criticized ABC's "Shindig," which put the Stones' gyrations on TV. The magazine also will blast NBC's "Hullabaloo" in its September issue. "Soloists, male and female, moan, groan and grimace in the sick songs, and lyric agonies of frustrated love," the guide complains. "Whatever this program may represent psychologically, sociologically and economically, esthetically it is ugly, grotesque and revolting."

Some DJ's, however, suggest that commercial rock 'n' roll is full of sound and fury—signifying nothing. Boston's Arnie ("Woo Woo") Ginsberg of WMEX claims that "a popular song is only successful because of the total sound. Words aren't that important." And a

Cleveland teen-ager confirms this opinion. Asked about a "suggestive word," she replied: "Words? What words?"

Rhythm, Riots and Revolution

REV. DAVID A. NOEBEL

As the power of rock music grew within the counterculture and the movements, so, too, did the concern it evoked in traditional circles. An extreme reaction came in 1966 from Christian crusader David Noebel, who found communist political menace and Pavlovian manipulations embedded in rock 'n' roll.

America's very young are not the only targets of the Communists. Also included in their ingeniously conceived master music plan are America's teenagers. Since rhythmic activity music ceases to be effective by early adolescence, the music designed for high school students is extremely effective in aiding and abetting demoralization among teenagers, effective in producing degrees of artificial neurosis and in preparing them for riot and ultimately revolution to destroy our American form of government and the basic Christian principles governing our way of life.

The music has been called a number of things, but today it is best known as rock 'n' roll, beat music or simply Beatle-music. Even *Time* magazine admitted that "there was obviously something visceral" about the music since it has caused riots in countless communities. Riot-causing it is, but it is also a noise which causes teenagers to experience countless side-effects, detrimental not only to the community, but also to the individual and the country. We contend that it was so planned. . . .

Reprinted by permission, Billy James Hargis, President, Christian Crusade Publications.

Today all major record companies are flooding our teenagers with a noise that is basically sexual, un-Christian, mentally unsettling and riot-producing. The consequences of this type of "music" are staggering. In Jacksonville, Florida, 6,700 rock 'n' roll fans were sent into a "screaming, fighting frenzy in the Jacksonville coliseum. . . . Twenty police officers on duty at the show were swamped and called for reinforcements . . . they (according to one police officer) were like a herd of cows stampeding.". . .

Four young men, noted for their tonsils and tonsure, are also helping to overwhelm our youth with this destructive type of "music." When the Beatles presented their "concert" in Vancouver, British Columbia, a hundred persons were stomped, gouged, elbowed and otherwise assaulted during the twenty-nine minutes performance. Nearly 1,000 were injured in Melbourne, Australia. In Beirut, Lebanon, fire hoses were needed to disperse hysterical fans. In the grip of Beatle fever, we are told, the teenagers weep, wail and experience ecstasy-ridden hysteria that has to be seen to be believed. Also, we are told, teenagers "bite their lips until they bleed and they even get overexcited and take off their clothes." To understand what rock 'n' roll in general and the Beatles in particular are doing to our teenagers, it is necessary to return to Pavlov's laboratory. The Beatles' ability to make teenagers weep and wail, become uncontrollable and unruly, and take off their clothes and riot is laboratory tested and approved. It is scientifically induced artificial or experimental neurosis.

Ivan P. Pavlov, the eminent Russian physiologist, was invited to Moscow as the personal house guest of Nikolai Lenin, the father of the Bolshevik revolution. Pavlov expressed confidence that his findings on conditioned reflexes and inhibitions would be a blessing to mankind someday in its struggle against human ailments. Lenin had other plans. . . .

Pavlov, in his many experiments with animals and human beings, discovered specific scientific procedures to produce artificial neuroses in dogs and men. In studying and relating these experiments, one is immediately impressed with the almost perfect analogy between what our youngsters experience under Beatlemania and the technique inflicted on Pavlov's dogs to develop "artificial neurosis.". . .

We contend that rock 'n' roll, certainly a strong external stimulus, is producing this artificial type of neurosis in our teenagers, and

causing teenage mental breakdowns to reach an all time high. . . .
Rock 'n' roll, with its perverted music form, dulls the capacity for
attention and creates a kind of hypnotic monotony which blurs and
makes unreal the external world. "Earthly worries are submerged in
a tide of rising exaltation . . . the whole universe is compressed into
the medium of the beat, where all things unite and pound forward,
rhythmic, and regular." In the area of morals, "rock 'n' roll treats
the concept of love with a characteristic doubleness. . . . The lyrics
generally capitulate to the concept [of true love], *but the music itself
expresses the unspoken desire to smash it to pieces and run amuck."* This was
precisely what Dr. Ronald Sprenger, chief school medical officer of
Nottingham, England, had in mind when he referred to rock 'n' roll
as the cause of sexual delinquency among teenagers. He also said,
"Mass hysteria affects many to the stage of loss of consciousness and
lack of thought for their immediate welfare."

With the previously instilled inhibitions prohibiting the teenager
from committing acts of sexual and other delinquency, the external
excitatory music creates exactly the opposite desires. The ensuing
internal conflict causes a severe clash or collision of the two forces
and the teenager breaks down with a mental condition identifiable
as artificial neurosis.

And, the frightening—even terrifying—aspect of this mentally conditioned process is the fact that the young people, in this highly
excited, hypnotic state, can be told to do practically anything—and
they will.

The Beatles were in Seattle, Washington, for a "concert" in August
1964. According to the *Intelligencer,* the show began at 8:07. "First
came the Bill Black-Combo, then the Exciters, and after them the
Righteous Brothers. Next on the program was Jackie de Shannon,
who sang 'Needles and Pins'—and several other songs, as well as
having the audience sing 'Happy Birthday' to her."

Burt McMurtrie, a radio personality in the Northwest and a pro-
Beatle fan, had the following to say about those "entertainers": . . .
"That entire evening seemed *designed* to arouse every animal and sex
instinct in the audience up to uncontrollable pitch and just such did
it accomplish.

"It was the old, down-by-the-river religious pitch a thousand times
magnified. The sort of emotional lack of control, out-of-control found
in a savage jungle. And it is not healthy."

Dr. Bernard Saibel, child guidance expert for the Washington State division of community services, attended the Seattle performance of England's Beatles at the request of the *Seattle Times*. The following is Dr. Saibel's report.

"The experience of being with 14,000 teenagers to see the Beatles is unbelievable and frightening.

"And believe me, it is not at all funny, as I first thought when I accepted this assignment.

"The hysteria and loss of control go far beyond the impact of the music. Many of those present became frantic, hostile, uncontrolled, screaming, unrecognizable beings.

"If this is possible—and it is—parents and adults have a lot to account for to allow this to go on.

"*This is not simply a release*, as I at first thought it would be, *but a very destructive process* in which adults allow the children to be involved—allowing the children a mad, erotic world of their own without the reassuring safeguards of protection from themselves.

"The music is loud, primitive, insistent, strongly rhythmic, and releases in a disguised way (can it be called sublimation?) the all too tenuously controlled, newly acquired physical impulses of the teenager.

"Mix this up with the phenomena of mass hypnosis, contagious hysteria, and the blissful feeling of being mixed up in an all-embracing, orgiastic experience, and every kid can become 'Lord of the Flies' or the Beatles.

"Why do the kids scream, faint, gyrate and in general look like a primeval, protoplasmic upheaval and go into ecstatic convulsions when certain identifiable and expected trade-marks come forth, such as 'O yeah!' a twist of the hips or the thrusting out of an electric guitar?

"Regardless of the causes or reasons for the behavior of these youngsters, it had the impact of an unholy bedlam, the like of which I have never seen. It caused me to feel that such should not be allowed again, if only for the good of the youngsters.

"It was an orgy for teenagers."

7

"THE WHOLE WORLD IS WATCHING": 1968 . . . AND AFTER

The year 1968 witnessed periods of optimism followed by periods of despair and disillusion. At times movement activists felt that not only was their message penetrating mainstream America, but that the political tide was turning. These enthusiastic moments were often followed by tragedy, defeat, and pessimism. World events seemed to compress a lifetime into a year and a half. From the announcement in the fall of 1967 of a challenge to Lyndon Johnson within his own party to the Days of Rage of the SDS splinter group, the Weathermen, in the spring of 1969, events came to repeated crisis points in America and around the world. America reeled from its tragedies, its disillusionments, and its internal rifts.

By the end of 1967 the Democratic Party had been increasingly discredited by both the left and the right, with the former seeing it as the party of war and the latter as the party that threw money into failed social welfare programs and would not impose law and order (see chapter 6). But in the fall of that year antiwar forces within the party convinced Minnesota Senator Eugene McCarthy to stand against Lyndon Johnson for the presidential nomination in 1968. Initially viewed as a quixotic quest, McCarthy's challenge took on new energy early in 1968.

Despite optimistic appraisals by American leaders, the Tet offensive in Vietnam in early 1968 showed that the North Vietnamese and Vietcong were powerful and could still surprise the Americans with bold strikes (see chapter 4). The taking and holding of the American Embassy in South Vietnam's capital city of Saigon served as a symbolic example for the American people of enemy strength and resolve. More than ever, Americans became aware of the "credibility gap" that existed between optimistic government assessments and what millions saw each night on television or read in their newspapers.

Growing concern about the war fueled anti-Johnson sentiment. After a highly respectable showing by McCarthy in the New Hampshire primary in early March, New York Senator Robert Kennedy entered the race. And then in a stunning surprise, Lyndon Johnson withdrew on the eve of the Wisconsin primary at the end of the month. After years outside the political process, antiwar forces began to feel that they were having some effect. The remaining primary season for the Democrats became a test between McCarthy and Kennedy, while Vice President Hubert Humphrey, who entered the race too late to run in the primaries, sought to woo party bosses and Democrats once committed to LBJ.

The enthusiasm following Johnson's announcement was crushed the following week when Martin Luther King, Jr., was assassinated in Memphis. Setting off days of urban rebellion across the nation, the King murder reminded all Americans, and blacks in particular, of the violent underside of American life and of limited progress on racial matters since 1965. Black activists had become more militant, angry, and nationalist, and rebellions in urban ghettos became frequent summer occurrences (see chapter 3). The Black Panthers, praised for their self-determination and focus on selfdefense, emerged as a symbol of the changing perspective for many radicals, white as well as black. They also were a subject of interest for the media and of obsession by the Federal Bureau of Investigation.

Despite victories in the political arena, college students grew more militant on campuses across the country in the spring of 1968. One college after another erupted—mainly over antiwar and racial issues. Students around the world protested as well, aiming their critiques at their own governments and universities, but also at American involvement in Vietnam. From California and New York to Paris, Berlin, and Mexico City, students felt themselves a part of a loosely defined international movement aimed at changing their own societies and, perhaps, the world.

The optimism engendered by the early victories of the antiwar forces within the Democratic Party turned sour and tragic as, first, Robert Kennedy was murdered moments after declaring victory in the California primary (the fourth assassination of a national leader in five years, adding his name to those of John F. Kennedy, Malcolm X, and Martin Luther King, Jr.) and, second, Hubert Humphrey emerged as the front-runner despite having entered none of the primaries. The party's convention, held in Chicago in August, became not only an arena for nominating candidates, but a theater of protest and rage. With Humphrey's nomination seemingly assured, and with it a reaffirmation of Johnson's Vietnam policies, many delegates and demonstrators voiced their disappointment and anger. The tense atmosphere was heightened by clashes between antiwar forces and Chicago police, who had denied all parade permits and had armed themselves with riot-control weapons and armored vehicles. Aided by undercover FBI agents, the Chicago police bullied and assaulted demonstrators. While the marchers chanted "the whole world is watching," Americans viewing the convention on television saw police beat students, Chicago Mayor Richard Daley spit epithets at platform speakers who questioned the tactics of his police, and the Democrats unravel as the party of reform and peaceful social change. The election of Republican Richard Nixon in November confirmed the disillusionment.

Within the political movements, feelings of dispiritedness and anger began to unravel the umbrella that linked new left and antiwar groups. SDS, whose Port Huron Statement had helped begin the movement in the early sixties, saw groups break off and split apart. One segment, the Weathermen, advocated armed insurrection and violence as the only way American society could be changed. Drawing some of their inspiration from the Panthers, the Weathermen's influence grew much larger than their small numbers would suggest. They seemed to embody mounting disbelief in the possibility that American society would ever be changed voluntarily or democratically.

By 1969 most of the optimism that had characterized the early years of the sixties and had erupted periodically in 1968 had receded. Some could still find solace in events such as the gathering at Woodstock in the summer of 1969 (see chapter 9) or by scaling back their ambitions and joining rural communes in order to achieve a more measured personal salvation (see chapter 5). But for a great many, what remained were feelings of disillusion, hopelessness, and anger.

CAMPUS EXPLOSIONS

In 1968 and 1969 a wave of campus demonstrations erupted. Across the country and around the world students sought to take power into their own hands in order to address the injustices they felt existed on campus, in their communities, and in their countries.

Two, Three, Many Columbias

TOM HAYDEN

In the spring of 1968 Columbia University became the stage for a major confrontation between students and the college administration. The issues focused on the university's military-related research, and thus Vietnam, and on Columbia's racial policy vis-à-vis black students and the adjacent community of Harlem. Students demonstrated, occupied buildings, and eventually went on strike. The administration called in police to clear the protesters, many of whom were injured and arrested. Like Berkeley in 1964, Columbia became the center of national media attention.

Tom Hayden, active in the new left since the early 1960s, wrote the following statement about the demonstrations at Columbia University. He suggests why this was more radical than previous student strikes and calls for more actions following the Columbia model.

The goal written on the university walls was "Create two, three, many Columbias"; it meant expand the strike so that the U.S. must either change or send its troops to occupy American campuses.

At this point the goal seems realistic; an explosive mix is present on dozens of campuses where demands for attention to student views are being disregarded by university administrators.

The American student movement has continued to swell for nearly a decade: during the semi-peace of the early '60s as well as during Vietnam; during the token liberalism of John Kennedy as well as during the bankrupt racism of Lyndon Johnson. Students have responded most directly to the black movement of the '60s: from Mississippi Summer to the Free Speech Movement; from "Black Power" to "Student Power"; from the seizure of Howard University to the seizure of Hamilton Hall. As the racial crisis deepens so will the campus crisis. But the student protest is not just an offshoot of the black protest—it is based on authentic opposition to the middle-class world of manipulation, channeling and careerism. The students are in opposition to the fundamental institutions of society.

The students' protest constantly escalates by building on its achievements and legends. The issues being considered by seventeen-year-old freshmen at Columbia University would not have been within the imagination of most "veteran" student activists five years ago.

Columbia opened a new tactical stage in the resistance movement which began last fall: from the overnight occupation of buildings to permanent occupation; from mill-ins to the creation of revolutionary committees; from symbolic civil disobedience to barricaded resistance. Not only are these tactics already being duplicated on other campuses, but they are sure to be surpassed by even more militant tactics. In the future it is conceivable that students will threaten destruction of buildings as a last deterrent to police attacks. Many of the tactics learned can also be applied in smaller hit-and-run operations between strikes: raids on the offices of professors doing weapons research could win substantial support among students while making the university more blatantly repressive.

In the buildings occupied at Columbia, the students created what they called a "new society" or "liberated area" or "commune," a society in which decent values would be lived out even though university officials might cut short the communes through use of police. The students had fun, they sang and danced and wisecracked, but there was continual tension. There was no question of their constant awareness of the seriousness of their acts. Though there were a few violent arguments about tactics, the discourse was more in the form of endless meetings convened to explore the outside political situation, defense tactics, maintenance and morale problems within the group. Debating and then determining what leaders should do were alternatives to the remote and authoritarian decision-making of Columbia's trustees.

The Columbia strike represented more than a new tactical movement, however. There was a political message as well. The striking students were not holding onto a narrow conception of students as a privileged class asking for inclusion in the university as it now exists. This kind of demand could easily be met by administrators by opening minor opportunities for "student rights" while cracking down on campus radicals. The Columbia students were instead taking an internationalist and revolutionary view of themselves in opposition to the imperialism of the very institutions in which they have been groomed and educated. They did not even want to be included in the decision-making circles of the military-industrial complex that runs Columbia: *they want to be included only if their inclusion is a step toward transforming the university.* They want a new and independent university standing against the mainstream of American society, or they want no university at all. They are, in Fidel Castro's words, "guerrillas in the field of culture."

How many other schools can be considered ripe for such confrontations? The question is hard to answer, but it is clear that the demands of black students for cultural recognition rather than paternalistic tolerance, and radical white students' awareness of the sinister paramilitary activities carried on in secret by the faculty on many campuses, are hardly confined to Columbia. Columbia's problem is the American problem in miniature—the inability to provide answers to widespread social needs and the use of the military to protect the authorities against the people. This process can only lead to greater unity in the movement.

Support from outside the university communities can be counted on in many large cities. A crisis is foreseeable that would be too massive for police to handle. It can happen; whether or not it will be necessary is a question which only time will answer. What is certain is that we are moving toward power—the power to stop the machine if it cannot be made to serve humane ends.

American educators are fond of telling their students that barricades are part of the romantic past, that social change today can only come about through the processes of negotiation. But the students at Columbia discovered that barricades are only the beginning of what they call "bringing the war home."

Columbia Liberated

COLUMBIA STRIKE COORDINATING COMMITTEE

The following is a statement of the issues, demands, and events of the 1968 Columbia strike.

THE STRIKE IN CONTEXT

The most important fact about the Columbia strike is that Columbia exists within American society. This statement may appear to be a truism, yet it is a fact too often forgotten by observers, reporters, administrators, faculty members, and even some students. These people attempt to explain the "disturbances" as reaction to an unresponsive and archaic administrative structure, youthful outbursts of unrest much like panty raids, the product of a conspiracy by communist agents in national SDS or a handful of hard-core nihilists ("destroyers") on the campus, or just general student unrest due to the war in Vietnam.

But in reality, striking students are responding to the totality of the conditions of our society, not just one small part of it, the university. We are disgusted with the war, with racism, with being a part of a system over which we have no control, a system which demands gross inequalities of wealth and power, a system which denies personal and social freedom and potential, a system which has to manipulate and repress us in order to exist. The university can only be seen as a cog in this machine; or, more accurately, a factory whose product is knowledge and personnel (us) useful to the functioning of the system. The specific problems of university life, its boredom and meaninglessness, help prepare us for boring and meaningless work in the "real" world. And the policies of the university—expansion into the community, exploitation of blacks and Puerto Ricans, support for imperialist wars—also serve the interests of banks, corporations, government, and military represented on the Columbia Board of Trustees and the ruling class of our society. In every way, the university is "society's child." Our attack upon the university is really an attack upon this society and its effects upon us. We have never said otherwise.

The development of the New Left at Columbia represents an organized political response to the society. We see our task, first as identifying for ourselves and for others the nature of our society—who controls it and for what ends—and secondly, developing ways in which to transform it. We understand that only through struggle can we create a free, human society, since the present one is dominated by a small ruling class which exploits, manipulates, and distorts for its own ends—and has shown in countless ways its determination to maintain its position. The Movement at Columbia began years ago agitating and organizing students around issues such as students' power in the university (Action), support of the civil rights movement (CORE), the war in Vietnam (the Independent Committee on Vietnam). Finally, Columbia chapter Students for a Democratic Society initiated actions against many of the above issues as they manifest themselves on campus. Politically speaking, SDS, from its inception on campus in November, 1966, sought to unite issues, "to draw connections," to view this society as a totality. SDS united the two main themes of the movement—opposition to racial oppression and to the imperialist war in Vietnam—with our own sense of frustration, disappointment, and oppression at the quality of our lives in capitalist society.

One of the most important questions raised by the strike was who controls Columbia, and for what ends? SDS pointed to the Board of Trustees as the intersection of various corporate, financial, real-estate, and government interests outside the university which need the products of the university—personnel and knowledge—in order to exist. It is this power which we are fighting when we fight particular policies of the university such as expansion at the expense of poor people or institutional ties to the war-machine. We can hope for and possibly win certain reforms within the university, but the ultimate reforms we need—the elimination of war and exploitation—can only be gained after we overthrow the control of our country by the class of people on Columbia's Board of Trustees. In a sense, Columbia is the place where we received our education—our revolutionary education. . . .

But why do students, predominantly of the "middle-class," in effect, reject the university designed to integrate them into the system and instead identify with the most oppressed of this country and the world? Why did the gymnasium in Morningside Park become an issue over which Columbia was shut down for seven weeks? Why pictures of Che Guevara, Malcolm X, and red flags in the liberated buildings?

Basically, the sit-ins and strike of April and May gave us a chance to express the extreme dissatisfaction we feel at being *caught in this "system."* We rejected the gap between potential and realization in this society. We rejected our present lives in the university and our future lives in business, government or other universities like this one. In a word, we saw ourselves as oppressed, and began to understand the forces at work which make for our oppression. In turn, we saw those same forces responsible for the oppression and colonization of blacks and Puerto Ricans in ghettos, and Vietnamese and the people of the third world. By initiating a struggle in support of black and third world liberation, we create the conditions for our own freedom—by building a movement which will someday take power over our society, we will free ourselves.

As the strike and the struggle for our demands progressed, we learned more about the nature of our enemy and his unwillingness to grant any of our demands or concede any of his power. Illusions disappeared: the moral authority of the educator gave way to police violence, the faculty appeared in all its impotent glory. On the other hand, tremendous support came in from community residents, black and white alike, from university employees, from high school students, from people across the country and around the world. Inevitably, we began to re-evaluate our goals and strategy. Chief among the lessons were (1) We cannot possibly win our demands alone: we must unite with other groups in the population; (2) The 6 demands cannot possibly be our ultimate ends: even winning all of them certainly would not go far enough toward the basic reforms we need to live as human beings in this society; (3) "Restructuring" the university, the goal of faculty groups, various "moderate" students, and even the trustees, cannot possibly create a "free" or "democratic" university out of this institution. (First, how can anyone expect any meaningful reforms when even our initial demands have not been met?) Secondly, we realize that the university is entirely synchronized with the society: how can you have a "free", human university in a society such as this? Hence the SDS slogan "A free university in a free society." The converse is equally true.

The basic problem in understanding our strike—our demands, tactics, and history—consists of keeping in mind the social context of the university and of our movement. If you understand that we are the political response to an oppressive and exploitative social and economic system, you will have no difficulty putting together the pieces. . . .

The six demands:

1. That the administration grant amnesty for the original "IDA 6" and for all those participating in these demonstrations.
2. That construction of the gymnasium in Morningside Park be terminated immediately.
3. That the university sever all ties with the Institute for Defense Analysis and that President Kirk and Trustee Burden resign their positions on the Executive Committee of that institution immediately.
4. That President Kirk's ban on indoor demonstrations be dropped.
5. That all future judicial decisions be made by a student-faculty committee.
6. That the university use its good offices to drop charges against all people arrested in demonstrations at the gym site and on campus.

As the fall begins, it is clear that Columbia will be the scene of much more radical political action. No demands have yet been met. The university is prosecuting in criminal court close to 1,100 people, most of whom are students. At least 79 students have been suspended, hundreds more placed on probation. Columbia's exploitation of the community and her support for the Government's imperialist policies continue. Most important, people now know that they are fighting the forces behind Columbia, the power of the ruling class in this society, not just the institution. And they have the commitment to keep fighting. The Democratic National Convention killed electoral politics for young people in this country and the Chicago Police Dept. provided an alternative—to fight. So did Columbia in the spring. So does it now, along with every other university in this country. The struggle goes on. Create two, three, many Columbias, that is the watchword!

List of Strike Demands

SAN FRANCISCO STATE: BLACK STUDENT UNION AND THIRD WORLD LIBERATION FRONT

The 1969 San Francisco State strike developed out of calls by students of color for changes in the racial policies of the university. The growth of Black Power and ideas about ethnic and racial identity led to demands for the development of black studies departments. These grew into central concerns of the San Francisco State conflict.

Following is a list of the fifteen strike demands as put forth by the Black Students Union and the Third World Liberation Front.

THE TEN BSU DEMANDS

1. That all Black Studies courses being taught through various other departments be immediately made part of the Black Studies Depart-

ment, and that all the instructors in this department receive full-
time pay.

2. That Dr. Nathan Hare, Chairman of the Black Studies Department,
receive a full professorship and a comparable salary according to
his qualifications.

3. That there be a Department of Black Studies which will grant a
Bachelor's Degree in Black Studies; that the Black Studies Department, the chairman, faculty, and staff have the sole power to hire
faculty and control and determine the destiny of its department.

4. That all unused slots for Black Students from Fall 1968 under the
Special Admissions Program be filled in Spring 1969.

5. That all Black students wishing so be admitted in Fall 1969.

6. That twenty (20) full-time teaching positions be allocated to the
Department of Black Studies.

7. That Dr. Helen Bedesem be replaced from the position of Financial
Aids Officer, and that a Black person be hired to direct it, that
Third World people have the power to determine how it will be
administered.

8. That no disciplinary action will be administered in any way to any
students, workers, teachers, or administrators during and after the
strike as a consequence of their participation in the strike.

9. That the California State College Trustees not be allowed to dissolve
the Black program on or off the San Francisco State College campus.

10. That George Murray maintain his teaching position on campus for
the 1968–69 academic year.

THE FIVE TWLF DEMANDS

1. That a school of Ethnic Studies for the ethnic groups involved in
the Third World be set up with the students in each particular ethnic
organization having the authority and control of the hiring and
retention of any faculty member, director and administrator, as well
as the curriculum in a specific area study.

2. That fifty (50) faculty positions be appropriated to the School of
Ethnic Studies, 20 of which would be for the Black Studies Program.

3. That in the Spring semester, the college fulfill its commitment to
the nonwhite students in admitting those that apply.

4. That, in the Fall of 1969, all applications of nonwhite students be
accepted.

5. That George Murray, and any other faculty person chosen by non-
white people as their teacher, be retained in their positions.

We Needed a Revolution

LEO LITWAK

A member of the English Department at San Francisco State, Litwak penned this prostrike article.

Returning from Europe after World War II, I joined the swarm of GI's seeking academic careers. The college campus seemed a likely place to find peace and security. But it was every man for himself. We pursued our degrees in competition with others: our grades against theirs, our ability to charm professors against theirs. The curriculum was designed mainly to weed out the less worthy, and our intellectual life existed mostly beyond the academic walls.

After 18 years, I was secure. I did my job. I had tenure, an adequate salary. I worked hard. Others made academic policy, but I didn't care. I was reconciled to the fact that my significant life was off-campus. I had no strong sentiments for my institution.

Then, last November, all this changed. The Black Students Union began a strike at San Francisco State College that ended my detachment and imperiled my security. The BSU came at us with nonnegotiable demands. It indicted the college as a racist institution, abused state and local officials as "racist pigs" and "slavemasters." Groups of militant blacks entered classrooms shouting, "On strike! Shut it down!" They jostled professors, shoved students, ordered classes dismissed. Some smashed windows, broke lab equipment and set off fire alarms.

The objective of the strike was to close the college until the BSU demands were met. A coalition of other minority groups, called the Third World Liberation Front, joined the revolt and tacked on more demands.

I felt that the intrusion of the blacks into the classrooms was outrageous, that their bellicose demands were irrational and therefore

Reprinted by permission, Leo E. Litwak

frightening. They wanted an autonomous Black Studies Department and an Ethnic Studies School, with minority-group faculty and students having sole authority to hire, fire and determine policy. I listened to the BSU strike leaders and was repelled by their rhetoric. "Power to the people!" Wasn't that a Maoist line? "Racist pigs!" Did they mean our innocuous deans and administrators? The crowd chanted simple slogans that turned me off. "Shove the puppets against the wall!" If they reduced men to puppets, they might indeed be able to shove them against the walls. I decided to stay clear of the mess. While I resented the strikers, I shared some of their grievances. I might become involved and imperil my cozy academic status.

Plainclothesmen were guarding campus buildings. Blacks held class everywhere. A black youth with a West Indian accent warned, "Don't think about returning this campus to normal. Your education is going on right now. We black students are your teachers." The subject they taught was Power. "For too long we've politely requested what should always have been ours. No one has the power to *give* us freedom. And we don't *request* you people for our rights. We *demand* them." The students considered talks with the local administration useless. "You people have no power to give us what we demand. We been talking to you for two years, and we got nothing. We just get tricked. Now we will only talk to educate you, but our demands are nonnegotiable. This strike will be over when our demands are met."

The faculty was powerless. The Governor and state legislature gave power to the Board of Trustees and the Chancellor's office. Little reached the college president and less went to the council of deans and department chairmen. There was nothing left for the faculty and students. In our time of crisis, we discovered that the system allowed us no solutions.

A general faculty meeting remained in session for several weeks and passed 70 resolutions with no visible influence on the strike. Instead, we were accused of being soft on student radicals. Superintendent of Public Instruction Max Rafferty and Gov. Ronald Reagan wanted these dissidents handled like a bunch of rowdies in an Old West saloon. Enough resolutions; enough talk; throw the bums out.

A small band of faculty militants called a short-lived strike against state interference, but a far larger group, while not joining that strike, had soured on the administration's unimaginative doctrine of "classes as usual." They wanted to suspend regular instruction, move out of the classrooms and onto the campus. I began to wonder why we couldn't use this scary energy for some new kind of education, rather than clamp a lid on it.

The majority of my colleagues, however, didn't want to surrender formal instruction. They asked, what about grades? What about teaching credentials? What about jobs that require a degree? Wasn't that what education was *really* about?

I decided, no. Not really. I questioned whether the contradiction between campus experience and community experience was any longer tolerable. I'd once welcomed the benign order of campus life. But did I want to continue paying the price for that security? I was subjected to educational policies that made no sense to me. I didn't feel there was anything sacred about our curriculum. On the contrary, it was my impression that most programs have no inherent justification but simply reflect campus politics. I agreed with those who wanted regular instruction suspended in favor of a different mode of encounter.

Only a minority of the faculty shared my view. There was considerable support for Prof. S. I. Hayakawa, who announced that no student would interfere with the conduct of his classes. He urged strong police measures, and strong police measures were what we got.

Leaving a faculty meeting about that time, I heard screams. Two officers from the Tactical Squad hauled a BSU leader across the campus through hundreds of milling students. Both cops had revolvers out. One wheeled around to cover everyone, including me. Dozens of reporters and television crews were watching. A half-dozen police found themselves in a tight spot. Suddenly, they lashed out. They beat a frail, bespectacled BSU leader to the ground. They swung their batons like baseball bats. They clobbered everyone in their way, including innocents. Soon I found myself aligned with colleagues trying to separate students and police. The Tac Squad photographer snapped my picture. Like it or not, I was involved.

The campus mayhem finally forced the faculty to suspend formal instruction, and the entire college was convoked to discuss the strike issues. Strike leaders confronted college faculty and administration on the stage of the main auditorium. All together—students and faculty—we faced the vital issues of our college.

The minority students presented a strong case in strong language. Could we be made to understand, they wondered, why they would never allow themselves to be absorbed into the traditional campus life while their people continued to suffer in the ghetto? They demanded an education that would enable them to serve their community. The existing curriculum was irrelevant to their purposes. They didn't balk at obscenity. They insulted their opposition and made open bids for audience sympathy. Our administrators responded to this passion with the tedious precision of accountants, citing the limitations of state codes, budgetary policy and a fiscal crisis.

The students, accusing the college administration of bad faith, brought the convocation to a premature end. Next, the trustees forced President Smith to resign and replaced him with Dr. Hayakawa, of the colorful tam-o'-shanter and hard line. Official California had chosen to ignore the basic dissatisfactions and possibilities for reform that lay beneath the rebels' furious rhetoric. The Governor—with popular support, it's true—wanted to restore the college of his Hollywood fantasies, a benign place for cheerleaders and absentminded professors.

Acting President Hayakawa declared all assemblies illegal unless authorized by him. Professors who did not hold classes as scheduled risked being fired. He announced that all necessary force would be employed to keep the campus open. He refused to negotiate with those he regarded as hooligans. Both sides chose *High Noon* as the kind of confrontation they preferred.

Six hundred cops assembled near the campus. Three thousand students gathered on the commons. Dr. Hayakawa piped from loudspeakers to everyone, "This is a warning. All innocent bystanders leave this vicinity. Go to your classes. Go to the library. Leave the troublemakers to the police. Those of you who want trouble, stay there; the police will see that you get it." For two weeks, there were daily confrontations. The script never changed. The cops approach; students taunt them; clods of turf and pinecones are flung. Suddenly, a cop lets go and flails away, and the movement spreads down the line. When they swing, they put their weight behind the sticks. I see them still flailing away after the kid is downed.

One of my colleagues, protesting a brutal arrest, was thrown down, handcuffed, led away with a riot stick pressed to his throat. An officer squirted Mace in his eyes. Another came from behind—"How do you like this, you fancy-pants professor?"—and cut his head open with a blow from a riot stick that knocked him cold. The professor was charged with resisting and interfering with an arrest.

One of my students told me she was striking "because of the PIGS!" Her boyfriend had been photographing arrests behind the gym. A cop seized his camera and stripped the film. Another said, "No one's looking." They fractured his ribs, damaged a lung, thrust a riot stick under his genitals and hoisted up and down. They charged the boy with attempted murder. PIGS!

Hayakawa announced after a particularly bloody day: "This has been the most exciting day since my tenth birthday, when I rode a roller coaster for the first time." It was a callous statement. Yet it reflected what everyone experienced, a new energy that changed our connections to each other and to our institution. What a loss if we simply resumed teaching as before and didn't profit from these new connections. Should we simply repair broken windows, wash away strike slogans from building façades and plant flowers? Should we get back to Keats and California state history, and drama classes, and allow the performance of *Little Me* that had been interrupted by strike action? If students wished to participate in the fundamental design of my courses, why not? If my work could become relevant to my experience and theirs, perhaps teaching and learning could become more joyful.

Those of us who wanted to profit from the new energies on campus had no alternative but to join the American Federation of Teachers strike. We had no illusions that we could defeat the overwhelming power the state would muster against us. We were a minority of the faculty. Public sentiment strongly favored repressive measures. We were the villains; Hayakawa was the hero. But we felt that submitting to the old routines without any resistance would be degrading. We had everything to lose—rank, tenure, jobs, homes—yet we struck. We established a picket line around campus and marched through one of the wettest winters in San Francisco history. At times, we were frightened; often, we were exhilarated. Yet we became united, with a new commitment to our work and to our institution.

The strike finally ended, but a volatile situation remains. The administration is still intransigent. But we are changing things in our classrooms. Students are collaborating in the design of courses. In some departments, we are moving away from the old hierarchical structure toward more democratic participation. Perhaps, through our strikes, we faculty and students have chosen a new and hopeful direction for higher education in America.

Harvard: The Rulers and the Ruled

The Harvard student strike captured national attention, as police were called in to clear demonstrators from Harvard Yard. As part of their charges against the university, students included Harvard's incorporation into the military-industrial complex, reproducing antiwar movement arguments about the university.

Harvard University is an ivory tower: an ivory tower atop a castle which is part of a kingdom which, in turn, directs a far-reaching empire. What was long ago clear to the business and political directors of "American Civ." is today clear to everybody else: American universities—including their historic and elite quintessence, Harvard—are no ethereal communities of scholars. The proverbial absent-minded professors, the archive rats, the bohemians, and the assorted academic odd-balls who are still found on numerous campuses are only the sad but noble remnants of an utterly shattered classical bourgeois ideal of *Universitas*. Today, far from being cut off from the "real world outside," American universities are absolutely central components of the social system of technological warfare-welfare capitalism. The functions, goals, structure, and organization of the universities are directly and indirectly determined by the needs and perspectives of that social system.

Thus it is not really surprising to find that the members of universities' ruling bodies are simultaneously corporation and bank directors, state functionaries, and military chiefs. Nor is it surprising that universities not only tend, increasingly, to *look* like, but actually are key centers of business and military activity. Nor, further, is it particularly amazing that daily life in nearly all universities is bureaucratized, fragmented, mechanized, and mechanical; and that it reproduces itself in the new directors, service personnel, and consumers it "educates."

To be certain, American universities, particularly Harvard, do not contain the systematic and coordinated terror and regimentation of military barracks, concentration camps, or industrial factories. Universities are, most of them, "liberal institutions." This is true in the sense that they are part of the theory and practice of liberal corporate capitalism whose contemporary historical role began with the Open Door policy in Asia at the turn of the century and Wilson's make-the-world-safe-for-democracy intervention against social revolution in Russia and Eastern Europe. It is also true in the sense that universities do indeed function as forums of intellectual debate, dissent, and critical thinking. To equate this latter set of facts with "the University," however, is to confuse a part with the whole—the whole which students are educated to be blind to. For *one* of the central functions of the forum-dialogue-criticism aspect of the university is to weave a democratic veil which enshrouds a concentrated, highly organized, and totally undemocratic system of wealth and power. From the point of view of the university as a structure of power and control, debate, dissent, and criticism are healthy and productive only so long as they leave the power structure untouched. This is a system of dual power in which one side has no power. It is the truth of the phrase: "the market place of ideas," in which ideas and men of ideas are transformed into commodities.

Harvard University Strike Poster

On a poster created and produced by students on strike at Harvard's Graduate School of Design, reasons for participation are spelled out in the most direct way.

STRIKE FOR THE EIGHT
DEMANDS STRIKE BE
CAUSE YOU HATE COPS
STRIKE BECAUSE YOUR
ROOMMATE WAS CLUBBED
STRIKE TO STOP EXPANSION
STRIKE TO SEIZE CONTROL
OF YOUR LIFE STRIKE TO
BECOME MORE HUMAN STR
IKE TO RETURN PAINE HALL
SCHOLARSHIPS STRIKE BE
CAUSE THERE'S NO POETRY
IN YOUR LECTURES
STRIKE BECAUSE CLASSES
ARE A BORE STRIKE FOR
POWER STRIKE TO SMASH THE
CORPORATION STRIKE TO MAKE
YOURSELF FREE STRIKE TO
ABOLISH ROTC STRIKE BECAUSE
THEY ARE TRYING TO SQUEEZE
THE LIFE OUT OF YOU STRIKE

Early in the decade, campuses such as the University of California, Santa Barbara, and the University of Illinois had been quiet. Within the UC system, Berkeley and UCLA were the scenes of political action, while among Big Ten schools, Michigan and Wisconsin seemed the most political. By the end of the sixties, many previously calm colleges and universities, like these two, erupted.

Santa Barbara

More than 1,000 kids seized a three-block business district in a student neighborhood near the University of California at Santa Barbara Wednesday night, Feb. 25, held it from police for six hours, smashed windows, set fire to a police car, and burned a plush Bank of America office to the ground, doing more than a quarter of a million dollars damage to the bank alone.

Five hundred national guardsmen were called out Friday, Feb. 27, and another 2,500 placed on standby alert after students drove 300 police out of their neighborhood three nights in a row. Two inches of rain plus a student decision not to fight the Guard quieted the area Friday and Saturday nights. "We don't have any quarrel with them," a spokesman said.

But sheriff's officers worried that renewed demonstrations would follow the pull-out of the Guard on Sunday and Monday. "It scares me," said Sheriff Lieut. William Chickering. "We've been told that the demonstrators are going to wait until the National Guard pulls out and do it to us again."

A total of 141 persons were arrested in five nights. At least 34 policemen were injured. Other casualties included a 35-year-old university employee, who was shot in the shoulder when he accidentally drove through a police roadblock, and a 21-year-old student, who was hospitalized after being run down by a police car Thursday night.

Gov. Ronald Reagan flew to Santa Barbara on Thursday morning. He called the demonstrators "cowardly little bums," declared a "state of extreme emergency," and placed National Guard units on alert. He also said he would declare martial law if necessary. County officials ordered a 6 P.M. to 6 A.M. curfew, and police were ordered to "prohibit loitering on public streets" and to "break up assemblies of more than three persons."

Students defied the orders, and a combined force of 300 police, California Highway Patrolmen and sheriff's deputies was gathered from three counties Thursday night. They fought students for six hours and were forced to withdraw at 11:30 P.M.

The most spectacular destruction occurred Wednesday night. One thousand demonstrators began pelting sheriff's cars with rocks. At

9:45 P.M. they captured one car, forcing two deputies to flee and then setting the car afire. The flames were 30 feet high. Windows were smashed; the plywood used to board up the Bank of America's windows, smashed the day before, was torn down and set afire; demonstrators then surged into the bank.

An observer said that the group inside "hurled chairs into windows, overturned desks, created snowfalls of envelopes from an upstairs office and tore up anything they could reach." Then some people got a big trashcan, set it on fire, and ran it through the front doors and pushed it against the drapery.

The police were informed that a manager was inside the burning bank. Seventy sheriff's deputies, in full riot gear, were sent to free the manager, but when they arrived they found they had fallen into a trap. There was no manager inside but there were hundreds of students surrounding the cops, throwing rocks.

The police fought their way out and withdrew completely, surrendering the area to the students until 2:15 A.M., when a force of 240 cops returned to clear the streets.

After the police withdrawal, firemen were unable to reach the bank. Some fraternity members tried to put out the fire, but it was ignited again and the whole place was gone in 45 minutes. A few charred beams were all that remained the next morning; bank officials said $275,000 damage was done.

One veteran radical said, "While the students held the shopping center, there wasn't an atmosphere of 'wild in the streets.' The group was calm and highly political—explicitly anti-capitalist. Targets of window-breaking were chosen carefully: the Bank, the real estate offices which gouge students on rents, and the gas stations whose companies pollute Santa Barbara Bay with oil seepages. Small businesses were not touched."

The business district that was seized and held from police on three consecutive nights lies in the heart of Isla Vista, a suburb of Santa Barbara, with a population of 13,000. Of these, 9,000 are students of the University of California branch here.

The students had been united by a series of on-campus demonstrations which began in January, when Bill Allen, a popular anthropology professor, was denied tenure. Three-fourths of the school's 14,000 students took part in one demonstration or another. Two-thirds of the student body signed a petition in support of Allen.

"This was the first time radical politics made an appearance at the University of California at Santa Barbara," one veteran radical said. "In the campus demonstrations there was a feeling of the early 'sixties—they were non-violent and not confrontation demonstrations."

In spite of the peaceful character of the campus demonstrations, police arrested 19 people, dragging many of them out of bed in the middle of the night. The demand to re-hire Allen was not met, and a massive residue of frustration and hostility to the police was left.

The Chicago conspiracy defendants became immensely popular among Santa Barbara students. Tom Hayden gave a speech at the university in early January, drawing an enthusiastic crowd of 1,200, the largest audience ever assembled for a political event on the campus up to that time. In February, the official student government invited Defense Attorney William Kunstler to speak on campus, offering him $2,000 of student funds, plus a percentage of the gate, plus a passing of the hat. He appeared Wednesday afternoon, February 25, in the football stadium, where 7,000 people paid 50¢ each to hear him.

The night after his speech the bank was burned. Gov. Reagan suggested that Kunstler had violated the "Rap Brown act"—saying he crossed a state line to incite violence (this is the law the Chicago defendants were convicted under).

Student leaders pleaded with newsmen not to say Kunstler incited the violence, pointing out that the windows of the bank had been broken the night before his appearance on campus.

The Bank of America, whose offices have been attacked during the past week in Berkeley, San Francisco and Los Angeles, has offered a $25,000 reward for the Santa Barbara arsonists. Board Chairman Louis B. Lundborg reported that "we have not been able to open the vault doors since the fire, but we assume that the bank's funds and records are safe." He said the bank was "proud to be a symbol of the establishment in the real sense of that word: established law and order, established orderly process."

University of Illinois

It started with a small, peaceful rally Monday, March 2. Within four days, the University of Illinois campus here [Champaign] had become a scarred battlefield, an occupied, curfewed zone—a Day After.

The outburst of student rage, which eventually saw thousands of people battling with every size, shape and brand of cop the state could muster, and which caused 900 National Guardsmen to be brought onto the campus, was sparked by the Monday rally called by the Radical Union to protest the presence of General Electric recruiters on the campus. At the rally, students who had been working at the GE plant in Danville, 30 miles away, explained GE's double-edged profiteering: its underpayment of its own workers and, as the nation's second largest defense contractor, its lucrative involvement in the deadly exploitation of the Third World.

After the rally several hundred demonstrators moved to the Electrical Engineering building where GE was recruiting on the third floor. They found all entrances guarded by police—one could visit the GE men "by appointment only."

Fifty students pulled down a fire escape and surged up to the third floor where they scuffled briefly with police. One cop was knocked out by a well-swung bookbag. Several people were arrested inside the building, others were clubbed and arrested outside. GE recruiting stopped for the day.

That afternoon the Board of Trustees of the university cancelled Conspiracy lawyer Bill Kunstler's speaking engagement for Tuesday night, branding him "a clear and present danger" to the campus.

An angered crowd rallied in the Student Union at 7 P.M. and then, 5,000 strong, they swarmed through the campus hitting selected targets. Two-thirds of the windows of the huge oval Armory which houses the University of Illinois ROTC program were broken. Windows in the Administration Building, the Chancellor's office, the Electrical Engineering Building, the Math Department and three nearby rip-off stores were also smashed.

Four hundred university, Champaign, Urbana and State police exercised little control over the crowd, merely picking up (with the assistance of frat men and jocks) isolated students here and there. By midnight when the crowd dispersed, they had arrested 24 students on charges including mob action, criminal damage, criminal trespass, resisting arrest and disorderly conduct.

After a fairly peaceful Tuesday—with the campus swarming with hundreds of police and National Guardsmen—the students came to campus Wednesday to learn that General Motors, Standard Oil, Lockheed and U.S. Steel were recruiting on the third floor of their own Student Union. (Students later found out that Dow Chemical had been recruiting secretly the same day in another building.)

Three hundred students moved up to the third floor and sat-in in the corridor. Some recruiters came out from behind their locked doors and left the building. When Champaign and State police were called in, the sit-inners tried to leave peacefully, but the cops began pushing people down the stairs. One student tried to save his friend from arrest and got a six-inch split clubbed into his skull for his efforts.

A crowd of 2,000 people milled around the campus Wednesday afternoon, alternately confronting police and retreating or being clubbed back. Several people were seriously hurt. The windows of the nearby Bell Telephone Company were smashed.

After the 10:30 P.M. curfew, police rounded up three busloads of curfew violators, pulled demonstrators out of dormitories and private houses, and refused to let injured people into the school's medical center. A 13-year-old boy was run over by a police car during the wipe-up operation. Wednesday saw 147 arrests.

The National Guard is still in Champaign. You still have to be off the streets at 10:30. It isn't over yet.

International Protests

Voices

RONALD FRASER

Student demonstrations were not restricted to the United States. The student movement was an international one. For his book on 1968, Ronald Fraser collected voices and slogans from around the globe.

My most vivid memory of May '68: The new-found ability for everyone to *speak*—to speak of anything with anyone. In that month of talking during May you learnt more than in the whole of your five years of studying. It was really another world—a dream world perhaps—but that's what I'll always remember: the need and the right for everyone to speak—*René Bourrigaud, student at the Ecole Supérieure d'Agriculture, Angers, France*

Freedom is the consciousness of our desires—*French slogan*

People were learning through doing things themselves, learning self-confidence. It was magic, there were all these kids from nice middle-class homes who'd never done or said anything and were now suddenly speaking. It was democracy of the public space in the market place, a discourse where nobody was privileged. If anything encapsulated what we were trying to do and why, it was that. . . .—*Pete Latarche, leader of the university occupation at Hull, England, 1968*

It's a moment I shall never forget. Suddenly, spontaneously, barricades were being thrown up in the streets. People were building up the cobblestones because they wanted—many of them for the first time—to throw themselves into a *collective,* spontaneous activity. People were releasing all their repressed feelings, expressing them in a festive spirit. Thousands felt the need to communicate with each other, to love one another. That night has forever made me optimistic about history. Having lived through it, I can't ever say, "It will never happen. . . ."—*Dany Cohn-Bendit, student leader at Nanterre University, on the night of the Paris barricades, 10/11 May 1968*

The unthinkable happened! Everything I had ever dreamt of since childhood, knowing that it would never happen, now began to become real. People were saying, fuck hierarchy, authority, this society with its cold rational elitist logic! Fuck all the petty bosses and the mandarins at the top! Fuck this immutable society that refuses to consider the misery, poverty, inequality and injustice it creates, that divides people according to their origins and skills! Suddenly, the French were showing they understood that they had to refuse the state's authority because it was malevolent, evil, just as I'd always thought as a child. Suddenly they realized that they had to find a new sort of solidarity. And it was happening in front of my eyes. That was what May '68 meant to me!—*Nelly Finkielsztejn, student at Nanterre University, Paris*

For most of us the issue is not what's right and wrong. Most of us have a pretty clear sense of that. The issue is, what am I going to do? Am I going to do what's right, or am I going to do what's expedient? Because often to do what's right means you just get blown away, you know. So when somebody finds a way to do what is right and be effective at the same time, people just go OOOF! Because now they're liberated, now they can do what's right!—*John O'Neal, Student Nonviolent Coordinating Committee (SNCC) activist during the civil rights campaign in the American South*

My world had been very staid, very traditional, very frightened, very middle-class and respectable. And here I was doing these things that six months before I would have thought were just horrible. But I was in the midst of an enormous tide of people. There was so much constant collective reaffirmation of it. The ecstasy was stepping out of time, out of traditional personal time. The usual rules of the game in capitalist society had been set aside. It was phenomenally liberat-

ing. . . . At the same time it was a political struggle. It wasn't just
Columbia. There *was* a fucking war on in Vietnam, and the civil rights
movement. These were profound forces that transcend that moment.
1968 just cracked the universe open for me. And the fact of getting
involved meant that never again was I going to look at something
outside with the kind of reflex condemnation or fear. Yes, it was the
making of me—or the unmaking.—*Mike Wallace, occupation of Columbia
University, New York, April 1968*

Hey Hey L. B. J.
How Many Kids Did You Kill Today?—*American anti-Vietnam War chant
                                    directed at President Lyndon B. Johnson*

We'd been brought up to believe in our hearts that America fought
on the side of justice. The Second World War was very much ingrained
in us, my father had volunteered. So, along with the absolute horror
of the war in Vietnam, there was also a feeling of personal betrayal.
I remember crying by myself late at night in my room listening to
the reports of the war, the first reports of the bombing. Vietnam was
the catalyst. . . .—*John Levin, student leader at San Francisco State College*

I was outraged, what shocked me most was that a highly developed
country, the super-modern American army, should fall on these Vietnamese peasants—fall on them like the conquistadores on South
America, or the white settlers on the North American Indians. In my
mind's eye, I always saw those bull-necked fat pigs—like in Georg
Grosz's pictures—attacking the small, child-like Vietnamese.—*Michael
von Engelhardt, German student*

The resistance of the Vietnamese people showed that it could be
done—a fight back was possible. If poor peasants could do it well why
not people in Western Europe? That was the importance of Vietnam,
it destroyed the myth that we just had to hold on to what we had
because the whole world could be blown up if the Americans were
"provoked." The Vietnamese showed that if you were attacked you
fought back, and then it depended on the internal balance of power
whether you won or not.—*Tariq Ali, a British Vietnam Solidarity Campaign leader*

We won't ask
We won't demand
We will take
and occupy
—*French slogan*

So we started to be political in a totally new way, making the connection between our student condition and the larger international issues. A low mark in mathematics could become the focal point of an occupation by students who linked the professor's arbitrary and authoritarian behaviour to the wider issues, like Vietnam. Acting on your immediate problems made you understand better the bigger issues. If it hadn't been for that, perhaps the latter would have remained alien, you'd have said "OK, but what can *I* do?"—*Agnese Gatti, student at Trento Institute of Social Sciences, Italy*

Creating a confrontation with the university administration you could significantly expose the interlocking network of imperialism as it was played out on the campuses. You could prove that they were working hand-in-hand with the military and the CIA, and that ultimately, when you pushed them, they would call upon all the oppressive apparatus to defend their position from their own students.—*Jeff Jones, Students for a Democratic Society (SDS), New York regional organizer*

We Are The People Our Parents Warned Us Against
—*J. J. Jacobs, SDS, during the Columbia University occupation*

Those who are disgusted with the inhuman aspects of their society should D R O P O U T of it and give themselves full time to making this world a more beautiful place with their every act. If all of us would stop spending our time and energy trying to save America from within and would instead unite in our own society to set an example, all of the really stupid things that are going on would be effectively pointed out to the rest of the people.—*John Sinclair, counter-culture leader, Detroit*

Everybody was terribly young and didn't know what was going on. One had a sort of megalomaniac attitude that by sheer protest and revolt things would be changed. It was true of the music, of the hallucinogenics, of politics, it was true across the board—people threw themselves into activity without experience. The desire to do something became tremendously intense and the capacity to do it diminished by the very way one was rejecting the procedures by which things could be done. It led to all sorts of crazy ideas. *Anthony Barnett, sociology student, Leicester University, England*

> Ho! Ho! Ho Chi Minh!
> Dare to Struggle, Dare to Win!
> *—American slogan*

There was a readiness for violence which came from an enormous anger, a rage. If it hadn't been so, we wouldn't have built barricades with other people's cars, without thinking for a moment to ask their owners. Wouldn't have overturned a bus as a matter of course and set fire to it. Yes, emotionally, we were out for war now, civil war. . . .—*Barbara Brick, student at Munich University after the assassination attempt on the West German student leader Rudi Dutschke, in April 1968*

The CS gas made you vomit. But I believed you could vomit just as well going forward as back. I kept telling people, "If you don't breathe through your nose, the gas won't do you any harm." I may have even believed it myself for a time! But it was the kids who showed us the only thing that worked. With a bit of rag or blanket in their hand, they'd pounce on the cannisters the moment they landed and throw them back. It was unbelievable! And although it didn't stop them choking, at least it made the police choke as well.—*Bernadette McAliskey* (née *Devlin*), *Derry riots, Northern Ireland, August 1969*

Two cops came around the corner. They put their .327 Magnums up to my head and cocked the hammers. It was raining and I had my hands in my trench coat. We were armed at different times, but I wasn't armed then. They said, "Take your hands out of your pockets real slow." I was a goner if I did, I knew they'd say you were going for your gun. I couldn't make my hands come up. I kept telling them I didn't have one. What was racing through my mind was that it would be really stupid for the ruling class to do this right now, at the height of the strike. And then another part of my mind was saying that these two cops had probably never heard of the ruling class. They're just going to kill the straight-haired nigger, as the tactical squad called me.—*Hari Dillon, student at San Francisco State during the strike, November 1968–April 1969*

I began to realize what it was all about. The state had mobilized. It taught me two lessons. Students by themselves would never get anywhere. Secondly, that the contribution of student activism, intelligence, humour and organizational ability had to go into the workers' movement in some way.—*Paul Ginsborg, research fellow, Cambridge, England*

The duty of a revolutionary is to make the revolution.—*Widely adopted slogan of Che Guevara, the Cuban revolutionary leader*

One talked about revolution to begin with because the Vietnamese were having a revolution, or because the Cubans had a revolution. Then, by analogy, which may not have been that sound but was certainly strong polemically, people would pose the question: How do we think about the black movement in the U.S. in terms of revolutionary models? Is there a paradigm of the revolutionary society? Of the revolutionary personality? As the discussion got heated, people more and more started to think, Well, what would we be if we were revolutionaries? If we students became revolutionary?—*Carl Oglesby, former president, SDS*

In all extraordinary situations, and none is more extraordinary than a revolutionary situation, the world seems open all of a sudden. The traditional barriers between "home" and "abroad" break down to some degree. It's not only the revolutionary's "extraordinary" state of mind, but the fact that the outside world changes. It becomes a matter of course to take part in unknown people's activities, whether at home or in a foreign country. Even normal, traditional people suddenly open their doors to strangers. That all this happened in 1968 and the following years indicates that there was at least a revolutionary climate if not a "revolutionary situation."—*Anna Pam, West German SDS*

You'd read about things like this happening in Russia in 1917. Now it was happening in our own streets. It was amazing! Here were barricades keeping the British army and police out of our streets, out of "Free Belfast." It wasn't as politically explosive as it could have been, but if you didn't make the best use of the occasion the first time—so what? You'd learn for the next time.—*Michael Farrell, People's Democracy student leader, on the uprising in Belfast, August 1969*

We had the idea that the social revolution had to start from daily life. Start from even the smallest unbearable aspects of daily life, like wearing a tie or make-up. Start to make our relationships of a different order to the existing one. Start to take things back into our hands, reappropriate what had been expropriated from us. The revolution must be a festival—the festival of the oppressed.—*Elsa Gili, researcher at Turin University*

THE DEMOCRATS DIVIDE

The 1968 presidential election grew into one of the most heated and confrontational contests in American history. By the time Richard Nixon defeated Hubert Humphrey in the fall, President Lyndon Johnson had declined to run for reelection, one candidate had been assassinated, and the Democratic Convention in Chicago had erupted into a chaos that deeply threatened the party.

The McCarthy Campaign

JEREMY LARNER

When Eugene McCarthy announced he would challenge Lyndon Johnson for the Democratic nomination on the issue of the war in Vietnam, many college students and political activists flocked to his cause. This excerpt from Jeremy Larner's memoir of that campaign, Nobody Knows, *reflects on the seriousness of the student volunteers and the meaning of McCarthy's strong showing in the New Hampshire primary.*

In New Hampshire, everyone was abjectly grateful to McCarthy just for entering. At last Johnson and Johnson's war were going to be challenged. It was forgivable, then, that the candidate was not going full throttle. It was laid to shyness, modesty, stiffness—all understandable in a man of such bearing and intelligence. Who could have explained at that point that worldly effort might lead to corruption, to the pressures of other people's expectations, perhaps to a showdown where one would be exposed and unbearably judged by common enthusiasts who had no right of judgment?

Yet it was frustrating, for those who cared, that much of the early campaign, before the final moments of New Hampshire, was vitiated by the candidate's reluctance to take practical responsibility for his spiritual decision. First of all, there was little interest in engaging a campaign staff. Curtis Gans and a few others who coordinated the New Hampshire campaign and brought in student canvassers were put on the payroll only at the last moment. McCarthy refused to phone more experienced people who were suggested for staff positions, and Blair Clark—a former newspaperman and CBS executive—was made campaign manager despite his own insistence that he was not a professional and must soon be replaced. McCarthy seemed to prefer nonpro-

Reprinted by permission, Jeremy Larner, Original source: Jeremy Larner, *Nobody Knows; Reflections on the McCarthy Campaign of 1968,* New York: Macmillan, 1970.

fessionals, who were shyer about bothering him. Blair Clark, for instance, stayed on as campaign manager till the end, and was instrumental, in fact, in McCarthy's decision to enter New Hampshire; while professionals who had worked for other candidates in the past were usually undermined and forced to quit the McCarthy effort. Three weeks before the New Hampshire primary, there was no campaign organization whatever. Thirteen offices had been opened in the state, but only three of them were staffed full-time. Back in Washington the mail piled up, the country was responding and for a long time there was no one even to open the envelopes.

The Dump Johnson managers were hoping the campaign would get off to a strong start on December 2, 1967, at the Conference for Concerned Democrats, where they had brought together Democratic politicians and officeholders from all over the country who were against the war. They were hoping McCarthy would announce his candidacy on that occasion, but he announced two days earlier in Washington. At the conference in Chicago, he insisted on sharing the platform with no one, though the organizers had hopes to make a show of support and strength. When McCarthy was late, Al Lowenstein spoke to hold the audience, and McCarthy was angry at him for speaking strongly. He shrank from Lowenstein's personal attack on Johnson—he had deep misgivings about a group of young rebels using him as a battering-ram against his party. McCarthy himself spoke with no particular substance or feeling, and afterwards refused to visit the overflow crowd of four thousand who had waited downstairs for three hours. He said he thought he had done enough; the organizers had to say he didn't know the people were down there.

McCarthy's attitude then and later was that he was doing his supporters a favor by "letting them use my name." Understandably, he had reservations about their inexperience and optimism. He knew as well as anyone that their purposes and values were not necessarily his. But it was all the more incongruous that he left it up to them to propose a campaign, and took the attitude that he for his part would accept whatever of it he could bear. At one point he agreed to a TV interview on *Face the Nation* only if his schedulers would cancel two days of New Hampshire.

Though it frustrated his campaign staff, McCarthy's demeanor was a great advantage with the young people who began to come to him in New Hampshire, mainly from the elite colleges of the East

Coast and the upper West Side of New York City. The students enjoyed McCarthy's respectability and wit as the outer signs of solidity, courage and wisdom. They didn't miss his not directing them: he was the permissive father who is really wonderful but who has to be explained to outsiders. And it seemed *he trusted them* to do the explaining. Unlike their real parents, he saw (they thought) that action belongs to youth, that "the new generation" is really going to save the world.

The dedication and seriousness of the students who canvassed for McCarthy was not only legendary but real. They truly were, as Robert Kennedy was later to point out, the "A" students in their high schools and colleges. Politically they were inclined to some romanticization of the NLF, Chè Guevara, and Malcolm X. But whether they came with beards to shave or not, these were kids who reacted against the violent anti-Americanism of the New Left, whom they far outnumbered. Though they hated the war and the draft, they still believed that America could be beautiful—if it would live up to its own principles. American optimists at heart, immune in the long run to ideology, they were terribly grateful to have a chance to do something real. Most of them had thought that chance would never come.

The campaign headquarters set up in Concord, a good safe 20 miles from the more indolent atmosphere of the candidate's entourage at the Wayfarer ski lodge in Manchester. Joel Feigenbaum and Matty Bornstein, a couple of graduate physics students from Cornell, set the canvassing process into motion with a statistical analysis of New Hampshire's population and political distribution—a technique they employed later on in Portland, Oregon. Another young academic named Ben Stavis divided New Hampshire into maps and charts by which he could keep precise accounts of the canvassing. A telephone system tracked ward-by-ward progress and routed incoming volunteers. By the last week, the young managers were turning volunteers away. They rang the doorbell of every Democrat and independent in the state—some two or three times. On the day before the election they delivered to every house a sample ballot marked with McCarthy's 24 electors.

I have heard tapes of some of the door-to-door conversations in New Hampshire and Wisconsin: the best of them were conducted in a tone of respect which must have surprised both parties. The canvassers were learning more than they were teaching—learning that whether or not people understood Vietnam, they knew that something had

gone very wrong with this country. The canvassers had been instructed
not to argue but to ask questions and let people talk. Often the
voters fumbled with personal discontents, burst out with hatred that
transcended its immediate objects—but many, many connected their
troubles with Lyndon Johnson, and some, amazingly, said just about
what the kids were saying. The canvassers could then suggest to them
a look at Gene McCarthy. A look would convince you he was a serious,
honest, careful person—if he were President, people would come
back to America again, just as we have. People could talk again, just
as we're talking now.

That was the mood, at least. The McCarthy kids loved McCarthy,
they loved each other, they loved New Hampshire and Wisconsin. No
wonder Bobby Kennedy admired them: it takes a hard case to turn
away from love. Especially when the lovers are smart and young
and healthy. . . .

American politics would never be quite the same after New Hampshire. First of all, there was the fact that a candidate of no prior
national fame had shaken an incumbent President without established
backing and without a political machine. If McCarthy had done only
that . . . we would be forever grateful. There could be such a thing
as issue politics on the Presidential level, the war in Vietnam was such
an issue, and when amateurs got together in a certain spirit, even the
President had better look out! Regardless of what happened thereafter, we had the suspicion that democracy could be made to work. No
matter who was President, we would know that government could
never be quite the closed room we had feared it was. There was a
point where history simply was not going to absolve a President. There
was a point where ordinary people could make a little history of
their own.

And the Johnson people had made it even sweeter for us by raising
the issue of patriotism. A McCarthy victory would bring joy in Hanoi,
they informed the public. Governor King said that McCarthy was "a
champion of appeasement and surrender." Senator McIntyre said
that McCarthy was good news for "draft-dodgers and deserters." They
ran newspaper ads telling how Ho Chi Minh was counting on McCarthy in New Hampshire.

All of this only underscored the unprecedented nature of McCarthy's challenge. He had run against an American war while that war
was going on. He was more than a General Eisenhower who promised

peace with military prestige. He was a dove who asked whether the price of victory was worth it.

If you did it right, if you did it with McCarthy's kind of dignity, you could emerge with your reputation untarnished. And there was much to be said here for the self-imposed discipline of the youth corps. "Clean for Gene" was a policy of practical political sophistication. For several years the peace movement had been having a mixed effect on America. In New Hampshire it was possible for students to work effectively against the war and the assumptions behind the war without an exchange of hostility.

For McCarthy had begin to do much more than simply advocate peace. He was, to his lasting credit, the first Presidential candidate directly to challenge the American military and its role in the decision-making process. McCarthy did not invent this challenge from scratch: his comments fit into an increasing trend of criticism which he himself had been part of with his attacks from the Senate floor on foreign arms sales and the unchecked activities of the CIA. Other Senators, such as William Fulbright and George McGovern, had played more prominent roles in the burgeoning assault on the Pentagon; there were figures in national life, though not in Congress, who had made telling connections between the military and the American corporate economy. But it was McCarthy's singular achievement to develop an acceptable public diction for a criticism of American policy which up till then had been expressed only in a limited, academic context or in terms which the public rejected as eccentrically radical.

. . . The McCarthy campaign legitimized open and extensive attack on the military by respectable politicians, who learned in 1968 that it would not necessarily kill their public careers. In the Congress of 1968–69, for instance, there has been full-scale opposition to the Nixon-backed anti-ballistic missile proposal, including an open challenge to the Pentagon's reliability and honesty. Senator Edward Kennedy, among others, has gone further on this issue than either he or his brother were willing to venture before 1968. Clearly we have come some distance from the days when Congress merely rubber-stamped the Pentagon. McCarthy was not the only leader in this process. But he was the first to judge that the issue could be presented in a national campaign, and the first to find a way to do it.

For all of these achievements, McCarthy's conservative manner and lack of zeal were a political asset. He put his criticisms into a context of restoring institutions rather than transforming them. Thus

he was able to criticize the government without scaring people with
plans for structural change. On this score, his analysis and his vocabulary did not go to the roots of America's social and political crisis.
McCarthy spoke always of restoring balance rather than creating a
new sort of society in America. The great paradox of his candidacy
is that this approach had the political impact to give hope once more
to those who believed that only deep changes could save their country.

An American Melodrama

LEWIS CHESTER, GODFREY HODGSON, AND BRUCE PAGE

*Three British journalists covering the 1968 election capture the feelings of a
week that began with Lyndon Johnson's withdrawal from the reelection campaign and ended with the assassination of Martin Luther King, Jr.*

Lyndon Johnson stared toward the television camera. He was not
looking straight into the lens, but at a teleprompter screen just below
it. This useful device, flashing the words of his script to him at a
suitable rate for his slow and impressive rate of reading, had enabled
him to get through a speech nine thousand words long without once
dropping his eyes to the desk in front of him. Eighty-five million of
his fellow citizens had thus been able to watch the powerful emotions
registered on his familiar face.

It was nine-thirty-five P.M. in Washington, on March 31, 1968. The
President had just read, "I would ask all Americans, whatever their
personal interest or concern, to guard against divisiveness and all its
ugly consequences." He glanced across at his wife, and raised his

right arm. It was a prearranged signal that he would, after all, read some additional words which had been prepared for the machine later than the rest. Mrs. Johnson, and very few other people, knew what those words would be.

"Fifty-two months and ten days ago," the President read, "in a moment of tragedy and trauma, the duties of this office fell upon me." Many of his watchers divined now that he was off on another tack, away from the discussion of Vietnam which had been the main burden of his speech. Where on earth was he headed now? "I have concluded," Johnson said, "that I should not permit the Presidency to become involved in the partisan divisions that are developing in this political year." It was a startling proposition—to take out of politics the most important elective office in the Western world. But it prepared the way for his next statement, which—for theatrical effect if nothing else—must compare with anything that any President has ever said: "Accordingly, I shall not seek, and I will not accept, the nomination of my party for another term as your President."

The President had been tired . . .

The fact of the President's exhaustion was well known in Washington in the spring of 1968. When he made his telecast on March 31, it showed in the movements of his hands. Once or twice, tears stood in his eyes. But until the telecast, there remained an almost superstitious belief in his demonic energy. Surely he would refresh his energy from some inner well and gird himself again to scatter his enemies. And one enemy, of course, in particular.

There were some in Washington who, without actual knowledge, had long suspected that the President would decide not to run again. One of these people, a close personal friend of Johnson's, was asked in late March whether he still thought the President would not run. The friend laughed and said, "With Robert Kennedy in the race, he won't be able to resist running against him!"

It was characteristic of the tempo of American politics that of the four men then openly competing for the Presidency two were in the air when Lyndon Johnson made his move. Richard Nixon was in his own campaign plane, a Boeing 727 jet, about twenty minutes out of New York on a trip from Milwaukee. Robert Kennedy was in an American Airlines Astrojet making its approach to John F. Kennedy Airport, New York, incoming from Phoenix, Arizona.

Eugene McCarthy was finishing a speech in Waukesha, Wisconsin.

And the fourth candidate, George Wallace, was immobilized for the moment. He was in Montgomery, Alabama, with his wife Lurleen, then shortly to undergo her last operation for cancer.

Two days after Johnson announced his decision, on April 2, the primary election in Wisconsin would fall due. When he spoke, Johnson already knew he was going to be badly beaten, and perhaps humiliated, in that election by Eugene McCarthy.

Before the New Hampshire primary on March 12, the President and James H. Rowe, a Washington lawyer whom he had chosen to run his campaign, had expected no trouble in Wisconsin. Ten days before the vote, Rowe began to worry. He sent out half a dozen tried political operators to make the state safe. One of them was Neil Staebler, a veteran politician from Michigan. Every night, they called the White House and told the President's aides what they had found. There was no organization and too little money, and McCarthy was riding on a wave of enthusiasm. In the end, Staebler flew to Washington and gave it to Jim Rowe without varnish. "I told him," he says, "that it was quite evident that the President would be beaten.". . .

These reports came at a moment when the President already knew that the Gallup poll was going to publish, on March 31, figures showing that the percentage of voters who supported his actions as President had dwindled to thirty-five. After New Hampshire and Wisconsin, there were other important primaries to come, in most of which the President—or his representative—would be compelled by law or by practice to compete. There was scarcely one of them in which he could hope to avoid comprehensive and humiliating defeat by Eugene McCarthy or, what was worse, by Robert Kennedy.

Primary elections are not everything, of course. As the leader of his party, the President could still hope to command the allegiance of a majority of the delegates to the convention. But even here, the little-noticed fact that Lyndon Johnson, the great legislator, was a poor party manager, made his grasp uncertain. It was entirely possible by late March that the incumbent President might fail to win the Presidential nomination of his own party.

No doubt for such a proud man the prospect and even the danger of such a humiliation was anguish. But there was an even greater risk. Short of death or impeachment, Johnson still had nine months to serve as President. The shadow of domestic revolt had already compromised his authority. The disastrous turning of an intensely unpopular foreign war now threatened to destroy it completely.

Only a few days before his announcement, he had been debating with his generals such alarming "options" as the invasion of Laos and the invasion of North Vietnam. Confronted by their estimate that such drastic policies to end the war would demand the sending of two hundred thousand more American troops to Vietnam, he had chosen to keep the war "limited." But that meant a daily struggle against the intrinsic momentum of the war. And he had chosen to negotiate. Apart from his strong feeling that it was improper to divert time and energies to campaigning from the supervision of the war and the peace talks, there was the realization that the two roles might well prove irreconcilable. His White House adviser, Walt Rostow, might argue with jesuitical ingenuity that the Tet offensive had been "the greatest blunder of Ho Chi Minh's career." The President might even believe, as he told the Australian Cabinet in December, that after a cold winter the war would be won. But he knew how hard it would be to sell those arguments on the hustings. Least of all could they be sold there by Lyndon Johnson, whose mere appearances seemed only too likely to provoke civil disorder.

If Johnson were to fight and lose in the primaries, he could hope to keep the nomination only by the most ruthless demands on the loyalty of the party machine. And that effort was likely to be self-defeating. It might make him so disastrous an electoral liability that the politicians would turn to Kennedy in sheer self-defense. To put it at its simplest, Johnson was losing control of his party. . . .

At suppertime on Thursday, April 4, Martin Luther King stepped out of his room on the second floor of the Lorraine Motel in Memphis. He had spent most of the day in the room with his disciples, Jesse Jackson, Andrew Young, Ralph Abernathy. They were all young black clergymen whose toughness and militancy had been hardened by years of nonviolent campaigning in the streets, the black churches, and the white jails of the South. They had seen how, in Birmingham in 1963 and in Selma in 1965, King had been able to use the technique of nonviolent confrontation to keep the Negro's demands at the top of the agenda for white America. But now they were wavering about nonviolence. King himself knew as well as any of them how hard it was going to be to restrain the anger of their people and to compete with those who sneered at his creed and wanted to brush it aside. Only the Sunday before, in the National Cathedral in Washington, a few hours before the President's announcement, he had said, "I don't like to predict violence, but if nothing is done between now and June to raise ghetto hope, I feel that this summer will not only be as bad, but worse than last year."

Now, in the close motel room, he preached his philosophy to his friends as he had done so often before. He spoke of Jesus and of Gandhi, and he told them in his slow, quiet voice, "I have conquered the fear of death." In substance, he repeated to them the sermon he had given the night before in a Memphis church, ending with these words: "Like anybody, I would like to live a long life. Longevity has its grace. But I'm not concerned about that now. I just want to do God's will. And he's allowed me to go up to the mountain. And I've looked over, and I've seen the promised land."

He stepped out of room 306 to the balcony. Jesse Jackson pointed out to him the organist who was going to play at the church where he was to speak that night. "Oh, yeah," said King. "He's my man." And he leaned over the railing. "Tell him to play 'Precious Lord,' and play it real pretty!"

Two hundred and five feet away, across the motel courtyard, across the unmended back-street roadway and the scrubby, untended gardens of a row of sleazy brick houses, a man was watching. He was white. He had been watching for two hours, his feet in a dingy bathtub, his left hand braced against the window, and his right eye to the telescopic sight of a rifle. It was a .30-'06 pump-action Remington, but at that range, with a scope, there was no question of missing with any weapon. As Dr. King straightened up to go, the man fired. . . .

To be a garbage collector in Memphis is a Negro job. The city of Memphis did not recognize the garbage-collectors' union, the American Federation of State, County and Municipal Employees. On February 12, more than a thousand garbage men, virtually all Negro, went on strike. They had two main demands: recognition of their union and the city's agreement to deduct union dues from their pay packets. The mayor, a shopkeeper called Henry Loeb, flatly refused both requests and began to hire white strikebreakers. By February 22, the strikers were angry enough to march on the auditorium where the city council was meeting to discuss a compromise. The council turned the plan down, and the police dispersed the demonstrating strikers with truncheons and tear gas. . . .

There were sit-ins, and silent single-file marches down Main Street by black sandwich men whose boards proclaimed simply I AM A MAN.

The Negroes in Memphis had long been leaderless and divided into middle class, working class, and the unemployed at the bottom of the heap. . . .

On March 14, nine thousand Memphis Negroes listened to speeches of encouragement from two of the most powerful—and moderate—of the national Negro leaders: Bayard Rustin, and Roy Wilkins, of the National Association for the Advancement of Colored People. And on March 16, Martin Luther King came to Memphis. . . . He had been in Mississippi recruiting enthusiasm for the Poor People's Crusade he was planning to take to Washington in the summer. He stopped in Memphis, and agreed to come back on March 28.

Technically and politically, as an exercise in nonviolent protest, the March 28 march can only be called a disaster. . . .

The marchers met at Clayborne Temple, a large gray-brick Negro church. They were surrounded from the start by burly, unsympathetic police in full riot kit. King arrived late, and Lawson was never quite able to channel the milling mass into an orderly column. The demonstrators had been given I AM A MAN banners, mounted on stout wooden poles. From the outset, twenty or thirty young militants tore off the banners and used the poles to smash in shop windows.

For a while, the police did nothing. Then, as the head of the column was wheeling out of Beale Street into Main Street and toward the white part of town, some of the young men began to javelin their poles clear over the marchers' heads into the windows on the other side of the street. The police waded into them, and a riot became inevitable.

The black leaders began to be afraid for King's life. They had already had threats, both from white racists and from Black Power militants. Lawson took a bullhorn and turned the column around. When they got back to the church, the older people dispersed as they were asked to do, but the young wouldn't go. They grabbed sticks and bottles and began to throw them at the police. Stupidly, the police used tear gas to herd them into the church, where firebrand Black Power orators were lashing them back into the fight. All hell broke loose. Young Negroes started to throw Molotov cocktails, and the police opened fire.

Before the night was over, King had suffered the worst defeat of his career. He called a press conference and said he would not come back to Memphis. Some newspapers openly reported that he fled. But it was not his courage that had failed. What had happened was a terrible setback to his faith in that self-discipline under provocation which, he had always argued, could alone give nonviolent protest its power to persuade.

Lawson went on with his daily demonstrations, and King was persuaded to change his mind. His lieutenants began to work with Lawson on careful preparations for a second march. On Wednesday, April 3, King came back to lead it. He had been criticized for living in luxurious white motels, so this time he checked into the Lorraine Motel, room 306. . . .

King was shot a few seconds after six o'clock, Memphis time, which is seven o'clock on the East Coast. Within a quarter of an hour, blacks in Harlem and the south side of Chicago and on upper Fourteenth Street in Washington had heard the news on their transistor radios. The wire-service copy was handed to the President in his oval office as he was talking about the Vietnam peace negotiations with his ambassador to Moscow, Llewellyn Thompson. A few minutes later Johnson's secretary, Juanita Roberts, typed a second message on a slip of paper and handed it to him. "Mr. President," it read, "Martin Luther King is dead."

The President was scheduled to leave that night for Hawaii to talk about the war and his new initiative for peace with his generals. That afternoon, he had held a surprise meeting with U Thant at the United Nations. All that must now be laid aside. He sat down and wrote out a short statement and read it into the television cameras.

"America is shocked and saddened by the brutal slaying tonight of Dr. Martin Luther King," he began, in a voice heavy with sorrow and concern. "I ask every citizen to reject the blind violence that has struck Dr. King. . . . We can achieve nothing by lawlessness and divisiveness among the American people. . . ."

At Fourteenth and U Streets, less than a mile to the north, his voice was coming over the radio in the People's Drugstore. Black staff and customers gathered round to listen to their President. "Honky!" shouted one man. "He's a murderer himself," said another. "This will mean a thousand Detroits," said a third.

Within two hours, the prophecy was well on the way to fulfillment. In Washington, an angry black river poured into the streets. At Fourteenth and U, at the heart of the crowded, dingy black city of slums which mocks the pompous monuments and cool green spaces of the white capital, a middle-aged man began to shout. There were tears in his eyes. He picked up a trash can and hurled it through a drug-store window.

"This is it, baby," said another man. "The shit is going to hit the fan now. We ought to burn the place down right now." And to the best of their ability, that is just what they did. "Man!" said a militant leader—one who had helped to set the fires with Molotov cocktails and dynamite—"when that window broke, that was like—the shot that was heard round the world when the honkies were fighting their own people!"

In Chicago, with more than eight hundred thousand Negroes, violence was slower to start. But before it was over, twenty blocks of West Madison Street had been burned and Federal troops had been called in. Mayor Daley was so shaken and so angry that he ordered his policemen, if it ever happened again, to "shoot to kill arsonists, and shoot to maim looters."

There were rioting and arson, shooting by snipers and by police—in New York, Detroit, Newark, Cincinnati. In Baltimore, the Republican governor took the outbreak of rioting almost as a personal affront. His name was Spiro T. Agnew.

By the end of the week, thirty-seven people had been killed and there had been riots in more than a hundred cities. For the first time in history, the situation room in the basement of the west wing of the White House was plotting the course of a domestic crisis. Into that nerve center of America as a great power there flowed reports of fighting—not in Khe Sanh or on the Jordan, but on Sixty-third Street in Chicago, One hundred twenty-fifth Street in New York, Fourteenth Street in Washington: the White House is on Sixteenth Street. . . .

And there was Robert Kennedy. When he heard that King was dead, he went out onto a street corner in Indianapolis and told the small crowd of Negroes who gathered what had happened. Standing under a street lamp, he waited until the shouts of the men and the wails of the women had died away. Then he quoted Aeschylus: "Even in our sleep, pain which cannot forget falls drop by drop upon the heart, until in our despair, against our own will, comes wisdom through the awful grace of God."

The Kerner Report

In the midst of an already tumultuous political year, the Presidential Commission on Urban Disorders, headed by former Illinois Governor Otto Kerner, issued its report. In a statement that was widely quoted, it cautioned America about its racial divisions: "Our nation is moving toward two societies, one black, one white—separate and unequal." Below is the brief summary that introduces the commission's long report.

The summer of 1967 again brought racial disorders to American cities, and with them shock, fear and bewilderment to the nation.

The worst came during a two-week period in July, first in Newark and then in Detroit. Each set off a chain reaction in neighboring communities.

On July 28, 1967, the President of the United States established this Commission and directed us to answer three basic questions:

What happened?

Why did it happen?

What can be done to prevent it from happening again?

To respond to these questions, we have undertaken a broad range of studies and investigations. We have visited the riot cities; we have heard many witnesses; we have sought the counsel of experts across the country.

This is our basic conclusion: Our nation is moving toward two societies, one black, one white—separate and unequal.

Reaction to last summer's disorders has quickened the movement and deepened the division. Discrimination and segregation have long permeated much of American life; they now threaten the future of every American.

This deepening racial division is not inevitable. The movement apart can be reversed. Choice is still possible. Our principal task is to define that choice and to press for a national resolution.

To pursue our present course will involve the continuing polarization of the American community and, ultimately, the destruction of basic democratic values.

The alternative is not blind repression or capitulation to lawlessness. It is the realization of common opportunities for all within a single society.

This alternative will require a commitment to national action—compassionate, massive and sustained, backed by the resources of the most powerful and the richest nation on this earth. From every American it will require new attitudes, new understanding, and, above all, new will.

The vital needs of the nation must be met; hard choices must be made, and, if necessary, new taxes enacted.

Violence cannot build a better society. Disruption and disorder nourish repression, not justice. They strike at the freedom of every citizen. The community cannot—it will not—tolerate coercion and mob rule.

Violence and destruction must be ended—in the streets of the ghetto and in the lives of people.

Segregation and poverty have created in the racial ghetto a destructive environment totally unknown to most white Americans.

What white Americans have never fully understood—but what the Negro can never forget—is that white society is deeply implicated in the ghetto. White institutions created it, white institutions maintain it, and white society condones it.

It is time now to turn with all the purpose at our command to the major unfinished business of this nation. It is time to adopt strategies for action that will produce quick and visible progress. It is time to make good the promises of American democracy to all citizens—urban and rural, white and black, Spanish-surname, American Indian, and every minority group.

Our recommendations embrace three basic principles:

- To mount programs on a scale equal to the dimension of the problems;
- To aim these programs for high impact in the immediate future in order to close the gap between promise and performance;
- To undertake new initiatives and experiments that can change the system of failure and frustration that now dominates the ghetto and weakens our society.

These programs will require unprecedented levels of funding and performance, but they neither probe deeper nor demand more than the problems which called them forth. There can be no higher priority for national action and no higher claim on the nation's conscience.

We issue this Report now, five months before the date called for by the President. Much remains that can be learned. Continued study is essential.

As Commissioners we have worked together with a sense of the greatest urgency and have sought to compose whatever differences exist among us. Some differences remain. But the gravity of the problem and the pressing need for action are too clear to allow further delay in the issuance of this Report.

The Chicago Democratic Convention

JEREMY LARNER

The Democratic Convention in Chicago in August 1968 exploded into confrontations inside and outside the hall. Robert Kennedy's presidential bid had ended when he was killed in California in June. Vice President Hubert Humphrey, the eventual nominee, had not entered a single primary and based his bid on the support of party bosses and the Johnson faithful. The McCarthy campaign brought many of its young supporters to Chicago to lobby for the Minnesota senator. The National Mobilization to End the War in Vietnam ("The Mobe") organized large demonstrations throughout convention week. The Yippies planned street theatre and demonstrations, including nominating an actual pig for president to mock the Democrats. And Chicago Mayor Richard Daley planned to confront any problems by reinforcing his police force with armored vehicles and additional men, and by denying all parade permits.

In Jeremy Larner's memoir of the McCarthy campaign, another part of which is reprinted above, he describes the Democratic Convention and his disillusionment with American politics.

Reprinted by permission, Jeremy Larner. Original source: Jeremy Larner, *Nobody Knows; Reflections on the McCarthy Campaign of 1968*, New York: Macmillan, 1970.

On Wednesday night I went across the street and walked among the demonstrators in Grant Park. They were survivors of the battle in Lincoln Park, and they were bitter, but most of them seemed like gentle college kids come to town for a piece of history. The majority who hated the cops should not be confused with the minority who actively provoked them, or the smaller minority who attacked. According to the Walker Report, 5000 of the young people were from the Chicago area and 500 more came from out of town. Sam Brown estimated that 40 percent were "McCarthy kids" who had formerly worked as volunteers in one area or another. "The Mobilization" had fallen far short of its call for 100,000 revolutionary troops, and must have been worried at first about a public embarrassment.

I walked down the line where the cops stood holding their clubs and glaring into the park with incredible hostility. Occasionally someone would come up and taunt them as if the cops embodied all the forces above and beyond them. Huge TV floodlights bathed the park in an eerie dead white, like moonlight in the middle of the ocean. People moving cast deep shards of shadow through the crowd and into the dark trees. We were in an enchanted circle. If the moon went out, the shadows would engulf us, the wall of blue would break upon us, and we would drown in a sea of fury.

Most of the demonstrators sat on the ground talking and singing. Their favorite song was "We Shall Overcome." A few wore helmets and were dressed for battle—these were the ones who stood in line for the microphone and sent long harangues into the dark. A few kids lay stoned not five feet from the straining line of cops. Here and there a couple of young black men or lower-class hoods stood on the margins of the light in a kind of hostile sympathy.

Suddenly someone called me. Two former students of mine, sweeter girls you could not find. A year ago they had no interest in politics whatsoever. I met some grad students who'd driven down from Madison, sensible people who hate the war but also hate to get hurt. A Chicago housewife I'd known in college. Finally a youngster from New York, stretched out happily on the grass. "Hey, man! I've been talking to delegates!" Turns out he really has, he met them in the park. And that's why he came to Chicago: to talk to delegates and convince them to vote for McCarthy. At three in the morning, there must be fifty delegates sitting with the kids in Grant Park. From time to time a chant goes up to the people in the Hilton: "We want Gene! Dump the Hump!"

From what I saw, most of the kids who came to Chicago wanted change, but were not dedicated revolutionaries. They wanted the system to start working, and many of them believed that the Chicago convention was its last chance. They thought if the Democratic Party wouldn't represent those who were against the war and in favor of a new kind of racial and economic justice in America, then a revolution might be inevitable. But they thought that the revolution would be made by forces far larger than themselves. Some of them thought that violence in the end might be the only way, but only a very few of them were personally violent. They identified with the victims of violence—which turned out to be not so unreasonable.

THINK OF YOUR DESIRES AS REALITY says a slogan in one of the underground papers they distributed that week. A childish indulgence on first reading. But wasn't that what we all were doing during 1968? And what could we have done without it?

On Thursday the kids were bent on committing the terrible crime of marching without a permit. Some of them took a hill in the park and planted a Vietcong flag there, so naturally the brave policemen had to chase them and gas them. Looking out a window of the Hilton I saw white puffs of gas far up Michigan Avenue. In five minutes we were crying up on the 23rd floor.

A call came from the Ampitheater: Julian Bond would second McCarthy's nomination in an hour, but he didn't have a speech. A speech was quickly written. It ended: "When others held back, Gene McCarthy assumed that the American people could bear the truth—and we learned that not only could they bear it—they were hungry for truth, starving for frankness and honesty—and hoping and praying for a candidate who would speak freely and openly. . . .

"Fellow delegates, the people of America are watching us now— as indeed the whole world is watching us. They are looking to the Democratic Party to honor their faith in democracy. . . . It is not too late. . . ." etc.

Of course it was too late, or it would have been harder to write the speech.

It was too late also for me to risk a drive to the Amphitheater; the hotel was surrounded by surging crowds and cops. We had to get the speech on the teletype, but the machine kept breaking down. While I waited I looked out the window from the 15th floor. Gorgeous afternoon, the lake a flawless blue. But tear gas still hung in the air, and up Michigan Avenue the street suddenly filled with people coming our way.

The cops set up a line at the intersection and blockaded them away from the Hilton. I saw the Poor People's mule train being drawn through the line, past the Hilton and around the corner, and I caught my breath. Sure enough, they weren't going to permit the crime of blocking traffic. The line of cops moved forward to clear the street. Here and there an individual resisted, or stumbled—and in an instant the cops were lunging forward and clubbing heads with all their might. You could hear the sodden *thuck* of club on skull clear up to the 15th floor.

It was worse than anything I later saw on television. Cops chased kids off into the park and out of sight among the trees, emerged with one cop dragging a boy or girl by the leg and another cop running alongside clubbing in the groin. A man tried to carry a bleeding woman into the hotel and they were both clubbed and thrown into the wagon. People ran up to plead with cops beating kids on the ground and the cops turned around and clubbed them. They clubbed men in white who knelt to carry off the fallen and clubbed anyone with a camera on his neck. They charged people on the sidewalk and smashed them up against the building as we heard terrible screams. Very few were fighting back; I saw none with weapons. What I saw was blue helmets surging forward in waves, clubbing and clubbing and clubbing.

All at once I was angrier than I would ever have believed. Down in the street I saw what we'd been waiting for all summer. The same violence that burnt villages, the violence that smashed up anything it couldn't understand. I was raging with the force of everything I'd held down day by day working against my pride for the sake of some damn imaginary cause which was a losing cause anyway. Which could be wiped out at any moment by blue helmets who took the right to club.

The blues were clustered now straight underneath the window. I reached for a heavy lamp—and some teen-age girls rushed to stop me. "You'll be as bad as they are!"

"You're right," I said. I pulled back from the window. But I knew if I'd had a machine gun then I'd have mowed them down.

Later, when that knowledge sunk in, I was sick and scared of more than just the cops. . . .

I was given a lift to the airport by Bob Scheer. I was so tired and depressed I couldn't talk straight, but Scheer was elated. "This has been a good thing for us," he gloated. "Thousands of kids have been radicalized by what happened here."

I wasn't sure. I remembered the kids in the park chanting for Gene even after the clubbings and the nomination. But Scheer had ten examples for every one of mine—and sure enough the newspapers and magazines soon backed him up. Youth now reads that it was "radicalized" at Chicago, and may even be ready to buy that image.

But I still don't know what that word means in terms of politics. McCarthy's student volunteers were already radical in wanting to change the American political structure rather than slowly reform it, radical in wanting to redistribute power. But in context, "radicalization" seemed to mean the abandonment of politics in favor of violence. Scheer had with him a gleeful SDS kid who was predicting that he and his would break up everything in sight. Like the cops I talked to, he was still high from the violence.

Since Chicago I've found that most student activists no longer feel they can make an absolute argument against the use of force. They talk sometimes as if democratic methods are washed up in this country. But I know too that if a liberal Democrat against the war—even one of the regular party men like George McGovern or Ted Kennedy or Harold Hughes—took the initiative in leading a campaign to turn this country around, most of the students would work for him. There would be a tendency for an autonomous student movement to develop around such a campaign, and it would probably push toward goals beyond the scope of its candidate.

The problem is not the students—an overwhelming majority of them are ready to work for the ideals they were taught in their high school civics classes. The problem is the rest of the country, and by the middle of 1969 Richard Nixon was betting they weren't ready.

Rights in Conflict

THE WALKER COMMISSION

The commission appointed to investigate the events surrounding the Chicago convention was headed by Daniel Walker, later governor of Illinois. Among the most significant findings of the Walker Commission was that the Chicago police had provoked the crowd, encouraged by Major Richard Daley. They had engaged in what the commission referred to as a "police riot." The following is excerpted from the summary of the report.

During the week of the Democratic National Convention, the Chicago police were the targets of mounting provocation by both word and act. It took the form of obscene epithets, and of rocks, sticks, bathroom tiles and even human feces hurled at police by demonstrators. Some of these acts had been planned; others were spontaneous or were themselves provoked by police action. Furthermore, the police had been put on edge by widely published threats of attempts to disrupt both the city and the Convention.

That was the nature of the provocation. The nature of the response was unrestrained and indiscriminate police violence on many occasions, particularly at night.

That violence was made all the more shocking by the fact that it was often inflicted upon persons who had broken no law, disobeyed no order, made no threat. These included peaceful demonstrators, onlookers, and large numbers of residents who were simply passing through, or happened to live in the areas where confrontations were occurring.

Newsmen and photographers were singled out for assault, and their equipment deliberately damaged. Fundamental police training was ignored; and officers, when on the scene, were often unable to control their men. As one police officer put it: "What happened didn't have anything to do with police work."

The violence reached its culmination on Wednesday night.

A report prepared by an inspector from the Los Angeles Police

Department, present as an official observer . . . :

> There is no question but that many officers acted without restraint and exerted force beyond that necessary under the circumstances. The leadership at the point of conflict did little to prevent such conduct and the direct control of officers by first line supervisors was virtually non-existent.

He is referring to the police-crowd confrontation in front of the Conrad Hilton Hotel. Most Americans know about it, having seen the 17-minute sequence played and replayed on their television screens.

But most Americans do not know that the confrontation was followed by even more brutal incidents in the Loop side streets. Or that it had been preceded by comparable instances of indiscriminate police attacks on the North Side a few nights earlier when demonstrators were cleared from Lincoln Park and pushed into the streets and alleys of Old Town.

How did it start? . . .

Government—federal, state and local—moved to defend itself from the threats, both imaginary and real. The preparations were detailed and far ranging: from stationing firemen at each alarm box within a six block radius of the Amphitheatre to staging U.S. Army armored personnel carriers in Soldier Field under Secret Service control. Six thousand Regular Army troops in full field gear, equipped with rifles, flame throwers, and bazookas were airlifted to Chicago on Monday, August 26. About 6,000 Illinois National Guard troops had already been activated to assist the 12,000 member Chicago Police Force. . . .

. . . On August 18, 1968, the advance contingent of demonstrators arrived in Chicago and established their base, as planned, in Lincoln Park on the city's Near North Side. Throughout the week, they were joined by others—some from the Chicago area, some from states as far away as New York and California. On the weekend before the convention began, there were about 2,000 demonstrators in Lincoln Park; the crowd grew to about 10,000 by Wednesday.

There were, of course, the hippies—the long hair and love beads, the calculated unwashedness, the flagrant banners, the open lovemaking and disdain for the constraints of conventional society. In dramatic effect, both visual and vocal, these dominated a crowd whose members actually differed widely in physical appearance, in motivation, in political affiliation, in philosophy. The crowd included Yippies come to "do their thing," youngsters working for a political candidate, professional people with dissenting political views, anarchists and determined revolutionaries, motorcycle gangs, black activists, young thugs, police and secret service undercover agents. There were demonstrators waving the Viet Cong flag and the red flag of revolution and there were the simply curious who came to watch and, in many cases, became willing or unwilling participants.

To characterize the crowd, then, as entirely hippy-Yippie, entirely "New Left," entirely anarchist, or entirely youthful political dissenters is both wrong and dangerous. The stereotyping that did occur helps to explain the emotional reaction of both police and public during and after the violence that occurred.

Despite the presence of some revolutionaries, the vast majority of the demonstrators were intent on expressing by peaceful means their dissent either from society generally or from the administration's policies in Vietnam.

Most of those intending to join the major protest demonstrations scheduled during convention week did not plan to enter the Amphitheatre and disrupt the proceedings of the Democratic convention, did not plan aggressive acts of physical provocation against the authorities, and did not plan to use rallies of demonstrators to stage an assault against any person, institution, or place of business. But while it is clear that most of the protesters in Chicago had no intention of initiating violence, this is not to say that they did not expect it to develop.

It was the clearing of the demonstrators from Lincoln Park that led directly to the violence: symbolically, it expressed the city's opposition to the protesters; literally, it forced the protesters into confrontation with police in Old Town and the adjacent residential neighborhoods.

The Old Town area near Lincoln Park was a scene of police ferocity exceeding that shown on television on Wednesday night. From Sunday night through Tuesday night, incidents of intense and indiscriminate violence occurred in the streets after police had swept the park clear of demonstrators.

Demonstrators attacked too. And they posed difficult problems for police as they persisted in marching through the streets, blocking traffic and intersections. But it was the police who forced them out of the park and into the neighborhood. And on the part of the police there was enough wild club swinging, enough cries of hatred, enough gratuitous beating to make the conclusion inescapable that individual policemen, and lots of them, committed violent acts far in excess of the requisite force for crowd dispersal or arrest. To read dispassionately the hundreds of statements describing at firsthand the events of Sunday and Monday nights is to become convinced of the presence of what can only be called a police riot.

Here is an eyewitness talking about Monday night:

> The demonstrators were forced out onto Clark Street and once again a traffic jam developed. Cars were stopped, the horns began to honk, people couldn't move, people got gassed inside their cars, people got stoned inside their cars, police were the objects of stones, and taunts, mostly taunts. As you must understand, most of the taunting of the police was verbal. There were stones thrown of course, but for the most part it was verbal. But there were stones being thrown and of course the police were responding with tear gas and clubs and every time they could get near enough to a demonstrator they hit him.
>
> But again you had this police problem within—this really turned into a police problem. They pushed everybody out of the park, but this night there were a lot more people in the park than there had been during the previous night and Clark Street was just full of people and in addition now was full of gas because the police were using gas on a much larger scale this night. So the police were faced with the task, which took them about an hour or so, of hitting people over the head and gassing them enough to get them out of Clark Street, which they did.

But police action was not confined to the necessary force, even in clearing the park:

A young man and his girl friend were both grabbed by officers. He screamed, "We're going, we're going," but they threw him into the pond. The officers grabbed the girl, knocked her to the ground, dragged her along the embankment and hit her with their batons on her head, arms, back and legs. The boy tried to scramble up the embankment to her, but police shoved him back in the water at least twice. He finally got to her and tried to pull her in the water, away from the police. He was clubbed on the head five or six times. An officer shouted, "Let's get the fucking bastards!" but the boy pulled her in the water and the police left.

Like the incident described above, much of the violence witnessed in Old Town that night seems malicious or mindless:

> There were pedestrians. People who were not part of the demonstration were coming out of a tavern to see what the demonstration was . . . and the officers indiscriminately started beating everybody on the street who was not a policeman.

Another scene:

> There was a group of about six police officers that moved in and started beating two youths. When one of the officers pulled back his nightstick to swing, one of the youths grabbed it from behind and started beating on the officer. At this point about ten officers left everybody else and ran after this youth, who turned down Wells and ran to the left.
>
> But the officers went to the right, picked up another youth, assuming he was the one they were chasing, and took him into an empty lot and beat him. And when they got him to the ground, they just kicked him ten times—the wrong youth, the innocent youth who had been standing there.

A federal legal official relates an experience of Tuesday evening.

> I then walked one block north where I met a group of 12–15 policemen. I showed them my identification and they permitted me to walk with them. The police walked one block west. Numerous people were watching us from their windows and balconies. The police yelled profanities at them, taunting them to come down where the police would beat them up. The police stopped a number of people on the street demanding identification. They verbally abused each pedestrian and pushed one or two without hurting them. We walked back to Clark Street and began to walk north where the police stopped a number of people who appeared to be protesters, and ordered them out of the area in a very abusive way. One protester who was walking in the opposite direction was kneed in the groin by a policeman who was walking towards him. The boy fell to the ground and swore at the policeman who picked him up and threw him to the ground. We continued to walk toward the command post. A derelict who appeared to be very intoxicated, walked up to the policeman and mumbled something that was incoherent. The policeman pulled from his belt a tin container and sprayed its contents into the eyes of the derelict, who stumbled around and fell on his face.

It was on these nights that the police violence against media representatives reached its peak. Much of it was plainly deliberate. A newsman was pulled aside on Monday by a detective acquaintance of his who said: "The word is being passed to get newsmen." Individual newsmen were warned, "You take my picture tonight and I'm going to get you." Cries of "get the camera" preceded individual attacks on photographers. . . .

A network cameraman reports that on the same night:

> I just saw this guy coming at me with his nightstick and I had the camera up. The tip of his stick hit me right in the mouth, then I put my tongue up there and I noticed that my tooth was gone. I turned around then to try to leave and then this cop came up behind me with his stick and he jabbed me in the back.
>
> All of a sudden these cops jumped out of the police cars and started just beating the hell out of people. And before anything else happened to me, I saw a man holding a Bell & Howell camera with big wide letters on it, saying "CBS." He apparently had been hit by a cop. And cops were standing around and there was blood streaming down his face. Another policeman was running after me and saying, "Get the fuck out of here." And I heard another guy scream, "Get their fucking cameras." And the next thing I know I was being hit on the head, and I think on the back, and I was just forced down on the ground at the corner of Division and Wells.

Out of 300 newsmen assigned to cover the parks and streets of Chicago during convention week, more than 60 (about 20%) were involved in incidents resulting in injury to themselves, damage to their equipment, or their arrest. Sixty-three newsmen were physically attacked by police; in 13 of these instances, photographic or recording equipment was intentionally damaged.

The violence did not end with either demonstrators or newsmen on the North Side on Sunday, Monday and Tuesday. It continued in Grant Park on Wednesday. It occurred on Michigan Avenue in front of the Conrad Hilton Hotel, as already described. A high-ranking Chicago police commander admits that on that occasion the police "got out of control." This same commander appears in one of the most vivid scenes of the entire week, trying desperately to keep individual policemen from beating demonstrators as he screams, "For Christ's sake, stop it!"

Thereafter, the violence continued on Michigan Avenue and on the side streets running into Chicago's Loop. . . .

Police ranged the streets striking anyone they could catch. To be sure, demonstrators threw things at policemen and at police cars; but the weight of violence was overwhelmingly on the side of the police. A few examples will give the flavor of that night in Chicago:

"At the corner of Congress Plaza and Michigan," states a doctor, "was gathered a group of people, numbering between thirty and forty. They were trapped against a railing [along a ramp leading down from Michigan Avenue to an underground parking garage] by several policemen on motorcycles. The police charged the people on motorcycles and struck about a dozen of them, knocking several of them down. . . ."

A UPI reporter witnessed these attacks, too. He relates in his statement that one officer, "with a smile on his face and a fanatical look in his eyes, was standing on a three-wheel cycle, shouting, 'Wahoo, wahoo,' and trying to run down people on the sidewalk." The reporter says he was chased thirty feet by the cycle. . . .

"A well-dressed woman saw this incident and spoke angrily to a nearby police captain. As she spoke, another policeman came up from behind her and sprayed something in her face with an aerosol can. He then clubbed her to the ground. . . ."

"A wave of police charged down Jackson," another witness relates. "Fleeing demonstrators were beaten indiscriminately and a temporary, makeshift first aid station was set up on the corner of State and Jackson. Two men lay in pools of blood, their heads severely cut by clubs. A minister moved amongst the crowd, quieting them, brushing aside curious onlookers, and finally asked a policeman to call an ambulance, which he agreed to do. . . ."

Police violence was a fact of convention week. Were the policemen who committed it a minority? It appears certain that they were—but one which has imposed some of the consequences of its actions on the majority, and certainly on their commanders. There has been no public condemnation of these violators of sound police procedures and common decency by either their commanding officers or city officials. Nor (at the time this Report is being completed—almost three months after the convention) has any disciplinary action been taken against most of them. That some policemen lost control of themselves under exceedingly provocative circumstances can perhaps be understood; but not condoned. If no action is taken against them, the effect can only be to discourage the majority of policemen who acted responsibly, and further weaken the bond between police and community.

Although the crowds were finally dispelled on the nights of violence in Chicago, the problems they represent have not been. Surely this is not the last time that a violent dissenting group will clash head-on with those whose duty it is to enforce the law. And the next time the whole world will still be watching.

The Trial

TOM HAYDEN

Despite the Walker Commission's report asserting the culpability of the police, Chicago authorities arrested eight antiwar and radical leaders and put them on trial for conspiracy to incite a riot. Tom Hayden, one of those arrested, recounts his experiences during a trial that gained national attention. The courtroom exploded on numerous occasions, defendants shouted at the judge, and lawyers were held in contempt. Black Panther Bobby Seale was gagged and chained to his chair by order of the judge. His case was ultimately separated from the other seven.

> Our kids don't understand that we don't mean anything when we use the word "nigger" ... they just look at us like we were a bunch of dinosaurs ... we've lost our kids to the freaking fag revolution.
>   —Prosecuting Attorney Thomas Foran
>   in a speech after the trial

Our crime was our identity.

Even the sympathetic press misunderstood, billing our case as one of "dissent on trial." So did Bill Kunstler in the beginning, when he spoke of repression of "the spectrum of dissent" and implied that

Reprinted by permission, Tom Hayden.

we differed from other Americans only in our political opinions. Although there was a certain amount of obvious truth in this claim, it always seemed superficial to us.

The vague nature of the government's case made us feel we were on trial for something deeper and unspoken. The charges against us made no sense. We spent endless hours trying to comprehend what the case was all about.

Against our common sense the government kept insisting that the trial was not "political," not about the Vietnam war, not about the Black Panther Party, but simply the prosecution of a criminal indictment. It was, for the government, a question of whether we had conspired to cross state lines with the intention of organizing, promoting, or encouraging a riot. To prove its case it relied on evidence from Chicago policemen, undercover and FBI agents, Army and Navy personnel, two *Chicago Tribune* reporters, and only two civilians with no apparent police connections. . . .

We became the Conspiracy not because we did anything together in 1968 but simply because we were indicted together. We became closely knit because of the trial, and perhaps the government was relying on this very process for its proof. By intertwining our names through the testimony (as if the words and evidence reflected the reality of 1968) while we sat together at the defense table for five months, it might begin to appear to a jury that we always had been an interconnected unit. But evidently it never convinced the jury, and it certainly made us feel strange, like survivors of a shipwreck getting to know one another because we shared the same raft.

As for concrete evidence of lawbreaking activity, the government puzzled us further by introducing almost nothing. . . .

Since the evidence of conspiracy and concrete illegal activity was so weak, the thrust of the government's attack had to be carried out against our "state of mind." As we sat through the months of testimony about our consciousness, we began to realize that the charges against us were really just as *total* as the changes we wanted to make in American society. On the surface there was evidence of conversations, speeches, and plots hatched in the presence of undercover government agents. Many of these were wholly fabricated; others were twisted accounts. The accurate ones—those recorded on tape—were never difficult to justify legally. But just below the surface of the testimony there was always the implication that we were dangerous and alien to the America of the jury. . . .

Our underlying crime, the evidence of which was revealed every day in the courtroom, was that we were beginning to live a new life style beyond that of capitalist America. Our defense table was a "liberated zone" right in front of the jury's eyes. The room itself was a sterile horror, shaped like a box, the doors smoothly tucked into the walls, neon lighting casting illumination without shadow, as if people did not exist. Paintings of British and American historical figures hung above the bench and just below the Great Seal of the United States. It was a heavy decorum. As many as twenty federal marshals kept "order," instructing spectators that they could not laugh, fall asleep, read, or go to the bathroom without forfeiting their seats. The government's table, nearer the jury, was impeccably clean, the four-member team invariably dressed in gray flannel or, in the case of Foran, sporty gabardine suits. The jury, dressed neatly as well, obeyed their orders to say good morning to the judge but otherwise remained quiet and expressionless throughout the proceedings. The judge, his old man's head attached to his floating robe like a bizarre puppet, called for respect in his gravely, sonorous, vain tone. And there we were, supposedly the victims but somehow the center of everything: our hair growing longer with each passing month; our clothes ranging from hip to shabby; joking, whispering seriously, passing notes, reading newspapers, and ignoring testimony and the rules of the judge; occasionally looking for friendly jurors' faces but eventually giving up and just being ourselves. This behavior was the ultimate defiance of a court system that demands the repression of people into well-behaved clients, advocates, and jurors.

The conflict of life styles emerged not simply around our internationalism but perhaps even more around "cultural" and "psychological" issues. For instance, music. When Arlo Guthrie, Judy Collins, Phil Ochs, Country Joe, Pete Seeger, and others tried to sing for the jury, they were admonished that "this is a criminal trial, not a theater." No one, including the press, understood what was going on. From the judge to the most liberal journalist there was a consensus that we were engaged in a put-on, a further "mockery of the court." They seemed incapable of coming to terms with the challenge on any deeper level. The court's concession was that the words to the songs, but not the singing of them, were admissible. But this was a compromise that missed the entire point. The words of "Alice's Restaurant,"

"We Ain't A-Marchin' Any More," "Vietnam Rag," "Where Have All
the Flowers Gone," and "Wasn't That a Time" may be moving even
when they are spoken, but the words gained their meaning in this
generation because they were *sung*. To understand their meaning
would be to understand the meaning of music to the new consciousness. From the beginning of rock and roll, there has grown up a
generation of young whites with a new, less repressed attitude toward
sex and pleasure, and music has been the medium of their liberation.
When Phil Ochs sang "We Ain't A-Marchin' Any More" in Chicago
during the Convention, it provoked a pandemonium of emotion, of
collective power, that spoken words could not have done. Singing in
that courtroom would have jarred its decorum, but that very decorum
was oppressing our identity and our legal defense.

Or, for instance, sex. Government attorney Tom Foran's post-trial
statement about the "freaking fag revolution" merely confirmed what
we could see throughout. Foran represented imperialist, aggressive
man, while we, for all our male chauvinist tendencies, represented a
gentler, less aggressive type of human being. Schultz kept returning
to the phrase "public fornication" as though the words themselves
were a crime, since the government introduced no testimony to show
that Yippies had acted on this threat (except once in a tree, according
to an undercover agent). Allen Ginsberg was cross-examined as to
whether he had "intimate" relationships with Abbie and Jerry. Physical affection between the defendants and their friends and witnesses
was always noted by either the judge or the prosecution for the record.
The scene of Bill Kunstler hugging Ralph Abernathy was particularly
offensive to the judge, who declared that he had never seen so much
"physical affection in my courtroom."

The conflict of identity on this level was sharpest during Ginsberg's
testimony. . . . The conflict came out into the open during Foran's
cross-examination. Instead of questioning Allen about anything he
had testified to—such as pre-Convention planning by the Yippies and
permit negotiations—Foran asked him to recite and explain three
sexual poems apparently selected by the Justice Department agent at
the table, a young, bespectacled, high-voiced, short-haired, blue-eyed
young man named Cubbage. The first was about a wet dream, the
second about a self-conscious young man at a party who discovers
that he is eating an asshole sandwich, the third about a fantasy of
sleeping between a man and a woman on their wedding night. At

Foran's request Allen recited each one calmly and seriously and then
tried to answer the prosecutor's sarcastic query about their religious
significance. . . . When Allen left the stand we were in tears. Court
recessed a few minutes later, and Foran stared at Allen and said,
"Damn fag."

A third example of the cultural conflict revolved around language.
The government's case was a massive structure of obscene and provocative language attributed to us by police informers, language that the
jury was supposed to imagine coming from our mouths as they stared
at us across the courtroom. Some of the language was pure invention;
most of it was a twisting of words that had once been used by us.
Through the testimony over language, we came to the essence of the
supposed "communication gap" between the generations.

The language of the Establishment is mutilated by hypocrisy. When
"love" is used in advertising, "peace" in foreign policy, "freedom"
in private enterprise, then these words have been stolen from their
humanist origins, and new words become vital for the identity of
people seeking to remake themselves and society. Negroes become
"blacks," blacks become "Panthers," the oppressors become "pigs."
Often the only words with emotional content are those that cannot
be spoken or published in the "legitimate" world: fuck, motherfucker,
shit, and other "obscenities." New words are needed to express feelings: right on, cool, outta sight, freaky. New language becomes a
weapon of the Movement because it is mysterious, threatening to
conventional power: "We're gonna off the pig"; "We're gonna freak
the delegates.". . .

Filtered through the mind of the police agent, language becomes
criminal. The agent is looking for evidence; in fact, he has a vested
interest in discovering evidence and begins with the assumption of
guilt. Any reference to violence or blood, by an automatic mechanism
in the police mind, means an offensive attack on constituted authorities. Our language thus becomes evidence of our criminality because
it shows us to be outside the system. Perhaps our language would be
acceptable if it were divorced from practice. Obscenity has always
been allowed as part of free speech; it is the fact that our language
is part of our action that is criminal. A jury of our peers would truly
have been necessary for our language to have been judged, or even
understood. Or at the very least, our middle-aged jury should have

heard the expert testimony of someone who could partly bridge the communication gap. . . .

Finally, the conflict of identities always involved the racism of the court toward Bobby.

THE NEW LEFT SPLINTERS: THE WEATHER UNDERGROUND

As the decade neared its end, the new left coalition began to come apart. One faction of SDS, the Weathermen, advocated guerrilla warfare and saw themselves, along with several black groups, as the vanguard of the revolution. They believed an international revolution of people of color was possible, and that one of their responsibilities was to confront white people about their racism. The following are two documents from the Weathermen, and a third that stands in opposition to their strategies.

Bring the War Home

This is the National Action brochure that the national office has produced. So far they have been going as fast as we can print them. They can be ordered from the n.o. at a price of $5 per thousand.

It will also be printed as a part of the mass newspaper that SDS will have ready within a week. Send in orders for the paper, too, and pass them both out wherever you go.

It has been almost a year since the Democratic Convention, when thousands of young people came together in Chicago and tore up pig city for five days. The action was a response to the crisis this system is facing as a result of the war, the demand by black people for liberation, and the ever-growing reality that this system just can't make it.

This fall, people are coming back to Chicago: more powerful, better organized, and more together than we were last August.

SDS is calling for a National Action in Chicago on October 11. We are coming back to Chicago, and we are going to bring those we left behind last year.

LOOK AT IT: AMERICA, 1969

The war goes on, despite the jive double-talk about troop withdrawals and peace talks. Black people continue to be murdered by agents of the fat cats who run this country, if not in one way, then in another: by the pigs or the courts, by the boss or the welfare department. Working people face higher taxes, inflation, speed-ups, and the sure knowledge—if it hasn't happened already—that their sons may be shipped off to Vietnam and shipped home in a box. And young people all over the country go to prisons that are called schools, are trained for jobs that don't exist or serve no one's real interest but the boss's, and, to top it all off, get told that Vietnam is the place to defend their "freedom."

None of this is very new. The cities have been falling apart, the schools have been bullshit, the jobs have been rotten and unfulfilling for a long time.

What's new is that today not quite so many people are confused, and a lot more people are angry: angry about the fact that the promises we have heard since first grade are all jive; angry that, when you get down to it, this system is nothing but the total economic and military put-down of the oppressed peoples of the world.

And more: it's a system that steals the goods, the resources, and the labor of poor and working people all over the world in order to fill the pockets and bank accounts of a tiny capitalist class. (Call it imperialism.) It's a system that divides white workers from blacks by offering whites crumbs off the table, and telling them that if they don't stay cool the blacks will move in on their jobs, their homes, and their schools. (Call it white supremacy.) It's a system that divides men from women, forcing women to be subservient to men from childhood, to be slave labor in the home and cheap labor in the factory. (Call it male supremacy.) And it's a system that has colonized whole nations within this country—the nation of black people, the nation of brown people—to enslave, oppress, and ultimately murder the people on whose backs this country was built. (Call it fascism.)

But the lies are catching up to America—and the slick rich people and their agents in the government bureaucracies, the courts, the schools, and the pig stations just can't cut it anymore.

Black and brown people know it.

Young people know it.

More and more white working people know it.

And you know it.

LAST YEAR, THERE WERE ONLY ABOUT 10,000 OF US IN CHICAGO

The press made it look like a massacre. All you could see on TV were shots of the horrors and blood of pig brutality. That was the line that the bald-headed businessmen were trying to run down—"If you mess with us, we'll let you have it." But those who were there tell a different story. We were together and our power was felt. It's true that some of us got hurt, but last summer was a victory for the people in a thousand ways.

Our actions showed the Vietnamese that there were masses of young people in this country facing the same enemy that they faced.

We showed that white people would no longer sit by passively while black communities were being invaded by occupation troops every day.

We showed that the "democratic process" of choosing candidates for a presidential election was nothing more than a hoax, pulled off by the businessmen who really run this country.

And we showed the whole world that in the face of the oppressive and exploitative rulers—and the military might to back them up—thousands of people are willing to fight back. . . .

SDS IS CALLING THE ACTION THIS YEAR

But it will be a different action. An action not only against a single war or a "foreign policy," but against the whole imperialist system that made that war a necessity. An action not only for immediate withdrawal of all U.S. occupation troops, but in support of the heroic fight of the Vietnamese people and the National Liberation Front for freedom and independence. An action not only to bring "peace to Vietnam," but beginning to establish another front against imperialism right here in America—to "bring the war home."

We are demanding that all occupational troops get out of Vietnam and every other place they don't belong. This includes the black and brown communities, the workers' picket lines, the high schools, and the streets of Berkeley. No longer will we tolerate "law and order" backed up by soldiers in Vietnam and pigs in the communities and schools; a "law and order" that serves only the interests of those in power and tries to smash the people down whenever they rise up.

We are demanding the release of all political prisoners who have been victimized by the ever-growing attacks on the black liberation struggle and the people in general. Especially the leaders of the black liberation struggle like Huey P. Newton, Ahmed Evans, Fred Hampton, and Martin Sostre.

We are expressing total support for the National Liberation Front and the newly-formed Provisional Revolutionary Government of South Vietnam. Throughout the history of the war, the NLF has provided the political and military leadership to the people of South Vietnam. The Provisional Revolutionary Government, recently formed by the NLF and other groups, has pledged to "mobilize the South Vietnamese armed forces and people" in order to continue the struggle for independence. The PRG also has expressed solidarity with "the just struggle of the Afro-American people for their fundamental national rights," and has pledged to "actively support the national independence movements of Asia, Africa, and Latin America."

We are also expressing total support for the black liberation struggle, part of the same struggle that the Vietnamese are fighting, against the same enemy.

We are demanding independence for Puerto Rico, and an end to the colonial oppression that the Puerto Rican nation faces at the hands of U.S. imperialism.

We are demanding an end to the surtax, a tax taken from the working people of this country and used to kill working people in Vietnam and other places for fun and profit.

We are expressing solidarity with the Conspiracy 8 who led the struggle last summer in Chicago. Our action is planned to roughly coincide with the beginning of their trial.

And we are expressing support for GIs in Vietnam and throughout the world who are being made to fight the battles of the rich, like poor and working people have always been made to do. We support those GIs at Fort Hood, Fort Jackson, and many other army bases who have refused to be cannon fodder in a war against the people of Vietnam.

IT'S ALMOST HARD TO REMEMBER WHEN THE WAR BEGAN

But, after years of peace marches, petitions, and the gradual realization that this war was no "mistake" at all, one critical fact remains: the war is not just happening in Vietnam.

It is happening in the jungles of Guatemala, Bolivia, Thailand, and all oppressed nations throughout the world.

And it is happening here. In black communities throughout the country. On college campuses. And in the high schools, in the shops, and on the streets.

It is a war in which there are only two sides; a war not for domination but for an end to domination, not for destruction, but for liberation and the unchaining of human freedom.

And it is a war in which we cannot "resist"; it is a war in which we must fight.

On October 11, tens of thousands of people will come to Chicago to bring the war home. Join us.

Honky Tonk Women

In Cuba the imperialists were caught off guard; a small number of men overthrew Batista and drove American imperialism off the island within a short period of time. Cuban women, not involved in actual armed struggle, are now winning liberation in the Revolution. The fight in Vietnam has been the longest and fiercest yet, and the need to mobilize masses of people has produced the best Communist leadership. Under the NLF, with the vision of real equality and liberation, Vietnamese women took on major roles in their victorious war against the U.S. Now in North Vietnam and liberated zones of the South, the U.S. has been driven out, and Vietnamese women are winning formal equality in a process that began when they picked up the gun to destroy the U.S.

These revolutionary women are liberating themselves by fighting in a national struggle. But white women are part of Amerika, the white world-oppressor nation. As a nation, we have allowed a few rich men to exploit and plunder the rest of the world, and have used the wealth and privileges from their looting. The ruling class of this country has tried to buy our allegiance by creating material reasons for us to support them in Vietnam, Cuba and Latin America instead of the people fighting against them. The people of Vietnam, Cuba and other countries have fought wars for national identity, for self-determination. Our national identity is as the plunderers of the entire world. We must fight to destroy that national white oppressor identity and establish world communism—a job accomplished only by joining the people of the world, directly attacking and destroying imperialism with them. U.S. imperialism is our common enemy, and white women must join in this fight before they can win anything but empty transitional demands.

For white women to fight for "equal rights" or "right to work, right to organize for equal pay, promotions, better conditions . . ." while the rest of the world is trying to destroy imperialism, is racist. Those material improvements, like the rest of our privileges, are taken from the people of the world. These demands aren't directed toward the destruction of Amerika, but toward helping white people cope better with life in an imperialist system. (While Vietnamese and Cubans struggle daily in life-and-death encounters with our same enemy, white women should agitate for better working conditions in their work places!) All of recent history shows us that the imperialist pigs are willing to make great sacrifices, grant huge demands, to keep white people on their side. Any demand made by white people short of the total annihilation of imperialism can be granted by the pigs—and will be.

A real strategy for victory is not to get masses of people to fight with you for a few more crumbs—day-care centers for white women, equal pay with white men—but to fight with them against the source of our real oppression—pig Amerika. Our sad-eyed sisters' programs will never result in liberation for women. The strategy to win in Amerika is the strategy of international insurrection against imperialism, and we, with them, must become revolutionaries and join the fight.

Our liberation as individuals and as women is possible only when it is understood as a political process—part of the formation of an armed white fighting force. Political power grows out of the barrel of a gun, and the struggle to gain and use political power against the state is the struggle for our liberation.

Various political tendencies toward separatist women's movements do not recognize this reality. Our sad- but fiery-eyed sisters who proclaim that they—white women—can do it alone, do not see that a separatist strategy is doomed to failure. Imperialism draws its power from the control and exploitation of vast areas of the world—the oppression of white women is the source of only a tiny part of its power. They could easily grant our demands for a few improvements in our lives—demands which don't even answer or change the depth of our oppression—just as the pigs have done many times before. Only when we fight with the rest of the people of the world do we have any strategic power to destroy the pigs. Most of the separatist theories do not clearly define the enemy as US imperialism, so their programs do not focus on the source of our oppression.

Separatist women's movements have also formed mostly out of weakness and fear of men and "male strengths." By accepting the pigs' definition of what is male (and therefore, somehow, bad . . .), our sisters have ignored the need to formulate and criticize theory and strategy, the need to fight for our freedom. Because these skills are necessary to build the revolution, women too must develop and use them, changing ourselves, breaking out of our passivity and inexperience. Clearly men, too, must change—but this will happen only if we are openly Communist in our struggle with them, changing them as we make the revolution. Separatist programs and organizations have accepted the chauvinism of men as unchangeable—at least for the immediate future—and thus their strategy is to weaken men and revolutionary male leadership so that women (in the weakness they have accepted as unchangeable) can be equal or superior. By assuming that men can't change, women separatists accept their own defeat and inability to be transformed into Communists through our struggle. The only way we can win is to build a consciously Communist white movement, ready to ally and fight with the rest of the world's peoples. The pig role forced on men and women by Amerikan society has corroded our minds and strength—the only way to change that role is to destroy the pigs who want us to passively accept it. The way to win is to seize time and leadership by becoming Communists ourselves, and to show other people, especially men, the possibility and necessity for them to be Communists, too—to build a revolutionary Communist movement. This is our responsibility as revolutionary women, and we must take leadership in this struggle. . . .

We say to our comrades that we can do more than merely fight the painful effects of imperialism—but we must break out through the pigs' alternatives and definitions. We will undermine and smash the pigs themselves—the people and system of imperialism. Our victory will be political and military—so we must pick up the gun and use it until this system is dead. We must open and lead another armed front against Amerika—this time here, behind enemy lines—in the gut of the mother country. A woman who arms herself and fights the pig imperialists takes the first step toward becoming free, because she is fighting against what really keeps her down in a way that can win. What this means for us now is that we must begin building a strategy to engage in massive violence and armed struggle as soon as possible—to retaliate immediately when Fred Hampton is murdered, to make the pigs pay a high price for My Lai. This is the way we become revolutionaries—by making the revolution, by fighting to destroy the state. . . .

Male chauvinism still permeates society, and in many ways all of us. This is why women must often be together as women within any revolutionary white movement. Combatting our hatred and fear of

each other as women, and struggling together against male chauvinism in our comrades, we break down the pieces of Amerika still hidden
inside our minds and begin to become revolutionaries. Our new
strength comes out of understanding and destroying our oppression—both by fighting against its real source and by transforming
the misfits that it creates into whole people. The only reason for
separateness is to strengthen us in our fight against the state. It enables
us to fight together against our oppression, breaking out and overcoming it together through the struggle. The relationships that we build
between us after our self-hatred and competition are broken down
reflect the transformation that happens as we become revolutionaries.
Women sleeping with other women, developing full sexual and political relationships with each other, indicates that we are beginning to
really destroy the bourgeois values we have believed in for such a
long time, and apply revolutionary values to every facet of our lives.
As we break down these pig attitudes toward each other, and begin
to discover what revolutionary love is, we learn how to build satisfying
relationships with men too. But the basis of all relationships that we
have with each other—men and women both—must be the war that
we are making against the state. That is the reason that our old
imperialist values must break down—so we can become better revolutionaries, better able to make war and destroy the pig. That is the
reason monogamous relationships must be broken up—so that the
people involved, but especially the women, can become whole people,
self-reliant and independent, able to carry out whatever is necessary
to the revolution. . . .

Completely transformed from passive wimps, afraid of blood or
danger or guns, satisfied with the limitations set on us by hated slave
relationships with one man, we become revolutionary women—whole
people struggling in every way, at every level, to destroy the dying pig
system that has tried to keep us and the rest of the world under its
total control. But our leadership cannot be just exemplary, it must
also be strategic. In the past, few of us ever thought that we could
formulate strategy or theory. Learning these skills together with other
women, taking responsibility for our own political development, has
broken down our male chauvinism and self-hatred, preparing us to
better struggle with men's chauvinism toward us.

We have begun our fight against imperialism, the source of our
oppression. In the fight we become transformed—and must transform
ourselves—into revolutionaries in order to win, but this change is only

real when we are actually fighting and destroying Amerika, ripping her apart from the inside as the rest of the world destroys her from the outside. We are honky tonk women in the gut of the mother country. We demand—not "Bread and Roses" to make our lives a little better and shield us from struggle a little more—but bombs and rifles to join the war being fought now all over the globe to destroy the motherfuckers responsible for this pig world.

New Left, Old Traps

TODD GITLIN

Not all of SDS was drawn to the Weathermen. Todd Gitlin, an early new leftist and past president of SDS, criticizes much of what was happening within the left in late 1968 and 1969.

The New Left of the Sixties was specifically of the American Sixties. It was born in action and vision—action to create a decently responsible life in the twentieth century; vision to recover the nation's soul from the bankrupt imitative leftism and the end-of-ideology liberalism of the gray Fifties. Instead of the soapbox harangue, patient, everyday work *with* people; instead of frozen hierarchy, organization by real contributions, participation, democracy. "Put your body on the line" and "let the people decide" were rallying cries, from the Mississippi Delta to Berkeley and the Newark ghetto. New generations, born into affluence and cynicism, rattling around in the hollowness of the American Century, learned that the world was in revolution and that American power was finally the enemy of all dreams, discovered that blacks wanted out of their chains and felt unselfconscious in demanding that the society conform to their vision of a civilization beyond scarcity and in beginning to be that vision (traces of it at least) themselves.

The Good Old Days weren't all that good, although people did seem to care more about each other then. The New Left was elitist, narrowly built on the education acquired in the hated but elite educational factory itself. It was self-righteous and vague enough in its rhetoric to see the slogans of Port Huron and the Free Speech Movement co-opted by the Peace Corps and the university pacification programs; it was tentative at a time when everything began to cry for clear explanations.

The New Left had to discard its lingering illusions of American flexibility with every broken black body, every butchered Vietnamese and every broken white head. The radical disappointment with which we began the decade, the bitter discovery that America had defaulted on her own liberal promises, had to yield to something that felt like a revolutionary imperative. Suddenly in the middle of the decade, there was a mass resistance—resistance against the war, against the war university, against white supremacy. Finally, whether in so many words or not, against capitalism itself, against class society and the empire, which are its logical outgrowths. The very success of that mass resistance—a dead end against its own limits—has thrown the movement for a loop. The young radicals, increasingly the radical young, driven from all the institutions of control and management, had to make a new life, necessarily a life of political opposition, out there in the space between institutions.

The interface between "hippies" and "politicals" melted into a new creature: the hairy, anarchic, activist, implacable, creatively desperate "street person" whose life conditions admit to no chance of reform solutions, who says with his actions: "Your schools, your offices, your shops, your army have vomited me up, and now your cops come to mop me up, but you can't take from me the only place you have left me, the place where I live and breathe my being, the base from which I launch my assault on your barbarism; I *will fight*." He is a new creature living in a new political culture; he feels like a nigger and the coercive powers-that-be treat him like one.

Through all this, from Stop the Draft Week to Chicago, the Movement felt its strength in the streets. But precisely at the moment it discovered its strength, it also comprehended its weakness. Although it grew numerically as a social force, including high school kids and soldiers as well as "students" and "dropouts," and became recognizable, even to the universal sign of the flashed "V," it was still painfully far from even the shadow of revolutionary change. Not only that; at the peak of its energy it was more brutally attacked by the police, the courts, the entire repressive apparatus, than ever before. Moreover, first-hand encounters with Vietnamese and Cubans made imperialism and its Third World opposition concrete. The stakes of success or failure had never seemed so fatefully present.

In this sequence, most sharply at the time of the Chicago battles, an inescapable choice presented itself: Either the post-scarcity left would comprehend its own unprecedented identity as a social force, elaborate that identity into a vision and program for the campus and the youth ghettoes, and use its reality as a strength from which to encounter anti-colonial and working-class energy and to devise common approaches—or it would turn from its identity, throw the vision out with the narrowness of the class base, and seek an historically pre-packaged version of revolution in which students and *déclassés* intellectuals are strictly appendages or tutors to the "real" social forces. Either it would take itself seriously as a visionary force, conscious of post-scarcity potentials with revolutionary and democratic goals, or it would buy clarity on-the-cheap, taking refuge in mirror-models of the underdeveloped socialisms of Russia and the Third World. Either it would accept the awesome risk of finding new paths—or it would walk the beaten trails, pugnacious and sad. A grave choice, where the stakes are immense; but the pounding pressure of the State leaves no time for placid reflection.

Since Chicago, there has been a fundamental failure of nerve throughout the white movement, which is too widespread to be pinned on any agency, individual, or faction. We could obsess ourselves infinitely with the horror stories of this collective failure: assuming you are the revolution if you say so; getting to like the taste of the word "dictatorship" (of the proletariat, over the proletariat, over anyone); getting so pleased with being correct that you don't like being corrected; substituting rhetoric and slogans for analysis and appeals; kicking your friends as practice for your enemies. It is easier to obscure the real achievements of the past year (and it is again progress which is the property of no faction): the dozens of militant campus movements; the broaching of questions of class within the movement itself; the self-direction of a Women's Liberation movement which refuses to be pigeonholed; the development of the movement's own institutions, including the underground press, Newsreel, communes; the explosion of energy in the high schools and the stirrings in the working-class junior colleges; the identification of the enemy as the global imperialist system. But make no mistake. Most of that growth, numerical and political, is an enormous tribute to what Marxists call the objective conditions; much of the rest, like the weight of a tumor, is canceled out by the attending pathologies.

Fortunately, this impossible society creates the left faster than the organized left can destroy itself. Little question about it—regardless of the fate of the left, all signs are that the monster will continue to sap itself of its own strength, keep itself off-balance. It will lose the loyalty of students, blacks and other colonized minorities by failing to meet their most elemental needs. Soldiers will continue to desert, blacks to revolt, white students to reject the withering carrot and fight the big stick, millions of others to look, at least, for ways to make sense of the madness. Even deprived of its revolutionary scapegoats, this society will disrupt itself.

At the same time, the society digs the foundations of the police state. Not only the police, but all the skilled and privileged whites who are squeezed to finance the failures of capitalism, all those forced to occupy the front lines of racism while the Rockefellers and Cliffords are secure in their bunkers—they are the shock troops for a desperate system. Whether the left can survive is finally a question of whether it can inject its dreams so deeply into the lifestream of the society that millions of people across class and race lines will fight to vindicate the revolutionary promise. Right now it is a question of whether the living consciousness that a new world is possible—free of material misery, hierarchy, useless work—can encounter the more traditional needs of the rest of the American people and the rest of the world, without abandoning its integrity. For underneath the new, pre-packaged, clenched-teech optimism complete with symbols, language, heroes and unquestioning allegiances, is a fundamental despair about this country, whether it can make—or even *deserves*—its own revolution.

But that revolution, if fought with an international sensibility, would be the best contribution we could make to the rest of the world. If the wealth that America loots from the Third World, and wastes (on arms, packaging, trivial work, etc.) were liberated, how much of the economic pressure could be taken off the Third World, whose own best energies are now absorbed in the struggle for brute industrialization? How might the continents now entering history be spared the agonies of primitive capital accumulation? There are no answers yet because we have not asked urgently, because we have been satisfied to try to tie down American troops on domestic battlefronts—to break the will of the Leviathan by depriving it of the loyalty of its work force, its managerial apprentices, its reluctant soldiers and its literal children. Good; but not enough.

The left must be *conscious* of its visionary prerogative as well as of its privilege; it must find ways of working on the other side of both hope and despair because there is no other way to live and because Americans must be confronted with the practicality of a new way of life. It must make models of that life, like People's Park, while at the same time explaining itself and constantly probing outward from its roots in the middle classes. It must be patient while urgent, and it must do all this without transforming itself into a scatter of "vanguards," each defined by its imperious distance from the Americans from whom at least one piece of the world revolution is to be made.

Plainly, there is much more to be said. But the old civil rights song said the important thing: "Keep your eyes on the prize. Hold on."

8

"SHE'S LEAVING HOME" THE WOMEN'S LIBERATION MOVEMENT

The women's liberation movement did not spring suddenly to life in the late 1960s, but instead grew out of the political, economic, and social changes of the postwar period and, specifically, the civil rights, new left, and student movements. Developments such as the changing nature of work, women's increasing labor-force participation, and expansion of the universities meant that new opportunities were available for women in American society. Female activists in other political movements began to recognize that they were not being treated equally by their male peers (see chapter 1). As women considered their situations, they realized how often they found themselves serving men and providing dependable backup for the movements, and how seldom they were taken seriously as political activists or leaders.

Learning from the civil rights movement, both its political ideology and the women they encountered within it, these young, mostly white women wondered why they fought for other people's rights when they were subordinated in their own movements and communities. They developed analyses suggesting that American society treated women as inferiors, paying them less at work and discouraging them from goals other than motherhood, domesticity, and attracting men. As the arguments coalesced, the women's liberation movement quickly caught fire.

In 1963 Betty Friedan published *The Feminine Mystique,* a work of enormous influence on white, middle-class American women. The book explored the unhappiness of suburban housewives who appeared to have achieved everything they had ever desired. Friedan argued that these women were frustrated by their confinement to domestic roles and wanted to explore other aspects of their personalities and inclinations. Thus, even before young female student activists began to complain about males in the movement and before they had formed their own political groups, older women had begun to agitate—in associations such as the National Organization for Women (NOW)—to change discriminatory laws and practices that prevented women from realizing their full potential.

It was youthful women's focus on sexual politics, abortion, birth control, personal relationships, and sexual freedom, however, that captured the attention of thousands of young women. Through the vehicle of consciousness-raising groups, in which small groups of women shared personal experiences and recognized the common political and social sources of their problems, feminism spread. Housework, sexuality, sexual orientation, relationships, mothering, day care, and work became topics analyzed from the perspective of women. The conclusions drawn were that American society was patriarchal and sexist, depended on women's labor and love, and yet denigrated not only their activities but women themselves. Younger women began to recognize the structural discrimination against women and joined older women in the struggle to change laws and policies that perpetuated women's second-class citizenship.

The women's liberation movement of the late 1960s and early 1970s attracted a primarily—but not exclusively—white, middle-class following. Women in the nationalist movements—African-American, Asian-American, and Chicano—began to articulate feminist positions (see chapter 3, as well). Working-class women explored their differences from middle-class women. For the most part, however, white middle-class women emphasized the commonality of all American women, such as their lack of access to legal abortion, and often overlooked class, racial, and ethnic divisions among women. The women's liberation movement that developed in the late 1960s remains one of the most profound and far-reaching of sixties social movements, continuing into the present, and influencing the enactment of significant social, cultural, economic, and political changes within American society.

LIBERAL FEMINISM

The Problem That Has No Name

BETTY FRIEDAN

Betty Friedan's 1963 book The Feminine Mystique, *from which this essay is taken, is often identified as the work most responsible for bringing the restlessness among white middle-class women to public attention. It explored white women's discontent as mothers and housewives, their limited personal possibilities, and their confinement to domestic roles. It is widely seen as one of the major contributors to the development of sixties feminism.*

The problem lay buried, unspoken, for many years in the minds of American women. It was a strange stirring, a sense of dissatisfaction, a yearning that women suffered in the middle of the twentieth century in the United States. Each suburban wife struggled with it alone. As she made the beds, shopped for groceries, matched slipcover material, ate peanut butter sandwiches with her children, chauffeured Cub Scouts and Brownies, lay beside her husband at night—she was afraid to ask even of herself the silent question—"Is this all?"

For over fifteen years there was no word of this yearning in the millions of words written about women, for women, in all the columns, books and articles by experts telling women their role was to seek fulfillment as wives and mothers. Over and over women heard in voices of tradition and of Freudian sophistication that they could desire no greater destiny than to glory in their own femininity. . . . They were taught to pity the neurotic, unfeminine, unhappy women who wanted to be poets or physicists or presidents. They learned that truly feminine women do not want careers, higher education, political rights—the independence and the opportunities that the old-fashioned feminists fought for. . . .

By the end of the nineteen-fifties, the average marriage age of women in America dropped to 20, and was still dropping, into the teens. Fourteen million girls were engaged by 17. The proportion of women attending college in comparison with men dropped from 47 per cent in 1920 to 35 per cent in 1958. A century earlier, women had fought for higher education; now girls went to college to get a husband. By the mid-fifties, 60 per cent dropped out of college to marry, or because they were afraid too much education would be a marriage bar. Colleges built dormitories for "married students," but the students were almost always the husbands. A new degree was instituted for the wives—"Ph.T." (Putting Husband Through).

Then American girls began getting married in high school. And the women's magazines, deploring the unhappy statistics about these young marriages, urged that courses on marriage, and marriage counselors, be installed in the high schools. Girls started going steady at twelve and thirteen, in junior high. Manufacturers put out brassieres with false bosoms of foam rubber for little girls of ten. And an advertisement for a child's dress, sizes 3–6x, in the *New York Times* in the fall of 1960, said: "She Too Can Join the Man-Trap Set.". . .

In a New York hospital, a woman had a nervous breakdown when she found she could not breastfeed her baby. In other hospitals, women dying of cancer refused a drug which research had proved might save their lives: its side effects were said to be unfeminine. "If I have only one life, let me live it as a blonde," a larger-than-life-sized picture of a pretty, vacuous woman proclaimed from newspaper, magazine, and drugstore ads. And across America, three out of every ten women dyed their hair blonde. They ate a chalk called Metrecal, instead of food, to shrink to the size of the thin young models. Department-store buyers reported that American women, since 1939, had become three and four sizes smaller. "Women are out to fit the clothes, instead of vice-versa," one buyer said.

Interior decorators were designing kitchens with mosaic murals and original paintings, for kitchens were once again the center of women's lives. Home sewing became a million-dollar industry. Many women no longer left their homes, except to shop, chauffeur their children, or attend a social engagement with their husbands. Girls were growing up in America without ever having jobs outside the home. In the late fifties, a sociological phenomenon was suddenly remarked: a third of American women now worked, but most were no longer young and very few were pursuing careers. They were married women who held part-time jobs, selling or secretarial, to put their husbands through school, their sons through college, or to help pay the mortgage. Or they were widows supporting families. Fewer and fewer women were entering professional work. The shortages in the nursing, social work, and teaching professions caused crises in almost every American city. Concerned over the Soviet Union's lead in the space race, scientists noted that America's greatest source of unused brainpower was women. But girls would not study physics: it was "unfeminine.". . .

The suburban housewife—she was the dream image of the young American women and the envy, it was said, of women all over the world. The American housewife—freed by science and labor-saving appliances from the drudgery, the dangers of childbirth and the illnesses of her grandmother. She was healthy, beautiful, educated, concerned only about her husband, her children, her home. She had found true feminine fulfillment. As a housewife and mother, she was respected as a full and equal partner to man in his world. She was free to choose automobiles, clothes, appliances, supermarkets; she had everything that women ever dreamed of.

In the fifteen years after World War II, this mystique of feminine fulfillment became the cherished and self-perpetuating core of contemporary American culture. . . .

For over fifteen years, the words written for women, and the words women used when they talked to each other, while their husbands sat on the other side of the room and talked shop or politics or septic tanks, were about problems with their children, or how to keep their husbands happy, or improve their children's school, or cook chicken or make slipcovers. Nobody argued whether women were inferior or superior to men; they were simply different. Words like "emancipation" and "career" sounded strange and embarrassing; no one had used them for years. When a Frenchwoman named Simone de Beauvoir wrote a book called *The Second Sex,* an American critic commented that she obviously "didn't know what life was all about," and besides, she was talking about French women. The "woman problem" in America no longer existed.

If a woman had a problem in the 1950's and 1960's, she knew that something must be wrong with her marriage, or with herself. Other women were satisfied with their lives, she thought. What kind of a woman was she if she did not feel this mysterious fulfillment waxing the kitchen floor? She was so ashamed to admit her dissatisfaction that she never knew how many other women shared it. If she tried to tell her husband, he didn't understand what she was talking about. She did not really understand it herself. For over fifteen years women in America found it harder to talk about this problem than about sex. Even the psychoanalysts had no name for it. When a woman went to a psychiatrist for help, as many women did, she would say, "I'm so ashamed," or "I must be hopelessly neurotic." "I don't know what's wrong with women today," a suburban psychiatrist said uneasily. "I only know something is wrong because most of my patients happen to be women. And their problem isn't sexual." Most women with this problem did not go to see a psychoanalyst, however. "There's nothing wrong really," they kept telling themselves. "There isn't any problem."

But on an April morning in 1959, I heard a mother of four, having coffee with four other mothers in a suburban development fifteen miles from New York, say in a tone of quiet desperation, "the problem." And the others knew, without words, that she was not talking about a problem with her husband, or her children, or her home. Suddenly they realized they all shared the same problem, the problem that has no name. They began, hesitantly, to talk about it. Later, after they had picked up their children at nursery school and taken them home to nap, two of the women cried, in sheer relief, just to know they were not alone. . . .

Just what was this problem that has no name? What were the words women used when they tried to express it? Sometimes a woman would say "I feel empty somehow . . . incomplete." Or she would say, "I feel as if I don't exist." Sometimes she blotted out the feeling with a tranquilizer. Sometimes she thought the problem was with her husband, or her children, or that what she really needed was to redecorate her house, or move to a better neighborhood, or have an affair, or another baby. Sometimes, she went to a doctor with symp-

toms she could hardly describe: "A tired feeling . . . I get so angry
with the children it scares me . . . I feel like crying without any reason."
(A Cleveland doctor called it "the housewife's syndrome.") A number
of women told me about great bleeding blisters that break out on
their hands and arms. "I call it the housewife's blight," said a family
doctor in Pennsylvania. "I see it so often lately in these young women
with four, five and six children who bury themselves in their dishpans.
But it isn't caused by detergent and it isn't cured by cortisone.". . .

A mother of four who left college at nineteen to get married
told me:

> I've tried everything women are supposed to do—hobbies, gardening,
> pickling, canning, being very social with my neighbors, joining commit-
> tees, running PTA teas. I can do it all, and I like it, but it doesn't leave
> you anything to think about—any feeling of who you are. I never had
> any career ambitions. All I wanted was to get married and have four
> children. I love the kids and Bob and my home. There's no problem
> you can even put a name to. But I'm desperate. I begin to feel I have
> no personality. I'm a server of food and putter-on of pants and a
> bedmaker, somebody who can be called on when you want something.
> But who am I?

A twenty-three-year-old mother in blue jeans said:

> I ask myself why I'm so dissatisfied. I've got my health, fine children,
> a lovely new home, enough money. My husband has a real future as
> an electronics engineer. He doesn't have any of these feelings. He says
> maybe I need a vacation, let's go to New York for a weekend. But that
> isn't it. I always had this idea we should do everything together. I can't
> sit down and read a book alone. If the children are napping and I have
> one hour to myself I just walk through the house waiting for them to
> wake up. I don't make a move until I know where the rest of the crowd
> is going. It's as if ever since you were a little girl, there's always been
> somebody or something that will take care of your life: your parents,
> or college, or falling in love, or having a child, or moving to a new
> house. Then you wake up one morning and there's nothing to look
> forward to.

A young wife in a Long Island development said:

> I seem to sleep so much. I don't know why I should be so tired. This
> house isn't nearly so hard to clean as the cold-water flat we had when

I was working. The children are at school all day. It's not the work. I just don't feel alive.

In 1960, the problem that has no name burst like a boil through the image of the happy American housewife. In the television commercials the pretty housewives still beamed over their foaming dishpans and *Time's* cover story on "The Suburban Wife, an American Phenomenon" protested: "Having too good a time . . . to believe that they should be unhappy." But the actual unhappiness of the American housewife was suddenly being reported—from the *New York Times* and *Newsweek* to *Good Housekeeping* and CBS Television ("The Trapped Housewife"), although almost everybody who talked about it found some superficial reason to dismiss it. . . . Some said it was the old problem—education: more and more women had education, which naturally made them unhappy in their role as housewives. "The road from Freud to Frigidaire, from Sophocles to Spock, has turned out to be a bumpy one," reported the *New York Times* (June 28, 1960). . . .

Can the problem that has no name be somehow related to the domestic routine of the housewife? When a woman tries to put the problem into words, she often merely describes the daily life she leads. What is there in this recital of comfortable domestic detail that could possibly cause such a feeling of desperation? Is she trapped simply by the enormous demands of her role as modern housewife: wife, mistress, mother, nurse, consumer, cook, chauffeur; expert on interior decoration, child care, appliance repair, furniture refinishing, nutrition, and education? . . . She has no time to read books, only magazines; even if she had time, she has lost the power to concentrate. At the end of the day, she is so terribly tired that sometimes her husband has to take over and put the children to bed.

This terrible tiredness took so many women to doctors in the 1950's that one decided to investigate it. He found, surprisingly, that his patients suffering from "housewife's fatigue" slept more than an adult needed to sleep—as much as ten hours a day—and that the actual energy they expended on housework did not tax their capacity. The real problem must be something else, he decided—perhaps boredom. Some doctors told their women patients they must get out of the house for a day, treat themselves to a movie in town. Others prescribed tranquilizers. Many suburban housewives were taking tranquilizers like cough drops. . . .

It is easy to see the concrete details that trap the suburban house-wife, the continual demands on her time. But the chains that bind her in her trap are chains in her own mind and spirit. They are chains made up of mistaken ideas and misinterpreted facts, of incomplete truths and unreal choices. They are not easily seen and not easily shaken off.

How can any woman see the whole truth within the bounds of her own life? How can she believe that voice inside herself, when it denies the conventional, accepted truths by which she has been living? And yet the women I have talked to, who are finally listening to that inner voice, seem in some incredible way to be groping through to a truth that has defied the experts. . . .

I began to see in a strange new light the American return to early marriage and the large families that are causing the population explosion; the recent movement to natural childbirth and breastfeed-ing; suburban conformity, and the new neuroses, character patholo-gies and sexual problems being reported by the doctors. I began to see new dimensions to old problems that have long been taken for granted among women: menstrual difficulties, sexual frigidity, promis-cuity, pregnancy fears, childbirth depression, the high incidence of emotional breakdown and suicide among women in their twenties and thirties, the menopause crises, the so-called passivity and immaturity of American men, the discrepancy between women's tested intellectual abilities in childhood and their adult achievement, the changing inci-dence of adult sexual orgasm in American women, and persistent problems in psychotherapy and in women's education.

If I am right, the problem that has no name stirring in the minds of so many American women today is not a matter of loss of femininity or too much education, or the demands of domesticity. It is far more important than anyone recognizes. It is the key to these other new and old problems which have been torturing women and their hus-bands and children, and puzzling their doctors and educators for years. It may well be the key to our future as a nation and a culture. We can no longer ignore that voice within women that says: "I want something more than my husband and my children and my home."

Job Discrimination and What Women Can Do about It

ALICE ROSSI

An early feminist essay about discrimination against women in the labor market, this appeared in 1970 in one of the first anthologies of feminist writing. Alice Rossi, a sociologist, straightforwardly outlines the situation in which many women find themselves, and predicts a militant women's movement if job discrimination is not eliminated.

It is extremely difficult to obtain data on the operation and incidence of job discrimination against women. Employers do not put up signs saying "No women need apply" even when this is the unstated policy of their gatekeeping personnel managers. Some women are unaware that their ambitions are being arbitrarily thwarted, and many others are reluctant to discuss the painful and infuriating encounters they have had with job discrimination. Those of us who research and write about the status of women, or who are active in women's rights organizations, frequently hear confidential stories of women's experiences with discrimination in the job world.

My own files of such accounts have expanded enormously in recent years as a result of the growing concern for and assertiveness of women on this issue. Here are only a few illustrations, in the words of the women themselves, of certain types of discrimination that they have experienced. An engineering student at M.I.T. reports:

> For years I have had to fight to retain my interest in aeronautics. My high school teacher thought I was crazy to even think of going into aeronautical engineering. My mother said I'd never find a man willing to marry a woman who likes to "tinker with motors," as she put it. My

Reprinted by permission, Alice E. Rossi. This article originally appeared in *The Atlantic Monthly*.

professors say I won't get a job in industry and should switch to another engineering specialty.

A graduate student in musicology writes:

> All through college my professors tried to push me toward the good old reliable field of teaching music at the grade school level. I have resisted this, but it wasn't easy, and I know many women who just gave up and are now teaching at the lower grade level instead of becoming a composer, musician, or musicologist.

An older woman who returned to the university to work toward a doctorate in economics after years in business reported:

> My first day in graduate school I was greeted with the comment of an economics professor: "Women have no place in economics." He refused to mark the papers of the women students. We protested to the department but they upheld the prerogative of the faculty. The man in question was a visiting professor and they didn't want to "impose on him"! Never mind the effect on the women students!

These quotes all illustrate attempts on the part of parents and teachers to depress and redirect women away from their chosen professional ambitions. By far the larger emphasis in both my research and correspondence files concerns the experience of women in the job world itself. One woman who worked for a year in an architectural firm wrote:

> I never wanted to teach grade school children, which I am doing now. But I found so much prejudice and resentment against me in my first job in an architectural firm, where the men refused to take me seriously, that I couldn't take it. I left and switched to teaching art. At least I feel welcome in a school.

A woman interested in a career in college administration writes:

> I had the experience last year of seeing a job I had filled for two years upgraded when it was filled by a man, at double the salary I was paid for the same work. College-trained women are lumped with the secretarial and clerical staff, while college-trained men are seen as potential executives. A few years of this and everybody is behaving according to what is expected of them, not what they are capable of.

The reaction of these two women to covert discrimination against them was a quiet acceptance: one withdrew to another field, the other fumed but stayed put in her low-status administrative job. The next example shows goal restriction in the process of formation. Looking back on her three years of job experience since she graduated from college, one woman said:

> I've learned a lot of hard lessons since I left college. A woman must be competent in her present position, but she must not aspire to a higher one. If it is offered to her, she must show surprise and gratitude. If she shows ambition, the competition and general disdain toward women executives will cost her social acceptance. For a single woman, that social acceptance is important. I used to aim much higher than I do now, but I have learned the game, and try to accept the level at which women seem to be kept, without feeling too bitter about it all.

The net effect of such discouragement is expressed by an academic woman who has adopted the compliant female stance:

> Ask a man's opinion about your ideas, show gratitude for his help, make your points as questions, listen with respect and interest to his ideas, and in this way you may be accepted. Even the most insecure type of male will not resent your achievements if you are quiet about them.

What this woman does not realize is that she is caught in the "damned if you do and damned if you don't" vise typical of the situation of many women in professional fields. If they are vital and assertive, they are rejected as "aggressive bitches out to castrate men." If they are quiet and unassuming, they are rejected as "unlikely to amount to much." Women who try to ease their acceptance by male colleagues in a masculine profession with sweetness-and-light talk may be kept on in the particular low-status niche they occupy, but then find that they are rejected for promotion because they lack drive and ambition.

The women quoted thus far share a common characteristic; they experienced discrimination and did nothing about it. The devices used to keep them down are various forms of ridicule, social rejection, bypassing them to promote less competent men, or subtle forms of lowering their expectations. If supervisors express surprise when women do a job well and give a shrug of "What can you expect" when they do a mediocre job, and this is repeated often enough, many women eventually internalize these expectations and perform accordingly.

Fortunately, not all women have this reaction to discriminatory attempts to block their movement into "masculine" or administrative jobs. Some women do the bypassing themselves, by leaving the employers who prevent their advancement and setting themselves up as independent entrepreneurs. One woman with a degree in meteorological engineering gives this account of her career:

> I'm self-employed now. I am the boss, and no one can fire me. But it was a tough fight. When I graduated from M.I.T. I was told I'd never get anywhere in my field. But my advice to young women now is "don't listen to anybody's advice." When I found I was blocked from advancement in one firm, I simply took a job with another. Finally I reached a vice-presidency but found I couldn't become president there. I decided to leave and build my own firm. Now I have just that, and a client list of 100 firms we service as engineering consultants.

Another woman started out with a doctorate in education and tried to make her way in several business firms. She writes:

> As one of the few female presidents of public companies in the United States, I have had my share of battling with the male ego in the business world. After six years of being denied various professional positions because of my sex, I finally decided that the only way for a woman to succeed in business was to start her own company. My firm was incorporated last year, with big ideas and no money. Today it is a public company worth about five million dollars.

Nor has this woman executive forgotten the early difficulties she had as a woman in a man's world, for she goes on to explain:

> Half of my management staff is composed of young, brilliant women who are successfully combining their roles as wives, mothers, and professionals.

Not all women have either the qualities, the contacts, or the occupational interests appropriate to such shifts from a salaried employee to a self-employed business executive as these two women. They do, however, have numerical strength, and a growing number of women's rights organizations to assist them in tackling all levels of discrimination in employment. One of the most important legal assists in this regard is Title VII of the Civil Rights Act of 1964, which includes a sex-discrimination ban. . . .

In its annual report in 1967, the Equal Employment Opportunity Commission (EEOC) stated that *well over a third* of the complaints it received and analyzed in the first year of operations alleged discrimination based on sex, and many of its most difficult cases involved sex discrimination. Of the 2,432 cases of sex discrimination filed and analyzed by the EEOC in fiscal year 1966, the major problems, by order of frequency, were as follows: benefits; layoff, recall, and seniority; state labor laws for women, particularly restrictions on overtime work by women; job classification; hiring, of which complaints by women exceed complaints by men by a ratio of 4 to 1; promotion; and wage differentials. . . .

Court cases contesting the legality of state protective laws have been on the increase. In one important case, three women employees were fired by their Colgate-Palmolive employers on the ground that the law prevented women from lifting weights in excess of 35 pounds and the firm was replacing the women with men. The women first lost their case *(Sellers et al. v. Colgate-Palmolive)* in the Federal District Court for the Southern District of Indiana, but went on to win an appeal in the U.S. Court of Appeals for the 7th Circuit (Chicago) in 1969. The court reviewing the appeal ruled that the lower court's decision was "based on a misconception of the requirements of Title VII's antidiscrimination provisions."

The Court further ordered that Colgate had to notify all its workers that each of them who desired to do so would be given an opportunity to demonstrate ability to perform more strenuous jobs. When it is realized that on jobs previously reserved for men at the Indiana Colgate plant men were paid at wage rates which *began* at the *highest* rate payable to women, it is apparent that the effect of the court ruling is to give women equal opportunity to bid for better-paying jobs on the basis of their individual capabilities and desires, and to prohibit their exclusion from these jobs because of sex. It was a victory for the Colgate women workers in the case, for all women in industrial jobs, and for the volunteer women attorneys who represented the women workers (Human Rights for Women, Inc., Washington, D.C.).

One of the most pressing needs for legal change at the moment is to amend Section 702 of Title VII to exclude the current exemption of discrimination in the employment of teachers and administrative personnel of educational institutions. Teaching, from preschool through graduate and professional schools, is the single largest occupation college-trained American women enter, yet there is no federal legislation to protect women teachers against discrimination based on their sex. . . .

A second urgently needed amendment to Title VII is the inclusion of a prohibition against discrimination based on marital status. Whether an individual is single, married, divorced, or widowed is no proper concern of an employer, nor is it relevant to job performance if a spouse, a parent, or a sibling is already an employee. . . .

Women have a precarious hold on positions in the labor market. Like the blacks and the very young, they have traditionally been the expendable portion of the labor force which employers have been free to woo or reject in accordance with fluctuations in production, sales, patient, client, or student load. . . .

Should these protections against discrimination on the basis of sex not be enacted, we can predict increased militancy by American women. Such militancy among women, as among blacks, will not be evidence of psychological instability but a response to the frustration of rising expectations. Militant women in the 1970s may be spurned and spat upon as the suffragists were during the decade before the vote was won for women in 1920. But it must be recognized that such militant women will win legal, economic, and political rights for the daughters of today's traditional Aunt Bettys, just as our grandmothers won the vote that women can exercise today.

NOW Bill of Rights

The National Organization for Women (NOW) was organized in 1967 and became the central feminist association of middle-class women.

    I. Equal Rights Constitutional Amendment
    II. Enforce Law Banning Sex Discrimination in Employment
    III. Maternity Leave Rights in Employment and in Social Security Benefits
    IV. Tax Deduction for Home and Child Care Expenses for Working Parents
    V. Child Day Care Centers
    VI. Equal and Unsegregated Education
    VII. Equal Job Training Opportunities and Allowances for Women in Poverty
    VIII. The Right of Women to Control Their Reproductive Lives

WE DEMAND:

    I. That the U.S. Congress immediately pass the Equal Rights Amendment to the Constitution to provide that "Equality of rights under the law shall not be denied or abridged by the United States or by any State on account of sex," and that such then be immediately ratified by the several States.

    II. That equal employment opportunity be guaranteed to all women, as well as men, by insisting that the Equal Employment Opportunity Commission enforces the prohibitions against racial discrimination.

    III. That women be protected by law to ensure their rights to return to their jobs within a reasonable time after childbirth without loss of seniority or other accrued benefits, and be paid maternity leave as a form of social security and/or employee benefit.

    IV. Immediate revision of tax laws to permit the deduction of home and child-care expenses for working parents.

    V. That child-care facilities be established by law on the same basis as parks, libraries, and public schools, adequate to the needs of children from the pre-school years through adolescence, as a community resource to be used by all citizens from all income levels.

    VI. That the right of women to be educated to their full potential equally with men be secured by Federal and State legislation, eliminating all discrimination and segregation by sex, written and unwritten, at all levels of education, including colleges, graduate and professional schools, loans and fellowships, and Federal and State training programs such as the Job Corps.

    VII. The right of women in poverty to secure job training, housing, and family allowances on equal terms with men, but without prejudice to a parent's right to remain at home to care for his or her children; revision of welfare legislation and poverty programs which deny women dignity, privacy, and self-respect.

VIII. The right of women to control their own reproductive lives by removing from the penal code laws limiting access to contraceptive information and devices, and by repealing penal laws governing abortion.

What Would It Be Like if Women Win

GLORIA STEINEM

One of the best-known American feminists, Gloria Steinem, in 1970, advocates the relaxing of traditional sex roles for women and men and the abolition of sexist laws and practices, thereby leading to more gender fluidity and equality.

Any change is fearful, especially one affecting both politics and sex roles, so let me begin these utopian speculations with a fact. To break the ice.

Women don't want to exchange places with men. Male chauvinists, science-fiction writers and comedians may favor that idea for its shock value, but psychologists say it is a fantasy based on ruling-class ego and guilt. Men assume that women want to imitate them, which is just what white people assumed about blacks. An assumption so strong that it may convince the second-class group of the need to imitate, but for both women and blacks that stage has passed. Guilt produces the question: What if they could treat us as we have treated them?

That is not our goal. But we do want to change the economic system to one more based on merit. In Women's Lib Utopia, there will be free access to good jobs—and decent pay for the bad ones women have been performing all along, including housework. Increased skilled labor might lead to a four-hour workday, and higher wages would encourage further mechanization of repetitive jobs now kept alive by cheap labor.

With women as half the country's elected representatives, and a woman President once in a while, the country's *machismo* problems would be greatly reduced. The old-fashioned idea that manhood depends on violence and victory is, after all, an important part of our troubles in the streets, and in Vietnam. I'm not saying that women leaders would eliminate violence. We are not more moral than men; we are only uncorrupted by power so far. When we do acquire power, we might turn out to have an equal impulse toward aggression. Even now, Margaret Mead believes that women fight less often but more fiercely than men, because women are not taught the rules of the war game and fight only when cornered. But for the next 50 years or so, women in politics will be very valuable by tempering the idea of manhood into something less aggressive and better suited to this crowded, post-atomic planet. Consumer protection and children's rights, for instance, might get more legislative attention.

Men will have to give up ruling-class privileges, but in return they will no longer be the only ones to support the family, get drafted, bear the strain of power and responsibility. Freud to the contrary, anatomy is not destiny, at least not for more than nine months at a time. In Israel, women are drafted, and some have gone to war. In England, more men type and run switchboards. In India and Israel, a woman rules. In Sweden, both parents take care of the children. In this country, come Utopia, men and women won't reverse roles; they will be free to choose according to individual talents and preferences.

If role reform sounds sexually unsettling, think how it will change the sexual hypocrisy we have now. No more sex arranged on the barter system, with women pretending interest, and men never sure whether they are loved for themselves or for the security few women can get any other way. (Married or not, for sexual reasons or social ones, most women still find it second nature to Uncle-Tom.) No more men who are encouraged to spend a lifetime living with inferiors; with housekeepers, or dependent creatures who are still children. No more domineering wives, emasculating women, and "Jewish mothers," all of whom are simply human beings with all their normal ambition and drive confined to the home. No more unequal partnerships that eventually doom love and sex.

In order to produce that kind of confidence and individuality, child-rearing will train according to talent. Little girls will no longer be surrounded by airtight, self-fulfilling prophecies of natural passivity, lack of ambition and objectivity, inability to exercise power, and dexterity (so long as special aptitude for jobs requiring patience and dexterity is confined to poorly paid jobs; brain surgery is for males).

Schools and universities will help to break down traditional sex roles, even when parents will not. Half the teachers will be men, a rarity now at preschool and elementary levels; girls will not necessarily serve cookies or boys hoist up the flag. Athletic teams will be picked only by strength and skill. Sexually segregated courses like auto mechanics and home economics will be taken by boys and girls together. New courses in sexual politics will explore female subjugation as the model for political oppression, and women's history will be an academic staple, along with black history, at least until the white-male-oriented textbooks are integrated and rewritten.

As for the American child's classic problem—too much mother, too little father—that would be cured by an equalization of parental responsibility. Free nurseries, school lunches, family cafeterias built into every housing complex, service companies that will do household cleaning chores in a regular, businesslike way, and more responsibility by the entire community for the children: all these will make it possible for both mother and father to work, and to have equal leisure time with the children at home. For parents of very young children, however, a special job category, created by government and unions, would allow such parents a shorter workday.

The revolution would not take away the option of being a housewife. A woman who prefers to be her husband's housekeeper and/or hostess would receive a percentage of his pay determined by the domestic-relations courts. If divorced, she might be eligible for a pension fund, and for a job-training allowance. Or a divorce could be treated the same way that the dissolution of a business partnership is now.

If these proposals seem farfetched, consider Sweden, where most of them are already in effect. Sweden is not yet a working women's lib model; most of the role-reform programs began less than a decade ago, and are just beginning to take hold. But that country is so far ahead of us in recognizing the problem that Swedish statements on sex and equality sound like bulletins from the moon.

Our marriage laws, for instance, are so reactionary that women's lib groups want couples to take a compulsory written exam on the law, as for a driver's license, before going through with the wedding. A man has alimony and wifely debts to worry about, but a woman may lose so many of her civil rights that in the U.S. now, in important legal ways, she becomes a child again. In some states, she cannot sign credit agreements, use her maiden name, incorporate a business, or establish a legal residence of her own. Being a wife, according to most social and legal definitions, is still a nineteenth-century thing.

Assuming, however, that these blatantly sexist laws are abolished or reformed, that job discrimination is forbidden, that parents share financial responsibility for each other and the children, and that sexual relationships become partnerships of equal adults (some pretty big assumptions), then marriage will probably go right on. Men and women are, after all, physically complementary. When society stops encouraging men to be exploiters and women to be parasites, they may turn out to be more complementary in emotion as well. Women's lib is not trying to destroy the American family. A look at the statistics on divorce—plus the way in which old people are farmed out with strangers and young people flee the home—shows the destruction that has already been done. Liberated women are just trying to point out the disaster, and build compassionate and practical alternatives from the ruins.

What will exist is a variety of alternative life-styles. Since the population explosion dictates that childbearing be kept to a minimum, parents-and-children will be only one of many "families": couples, age groups, working groups, mixed communes, blood-related clans, class groups, creative groups. Single women will have the right to stay single without ridicule, without the attitudes now betrayed by "spinster" and "bachelor." Lesbians or homosexuals will no longer be denied legally binding marriages, complete with mutual-support agreements and inheritance rights. Paradoxically, the number of homosexuals may get smaller. With fewer overpossessive mothers and fewer fathers who hold up an impossibly cruel or perfectionist idea of manhood, boys will be less likely to be denied or reject their identity as males.

Changes that now seem small may get bigger:

Men's Lib. Men now suffer from more diseases due to stress, heart attacks, ulcers, a higher suicide rate, greater difficulty living alone, less adaptability to change and, in general, a shorter life-span than women. There is some scientific evidence that what produces physical problems is not work itself, but the inability to choose which work, and how much. With women bearing half the financial responsibility, and with the idea of "masculine" jobs gone, men might well feel freer and live longer.

Religion. Protestant women are already becoming ordained ministers; radical nuns are carrying out liturgical functions that were once the exclusive property of priests; Jewish women are rewriting prayers—particularly those that Orthodox Jews recite every morning thanking God they are not female. In the future, the church will become an area of equal participation by women. This means, of course, that organized religion will have to give up one of its great historical weapons: sexual repression. In most structured faiths, from Hinduism through Roman Catholicism, the status of women went down as the position of priests ascended. Male clergy implied, if they did not teach, that women were unclean, unworthy and sources of ungodly temptation, in order to remove them as rivals for the emotional forces of men. Full participation of women in ecclesiastical life might involve certain changes in theology, such as, for instance, a radical redefinition of sin.

Literary Problems. Revised sex roles will outdate more children's books than civil rights ever did. Only a few children had the problem of a *Little Black Sambo*, but most have the male-female stereotypes of "Dick and Jane." A boomlet of children's books about mothers who work has already begun, and liberated parents and editors are beginning to pressure for change in the textbook industry. Fiction writing will change more gradually, but romantic novels with wilting heroines and swashbuckling heroes will be reduced to historical value. Or perhaps to the sadomasochist trade. (*Marjorie Morningstar*, a romantic novel that took the 1950s by storm, has already begun to seem as unreal as its 1920s predecessor, *The Sheik*.) As for the literary plots that turn on forced marriages or horrific abortions, they will seem as dated as Prohibition stories. Free legal abortions and free birth control will force writers to give up pregnancy as the *deus ex machina*.

Manners and Fashion. Dress will be more androgynous, with class symbols becoming more important than sexual ones. Pro- or anti-Establishment styles may already be more vital than who is wearing them. Hardhats are just as likely to rough up antiwar girls as antiwar men in the street, and police understand that women are just as likely to be pushers or bombers. Dances haven't required that one partner lead the other for years, anyway. Chivalry will transfer itself to those who need it, or deserve respect: old people, admired people, anyone with an armload of packages. Women with normal work identities will be less likely to attach their whole sense of self to youth and appearance; thus there will be fewer nervous breakdowns when the first wrinkles appear. Lighting cigarettes and other treasured niceties will become gestures of mutual affection. "I like to be helped on with my coat," says one women's lib worker, "but not if it costs me $2,000 a year in salary."

For those with nostalgia for a simpler past, here is a word of comfort. Anthropologist Geoffrey Gorer studied the few peaceful human tribes and discovered one common characteristic: sex roles were not polarized. Differences of dress and occupation were at a minimum. Society, in other words, was not using sexual blackmail as a way of getting women to do cheap labor, or men to be aggressive.

Thus women's lib may achieve a more peaceful society on the way toward its other goals. That is why the Swedish government considers reform to bring about greater equality in the sex roles one of its most important concerns. As Prime Minister Olof Palme explained in a widely ignored speech delivered in Washington this spring [1970]: "It is *human beings* we shall emancipate. In Sweden today, if a politician should declare that the woman ought to have a different role from man's, he would be regarded as something from the Stone Age." In other words, the most radical goal of the movement is egalitarianism.

If women's lib wins, perhaps we all do.

RADICAL WOMEN

No More Miss America

In August 1968, young radical feminists demonstrated against the Miss America Pageant in Atlantic City. This was one of the important inaugural events of the women's liberation movement. While the organizers, in the invitation below, suggest throwing away bras (along with girdles, false eyelashes, and the like), no burning of bras took place. Nonetheless, this image was constructed by the media, connecting "bra burning" to draft-card burning and the "burn, baby, burn" image of urban rioting, all radical repudiations of the status quo.

On September 7th in Atlantic City, the Annual Miss America Pageant will again crown "your ideal." But this year, reality will liberate the contest auction-block in the guise of "genyooine" de-plasticized, breathing women. Women's Liberation Groups, black women, high-school and college women, women's peace groups, women's welfare and social-work groups, women's job-equality groups, pro-birth con-

trol and pro-abortion groups—women of every political persuasion—all are invited to join us in a day-long boardwalk-theater event,
starting at 1:00 P.M. on the Boardwalk in front of Atlantic City's Convention Hall. We will protest the image of Miss America, an image that
oppresses women in every area in which it purports to represent us.
There will be: Picket Lines; Guerrilla Theater; Leafleting; Lobbying
Visits to the contestants urging our sisters to reject the Pageant Farce
and join us; a huge Freedom Trash Can (into which we will throw
bras, girdles, curlers, false eyelashes, wigs, and representative issues
of *Cosmopolitan, Ladies' Home Journal, Family Circle,* etc.—bring any such
woman-garbage you have around the house); we will also announce a
Boycott of all those commercial products related to the Pageant, and
the day will end with a Women's Liberation rally at midnight when
Miss America is crowned on live television. Lots of other surprises are
being planned (come and add your own!) but we do not plan heavy
disruptive tactics and so do not expect a bad police scene. It should
be a groovy day on the Boardwalk in the sun with our sisters. In case
of arrests, however, we plan to reject all male authority and demand
to be busted by policewomen only. (In Atlantic City, women cops are
not permitted to make arrests—dig that!)

Male chauvinist-reactionaries on this issue had best stay away, nor
are male liberals welcome in the demonstrations. But sympathetic
men can donate money as well as cars and drivers.

Male reporters will be refused interviews. We reject patronizing
reportage. *Only newswomen will be recognized.*

THE TEN POINTS

We Protest:

1. *The Degrading Mindless-Boob-Girlie Symbol.* The Pageant contestants epitomize the roles we are all forced to play as women. The
parade down the runway blares the metaphor of the 4-H Club county
fair, where the nervous animals are judged for teeth, fleece, etc., and
where the best "specimen" gets the blue ribbon. So are women in
our society forced daily to compete for male approval, enslaved by
ludicrous "beauty" standards we ourselves are conditioned to take
seriously.

2. *Racism with Roses.* Since its inception in 1921, the Pageant has not had one Black finalist, and this has not been for a lack of test-case contestants. There has never been a Puerto Rican, Alaskan, Hawaiian, or Mexican-American winner. Nor has there ever been a *true* Miss America—an American Indian.

3. *Miss America as Military Death Mascot.* The highlight of her reign each year is a cheerleader-tour of American troops abroad—last year she went to Vietnam to pep-talk our husbands, fathers, sons and boyfriends into dying and killing with a better spirit. She personifies the "unstained patriotic American womanhood our boys are fighting for." The Living Bra and the Dead Soldier. We refuse to be used as Mascots for Murder.

4. *The Consumer Con-Game.* Miss America is a walking commercial for the Pageant's sponsors. Wind her up and she plugs your product on promotion tours and TV—all in an "honest, objective" endorsement. What a shill.

5. *Competition Rigged and Unrigged.* We deplore the encouragement of an American myth that oppresses men as well as women: the win-or-you're-worthless competive disease. The "beauty contest" creates only one winner to be "used" and forty-nine losers who are "useless."

6. *The Woman as Pop Culture Obsolescent Theme.* Spindle, mutilate, and then discard tomorrow. What is so ignored as last year's Miss America? This only reflects the gospel of our society, according to Saint Male: women must be young, juicy, malleable—hence age discrimination and the cult of youth. And we women are brainwashed into believing this ourselves!

7. *The Unbeatable Madonna-Whore Combination.* Miss America and Playboy's centerfold are sisters over the skin. To win approval, we must be both sexy and wholesome, delicate but able to cope, demure yet titillatingly bitchy. Deviation of any sort brings, we are told, disaster: "You won't get a man!!"

8. *The Irrelevant Crown on the Throne of Mediocrity.* Miss America represents what women are supposed to be: unoffensive, bland, apolitical. If you are tall, short, over or under what weight The Man prescribes you should be, forget it. Personality, articulateness, intelligence, commitment—unwise. Conformity is the key to the crown—and, by extension, to success in our society.

9. *Miss America as Dream Equivalent To—?* In this reputedly democratic society, where every little boy supposedly can grow up to be
President, what can every little girl hope to grow to be? Miss America.
That's where it's at. Real power to control our own lives is restricted
to men, while women get patronizing pseudo-power, an ermine cloak
and a bunch of flowers; men are judged by their actions, women by
their appearance.

10. *Miss America as Big Sister Watching You.* The Pageant exercises
Thought Control, attempts to scar the Image onto our minds, to
further make women oppressed and men oppressors; to enslave us
all the more in high-heeled, low-status roles; to inculcate false values
in young girls; to use women as beasts of buying; to seduce us to
prostitute ourselves before our own oppression.

NO MORE MISS AMERICA

Principles

NEW YORK RADICAL WOMEN

*This brief position statement sketches out a radical feminist perspective of the
late sixties.*

We take the woman's side in everything.

We ask not if something is "reformist," "radical," "revolutionary," or "moral." We ask: is it good for women or bad for women?

We ask not if something is "political." We ask: is it effective? Does
it get us closest to what we really want in the fastest way?

From *Sisterhood Is Powerful: An Anthology of Writings from the Women's Liberation Movement,*
edited by Robin Morgan. Copyright © 1970 by Robin Morgan. By permission.

We define the best interests of women as the best interests of the poorest, most insulted, most despised, most abused woman on earth. Her lot, her suffering and abuse is the threat that men use against all of us to keep us in line. She is what all women fear being called, fear being treated as and yet what we all really are in the eyes of men. She is Everywoman: ugly, dumb (dumb broad, dumb cunt), bitch, nag, hag, whore, fucking and breeding machine, mother of us all. Until Everywoman is free, no woman will be free. When her beauty and knowledge is revealed and seen, the new day will be at hand.

We are critical of all past ideology, literature and philosophy, products as they are of male supremacist culture. We are re-examining even our words, language itself.

We take as our source the hitherto unrecognized culture of women, a culture which from long experience of oppression developed an intense appreciation for life, a sensitivity to unspoken thoughts and the complexity of simple things, a powerful knowledge of human needs and feelings.

We regard our feelings as our most important source of political understanding.

We see the key to our liberation in our collective wisdom and our collective strength.

REDSTOCKINGS MANIFESTO

Redstockings, an important radical feminist organization based in New York, issued this 1969 manifesto.

I. After centuries of individual and preliminary political struggle, women are uniting to achieve their final liberation from male suprem-

Reprinted by permission, Redstockings Women's Liberation Archives for Action, P.O. Box 744, Stuyvesant Station, New York, NY 10009.

acy. Redstockings is dedicated to building this unity and winning our freedom.

II. Women are an oppressed class. Our oppression is total, affecting every facet of our lives. We are exploited as sex objects, breeders, domestic servants, and cheap labor. We are considered inferior beings, whose only purpose is to enhance men's lives. Our humanity is denied. Our prescribed behavior is enforced by the threat of physical violence.

Because we have lived so intimately with our oppressors, in isolation from each other, we have been kept from seeing our personal suffering as a political condition. This creates the illusion that a woman's relationship with her man is a matter of interplay between two unique personalities, and can be worked out individually. In reality, every such relationship in a *class* relationship, and the conflicts between individual men and women are *political* conflicts that can only be solved collectively.

III. We identify the agents of our oppression as men. Male supremacy is the oldest, most basic form of domination. All other forms of exploitation and oppression (racism, capitalism, imperialism, etc.) are extensions of male supremacy: men dominate women, a few men dominate the rest. All power structures throughout history have been male-dominated and male-oriented. Men have controlled all political, economic and cultural institutions and backed up this control with physical force. They have used their power to keep women in an inferior position. *All men* receive economic, sexual, and psychological benefits from male supremacy. *All men* have oppressed women.

IV. Attempts have been made to shift the burden of responsibility from men to institutions or to women themselves. We condemn these arguments as evasions. Institutions alone do not oppress; they are merely tools of the oppressor. To blame institutions implies that men and women are equally victimized, obscures the fact that men benefit from the subordination of women, and gives men the excuse that they are forced to be oppressors. On the contrary, any man is free to renounce his superior position provided that he is willing to be treated like a woman by other men.

We also reject the idea that women consent to or are to blame for their own oppression. Women's submission is not the result of brainwashing, stupidity, or mental illness but of continual, daily pressure from men. We do not need to change ourselves, but to change men.

The most slanderous evasion of all is that women can oppress men. The basis for this illusion is the isolation of individual relationships from their political context and the tendency of men to see any legitimate challenge to their privileges as persecution.

V. We regard our personal experience, and our feelings about that experience, as the basis for an analysis of our common situation. We cannot rely on existing ideologies as they are all products of male supremacist culture. We question every generalization and accept none that are not confirmed by our experience.

Our chief task at present is to develop female class consciousness through sharing experience and publicly exposing the sexist foundation of all our institutions. Consciousness-raising is not "therapy," which implies the existence of individual solutions and falsely assumes that the male-female relationship is purely personal, but the only method by which we can ensure that our program for liberation is based on the concrete realities of our lives.

The first requirement for raising class consciousness is honesty, in private and in public, with ourselves and other women.

VI. We identify with all women. We define our best interest as that of the poorest, most brutally exploited woman.

We repudiate all economic, racial, educational or status privileges that divide us from other women. We are determined to recognize and eliminate any prejudices we may hold against other women.

We are committed to achieving internal democracy. We will do whatever is necessary to ensure that every woman in our movement has an equal chance to participate, assume responsibility, and develop her political potential.

VII. We call on all our sisters to unite with us in struggle.

We call on all men to give up their male privileges and support women's liberation in the interest of our humanity and their own.

In fighting for our liberation we will always take the side of women against their oppressors. We will not ask what is "revolutionary" or "reformist," only what is good for women.

The time for individual skirmishes has passed. This time we are going all the way.

About My Consciousness Raising

BARBARA SUSAN

This Redstockings author describes the process of consciousness raising among small groups of women. Consciousness raising was considered one of the most important methods of changing the way in which women saw the world, enabling them to perceive and define their personal situations in social and political terms.

The first consciousness raising session that I attended was about house-work. We went around the room and each woman in turn told how she felt about housework and how she felt when she was standing over the dishes or stove, or what happened when she asked her husband or a man she was living with to do the dishes. It came to my turn and I explained how my husband always helped with the housework. If I was tired he'd cook dinner and sometimes even do the dishes. Yet I'd still start to boil every time I'd get in front of the sink or stove. I listened to other women also telling about how their men "helped" with the housework.

I began to get sick at the thought of these liberal men "helping" their wives with the housework. When we did other things like go to the beach or go out for ice cream he didn't help, he shared. It was only a matter of helping when it came to doing things that he didn't like to do. The group began to feel that something was wrong with the whole idea of men "helping" women with the housework. It meant that he was helping me with *my* job. Every time he'd help and I'd say "thank you" I was reinforcing the idea that it was my job! Regardless of whether I worked or not housekeeping was my job. It became pretty clear after hearing many women speak that this thing about helping was no petty detail of our personal lives. It became clear that it was a political fact. Listen to men talk about housework

Reprinted by permission, Barbara (Susan) Kaminsky.

or better yet ask them how they feel about it. I'll bet that most of them say that they "help out." This is not just a matter of semantics. It is important because it keeps us having the job of housework as our job . . . as woman's job. There were several things that were very surprising to me at this consciousness raising session, not the least of which was the conspicuous absence of men. It was quite pleasant to talk without them. There was no need to argue about whether or not the problems we felt were real. Also, that constant undercurrent of competition that almost all of us feel when in the presence of men was almost totally absent. We were able to begin to find new ways of relating to each other.

After doing consciousness raising for a while Redstockings developed a procedure for it that we find useful. We direct our talk to one particular question at a time in order to formulate an analysis based on our real experiences and so that any generalizations we might come to will be based on fact. We go around the room, each sister taking a turn. In this way everyone has a fair chance to speak and be totally heard. When a sister gives testimony the other women in the group can ask questions in order to clarify in their own minds what a sister is saying. Sometimes women interrupt a testimony to say how their own experiences are related directly to those of the woman speaking. When everyone has spoken we go around the room making generalizations and trying to find out what the connections are between our experiences and how they relate one to the other.

Consciousness raising is not a form of encounter group or psychotherapy. I've been involved in both and I can tell you they are very different. Therapy was useful to me in certain ways. It helped me develop a sense of self-worth and come to the understanding that I wasn't a bad person or useless. My experience in therapy helped me have a better image of myself and I even started to look better and dress in a more attractive way. In short I had more confidence in myself. . . .

In retrospect therapy had separated me from my sisters by calling them "most women" and me "special." It had neglected to tell me that my newly acquired feeling of self-worth was only going to propel me headlong into another struggle because although I felt worthy I was still a woman and very few other people were going to recognize my worth. Not only weren't they going to recognize my worth, but I was going to be penalized for fighting for my rights. I was labelled crazy, masochistic, etc. But this time I was not completely fooled.

I got into the women's movement and began to see that other women were also called crazy. The relief at finding I was not alone was incredible. I was stunned. Here were women who were strong. And what's more they were smart and had ideas about how things ought to be. It had been very effective in therapy calling me different from my sisters, trying to make me believe that I could find an individual solution without changing the external political conditions. It had effectively separated me from my sisters and even made me start to hate them. It put me in the position of not being able to identify with other women. I was identifying with men, which seems quite natural to me since they were the ones who got all the goodies.

In the women's movement and especially in consciousness raising I saw women who recognized that there was no such thing as a personal way of solving their problems so long as male supremacy in all its formal and informal forms still existed. Here were women looking for solutions based on their own collective experience. . . . They were talking about their personal experiences and analyzing them in terms of social structures rather than in terms of their own weaknesses. They were not, as therapy often does, blaming women for being passive and in a rut. They were trying to find out exactly what that rut was and how they were forced into it so that it could be changed. They were trusting to their own minds and experiences to understand oppression . . . not as an abstraction . . . not as something that happened to other women, but as a fact of their lives. . . .

Consciousness raising is a way of forming a political analysis on information we can trust is true. That information is our experience. It is difficult to understand how our oppression is political (organized) unless we first remove it from the area of personal problems. Unless we talk to each other about our so called personal problems and see how many of our problems are shared by other people, we won't be able to see how these problems are rooted in politics. When we talk about politics we don't mean in the limited sense of political parties such as the Democratic and Republican or economic systems like capitalism and socialism. We also see male supremacy as a political system in as much as all men are in collusion in forcing women into inferior and unproductive positions. Rare is the man who will support a woman vis-à-vis another man. There is a tacit agreement among men that women should do only certain kinds of work, (housework, childcare, nursing, clerical work, etc.) and that woman are incapable of controlling their own lives and therefore must be helped (controlled) by men. This "understanding" that men have is reinforced by our so called democratic legal system, prostitutes are criminals but their clients aren't (in New York State), women cannot accuse their husband of rape, etc.

In order for us to form a powerful political movement it must be a movement which answers to the needs of all women. We recognize that at the present time there are economic, class and racial differences among women which keep us from coming together politically. It is our hope that consciousness raising in groups of women who are not the same will help us to understand each other and help us all in building a movement which answers to the needs of more than just the most privileged woman. Our analysis is an expanding one, it changes as more and more women enter the movement and contribute their knowledge and experience thereby widening and correcting our understanding of oppression.

The Politics of Housework

PAT MAINARDI

In one of the best known early feminist pieces, published in 1969, Pat Mainardi recounts her personal experience of trying to equalize the work of daily life with her husband, and gives advice to women who want to share the housework with their male partners. The fact that there was a politics of housework proved eye opening.

Though women do not complain of the power of husbands, each complains of her own husband, or of the husbands of her friends. It is the same in all other cases of servitude; at least in the commencement of the emancipatory movement. The serfs did not at first complain of the power of the lords, but only of their tyranny.

—John Stuart Mill, *On the Subjection of Women*

Liberated women—very different from women's liberation! The first signals all kinds of goodies, to warm the hearts (not to mention other parts) of the most radical men. The other signals—*housework*. The first brings sex without marriage, sex before marriage, cozy housekeeping arrangements ("You see, I'm living with this chick") and the self-content of knowing that you're not the kind of man who wants a doormat instead of a woman. That will come later. After all, who wants that old commodity anymore, the Standard American Housewife, all husband, home and kids. The New Commodity, the Liberated Woman, has sex a lot and has a Career, preferably something that can be fitted in with the household chores—like dancing, pottery, or painting.

On the other hand is women's liberation—and housework. What? You say this is all trivial? Wonderful! That's what I thought. It seemed perfectly reasonable. We both had careers, both had to work a couple of days a week to earn enough to live on, so why shouldn't we share the housework? So I suggested it to my mate and he agreed—most men are too hip to turn you down flat. "You're right," he said. "It's only fair."

Then an interesting thing happened. I can only explain it by stating that we women have been brainwashed more than even we can imagine. Probably too many years of seeing television women in ecstasy over their shiny waxed floors or breaking down over their dirty shirt collars. Men have no such conditioning. They recognize the essential fact of housework right from the very beginning. Which is that it stinks. Here's my list of dirty chores: buying groceries, carting them home and putting them away; cooking meals and washing dishes and pots; doing the laundry, digging out the place when things get out of control; washing floors. The list could go on but the sheer necessities are bad enough. All of us have to do these things, or get some one else to do them for us. The longer my husband contemplated these chores, the more repulsed he became, and so proceeded the change from the normally sweet considerate Dr. Jekyll into the crafty Mr. Hyde who would stop at nothing to avoid the horrors of—*housework*. As he felt himself backed into a corner laden with dirty dishes, brooms, mops, and reeking garbage, his front teeth grew longer and pointier, his fingernails haggled and his eyes grew wild. Housework trivial? Not on your life! Just try to share the burden.

So ensued a dialogue that's been going on for several years. Here are some of the high points:

"I don't mind sharing the housework, but I don't do it very well. We should each do the things we're best at."
Meaning: Unfortunately I'm no good at things like washing dishes or cooking. What I do best is a little light carpentry, changing light bulbs, moving furniture *(how often do you move furniture?)*.
Also Meaning: Historically the lower classes (black men and us) have had hundreds of years experience doing menial jobs. It would be a waste of manpower to train someone else to do them now.
Also Meaning: I don't like the dull stupid boring jobs, so you should do them.

"I don't mind sharing the work, but you'll have to show me how to do it."
Meaning: I ask a lot of questions and you'll have to show me everything everytime I do it because I don't remember so good. Also don't try to sit down and read while I'm doing my jobs because I'm going to annoy hell out of you until it's easier to do them yourself.

"We used to be so happy!" (Said whenever it was his turn to do something.)
Meaning: I used to be so happy.
Meaning: Life without housework is bliss. *(No Quarrel here. Perfect agreement.)*

"We have different standards, and why should I have to work to your standards. That's unfair."
Meaning: If I begin to get bugged by the dirt and crap I will say "This place sure is a sty" or "How can anyone live like this?" and wait for your reaction. I know that all women have a sore called "Guilt over a messy house" or "Household work is ultimately my responsibility."

I know that men have caused that sore—if anyone visits and the place *is* a sty, they're not going to leave and say, "He sure is a lousy housekeeper." You'll take the rap in any case. I can outwait you.

Also Meaning: I can provoke innumerable scenes over the housework issue. Eventually doing all the housework yourself will be less painful to you than trying to get me to do half. Or I'll suggest we get a maid. She will do my share of the work. You will do yours. It's women's work.

"I've got nothing against sharing the housework, but you can't make me do it on your schedule."

Meaning: Passive resistance. I'll do it when I damned well please, if at all. If my job is doing dishes, it's easier to do them once a week. If taking out laundry, once a month. If washing the floors, once a year. If you don't like it, do it yourself oftener, and then I won't do it at all.

"I *hate* it more than you. You don't mind it so much."

Meaning: Housework is garbage work. It's the worst crap I've ever done. It's degrading and humiliating for someone of *my* intelligence to do it. But for someone of *your* intelligence . . .

"Housework is too trivial to even talk about."

Meaning: It's even more trivial to do. Housework is beneath my status. My purpose in life is to deal with matters of significance. Yours is to deal with matters of insignificance. You should do the housework.

"This problem of housework is not a man-woman problem! In any relationship between two people one is going to have a stronger personality and dominate."

Meaning: That stronger personality had better be *me*.

"In animal societies, wolves, for example, the top animal is usually a male even where he is not chosen for brute strength but on the basis of cunning and intelligence. Isn't that interesting?"

Meaning: I have historical, psychological, anthropological, and biological justification for keeping you down. How can you ask the top wolf to be equal?

"Women's liberation isn't really a political movement."
Meaning: The Revolution is coming too close to home.
Also Meaning: I am only interested in how *I* am oppressed, not how
I oppress others. Therefore the war, the draft, and the university are
political. Women's liberation is not.

"Man's accomplishments have always depended on getting help from
other people, mostly women. What great man would have accomplished what he did if he had to do his own housework?
Meaning: Oppression is built into the System and I, as the white
American male, receive the benefits of this System. I don't want to
give them up. . . .

Women's Political Action

*Two short reports published in early women's journals provide a sense of the
range of feminist political activities and the interconnection between feminism
and other political movements of the time.*

Women Support Panther Sisters

New Haven, Connecticut. On Saturday, November 22, a coalition of
Women's Liberation, the Black Panther Party and the Welfare Rights
Organization staged an inspiring demonstration in support of 14 New
Haven Panthers in prison. Led by members of Women's Liberation
and Welfare Rights, thousands of black and white radicals marched
through crowded streets of New Haven and held a militant rally in

front of the Court House. This was the first large action planned and led by Women's Liberation.

The 14 Panthers have spent the last 6 months in jail without a trial on charges of conspiracy, murder and kidnapping, in connection with the death of Alex Rackley, a former Panther, last May. The Panthers claim these are trumped-up charges designed to keep them off the street, out of their communities and away from the people they want to serve. There have been similar incidents all over the country.

Five of the 14 Panthers are women: 2 of the women—Rose Smith and Loretta Luckes—are pregnant; 1 woman—Frances Carter—recently gave birth under armed guard. Her physical condition was so poor, she spent 30 hours in labor and the baby was delivered by Caesarian section. The women have been denied the right to physical exercise, fresh air, and proper clothing. Rose has gained only 1 pound in the 6 months of her pregnancy spent in jail. They have not been able to sleep as lights have flooded their cells day and night. Their babies will be taken away from them by the state, denying the wishes of the Black Panther community to raise the children in a Panther commune.

The speakers at the rally were two Panther women, a Young Lord woman, and a woman from Women's Liberation. Their raps dealt with the specific issues of the demonstration, political repression, the true nature of the "system" and the relation of all these to women.

Throughout the march and rally cries of "Right On!" echoed in reply to exhortations to "Free Our Sisters, Free Ourselves, Power to the People!"; "Fuck Harvard, Fuck Yale, Get Those Panthers Out of Jail!"; "Out of the House, Out of the Ghetto, Out from Under, Women Unite!" and, in short, to make a revolution in America NOW!

Women conceived of and led the march and rally to support our sisters and brothers who are political prisoners and to raise the issues of the particular oppression of women in our society. We wanted to make the following points: 1) women are committed to the struggle to radically change America in solidarity with our brothers, black and white; 2) Women are committed to playing a leadership role in this struggle; 3) Women are committed to raising issues which are particularly relevant to women in the struggle.

Women Destroy Draft Files

An anti-war, anti-imperialist raid on a draft board took place in New York City in July. Destroyed were at least 6,500 l-A files, most of the cross reference system, and the "l" and "A" keys on typewriters. Pictures of one week's war dead were pasted up and a note was left to the workers at the draft board explaining that women had done the action and why they had done it.

The women then appeared, as they had promised they would, at a demonstration in Rockefeller Center on July 3. They stated that they wanted to make clear the connection between overseas corporate involvement and American military and political intrusions into the affairs of Asia, Africa, and Latin America; and that corporations such as Dow, Standard Oil, Shell, and Chase Manhattan bear much responsibility for U.S. domination of those areas from which we profit. Although the police knew which women were the participants in the action, six were arrested, including two who had nothing to do with the action. The women had been tossing shredded l-A files into the air amid lunchtime crowds.

Free Our Sisters, Free Ourselves

When seven Black Panther Party women were jailed in Connecticut in November 1969, accused of murder and conspiracy, women's groups as well as African-American organizations rallied to their defense.

Jean Wilson, Maude Francis, Peggy Hudgins, Erica Huggins, Francis Carter, Loretta Luckes and Rose Smith are being held, without bail, in Niantic State Prison Farm. They have not been tried or charged with any crime. Our sisters are young, black, and members of the Black Panther Party.

Francis Carter, Loretta Luckes, and Rose Smith are pregnant, and due to give birth in December.

WHAT'S BEING DONE TO THESE WOMEN?
They are deliberately kept in bad health; searchlights shine in their faces, sirens sound outside their windows day and night, so they can't sleep.

They are badly fed, denied fresh air and exercise, and were allowed maternity clothes only a month ago.

They are kept in solitary confinement, denied the right to speak to other women, or to choose lawyers to defend them.

They will be forced to give birth under armed guard, attended by prison doctors who don't care at all about them: Rose Smith weighed 133 when she was thrown into jail six months ago. She is now eight months pregnant, and has gained only one pound.

If the babies manage to be born alive, and survive under these conditions, the State of Connecticut intends to:
    call our sisters "unfit" mothers
    take away their babies
    decide who will raise their babies.

Francis Carter, Loretta Luckes and Rose Smith are being tortured because they are BLACK
        because they are PANTHERS
        because they are WOMEN

And what these women are suffering is an extension and reflection of generally how rotten things are for all women, like on the job, alone in the home.

WE DEMAND: *With the mothers, that the Black Panther Party be allowed to care for these children as is the desire of the Black Panther women and men.*
    We reject the State's definition of "fit" mother, family unit, and "suitable" home.
    The State, by its tortuous treatment of our Panther sisters has proved itself to be an "unfit" guardian for these children.

We insist that a mother is NOT "unfit" because she does not accept the status quo.

WE DEMAND: *That our three pregnant sisters be released on their own recognizance,* and that reasonable bail be set for all of the Panthers in jail.

WE DEMAND: An end to the torture of these women, adequate diet, exercise and clothing, an end to the isolation and sleepless nights.

WE DEMAND: Their right to prenatal and maternal care by doctors of their choice, their right to give birth without armed guard.

WE DEMAND: Immediate freedom for the Connecticut Panthers, and all political prisoners.

AND WHAT IS THEIR CRIME?
They have begun to construct concrete programs which help women.
—Free health programs
—Free Breakfast for Children programs
—Free day-care programs
—Free clothes for women and children who need them

These women had to stand up alone to begin these things. We will no longer have to stand up alone—*now when we rise up—we rise up together.*

We will show the prisons, the courts, and the state that we will not tolerate the oppression of our sisters anywhere, in any way, shape or form.

Goodbye to All That

ROBIN MORGAN

Robin Morgan, the well-known feminist author and editor of the extremely influential anthology Sisterhood Is Powerful, *wrote a scathing and furious essay in 1970, an excerpt of which is reprinted here, exposing the sexism of the white new left.*

By permission.

That's what I wanted to write about—the friends, brothers, lovers in the counterfeit male-dominated Left. The good guys who think they know what "Women's Lib," as they so chummily call it, is all about—and who then proceed to degrade and destroy women by almost everything they say and do: The cover on the last issue of *Rat* (front *and* back). The token "pussy power" or "clit militancy" articles. The snide descriptions of women staffers on the masthead. The little jokes, the personal ads, the smile, the snarl. No more, brothers. No more well-meaning ignorance, no more co-optation, no more assuming that this thing we're all fighting for is the same: one revolution under *man,* with liberty and justice for all. No more.

Let's run it on down. White males are most responsible for the destruction of human life and environment on the planet today. Yet who is controlling the supposed revolution to change all that? White males (yes, yes, even with their pasty fingers back in black and brown pies again). It just could make one a bit uneasy. It seems obvious that a legitimate revolution must be led by, *made* by those who have been most oppressed: black, brown, and white *women*—with men relating to that the best they can. A genuine Left doesn't consider anyone's suffering irrelevant or titillating; nor does it function as a microcosm of capitalist economy, with men competing for power and status at the top, and women doing all the work at the bottom (and functioning as objectified prizes or "coin" as well). Goodbye to all that. . . .

Let it all hang out. Let it seem bitchy, catty, dykey, frustrated, crazy, Solanisesque, nutty, frigid, ridiculous, bitter, embarrassing, man-hating, libelous, pure, unfair, envious, intuitive, low-down, stupid, petty, liberating. WE ARE THE WOMEN THAT MEN HAVE WARNED US ABOUT.

And let's put one lie to rest for all time: the lie that men are oppressed, too, by sexism—the lie that there can be such a thing as "men's liberation groups." Oppression is something that one group of people commits against another group specifically because of a "threatening" characteristic shared by the latter group—skin color or sex or age, etc. The oppressors are indeed *fucked up* by being masters (racism hurts whites, sexual stereotypes are harmful to men) but those masters are not *oppressed.* Any master has the alternative of divesting himself of sexism or racism—the oppressed have no alternative—for they have no power—but to fight. In the long run, Women's Liberation will of course free men—but in the short run it's going to *cost* men a lot of privilege, which no one gives up willingly or easily. Sexism is *not* the fault of women—kill your fathers, not your mothers. . . .

Goodbye, goodbye. The hell with the simplistic notion that automatic freedom for women—or non-white peoples—will come about ZAP! with the advent of a socialist revolution. Bullshit. Two evils predate capitalism and have been clearly able to survive and post-date socialism: sexism and racism. Women were the first property when the Primary Contradiction occurred: when one half of the human species decided to subjugate the other half, because it was "different," alien, the Other. From there it was an easy enough step to extend the Other to someone of different skin shade, different height or weight or language—or strength to resist. Goodbye to those simple-minded optimistic dreams of socialist equality all our good socialist brothers want us to believe. How liberal a politics that is! How much further we will have to go to create those profound changes that would give birth to a genderless society. *Profound,* Sister. Beyond what is male or female. Beyond standards we all adhere to now without daring to examine them as male-created, male-dominated, male-fucked-up, and in male self-interest. *Beyond all known standards,* especially those easily articulated revolutionary ones we all rhetorically invoke. Beyond, to a species with a new name, that would not dare define itself as Man.

I once said, "I'm a revolutionary, not just a woman," and knew my own lie even as I said the words. The pity of that statement's eagerness to be acceptable to those whose revolutionary zeal no one would question, i.e., any male supremacist in the counterleft. But to become a true revolutionary one must first become one of the oppressed (not organize or educate or manipulate them, but become one of them)—or realize that you *are* one of them already. No woman wants that. Because that realization is humiliating, it hurts. It hurts to understand that at Woodstock or Altamont a woman could be declared uptight or a poor sport if she didn't want to be raped. It hurts to learn that the Sisters still in male-Left captivity are putting down the crazy feminists to make themselves look okay and unthreatening to our mutual oppressors. It hurts to be pawns in those games. It hurts to try and change *each day of your life right now*—not in talk, not "in your head," and not only conveniently "out there" in the Third World (half of which is women) or the black and brown communities (half of which are women) but in your own home, kitchen, bed. No getting away, no matter how else you are oppressed, from the primary oppression of being female in a patriarchal world. It hurts to hear that the Sisters in the Gay Liberation Front, too, have to struggle continually against the male chauvinism of their gay brothers. It hurts that Jane Alpert was cheered when rapping about imperialism, racism, the Third World, and All Those Safe Topics but hissed and booed by a Movement crowd of men who wanted none of it when she began to talk about Women's Liberation. The backlash is upon us. . . .

It is the job of revolutionary feminists to build an ever stronger independent Women's Liberation Movement, so that the Sisters in counterleft captivity will have somewhere to turn, to use their power and rage and beauty and coolness in their own behalf for once, on their own terms, on their own issues, in their own style—whatever that may be. Not for us in Women's Liberation to hassle them and confront them the way their men do, nor to blame them—or ourselves—for what any of us are: an oppressed people, but a people raising our consciousness toward something that is the other side of anger, something bright and smooth and cool, like action unlike anything yet contemplated or carried out. It is for us to survive (something the white male radical has the luxury of never really worrying about, what with all his options), to talk, to plan, to be patient, to welcome new fugitives from the counterfeit Left with no arrogance but only humility and delight, to plan, to push—to strike.

There is something every woman wears around her neck on a thin chain of fear—an amulet of madness. For each of us, there exists somewhere a moment of insult so intense that she will reach up and rip the amulet off, even if the chain tears at the flesh of her neck. And the last protection from seeing the truth will be gone. Do you think, tugging furtively every day at the chain and going nicely insane as I am, that I can be concerned with the puerile squabbles of a counterfeit Left that laughs at my pain? Do you think such a concern is noticeable when set alongside the suffering of more than half the human species for the past 5,000 years—due to a whim of the other half? No, no, no, goodbye to all that.

Women are Something Else. This time, we're going to kick out all the jams, and the boys will just have to hustle to keep up, or else drop out and openly join the power structure of which they are already the illegitimate sons. Any man who claims he is serious about wanting to divest himself of cock privilege should trip on this: all male leadership out of the Left is the only way; and it's going to happen, whether through men stepping down or through women seizing the helm. It's up to the "brothers"—after all, sexism is their concern, not ours; we're too busy getting ourselves together to have to deal with their bigotry. So they'll have to make up their own minds as to whether they will be divested of just cock privilege or—what the hell, why not say it, *say* it?—divested of cocks. How deep the fear of that loss must be, that it can be suppressed only by the building of empires and the waging of genocidal wars!

Goodbye, goodbye forever, counterfeit Left, counterleft, male-dominated cracked-glass-mirror reflection of the Amerikan Nightmare. Women are the real left. We are rising, powerful in our unclean bodies; bright glowing mad in our inferior brains; wild hair flying, wild eyes staring, wild voices keening; undaunted by blood we who hemorrhage every twenty-eight days; laughing at our own beauty we who have lost our sense of humor; mourning for all each precious one of us might have been in this one living time-place had she not been born a woman; stuffing fingers into our mouths to stop the screams of fear and hate and pity for men we have loved and love still; tears in our eyes and bitterness in our mouths for children we couldn't have, or couldn't *not* have, or didn't want, or didn't want *yet*, or wanted and had in this place and this time of horror. We are rising with a fury older and potentially greater than any force in history, and this time we will be free or no one will survive. POWER TO ALL THE PEOPLE OR TO NONE. All the way down, this time.

FREE OUR SISTERS! FREE OURSELVES!

OUR BODIES, OUR SEXUALITY

The Myth of the Vaginal Orgasm

ANNE KOEDT

Anne Koedt provided one of the major essays of the early women's movement. Understanding their bodies and gaining a more secure connection to their own sexuality were crucial issues for the youthful feminists. This 1968 examination of how women's sexuality had been constructed by men with little regard for women's pleasure was received by feminists with amazement and excitement.

Whenever female orgasm and frigidity are discussed, a false distinction is made between the vaginal and the clitoral orgasm. Frigidity has generally been defined by men as the failure of women to have vaginal orgasms. Actually the vagina is not a highly sensitive area and is not constructed to achieve orgasm. It is the clitoris which is the center of sexual sensitivity and which is the female equivalent of the penis.

I think this explains a great many things: First of all, the fact that the so-called frigidity rate among women is phenomenally high. Rather than tracing female frigidity to the false assumptions about female anatomy, our "experts" have declared frigidity a psychological problem of women. Those women who complained about it were recommended psychiatrists, so that they might discover their "problem"—diagnosed generally as a failure to adjust to their role as women.

The facts of female anatomy and sexual response tell a different story. Although there are many areas for sexual arousal, there is only one area for sexual climax; that area is the clitoris. All orgasms are extensions of sensation from this area. Since the clitoris is not necessarily stimulated sufficiently in the conventional sexual positions, we are left "frigid."

Aside from physical stimulation, which is the common cause of orgasm for most people, there is also stimulation through primarily mental processes. Some women, for example, may achieve orgasm through sexual fantasies, or through fetishes. However, while the stimulation may be psychological, the orgasm manifests itself physically. Thus, while the cause is psychological, the *effect* is still physical, and the orgasm necessarily takes place in the sexual organ equipped for sexual climax—the clitoris. The orgasm experience may also differ in degree of intensity—some more localized, and some more diffuse and sensitive. But they are all clitoral orgasms.

All this leads to some interesting questions about conventional sex and our role in it. Men have orgasms essentially by friction with the vagina, not the clitoral area, which is external and not able to cause friction the way penetration does. Women have thus been defined sexually in terms of what pleases men; our own biology has not been properly analyzed. Instead, we are fed the myth of the liberated women and her vaginal orgasm—an orgasm which in fact does not exist.

What we must do is redefine our sexuality. We must discard the "normal" concepts of sex and create new guidelines which take into account mutual sexual enjoyment. While the idea of mutual enjoyment is liberally applauded in marriage manuals, it is not followed to its logical conclusion. We must begin to demand that if certain sexual positions now defined as "standard" are not mutually conducive to orgasm, they no longer be defined as standard. New techniques must be used or devised which transform this particular aspect of our current sexual exploitation. . . .

FREUD—A FATHER OF THE VAGINAL ORGASM

Freud contended that the clitoral orgasm was adolescent, and that upon puberty, when women began having intercourse with men, women should transfer the center of orgasm to the vagina. The vagina, it was assumed, was able to produce a parallel, but more mature, orgasm than the clitoris. Much work was done to elaborate on this theory, but little was done to challenge the basic assumptions. . . . It was Freud's feelings about women's secondary and inferior relationship to men that formed the basis for his theories on female sexuality.

Once having laid down the law about the nature of our sexuality, Freud not so strangely discovered a tremendous problem of frigidity in women. His recommended cure for a woman who was frigid was psychiatric care. She was suffering from failure to mentally adjust to her "natural" role as a woman. Frank S. Caprio, a contemporary follower of these ideas, states:

> . . . whenever a woman is incapable of achieving an orgasm via coitus, provided the husband is an adequate partner, and prefers clitoral stimulation to any other form of sexual activity, she can be regarded as suffering from frigidity and requires psychiatric assistance. (*The Sexually Adequate Female,* p. 64.)

The explanation given was that women were envious of men—"renunciation of womanhood." Thus it was diagnosed as an anti-male phenomenon.

It is important to emphasize that Freud did not base his theory upon a study of woman's anatomy, but rather upon his assumptions of woman as an inferior appendage to man, and her consequent social and psychological role. In their attempts to deal with the ensuing problem of mass frigidity, Freudians created elaborate mental gymnastics. Marie Bonaparte, in *Female Sexuality,* goes so far as to suggest surgery to help women back on their rightful path. . . . But the severest damage was not in the area of surgery, where Freudians ran around absurdly trying to change female anatomy to fit their basic assumptions. The worst damage was done to the mental health of women, who either suffered silently with self-blame, or flocked to psychiatrists looking desperately for the hidden and terrible repression that had kept from them their vaginal destiny.

LACK OF EVIDENCE

One may perhaps at first claim that these are unknown and unexplored areas, but upon closer examination this is certainly not true today, nor was it true even in the past. For example, men have known that women suffered from frigidity often during intercourse. So the problem was there. Also, there is much specific evidence. Men knew that the clitoris was and is the essential organ for masturbation, whether in children or adult women. So obviously women made it clear where *they* thought their sexuality was located. Men also seem suspiciously aware of the clitoral powers during "foreplay," when they want to arouse women and produce the necessary lubrication for penetration. Foreplay is a concept created for male purposes, but works to the disadvantage of many women, since as soon as the woman is aroused the man changes to vaginal stimulation, leaving her both aroused and unsatisfied.

It has also been known that women need no anesthesia inside the vagina during surgery, thus pointing to the fact that the vagina is in fact not a highly sensitive area.

Today, with existence knowledge of anatomy, with Kelly, Kinsey, and Masters and Johnson, to mention just a few sources, there is no ignorance on the subject. There are, however, social reasons why this knowledge has not been popularized. We are living in a male society which has not sought change in women's role. . . .

ANATOMICAL EVIDENCE

Rather than starting with what women *ought* to feel, it would seem logical to start out with the anatomical facts regarding the clitoris and vagina.

The Clitoris is a small equivalent of the penis, except for the fact that the urethra does not go through it as in the man's penis. Its erection is similar to the male erection, and the head of the clitoris has the same type of structure and function as the head of the penis. G. Lombard Kelly, in *Sexual Feeling in Married Men and Women,* says:

> The head of the clitoris is also composed of erectile tissue, and it possesses a very sensitive epithelium or surface covering, supplied with

> special nerve endings called genital corpuscles, which are peculiarly adapted for sensory stimulation that under proper mental conditions terminates in the sexual orgasm. No other part of the female generative tract has such corpuscles. (Pocketbooks; p. 35.)

The clitoris has no other function than that of sexual pleasure.

The Vagina—Its functions are related to the reproductive function. Principally, 1) menstruation, 2) receive penis, 3) hold semen, and 4) birth passage. The interior of the vagina, which according to the defenders of the vaginally caused orgasm is the center and producer of the orgasm, is:

> like nearly all other internal body structures, poorly supplied with end organs of touch. The internal entodermal origin of the lining of the vagina makes it similar in this respect to the rectum and other parts of the digestive tract. (Kinsey, *Sexual Behavior in the Human Female*, p. 580.)

The degree of insensitivity inside the vagina is so high that "Among the women who were tested in our gynecologic sample, less than 14% were at all conscious that they had been touched." (Kinsey, p. 580.)

Even the importance of the vagina as an *erotic* center (as opposed to an orgasmic center) has been found to be minor.

Other Areas—Labia minora and the vestibule of the vagina. These two sensitive areas may trigger off a clitoral orgasm. Because they can be effectively stimulated during "normal" coitus, though infrequently, this kind of stimulation is incorrectly thought to be vaginal orgasm. However, it is important to distinguish between areas which can stimulate the clitoris, incapable of producing the orgasm themselves, and the clitoris:

> Regardless of what means of excitation is used to bring the individual to the state of sexual climax, the sensation is perceived by the genital corpuscles and is localized where they are situated: in the head of the clitoris or penis. (Kelly, p. 49.)

Psychologically Stimulated Orgasm—Aside from the above mentioned direct and indirect stimulations of the clitoris, there is a third way an orgasm may be triggered. This is through mental (cortical) stimulation, where the imagination stimulates the brain, which in turn stimulates the genital corpuscles of the glans to set off an orgasm.

WOMEN WHO SAY THEY HAVE VAGINAL ORGASMS

Confusion—Because of the lack of knowledge of their own anatomy, some women accept the idea that an orgasm felt during "normal" intercourse was vaginally caused. This confusion is caused by a combination of two factors. One, failing to locate the center of the orgasm, and two, by a desire to fit her experience to the male-defined idea of sexual normalcy. Considering that women know little about their anatomy, it is easy to be confused.

Deception—The vast majority of women who pretend vaginal orgasm to their men are faking it to "get the job." In a new bestselling Danish book, *I Accuse,* Mette Ejlersen specifically deals with this common problem, which she calls the "sex comedy." This comedy has many causes. First of all, the man brings a great deal of pressure to bear on the woman, because he considers his ability as a lover at stake. So as not to offend his ego, the woman will comply with the prescribed role and go through simulated ecstasy. In some of the other Danish women mentioned, women who were left frigid were turned off to sex, and pretended vaginal orgasm to hurry up the sex act. Others admitted that they had faked vaginal orgasm to catch a man. In one case, the woman pretended vaginal orgasm to get him to leave his first wife, who admitted being vaginally frigid. Later she was forced to continue the deception, since obviously she couldn't tell him to stimulate her clitorally.

Many more women were simply afraid to establish their right to equal enjoyment, seeing the sexual act as being primarily for the man's benefit, and any pleasure that the women got as an added extra.

Other women, with just enough ego to reject the man's idea that they needed psychiatric care, refused to admit their frigidity. They wouldn't accept self-blame, but they didn't know how to solve the problem, not knowing the physiological facts about themselves. So they were left in a peculiar limbo.

Again, perhaps one of the most infuriating and damaging results of this whole charade has been that women who were perfectly healthy sexually were taught that they were not. So in addition to being sexually deprived, these women were told to blame themselves when they deserved no blame. Looking for a cure to a problem that has none can lead a woman on an endless path of self-hatred and insecurity. For she is told by her analyst that not even in her own role allowed in a male society—the role of a woman—is she successful. She is put on the defensive, with phony data as evidence that she'd better try to be even more feminine, think more feminine, and reject her envy of men. That is, shuffle even harder, baby.

WHY MEN MAINTAIN THE MYTH

1. *Sexual Penetration Is Preferred*—The best stimulant for the penis is the woman's vagina. It supplies the necessary friction and lubrication. From a strictly technical point of view this position offers the best physical conditions, even though the man may try other positions for variation.

2. *The Invisible Woman*—One of the elements of male chauvinism is the refusal or inability to see women as total, separate human beings. Rather, men have chosen to define women only in terms of how they benefited men's lives. Sexually, a woman was not seen as an individual wanting to share equally in the sexual act, any more than she was seen as a person with independent desires when she did anything else in society. Thus, it was easy to make up what was convenient about women; for on top of that, society has been a function of male interests, and women were not organized to form even a vocal opposition to the male experts.

3. *The Penis as Epitome of Masculinity*—Men define their lives primarily in terms of masculinity. It is a universal form of ego-boosting. That is, in every society, however homogeneous (i.e., with the absence of racial, ethnic, or major economic differences) there is always a group, women, to oppress.

The essence of male chauvinism is in the psychological superiority men exercise over women. This kind of superior-inferior definition of self, rather than positive definition based upon one's own achievements and development, has of course chained victim and oppressor both. But by far the most brutalized of the two is the victim.

An analogy is racism, where the white racist compensates for his feelings of unworthiness by creating an image of the black man (it is primarily a male struggle) as biologically inferior to him. Because of his power in a white male power structure, the white man can socially enforce this mythical division.

To the extent that men try to rationalize and justify male superiority through physical differentiation, masculinity may be symbolized by being the *most* muscular, the most hairy; having the deepest voice, and the biggest penis. Women, on the other hand, are approved of (i.e., called feminine) if they are weak, petite; shave their legs; have high soft voices, and no penis.

Since the clitoris is almost identical to the penis, one finds a great deal of evidence of men in various societies trying to either ignore the clitoris and emphasize the vagina (as did Freud), or, as in some places in the Mideast, actually performing clitoridectomy. Freud saw this ancient and still practiced custom as a way of further "feminizing" the female by removing this cardinal vestige of her masculinity. It should be noted also that a big clitoris is considered ugly and masculine. Some cultures engage in the practice of pouring a chemical on the clitoris to make it shrivel up into "proper" size.

It seems clear to me that men in fact fear the clitoris as a threat to masculinity.

4. *Sexuality Expendable Male*—Men fear that they will become sexually expendable if the clitoris is substituted for the vagina as the center of pleasure for women. Actually this has a great deal of validity if one considers *only* the anatomy. The position of the penis inside the vagina, while perfect for reproduction, does not necessarily stimulate an orgasm in women because the clitoris is located externally and higher up. Women must rely upon indirect stimulation in the "normal" position.

Lesbian sexuality could make an excellent case, based upon anatomical data, for the extinction of the male organ. Albert Ellis says something to the effect that a man without a penis can make a woman an excellent lover.

Considering that the vagina is very desirable from a man's point of view, purely on physical grounds, one begins to see the dilemma for men. And it forces us as well to discard many "physical" arguments explaining why women go to bed with men. What is left, it seems to me, are primarily psychological reasons why women select men at the exclusion of women as sexual partners.

5. *Control of Women*—One reason given to explain the Mideastern practice of clitoridectomy is that it will keep the women from straying. By removing the sexual organ capable of orgasm, it must be assumed that her sexual drive will diminish. Considering how men look upon

their women as property, particularly in very backward nations, we should begin to consider a great deal more why it is not in men's interest to have women totally free sexually. The double standard, as practiced for example in Latin America, is set up to keep the woman as total property of the husband, while he is free to have affairs as he wishes.

6. *Lesbianism and Bisexuality*—Aside from the strictly anatomical reasons why women might equally seek other women as lovers, there is a fear on men's part that women will seek the company of other women on a full, human basis. The establishment of clitoral orgasm as fact would threaten the heterosexual *institution*. For it would indicate that sexual pleasure was obtainable from either men *or* women, thus making heterosexuality not an absolute, but an option. It would thus open up the whole question of *human* sexual relationships beyond the confines of the present male-female role system.

An Abortion Testimonial

BARBARA SUSAN

One of the most significant political campaigns waged by feminists was to legalize abortion, ultimately successful in the 1973 Roe v. Wade *Supreme Court ruling. Talking publicly about and testifying to one's experiences were central to the movement to change abortion laws. This testimony by Barbara Susan was given before the New York State legislature considering changes in state law.*

I became pregnant. I had incomplete knowledge of contraception. I was sane and healthy, therefore ineligible for a legal abortion. Not

Reprinted by permission, Barbara (Susan) Kaminsky.

being criminal or sophisticated I had no access to illegal means of abortion. I asked my mother for money to cover the cost of a trip to Japan where abortion was legal. She was not wealthy. She refused. She became hysterical. I became hysterical. Twenty-four hours later I was married. Eight months later I was delivered of an infant. Shortly afterwards the child was adopted and my marriage dissolved.

At the time of conception I was capable of a love relationship but not a parent-child relationship. The state forced me into becoming a parent by denying me the right to a legal abortion. I would like to sue the state for damages resulting from that maternity.

I was forced into a marriage relationship through pressure from my family. Pressure, which since I was in a vulnerable position, I was unable to resist. My husband had no money. I left college and took a full-time job. By taking a leave of absence from college I forfeited a regents scholarship (which was the only reason I was able to attend school). Also, the school had a rule which did not allow pregnant women to register. In effect, I had no freedom to pursue the goals which I had set up for myself. The state was punishing me for my sexual behavior. I no longer had control of my life. At seventeen years of age it had been interrupted by forced maternity.

I decided to give the child up for adoption. I had to defend that decision against family and friends who had been so influenced by the legal sanctions given to motherhood that they found it impossible to accept my decision. They tried to convince me to stay married and become a mother. I was unprepared for motherhood financially, emotionally, and morally.

I decided to dissolve the marriage. After the birth of the child I returned to school. I was also working at that time to pay off legal bills, medical bills, and to support myself. (I had been fired from my previous job when they discovered I was pregnant.) After one term I left school and got a full-time job. My present occupation as an art teacher and a painter is not a very lucrative one, and can barely support me, let alone enable me to return to school.

When I tried to take control of my life (have an abortion), I faced opposition. The state was on the side of the opposition. I feel it is unconstitutional for the state to have taken any position in relation to the moral and emotional way in which I chose to conduct my life. The state should compensate me for the emotional ordeal it put me through. Moreover, the state should be made to support me while I finish my education.

The Woman-Identified Woman

RADICALESBIANS

In this early statement of feminist lesbianism, the authors (Artemis March, Ellen Shumsky, Rita Mae Brown, Cynthia Frank, Lois Hart, and Barbara Gladstone) argue that lesbianism is not being dealt with in the women's movement. They define lesbianism as the centrality of women for women, a rejection of always defining themselves in relation to men and of considering only relationships with men as significant. They argue that accusations of lesbianism have traditionally been used to disempower women.

What is a lesbian? A lesbian is the rage of all women condensed to the point of explosion. She is the woman who, often beginning at an extremely early age, acts in accordance with her inner compulsion to be a more complete and freer human being than her society—perhaps then, but certainly later—cares to allow her. These needs and actions, over a period of years, bring her into painful conflict with people, situations, the accepted ways of thinking, feeling and behaving, until she is in a state of continual war with everything around her, and usually with herself. She may not be fully conscious of the political implications of what for her began as personal necessity, but on some level she has not been able to accept the limitations and oppression laid on her by the most basic role of her society—the female role. The turmoil she experiences tends to induce guilt proportional to the degree to which she feels she is not meeting social expectations,

Reprinted by permission, Artemis March.

and/or eventually drives her to question and analyze what the rest of her society more or less accepts. She is forced to evolve her own life pattern, often living much of her life alone, learning usually much earlier than her "straight" (heterosexual) sisters about the essential aloneness of life (which the myth of marriage obscures) and about the reality of illusions. To the extent that she cannot expel the heavy socialization that goes with being female, she can never truly find peace with herself. For she is caught somewhere between accepting society's view of her—in which case she cannot accept herself—and coming to understand what this sexist society has done to her and why it is functional and necessary for it to do so. Those of us who work that through find ourselves on the other side of a tortuous journey through a night that may have been decades long. The perspective gained from that journey, the liberation of self, the inner peace, the real love of self and of all women, is something to be shared with all women—because we are all women.

It should first be understood that lesbianism, like male homosexuality, is a category of behavior possible only in a sexist society characterized by rigid sex roles and dominated by male supremacy. Those sex roles dehumanize women by defining us as a supportive/serving caste *in relation to* the master caste of men, and emotionally cripple men by demanding that they be alienated from their own bodies and emotions in order to perform their economic/political/military functions effectively. Homosexuality is a by-product of a particular way of setting up roles (or approved patterns of behavior) on the basis of sex; as such it is an inauthentic (not consonant with "reality") category. In a society in which men do not oppress women, and sexual expression is allowed to follow feelings, the categories of homosexuality and heterosexuality would disappear.

But lesbianism is also different from male homosexuality, and serves a different function in the society. "Dyke" is a different kind of put-down from "faggot," although both imply you are not playing your socially assigned sex role . . . are not therefore a "real woman" or a "real man." The grudging admiration felt for the tomboy, and the queasiness felt around a sissy boy point to the same thing: the contempt in which women—or those who play a female role—are held. And the investment in keeping women in that contemptuous role is very great. Lesbian is the word, the label, the condition that holds women in line. When a woman hears this word tossed her way, she knows she is stepping out of line. She knows that she has crossed the terrible boundary of her sex role. She recoils, she protests, she reshapes her actions to gain approval. Lesbian is a label invested by the Man to throw at any woman who dares to be his equal, who dares to challenge his prerogatives (including that of all women as part of the exchange medium among men), who dares to assert the primacy of her own needs. To have the label applied to people active in women's liberation is just the most recent instance of a long history; older women will recall that not so long ago, any woman who was successful, independent, not orienting her whole life about a man, would hear this word. For in this sexist society, for a woman to be independent means she *can't* be a *woman*—she *must* be a *dyke*. That in itself should tell us where women are at. It says as clearly as can be said: women and person are contradictory terms. For a lesbian is not considered a "real woman." And yet, in popular thinking, there is really only one essential difference between a lesbian and other women: that of sexual orientation—which is to say, when you strip off all the packaging, you must finally realize that the essence of being a "woman" is to get fucked by men.

"Lesbian" is one of the sexual categories by which men have divided up humanity. While all women are dehumanized as sex objects, as the objects of men they are given certain compensations: identification with his power, his ego, his status, his protection (from other males), feeling like a "real woman," finding social acceptance by adhering to her role, etc. Should a woman confront herself by confronting another woman, there are fewer rationalizations, fewer buffers by which to avoid the stark horror of her dehumanized condition. Herein we find the overriding fear of many women towards exploring intimate relationships with other women: the fear of being used as a sexual object by a woman, which not only will bring her no male-connected compensations, but also will reveal the void which is woman's real situation. This dehumanization is expressed when a straight woman learns that a sister is a lesbian; she begins to relate to her lesbian sister as her potential sex object, laying a surrogate male role on the lesbian. This reveals her heterosexual conditioning to make herself into an object when sex is potentially invoked in a relationship, and it denies the lesbian her full humanity. For women, especially those in the movement, to perceive their lesbian sisters through this male grid of role definitions is to accept this male cultural conditioning and to oppress their sisters much as they themselves have been oppressed by men. Are we going to continue the male classification system of defining all females in *sexual relation* to some *other* category of people? Affixing the label "lesbian" not only to a woman who aspires to be a person, but also to any situation of real love, real solidarity, real primacy among women is a primary form of divisiveness among women: it is the condition which keeps women within the confines of the feminine role, and it is the debunking/ scare term that keeps women from forming any primary attachments, groups, or associations among ourselves.

Women in the movement have in most cases gone to great lengths to avoid discussion and confrontation with the issue of lesbianism. It puts people up-tight. They are hostile, evasive, or try to incorporate it into some "broader issue." They would rather not talk about it. If they have to, they try to dismiss it as a "lavender herring." But it is no side issue. It is absolutely essential to the success and fulfillment of the women's liberation movement that this issue be dealt with. As long as the label "dyke" can be used to frighten a woman into a less militant stand, keep her separate from her sisters, keep her from giving primacy to anything other than men and family—then to that extent she is controlled by the male culture. Until women see in each other the possibility of a primal commitment which includes sexual love, they will be denying themselves the love and value they readily accord to men, thus affirming their second-class status. As long as male acceptability is primary—both to individual women and to the movement as a whole—the term "lesbian" will be used effectively against women. Insofar as women want only more privileges within the system, they do not want to antagonize male power. They instead seek acceptability for women's liberation, and the most crucial aspect of the acceptability is to deny lesbianism—i.e., deny any fundamental challenge to the basis of the female role.

It should also be said that some younger, more radical women have honestly begun to discuss lesbianism, but so far it has been primarily as a sexual "alternative" to men. This, however, is still giving primacy to men, both because the idea of relating more completely to women occurs as a *negative reaction to men,* and because the lesbian relationship is being characterized simply by sex which is divisive and sexist. On one level, which is both personal and political, women may withdraw emotional and sexual energies from men, and work out various alternatives for those energies in their own lives. On a different political/psychological level, it must be understood that what is crucial is that women begin disengaging from male-defined response patterns. In the privacy of our own psyches, we must cut those cords to the core. For irrespective of where our love and sexual energies flow, if we are male-identified in our heads, we cannot realize our autonomy as human beings.

But why is it that women have related to and through men? By virtue of having been brought up in a male society, we have internalized the male culture's definition of ourselves. That definition views us as relative beings who exist not for ourselves, but for the servicing, maintenance and comfort of men. That definition consigns us to sexual and family functions, and excludes us from defining and shaping the terms of our lives. In exchange for our psychic servicing and for performing society's nonprofit-making functions, the man confers on us just one thing: the slave status which makes us legitimate in the eyes of the society in which we live. This is called "femininity" or "being a real woman" in our cultural lingo. We are authentic, legitimate, real to the extent that we are the property of some man whose name we bear. To be a woman who belongs to no man is to be invisible, pathetic, inauthentic, unreal. He confirms his image of us—of what we have to be in order to be acceptable by him—but not our real selves; he confirms our womanhood—as he defines it, in relation to him—but cannot confirm our personhood, our own selves as absolutes. As long as we are dependent on the male culture for this definition, for this approval, we cannot be free.

The consequence of internalizing this role is an enormous reservoir of self-hate. This is not to say the self-hate is recognized or accepted as such; indeed most women would deny it. It may be experienced as discomfort with her role, as feeling empty, as numbness, as restlessness, a paralyzing anxiety at the center. Alternatively, it may be expressed in shrill defensiveness of the glory and destiny of her role. But it does exist, often beneath the edge of her consciousness, poisoning her existence, keeping her alienated from herself, her own needs, and rendering her a stranger to other women. They try to escape by identifying with the oppressor, living through him, gaining status and identity from his ego, his power, his accomplishments. And by not identifying with other "empty vessels" like themselves. Women resist relating on all levels to other women who will reflect their own oppression, their own secondary status, their own self-hate. For to confront another woman is finally to confront one's self—the self we have gone to such lengths to avoid. And in that mirror we know we cannot really respect and love that which we have been made to be.

As the source of self-hate and the lack of real self are rooted in our male-given identity, we must create a new sense of self. As long as we cling to the idea of "being a woman," we will sense some conflict with that incipient self, that sense of I, that sense of a whole person. It is very difficult to realize and accept that being "feminine" and being a whole person are irreconcilable. Only women can give each other a new sense of self. That identity we have to develop with reference to ourselves, and not in relation to men. This consciousness is the revolutionary force from which all else will follow, for ours is an organic revolution. For this we must be available and supportive to one another, give our commitment and our love, give the emotional support necessary to sustain this movement. Our energies must flow toward our sisters, not backwards toward our oppressors. As long as women's liberation tries to free women without facing the basic heterosexual structure that binds us in one-to-one relationship with our own oppressors, tremendous energies will continue to flow into trying to straighten up each particular relationship with a man, how to get better sex, how to turn his head around—into trying to make the "new man" out of him, in the delusion that this will allow us to be the "new woman." This obviously splits our energies and commitments, leaving us unable to be committed to the construction of the new patterns which will liberate us.

It is the primacy of women relating to women, or women creating a new consciousness of and with each other which is at the heart of women's liberation, and the basis for the cultural revolution. Together we must find, reinforce and validate our authentic selves. As we do this, we confirm in each other that struggling, incipient sense of pride and strength, the divisive barriers begin to melt, we feel this growing solidarity with our sisters. We see ourselves as prime, find our centers inside of ourselves. We find receding the sense of alienation, of being cut off, of being behind a locked window, of being unable to get out what we know is inside. We feel a realness, feel at last we are coinciding with ourselves. With that real self, with that consciousness, we begin a revolution to end the imposition of all coercive identifications, and to achieve maximum autonomy in human expression.

RACE, ETHNICITY, AND CLASS: FEMINIST ISSUES

To My White Working-Class Sisters

DEBBY D'AMICO

According to the author, writing in 1970, feminism was not just for the middle class. Working-class and poor women must recognize their worth in a culture that glorifies wealth and success. They and all people of color have been made to feel inferior. This is a common bond among them—stronger than their ties to rich white women.

We are the invisible women, the faceless women, the nameless women . . . the female half of the silent majority, the female half of the ugly Americans, the smallest part of the "little people." No one photographs us, no one writes about us, no one puts us on TV. No one says we are beautiful, no one says we are important, very few like to recognize that we are *here*. We are the poor and working-class white women of America, and we are cruelly and systematically ignored. All

Reprinted by permission, Deborah D'Amico.

of our lives we have been told, sometimes subtly, sometimes not so subtly, that we are not worth very much. This message has been put across to me, a white working-class woman, all my life. I think the time has come to speak out against these insults, and so I have decided to write about parts of my life and my ideas. I am doing this for all my sisters who have been made to feel that they are not worth writing about, and for all those people who have to be convinced of poor white existence, those same people who told us that because we are all white our lives are the same as those of the middle and upper class.

When I was in the second grade, we were given a sample aptitude test to accustom us to the test-taking rut that would ultimately determine whether we would be programmed toward college or a dead-end job. After we had answered several multiple-choice questions, the teacher had us check our answers against the "right" ones. One of the questions pictured a man in a tuxedo, a man in a suit, and a man in overalls. The question read: "Which man is going to work?" The "correct" answer was: the man in the suit. I can still feel the shame that came with the realization that what went on in my home was marked "incorrect." I responded the way oppressed people often respond—by secretly hating myself and my family. I remember constantly begging my father to put on a suit—my father who worked an average of 65 to 80 hours a week driving trucks, checking out groceries in a supermarket, and doing any of the other deadening jobs which came his way. My mother didn't escape my judgments either. The unreal Dick, Jane, and Sally world our school books presented as the "right" way of life, reinforced by TV and middle-class schoolmates' homes, made me viciously attack her grammar whenever she spoke and ask her questions like: "How come *you* never wear dresses or get your hair done?" The world of my home gave me concrete answers: at the time my mother had three kids in diapers and another on the way, hardly a life-style that called for a well-dressed mannequin. But the middle-class world of America was bigger than my home and I was overcome by its judgments.

As I went on through school, I continued to be taught about an America that had little to do with me. The picture of American life drawn in history books was almost always a comfortable one, with exceptions like wars and the Depression (hardships which the middle class participated in and thus wanted to talk about). Working-class sisters, wake up! Black people were not the only ones left out of history books. George Washington is no relative of yours; neither is Henry Ford, or Nixon and Agnew. While George Washington was relaxing at his Mt. Vernon estate, *your* ancestors may have been among the two-thirds majority of white settlers who served as indentured servants for Master George and others like him. They may have been servants who were kidnapped from the slums of England and Ireland and brought here in chains to be sold to the highest bidder. Your grandmother might have been one of the "huddled masses yearning to breathe free," who came to America and wound up in a tenement where free air never blew, working from can see to can't see, made to feel alien and ashamed of an Old World culture infinitely more alive and colorful than the drab, Puritan, "Mr. Clean" ways of America. I have listened to the old folks in my family talk about how they "came over," and how they survived, the first Italians in an all-Irish neighborhood. That is *my* history. While Mr. Pullman was amassing his fortune, our people were fighting and dying for the rights of working men and women, our people were being shot and beaten for what they believed. I was not taught this in school but learned it later on my own. In high school I continued to learn middle-class ways. I spent years learning to talk like them, eat like them, look like them. I learned a language that had little to do with the concrete terms of my life or the lives of my family and fellow workers.

At the same time that books were deluging me with middle-class culture, I began to feel the pinch of unworthiness in other ways. I attended a parochial high school for one year which was upper-middle-class dominated. If your family had no influential friends to take out $50 ads in the yearbook, you were punished—shame on you! they said, for your failure to measure up in America, shame on you because you haven't made it in the land of the free and the home of the brave.

During my high school years I entered the great rat race of women who were dedicated to snagging any and all men considered desirable. I was again led by middle-class values, and so I rejected the knit-shirted, "greasy"-haired, dark-skinned Italians I grew up with and made a mad dash for the Brylcreem man. All the while, of course, feeling I could never get him, because I wasn't the *girl* in the Brylcreem commercial. I read all the middle-class fashion and glamour magazines and tried to look like people who were able to look that way because of a life-style that included a closet full of clothes I couldn't afford and a leisurely existence that allowed them to look cool and unruffled all the time. And there I was working in a luncheonette so shabby I never mentioned it to anyone for a lousy six dollars a Saturday that I immediately spent in vain efforts to make myself "acceptable"-looking. During the day I gossiped condescendingly about the way people dressed, playing at being the glorious magazine girl, and at night I sulked off to the phone company to be bitten by cord lice and told all night that I was either very slow or innately stupid.

And people, in social and job situations, have been saying that ever since. In social situations it is said as I sit quietly by and watch well-dressed, slick, confident women of the upper classes, America's idea of beauty, steal the eyes, applause, and the image of woman from me. It is said in many ways on the job: at my last job I was mimeographer at a school, a "liberal, progressive" school at that. I once spoke up at a staff meeting and the first remark to follow the stunned silence was, "Why doesn't someone put her on the faculty?" Yes, put me among the educated middle class because you absolutely can't deal with a worker who thinks and has ideas. After I mentioned this, I was told that it was a compliment and that I should be *grateful*. Grateful that they thought I was as good as them. At the same school I was once asked, "Are you the switchboard?" Naturally—since we are looked on as extensions of the machines we operate, not as human beings.

What all this has done to us is create a deep, deep sense of unworthiness, a sense so deep it dooms us. I have a thirteen-year-old friend who is well on the way to life either in prison or on heroin. We, *as a people,* have nothing that says to him, "You shouldn't ruin your life. You're a good, worthwhile person." If or when he does go to jail, there will be no Black Muslims to tell him he is a worthwhile person just because of what he is. No one will be there to give him the respect and support of an alternate culture that respects what he is. That is what the judgment of middle-class America has done to us.

Why has this happened to us? It has happened because we believed in the American dream, in the dream that *anyone* can be *anything* if he only tries, works hard, and if he doesn't make it, it's only because something about *him* is rotten. Since we don't have much to begin with, we're made to feel we don't deserve much. And we believe it—even though the truth of our lives tells us that we have worked, and damned hard, but we still didn't have the kinds of lives we read about and saw on TV. And America has kept us out of magazines and off TV *because* our faces and voices are full of this truth. We have hated black people, but we have hated ourselves more. By believing black people are inferior, we have kept the truth about ourselves from each other—that the people who have the power and money in America never intend to raise our incomes or those of black people, not because we aren't worthy, but because it would cut into their profits to do so. We believed black people were so inferior that they weren't supposed to make it—we believed we were superior and could make it—but we never did and we blame ourselves. As white people who haven't made it, we are the living proof of the American lie and we hate ourselves for it.

What can we do about all this? As poor and working-class women, we can *start* asking what is wrong with America and *stop* asking what is wrong with ourselves. In a culture where women are often judged by beauty alone, the standard of beauty does not fit us. We, as *ourselves*, as we go to work or wash dishes, we, *in our daily lives*, are never called beautiful. Black women have told themselves that they are beautiful in their natural lives, and we need to do the same for ourselves. We must begin to see ourselves as beautiful in our ability to work, to endure, in our plain, honest lives, and we must stop aspiring to a false-eyelash existence that is not and never has been for us. We are not the women in *Vogue, Glamour,* or *As The World Turns,* nor should we want to be. We are the women who have dealt all our lives with the truths and tragedies of real life, because we never had the option of the armchair-beautiful-people existence. We are the people who have no maids or therapists to dump our troubles on. We know what it is to work hard and we are not guilty of wearing silks while others wear rags. We should never admire the women in *Vogue,* because there is something undeniably ugly about women who wear minks while others can't afford shoes—and no amount of $20-an-ounce makeup can hide that brand of ugliness. We must start learning that other people have been victims of this middle-class culture aping the rich. Black and Puerto Rican, Mexican and Indian, Chinese and Japanese people have had their true history concealed and their faces scorned by TV and magazines. We must see that those who share the hardships we share are not the white middle and upper classes, but the black and brown people who work at our sides. As white working-class and poor people we must begin to be proud of ourselves, our histories, and each other; we must unite and support ourselves as a people. Once we respect ourselves, we will find it necessary to struggle with a society and with jobs which tell us we are worthless. In that struggle we will learn that the anger of black and brown people which we have feared for so long has the same direction as our anger, that their enemies are our enemies, and their fight our fight.

Double Jeopardy: To Be Black and Female

FRANCES BEAL

This is an important early statement of the multiple oppressions suffered by black women and of the necessity for the white women's movement to confront racism and imperialism. Beal argues that feminism must be relevant to the lives of poor and working-class black women.

In attempting to analyze the situation of the black woman in America, one crashes abruptly into a solid wall of grave misconceptions, outright distortions of fact and defensive attitudes on the part of many. The system of capitalism (and its afterbirth, racism) under which we all live, has attempted by many devious ways and means to destroy the humanity of all people, and particularly the humanity of black people. This has meant an outrageous assault on every black man, woman and child who resides in the United States.

In keeping with its goal of destroying the black race's will to resist its subjugation, capitalism found it necessary to create a situation where the black man found it impossible to find meaningful or productive employment. More often than not, he couldn't find work of any kind. And the black woman likewise was manipulated by the system, economically exploited and physically assaulted. She could often find work in the white man's kitchen, however, and sometimes became the sole breadwinner of the family. This predicament has led to many psychological problems on the part of both man and woman and has contributed to the turmoil that we find in the black family structure.

Unfortunately, neither the black man nor the black woman understood the true nature of the forces working upon them. Many black women tended to accept the capitalist evaluation of manhood and womanhood and believed, in fact, that black men were shiftless and lazy, otherwise they would get a job and support their families as they ought to. Personal relationships between black men and women were thus torn asunder and one result has been the separation of man from wife, mother from child, etc.

America has defined the roles to which each individual should subscribe. It has defined "manhood" in terms of its own interests and "femininity" likewise. Therefore, an individual who has a good job, makes a lot of money and drives a Cadillac is a real "man" and conversely, an individual who is lacking in these "qualities" is less of a man. The advertising media in this country continuously informs the American male of his need for indispensable signs of his virility—the brand of cigarettes that cowboys prefer, the whiskey that has a masculine tang or the label of the jockstrap that athletes wear.

The ideal model that is projected for a woman is to be surrounded by hypocritical homage and estranged from all real work, spending idle hours primping and preening, obsessed with conspicuous consumption, and limiting life's functions to simply a sex role. We unqualitatively reject these respective models. A woman who stays at home, caring for children and the house, often leads an extremely sterile existence. She must lead her entire life as a satellite to her mate. He goes out into society and brings back a little piece of the world for her. His interests and his understanding of the world become her own and she cannot develop herself as an individual, having been reduced to only a biological function. This kind of woman leads a parasitic existence that can aptly be described as "legalized prostitution."

Furthermore, it is idle dreaming to think of black women simply caring for their homes and children like the middle-class white model. Most black women have to work to help house, feed and clothe their families. Black women make up a substantial percentage of the black working force and this is true for the poorest black family as well as the so-called middle-class family.

Black women were never afforded any such phony luxuries. Though we have been browbeaten with this white image, the reality of the degrading and dehumanizing jobs that were relegated to us quickly dissipated this mirage of womanhood. . . .

Unfortunately, there seems to be some confusion in the movement today as to who has been oppressing whom. Since the advent of black power, the black male has exerted a more prominent leadership role in our struggle for justice in this country. He sees the system for what it really is for the most part, but where he rejects its values and mores on many issues, when it comes to women, he seems to take his guidelines from the pages of the *Ladies' Home Journal.* Certain black men are maintaining that they have been castrated by society but that black women somehow escaped this persecution and even contributed to this emasculation.

Let me state here and now that the black woman in America can justly be described as a "slave of a slave." By reducing the black man in America to such abject oppression, the black woman had no protector and was used, and is still being used in some cases, as the scapegoat for the evils that this horrendous system has perpetrated on black men. Her physical image has been maliciously maligned; she has been sexually molested and abused by the white colonizer; she has suffered the worst kind of economic exploitation, having been forced to serve as the white woman's maid and wet nurse for white offspring while her own children were more often than not starving and neglected. It is the depth of degradation to be socially manipulated, physically raped, used to undermine your own household, and to be powerless to reverse this syndrome.

It is true that our husbands, fathers, brothers and sons have been emasculated, lynched and brutalized. They have suffered from the cruellest assault on mankind that the world has ever known. However, it is a gross distortion of fact to state that black women have oppressed black men. The capitalist system found it expedient to enslave and oppress them and proceeded to do so without consultation or the signing of any agreements with black women.

It must also be pointed out at this time that black women are not resentful of the rise to power of black men. We welcome it. We see in it the eventual liberation of all black people from this corrupt system of capitalism. Nevertheless, this does not mean that you have to negate one for the other. This kind of thinking is a product of miseducation: that either it's X or it's Y. It is fallacious reasoning that in order for the black man to be strong, the black woman has to be weak.

Those who are exerting their "manhood" by telling black women to step back into a domestic, submissive role are assuming a counter-revolutionary position. Black women likewise have been abused by the system and we must begin talking about the elimination of all kinds of oppression. If we are talking about building a strong nation, capable of throwing off the yoke of capitalist oppression, then we are talking about the total involvement of every man, woman, and child, each with a highly developed political consciousness. We need our whole army out there dealing with the enemy and not half an army.

There are also some women who feel that there is no more productive role in life than having and raising children. This attitude often reflects the conditioning of the society in which we live and is adopted from a bourgeois white model. Some young sisters who have never had to maintain a household and accept the confining role which this entails, tend to romanticize (along with the help of a few brothers) this role of housewife and mother. Black women who have had to endure this kind of function are less apt to have these utopian visions.

Those who project in an intellectual manner how great and rewarding this role will be and who feel that the most important thing that they can contribute to the black nation is children, are doing themselves a great injustice. This line of reasoning completely negates the contributions that black women have historically made to our struggle for liberation. These black women include Sojourner Truth, Harriet Tubman, Mary McLeod Bethune and Fannie Lou Hamer, to name but a few.

We live in a highly industrialized society and every member of the black nation must be as academically and technologically developed as possible. To wage a revolution, we need competent teachers, doctors, nurses, electronics experts, chemists, biologists, physicists, political scientists, and so on and so forth. Black women sitting at home reading bedtime stories to their children are just not going to make it. . . .

Much has been written recently about the women's liberation movement in the United States and the question arises whether there are any parallels between this struggle and the movement on the part of black women for total emancipation. While there are certain comparisons that one can make, simply because we both live under the same exploitive system, there are certain differences, some of which are quite basic.

The white women's movement is far from being monolithic. Any white group that does not have an anti-imperialist and antiracist ideology has absolutely nothing in common with the black woman's struggle. In fact, some groups come to the incorrect conclusion that their oppression is due simply to male chauvinism. They therefore have an extremely antimale tone to their dissertations. Black people are engaged in a life and death struggle and the main emphasis of black women must be to combat the capitalist, racist exploitation of black people. While it is true that male chauvinism has become institutionalized in American society, one must always look for the main enemy—the fundamental cause of the female condition.

Another major differentiation is that the white women's liberation movement is basically middle class. Very few of these women suffer the extreme economic exploitation that most black women are subjected to day by day. This is the factor that is most crucial for us. It is not an intellectual persecution alone; it is not an intellectual outburst for us; it is quite real. We as black women have got to deal with the problems that the black masses deal with, for our problems in reality are one and the same.

If the white groups do not realize that they are in fact fighting capitalism and racism, we do not have common bonds. If they do not realize that the reasons for their condition lie in the system and not simply that men get a vicarious pleasure out of "consuming their bodies for exploitive reasons" (this kind of reasoning seems to be quite prevalent in certain white women's groups), then we cannot unite with them around common grievances or even discuss these groups in a serious manner because they're completely irrelevant to the black struggle.

The black community and black women especially must begin raising questions about the kind of society we wish to see established. We must note the ways in which capitalism oppresses us and then move to create institutions that will eliminate these destructive influences.

The new world that we are attempting to create must destroy oppression of any type. The value of this new system will be determined by the status of the person who was low man on the totem pole. Unless women in any enslaved nation are completely liberated, the change cannot really be called a revolution. If the black woman has to retreat to the position she occupied before the armed struggle, the whole movement and the whole struggle will have retreated in terms of truly freeing the colonized population. . . .

To Whom Will She Cry Rape?

ABBEY LINCOLN

The celebrated jazz singer Abbey Lincoln decries racism and painfully describes the position and representation of the black woman in American society, including their mistreatment by black men.

My mother is one of the most courageous people I have ever known, with an uncanny will to survive. When she was a young woman, the white folks were much further in the lead than they are now, and their racist rules gave her every disadvantage; yet, she proved herself a queen among women, any women, and as a result will always be one of the great legends for me.

But strange as it is, I've heard it echoed by too many Black full-grown males that Black womanhood is the downfall of the Black man in that she (the Black woman) is "evil," "hard to get along with," "domineering," "suspicious," and "narrow-minded." In short, a black, ugly, evil you-know-what.

As time progresses I've learned that this description of my mothers, sisters, and partners in crime is used as the basis and excuse for the further shoving, by the Black man, of his own head into the sand of oblivion. Hence, the Black mother, housewife, and all-round girl

Reprinted by permission, Abbey Lincoln.

Thursday is called upon to suffer both physically and emotionally every humiliation a woman can suffer and still function.

Her head is more regularly beaten than any other woman's, and by her own man; she's the scapegoat for Mr. Charlie; she is forced to stark realism and chided if caught dreaming; her aspirations for her and hers are, for sanity's sake, stunted; her physical image has been criminally maligned, assaulted, and negated; she's the first to be called ugly and never yet beautiful, and as a consequence is forced to see her man (an exact copy of her, emotionally and physically), brainwashed and wallowing in self-loathing, pick for his own the physical antithesis of her (the white woman and incubator of his heretofore arch enemy the white man). Then, to add guilt to insult and injury, she (the Black woman) stands accused as the emasculator of the only thing she has ever cared for, her Black man. She is the scapegoat for what white America has made of the "Negro personality."

Raped and denied the right to cry out in her pain, she has been named the culprit and called "loose," "hot-blooded," "wanton," "sultry," and "amoral." She has been used as the white man's sexual outhouse, and shamefully encouraged by her own ego-less man to persist in this function. Wanting, too, to be carried away by her "Prince Charming," she must, in all honesty, admit that he has been robbed of his crown by the very assaulter and assassin who has raped her. Still, she looks upon her man as God's gift to Black womanhood and is further diminished and humiliated and outraged when the feeling is not mutual.

When a white man "likes colored girls," his woman (the white woman) is the last one he wants to know about it. Yet, seemingly, when a Negro "likes white girls," his woman (the Black woman) is the first he wants to know about it. White female rejects and social misfits are flagrantly flaunted in our faces as the ultimate in feminine pulchritude. Our women are encouraged by our own men to strive to look and act as much like the white female image as possible, and only those who approach that "goal" in physical appearance and social behavior are acceptable. At best, we are made to feel that we are poor imitations and excuses for white women.

Evil? Evil, you say? The Black woman is hurt, confused, frustrated, angry, resentful, frightened and evil! Who in this hell dares suggest that she should be otherwise? These attitudes only point up her perception of the situation and her healthy rejection of same.

Maybe if our women get evil enough and angry enough, they'll be moved to some action that will bring our men to their senses. There is one unalterable fact that too many of our men cannot seem to face. And that is, we "black, evil, ugly" women are a perfect and accurate reflection of you "black, evil, ugly" men. Play hide and seek as long as you can and will, but your every rejection and abandonment of us is only a sorry testament of how thoroughly and carefully you have been blinded and brainwashed. And let it further be understood that when we refer to you we mean, ultimately, us. For you are us, and vice versa.

We are the women who were kidnapped and brought to this continent as slaves. We are the women who were raped, are still being raped, and our bastard children snatched from our breasts and scattered to the winds to be lynched, castrated, de-egoed, robbed, burned, and deceived.

We are the women whose strong and beautiful Black bodies were—and are—still being used as a cheap labor force for Miss Anne's kitchen and Mr. Charlie's bed, whose rich, black, and warm milk nurtured—and still nurtures—the heir to the racist and evil slavemaster.

We are the women who dwell in the hell-hole ghettos all over the land. We are the women whose bodies are sacrificed, as living cadavers, to experimental surgery in the white man's hospitals for the sake of white medicine. We are the women who are invisible on the television and movie screens, on the Broadway stage. We are the women who are lusted after, sneered at, leered at, hissed at, yelled at, grabbed at, tracked down by white degenerates in our own pitiable, poverty-stricken, and prideless neighborhoods.

We are the women whose hair is compulsively fried, whose skin is bleached, whose nose is "too big," whose mouth is "too big and loud," whose behind is "too big and broad," whose feet are "too big and flat," whose face is "too black and shiny," and whose suffering and patience is too long and enduring to be believed.

Who're just too damned much for everybody.

We are the women whose bars and recreation halls are invaded by flagrantly disrespectful, bigoted, simpering, amoral, emotionally unstable, outcast, maladjusted, nymphomaniacal, condescending white women . . . in desperate and untiring search of the "frothing-at-the-mouth-for-a-white-woman, strongbacked, sixty-minute hot black." Our men.

We are the women who, upon protesting this invasion of our privacy and sanctity and sanity, are called "jealous," and "evil," and "small-minded," and "prejudiced." We are the women whose husbands and fathers and brothers and sons have been plagiarized, imitated, denied, and robbed of the fruits of their genius, and who consequently we see emasculated, jailed, lynched, driven mad, deprived, enraged, and made suicidal. We are the women whom nobody, seemingly, cares about, who are made to feel inadequate, stupid and backward, and who inevitably have the most colossal inferiority complexes to be found.

And who is spreading the propaganda that "the only free people in this country are the white man and the Black woman?" If this be freedom, then Heaven is Hell.

Who will revere the Black woman? Who will keep our neighborhoods safe for Black innocent womanhood? Black womanhood is outraged and humiliated. Black womanhood cries for dignity and restitution and salvation. Black womanhood wants and needs protection, and keeping, and holding. Who will assuage her indignation? Who will keep her precious and pure? Who will glorify and proclaim her beautiful image? To whom will she cry rape?

The Mexican–American Woman

ENRIQUETA LONGAUEX Y VASQUEZ

One of the first articles to deal with the Chicana, this 1970 piece opened floodgates of reflection and awareness about the situation of women in Chicano history, contemporary life, and the Chicano movement.

While attending a Mexican-American conference in Colorado this year, I went to one of the workshops that were held to discuss the role of the Chicana—the Mexican-American woman, the woman of La Raza. When the time came for the women to report to the full conference, the only thing that the workshop representative had to say was this: "It was the consensus of the group that the Chicana woman does not want to be liberated."

As a woman who has been faced with living as a member of the Mexican-American minority group, as a breadwinner and a mother raising children, living in housing projects, and having much concern for other humans plus much community involvement, I felt this as quite a blow. I could have cried. Surely we could at least have come up with something to add to that statement. I sat back and thought, Why? Why? Then I understood why the statement had been made and I realized that going along with the feelings of the men at the convention was perhaps the best thing to do at the time.

Looking at the history of the Chicana or Mexican woman, we see that her role has been a very strong one—although a silent one. When the woman has seen the suffering of her people, she has always responded bravely and as a totally committed and equal human. My mother told me of how, during the time of Pancho Villa and the revolution in Mexico, she saw the men march through the village continually for three days and then she saw the battalion of women marching for a whole day. The women carried food and supplies; also, they were fully armed and wearing loaded *Carrilleras*. In battle, they fought alongside the men. Out of the Mexican Revolution came the revolutionary personage "Adelita," who wore her *rebozo* crossed at the bosom as a symbol of the revolutionary women in Mexico.

Then we have our heroine Juana Gallo, a brave woman who led her men to battle against the government after having seen her father and other villagers hung for defending the land of the people. She and many other women fought bravely with their people. And if called upon again, they would be there alongside the men to fight to the bitter end.

Today, as we hear the call of La Raza and as the dormant, "docile," Mexican-American comes to life, we see again the stirring of the people. With that call, the Chicana woman also stirs and I am sure that she will leave her mark upon the Mexican-American movement in the Southwest.

How the Chicana woman reacts depends totally on how the *macho* Chicano is treated when he goes out into the "mainstream of society." If the husband is so-called successful, the woman seems to become very domineering and demands more and more in material goods. I ask myself at times, Why are the women so demanding? Can they not see what they make of their men? But then I realize: this is the price of owning a slave.

A woman who has no way of expressing herself and of realizing herself as a full human has nothing else to turn to but the owning of material things. She builds her entire life around these, and finds security in this way. All she has to live for is her house and family; she becomes very possessive of both. This makes her a totally dependent human. Dependent on her husband and family. Most of the Chicana women in this comfortable situation are not particularly involved in the movement. Many times it is because of the fear of censorship in general. Censorship from the husband, the family, friends, and society in general. For these reasons she is completely inactive.

Then you will find the Chicana whose husband was not able to fare so very well in society, and perhaps has had to face defeat. This is the Chicana who really suffers. Quite often the man will not fight the real source of his problems, be it discrimination or whatever, but will instead come home and take it out on his family. As this continues, his Chicana becomes the victim of his *machismo* and woeful are the trials and tribulations of that household.

Much of this is seen, particularly in the city. The man, being head of the household but unable to fight the System he lives in, will very likely lose face and for this reason there will often be a separation or divorce in a family. It is at this time that the Chicana faces the real test of having to confront society as one of its total victims.

There are many things she must do. She must: 1) find a way to feed and clothe the family; 2) find housing; 3) find employment; 4) provide child care; and 5) find some kind of social outlet and friendship.

1) In order to find a way to feed and clothe her family, she must find a job. Because of her suppression she has probably not been able to develop a skill. She is probably unable to find a job that will pay her a decent wage. If she is able to find a job at all, it will probably be sought only for survival. Thus she can hope just to exist; she will hardly be able to live an enjoyable life. Here one of the most difficult

problems for the Chicana woman to face is that of going to work. Even if she does have a skill, she must all at once realize that she has been living in a racist society. She will have much difficulty in proving herself in any position. Her work must be three times as good as that of the Anglo majority. Not only this, but the competitive way of the Anglo will always be there. The Anglo woman is always there with her superiority complex. The Chicana woman will be looked upon as having to prove herself even in the smallest task. She is constantly being put to the test. Not only does she suffer the oppression that the Anglo woman suffers as a woman in the market of humanity, but she must also suffer the oppression of being a minority person with a different set of values. Because her existence and the livelihood of the children depend on her conforming, she tries very hard to conform. Thus she may find herself even rejecting herself as a Mexican-American. Existence itself depends on this.

2) She must find housing that she will be able to afford. She will very likely be unable to live in a decent place; it will be more the matter of finding a place that is cheap. It is likely that she will have to live in a housing project. Here she will be faced with the real problem of trying to raise children in an environment that is conducive to much suffering. The decision as to where she will live is a difficult matter, as she must come face-to-face with making decisions entirely on her own. This, plus having to live them out, is very traumatic for her.

3) In finding a job she will be faced with working very hard during the day and coming home to an empty house and again having to work at home. Cooking, washing, ironing, mending, plus spending some time with the children. Her role changes to being both father and mother. All of this, plus being poor, is very hard to bear. On top of this, to have a survey worker or social worker tell you that you have to have incentive and motivations—these are tough pressures to live under. Few men could stand up under such pressures.

4) Child care is one of the most difficult problems for a woman to have to face alone. Not only is she tormented with having to leave the raising of her children to someone else, but she wants the best of care for them. For the amount of money that she may be able to pay from her meager wages, it is likely that she will be lucky to find anyone at all to take care of the children. The routine of the household is not normal at all. She must start her day earlier than an average

worker. She must clothe and feed the children before she takes them to be cared for in someone else's home. Then too, she will have a very hard day at work, for she is constantly worrying about the children. If there are medical problems, this will only multiply her stress during the day. Not to mention the financial pressure of medical care.

5) With all of this, the fact still remains that she is a human and must have some kind of friendship and entertainment in life, and this is perhaps one of the most difficult tasks facing the Mexican-American woman alone. She can probably enjoy very little entertainment, since she can not afford a babysitter. This, plus the fact that she likely does not have the clothes, transportation, etc. As she cannot afford entertainment herself, she may very often fall prey to letting someone else pay for her entertainment and this may create unwanted involvement with some friend. When she begins to keep company with men, she will meet with the disapproval of her family and often be looked upon as having loose moral values. As quite often she is not free to remarry in the eyes of the Church, she will find more and more conflict and disapproval, and she continues to look upon herself with guilt and censorship. Thus she suffers much as a human. Everywhere she looks she seems to be rejected.

This woman has much to offer the movement of the Mexican-American. She has had to live all of the roles of her Raza. She has had to suffer the torments of her people in that she has had to go out into a racist society and be a provider as well as a mother. She has been doubly oppressed and is trying very hard to find a place. Because of all this, she is a very, very strong individual. She has had to become strong in order to exist against these odds.

The Mexican-American movement is not that of just adults fighting the social system, but it is a total commitment of a family unit living what it believes to be a better way of life in demanding social change for the benefit of humankind. When a family is involved in a human rights movement, as is the Mexican-American family, there is little room for a woman's liberation movement alone. There is little room for having a definition of woman's role as such. Roles are for actors and the business at hand requires people living the examples of social change. The Mexican-American-movement demands are such that, with the liberation of La Raza, we must have a total liberation. The woman must help liberate the man and the man must look upon this liberation with the woman at his side, not behind him, following, but alongside of him, leading. The family must come up together.

The Raza movement is based on brother- and sisterhood. We must look at each other as one large family. We must look at all of the children as belonging to all of us. We must strive for the fulfillment of all as equals, with the full capability and right to develop as humans. When a man can look upon a woman as human, then, and only then, can he feel the true meaning of liberation and equality.

Conference of Mexican Women: Un Remolino

FRANCISCA FLORES

In this article published in an early Chicano magazine, Flores describes one of the first national Chicana women's meetings.

The Conferencia de Mujeres Por La Raza held in Houston, Tejas over Memorial Day week-end was the beginning of a chubasco to say the least. Like the Chubascos that threaten La Paz [Baja, California] from time to time, the Women's Conference represented such force and potential for a breakthrough against existing stumbling blocks and obstacles in the women's struggle for equality . . . that persons within the movement who disagree with this direction, urged and supported some women to form a flank within the groundswell of the Conference in order to break it.

Close to 600 women participated in the workshops held at the Magnolia Branch of the Houston YWCA. Some of the workshops held on Saturday were so large that only the most vocal and most aggressive could be heard discussing issues that interest women but which are shaking the men who feel threatened by women in action, women in leadership roles, women who are literally out of reach of the masculine dictum.

The three workshops which received the greatest and the hottest discussion were: Sex and the Chicana–Noun and Verb; Marriage: Chicana Style; and the Feminist Movement: Do We Have a Place In It? In these workshops the question of the role of women in relation to men, and to the Anglo society were raised. The waves raised by these issues split over into the afternoon workshops and the discussion and controversies which developed continued through the night. By Sunday morning the women who believe that women in the Chicano community must submit to the dominance of the men walked out. Much of their rationale was superficial . . . charging that the YWCA was using the women to further their own program to wipe out racism . . . that women of the barrio were not invited . . . that men were not allowed to attend, although there were "gringas" present, etc. . . .

SCRATCH THE SURFACE

Beneath the rhetoric, such as so many people use these days, and which the most outspoken participants engaged in, were the fundamental issues of: the right of self determination by Mexican women over questions affecting her body. The issue of birth control, abortions, information on sex and the pill are considered "white" women's lib issues and should be rejected by Chicanas according to the Chicano philosophy which believes that the Chicana women's place is in the home and that her role is that of a mother with a large family. Women who do not accept this philosophy are charged with betrayal of "our culture and heritage." OUR CULTURE HELL! Many of the women who insist that the woman's place is in the home are college students or graduates.

Mexican women who bear (large) families beyond the economic ability to support them, suffer the tortures of damnation when their children die of malnutrition, of tuberculosis and other illnesses which wipe out families in poverty stricken or marginal communities in the Southwest. The young people, as well as others, who promote such theoretical absurdities do not know what they are saying. IF A WOMAN WANTS A LARGE FAMILY . . . NO ONE WILL INTERFERE WITH HER RIGHT TO HAVE ONE . . . even if they cannot personally afford it . . . that is their right. However, to stipulate this right as a tenet of La Causa for all women of La Raza is to play a dangerous game with the movement. It means—stripped of its intellectual romanticism—that Chicanas are being condemned to wash diapers and stay home all of their youth . . . something which the girls in college are not doing and yet some of them are the ones insisting that their hermanas de raza do so because this "is their role."

There are some strong women who can handle a family and a career at the same time. Some can make motherhood a career by giving birth to many children in an equal number of years. However, most women cannot. In the course of many pregnancies many mothers and children do not make it. The toll in human life is very great. If the promulgators of the "Chicana's role is in the home having large families" also projected concern with the health problems of abnormal or self-induced abortions and stillborn births, we might accept their contentions as a basis for discussion. As it stands, however, we have to conclude that their belief in the role of the Mexican women is based on erroneous cultural and historical understanding of what is meant by "our cultural heritage," as it relates to the family.

WHAT WE SAY

As stated before, the question of large families is the choice each person or family will make for themselves. That is their inalienable right. A woman who wants a large family should not be denied. *What we are saying is that the woman should have the right to participate in making that decision.* And if she chooses to have a large family she should enjoy all of the protection and benefits necessary for her and her children's health and economic well-being. This means that the health and well being of her husband is very important . . . otherwise, the family is jeopardized . . . if they are left to shift for themselves economically. It can devastate a family. In East Los Angeles, Ca., it is estimated that 20% of the heads of family are women. This is 1/5 of all Mexican households. The men, formerly, heads of these families have real problems. And these problems must be taken into account when discussing the role of individuals in a family. The cry of machismo will not answer these problems.

The women who advocate that the woman's place is in the home and that they should raise large families should contemplate long and seriously the ramifications of their theory and develop a program to fit the needs of women who stay home and raise large families. These needs cannot be filled with rhetorical abstracts—stripped of its verbiage—which means continued inequality and suppression of women. Further, those who promote backward and reactionary theories cannot cleanse themselves by engaging in diversionary tactics . . . blaming all who do not agree with them—as being WOMEN'S LIB! The tactics of reaction used to be red-baiting . . . now we have women-baiting. Women's Lib. INDEED!

A WEEK-END LONG TO BE REMEMBERED

The influence and impact of the Houston Conference of Mujeres Por La Raza many not be fully realized for many years to come. It has given greater impulse to discussion on the role of Mexican women which has been going on for the last two or three years. There have been numerous attempts, on the part of women in general Chicano organizations to express themselves as a group. However, men have been mildly interested and amused by their efforts. A couple of years ago, the women attending the Denver Youth Conference met in a workshop to discuss their role within this movement . . . however, they returned to report: "It was the consensus of the group that the Chicana woman does not want to be liberated."

Last year, the women in MAPA, Mexican American Political Association attempted to establish a women's caucus at their annual convention. The caucus only functioned during the course of the convention. Women attending the Latino Conference held in Wisconsin, last year, also held a workshop on women. One of the proposals voted out was that 1/3 of the leadership of the organization be made up from women. It is not known if their organizational efforts continue in effect or if they have become lost in the general policy that the women's first responsibility is to the men and to keep the family together.

Other organizations have dealt differently with women. Some have auxiliaries which meet separately but function together on issues of over-all concern. Women in these types of organizations usually do the housekeeping tasks of the men's organizations. Last year, the Mexican American National Issues Conference, meeting in Sacramento, included a Workshop on Women. This workshop voted to become the Comision Feminil Mexicana and functions as an independent organization affiliated to the Mexican American National Issues Conference. (Femenil, for those who do not understand Spanish, means feminine or womanly.)

Resolution

The effort and work of Chicana/Mexican women in the Chicano movement is generally obscured because women are not accepted as community leaders either by the Chicano movement or by the Anglo establishment.

The existing myopic attitude does not, however, prove that women are not capable or willing to participate. It does not prove that women are not active, indispensible (representing over 50% of the population), experienced and knowledgeable in organizing, tactics and strategy of a people's movement.

THEREFORE, in order to terminate exclusion of female leadership *in the Chicano/Mexican movement* and in the community, be it RESOLVED that a Chicana/Mexican Women's Commission be established at this Conference which will represent women, in all areas where Mexicans prevail, and:

That this commission be known as the Comision Femenil Mexicana, and;

That the Comision direct its efforts to organizing women to assume leadership positions *within* the Chicano movement and in community life, and;

That the Comision disseminate news and information regarding the work and achievement of Mexican/Chicana women, and;

That the Comision concern itself in promoting programs which specifically lend themselves to help, assist and promote *solutions to female type problems and problems confronting the Mexican family*, and;

That the Comision spell out issues to support, and explore ways to establish relationships with other women's organizations and movements.

VIVA LA CAUSA!

What Is Reality?

FRANCISCA FLORES

Flores presents the dilemmas of young Chicana women regarding sex and sexuality.

The phrase, "It is not our cultural heritage" used to reject issues or philosophies we do not agree with is being used more and more these days. Presently, with the greater interest and action by Mexican women in La Causa and the greater degree of attention being paid by the media on "women's liberation movement," it is being used to cover many sins. Primarily, it is being advanced to reject the "white middle class" dogma of social values, however, it also serves to keep hidden some very important problems being faced by our young women.

One issue, being "swept under the rug" is the increased number of abortions and V.D. infections current among Mexican youth. The young women in East Los Angeles are dramatically refusing to take the pill as a preventative measure or to enroll in birth control programs. Their refusal to face the facts is demonstrated by their preference to accept an abortion rather than to take "the pill." The young women (13 years and up) have many reasons why they refuse to take the pill. "It forms cancer . . ." said one girl while lighting up a cigarette. This phenomena in the Mexican community . . . abortions

Reprinted by permission, Francisca Flores.

rather than prevention, is not true in other communities . . . white or black. Therefore, the element which is different . . . "cultural heritage" must be examined and discussed. It must be dealt with, if the physical and mental health of young Chicanas is to be preserved. This is not a question of Mexican girls engaging in more sex than others . . . it lies in their group's refusal to take the pill or other preventative measures. Why is this so? Is it the teachings of the church . . . is it that their personal guilt feelings run deeper or that this guilt involves more persons than just themselves?

In a way, it's like having committed a crime . . . an aberration which causes the mind to refuse admission of the act because it is looked upon with such deep disfavor. In other words, "young ladies do not engage in sex without marriage vows." So, if a girl submits to birth control . . . she is admitting "pre-meditation" of sex, and this can never be the case, because "our culture" does not permit it. And if she gets caught becoming pregnant . . . it must have been an act that she could not control . . . a situation which occurred against her will. Therefore, birth control information is out . . . and the pill cannot be taken. What is happening in today's scene of high degree of sexual activity by the very young, is that ABORTIONS ARE BEING SUBSTI-TUTED as the answer. Some girls, not yet 20 years old are already facing the prospect of an abortion for the third time.

RATIONALE

All rationale, rhetoric being given for opposing a movement for women's rights must be exposed, in order to allow for needed change in attitudes. Otherwise, the youth are going to pay heavily in mental and physical health.

Graciela Olivarez, in her speech at the Houston Conference of Mujeres Mexicanas pointed out that the real problem faced by women (and men) in relation to machismo is that they both suffer from a "Virgin Image and a Mother Complex. The young men," she pointed out, "look up to their mothers as saints, as virgins (all women worthy of marriage must be virgins). The mother is placed on a pedestal. The young man cannot face the fact that his mother had to have intercourse with his father in order to give birth to him." Therefore, the Mexican woman . . . lindisima mujer . . . in the mind of the male, must be a virgin when he marries her. How can a girl admit premarital sex to anyone, even to herself, under these circumstances. NO! The family, the Church, but most important, the attitude of the men, and the girl's own sense of guilt does not allow her to face the reality that sex involvement requires preventative measures, if unwanted pregnancies are to be avoided. Abortion may seem the way out for these young women, but the price they will have to pay later, may be fatal. All because we insist that "our cultural heritage" implies that the woman must be placed on a pedestal, without examining the reason for this attitude, its inevitable consequences and its effect on the youth. We must bring this issue out into the open . . . discuss it and its psychological implications upon our community. Only in this way will it be possible to lift the burden it is placing on our women.

The Young Lords Party

DENISE OLIVER

A young women in the Puerto Rican Young Lords Party states her opposition to machismo *and decries the secondary position of women in Puerto Rican society and in the movement.*

Within the Party, one of our Thirteen Points is that we want equality for women. We oppose *machismo,* and the way we're dealing with it is by actually clarifying what it is, how we sense it as women, and how to combat it within the revolutionary struggle. It is going to be very difficult because the brainwashing has been so heavy. Women have been brainwashed into believing that they are weak, that they are not

Reprinted by permission, McGraw-Hill. Original source: M. Abramson, *Palante: Young Lords Party,* New York: McGraw-Hill, 1971.

fighters, that they are not capable of picking up guns—in fact, they're supposed to be afraid of guns, afraid of anything mechanical.

Our role is to educate sisters so that they can be a vital part of the revolution. Since we see the struggle in this country as basically being one of urban guerrilla warfare, the woman must take a major role because of the mobility she has—a much greater mobility than a man's. The fact is that pigs are male chauvinists, so they may not be as inclined to shoot a woman walking down the street with her children, a pocketbook, and some bundles of groceries that may contain bombs; they may not be as brutal toward a woman when she's arrested. We have to *use* that kind of chauvinism.

We also don't want a revolution to happen *after* the revolution. We don't want to say, "Well, we want a socialist society, we want to have armed struggle," and after all that's over, still have to deal with the fact that women are oppressed.

In the Algerian Revolution, women were the carriers of weapons—they couldn't actually use them. And the position of women in Algeria today is still an inferior one. The revolution in Cuba was also one in which the woman in most cases did not play a role as fighter, and today there's a big women's liberation struggle going on inside the country.

Now, in the Vietnamese struggle the sisters are probably the most liberated women in the world. That's because all the sisters in North Vietnam are fighting, and they're fighting right alongside the brothers, and sometimes in front of them. We want that kind of thing to happen here.

The whole concept of *machismo*—that man is superior in all ways—has developed among our people because the Third World man is so oppressed by outside forces—by the system, by capitalism—that he's taught to believe that the only way he can get back at this is by being superior to women.

Machismo is a word that is used to depict a certain tendency among Latin males. It doesn't mean that *machismo* doesn't exist among white males—it's just that it's not as obvious. Among white men, their whole *machismo* thing is, like, who can make better business deals or take over a large corporation. A man is respected by virtue of the money he has. But since the Third World man doesn't have any money, he's respected by his fellows for how much balls he's got, and how much he can oppress women, and how many women he can take to bed and use and fuck over. So that although *machismo* is not just a Latin thing—and we'd like to make sure that idea gets corrected—it is more apparent in oppressed communities.

When you look to any group to find out who's the most oppressed, it's always gonna be the women. Whether it's in the bourgeoisie, or the working class or *lumpen proletariat,* it doesn't make any difference. Just look at a woman and you'll find the story of real oppression in this society. In our case, our oppression is threefold. It's first the oppression under capitalism that affects all people of the Third World; secondly, there's the oppression under capitalism that affects women in terms of jobs and things like that; and thirdly, there's the oppression that we receive from our own men.

In Puerto Rican society, the woman is taught to cater to the needs of her family, in particular to the demands of her father or husband. She's taught that she is inferior in her own ways. Like, sometimes she is taught not to enjoy sex. The man, of course, can go out and enjoy it—this is being very *macho.* . . .

We have to have the kind of society where a woman can determine for herself whether or not she wants to have a child—not on the basis of whether that child will eat, because all children will be eating and will be well-clothed and well-educated, but just on the basis of how many children she feels like having at that time. Also, in a system such as ours, where abortion is kind of a forced thing—sisters have to have abortions in hospitals where they may die. Carmen Rodriguez, one of our sisters, was the first woman to die of an abortion after the abortion law was passed in New York State. She died in Lincoln Hospital because she was operated on in the supply room in a hospital overrun with garbage, filth and decay, where the electrical wiring is all hanging out loose. She died because the doctor that did the abortion has to do too many a day—so that after doing several he's very overtired, and very fuzzy about what he's doing. This is the kind of thing that happens under a system where health care is not taken care of, in a system that gives individuals totally unequal treatment. . . .

An individual woman, you know, has the right to control her own body. Obviously, any kind of control over your own body, by physical means or through things like forced abortion, on the one hand, or not allowing women to have abortions, on the other, is a form of slavery. But if we're gonna talk about that kind of liberation, I think that before a woman can really control her own body, she has to liberate her mind—and before a woman can liberate her mind, both brothers and sisters have to have their minds liberated. . . .

When the Party got started, there were very few sisters. It was mostly brothers, and those sisters that were in the Party got vamped on constantly. We didn't have a chance to contribute politically, we weren't growing or developing, we were not in leadership positions at all. We were relegated to doing office work, typing, taking care of whatever kids were around, being sex objects. When a new sister would come in the door, all the brothers would crowd around her and say, "Hey, baby, what's happening? You really are fine, wow!" and all this stuff. We objected to that. We saw that we really weren't gonna be able to do any kind of constructive organizing in the community without sisters actively involved in the Party, because most of the people that we're organizing are women with children, through the free-breakfast program and through the free-clothing drive and the health care programs. So, we brought this up to Central Committee and it was decided that a women's caucus would be formed for our own political development, and because a lot of sisters were not at the point where they could discuss a lot of the things that bothered them in the presence of brothers, and they needed that kind of solidarity with other sisters in the Party for strength.

From the caucus, we developed an awareness of what Women's Liberation is all about and the role of the woman in the revolution. As we began to grow and develop politically, we started to force the brothers to deal with us within the Party. One thing we realized was that although the Thirteen Point Program said, "We want equality for women. *Machismo* must be revolutionary and not oppressive," *machismo* was never gonna be revolutionary. Saying "revolutionary *machismo*" is like saying "revolutionary fascism" or "revolutionary racism"—it's a contradiction. And so, through our political growth and development, that point in the program was changed.

We also started correcting and disciplining the brothers for their male chauvinism, because then we understood it wasn't just about a brother beating up a sister, but that in a political party it could be much more subtle. For example, the Defense Ministry was made up only of brothers, even though the Party said that the Defense Ministry is not to be looked upon as a goon squad; it's not about how many muscles you have—it's about how sharp and intelligent, quick-thinking, fast-acting you are, how well you can deal with strategy and tactics.

So through Women's Caucus there are now sisters who play a major role in Defense.

After a while, we were faced with a real contradiction. Here we were growing in the Women's Caucus and getting much more political and jumping on brothers who didn't understand a lot of times where we were coming from. A lot of brothers in the Party are off the street, and they don't know about male chauvinism from a hole in the wall. They were getting very uptight behind the fact that they were getting disciplined every time they opened their mouths. So that one of the things that we pushed for was the establishment of the Men's Caucus to correct that. Now the men in the Party meet at the same time that the women do. They discuss the fucked-up things that society has put in their heads. They're dealing with "What is a man?" After several months of having separate caucuses, we're now having brothers and sisters meet together at each branch to discuss sexism, because we were tending toward a separation that we didn't want.

You know, I don't believe in the concept of just a liberated woman; I believe that there has to be a liberated man too—that a liberated woman without a liberated man is not gonna be a liberated woman, that men have to get away from this whole hangup on their masculinity being their penis. 'Cause that's not what it's about—there are very few differences between male and female, other than biological ones, and we have to get to that level of understanding.

Yes, there is still male chauvinism in the Party—it's a difficult struggle for a man to liberate himself after twenty-three or twenty-four or twenty-five years of being a *macho*. But there is a new man evolving, just like there is a new woman evolving. It's not just the women who are pointing out male chauvinism, the men are even disciplining other men because of it. It's gonna be very gradual, but I can see it, it's happening. . . .

The next two documents, written in 1971 by Asian-American women, argue for female equality in American society and within the Asian-American movement itself.

Asian Women as Leaders

American society is broken up into different levels based on economic income, education, politics, color and sex. Each level has a prescribed set of rules for action and interplay—roles that are enforced by the levels above. At the bottom of these varying gradations are women of color. Third World women face domination by both racism and sexism (discrimination based on sex). Both racism and sexism are means by which American society controls and oppresses everyone. Everyone is forced to conform to the values and roles established by the dominant group in order to "succeed." For the Asian movement to progress, it must have a clear understanding of sexism, racism, and imperialism; and deal with them simultaneously.

For Asian women in general, the stereotypes or roles have been of two major kinds: either docile, submissive Oriental dolls who will cater to the whims of any man; or the Suzie Wong, sex-pot, exotic bitch-body. Between these two are the efficient secretary, sexy stewardess, the good housekeeper and domestic, the girl any guy would like to marry.

Women in the Asian movement find that these stereotypes are still hovering over their heads. Not only these but new stereotypes, too: i.e., Asian men have tried to define for "their women" what it means to be "heavy." Men in the Asian movement also find themselves tied down to stereotypes. Perhaps they may feel that to be a MAN one must have authority and responsibility. In the same light, they will frown on women who take on a lot of responsibility (and the authority that goes along with it), labelling them as "unfeminine."

Women then tend to fear this loss of "femininity" and so they do the clerical work and the cleaning up, activities for which intellect is not essential or expected. Women may also fulfill these jobs because they do them best: And why do they do them the best? Because women are never encouraged to do anything else; women's potential abilities as a leader are left untapped and undeveloped. She loses her confidence in being able to handle such responsibility.

The sisters who have achieved a position of authority in the movement are a minority and are still trapped by the stereotypes that society has created. It is a struggle for women to attain the top leadership positions. Women who "make it" into such positions have had to reject the stereotypes already imposed upon them. But because the new definition of "the Asian woman" has not get evolved, women find themselves in a "limbo." Some find themselves being labelled as Bitches—women who speak out loudly and strongly; who are authoritarian, who boss people around, and command some form of respect. Some must resort to being overly diligent and efficient to prove themselves as worthy of the same leadership positions as the men. Others gain respect by appearing to accomplish work in a multitude of projects but actually only completing a few tasks. And still others attain their leadership positions as token gestures. Some women can gain respect only by putting up with put-downs on other women, i.e., "you're not one of those bird-brained little girls," or "You're as strong as a man!"

Once women do get into leadership positions, they find that their ideas are usurped by the men, who then take credit for the idea as being their own. Women are often heard but not listened to. Many times, the woman must play her old role in order to get things done: "Oh, please, can you help me carry this. It's much too heavy for little old me. . . ."

How can these problems be solved? People must recognize that women are half of the working force in the movement against oppression, exploitation, and imperialism. They are half of the working force in creating the new revolutionary lifestyle. Men and women in the movement must therefore begin to live the ideals and goals they are working for. To do this, they must not let chauvinist acts slide by. People cannot work together effectively if there are hidden tensions or if people let little annoyances build up inside themselves. They must deal with racism or imperialism. They must be able to develop as human beings, not subject to categorizations and stereotypes. Developing as people confident in themselves, in their ideas, they will not be afraid of criticism; they will see the need for criticism, self-criticism in order to move forward. The struggle is not men against women nor women against men, but it is a united front striving for a new society, a new way of life.

> If I go forward,
> Follow me.
> Push me if I fall behind.
> If I betray you,
> If they take me,
> Avenge me then in kind.

Politics of the Interior

Women cannot define themselves without society imposing its images and stifling them with sex roles. Women should be considered as human beings, not categorized or defined because of their sex. Women should not be considered as physically and intellectually weak, incompetent creatures inferior to men. They must not be deprived of equal pay for equal work. Furthermore, division of labor in offices, factories, and homes should not automatically be sex-assigned.

CAPITALISM

It is the social system, not men, which is the enemy. Under the oppressive capitalist system, men feel that their social status depends on the amount of material wealth, physical prowess, and their owner-

© 1971 University of California, Berkeley, *Asian Women* Journal Staff (Emma Gee, Susan Fong, Diana Gong, Jean Quan, Carolyn Yee). Reprinted 1975 UCLA Asian American Studies Center.

ship of consumer status symbols. Men are counted as failures if they do not live up to this role, as are women who do not live up to theirs, of catching the economically successful man. Both men and women are sacrificed for the System.

In order to be aware of this, women should support one another emotionally and not rely exclusively on the "traditional male support." The relationship between the sexes must be re-defined. Women must begin to define themselves. By recognizing ourselves as capable of giving support to other sisters, the nature of sexual oppression will be realized, and united action with men can be taken to overthrow the system which oppresses both women and men.

Radical feminism plays an important role in the liberation of all people.

BIRTH CONTROL

Birth control is one of the most publicized issues of the women's movement. Yet, remember that because birth control itself is essentially assigned a social value, it must be subject to critical evaluation. Society and the men who rule society have always controlled the use of birth control. This results in depriving women control over their own bodies. Birth control by our society is used as an oppressive means of subjecting women to unnecessary physical and emotional hardship. It is women who bear the burden of unwanted children.

Most contraceptive methods are designed for women and even the most effective methods such as the pill and IUD can be detrimental to her health. Improvement is needed, but development of safe, effective contraception as well as abortion are not placed as a high priority by men who make our laws. Our society's sexist bias is reflected in the lack of medical research on new birth control methods for men and in that experimental subjects are usually non-white, Third World women. Birth control practices are also racist.

Ironically, women who seek illegal abortions not only face the threat of serious physical injury or death but also criminal prosecution. When seeking a legal abortion, women must face male-staffed abortion boards and social and religious condemnation by our society.

In addition, the "sexual revolution" which has emerged from the publicity of the birth control issue has only contributed to emphasizing the woman as a "sexual object" rather than allowing her to utilize birth control as a means of elevating her status as a self-defined human being.

As women who recognize birth control as a means of self-determination and the liberation for all women from unwanted children, we demand that:

1. the condescending moralistic attitudes which often accompany birth control and abortions be eliminated;
2. responsibility for birth control be shared also by men;
3. more facilities, information as well as financial support, be provided for birth control.

Although we recognize that these alone will not alleviate the massive social and economic conditions which cause other forms of subjugation of women, we feel that birth control must be treated as a necessary step to our self-determination.

GAY QUESTION

It is difficult to take a "stand" on the gay question from our perspective as "straight" sisters. For many of us, the issue, in terms of ourselves, is an unreality because a lack of awareness informationally, because it is totally out of our experience, and because of not having resolved the issue as well as many others in our meetings. Yet, we recognize that as an oppressed people—economically, legally (it is against the law to be gay), and psychologically (in terms of being labeled sick)—gay women must also have the right to self-definition.

The gay movement has provided one of the most challenging criticisms of the radical movement for it has questioned the basic issues of chauvinism within the movement as well as the alienation of gay women from women's groups. "Lesbianism" can be seen as revolutionary in that it is a challenge to the basic assumptions of the present system, representing an alternative life style.

As revolutionary women seeking the liberation of all women, we support a united front with our sisters against all arbitrary and rhetorical social standards.

ASIAN WOMAN AND THE MOVEMENT

Asian-American women are faced with a double contradiction—their struggle as a Third World people in a racist nation and their role as women in a sexist society. In even the most progressive elements of the Asian community, Asian women too often receive little support in resolving their problems.

Part of the confusion lies in the emerging nationalism of the Asian-American movement and its search for models. Asian-Americans have turned to Asia and to the traditional and revolutionary values of China and Vietnam. However, there are problems inherent in the uncritical adoption of the "Asian" values for Asian-American women. The role of Asian women in the traditional Asian societies being always subordinate is antithetical to the entire concept of self-determination. On the other hand, the liberation of our revolutionary sisters in China and Vietnam has taken place within socialist revolutions. Conditions are different from America and alien to the Asian-American experience.

In America, Asian-Americans find affinity with Third World groups. Yet, only within few Third World or white movements has the role of women been satisfactorily resolved. Women's concern for sexual self-determination is often rejected or isolated as "bourgeois" or secondary to the greater struggle. Such attitudes evade the issue.

Unless the Asian-America movement deals seriously with the women question, Asian women may often feel compelled to choose between her people and her liberation as a woman.

In finding solutions, we must first define our problem. Because Asian women face the double oppression of racism and sexism, our first priority is within our communities, but the definition of Asian womanhood must be part of a "whole" Asian Movement. Though men do not always realize the needs of women because they hold a comfortable position, we remind men that women are one half of humanity, and no movement can be successful unless it includes women.

The women question must not be ignored but seen in the context of priorities, communities and progressive insight. Divisions cannot afford to exist in the struggle of our people.

We demand:

1. men take responsibility for re-educating themselves about their sexism, subtle or overt. Too often men thrust the responsibility on women to explain all;
2. women's groups be encouraged without paternalism, unspoken distrust, or hostility;
3. re-evaluation of leadership structure, women encouraged to take leadership positions traditionally assigned to men;
4. reappraisal of projects and facilities to examine whether they serve the needs of women—abortion counseling, health facilities, daycare, etc; and
5. domestic responsibilities to be done collectively by women and men—liberating women to participate more fully in activities.

Women also have the responsibility to understand the differences which go beyond sex and culture. We must make a special effort to realize the differences between generations and economic classes. If we can understand and respect differences, and unify in our struggle, radical feminism will be a powerful force in the liberation of our people.

RELATIONSHIP TO THIRD WORLD WOMEN AND WHITE WOMEN

Of course, as Asian women we feel a special closeness with other Third World women that we do not feel with white women, for we experience the same racism that all Third World women feel. Third World women in the U.S. understand the double jeopardy of color and sex. For example, employment practices indicate that the median income of white women, employed full time is lower than that of black men, employed full time. The median income of black women is lower still, but the median education of both groups of women is higher than that of their male counterparts. More white women work full-time year round than all black men and women working full and part time combined. So black women earn the least and are employed the least often.

We must not be divided from other Third World women or deny the value of our fight for freedom—freedom as women as well as people of color. When we fight for the freedom of Third World people, we must also press for the equality of women. As Third World women we play an integral part in the fight for freedom of all people. (As stated by the Young Lords Party, "the women's struggle is the revolution within the revolution.")

The same oppressive mentality which subjugates Third World people abuses white women also. Thus we, as Asian women, must also develop unity and understanding with white women. But, the ties between ourselves and white women are presently loose because the education system in this country re-enforces the belief in the "inferiority of colored people." This notion is unavoidable in the educating process whose assumptions we all learn. Together we can combat that assumption, but even there is a limit to our obligation to white women, for we must all be responsible for our own education in order to combat racism and self-debasement.

If we as women are willing to combat and root-out racism as well as sexism, the bonds between Third World women and white women will unite them in a common cause with a common idea.

All people who are oppressed must not only recognize the causes of their oppression but also recognize the validity of other struggles. We cannot underestimate the realities of factors which contribute to and re-enforce oppression. We must always be prepared for the struggle, to strengthen ourselves both in character and in the rightness of our position, and to realize that sisterhood *is* powerful.

9

"WHEN THE MUSIC'S OVER": ENDINGS AND BEGINNINGS

It is not difficult to think of the end of the 1960s in symbolic or apocalyptic terms. Despite Richard Nixon's pledge to end it, the war in Vietnam dragged on and even intensified, with more extreme bombing of North Vietnam than ever before. In 1970 the United States invaded Cambodia and students across the country demonstrated in despair. At Kent State University in Ohio, National Guardsmen, ordered to campus to quell demonstrators, shot and killed four students. A National Student Strike followed in which thousands of high school and college students across the country walked out of classes and schools. Many college students never finished the academic year, as administrators canceled classes and final exams in the hope of avoiding more violence and parents insisted that their children return home. At Jackson State University in Mississippi, police opened fire on students, killing two more. The fact that police and National Guard forces were now shooting students, as well as poor ghetto residents and Black Panthers (see chapter 3), seemed to symbolize in the starkest terms the generational rupture and the fury that had been unleashed by the counterculture and by the student, antiwar, and Black Power movements. Civil war did not seem a wholly inappropriate image.

In Berkeley, site of the most famous early student protest, the Free Speech Movement (see chapter 2), an attempt to create a community park ended in violence and death the year before Kent State and Jackson State. Hundreds of students and community residents had become involved in developing a people's park on an unused lot owned by the University of California. The makeover of the property into an attractive and communal public space seemed to embody the creativity, beauty, and cooperativeness of the movement. University officials warned, however, that the property belonged to the school and, after a series of confrontations, sealed the park and destroyed it. In the ensuing demonstrations and conflict, one student was killed and another blinded. Police dropped tear gas from helicopters, suggesting symbolically to many that the war in Southeast Asia had come home. The imagery of People's Park, Kent State, and Jackson State, the sorrow and rage and symbolism of destruction and death, all merged with the bitterness of a war that never seemed to end and a decade that was about to.

Two rock 'n' roll events of 1969, at Woodstock and Altamont, eerily represented the extremes of the decade. At Woodstock, half a million people came together in New York State to listen peacefully and lovingly to the music of the sixties. Woodstock became a symbol of the love, peace, drugs, and music of the counterculture at its best. At Altamont, in Northern California, a free concert sponsored by the Rolling Stones turned violent when Hell's Angels, hired to guard the stage, brutalized a number of concertgoers and stabbed one member of the audience to death. These two events epitomized the optimistic and pessimistic sides that coexisted in the counterculture by late in the decade. Violence seemed pervasive—from Southeast Asia to college campuses to rock concerts—and generational, cultural, and political rifts endemic to American society.

New groups emerged as others declined or splintered. In addition to feminism (see chapter 8), two other enduring movements of the decade grew in the late 1960s. In June 1969 police raided a gay men's bar in New York City, the Stonewall Inn. Atypically, the patrons fought back. Days of rioting in Greewich Village followed. The Stonewall Rebellion is usually identified as the beginning of the gay liberation movement. In the months and years that followed, the repression of gays and lesbians became an issue throughout the nation. The question of homosexual rights and acceptance proved explosive within some of the political movements as well. In the women's movement, for example, lesbians accused heterosexual feminists of hostility and homophobia. Throughout the 1970s and 1980s, gay and lesbian liberation continued to be on the national political agenda, raising consciousness and gaining strength while simultaneously eliciting a conservative backlash.

Similarly, the environmental movement that gained national attention in the late 1960s continued to draw adherents and critics over the next decades. Many in the counterculture had rejected the commercialism and destructiveness of American capitalism and its apparent disregard for nature. Their response was often a turn to organic gardening and more healthful foods. This was especially true after the initial utopian phase of the counterculture gave way to more limited and personal approaches in the late decades (see chapter 5). Other Americans, as well, grew concerned about environmental questions—especially the large-scale poisoning of air, water, soil, and food, as well as the implications of a rapidly expanding world population. An array of potential solutions, from creation of the Environmental Protection Agency to the movement for zero population growth, sprang up as individuals confronted the results of human disregard for the earth.

It is probably simplistic to see the end of the sixties solely in apocalyptic terms or as initiating the political agenda for future decades. Both images are accurate. Antiwar activism continued as long as the war itself. The women's, gay and lesbian, and environmental movements expanded in the following years. As economic instability created new concerns among many Americans, the youthful idealism and utopianism of the decade receded, to be replaced by a more measured and cautious approach to problems. The Watergate crisis injected a large dose of cynicism into Americans' political outlook.

With a more moderate—some said more mature—tone, many individuals aimed to confront problems anew. Older activists tried to rekindle the spirit that had first sparked the movements in the early decade. Younger individuals sought to gain the same sense of commitment and enthusiasm their older brothers and sisters had achieved. "We had a dream and we are losing it," black activist Julius Lester wrote at the end of the decade. The problems were no less real. In fact, they appeared more complex. "In the beginning it was easy to maintain the dream," Lester observed. Now it was much more difficult. But no matter how difficult, the dream was necessary. "Without the dream, there is no revolution."

PEOPLE'S PARK

The attempt in 1969 by residents of Berkeley to build a community park on unused property owned by the University of California led to serious confrontation.

The Meaning of People's Park

JOHN OLIVER SIMON

Poet and Berkeley resident John Oliver Simon explores the meaning of the park project and the university's aggressive reaction.

What is it about People's Park in Berkeley? Meanings proliferate: the escalation in systematic counter-insurgency, Vietnam coming home, the nationally-coordinated repression, the raising of the question of private property, Berkeley as weapons-testing ground. But from a few weeks' distance, the most distinctive meaning seems to me something different. We are still inside the events though, and these notes are not intended to have finality.

For the first time the white left and street movements have fought to defend something they made themselves rather than to win demands from the Authorities. When the Park-makers talk about the Park, they glow: when they talk about the fence, they become grave. The Park is physically, touchably, verifiably *there*, not just for its makers but for any eyes and hands. "Serving the people" requires physical proof, and the Park was that. Straight people were welcome, and they used the Park.

Public need and vision collided with property. The friction between irrepressible need and immovable institutions ignited a war.

The Mayor of Berkeley said the trouble was that the street people had not asked the University's permission. Disingenuous or not (there was no sign the University would grant anything), this Jeffersonian relic, caricature of the petit-bourgeois antihero, had put his finger on something. Indeed no permission had been solicited. A number of Telegraph Avenue revolutionaries had simply moved onto the land, to use and defend it in the spirit, they said, of the Costanoan Indians who had owned the land before Spanish missionaries, Mexican troops, American settlers, the U.S. government, and the University of California in turn had expropriated it. Squatting, whether enshrined in ruling-class law or outside it, is one of the few uniformities in American custom. The difference was that the Park-makers applied the standard of good use. Had the University enriched the community when it seized private property (yes!) from small landlords who hadn't wanted to sell, the Park-makers could not have made an appealing case for their use of the plot. As it was, the University had planned lucrative and authoritarian dormitories—for students who don't want to live in the ones that exist—and later, after the Park was started, had scraped together a scheme for playing fields—for students who don't use the present ones. Meantime, the land was a muddy parking lot.

As substance and sign of a possible participatory order, as the living and hand-made proof that necessary institutions need not be overplanned, absentee-owned, hierarchical—as such the Park came to stand in many minds as one tantalizing trace of a good society, as the practical negation of American death, as a redemption worth fighting for. Suddenly, almost inescapably, citizens were asked to choose between the splendid, self-ordered reality of People's Park and images of Chancellor Roger Heyns with his committees and charts and literally murderous lies. At a Regent's committee meeting June 7, the question kept coming up, "What would you do if another group came onto the land and claimed it?" One member of the Park negotiating committee answered, "We'd talk it over with them, work something out." Another member said later he wished he'd had the chance to say: "We know we wouldn't shoot them, the way you did." As the real-world choices shrink to two, soulful socialism and the police state, could they be any clearer?

The point is that the Park began to embody, not just the negation of capitalist principles of property and land-use, but some glimmering of the method and substance of a consciously visionary socialism rising from the ashes and the mud. It "educated" more people than a million anti-imperialist and anti-captialist slogans. In the eyes of students and townspeople it discredited the University as dozens of transient, strictly-oppositional movements had failed to. "Yes, of course! Why *should* land be traded like paper? What is land for anyway?" The same principles here as in the Black Panther Party's program of Breakfast for Children, about which Jesse Unruh complained that the Panthers were feeding more California children than the Government of the United States of America. Bobby Seale worked in the Park, praised it, instantly comprehended its meaning. . . .

Meanwhile, people from all classes worked in People's Park and in the subsequent People's Park Annex, and then fought for them. Many working-class people, including National Guardsmen, could understand the Park as well, and what they didn't understand could become an opening wedge into a discussion of property. . . .

But in People's Park the white movement gave body to its vision, blended construction into destruction; and thousands of people responded, in their own fashion—PTAs, unions, and the rest. Thousands of prior Reagan supporters turned on him and decided not to be "good Germans." The ruling class itself was substantially split, and the paltry parliamentary democracy of the Berkeley City Council discredited. (Even their halting vote to ask Reagan to withdraw his troops was ignored.) Had Berkeley been America, a contest for power would have become a plausible prospect, and we could have begun choosing the means to translate the popular will into a new system. . . .

Marvin Garson had the insight at the time that two theories of the street were at war. In the bourgeois theory of the street, a person has three essential functions in life: working, buying, and "living." The cement of the system is traffic, especially car traffic. The street has value as the route between home and office, office and store, store and home. When the authorities say traffic must be kept moving, they mean it. This is the simple and monstrous logic behind the defacing of all American land, behind a legislative committee's recently-announced call for 1400 *more* miles of freeway in the San Francisco Bay Area by 1990. Meanwhile, the street people were saying that they are whoever they are wherever they are; that life is not segmented; that the street is for being, and that being takes precedence over traffic.

Those two theories crashed head-on. But last year the community was not ready for much beyond its still vague and abstract right to the street. So factions quarreled about "demands," "leadership" separated from the mass, and it all ended July 4 with a giant Avenue celebration. Few talked about a program that groups of people, "affinity groups," could themselves begin to implement from the stuff of their organic need. . . .

Like who knows how many thousand others, I got involved in the battle of People's Park when somebody handed me a shovel and said, "over there, we're breaking it up so we can lay sod down." Packed by weight of years of houses and months of cars, the hard earth barely yielded to any tool, had an oily blue sheen in the sunlight where it was cut. This was Sunday, April 20, behind Telegraph Avenue in Berkeley. . . .

I worked steadily for 20 minutes, then wandered through the diligent crowd. "Now I see how the Chinese build dams." No idle tools, and some dude in a cowboy hat was grading the bumps and hollows on a rented bulldozer. Wine bottles passed, lemonade, and joints from hand to hand. By dusk a rock band was playing and several hundred square yards of park had been laid down under old trees.

In the next three weeks I came back time after time, bringing trees, poems and most of the children on my block. Now there is a brown dusty lot there, patrolled by Burns detectives, who replaced the National Guard behind that cyclone fence. I suppose that in the national mind, if any, the whole issue seems a little silly, cross between the spring dreams of flower children and the devious plots of SDS-inspired revolutionaries. Some factions of SDS, at least, share this view.

But we find it impossible to deny that the park is at the very center of our struggle. The revolution is about the opening of time and space for human beings, inevitably the total liberation of the ecology. "The most revolutionary consciousness," says Gary Snyder, "is to be found among the most oppressed classes—animals, trees, grass, air, water, earth." The park has brought the concept of the Whole Earth, the Mother Earth, into the vocabulary of revolutionary politics. The park has raised sharply the question of property and use; it has demonstrated the absurdity of a system that puts land title above human life; and it has given the dispossessed children of the tract homes and the cities a feeling of involvement with the planet, an involvement proved through our sweat and our blood.

The park has joined international antagonists in battle. The owner of title is the University of California, the prototype Multiversity, up to its ears in war research and with a Rand systems analyst for its president. The park people are the students, quasi-students and street people who made a Free Speech Movement, a Vietnam Day Committee, a Stop the Draft Week, who declare themselves to be the brothers of the Black Panthers, the Cubans, the Vietcong.

The land of the park used to be nice "substandard" houses where students and street people lived. The University, spreading its holdings particularly in the south campus hip ghetto, acquired the land via eminent domain for $1.3 million with the claim that it had become "a scene of hippie concentration and rising crime," and demolished the houses in the summer of 1968. Then the lot was empty, cars stuck in the winter rain and mud, glass, litter.

Central to previous Berkeley crises was the theme of protest, disruption of the public obscenities that maim our society. The park crisis started because people went ahead and did something for which there was no legal convention, building a new society on the vacant lots of the old. The park was born April 20, and it lived three and a half weeks. It is difficult to go back to the spirit of those days, when at first even the police were reasonably friendly. Decisions were made by the people who wanted to work, to lay sod here and plant a revolutionary corn garden there. There was a play area with several swings and a sandbox, but the favorite children's thing was a set of 7-foot high wooden letters spelling K N O W which could be crawled through. A platform festooned with prayer flags, brick walls, a maypole, a fire pit surrounded at night by the young passive drifters, far gone and not coming home.

Thursday morning, May 15, 300 police in battle gear surrounded the park at 4:45 A.M. and ordered us out. Hopelessly outnumbered, we stumbled through their lines to watch workmen putting up the fence. Exhausted, tears of rage, tears of grief. And then at noon 5000 people whooped down the Avenue from campus to do battle. Everybody knows about Bloody Thursday, the shotguns, the death of

James Rector. The days became indeterminate ages of confrontation, continual fear, meetings to all hours; too close to it to be a historian, I can offer an incident or two to give a sense of how it was:

Late afternoon, Bloody Thursday, quiet south campus street, woman with baby carriage, telephone repairman, street brother grazed earlier by pellets tells girl on lawn "they're shooting people on telegraph." "Are you sure?" then Blue Meanie (Alameda country sheriff) pokes his head around the corner and lets fly, wounding the brother again, missing the baby carriage and grazing the phone man who doesn't understand, "lemme go get his badge number" he cries and has to be held back gently, "no, he's not wearing a badge and if you go up there they'll shoot you again.". . .

Gatherings, marches, loitering is illegal at the discretion of the pigs; every day the people gather, march, loiter; dispersed, they regroup and come back for more; downtown Berkeley is closed down nine days in a row. Cut off from the main body, a group of 50 blocks a busy intersection for ten minutes; one brother is nearly run down by a young black gunning in a sports car. Then come a dozen cops and the people slowly yield, one boy a little too slow and he is thrown down, the clubs rise and fall but somehow he is up again and running free, pursued as rocks fly from the crowd, the first cop trips and helmet, club shoots loose, he has to retreat—combing his trained blonde hair. . . .

Every day three helicopters circle the city from first light. One day a trapped crowd is gassed on campus by a copter. The afternoons go and on, the people still unused to violence and untrained, intermittently ready to go down for each other, not really sure how much they mean by revolution, not yet a military quantity. Thursday the 22nd nearly 500 are herded into a parking lot and busted, then subjected to incredible humiliations at the concentration camp known as Santa Rita; when I see friends on their release next day, they are whispering, shaken and bent.

The confrontations quieted before the big march on Memorial Day. Thirty thousand people, mostly scared to death; Telegraph Avenue is closed off by barbed wire, machine guns are on the roofs; liberal nonviolent monitors with white armbands are circulating in the crowd, at intersections they link arms between the people and the police, continually they cry KEEP MOVING. The official park monitors in green helmets are very far between. Everyone expects a massacre. At the park, the march slows; a few continue around the city-assigned route, others sprawl off into side streets, frustrated by the fence and the incongruous picnic atmosphere. A band arrives on a flatbed truck, grass is laid down in the street and freaks with hoses begin to jump up and down, screaming and spraying the crowd. The tension dissolves into an incomplete orgy; behind the fence, the Guard is watching, roasting in their flak jackets, impassive, feelings masked. Late afternoon, a thousand people follow the band through the streets, dancing whooping and hollering WE ARE FREE a block away from the scene of the big bust. "Not yet."

On the day of the march a 13-point "Berkeley Liberation Program" appeared in the *Berkeley Barb*. Drawn up after weeks of discussion among many Berkeley radicals, it represents a common point of departure for the community, and already has become a focus for right-wing hysteria. Reagan has cited it as evidence of What They Really Want, and the conservative Berkeley Gazette, viewing it as "a declaration of war," editorialized "there is no gentle way to deal with the Berkeley Liberation Program." And yet it is a curiously modest document, raising almost no ideas that have not been raised before. It does not appear to be a blueprint for a revolutionary society; at most it is a plan for survival in a dangerous period, a list of not impossible priorities. . . .

The points call for the south campus ghetto to become "a strategic free territory for revolution," speak to the flowering of revolutionary culture and working out a humane community through communal services, housing councils, tax reform and a government of "people in motion around their own needs." The schools are to become "training grounds" of struggle, while open war is declared on the University as "a major brain center for world domination." The document demands the full liberation of women and defends "the liberating potential of drugs." It announces alliance with the Black Panther Party and "all Third World Liberation movements" and criticizes sectarian groups as "supposed vanguards seeking to manipulate mass movements." The tenth section says "we will defend ourselves against law and order" and suggests that the people must be armed and skilled in self defense and street fighting. Finally, "liberation committees" of people who can trust each other are put forward as an alternative to traditional organizing techniques.

The Liberation Program is important because Berkeley represents probably the only place in America where white revolutionaries live in a territory in which it makes sense to say they are the people, *now.* Unlike the hip enclaves in New York, Chicago, San Francisco and so on, the south campus is a valid community to itself and does not have to cope with enveloping and hostile working-class neighbors. Within this territory the people have risen and fought the police four times now in the last year. Although the future of People's Park remains unclear, people have begun to look towards many ways of implementing the basic principles of the park: community, spontaneity, and opening of time, space and life in relation to the environment. The Liberation Program speaks to the possibility of maintaining a "zone of struggle and liberation" in Berkeley. An International Liberation School is opening this month, which will teach basic survival skills: self defense, first aid, legal defense and communications. People are talking now about breakfasts for children, legal collectives, free clinics. Some are beginning to see that this is not an easy matter, it will last years, last our lives.

The next set of documents represents some of the many manifestos, proclamations, letters, speeches, and newspaper articles about People's Park. They evidence the passion the park inspired and the sense of community that was created both by the building of the park and by its destruction at the hands of university officials.

Who Owns the Park?

FRANK BARDACKE

Frank Bardacke, longtime Berkeley activist, Free Speech Movement veteran, and antiwar organizer, penned this unsigned proclamation.

Reprinted by permission, Frank Bardacke.

Someday a petty official will appear with a piece of paper, called a land title, which states that the University of California owns the land of the People's Park. Where did that piece of paper come from? What is it worth?

A long time ago the Costanoan Indians lived in the area now called Berkeley. They had no concept of land ownership. They believed that the land was under the care and guardianship of the people who used it and lived on it.

Catholic missionaries took the land away from the Indians. No agreements were made. No papers were signed. They ripped it off in the name of God.

The Mexican Government took the land away from the Church. The Mexican Government had guns and an army. God's word was not as strong.

The Mexican Government wanted to pretend that it was not the army that guaranteed them the land. They drew up some papers which said they legally owned it. No Indians signed those papers.

The Americans were not fooled by the papers. They had a stronger army than the Mexicans. They beat them in a war and took the land. Then they wrote some papers of their own and forced the Mexicans to sign them.

The American Government sold the land to some white settlers. The Government gave the settlers a piece of paper called a land title in exchange for some money. All this time there were still some Indians around who claimed the land. The American army killed most of them.

The piece of paper saying who owned the land was passed around among rich white men. Sometimes the white men were interested in taking care of the land. Usually they were just interested in making money. Finally some very rich men, who run the University of California, bought the land.

Immediately these men destroyed the houses that had been built on the land. The land went the way of so much other land in America—it became a parking lot.

We are building a park on the land. We will take care of it and guard it, in the spirit of the Costanoan Indians. When the University comes with its land title we will tell them: "Your land title is covered with blood. We won't touch it. Your people ripped off the land from the Indians a long time ago. If you want it back now, you will have to fight for it again."

Human Values and People's Park

DENISE LEVERTOV

Poet Denise Levertov, then teaching at Berkeley, addressed this open letter to fellow faculty members in the student newspaper, The Daily Californian, *May 16, 1969.*

Yesterday with some young poets (students) I was at People's Park shoveling up garbage into a truck and taking it away to the city dump. Around us others were digging, planting flowers, enjoying the sun and good fellowship, playing with children, peacefully rapping. The Park was a little island of Peace and hope in a world made filthy and hopeless by war and injustice.

Early this morning my husband and I were awakened by the familiar, ominous sound of a police helicopter zooming back and forth over the streets of Berkeley. By 7:30 A.M., when we got to the Park, the bulldozers were already destroying the happy place human beings had begun to construct for each other, and a different kind of garbage—the concrete around the bases of fence posts—was being poured into it, in place of what we had removed the day before.

A university is supposed to teach, among other things, the Humanities. Are you, brothers and sisters who teach, going to let this inhumane thing happen, in your name—our name—the name of the University of which we, the Faculty, are a part—without a squeak? Do we believe in humane values, in constructive, creative life, or don't we? Or does the average professor—as many of the kids believe, or at least suspect—consider Property as sacred, and people and their needs and aspirations as dispensable?

Reprinted courtesy of *The Daily Californian* and the author, Denise Levertov.

Their Foe Is Ours

The following letter, dated May 23, 1969, was signed by the Third World Liberation Front.

To the People of People's Park:

It is in the spirit of brotherhood that we write to you. You have shown through courageous and consistent action that you, like us, are frustrated, tired of and disgusted with the forces that conspire against us all.

We have learned in the past that you do not judge a person by what he says, or what he thinks, but by what he does. You have fought. You have been hurt. The REAL TEST IS YET TO COME. WILL YOU COME BACK? We do not suggest that you come again, unorganized, naive, and with only your moral indignation. COME BACK ORGANIZED, PREPARED TO GIVE AS WELL AS RECEIVE—COME BACK A MILLION.

And to Brother Rector, because in his death he gained a brotherhood with all oppressed people, we express our sympathies to his memory and family. AND TO YOU—ORGANIZE.

TO PEOPLE OF COLOR ON THIS CAMPUS. IT IS ALL TOO CLEAR THAT THOSE WHO TAKE A PARK AWAY ARE OF THE SAME FAMILY THAT BRUTALIZE OUR COMMUNITIES, TERRORIZE OUR WOMEN, AND DESTROY THE ESSENCE OF FREEDOM ITSELF. JOIN IN THIS STRUGGLE, WE MUST SEE THAT THEIR FOE IS OURS.

POWER TO THE PEOPLE
POWER TO THE PEOPLE OF COLOR
POWER TO THE PEOPLE OF JUSTICE

T.W.L.F. Steering Committee

Pig's Park

In December 1969 the new left magazine Hard Times *reported on the fate of the land that had once been People's Park.*

They make a desert, pave it, and call it an athletic field. Despite the Regents' plans, the land everyone knows as People's Park goes unused. The plot of Berkeley land, so bitterly fought over . . ., is now known as "Haste Field."

During the summer, under pressure from its young staff members, a University-hired architectural firm refused to design housing for the cyclone-fenced field. No other local firm will accept the contract.

The University administration has tried to lease the larger of the two parking lots to the City of Berkeley. When the City backed out, UC offered a profitable deal to a black OEO group; they could lease the land for $10 and pocket all parking fees. Now the group has backed out. "The scheme must be exposed for what it is," said their release. "Namely, a divisive tactic and possibly a planned confrontation which could end in the slaughter of many black and street people, by each other, or ultimately by the police or National Guard."

At the same time, the campus Interfraternity Council voted 30 to 1 to boycott the field. Intramural teams will not play there.

"The Regents want it to be a sports field and parking lot," a University spokesman told the Berkeley Tribe. "Whether anyone uses it is another matter."

KENT STATE AND JACKSON STATE

The American invasion of Cambodia in May 1970 prompted demonstrations across the country, including those on the campus of Kent State University in Kent, Ohio. When National Guardsmen opened fire on Kent State demonstrators on Monday, May 4, antagonism over the war seemed to reach its logical extreme, with armed forces of the American military establishment shooting and killing American antiwar protesters.

Kent State

THE PRESIDENT'S COMMISSION ON CAMPUS UNREST

The events at Kent State, followed by the shootings at Jackson State ten days later, led to the appointment of a Presidential Commission on Campus Unrest, which looked at a number of questions including these two campus incidents. Despite the dispassionate tone with which the commission's report details events at Kent, a sense of the mounting tension and the horror of the killings emanates from its description.

The first disturbance began Friday evening on North Water Street, a downtown area where six bars, popular with young people, are located. Some of these bars feature rock bands. . . .

May 1 was one of the first warm Friday nights of the spring. A sizable crowd of young people, some of whom were discussing Cambodia, gathered in and around the bars. About 11:00 P.M., they began to jeer passing police cars.

Kent's small police force had fewer than 10 men on duty when the disturbance began. Four of these men in two patrol cars were specifically assigned to North Water Street.

The crowd grew increasingly boisterous. They began to chant slogans, and a motorcycle gang called the "Chosen Few" performed some tricks with their bikes. Shortly before 11:30 P.M., someone threw a bottle at a passing police car. The Kent city police ceased efforts to patrol the street and waited for reinforcements from the day shift and from other law enforcement agencies.

Some of the crowd, which had grown to about 500, started a bonfire in the street. Soon the crowd blocked the street and began to stop motorists to ask their opinion about Cambodia. . . .

Some demonstrators began to break store windows with rocks. A few items were stolen from the display windows of a shoe store and a jewelry store. A fertilizer spreader was taken from a hardware store and thrown through the window of a bank. In all, 47 windows in 15 establishments were broken, and two police officers were cut by thrown missiles.

At 12:30 A.M., after the trashing had begun, Kent Mayor LeRoy M. Satrom declared a state of emergency and ordered the bars closed. The assembled force of city police and sheriff's deputies then moved to clear the street, which became even more crowded as evicted patrons poured out of the bars. . . .

Fifteen persons, all with Ohio addresses, were arrested that night, most of them on charges of disorderly conduct.

SATURDAY, MAY 2

Against the background of Friday night's activities, rumors proliferated. . . .

When 40 uniformed ROTC cadets gathered early Saturday morning at the ROTC building to be transported to a rifle range, students who saw them spread a report that the National Guard was on campus. . . .

In the wake of Friday night's window-breaking in Kent, the university administration launched a strenuous effort to restore order among students. . . .

At the university, a crowd had assembled on the Commons around the Victory Bell by 7:30 P.M. The group appeared to be an idle collection of students whom the curfew had prevented from going downtown. . . .

On the Commons, a young man is reported to have jumped up on the brick structure from which the Victory Bell is suspended and to have said, "They're trying to keep the kids penned up in the dorms. Let's go."

The crowd soon moved off toward Tri-Towers, a complex of dormitories where one of the specially arranged dances was being held. Faculty marshals observed them as they followed the usual student parade route around the dormitories, picking up new recruits as they went. By the time they headed back toward the Commons, the crowd had grown to around 1,000, and some were chanting, "Ho, Ho, Ho Chi Minh," and "One, two, three, four, we don't want your fucking war." As they crossed the Commons near the ROTC building, some shouted, "Get it," "Burn it," and "ROTC has to go.". . .

The ROTC building was an obvious target. It was a two-story wooden structure—an old World War II-type Army barracks—and it looked easy to ignite. Many students saw it as evidence that the university supported the Vietnam war effort by maintaining a military training program on campus.

About 8:10 P.M., a few students began to throw rocks at the ROTC building. In a short while, flying rocks had broken some of the building's windows. A few in the crowd appeared to have brought bags of rocks to the scene. A group used an ash can as a battering ram to break in a window; some started throwing lighted railroad flares into and onto the building. A curtain caught fire. In the crowd, someone burned a miniature American flag. . . .

Finally, a young man dipped a cloth into the gasoline tank of a parked motorcycle. Another young man ignited it and set the building afire. The building began to burn about 8:45 P.M. . . .

As the campus police marched up in riot gear, someone shouted, "Here come the pigs." The police fired tear gas at the crowd, which then left the ROTC building area and moved across the Commons. . . .

Aware of the turmoil on campus, Mayor Satrom had called General Del Corso's office at 8:35 P.M. to renew his request for troops. He spoke to Colonel Simmons. Acting under the directions left him by General Del Corso, Simmons called the Akron bivouac and ordered the troops to Kent. . . .

SUNDAY, MAY 3

At 10:00 A.M. Sunday, while Kent State President White was on his way home from Iowa by plane, Governor Rhodes arrived in Kent and held a news conference. . . .

Governor Rhodes called the Kent disturbances "probably the most vicious form of campus-oriented violence yet perpetrated by dissident groups and their allies in the state of Ohio" and told his listeners that "we are going to employ every force of law that we have under our authority.". . .

Students began gathering on the Commons about 8:00 P.M. The crowd was peaceful and included a group of coeds kicking a soccer ball around. But by 8:45 P.M., it had grown so large that campus police and the Highway Patrol suggested to Colonel Finley that the 1:00 A.M. campus curfew be cancelled and an immediate curfew imposed. As a result, shortly before 9:00 P.M., Major Jones read the Ohio Riot Act to the crowd on the Commons and gave them five minutes to disperse. When they did not, police proceeded to disperse them with tear gas. . . .

Fifty-one persons were arrested Sunday night, most of them for curfew violations. This brought the total of arrests to more than 100 since the disturbances had begun. . . .

MONDAY, MAY 4

As they lined up opposite students on the Commons shortly before noon, the three National Guard units involved in the Kent State shooting had had an average of three hours of sleep the night before. . . .

A call for a noon rally on the Commons was passed around the campus by word of mouth and by announcements chalked on class-room blackboards. The precise purpose was not made clear, but most students assumed it was to protest the presence of the National Guard, which by now was resented by many students, even by many who held no deep political beliefs.

General Canterbury called a meeting for 10:00 A.M. Monday to discuss plans for the day and to reduce confusion over the curfew hours. He attended the meeting in civilian clothes to avoid attracting attention. . . .

Canterbury testified before the Commission that he first learned about the rally during this meeting. When he asked White if it should be permitted, White replied, "No, it would be highly dangerous."

Throughout the morning, guardsmen patrolled the campus without notable incident.

About 11:00 A.M., students began gathering on the Commons, apparently for a variety of reasons. Some had heard vaguely that a rally would be held. Some came to protest the presence of the Guard. Some were simply curious, or had free time because their classes had been cancelled. Some students stopped by on their way to or from lunch or class. The Commons is a crossroads between several major university buildings.

Many students who described themselves as "straight," or conservative, later attributed their presence at the rally to a desire to protest against the National Guard. This attitude was reflected in the testimony of one Kent State coed before the Commission:

> I just really couldn't believe it. It was a very unreal feeling to walk up on your Front Campus and see these armed troops. You know, like you had been invaded, in a way. . . .
>
> I had my books with me and I had a report due in the next hour and I intended to go to class. It was when I found I couldn't go across campus, I decided to go to the rally. . . .
>
> I just couldn't believe the Guards were on campus. It was mostly, just outrage and disgust and fear, and all sorts of crazy things. I just couldn't believe that my campus had been taken over by Guards. You know, they said I couldn't cross the campus, they said we can't assemble on the campus. I stood on the Commons. I was watching the Guards and thinking, they are telling us to leave, but this is our campus, we belong here and they don't. That is why I stayed mostly.

This coed was gassed on the Commons, moved back over Blanket Hill to the Prentice Hall parking lot, and was within three feet of Allison Krause when Miss Krause was killed. . . .

By 11:45 the crowd had grown to more than 500. The principal group gathered around the Victory Bell about 170 yards across the Common from the burned-out ROTC building, where the guardsmen were stationed. Canterbury ordered the crowd dispersed.

[Lt. Col. Charles] Fassinger then ordered troops to form up by the ruins of the ROTC building. Some 40 to 50 men from Company A, about 35 to 45 men from Company C, and 18 men from Troop G were hurriedly assembled. Those who had not already done so were ordered to "lock and load" their weapons. By this process an M-1 rifle is loaded with an eight-round clip of .30 caliber ball ammunition, and one bullet is moved up into the chamber ready to fire. The weapon will then fire immediately after the safety mechanism is disengaged and the trigger is pulled. Throughout the weekend, whenever guardsmen were on duty, their weapons were locked and loaded.

A Kent State policeman, Harold E. Rice, stood near the ROTC ruins and, using a bullhorn, ordered the students to disperse. It is doubtful that Rice was heard over the noise of the crowd. A jeep was brought up. Rice, a driver, and two Guard riflemen drove out across the Commons toward the crowd. Rice gave the dispersal order again.

The students responded with curses and stones. Some chanted "Pigs off campus" and "One, two, three, four, we don't want your fucking war." Rocks bounced off the jeep, and Rice said the occupants were hit several times.

Specialist Fifth Class Gordon R. Bedall, who was in the jeep, said Rice saw a student in the crowd who, Rice believed, was one of the instigators of the weekend disturbances. Rice asked the driver to direct the jeep into the crowd so that he could pick up this young man and take him back. According to the driver, a shower of rocks from several students forced the jeep back twice. Major Jones was dispatched from the Guard lines to order the jeep to return.

At 11:58 A.M., as the jeep returned, Canterbury ordered the 96 men and seven officers to form a skirmish line, shoulder to shoulder, and to move out across the Commons toward the students. Each man's weapon was locked and loaded. Canterbury estimated the size of the crowd on the Commons at about 800; another 1,000 or more persons were sitting or milling about on the hills surrounding the Commons. His goal as he moved out was to disperse the crowd. . . .

Shortly before noon, students began to ring the Victory Bell. Two generalized emotions seemed to have prevailed among the 2,000 or so young persons who were now on or near the Commons. One was a vague feeling that something worth watching or participating in would occur, that something was going to happen and that the Guard would respond. The other was antipathy to the Guard, bitter in some cases, accompanied by the feeling that the Guard, although fully backed by official pronouncements, was somehow "trespassing" on the students' own territory.

A majority of the crowd was watching the tableau from the patio of Taylor Hall and from the slopes around the adjacent buildings. . . . Most of the onlooking students could not be described as neutral: in almost any quarrel between students and guardsmen, they would take the side of their fellow students.

The troops lined up with fixed bayonets across the northwestern corner of the Commons. On orders from Canterbury relayed by Fassinger, eight to ten grenadiers with M-79 grenade launchers fired two volleys of tear gas canisters at the crowd, which began to scatter. . . .

The day was bright and sunny, and a 14-mile-an-hour breeze was blowing. The tear gas did not at first scatter all the students: the wind blew some of the gas away; the aim of some of the grenadiers was poor, causing many who were only spectators to be gassed; and some of the students picked up the tear gas canisters and threw them back. Canterbury ordered the troops to move out. . . .

The guardsmen marched across the flat Commons, the students scattering before them up a steep hill beyond the Victory Bell. Canterbury's original plan was to march to the crest of Blanket Hill, a knoll beyond the bell, between the northern end of Johnson Hall and southern end of Taylor Hall. When some of the students ran to the north end of Taylor Hall, he sent a contingent of men around there to disperse them. He had hoped, after clearing the Commons, to withdraw his troops to the ROTC building.

When Canterbury reached the crest of Blanket Hill, however, he concluded that it would be necessary to push the students beyond a football practice field which lay about 80 yards below the crest of Blanket Hill.

By this time the crowd seemed more united in mood. The feeling had spread among students that they were being harassed as a group, that state and civic officials had united against them, and that the university had either cooperated or acquiesced in their suppression. They reacted to the guardsmen's march with substantial solidarity. They shouted, "Pigs off campus," and called the guardsmen "green pigs" and "fascist bastards."

Rocks flew as the guardsmen marched across the Commons. Capt. Snyder, the C Company commander, said a young man near Taylor

Hall struck him twice with stones. When the young man refused Snyder's order to put the rocks down, Snyder knocked him down with his baton. The youth scrambled to his feet and ran away.

The antagonism between guardsmen and students increased. The guardsmen generally felt that the students, who had disobeyed numerous orders to disperse, were clearly in the wrong. The razing of the ROTC building had shown them that these noisy youths were capable of considerable destruction.

Many students felt that the campus was their "turf." Unclear about the authority vested in the Guard by the governor, or indifferent to it, some also felt that their constitutional right to free assembly was being infringed upon. As they saw it, they had been ordered to disperse at a time when no rocks had been thrown and no other violence had been committed. Many told interviewers later, "We weren't doing anything."

The guardsmen marched down the east slope of Blanket Hill, across an access road, and onto the football practice field, which is fenced in on three sides. The crowd parted to let them down the hill to the field and then reformed in two loose groups—one on Blanket Hill, above the football field, and the other in the Prentice Hall parking lot at the north end of the field. The crowd on the parking lot was unruly and threw many missiles at guardsmen on the football field. It was at this point that the shower of stones apparently became heaviest. Nearby construction projects provided an ample supply of rocks.

Tear gas canisters were still flying back and forth; after the Guard would shoot a canister, students sometimes would pick it up and lob it back at the guardsmen. In some cases, guardsmen would pick up the same canister and throw it at the students. Some among the crowd came to regard the situation as a game—"a tennis match" one called it—and cheered each exchange of tear gas canisters. Only a few students participated in this game, however. One of them was Jeffrey Glenn Miller. A few minutes later, Miller was fatally shot.

As the confrontation worsened, some students left the scene. Among those who departed was a student who had gone to the rally with a classmate, William Schroeder. Subsequently, Schroeder was killed.

While on the football field, about a dozen guardsmen knelt and pointed their weapons at the students in the Prentice Hall parking lot, apparently as a warning or a threatening gesture. Whether any shot was fired on the field is in dispute.

Richard A. Schreiber, an assistant professor of journalism at Kent State, said he was watching the action through binoculars from the balcony of Taylor Hall when he saw an officer fire one shot from a .45 caliber automatic pistol at a 45-degree angle over the heads of rock-throwers in a nearby parking lot. . . .

As the guardsmen withdrew from the field, many students thought either that they had run out of tear gas or that there was nothing more they could do in their strategically weak position. Many felt a sense of relief, believing all danger was over. Most expected the Guard to march back over Blanket Hill to the ROTC building. . . .

The movements of the crowd in the last minute or two before the firing are the subject of considerable dispute. . . . General Canterbury:

> As the troop formation reached the area of the Pagoda near Taylor Hall, the mob located on the right flank in front of Taylor Hall and in the Prentice Hall parking lot charged our right flank, throwing rocks, yelling obscenities and threats, "Kill the pigs," "Stick the pigs." The attitude of the crowd at this point was menacing and vicious.

General Canterbury also testified that the closest students were within four to five yards of the Guard. . . . The nearest person wounded, Joseph Lewis, Jr., who was 20 yards away, said there was no one between him and the Guard. The closest person killed, Jeffrey Glenn Miller, was at least 85 yards away.

An 8-millimeter motion picture film, taken by an amateur cameraman from a point approximately 500 yards northeast of the firing line, indicates that the main body of aggressive students was about 60 to 75 yards away, at the foot of the hill near the corner of the Prentice Hall parking lot.

Movie film and testimony indicate that as guardsmen reached the top of the hill, some students surged from the east face of Taylor Hall and the southern end of the parking lot up toward the guardsmen on Blanket Hill. The film is too indistinct to tell how many of the students involved in this movement were throwing rocks. The leading edge of this crowd appears to have advanced to a point no closer than 20 yards from the guardsmen, with the main body 60 to 75 yards away, before the gunfire began and they reversed their direction. It is possible that some of them had no aggressive intent but instead began running up the hill in the direction of the Guard to get a good vantage point on Blanket Hill after, as they expected, the guardsmen retreated down the far side of the slope.

Near the crest of Blanket Hill stands the Pagoda, a square bench made of 4-by-4 wooden beams and shaded by a concrete umbrella. The events which occurred as the Guard reached the Pagoda, turned, and fired on the students, are in bitter dispute.

Many guardsmen said they had hard going as they withdrew up the hill. Fassinger said he was hit six times by stones, once on the shoulder so hard that he stumbled.

Fassinger had removed his gas mask to see more clearly. He said the guardsmen had reached a point between the Pagoda and Taylor Hall, and he was attempting to maintain them in a reasonably orderly formation, when he heard a sound like a shot, which was immediately followed by a volley of shots. He saw the troops on the Taylor Hall end of the line shooting. He yelled, "Cease fire!" and ran along the line repeating the command.

Major Jones said he first heard an explosion which he thought was a firecracker. As he turned to his left, he heard another explosion which he knew to be an M-1 rifle shot. As he turned to his right, toward Taylor Hall, he said he saw guardsmen kneeling (photographs show some crouching) and bringing their rifles to their shoulders. He heard another M-1 shot, and then a volley of them. He yelled, "Cease fire!" several times, and rushed down the line shoving rifle barrels up and away from the crowd. He hit several guardsmen on their helmets with his swagger stick to stop them from firing.

General Canterbury stated that he first heard a single shot, which he thought was fired from some distance away on his left and which in his opinion did not come from a military weapon. Immediately afterward, he heard a volley of M-1 fire from his right, the Taylor Hall end of the line. The Guard's fire was directed away from the direction from which Canterbury thought the initial, nonmilitary shot came. His first reaction, like that of Fassinger and Jones, was to stop the firing.

Canterbury, Fassinger, and Jones—the three ranking officers on the Hill—all said no order to fire was given.

Twenty-eight guardsmen have acknowledged firing from Blanket Hill. Of these, 25 fired 55 shots from rifles, two fired five shots from .45 caliber pistols, and one fired a single blast from a shotgun. Sound tracks indicate that the firing of these 61 shots lasted approximately 13 seconds. The time of the shooting was approximately 12:25 P.M.

Four persons were killed and nine were wounded. . . .

Of the casualties, two were shot in the front, seven from the side, and four from the rear. All 13 were students at Kent State University. . . .

Sandra Lee Scheuer, 20, a junior, is believed to have been on her way to a 1:10 P.M. class in the Music and Speech Building when she was struck. She has not been identified in any available photographs as having attended the prohibited noon rally on the Commons.

Allison B. Krause, 19, a freshman, was among the group of students gathered on the Commons by the Victory Bell shortly before noon. After her death, small fragments of concrete and cinder block were found in the pockets of her jacket.

Jeffrey Glenn Miller, 20, a junior, was present in the crowd on the Commons when the dispersal order was given and made obscene gestures with his middle fingers at guardsmen. He also threw back a tear gas canister at the Guard while it was on the football practice field.

William K. Schroeder, 19, a sophomore, was an ROTC cadet. A photograph shows him retreating up Blanket Hill from the rally on the Commons, but he is not shown taking part in any of the harassment of the Guard.

Get Off Our Campus

TOM GRACE

One of the Kent students hit by National Guard bullets, Tom Grace recounts that Monday morning.

The crowd had grouped around the victory bell, which had been historically used to signal victories in Kent State football games, and the bell was being sounded to signal students to congregate. There were at the very least another thousand or so observers and onlookers ringing the hills that surround this part of the commons. . . .

At that point, a campus policeman in a National Guard jeep ordered the crowd, through the use of a bullhorn, to disperse and go to their homes. . . . We felt that this was our campus, that we were doing nothing wrong, and that they had no right to order us to disperse. If anyone ought to leave, it's them, not us. That's how I felt.

I was standing there yelling and screaming along with everyone else, and then someone flung either a rock or a bottle at the jeep, which bounced harmlessly off the tire. I don't think it was necessarily meant to bounce off the tire; fortunately the person was not a very good shot. That, of course, alarmed the occupants of the jeep. I think they realized at that point—because of the crescendo the chants had reached, and also the fact that people were pitching objects in their direction—that we weren't going to leave.

So the jeep drove back to the National Guard lines which had formed on the other side of the commons in front of the remains of the burned ROTC building. Then the National Guardsmen leveled their bayonets at us and started to march across the commons in our direction, shooting tear gas as they came. . . .

I retreated to a girls' dormitory where there were some first-floor restrooms. The female students had opened up the windows and were passing out moistened paper towels so people could relieve the effects of the tear gas. So I went and I cleansed my eyes to the best of my ability, and that seemed to take care of me at the moment. . . .

Then I remember that the National Guard troop seemed to get into a little huddle before leaving the practice football field. They reformed their lines and proceeded back up the hill. It was almost like the parting of the Red Sea. The students just moved to one side or the other to let the National Guardsmen pass, because no one in their right mind would have stood there as bayonets were coming.

A lot of people were screaming, "Get out of here, get off our campus," and in the midst of all this were some students, oddly enough, who were still wandering through the area with their textbooks, as if they were completely unaware of all that was taking place. I felt that I was still keeping a safe distance. I was 150, 165 feet away. I know that because it's since been paced off.

When the National Guardsmen got to the top of the hill, all of a sudden there was just a quick movement, a flurry of activity, and then a crack, or two cracks of rifle fire, and I thought, Oh, my God! I turned and started running as fast as I could. I don't think I got more than a step or two, and all of a sudden I was on the ground. It was just like somebody had come over and given me a body blow and knocked me right down.

The bullet had entered my left heel and had literally knocked me off my feet. I tried to raise myself, and I heard someone yelling, "Stay down, stay down! It's buckshot!". . .

So I threw myself back to the ground and lay as prone as possible to shield myself as much as I could, although like most people I was caught right in the open. I couldn't run, because I had already been hit. There was no cover. I just hugged the ground so as to expose as little of my body as possible to the gunfire.

It seemed like the bullets were going by within inches of my head. I can remember seeing people behind me, farther down the hill in the parking lot, dropping. I didn't know if they were being hit by bullets or they were just hugging the ground. We know today that it only lasted thirteen seconds, but it seemed like it kept going and going and going. And I remember thinking, When is this going to stop?

So I was lying there, and all of a sudden this real husky, well-built guy ran to me, picked me up like I was a sack of potatoes, and threw me over his shoulder. He carried me through the parking lot in the direction of a girls' dormitory. We went by one body, a huge puddle of blood. Head wounds always bleed very badly, and his was just awful.

The female students were screaming as I was carried into the dormitory and placed on a couch, bleeding all over the place. A nursing student applied a tourniquet to my leg. I never really felt that my life was in danger, but I could look down at my foot and I knew that I had one hell of a bad wound. The bullet blew the shoe right off my foot, and there was a bone sticking through my green sock. It looked like somebody had put my foot through a meatgrinder.

The ambulances came. Some attendants came in, put me on a stretcher, and carried me outside. The blood loss had lessened because of the tourniquet that was on my leg. I remember having my fist up in the air as a sign of defiance. They put me into the top tier in the ambulance rather than the lower one, which was already occupied. I remember my foot hitting the edge of the ambulance as

I went in. From that moment on, until the time that I actually went under from the anesthesia at Robinson Memorial Hospital, I was probably in the most intense pain that I've ever experienced in my life.

They had the back doors closed by this time, and the ambulance was speeding away from the campus. I looked down and saw Sandy Scheuer. I had met Sandy about a week or two beforehand for the first and only time. She had been introduced to me by one of the guys who lived downstairs in my apartment complex. They were casual friends, and she struck me as being a very nice person.

She had a gaping bullet wound in the neck, and the ambulance attendants were tearing away the top two buttons of her blouse and then doing a heart massage. I remember their saying that it's no use, she's dead. And then they just pulled up the sheet over her head.

What Did They Expect, Spitballs?

JAMES MICHENER

James Michener, the best-selling novelist, wrote a nonfiction account of the events at Kent. Among his interviews are several reactions from townspeople and others that clearly display the extraordinary hostility engendered by antiwar demonstrators, student activists, and hippies. This is merely a brief sampling of these reactions.

Authority, law and order are the backbone of our society, for its protection. Would you want authorities to stand by if your home were threatened? Well, Kent State is my home by virtue of taxes spent funding it. What's more, it's their home by virtue of tuition paid. Playful children destroying a disenchanting toy.

How dare they! I stand behind the action of the National Guard! I want my property defended. And if dissenters refuse to obey the final warning before the punishment, hurling taunts, rocks (stones, they say), sticks, brandishing clubs with razor blades imbedded, then the first slap is a mighty sting.

Live ammunition! Well, really, what did they expect, spitballs? How much warning is needed indeed.

Hooray! I shout for God and Country, recourse to justice under law, fifes, drums, martial music, parades, ice cream cones—America, support it or leave it.

Ravenna [Ohio] housewife

When radical students are allowed to go through a town smashing windows, terrifying the citizens, and are allowed to burn buildings belonging to the taxpayers to the ground, I think it is high time that the Guard be brought in to stop them—and stop them in any way they can.

The sooner the students of this country learn that they are not running this country, that they are going to college to learn, *not teach*, the better.

If those students don't like this country or our colleges, why don't they go to the country from which they are being indoctrinated?

Concerned citizen

We are paying a large percentage of our hard-earned money to support and educate these young people. For what? To let them burn and destroy property that more of our tax money has paid for? Who paid for the hose that was cut while our firemen were trying to stop a fire, set deliberately, all the while being pelted with rocks. Some innocent person's home could very well have burned while our firemen were busy fighting a fire on campus.

Concerned resident

Some have questioned the need of the National Guard on campus and throughout our city. However, I shudder to think of the condition of our city today had they had not been present to protect and preserve what so many have labored endlessly to build.

Kent citizen

Congratulations to the Guardsmen for their performance of duty on the Kent University Campus. I hope their actions serve as an example for the entire nation. The governors of our states cannot waste the taxpayers' money playing games. These men were alerted as a last resort to control mob action.

I extend appreciation and whole-hearted support of the Guard of every state for their fine efforts in protecting citizens like me and our property.

Mother of Guardsman

I have one possible solution to the problem. Build a fence completely around KSU, put President White and his 550 faculty members inside along with all the agitators that they understand so well and let them do their thing. We could also change the name from KSU to "Idiot Hill." Then Dr. White and his faculty and students could assemble and throw rocks at each other and play with matches and burn things down, because they understand each other's reasoning and don't want to be bothered.

So be it! I have more ideas, but what's the use. In fact, who needs KSU? Not me.

Kent taxpayer

Kent has tolerated these so-called misunderstood students long enough. The city of Kent should be off-limits to students. Keep them on the university grounds, and when they have completely destroyed it, they can go home and we will be rid of them.

If the National Guard is forced to face these situations without loaded guns, the silent majority has lost everything. The National Guard made only one mistake—they should have fired sooner and longer.

As for the parents of the dead students, I can appreciate their suffering, they probably don't know the truth. A dissident certainly isn't going to write home about his demonstration activities. Parents are learning the hard way and others should take heed. The high school photos that appeared in the paper were all very nice, but how do you explain the mother who refused to identify her own son at the hospital because of his appearance. This same boy had refused to go home on holidays.

I only hope the National Guard will be there the next time we need them. I am fully prepared to protect what is mine—property, home and life—at any cost against these mobs of dissidents in the event our law enforcement is prohibited to do what is necessary.

Ravenna citizen

It is too bad that a small minority of students feel that these damnable demonstrations must take place. If the slouchily dressed female students and the freakishly dressed, long-haired male students would properly dress and otherwise properly demean themselves as not to make show-offs of themselves, such trouble could be and would be avoided. It is difficult to understand why female students must get out and make such fools of themselves as they do, but it is understandable that male students do so largely to get their screwball mugs on television and in the press.

If the troublemaking students have no better sense than to conduct themselves as they do on our university and college campuses, such as throwing missiles, bottles and bullets at legally constituted police authority and the National Guard, they justly deserve the consequences that they bring upon themselves, even if this does unfortunately result in death.

Attorney-at-law

Jackson State

THE PRESIDENT'S COMMISSION ON CAMPUS UNREST

Ten days after the shootings at Kent State, National Guard and police forces in Jackson, Mississippi, fired on students at Jackson State University. Again, as the President's Commission report describes the events, the profound impact emerges from the disinterested presentation of the facts. For many Americans, especially those within the antiwar movement, two campus shootings within days of each other seemed to signal a new and violent turn in the politics of confrontation.

Disturbances began shortly after dusk on Wednesday, May 13. The triggering incident is undetermined, but by 9:00 P.M. rocks were being thrown at white motorists from a crowd of about 100 persons gathered on both sides of Lynch Street in front of Alexander Hall. Shortly thereafter, a Jackson City Police patrol car traveling west on Lynch Street was struck by a missile. By 9:45 P.M., there were approximately 150 persons, both men and women, in the Alexander Hall area. Most of them were students, and more than three fourths of those present were passive onlookers.

At approximately 10:00 P.M., Jackson City Police units established roadblocks on Lynch Street and on Pearl Street to seal off the campus. The rock-throwing stopped. . . .

At approximately 10:15 P.M. Edward Curtis, Dean of Men, accompanied by Sergeant M. P. Stringer of the security force, informed the crowd in front of Alexander Hall that President Peoples had imposed a 10:30 P.M. curfew. Some students went toward their dormitories, but many remained on the street. Little was done to enforce the curfew.

Jackson's Mayor Russell Davis spoke with the governor at about this time and requested that the National Guard be mobilized and the Mississippi Highway Patrol placed on standby.

At about 10:30 P.M. security officer George Jones was driving onto the campus in his pickup truck. A rock struck and shattered his left vent window as he passed in front of Stewart Hall, where about 200 persons were massed. Some in the crowd moved toward the truck. Jones fired three shots into the air with his revolver and then drove quickly to security police headquarters. . . .

As the evening progressed, security officers increasingly heard reports that the students intended to march on the college ROTC building located some 150 yards south of Stewart Hall. At about 10:45 P.M. approximately 100 students and neighborhood youths broke from the crowd in the vicinity of Stewart Hall and moved toward the ROTC building. Dean Curtis and security officer Stringer went to the area, where they were joined by the commanding officer of the ROTC unit. With assistance from student leaders, they managed to quiet and disperse most of the crowd. . . .

The city police and highway patrol units linked up before 11:30 P.M. They moved on foot to the ROTC building. As they passed Stewart Hall, the combined units were jeered by a crowd estimated at 250 to 300 persons. Rocks and other objects were thrown at them, but there were no injuries. Obscenities were shouted.

Martel Cook, a black reporter and part-time student at Jackson State, came from the campus area to the barricade. He informed the mayor that the situation was quieting down. Cook advised that there might be bloodshed if the police went in. Two other students also urged the mayor not to send the police back to the campus. . . .

Sometime after midnight, the crowd gradually began to disperse. By the early hours of the morning the disturbance was over and the campus was quiet. . . .

At about 3:00 A.M. the Adjutant General of Mississippi, Major General Walter Johnson, visited Dr. Peoples at his home and informed him that the Mississippi National Guard had been placed on alert. He told Dr. Peoples that tear gas probably would be used if disorders developed on the following day. Dr. Peoples was advised that gas masks would be brought to his home for him and members of his family. . . .

EVENTS OF MAY 14, 1970

There was some apprehension at Jackson State College Thursday, May 14, but the campus was quiet and class attendance was normal. . . .

At 7:30 P.M., a National Guard log recorded that 647 guardsmen were on duty and stationed at an armory in Jackson. The armory was more than a 20-minute drive from the campus.

Around 9:30 P.M., a small group in the vicinity of Stewart Hall began throwing rocks at passing white motorists. Lynch Street soon was sealed off as it had been the night before. The crowd swelled to between 100 and 200 persons, most of them onlookers who cheered the rock-throwers. . . .

Reports were coming in to the Jackson police department that the situation on campus was worsening. Around 10:15 P.M. a policeman gave a radio order: "Call that security guard out there at Jackson State and see if they can't scatter them niggers."

At the National Guard armory, an officer was monitoring the police radio reports. At some point between 10:30 P.M. and 11:00 P.M. he suggested to General Johnson that National Guardsmen be put on trucks, ready to roll onto the campus. After General Johnson listened to the police radio for a few minutes, he ordered the guardsmen to move to positions on Lynch Street near both ends of the campus. If called in, he wanted to be ready to move onto the campus at once. It was around 11:00 P.M. . . .

The crowd at Stewart Hall grew in size. Students from the dormitory joined the demonstrators in jeering and yelling insults and obscenities. . . . Rocks and pieces of brick were thrown, but there were no serious injuries to firemen or police officers. . . .

There were conflicting reports of small caliber gunfire from the area of Stewart Hall. Some highway patrolmen chased a group of persons into an alleyway adjoining Stewart Hall. Objects were thrown at them, and a patrolman fired a shotgun blast into a fourth-story window. No one was struck by the shot.

The gunfire from the highway patrol disturbed General Johnson, and he decided the National Guard should move onto the campus and relieve the highway patrol and city police. . . .

The National Guard was armed with special riot shotguns that hold seven rounds. The first four rounds are No. 9 birdshot, the smallest pellet used in shotguns, backed up by three rounds of double-O buckshot, the heaviest used in shotguns. City police carried shotguns loaded with heavy No. 1 buckshot. Most highway patrolmen were armed with shotguns loaded with double-O buckshot, others carried personally owned rifles or carbines, and two were armed with loaded submachine guns.

The National Guard and city police each had men specially assigned for antisniper duty, senior sharpshooters armed with rifles. Although the highway patrol manual indicates formal procedures for controlling sniper fire, Jones and a majority of his men considered each individual officer authorized to shoot any time he saw a sniper if he believed lives were threatened.

After reaching Alexander Hall, the tank stopped in front of or slightly east of the west wing. With few exceptions, the city police were in a line south and east of the tank, and the highway patrolmen were in a line north and west of the tank, nearer the crowd. There were highway patrolmen within 20 feet of the nearest member of the crowd, most of whom had moved behind a 3 1/2-foot high chain-link fence along a sidewalk

Estimates of the size of the crowd range all the way from 40 to 400. Along the fence in front of Alexander Hall, a campus security officer was urging students to disperse. There were jeers, obscene epithets, and a chant of "Pigs! Pigs!" Many girls inside the dormitory watched from their rooms and from stairwell landings in the west wing. Behind the police—on the south side of the street—a smaller group of demonstrators and onlookers stood near Roberts Dining Hall behind a chain-link fence which runs on top of a concrete retaining wall.

Soon after the peace officers and their tank stopped, the insults grew louder. Two TV newsmen, Bert Case and Jack Hobbs, moved into the area of the skirmish line. . . .

Someone threw a bottle from the lawn behind the fence in front of Alexander Hall. Almost simultaneously, another bottle was lobbed from behind the retaining wall across the street, to the rear of the police line. One line of city police had turned to face that direction after some objects were thrown. . . .

Almost instantaneously, a general barrage of shotgun, carbine, rifle, and submachine gun fire began. Case, standing beside Hobbs, recalled that "the bottle crashed and the next thing I remember, they were firing."

Case looked toward the officers, saw their guns pointed upward, and his first impression was that the officers were firing into the air over Alexander Hall or possibly shooting tear gas.

When Case heard the shattering of glass in Alexander Hall, he realized that the officers were actually firing into the building. To him, it appeared they "systematically" shot into the windows from the top floor down to the bottom.

A college official who was standing a block away later said, "The whole sky lighted up."

The students at first thought that blanks or tear gas were being fired. Those outside began running for the hallway entrance, then began diving for cover.

In the doorway in front of the officers, one student, then others, fell. The entrance was blocked, as students struggled to find shelter.

Phillip Gibbs, a married 20-year-old junior and father of an 18-month-old son, was struck by a shotgun blast about 50 feet east of the west wing doorway of Alexander Hall. One buckshot pellet entered his left underarm area and two more entered his head, one just beneath the left eye, fatally penetrating the brain.

James Earl Green was standing in front of Roberts Hall, across Lynch Street from Alexander Hall. A student saw him run to the side of Roberts Hall, stop suddenly, and fall. He was killed by a buckshot slug which entered his side and traveled through his liver, left lung, and heart. Green was a high school student. . . .

Bert Case made a tape recording of the gunfire. The fusillade lasted 28 seconds.

Many of the officers emptied shotguns containing four rounds of buckshot. One patrolman, who fired four rounds, reloaded and fired four more, and reloaded and fired again. He told a Commission staff investigator he did not know "how many times" he reloaded and emptied his gun.

In all, more than 150 rounds were fired. Most were fired into the air, but FBI investigation showed that nearly 400 bullets or pieces of buckshot struck Alexander Hall. . . .

At the scene of the shooting, two newsmen recalled, the atmosphere among the officers was one of "some levity," and many officers engaged in casual small talk. Inspector Jones reported that two students were "10-7," radio code for "Out of Service." The radio tape continued:

Got one more female shot here—think it's serious.

A total of six injured there?

No, we got two more males, they say.

I think there are about three more nigger males over there, one of 'em shot in the arm, one of 'em shot in the leg, and one of 'em somewhere else. They ain't hurt all that bad. Them gals, it was two nigger gals, two more nigger gals from over there shot in the arm I believe. One of 'em is over there in the east end. I told . . . there two nigger females and three males we just discovered, that's a total of ten. . . . Here's another one, let me see what is this.

All persons killed or injured by gunshot were black.

GAY LIBERATION

Discrimination and overt hostility toward homosexuals were prevalent in American society and were not issues on the agenda of straight Americans, even those working for the civil rights of minorities and women. In the late 1960s, however, gays and lesbians began the movement aimed at legitimizing their claims for equal treatment. This effort continues into the 1990s.

Gay Power Comes to Sheridan Square

LUCIAN K. TRUSCOTT

The confrontation between police and gay men at the gay bar, the Stonewall Inn, on June 27, 1969, is considered the first public eruption of the movement for gay rights. The following assessment initially appeared in The Village Voice. *Written on a three-hour deadline, it was only the third story Truscott had ever written for publication.*

Sheridan Square this weekend looked like something from a William Burroughs novel as the sudden specter of "gay power" erected its brazen head and spat out a fairy tale the likes of which the area has never seen.

The forces of faggotry, spurred by a Friday night raid on one of the city's largest, most popular, and longest lived gay bars, the Stonewall Inn, rallied Saturday night in an unprecedented protest against the raid and continued Sunday night to assert presence, possibility, and pride until the early hours of Monday morning. "I'm a faggot, and I'm proud of it!" "Gay power!" "I like boys!"—these and many other slogans were heard all three nights as the show of force by the city's finery met the force of the city's finest. The result was a kind of liberation, as the gay brigade emerged from the bars, back rooms, and bedrooms of the Village and became street people.

It began as a small raid—only two patrolmen, two detectives, and two policewomen were involved. But as the patrons trapped inside were released one by one, a crowd started to gather on the street. It was initially a festive gathering, composed mostly of Stonewall boys who were waiting around for friends still inside. Cheers went up as favorites emerged from the door, striking a pose and swishing by the detective with a "Hello there, fella." Wrists were limp and hair was primped. The stars were in their element.

Suddenly a paddywagon arrived and the mood of the crowd changed. Three of the more blatant queens—in full drag—were loaded inside, along with the bartender and doorman, to a chorus of catcalls and boos from the crowd. A cry went up to push the paddywagon over, but it drove away before anything could happen. The next person to come out was a dyke, and she put up a struggle. At that moment, the scene became explosive. Limp wrists were forgotten. Beer cans and bottles were heaved at the windows, and a rain of coins descended on the cops. At the height of the action, a bearded figure was plucked from the crowd and dragged inside. It was Dave Van Ronk, who had come from the Lion's Head to see what was going on. He was charged with throwing an object at the police.

Almost by signal the crowd erupted into cobblestone and bottle heaving. The trashcan I was standing on was nearly yanked out from under me as a kid tried to grab it for use in the window smashing melee. From nowhere came an uprooted parking meter—used as a battering ram on the Stonewall door. I heard several cries of "Let's get some gas," and a blaze soon appeared in the window of the Stonewall. As the wood barrier behind the glass was beaten open, the cops inside turned a firehose on the crowd. By the time the fags were able to regroup, several carloads of police reinforcements had arrived and the streets were cleared.

A visit to the 6th Precinct revealed that 13 people had been arrested on charges that ranged from Van Ronk's felonious assault of a police officer to the owners' illegal sale and storage of alcoholic beverages without a license. Two police officers had been injured in the battle with the crowd. By the time the last cop was off the street Saturday morning, a sign was going up announcing that the Stonewall would reopen that night. It did.

Protest set the tone for "gay power" activities on Saturday. The afternoon was spent boarding up the windows of the Stonewall and chalking them with signs of the new revolution: "We are Open," "There is all college boys and girls in here," "Support Gay Power—C'mon in, girls." Among the slogans were two carefully clipped and bordered copies of the *Daily News* story about the previous night's events, which was anything but kind to the gay cause. But the real action was in the street. Friday night's crowd had returned, led by a group of gay cheerleaders. "We are the Stonewall girls," they chanted. "We wear our hair in curls. We have no underwear. We show our pubic hairs!" The scene was a command-performance for queers. If Friday had been pick-up night, Saturday was date night. Hand-holding, kissing, and posing accented each of the cheers with a homosexual liberation that had appeared only fleetingly on the street before. Radio news announcements about the previous night's "gay power" chaos had brought half of Fire Island's Cherry Grove running back to see what they had left behind. The generation gap existed even here. Older boys had strained looks on their faces and talked in concerned whispers as they watched the up-and-coming generation take being gay and flaunt it.

As the chants on the street rose in frequency and volume, the crowd grew restless. "Let's go down the street and see what's happening, girls," someone yelled. And down the street went the crowd, smack into the Tactical Patrol Force. Formed in a line, the TPF swept the crowd back to the corner of Waverly Place where they stopped.

A stagnant situation there brought on some gay tomfoolery in the form of a chorus line facing the helmeted and club-carrying cops. Just as the line got into a full kick routine, the TPF advanced again and cleared the crowd of screaming gay-powerites down Christopher to Seventh Avenue. The cops amused themselves by breaking up small groups of people, till the crowd finally dispersed around 3:30 A.M.

Sunday was a time for watching and rapping. Gone were the "gay power" chants of Saturday, but not the new and open brand of exhibitionism. Steps, curbs, and the park provided props for what amounted to the Sunday fag follies as returning stars from the previous night's performances stopped by to close the show for the weekend.

Around 1 A.M. a non-helmeted version of the TPF made a sweep of the area. That put a damper on posing and primping, and as the last buses were leaving Jerseyward, the crowd grew thin. Allen Ginsberg and Taylor Mead walked by to see what was happening and were filled in by some of the gay activists. "Gay power! Isn't that great!" Allen said. He expressed a desire to visit the Stonewall—"You know, I've never been in there"—and ambled on down the street, flashing peace signs and helloing the TPF. It was a kind of joy to see him on the street, with his laughter and quiet commentary on consciousness, "gay power" as a new movement, and the implications of what had happened. I followed him into the Stonewall, where rock music blared from speakers all around a room that might have come right from a Hollywood set of a gay bar. He was immediately bouncing and dancing wherever he moved.

Ginsberg left, and I walked east with him. Along the way, he described how things used to be. "You know, the guys there were so beautiful—they've lost that wounded look that fags all had 10 years ago." It was the first time I had heard this crowd described as beautiful.

We reached Cooper Square, and as Ginsberg turned to head toward home, he waved and yelled, "Defend the fairies!" and bounced on across the square. He is probably working on a manifesto for the movement right now. Watch out. The liberation is under way.

What We Want, What We Believe

THIRD WORLD GAY LIBERATION

The following statement, written in 1971, links the liberation of Third World people, gays and lesbians, and women. A revolutionary manifesto, it calls for the end of capitalism, freedom for gays and lesbians as well as Third World people, and abolition of the nuclear family and institutionalized religion. In short, this program would have ended society as it was known.

Our straight sisters and brothers must recognize and support that we, gay women and men, are equal in every way within the revolutionary ranks.

We each organize our people about different issues, but our struggles are the same against oppression, and we will defeat it together. Once we understand these struggles, and gain a love for our sisters and brothers involved in these struggles, we must learn how best to become involved in them. . . .

The struggles of the peoples of the world are our fight as well; their victories are our victories and our victories are theirs. Our freedom will come only with their freedom.

Together, not alone, we must explore how we view ourselves, and analyze the assumptions behind our self-identity. We can then begin to crack the barriers of our varying illnesses, our passivity, sexual chauvinism—in essence, our inability to unabashedly love each other, to live, fight, and if necessary, die for the people of the earth.

As we begin to understand our place in this international revolution, and join with others in this understanding, we must develop the skills necessary to destroy the forces of repression and exploitation, so as to make it possible for a new woman and man to evolve in a society based on communal love.

While we understand that in the United States our main enemy is the socio-economic-political system of capitalism and the people

Reprinted by permission, Karla Jay and Allen Young.

who make profits off our sufferings, fights and divisions, we also recognize that we must struggle against any totalitarian, authoritarian, sex-controlled, repressive, irrational, reactionary, fascist government or government machine.

WHAT WE WANT: WHAT WE BELIEVE:

1. We want the right of self-determination for all Third World and gay people, as well as control of the destinies of our communities.

We believe that Third World and gay people cannot be free until we are able to determine our own destinies.

2. We want the right of self-determination over the use of our bodies: the right to be gay, anytime, anyplace; the right to free physiological change and modification of sex on demand; the right to free dress and adornment.

We believe that these are human rights which must be defended with our bodies being put on the line. The system as it now exists denies these basic human rights by implementing forced heterosexuality.

3. We want liberation for all women: We want free and safe birth control information and devices on demand. We want free 24-hour child care centers controlled by those who need and use them. We want a redefinition of education and motivation (especially for Third World women) towards broader educational opportunities without limitations because of sex. We want truthful teaching of women's history. We want an end to hiring practices which make women and national minorities 1) a readily available source of cheap labor; and 2) confined to mind-rotting jobs under the worst conditions.

We believe that the struggles of all oppressed groups under any form of government which does not meet the true needs of its people will eventually result in the overthrow of that government. The struggle for liberation of women is a struggle to be waged by all peoples. We must also struggle within ourselves and within our various movements to end this oldest form of oppression and its foundation—male chauvinism. We cannot develop a truly liberating form of socialism unless we fight these tendencies.

4. We want full protection of the law and social sanction for all human sexual self-expression and pleasure between consenting per-

sons, including youth. We believe that present laws are oppressive to Third World people, gay people, and the masses. Such laws expose the inequalities of capitalism, which can only exist in a state where there are oppressed people or groups. This must end.

5. We want the abolition of the institution of the bourgeois nuclear family.

We believe that the bourgeois nuclear family perpetuates the false categories of homosexuality and heterosexuality by creating sex roles, sex definitions and sexual exploitation. The bourgeois nuclear family as the basic unit of capitalism creates oppressive roles of homosexuality and heterosexuality. All oppressions originate in the nuclear family structure. Homosexuality is a threat to this family structure and therefore to capitalism. The mother is an instrument of reproduction and teaches the necessary values of capitalist society, i.e., racism, sexism, etc., from infancy on. The father physically enforces (upon the mother and children) the behavior necessary in a capitalist system: intelligence and competitiveness in young boys and passivity in young girls. Further, it is every child's right to develop in a non-sexist, non-racist, non-possessive atmosphere which is the responsibility of all people, including gays, to create.

6. We want a free non-compulsory education system that teaches us our true identity and history, and presents the entire range of human sexuality without advocating any one form or style; that sex roles and determination of skills according to sex be eliminated from the school system; that language be modified so that no gender takes priority; and that gay people must share in the responsibilities of education.

We believe that we have been taught to compete with our sisters and brothers for power, and from that competitive attitude grows sexism, racism, male and national chauvinism and distrust of our sisters and brothers. As we begin to understand these things within ourselves, we attempt to free ourselves of them and are moved toward a revolutionary consciousness.

7. We want guaranteed full equal employment for Third World and gay people at all levels of production.

We believe that any system of government is responsible for giving every woman and man a guaranteed income or employment, regardless of sex or sexual preference. Being interested only in profits, capitalism cannot meet the needs of the people.

8. We want decent and free housing, fit shelter for human beings. We believe that free shelter is a basic need and right which must not be denied on any grounds. Landlords are capitalists, and, like all capitalists, are motivated only by the accumulation of profits, as opposed to the welfare of the people.

9. We want to abolish the existing judicial system. We want all Third World and gay people when brought to trial, to be tried by people's court with a jury of their peers. A peer is a person from similar social, economic, geographical, racial, historical, environmental, and sexual background.

We believe that the function of the judicial system under capitalism is to uphold the ruling class and keep the masses under control.

10. We want the reparation for and release of all Third World gay and all political prisoners from jails and mental institutions.

We believe that these people should be released because they have not received fair and impartial trials.

11. We want the abolition of capital punishment, all forms of institutional punishment, and the penal system.

We want the establishment of psychiatric institutions for the humane treatment and rehabilitation of criminal persons as decided by the people's court. We want the establishment of a sufficient number of free and non-compulsory clinics for the treatment of sexual disturbances, as defined by the individual.

12. We want an immediate end to the fascist police force.

We believe that the only way this can be accomplished is by putting the defense of the people in the hands of the people.

13. We want all Third World and gay men to be exempt from compulsory military service in the imperialist army. We want an end to military oppression both at home and abroad.

We believe that the only true army for oppressed people is the people's army, and Third World, gay people, and women should have full participation in the People's Revolutionary Army.

14. We want an end to all institutional religions because they aid in genocide by teaching superstition and hatred of Third World people, homosexuals and women. We want a guarantee of freedom to express natural spirituality.

We believe that institutionalized religions are an instrument of capitalism, therefore an enemy of the People.

15. We demand immediate non-discriminatory open admission/

membership for radical homosexuals into all left-wing revolutionary groups and organizations and the right to caucus.

We believe that so-called comrades who call themselves "revolutionaries" have failed to deal with their sexist attitudes. Instead they cling to male supremacy and therefore to the conditioned role of oppressors. Men still fight for the privileged position of man-on-the-top. Women quickly fall in line behind-their-men. By their counterrevolutionary struggle to maintain and to force heterosexuality and the nuclear family, they perpetuate decadent remnants of capitalism. To gain their anti-homosexual stance, they have used the weapons of the oppressor, thereby becoming the agent of the oppressor.

It is up to men to realistically define masculinity, because it is they, who, throughout their lives, have struggled to gain the unrealistic roles of "men." Men have always tried to reach this precarious position by climbing on the backs of women and homosexuals. "Masculinity" has been defined by capitalist society as the amount of possessions (including women) a man collects, and the amount of physical power gained over other men. Third World men have been denied even these false standards of "masculinity." Anti-homosexuality fosters sexual repressions, male-supremacy, weakness in revolutionary drive, and results in an inaccurate non-objective political perspective. Therefore, we believe that all left-wing revolutionary groups and organizations must immediately establish non-discriminatory, open admission/ membership policies.

16. We want a new society—a revolutionary socialist society. We want liberation of humanity, free food, free shelter, free clothing, free transportation, free health care, free utilities, free education, free art for all. We want a society where the needs of the people come first.

We believe that all people should share the labor and products of society, according to each one's needs and abilities, regardless of race, sex, age, or sexual preferences. We believe the land, technology, and the means of production belong to the people, and must be shared by the people collectively for the liberation of all.

Lesbians and the Ultimate Liberation of Women

GAY LIBERATION FRONT WOMEN

This 1970 call argues for the end of homosexual oppression, focusing particularly on the failures of the women's liberation movement to defend and support lesbianism as central to women's freedom.

Gay Liberation Front women welcome all women. In meetings and activities we maintain a flexible way of doing things to encompass our sisters of different social, economic, racial, religious, and political interests, and to permit individual freedom in actions and activities, both inside and outside of GLF.

We provide an opportunity for women to relate to other women— through political activities and community social activities, beginning with dances and moving out into new forms of socializing and communicating with our sisters.

GLF was the first group in New York to come together specifically to fight homosexual oppression. GLF Women, a caucus of GLF, are lesbian activists fighting oppression on two fronts: As homosexuals, we work with our gay brothers to fight oppression based on society's exclusion of individuals who love members of the same sex. As women, we work with women's liberation to fight the oppression of all women.

Our strongest common denominator and greatest oppression lie with society's injustice against us as homosexuals. We are discriminated against as women, but lesbians who live openly are fired from jobs, expelled from schools, banished from their homes, and even beaten. Lesbians who hide and escape open hostility, suffer equal oppression through psychic damage caused by their fear and guilt. With this understanding, we focus on gay liberation, giving priority to gay issues and gay problems. We are part of the revolution of

Reprinted by permission, Karla Jay and Allen Young.

all oppressed people, but we cannot allow the lesbian issue to be an afterthought.

GLF Women are dedicated to changing attitudes, institutions, and laws that oppress lesbians, using all or any methods from reform to revolution. Actions and consciousness-raising achieve this goal. Gay liberation is a movement and a state of mind challenging history's basic legal and social assumptions about homosexuality. Openly proclaiming ourselves lesbians is a revolutionary act and a threat to the prevailing society, which excludes people who live outside the norm. We work for a common understanding among all people that lesbianism is the most complete and fulfilling relationship with another woman and a valid life style.

Gay consciousness-raising is a primary interest:

1. So that our lesbian sisters understand our oppression and fight against it. To be effective the lesbian movement must be a grass roots effort. We denounce the fact that society's rewards and privileges are only given to us when we hide and split our identity. We encourage self-determination and will work for changes in the lesbian self-image, as well as in society, to permit the "coming out" of each gay woman into society as a lesbian. The new self-image or "gay consciousness" refers to our sense of pride, unity, life-style, and community.

2. Raising consciousness of people in all movements—to be aware of their sexism.

3. Raising the consciousness of our sisters active in women's liberation to openly acknowledge and actively support lesbians, with the attitude of solidarity and not reciprocity. We denounce the use of the word "lesbian" to divide us from our sisters, who should be united with us in our common struggle for the liberation of all women. We feel that the core oppression of women is the lesbian's oppression and the ultimate liberation of women is through the liberation of lesbians. Real freedom for lesbians will mean the end of all oppressive relationships based on male dominance and the compulsion women feel to seek male approval and support.

Women's liberation groups must undertake consciousness-raising on lesbianism. They must accept among their leadership admitted and publicly known lesbians. They must make explicit their acceptance of the lesbian life-style now implicit in their analysis.

    a) Feminists speak of rejecting role-playing, but fail to see the pressures in society during children's formative years to love men over women.

b) They say that women should be free to govern their own bodies, but fail to grant freedom of sexual preference.

c) They denounce stereotyped male and female attitudes and characteristics, but fail to accept as natural the so-called masculine female and so-called feminine male.

d) They talk about being independent from men, but do not see that the lesbian life style is the ultimate form of independence.

e) They talk of love among women, but do not include physical expression of that love.

4. Education of the public to recognize homosexuals as an oppressed minority and to destroy stereotyped images based on and perpetuated by society's hostility. To fight prejudice with reason and love. *Gay is Good.* Sexuality is basic to all human beings, and homosexuality is as natural as heterosexuality. To teach children from the earliest years about homosexuality without bias.

To effect change, we advocate an open media policy, with media defined as lectures, demonstrations, leaflets, consciousness-raising, dances, and rapping in bars, as well as the press.

WOODSTOCK AND ALTAMONT

A Fleeting, Wonderful Moment of "Community"

The rock festival that took place on farmland near Bethel, New York, in August 1969 entered the American cultural legacy. Woodstock became more than three days of music and counterculture lifestyle. It seemed to symbolize the possibility of a community built on love, rock 'n' roll, drugs, and a communal approach to life itself. The New Yorker *offered this casual report from one of those in attendance.*

We talked with a younger friend of ours—a nineteen-year-old—who had been to the Festival, and he told us he was indignant and discouraged by what the *Times* had had to say about the event. In an editorial headed "Nightmare in the Catskills,"the *Times* said, "The dreams of marijuana and rock and roll music that drew 300,000 fans and hippies to the Catskills had little more sanity than the impulses that drive the lemmings to march to their deaths in the sea. They ended in a nightmare of mud and stagnation. . . . What kind of culture is it that can produce so colossal a mess?" "It wasn't a nightmare," our friend told us. "The mud didn't matter, and it was one of the most remarkable experiences I've ever had. The big point was not that pot was passed around openly but that because there was a minimum of force and restriction—the cops were few, and they were friendly—a huge crowd of people handled itself decently. There were no fights, no hassles, no pushing, no stealing. Everybody shared everything he had, and I've never seen such consideration for others. People volunteered for all kinds of jobs—picking up trash, carrying stuff, doing whatever was needed. It was the most extraordinary demonstration of how good people can be—really *want* to be, if they are let alone. It was an ethic shared by a huge mass of people. The *Times* wants to know what kind of culture produces this. In a broad sense, Christian culture produced it."

We asked our young friend, who attends the University of Chicago and has hair neither very short nor very long, to jot down some further notes on his experience. . . .

"I went rather casually," he wrote, "partly because I wanted to hear the music, and partly because I knew, by word of mouth, that there would be a tremendous mass of people my age, and I wanted to be part of it. Of course, there was going to be a terrific assemblage of artists—the best this kind of event has to offer—but the main thing was that by listening to the grapevine you could tell the Festival was going to be above and beyond that. . . . We heard that there wouldn't be any reserved seats, that we'd be free to wander, and that the townspeople weren't calling out the militia in advance. I went, like the others, to meet people, to sit on the grass and play guitars, and to be together. I also knew that people were coming from thousands of miles away, but I had no idea how tremendous the event would be. . . .

"I drove from Rhode Island with a group of friends. When we got on the New York Thruway, we began to see the first signs of how huge it would be—Volkswagens full of kids, motorcycles, hitchhikers carrying signs. Everybody waving at everybody else as people passed. The first traffic jam—about twenty miles from White Lake, on 17B—set the tone. It was a cheerful traffic jam. People talked from car to car. People came up and asked to sit on your hood. Somebody in our car spoke to a girl in a blue Volks next to us and, not having yet caught the tone, remarked that the jam was a drag. 'Oh, no,' she said quickly. 'Everyone here is so beautiful.' She gave us some wine, and we handed over peaches in exchange. . . .

"Finally, we got to a huge parking lot. It cost five dollars and it was already full. We were the last car in. We parked and started walking. This was 10 P.M. Thursday. There would be no music until Friday afternoon. We walked along in a stream, exchanging comments with every passerby. There were no houses, no local folks staring at us. People became aware of the land around us. Somebody said, 'It's like being part of an encamped army that has won.' We felt as though it were liberated territory. We came to the top of a hill and looked down on a huge meadow—a natural amphitheatre—where the Festival would be. In the center, people were building the stage. People were lying around in sleeping bags or sitting around little fires. The grass was fresh with dew, and the stars were bright. It was wonderful. We went on and found a campground, full of people sitting around or sleeping or eating. We unpacked our gear. For fifty cents, we bought 'macroburgers' that some communal people from California had cooked. They were made of soybeans, rice, and vegetables—no meat —between slices of rye bread. The California people also gave us slices of huge cucumbers they had grown themselves. It all tasted good. The girl serving the macroburgers gave us water in a plastic cup. She said, 'Save the cup. Somebody else may want it.' The campground was full of the most ingenious shelters. One huge canopy was made of scraps of polyethylene fastened to scraps of wood. Beneath it about forty people were lying down, snuggled against each other, singing and playing music. There was a fence across the campground, and one tough guy—the only tough guy I saw—started to tear down the fence, but people remonstrated with him. They told him it was the farmer's fence and it wasn't necessary to take it down. He was only allowed to take down one panel to make an exit. It was like that through the whole Festival. Where the mass needed an opening, an opening was made. There was no needless destruction. It was a functional thing. There was a woods between us and the amphitheatre. Two paths through the woods had been marked with strings of Christmas lights. One was called the Gentle Path and the other the Groovy Way. Nobody knows who named them. Late that night, we went to sleep in our sleeping bags with the sound of singing and guitars and voices all around us. I slept well.

"In the morning, it was raining lightly, but it didn't last. I went looking for water. I found a tank truck, and there I met a Rhode Island girl I knew who was there brushing her teeth. She hugged me, and the crowd laughed. We breakfasted with some people from the Santa Fe Hog Farm Commune. They were serving out of a great vat of boiled wheat and raisins, scooped onto a paper plate with a dollop of honey on it. It was delicious. It held me all day.

"That day, I just wandered around. I found a group of people who were blowing up a red balloon five feet across, so that their friends could find them, but lots of other people had the same balloons, so these huge red globes dotted the fields. Various groups of people had put up amusement devices for everybody to use free. One was called the Bumblebee Nest. It consisted of forked branches ingeniously fastened together with wooden pegs to support a platform of hay. It was just for the pleasure of sitting on. Somebody had an enclosure of chickens and had brought chicken feed. It was fun to feed the chickens. Somebody else had brought rabbits and made a big pen with benches in it, so you could sit and watch the rabbits and feed them. There was a huge tepeelike construction with a flat stone hung from ropes that you could stand on to swing. All these were free things that people had taken the trouble to provide for others. Most of the day, people wandered around and talked. I read and played cards. In the late afternoon, the music began. The amphitheatre was a mass of people, but there was no pushing. The sound system was excellent. We listened all afternoon and evening. The music was great, and the audience sang and clapped the rhythm. The performers loved it. There was a terrific feeling of unity between the crowd and the stage.

"The next morning, we woke to find it raining hard. Some boys who had got soaked took off their clothes and walked around naked. It didn't bother anyone. It brought home the idea that this was our land. Nobody was busting them. I was struck by how harmless it was—how the violence of sexuality was missing. The naked boys looked harmless and innocent.

"The concessionaires—hot-dog stands and so on—started out with prohibitive prices, and the kids complained to the management. All day, there were announcements from the stage about where to get free food. Eventually, there was an announcement that the concessionaires had knocked their prices down to cost.

"It rained hard the early part of the day, but the reaction of the crowd was 'Don't fight it.' We sat and listened, soaking wet. The rain really did something to reinforce the spirit. There were radios on the campground, and we began to hear news reports that we were in the midst of a mass disaster. At every report, the crowd around the radio laughed. It was such a splendid example of the division between us and the outside world. It dramatized the whole crazy split that the world thought we were having a disaster and we knew we were having no such thing.

"About three o'clock, the sun came out. Everyone took off his clothes to dry. I stripped to my shorts. We lay in the sun and listened to fantastic music. The most popular song was against the Vietnam war. Just as it finished, an Army helicopter flew over. The whole crowd—all those hundreds of thousands of people—looked up and waved their forefingers in the peace sign, and then gave a cheer for themselves. It was an extraordinary thing. Soon after that, the farmer who owned the land was introduced, and he got a huge cheer, too.

"Late that afternoon, a 'free stage' began acting as a travellers' aid, where volunteers arranged free rides for people and helped to solve problems. They took up a collection for a ten-year-old boy who had lost his money. They returned a lost child to her mother. They asked for volunteers to pick up garbage, and they made announcements warning those leaving to be careful on the way out—not to take grass with them, because of busts on the highway, and so on.

"There was still another day to go, but I had to leave. We got our stuff together and jammed three hitchhikers into our car and drove it out of the mud. As we went out, people called to us, 'Don't leave! Don't leave!' Nobody wanted to let go of what we'd had there. What we'd had was a fleeting, wonderful moment of what you might call 'community.' "

Coming of Age in Aquarius

ANDREW KOPKIND

For many, the example of Woodstock pointed beyond those few days of music to the possibility of a new era. Yippie founder Abbie Hoffman later wrote of a "Woodstock Nation." New left journalist Andrew Kopkind assesses both the limits and possibilities of the event in Hard Times.

The Woodstock Music and Art Fair wasn't held in Woodstock; the music was secondarily important and the art was for the most part unproduced; and it was as much of a fair as the French Revolution or the San Francisco earthquake. What went down on Max Yasgur's farm in the low Catskills last weekend defied casual categories and conventional perceptions. Some monstrous and marvelous metaphor had come alive, revealing itself only in terms of its contradictions: paradise and concentration camp, sharing and profiteering, sky and mud, love and death. The urges of the ten years' generation roamed the woods and pastures, and who could tell whether it was some rough beast or a speckled bird slouching towards its Day-Glo manger to be born?

The road from the Hudson River west to White Lake runs through hills like green knishes, soft inside with good earth, and crusty with rock and wood on top. What works of man remain are rural expressions of an Other East Village, where the Mothers were little old ladies with sheitls, not hip radicals with guns. There's Esther Manor and Siegel's Motor Court and Elfenbaum's Grocery: no crash communes or head shops. Along that route, a long march of freaks in microbuses, shit-cars and bikes—or on thumb and foot—passed like movie extras in front of a process screen. On the roadside, holiday-makers from the Bronx looked up from their pinochle games and afghan-knitting and knew that the season of the witch had come.

Reprinted by permission, James Ridgeway.

"Beatniks out to make it rich": Woodstock was, first of all, an environment created by a couple of hip entrepreneurs to consolidate the culture revolution and (in order to?) extract the money of its troops. Michael Lang, a 25-year-old former heavy dealer from Bensonhurt dreamed it up; he then organized the large inheritance of John Roberts, 26, for a financial base, and brought in several more operatives and financiers. Lang does not distinguish between hip culture and hip capital; he vowed to make a million before he was 25, beat his deadline by two years, and didn't stop. With his Village/Durango clothes, a white Porsche and a gleaming BSA, he looks, acts and *is* hip; his interest in capital accumulation is an extension of every hippie's desire to rip off a bunch of stuff from the A& P. It's a gas. . . .

By early summer, Woodstock looked to be the super rock festival of all time, and promoters of a dozen other summertime festivals were feverishly hyping up their own projects to catch the overflow of publicity and enthusiasm: Rock music (al fresco or recorded) is still one of the easiest ways to make money off of the new culture, along with boutique clothes and jewelry, posters, drugs and trip-equipment, Esquire magazine, Zig-Zag papers and Sara Lee cakes. But the Woodstock hype worried the burghers of Wallkill, and the law implemented their fears by kicking the bash out of town. Other communities, however, were either less uptight or more greedy; six hard offers for sites came to the promoters the day Wallkill gave them the boot. With less than a month to get ready, Woodstock Ventures, Inc., chose the 600-acre Yasgur farm (with some other parcels thrown in) at White Lake, N.Y.

Locals there were divided on the idea, and Yasgur was attacked by some neighbors for renting (for a reported $50,000) to Woodstock. But in the end, the profit motive drove the deal home. One townsman wrote to the Monticello newspaper: "It's none of their business how Max uses his land. If they are so worried about Max making a few dollars from his land they should try to take advantage of this chance to make a few dollars themselves. They can rent camping space or even sell water or lemonade." Against fears of hippie horrors, businessmen set promises of rich rewards: "Some of these people are shortsighted and don't understand what these children are doing," one said. "The results will bring an economic boost to the County, without it costing the taxpayer a cent."

The vanguard of freaks started coming a week or more before opening day, and by Wednesday they were moving steadily down Route 17-B, like a busy day on the Ho Chi Minh Trail. The early comers were mostly hard-core, permanent dropouts: Their hair or their manner or their rap indicated that they had long ago dug into their communes or radical politics or simply into oppositional lifestyles. In the cool and clear night they played music and danced, and sat around fires toasting joints and smoking hashish on a pinpoint. No busts, pigs or hassle; everything cool, together, outasight.

By the end of the next day, Thursday, the ambience had changed from splendor in the grass to explosive urban sprawl. Light and low fences erected to channel the crowds without actually seeming to oppress them were toppled or ignored; cars and trucks bounced over the meadows; tents sprung up between stone outcroppings and cow plop. Construction went on through the night, and already the Johnny-on-the-Spot latrines were smelly and out of toilet paper, the food supply was spotty, and long lines were forming at the water tank. And on Friday morning, when the population explosion was upon us all, a sense of siege took hold: Difficult as it was to get in, it would be almost impossible to leave for days.

From the beginning, the managers of the festival were faced with the practical problem of control. Berkeley and Chicago and Zap, N.D., were the functional models for youth mobs rampaging at the slightest provocation—or no provocation at all. The promoters interviewed 800 off-duty New York City policemen for a security guard (Sample question: "What would you do if a kid walked up and blew marijuana smoke in your face?" Incorrect answer: "Bust him." Correct answer: "Inhale deeply and smile."), chose 300 or so, and fitted them with mod uniforms. But at the last minute they were withdrawn under pressure from the Police Department, and the managers had to hire camp counselors, phys ed teachers and stray straights from the surrounding area.

The guards had no license to use force or arrest people; they merely were to be "present," in their red Day-Glo shirts emblazoned with the peace symbol, and could direct traffic and help out in emergencies if need be. The real work of keeping order, if not law, was to be done by members of the Hog Farm commune, who had been brought from New Mexico, along with people from other hippie retreats, in a chartered airplane (at $16,000) and psychedelic buses from Kennedy Airport.

Beneath the practical problem of maintaining order was the principal contradiction of the festival: how to stimulate the energies of the new culture and profit thereby, and at the same time control them. In a way, the Woodstock venture was a test of the ability of avant-garde capitalism at once to profit from and control the insurgencies which its system spawns. . . . The microcosmic system would "fail" if Woodstock Ventures lost its shirt, or if the control mechanisms broke down.

The promoters must have sensed the responsibility they carried. They tried every aspect of cooperation theory. SDS, Newsreel and underground newspapers were handed thousands of dollars to participate in the festival, and they were given a choice spot for a "Movement City"; the idea was that they would give hip legitimacy to the weekend and channel their activities "within the system." (They bought the idea.) Real cops were specifically barred from the camp grounds, and the word went out that there would be no busts for ordinary tripping, although big dealers were discouraged. There would be free food, water, camping facilities—and, in the end, free music, when attempts at crowd-channeling failed. But the Hog Farmers were the critical element. Hip beyond any doubt, they spread the love/groove ethic throughout the farm, breaking up incipient actions against "the system" with cool, low-key hippie talk about making love not war, the mystical integrity of earth, and the importance of doing your own thing, preferably alone. On the other hand—actually, on the same hand—they were the only good organizers in camp. They ran the free food operation (oats, rice and bulgar), helped acid-freaks through bad trips without Thorazine, and (with Abbie Hoffman) ran the medical system when that became necessary.

The several dozen Movement organizers at the festival had nothing to do. After Friday night's rain there was a theory that revolt was brewing on a mass scale, but the SDS people found themselves unable to organize around the issue of inclement weather. People were objectively trapped; and in that partial aspect, the Yasur farm was a concentration camp—or a hippie reservation—but almost everyone was stoned and happy. Then the rain stopped, the music blared, food and water arrived, and everyone shared what he had. Dope became plentiful and entirely legitimate; in a soft cool forest, where craftsmen had set up their portable headshops, dealers sat on tree stumps selling their wares: "acid, mesc, psilocybin, hash. . . ." No one among the half-million could not have turned on if he wanted to; joints were passed from blanket to blanket, lumps of hashish materialized like manna, and there was Blue Cheer, Sunshine acid and pink mescaline to spare.

Seen from any edge or angle, the army strung out against the hillside sloping up from the stage created scenes almost unimaginable in commonplace terms. No day's demonstration or political action had brought these troops together; no congress or cultural event before produced such urgent need for in-gathering and self-inspection. The ambiguities and contradictions of the imposed environment were worrisome; but to miss the exhilaration of a generation's arrival at its own campsite was to define the world in only one dimension.

Although the outside press saw only masses, inside the differentiation was more impressive. Maybe half the crowd was weekend-hip, out from Long Island for a quick dip in the compelling sea of freaks. The other half had longer been immersed. It was composed of tribes dedicated to whatever gods now seem effective and whatever myths produce the energy needed to survive: Meher Baba, Mother Earth, street-fighting man, Janis Joplin, Atlantis, Jimi Hendrix, Che.

The hillside was their home. Early Saturday morning, after the long night of rain—from Ravi Shankar through Joan Baez—they still had not abandoned the turf. Twenty or forty thousand people (exactitude lost its meaning: it was that sight, not the knowledge of the numbers that was so staggering) sat stonily silent on the muddy ground, staring at a stage where no one played: petrified playgoers in the marble stands at Epidaurus, thousands of years after the chorus had left for the last time.

No one in this country in this century had ever seen a "society" so free of repression. Everyone swam nude in the lake, balling was easier than getting breakfast, and the "pigs" just smiled and passed out the oats. For people who had never glimpsed the intense communitarian closeness of a militant struggle—People's Park or Paris in the month of May or Cuba—Woodstock must always be their model of how good we will all feel after the revolution.

So it was an illusion and it wasn't. For all but the hard core, the ball and the balling is over; the hassles begin again at Monticello. The repression-free weekend was provided by promoters as a way to increase their take and it will not be repeated unless future profits are guaranteed. (It's almost certain now that Woodstock Ventures lost its wad.) The media nonsense about death and O.D.s didn't change; it just accommodated the freaks for the weekend.

What is not illusionary is the reality of a new culture of opposition. It grows out of the disintegration of the old forms, the vinyl and aerosol institutions that carry all the inane and destructive values of privatism, competition, commercialism, profitability and elitism. The new culture has yet to produce its own institutions on a mass scale; it controls none of the resources to do so. For the moment, it must be content—or discontent—to feed the swinging sectors of the old system with new ideas, with rock and dope and love and openness. Then it all comes back, from Columbia Records or Hollywood or Bloomingdale's in perverted and degraded forms. But something will survive, because there's no drug on earth to dispel the nausea. It's not a "youth thing" now but a generational event; chronological age is only the current phase. Mass politics, it's clear, can't yet be organized around the nausea; political radicals have to see the cultural revolution as a sea in which they can swim, like black militants in "black culture." But the urges are roaming, and when the dope freaks and nude swimmers and loveniks and ecological cultists and music groovers find out that they have to fight for love, all fucking hell will break loose.

The Rolling Stones–At Play in the Apocalypse

MICHAEL LYDON

If Woodstock demonstrated the possibilities of a community built on love and rock, the December 1969 concert by the Rolling Stones at the Altamont raceway in Northern California presented the negative side of the image. After a success-

ful American tour, the Stones planned a free outdoor concert as a culmination.
A number of San Francisco-area bands played as well. Hiring members of the
motorcycle gang Hell's Angels to provide security and guard the stage resulted
in mayhem and violence. A number of fights and beatings developed, and
one concertgoer was killed. Rock critic Michael Lydon reported on the event
in Ramparts.

It all came down at Altamont on that strange day. A cold sun alternated
with bright clouds, and 300,000 young Americans stepped into the
future (or was it?), looked at each other, and were frightened by what
they saw. It was the biggest gathering in California (the population
of San Francisco is 756,000) since the Human Be-In three years before,
not only in numbers but in expectation. In common with all the
voluntary mass events of the '60's—was the Sproul Hall sit-in the
first?—it would, all believed, advance the trip, i.e., reveal some important lesson intrinsic to and yet beyond its physical fact. The
300,000, all in unspoken social contract, came not only to hear music,
but to bear living testimony to their own lives.

The Stones as well as the audience—and whether such a distinction
would or could be made was one of the day's questions—had wanted
it to be in San Francisco's Golden Gate Park, their gift to the city and
its culture. As their long hair, outrageous manners, and music had
helped make San Francisco possible, San Francisco had helped make
the past three years possible. Like thousands before them, the Stones
were coming to say thank you. They hoped it would be in all senses
a free concert, an event spiritually outside the commercial realm of
the tour. It both was and was not.

The scores of equipment trucks got to Altamont, 15 miles east of
Berkeley by early Friday evening; a huge volunteer crew worked like
ants under blue floodlights amid a growing tangle of wires, planking
and staging. "No one will be allowed on the grounds until seven A.M.
Saturday, so *stay home*," was the broadcast word, but by midnight there
were traffic jams miles from the site. At seven A.M. the gates are
opened. Over the hill and down into the hollow by the stage comes
a whooping, running, raggletaggle mob. In minutes the meadow is a
crush of bodies pressed so close that it takes ten minutes to walk 50
yards. On and on comes the crowd; by ten it spreads a quarter mile
back from the stage, fanning out like a lichen clinging to a rock.

There are the dancing beaded girls, the Christ-like young men, and smiling babies familiar from countless stories on the "Love Generation," but the weirdos too, whose perverse and penetrating intensity no camera ever captures. Speed freaks with hollow eyes and missing teeth, dead-faced acid heads turned out by countless flashes, old beatniks clutching gallons of red wine, Hare Krishna chanters with shaved heads and acned cheeks.

Face by face, body by body, the crowd is recognizable, comprehensible. As ugly beautiful mass, it is bewilderingly unfamiliar—a timeless lake of humanity climbing together through the first swirling, buzzing, euphoric-demonic hours of acid. Is this Bosch or Cecil B. DeMille; biblical, medieval, or millennial? Are we lost or found? Are we *we,* and if we are, who are we?

Whoever or whatever, we are *here, all* here, and gripped by the ever-amazing intensity of psychedelics, we *know* that this being here is no accident but the inevitable and present realization of our whole lives until this moment. One third of a million post-war boom babies gathered in a Demolition Derby junkyard by a California freeway to get stoned and listen to rock 'n' roll—is that what it has been all about?

Some call us Woodstock West, but we are not. Woodstock was a three-day encampment at which cooperation was necessary for survival; it was an event only because it became an event. The Altamont crowd is *demanding* that an event come to pass, be delivered, in a single day; should it go bad—well, it'll be over by evening.

It isn't that the morning is not a groove; it is, friendly enough and loose. But ... but what? There is too much of something; is it the people, the dope, the tension? Maybe it is the *wanting,* the concentration, not just of flesh, but of unfulfilled desire, of hope for (or is it fear of) deliverance. "There must be some way out of here, said the joker to the thief; there's too much confusion, I can't get no relief." What is our oppression that in escaping it we so oppress ourselves? Have we jammed ourselves together on these sere hills miles from home hoping to find a way out of such masses? If that is our paradox, is Altamont our self-made trap? And yet ... might we just be able, by acting out the paradox so intensely, to transcend it?

The Jefferson Airplane are on stage, knocking out "3/5's of a Mile in 9/10's of a Second" with a mad fury—

> Do away with people blowing my mind,
> Do away with people wasting my precious time,
> Take me to a simple place
> Where I can easily see my face . . .

That place is not Altamont—when suddenly all eyes rivet on an upraised pool cue. It is slashing downward; held by a mammoth Hell's Angel, and when it hits the unseen target there is a burst of water as if it had crushed a jellyfish. A wave of horror ripples madly across the crowd. The music stops and the stage is full of Angels in raunchy phalanx. The music starts, falters, stops. Thousands hold their breath and wave pathetic V signs. No one wants the Angels. A few scream "Pigs, pigs." The odds against the Angels are maybe 5000 to one, but the crowd is passive and afraid. The Angels stay on stage, sure of their power.

Now something is definitely wrong, but there is no time or space to set it right. The Angels become the villains, but why are they here? They just came, of course, as they always do, but we hoped, as friends. Since Ken Kesey faced them down and turned them on, San Francisco has had a sentimental romance with the Angels: the consummate outlaws, true rolling stones, street fighting men: they're so bad they're good, went the line. It turns out later that they were actually hired by the Stones on the suggestion of the Dead; their fee, $500 worth of beer. But now their open appetite for violence mocks our unfocussed love of peace: their grim solidarity, our fearful hopes of community.

Community? It just doesn't feel like that anymore. . . .

The day drags on. Many leave: as many more arrive. Invisibly and inevitably the crowd squeezes toward the stage until the first 50 yards around it are suffocatingly dense. . . .

Darkness begins to fall. "The Stones are here." "I saw their helicopter." "Somebody said they're not gonna show." The lights come on, and a new wave sweeps thousands more towards the stage. The stage itself is so full that it is sagging in the center. The Angels continue their random attacks. "The Stones are here." "That's why they turned on the lights."

In fact, they are—packed into a tiny trailer filled with stale smoke and spilled food. Charley's happy; he just needs to get through this final set and he can go home to Shirley and Serafina. Mick is upset:

as he got off the helicopter a freak had rushed him, screaming, "I hate you, I hate you," then punched him in the face. For all his presence, Mick Jagger is not fearless; on tour, when the engine of one small chartered plane had flamed briefly as it coughed to a start, Mick leapt from his seat, crying that the plane was about to explode. Keith, up all night and in the trailer all day, is exhausted. Crying girls peer and shout through the small screen windows. . . .

It is time. Surrounded by security men, they squeeze the few yards to a tent directly behind the stage. Mick Taylor, Keith and Bill tune up. A dozen Angels stand guard, punching at faces that peek through holes in the canvas. They are ready. The Angels form a wedge; they file between two equipment trucks, up four steps, and they are there. It is fully dark now but for the stage; in its incandescence, the Rolling Stones are as fine as ever. Mick bows low, sweeping his Uncle Sam hat wide in an ironic circle, and on Keith's signal, the band begins "Jumping Jack Flash." That incredible moment is there again. In those first seconds when Keith's shirt is sparkling, and Charley has just set his big cymbal shimmering with a snap of his right wrist, and Mick bends forward biting out the first defiant words, that enormous pressure of wants, material and spiritual, dissolves—phisst! like that in thin air. For it is just that moment, that achievement of perfect beauty after impossible trial, which is the object of all those longings.

> "Cause it's all right now,
> In fact it's a gas.
> I'm Jumping Jack Flash,
> It's a gas gas gas!

And then it is irrevocably gone. Four Angels flash from behind the amps, one vaulting almost over Charley's head. One jumping from the stage, and the crowd scatters into itself in total panic. There appears to be a fight. Then it seems to be over. The music goes on. Again: more Angels, this time wandering around among the Stones. They stop playing.

"Fellows, fellows," says Mick, "move back, won't you, fellows?" His sarcasm gets him through, and they start again. Trouble for the third time, and it's serious. Two Angels (I saw two) wade deep into the crowd. There are screams. Rows of faces fishtail away before these thugs from some very modern nightmare. Boos rise from the mass of the crowd who can't see what's wrong and who just want the show to go on. The band starts again but something unmistakably weird is still going on down in front. A few kids escape to the stage, streaking to the safety of its far corners. . . .

"This is an important announcement. Someone has been hurt and a doctor is leaving the stage right now; that's him with his arms raised, he's got a green jacket on. Will you please let him through. Someone has been badly hurt."

Security men are begging that all those who do not absolutely need to be on stage leave it. I leave, not unhappily, and walk through the burnt-out campfires, small piles of trash and rakishly tilted motor-cycles behind the stage, then up a slope where the kids are standing on cars, maybe 30 to a car. A girl comes by asking for her friends: she says she has cut her leg on barbed wire and wants to go home, but she lost her friends with the car at noon.

The Stones are going again, and the crowd is with them. We can't see them, but the music sounds good—not great, not free festival great, but no one hopes for that anymore. It is enough that it is here. Around me a few people are dancing gently. The morning's dope is wearing off: all the trips are nearly over. We do glimpse the basket flying through the air, trailing petals. We all cheer one last massive cheer. Friends find friends: the crowd becomes fragments that get into their cars that back up on the freeway for miles and for hours. Luckily it is only about eight: but it feels like the very end of the night when the only want is for rest. I realize that the Grateful Dead did not get a chance to play and figure that I won't go to any more of these things.

In the days that follow, the free concert becomes "the disaster at Altamont." There is wide disagreement on what happened and what it meant: everyone, it seems, had their own day, and that was, we all say, one of the problems. The only common emotion is disappoint-ment and impotent sorrow. "If only . . . if only . . ." The papers report that there were three births (though later the figure cannot be substantiated) and four deaths. Mark Feiger, 22, and Richard Savlov, 22, friends who had recently moved to Berkeley from New Jersey, were killed when a car on its way out to the freeway plowed into their campfire hours after the concert was over. A young man with long hair, mustache and sideburns, with a metal cross through his pierced right ear, still listed as "John Doe," stumbled stoned into an irrigation canal and drowned. Another, a young black man, Meredith Hunter, was stabbed, kicked and beaten by Angels right before the stage while the Stones were playing. His body was battered so badly that doctors knew, the moment they reached him, there was no chance to save him.

THE ENVIRONMENTAL MOVEMENT

The desire for a lifestyle more in keeping with nature meshed with growing concerns about the impact of human existence on the earth. Out of this emerged the beginnings of the environmental movement. The questions and issues raised in these years have continued throughout subsequent decades.

Lake Erie Water

BARRY COMMONER

Pollution of our natural resources became an important theme in the emerging environmental movement. Barry Commoner's 1971 The Closing Circle *details the destruction underway, as in this discussion of the serious condition of one of the Great Lakes.*

The most blatant example of the environmental crisis in the United States is Lake Erie, a huge inland sea large enough to symbolize the

Reprinted by permission, Barry Commoner. Original source: Barry Commoner, *The Closing Circle: Nature, Man, and Technology*, New York: Knopf, 1971.

permanence of nature. Lake Erie has been a major natural resource for a rich region comprising a half dozen large cities with a population of thirteen million, a huge and varied industry, lush farm lands, and profitable fisheries. But in the process of creating this wealth, the lake has been changed, so polluted that the original biological systems that maintained the social value of the lake have largely been killed off. The fate of Lake Erie is a measure of the damage we inflict on our natural resources in order to create the nation's wealth.

In the last decade, the people living near Lake Erie have had ample evidence of its deterioration. Nearly all the beaches they once enjoyed have been closed by pollution; each summer huge mounds of decaying fish and algae pile up on the shore; the once sparkling water is dense with muck; oil discharged into one of its tributary rivers has burst into flame. Lake Erie's living balance has been upset and if the lake is not yet "dead," it certainly appears to be in the grip of a fatal disease.

Lake Erie is about 12,000 years old. It was created by the great advancing ice sheet that gouged out the beds of the Great Lakes and later melted, filling the newly made depressions with clear water. Minerals from the surrounding rocks dissolved in the water of the newborn lake and streams carried into it material washed out of the soil of the adjacent lands. Now the biological life of the lake could begin. Microscopic plants—algae—grew and reproduced, creating their living substance from hydrogen taken from water, nitrogen and phosphorus provided by dissolved nitrate and phosphate salts, and carbon derived from the carbon dioxide of the air.

Once algae grow in it, a body of water can sustain a complex web of life: the small animals that eat the algae; the fish that feed on them; the bacteria of decay that return organic animal wastes to their inorganic forms—carbon dioxide, nitrate, and phosphate—which can then support the growth of fresh algae. This makes up the basic, fresh-water ecological cycle.

When the first observations of Lake Erie were recorded in the seventeenth century, it supported a large and varied population of fish. The waters of the lake were clear and sparsely populated with algae, for the nutrient salts leaching into the lake were only enough to produce a limited plant crop, which was also kept in check by the animals that fed on the algae. For two hundred years Lake Erie continued in this state of biological balance.

But beginning at the turn of this century, reports from Lake Erie fisheries revealed sudden changes in the life of the lake. First, there was the near disappearance of the lake sturgeon, a delectable, valuable fish long common in the lake. Before 1900, Lake Erie yielded a million-pound annual crop of sturgeon, but ten years later the yield had fallen to 77,000 pounds, never to recover again; in 1964 only 4,000 pounds of sturgeon were taken. In 1920 northern pike, which had until then yielded million-pound catches, all but disappeared. In the 1930's the cisco, which once represented half the total fish crop of Lake Erie, dropped from a yield of 14,000,000 pounds to 764,000 pounds and never recovered; from 1960 to 1964 the annual cisco catch was 8,000 pounds. In 1940 the Sauger-pike crop suddenly became reduced, reaching a scant 1,000 pounds in the years 1960 to 1964. A few years later the whitefish abruptly disappeared from the lake, and in the 1960's the blue pike met the same fate. The total fish catch, in pounds, is now not much different from what it was in 1900, but the valuable fish have been replaced by "rough" fish—perch, sheepshead, catfish, and carp, and by the sudden invasion of smelt from the ocean in the 1950's. The money value of the catch has declined sharply.

The fish, then, gave the first warning that the biology of Lake Erie was changing and fixed the start of the change at roughly 1900. . . .

The total mass of organic waste that reaches Lake Erie each year requires, for its conversion to inorganic salts, the consumption of about 180 million pounds of oxygen. A possible explanation of the recent oxygen deficits in the lake is the withdrawal of oxygen from lake water by the action of bacteria on this organic material. . . .

All this means that in using Lake Erie as a dumping ground for municipal and industrial organic wastes and for agricultural fertilizer drainage, there has accumulated—in the bottom mud—a huge and growing oxygen deficit. . . . As a result, in some future especially hot and windless summer, Lake Erie may be faced with a sudden demand to repay a century's accumulated oxygen debt. This would be a biological cataclysm that could possibly exhaust, for a time, most of the oxygen in the greater part of the lake waters. Such a catastrophe would make the lake's present plight seem slight by comparison. . . .

Human intervention—not enhancement of supposedly natural eutrophication—is wholly responsible for the present deterioration of Lake Erie and for its grimly uncertain future. The guilt is all ours. . . .

Lake Erie dramatizes the massive destruction of natural resources by environmental pollution. It is not unique; ecological changes similar to those that have occurred in Lake Erie are under way in Lake Michigan, Lake Ontario, and Lake Constance; early stages of manmade eutrophication have been detected in the Baltic Sea, and even in Lake Baikal, which is the least eutrophic lake in the world. Massive as it is, the pollution of Lake Erie warns of even greater ecological destruction to come.

Perhaps one of the most meaningful ways to sense the impact of the environmental crisis is to confront the question which is always asked about Lake Erie: how can we restore it? I believe that the only valid answer is that no one knows. For it should be clear that even if overnight all of the pollutants now pouring into Lake Erie were stopped, there would still remain the problem of the accumulated mass of pollutants in the lake bottom. To my knowledge, no one has proposed a means of solving that problem which is even remotely feasible. It is entirely likely, I believe, that practically speaking Lake Erie will *never* be returned to anything approximating the condition it was in, say, twenty-five to fifty years ago.

This, then, is the outcome of our assault on Lake Erie: we have grossly, irreversibly changed the biological character of the lake and have greatly reduced, now and for the foreseeable future, its value to man. Clearly we cannot continue on this course much longer.

Diet for a Small Planet

FRANCES MOORE LAPPÉ

Part of the convergence between the growing environmental movement and the focus of counterculture life on a more natural existence was the growth of interest in more healthy and ecologically minded eating. Francis Moore Lappé's Diet for a Small Planet calls for people to "eat lower on the food chain," which would benefit both the individual and the earth. Her theoretical discussion, a small portion of which in reprinted here, is supplemented by extensive menus and recipes.

This book is about PROTEIN—how we as a nation are caught in a pattern that squanders it; and how you can choose the opposite—a way of eating that makes the most of the earth's capacity to supply this vital nutrient. In the pages that follow I propose that our heavily meat-centered culture is at the very heart of our waste of the earth's productivity; and I invite you to explore the varied possibilities of nonmeat sources of protein.

Why has the information I have gathered not been easily available long before now? And why now is it being presented by someone who is neither a nutritionist nor an ecologist? Perhaps the answer is that we have neglected vital questions because of fixed cultural attitudes which relegate nonmeat protein sources to an inferior position. The fact that the first comprehensive research in plant protein became available only six months ago illustrates this meat-centered bias. As you are reading, you may discover that many of your beliefs about protein have been culturally conditioned. I know that mine were, and that just getting the facts has been marvelously freeing. When a meal was no longer rigidly defined as meat-vegetable-potatoes, many new and exciting culinary experiences became possible....

Reprinted by permission, Frances Moore Lappé. Original Source: Frances Lappé, *Diet for a Small Planet*, New York: Ballantine Books, 1971.

When your mother told you to eat everything on your plate because people were starving in India, you thought it was pretty silly. You knew that the family dog would be the only one affected by what you did or didn't waste. Since then you've probably continued to think that making any sort of *ethical* issue about eating is absurd. You eat what your family always ate, altered only perhaps by proddings from the food industry. It's probably a pretty unconscious affair, and you like it that way. But eating habits can have a meaning, a meaning that not only feels closer to you than an abstract ethic but brings you pleasure too. What I am about to describe to you may sound at first like just another ethical rule for eating, but to me it feels like common sense far removed from the abstract.

The act of putting into your mouth what the earth has grown is perhaps your most direct interaction with the earth. But, depending on the eating habits of a culture, this interaction can have very different consequences—for mankind, and for the earth. What I will be suggesting in this book is a guideline for eating from the earth that both maximizes the earth's potential to meet man's nutritional needs and, at the same time, minimizes the disruption of the earth necessary to sustain him. It's as simple as that. . . .

In order to understand this very simple idea of making the most of the earth's productivity while doing the least damage, we must have a clear picture of our present practices and their consequences. Since the eating habits of this culture center so heavily on meat, the best place to start is with the United States livestock production. . . .

Think for a moment of a cow grazing. We see the cow as one link in a food chain of which man is the last link. Man is, therefore, the obvious beneficiary. The cow eats grass and we get steak. What could be a better arrangement! But before we acclaim our good fortune let's examine just how the conversion of plants to meat occurs in practice. You will see that in this country we have drastically altered this simple grass-to-meat equation.

Livestock could very well serve man as a "protein factory," converting humanly inedible substances, like cellulose, and low-quality protein in plants into high-quality protein for our benefit. Grazing livestock on rangeland of little agricultural value is clearly fulfilling this function. And, as we shall see later, some livestock can even produce protein with a diet based on as simple a molecule as urea! . . .

Fully *one-half* of the harvested agricultural land in the U.S. is planted with feed crops. We feed 78 percent of all our grain to animals. This is the largest percentage of any country in the world. In Russia, 28 percent of grains are fed to animals, while in developing countries, the percentage ranges from 10 to 0. . . .

But these figures acquire real meaning only when we take into account the efficiency of livestock in the conversion of "feed" into protein for us. It is widely accepted that the ratio of nutrients put into an animal to the nutrients recovered for human consumption is high. For example, the protein production ratio for beef and veal in North America is 21 to 1. This means that a cow must be fed 21 pounds of protein in order to produce 1 pound of protein for human consumption. Other types of animal protein conversion are somewhat more efficient. . . .

Considering all classes of livestock in the U.S., the average ratio of protein conversion is 8 to 1.

Another way of assessing the relative inefficiency of livestock is by comparison with plants in the amount of protein produced per acre. An acre of cereals can produce *five times* more protein than an acre devoted to meat production; legumes (peas, beans, lentils) can produce *ten times* more; and leafy vegetables *fifteen times* more. These figures are averages—some plants in each category actually produce even more. Spinach, for example, can produce up to twenty-six times more protein per acre than can beef. . . .

Now let us put these two factors together: the large quantities of humanly edible protein being fed to animals; and their inefficient conversion into protein for human consumption. Some very startling statistics result. If we exclude dairy cows, the average ratio for protein conversion by livestock in North America is 10 to 1. Applying this ratio to the 20 million tons of protein fed to livestock in 1968 in the U.S., we realize that only 10 percent (or 2 million tons) was retrieved as protein for human consumption. Thus, in a single year through this consumption pattern, 18 million tons of protein becomes inaccessible to man. This amount is equivalent to *90 percent of the yearly world protein deficit*—enough protein to provide 12 grams a day for every person in the world! . . .

By now most of us are familiar with the facts of environmental damage wrought by chlorinated pesticides like DDT: in predatory birds like pelicans and falcons, DDT and related pesticides like Dieldrin can disrupt reproductive processes, and in ocean-going fish like salmon, DDT can cause damage to the nervous system. What may be less familiar to you, and of greater importance to us here, is just *why* these particular species are being affected. A major reason is that these animals are at the top of long food chains in which pesticides accumulate as one organism is eaten by another. This process of accumulation results from the fact that organochlorine pesticides like DDT and Dieldrin are retained in animal and fish fat and are difficult to break down. Thus, as big fish eat smaller fish, or as cows eat grass (or feed), whatever pesticides they eat are largely retained and passed on. So if man is eating at the "top" of such food chains, he becomes the final consumer and thus the recipient of the highest concentration of pesticide residues.

But unlike most other predators (or "carnivores," if you like), man has a choice of what and how much he eats. We have already explored one of the reasons for choosing to be an "herbivore" that eats low on the food chain—it is simply less wasteful. Another consideration, the one we are going to evaluate here, is that herbivores are less likely to accumulate potentially harmful environmental contaminants than are carnivores. . . .

In the last twenty years crop yields in the U.S. have increased sharply. . . . A major result of these greater yields, if not part of the impetus for them, has been to increase the amount of our agricultural yield available to livestock as feed. Currently, one-half of the yield of our harvested acreage is fed to animals, in part making possible our increase in meat consumption. (Beef and veal consumption has doubled in the U.S. in the last thirty-five years.)

Here is where pesticides enter in. These increased crop yields are almost entirely due to the introduction of the new kinds of pesticides in the mid-1940s. We might well ask whether it has been worth the cost of the subsequent contamination of our environment. We can observe the damage from pesticide residues to wildlife and speculate on their hazard to man. Like the waste of protein and like the overtaxing of our agricultural land, the presence of pesticide residues in our diet can be seen as yet another price we are paying for our unquestioning acceptance of increased meat production and consumption as an unassailable good. How often have I heard well-informed friends with concern about protecting the environment la-ment the fact that pesticides are a necessity. Organic agriculture would be ideal, they will say, but we couldn't feed 200 million people that way! I am not claiming to be able to estimate exactly how many people could be well-fed without the use of pesticides. *But,* the knowledge that we can presently afford to feed half of the yield of our harvested acreage to animals with so little return leads me to believe that we have an enormous "margin of safety" (or, more accurately, "margin of waste") in feeding our population. . . .

THE END OF THE DECADE

To Recapture the Dream

JULIUS LESTER

By the end of the decade many within the movements felt tired, dispirited, and cynical. While some concerns—such as those of women, gay and lesbian rights, and the environment—seemed to be gathering momentum, other aspects and, more important, the sense of the movement as a whole seemed to be in decline. Many activists felt the absence of the enthusiasm and idealism that marked the decade and the movements in their most heady days. In the summer of 1969 Julius Lester offered this brief assessment. Not intended as a eulogy for the decade, his essay nonetheless captures what had been lost, as well as what had been gained, over the years.

What we know as "the Movement" had its beginnings in the late 1950s. In Afroamerica the beginning was the 1956 bus boycott in Montgomery, Alabama in which a twenty-six-year-old minister, Martin Luther King, Jr. introduced non-violent direct action as a means of attacking the problem of racial discrimination. The bus boycott was a sharp departure in political tactics for blacks. . . .

In America during this same period, similar tactics were being used, as pacifists in New York, San Francisco and other cities demonstrated against the testing of nuclear weapons, the appropriation of monies for bomb shelters and air raid drills in the schools. In other parts of America a phenomenon known as the "beat generation" established psychic liberation zones in New York, Denver, New Orleans, San Francisco, and Los Angeles, saying that they would not follow the "man in the gray flannel suit," that life did not consist of the balance in your bank account, but in the values by which you lived.

None of us who were a part of those beginnings in the Fifties could have then predicted the Sixties. The Sixties represent one of the most fantastic compressions of political ideas and action of any decade in American history. (As Jim Morrison of The Doors has pointed out: "A generation lasts only two or three years now.") To go from sit-in demonstrations at lunch counters in the South to the Black Panther Party, from pacifist demonstrations against nuclear testing to a mass anti-war movement, from the "beat generation" to a cultural revolution is a ten-year journey almost beyond comprehension. Yet, this is the journey which has been made.

It is a tragedy of the Sixties that too few of us know the journey on which we have been. We refer to "the movement" as if it were a political monolith. But what we now call "the movement" bears little resemblance to what we called "the movement" in 1963. In the early Sixties, "the movement" consisted of SNCC, CORE and SCLC in Afroamerica, SDS, various socialist groups and peace groups in America. At that time if one wanted to be a part of "the movement" one affiliated himself with one of those organizations.

Today, "the movement" is no longer an identifiable political entity, but we still refer to it as if it were. It is more a socio-political phenomenon encompassing practically all of Afroamerica and a good segment of the youth of America. It is exemplified by the high school dropout who knows why he's not in school, the long-haired youth whose life is lived in the streets, college students, SDS organizers, winos, blacks in daishikis and blacks in suits and blacks in black leather jackets and on and on and on. Indeed, most of the people who now consider themselves to be a part of "the movement" do not belong to any organization. Instead, there are loose groupings of people around the country who share a common outlook, common life-styles, and common aspirations.

Things happened in the Sixties. We didn't make them happen as much as one action produced ten other actions (but the progression was geometric) and we were swept along with it. By the mid-Sixties, it was practically impossible for an organization to adequately control and guide actions which it initiated. And to tell the truth, we were so excited seeing so much happen, that few tried to control or direct what was happening. We were not concerned with being conscious of the implications of what we were doing. We were merely conscious of doing.

The nature of "the movement" underwent a subtle change in the mid-Sixties. Until 1964, "the movement" had depended upon its own people to carry information from place to place. Meetings were small; "movement" publications were few and people depended upon direct contact with each other to keep informed and since there were always a fair number of people in motion, this was not difficult. However, with the Summer Project in 1964 and the murders of Chaney, Goodman and Schwerner, the media became more and more prominent as the carriers of "movement" information. (One of the reasons the Summer Project came into being was an attempt to break the media black-out on Mississippi.) It had always played an unconscious role in "spreading the word." A 14-year-old black youth who watched sit-in demonstrators getting beaten in 1960 via NBC was 19 at the time of the Watts Rebellion, and he had been politicized by NBC, not by meetings, rallies or "movement" propaganda. And a ten-year-old in Detroit who witnessed Watts via NBC was more than ready two years later. "The movement" took advantage of the media's new interest in it and began to consciously use and eventually depend upon the media to be the agent for information rather than upon its own people and organs. And as "the movement" grew, it became so loose and ill-defined in structure and constituency that a press conference was the most effective way of communicating with "the movement."

The media was also the principle agent of information for the cultural revolution, feeding itself and making news about be-ins, love-ins, hippies, rock groups, drugs, etc., and it took the Yippies to merge the cultural revolution with the political movement via NBC. Abbie Hoffman and Jerry Rubin consciously used the media to transmit concepts of the cultural revolution and to direct those concepts toward political ends. . . .

By the fall of 1966, "the movement," which had once been composed of a few political organizations, was becoming a separate society, with its own newspapers, its own life-style, its own morality. It became like a huge river with people jumping in at every point along its banks. Those who had been swimming in the river for several years suddenly found themselves surrounded by hundreds of new swimmers and while everyone admitted that there was a communication gap between the young and their parents, few recognized that there was a growing communication gap within what we still called "the movement." We used the same words and thought we were talking about the same things, but, in actuality, increasingly, we were not. The political perspective of someone who has been in "the movement" since 1960 (and how many are left?) was, of necessity going to be different from that of one who entered in 1968. The viewpoint of the former was not necessarily superior to that of the latter, but the differences between the two had to be recognized and understood. The "movement" veteran had a sense of "movement" history, having lived it. The "movement" neophyte did not. As far as he was concerned, "the movement" began when he became aware of it. . . .

"The movement" is no longer what it was when SDS issued the Port Huron statement or when the Jefferson Airplane used to perform in Golden Gate Park. Today "the movement" has several divisions, the most apparent being the black-white one. . . .

There is a need for a new analysis. The quality of any political movement can be no better than the quality of its ideas and the way in which those ideas are expressed. A political movement functions on the basis of revolutionary concepts and revolutionary morality. In the past year, there has been an alarming decline in the quality of concepts and morality within the political movement. When a hyena has been wounded, it will turn and eat its entrails. The political movement which began in the late Fifties and came to fruition in the

Sixties had a clear concept of where it was going and some idea of how to go there. Yet, the further it went, the more aware it became of the complexities of the problems and the less apparent were the solutions. The more complex the problems appeared, the more the political movement turned to solutions others had used with success, namely, Marxism-Leninism. While these solutions worked for other people, there was little questioning as to what degree, if and how these solutions might work in America. The ways in which Ho, Mao and Fidel each used Marxism-Leninism in different ways to suit their particular problems was over-looked and the fact that they used Marxism-Leninism became all important. The result has been an ever-increasing factionalism within the political movement, with each side saying it represents the one, true approach and throwing epithets of "counter-revolutionary" back and forth like the Chicago police throwing tear gas cannisters. He who disagrees with me is counter-revolutionary seems to be the current level of political analysis and acumen. This not only creates dissension but is demoralizing in the extreme.

The political movement has become so concerned with itself that it has ceased to grow. In and of themselves, organizations are very dangerous things. They are begun as the vehicle for social change, for the revolution. After a while, though, they unknowingly become mistaken for the revolution itself. Organizations have to have offices, printing equipment, mailing lists, etc., and generally, it seems that the more the power structure moves against an organization, the more it becomes concerned with saving its offices, equipment, mailing lists, i.e. in preserving itself. Its principle tasks become paying the office rent and phone bills and getting people out of jail. And the more it is attacked, the more it has only one issue to bring before people—defend the organization. When an organization's overwhelming concern becomes its own preservation, it is no longer waging a struggle. It has merely become an employer with so many on the payroll and bills to be paid. The organization begins to rule its members instead of the members using the organization as a means to the end.

One of the important tasks of the Seventies will be to examine and evaluate organizations and if necessary, disband many and create others. Our loyalties have to be to the struggle, not to any particular organization. Too many people have left an organization and thereby, left "the movement," thinking that an organization was synonymous with "the movement."

Intense involvement with organizational internal affairs can blind us to what we are supposed to be about—the creation of a society based upon values of humanity. Yet, we cannot be the vehicle for the creation of this society unless we ourselves are in the process of being transformed. If we become narrow in outlook, if we refuse to be open to criticism, to new concepts, we become the fascists we say we are fighting. If we become so self-righteous and self-important that we talk to no one and listen to no one who does not agree with the way we view the world, we are even less than those we are allegedly fighting because we are supposed to know better. If we continue to substitute the waving of the little red book for thought, if we continue to substitute the screaming of slogans for ideology, if we continue to divide and fight among ourselves, then "the movement" of the Seventies will be comprised of bitter, disillusioned idealists who lost the dream.

We must not mistake an organization, a gun, or even an ideology for the revolution. They are only means toward it. Revolution is first and foremost a question of morality, a question of values, a question of the inner life of people. If we lose sight of this, we can create a society in which everyone is well-fed, well-clothed, well-housed, and find a new generation of the young rising up and saying, "We want the world and we want it NOW!"

We had the dream and we are losing it. If we can regain the fervor and intensity of that dream in the next five years, that will be more than enough. To create a society in which each man has the opportunity to love himself and thereby, the opportunity to love his fellows. That is the dream. Before we can create the revolution which will make real the dream, we must begin to create it among ourselves. In the beginning it was easy to maintain the dream. Now, because the problems facing us are more complex than we ever imagined, maintaining the dream is that much more difficult. Letting that dream suffuse our every thought, word and deed is that much more difficult. Yet, that is what we must do, no matter how difficult it becomes. Without the dream, there is no revolution.